SPLENDOUR OF THE CLASSICAL DANCES OF ANDHRA PRADESH

SPLENDOUR OF THE CLASSICAL DANCES OF ANDHRA PRADESH

Kalaprapoorna Varalakshmi Janapathy

Publications

KALPAZ PUBLICATIONS

DELHI-110052

Splendour of the Classical Dances of Andhra Pradesh

Rs. 1800

ISBN : 81-7835-507-8

Published in 2007 in India by
Kalpaz Publications
C-30, Satyawati Nagar, Delhi-110052
Phone : 9212729499
E-mail : Kalpaz@hotmail.com

Laser Typesetting at : Master Computers, Delhi
Printed at : Salasar Imaging System, Delhi

A Figurine in a temple at Tadipatri Anantapur dt
(Vijayanagara Times)

Dedicated to

M.R.R.Y. Ch. V.P. Murthy *Raju Garu*

Art lover, well known Gandhian, Freedom Fighter and
Hon. Former Minister of Religious Endowments
(Government of Andhra Pradesh)
with Warm Regards

Contents

Dr. Vempati Chinna Satyam

#4, Greenways Road, Raja Annamalai Puram, Chennai– 600028
Phone No: (044)24937260, Fax No: (044)24938473, E-mail: vempati@kuchipudi.com.

FORWARD

Mrs.Varalakshmi Janapathy is well known to me for several years as a very good auther and orator.

Mrs.Varalakshmi met me at my residence in Chennai in the middle of 2005 and explained in detail on her research work and study on Kuchipudi dance with the title "KUCHIPUDI THE CLASSICAL STYLE OF ANDHRAS" and has given me a copy of the works for my comments on it.

After studying the matetial, I was so impressed for the zeal and affection Mrs.Varalakshmi is having towards our ancient Kuchipudi dance. The author has taken lot of pains by travelling extensively to various places to find facts and referred many books related to this Kuchipudi dance form in particular and dance in general.

I believe that this elaborate information and material about the Kuchipudi dance and facts in this book given by Mrs.Varalskhmi Janapathy will defenitely benefit the present and future generations of artistes.

Chennai-600 028
January 30, 2006.

Vempati Chinna Satyam
VEMPATI CHINNA SATYAM

Preface

Dance is a divine art. The only two institutions that patronised the art of dance are the temple and the palace in the ancient and medieval India. In the temples, dance was one of the shodasopacharas to the lord (Natyam Dharayamdi).

From the 7th century onwards, the temple vied with the court as more and more grants came in pouring to the temples. Simple place of worship spread into a vast establishment catering to the social and cultural needs of the community.

It is a very interesting story to study how in South India, temples began to play a major role in promoting fine arts like dance and music. It was the time when art and religion were intricately intertwined. Lord was considered to be the source of all arts and art was considered to be very sacred and spiritual. Performances should be given in his presence to please him and it was considered to be elevating the audience to spiritual heights.

Hence, grants of lands were given lavishly by kings, nobles and common people also to dancers, musicians in the temples. Natya mantapas were built specially in the premises of the temples. There was a dancing hall at Nagai called Natya-Salai in 1062 A.D.

A record dated 1425 A.D. from Tiruchendur speaks of the gifts for dancing girls during the Maha-Puja Andikkappu. Even during the Pallava times, the Mukteswara temple, Kanchi and the Adipuriswara temple at Tiruvathiyur maintained a large number of dancing women (Adigalmelar) and musicians for singing during festivals. Women who were dedicated to dancing were called 'Deveradiyal', Talicheri-Pendugal kumthis. These women on account of their proficiency in dancing were held in high esteem by the society.

This practice of employing dancers in the temples increased by the time of Chola and Vijayanagara kings. Raja Raja, the great who was a great patron of cultural and artistic activities, employed 400 dancing girls in the Brihadeeswara temple, he built at Tanjore. A long list of these girls is found in the inscriptions of the temple. A number of singers, drummers, dancing masters were also employed to assist them. Dance masters were called 'Nattuvanars'. Higher income was given to them and the lands granted to them, were called Nattuvakkani. In Andhra Pradesh, they were called 'manyams'.

The inscriptions also give details of various dance styles practised and exhibited by them. In the Ranganadha temple at Srirangam, members of some particular families called 'Araiyars' perform dances in the temple. This is known as 'Araiyav-Savai'.

In the temple sculptures, we see a number of illustrations of dance styles, known to our ancestors. They are found in groups also while performing different poses. The temples of Palampet and Warangal have many illustrations of such dancers living in Kakatiya times. The artists, as well as the devotees conceived Gods as masters of dance, as seen from the beautiful icons like Siva as Nataraja, Krishna as Kaliya Mardana, Nritta Ganapati, Natya Saraswati. Thus, a sense of divinity was attached to dance and the temples pulsated with dance forms.

Devadasi Nritya Sampradayad of Andhra Pradesh Temple is the centre for Hindu culture and fine arts. All our arts have taken birth in the temple in the pursuit of God Almighty and have found place in Asthanas and have travelled upto foreign countries and have touched the hearts of artists all over the world with a sense of spirituality and immortal joy.

Andhra Country was ruled by Satavahanas, Ikshvakus, Pallavas, Chalukyas, Kakatiyas, Vijayanagara kings, Nayak kings of Tanjore and Madhura, Gajapathis, Jagapathis, Sansthanadhis, Reddy kings and also *Velama* kings.

They have patronised vedic religion, Buddhism, Jainism, Saivism (Pasupathi Sampradaya) Veera Vaishnavism (Madhura Bhakti Sampradaya) also.

The dance traditions that were followed in those times can be divided into three categories. They are (1) Aradhana Nrityas that were performed in the temples for the sake of deities, (2) *Devadasi Nrityas* that were performed for the pleasure of kings, (3) Those that were performed for the sake of commoners, like Yakshaganas, performances of Bhagavatas.

All those traditions were performed in accordance with the rules laid down by Bharatarnava of Nandikeswara, Abhinaya darpana, and Natya Sastra in a Sastraic way.

(1) Aradhana Nrityas performed in accordance with vedic tradition were in adoration of the five elements like the sky, the earth, air, water and fire and some Jathis are still preserved. These Jathis are performed praising Vinayaka. When they sing with 'Swara', they appear to be like chanting vedas. (2) Buddhist and Jain religious. Due to several political and religions reasons, the texts that speak of the spread of culture of those times are not to be found. Therefore, these are no authoritative texts to know about the dance traditions of those times, that can be basis of those traditions. But pillars, whereas cave temples like in Nagarjuna Konda, Amaravathi, Ajanta and Ellora, speak of those times and are similar to the Karanas, Angaharas, Sthanikas, Rechakas mentioned in Bharatarnava. Even today, the dances performed in the temples of Balidweepa and Japan speak of the Buddhist art of dance, that was prevalent in Buddha yuga of India.

Veera Saivam (Pasupathi Sampradaya) : Kakatiya's religion was Veera Saivam and they were worshipping Rudra Deva for 6 times in a day. Dance flourished in their times and special Nritya Vedikas were constructed just opposite to the main deity. Deva Nartakis were performing Pooja Nrityas on these platforms. Such platforms are not to be found in any other place in India.

Jayappa Senani wrote Nritta Ratnavali in Sanskrit and it has great similarities with Nandikeswaras Bharatarnava and Sangeeta Ratnakara of Saranga Deva.

Several kinds of Marga, Desi dance traditions were disclosed in texts like Panditaradhya Charitra, Basava purana. Those Nartakis that form Nattuva Mela Sampradaya were performing in the temples following Marga Paddhati and were also exhibiting 'Kelika'—(Kacheri Natyam) an admixture of Marga and Desi traditions in the Raja durbars of kings. Natya Mela was performed by male members following Desi traditions, Yakshaganas, and several Bhagavatha kadhas. Following the religious traditions of those times, they were exhibiting the kinds of Siva Leela Nrutyas and stories as dance dramas.

Vaishnavs (Srivaishnavism—Madhura Bhakti Sampradaya). The Vaishnavism that was practised by Ramanuja charya after Adi Sankara's philosophical preachings, attracted greatly the people and that was Vaishnavism of Madhura Bhakti Sampradaya.

The only lord worshipped was Jagannadha. All the other living creatures were considered to be female characters. Worshipping Jagannadha with dance and music was the inner soul of this Bhakti Sampradaya. Accoding to the tradition, Annmacharya, Siddhendrayogi, Yati Narayana teerdha wrote the sacred stories of Jagannadha in the form of Yakshaganas, Padas, Tarangas and spread these Bhagavatha Kadhas among people.

Vallabha, who lived in Gujarat permanently preached this Madhura Bhakti and on account of his influence, Krishna leelas Jalakrudas, Jata Natakam, Bhama Kalapam, Padams relating to Sringara Nayikas took deep roots in those times.

Ramabhadramba, Rangajanima Madhura Vani, Jasirekha, well versed in Sanskrit and Telugu could wrote poetry. For the uplift of our Vaishnava tradition, Vaishnava yuga could help a lot. Such a

PART-IV : BHAGWATA MELA AND OTHER TRADITIONS OF ANDHRA PRADESH

PART-III : TECHNIQUES OF INDIAN CLASSICAL DANCES

resourceful tradition would not have taken deep roots if only the concept of Krishna as the great hero was not invented.

Thus two important traditions developed in Andhra Pradesh as (1) Natya Mela and 2) Nattuva Mela (performed by Devadasis).

Nattuva Mela had two divisions: (1) Natya Sampradaya that was performed before God in temples. (2) When lord is on the Kalyana Mantapa, the dances that were performed for the sake of people and in Rajasthanas.

Out of these two, the Alaya Kala that was performed in temples is more ancient and sastraic also.

Devadasis: In Andhra Pradesh, all Devadasis that learnt dance were not allowed to dance in temples. Only those who learnt Alaya Sampradayas according to Agama Sastras from childhood, Telugu and Sanskrit language, music and dance, after attaining puberty were tested by Pandits for their proficiency and after Mudra Dharana only—*i.e.*, if it is Vaishnava, Sampradaya, Sankha on the left and chakra on the right; if it is Saiva Sampradaya, Lingadharana was done to her, they were allowed to offer Kumbhaharati to God, do Nritya before Swamy and weave the fan which is one of the Shodasopachara Pujas, other dancers, however proficient they were, were not allowed in temples. They were allowed inRánditha Sabhas, in Rajasthanas but were not allowed to enter into the temple. So, the pious tradition of Devadasi Sampradaya, took to bad times and finally disappeared in course of time.

Who are these Devadasis?

What was the relationship between them and the Alaya Nritya Kala (The temple dance).

There is an interesting story about them. Nara and Narayana were performing penance in Badarikavana. Indra, out of jealousy sent Rambha to disturb them from penance. She was trying to disturb them with her dance and music. Narayana, with a view to teach a lesson to Indra, created a beautiful woman called Urvasi. Indra, who thought that their penance was stopped and the dance and music also stopped, came to Narayana and requested him to pardon him. People who gathered there were getting astonished about the beauty and charm of Urvasi. Since then Urvasi was shining as a jewel in Indra Loka and Devadasis were her children.

Devadasis are of two kinds : (1) Siva dasi (2) Vishnu dasi.

Sivadasi's dance was full of Nritya Pradhanya, and exhibiting 'Ganbhira Bhava' (serious thought) and was also full of Karananga hara Vinyasa.

Vishnu Dasi's Natyam was full of delicate Bhava Prakatana, delicate Karavanagahara Vinyasa.

Devadasis were performing before God in temples, 'Kavutas', 'Asta Dikpalaka Natyas', Sapta lasyas'. They were exhibiting in Swamy's durbar, Nritta Nritya and Abhinaya, which is called 'Kelika'.

Kavutams were stotra geetas of various gods mixed with Mridanga Jathis written specially for the performance. They were in several Apurva talas (Vinayaka, Lakshmi, Brahma, Rudra and were played with Guru, Laghu plutadi vinyasa.

Navasandhi Astadikpalaka Baliharana Natyas, on special occasions when Astadighandhana was done, the dance that was done was called Navasandhi Natyam, inviting vividha Dikpalakas and to please them, Navasandhi is of two kinds.

(1) Stotra Nritya at the time of pooja (worship) (2) Prahari—during night after Pavalimpuseva, inviting Gods to protect the temple.

There are 7 kinds of lasyas: (1) Suddha (2) Desi (3) Perini (4) Prenkhana (5) Dandika (6) Kundali and (7) Kalasa. Karangahara Vinyasa performed by Parvati when Siva performed Seven Tandavas in the Kailasagiri in full of these seven lasyas.

For entertainment, Kelika is performed. This is a special 'pradarsana' of perini paddhati of the above seven lasyas. On this, Nritta, Nritya and Abhinaya are exhibited with discipline.

Garbhava, Vishama, Bhavasraya, Kavivaraka, Geeta are embodied in perini.

Nritya Pooja: After the Kumbha Harati, the Deva Nartaki receiving flowers of the temple priest, recites churnikas and offers pushpanjali to God. Afterwards, the Vadya brinda do 'Ambara Vinyasa'. Wind instruments like flute, Veena are played before the beginning of the dance and this is called 'Ambara'. According to this Ambara exhibition of 'Ayitta' is done. Ayitta means, with the sound of instruments, 'raga' and 'tala' are tuned with the delicate Mridanga. Later on, Alapachari 'Addi', Mehana, in Jhampa Tala, singing in 'Nata Raga' does Nritta. After completing Addika, Nandi, 'Sabdam' is played. This Nandi started with Mridanga Tattis is completed with Geetas and Teermanas.

Before this Nandi, if it is Siva temple, Bhujanga Trasa Bhujanga Nartanas are played. If it is Vaishna temple, Bikrama Nartana, Kemala Nartana are performed. After 'Nandi', Kavutams are performed and some of the Sapta Lasyas are also done. Finally this Nrityaradhana is completed with 'deeparadhana'.

Nritta ganas performed for pleasing Dikpalakas to please Vishnu—Bhramara Nritya is performed. Malihara raga, Brahma, Aditala, Yadanada Madhyam (1) Siva—Bhujanga Trasa Nrityamu. Sankarabhavana Raagamu—Adi—Rudra Talamu—Matrukananda Vadyamu (3) Indra—Lalitha Nrityamu Deva Gandhari—Nadanama Kriya Ragas—Samagaja Leela Talas: Meghanadha Vadyamu (4) Agni—Kalinga Nrityamu—Nata, Lalita Ragas: Adhyasana—Veena Vikrama Talas Simha nada Vadyamu (5) Yama—Kartari Nrityamu, Kysika, Mahahari ragas, Bhrangini Raja Chudamani Talas, Sondananda Vadya (6) Niruti—Vidyat Nrityam, Kaisika, Bharavi Ragas, Malla—Rangapradeepa Talas;—Vijaya-Vijayananda Vadyamu (7) Varuna—Utsanga Nrityamu, Sriraga and Megharanjani Ragas Bhringari, Makaranda Talas, Mangala Vadyamu (8) Vayu—Survaraka Nrityam, Gould, Vasantha, Bharavirgas, Tankari, Vijaya Talas, Gambhirananda Vadyamu (9) Kubera—Sankarna Vadyamu Nata, Srinagas, Labhru—Turanga Leela Talas Susampata Vadyamu (10) Easanya—Dandapada Nrityamu, Kandola, Sankarabharana Nrityasvrisha—Nanda Leela Talas, Matrakananda Vadyamu.

It appears that the Nritya Sampradaya of Andhra Pradesh is dependent on Bharatarnava of Nandikeswara.

Abhinaya darpana is an abridged version of Bharatarnava.

Devadasi's E Ka Patra Nritya, Adavu, Jathi, Teermanam—The methods of exhibiting them Mridanga Jathis are also mentioned in detail in Bharatarnava under the head 'Srunga Vadya—Chari Alankara. Our Nritya is given shape according to this 'Paddhati'.

Those who follow Nattuva Mela Sampradaya give importance to Abhinaya Vidya as mentioned in Natya Sastra and to Nritta on Bharatarnava.

In Andhra particularly, the Bharata Sastra had been highly developed in the medieval times in the courts of Kakatiyas, Reddis, Rayas and Nayudu's of Warangal, Vijaya Nagara and Nagarjuna Konda. In the tradition, the Bhagavatars of Andhra preserved a considerable amount of the knowledge of Bharatasastra popular experts like the present one, of the ancient type of Bharata and its contents will therefore be of particular value to students and enthusiasts in the field of traditional Natya in Andhra Pradesh". (Dr. Raghavan in his foreword on Natya Sastra by Sri PSR Appa Rao).

Details about the development of classical dances at the time of Sata Vahanas, Vishnu Kundins, Cholas, Pallavas are not available unfortunately.

Some cultural evidences of Amaravati speak of the art of dance of the 2nd century and the 'pindibandhas' shown in the various poses of Amravathi speak of the classical excellence of Satavahanas. Much of this wealth is taken away by the Britishers, and is available in Kingston Museum in London, which I had an occassion to see in 1982. Some are still available in Madras Museum.

After Satavahanas, Ikshvakus and Salankayaras and Vishnukundins, Pallavas ruled till the end of the 9th century and Cholas succeeded them Raja Raja I who ruled from AD 985 to AD 1016, was powerful in the south. In the middle of the 11th century, when Raja Raja Narendra ruled, several temples were built and he patronised all the art forms of Andhra.

All the above dynasties, encouraged construction of temples and developed various arts. They were patrons of classical arts. Numerous descriptions are there, written by Telugu poets about dance. Actually, Hindu culture especially Andhra culture is preserved in these art forms. There are many inscriptions in various temples on which various details are given as regards the gifts given by the dancers and gifts given to the dancers. In several inscriptions of Mukhalinga temple in Srikakulam district and Tripurantakam temple in Prakasam district, there are many about the noble role of dancers in gifting lands *etc.*

Dance traditions of Andhra Pradesh and their association with the temples is evident in the sculptures of the temples built by the Kakatiya rulers. Most noteworthy of these sculptures are those of the Ramappa temple of Palampet in Warangal district of Andhra Pradesh.

Dance and music had its high place in the sculptures of Chalukyas. Figures of Jammidoddi in Vijayawada, and sculptures of Bikkavolu, Bhimavaram speak of good dance operas and music festivals. Youngsters who play on veena, on 'pillana groiv' drummers, who play with hands, who play on Mridanga like Pambala some who play 'kolattam' some who open their mouth and sing appear to the dancing.

'Challavva', a Gandharva Vidya Visharada, was a vilasini in Chalakya Bhima's darbar. The king gave her gift of land in Attili village and 50 acres of nivesana land. Her father's name was Mallappa (SAMAGRA Andhra Sahityam—Arndra-page 119). (Attili Tamrasasna of Chalukya Bhima). Mallappa was praised as Tumtara in the Sasanananand her mother was like an Apsarasa by name Tondakka.

Reddy kings also patronised dance. Komara Reddy was writer of dance book entitled "Vasanta Rajee Yamu'. His lover was Lakuma and she was an expert who could dance in a thousand ways a single Bhava.

The Reddy kings were adherents of Agamic daily worship developed to a great extent. Errana, one of the famous Kavitraya and court-poet of Prolaya Vema Reddy has many references to dance in his works.

In Harivamsam (1 part-6-109) Errana depicts the falling of rain—the sky is the Kedika, when lightning has come to perform Gondili dance, clouds became the curtains and the hailstones formed as Pushpanjali. Nachana Somanadha, a contemporary of Errana, has also many references to dance in his uttara Harivamsam, Peda Komati Vema, Kumaragiri and Kataya Vema were not only great experts in the science of Natya but also great art critics. Halli Saka and Mattalli and many other forms of classical dances were in vogue at the time of Reddy kings and Srinadha mentions many of them in his works.

Kataya Vema the well-known commentator of Kalidasa's three dramas is styled as "Natya Vedarthavedinam"—the master of Natya veda or the science of dance. It is with his Kumaragirinajiyam commentary on Sakuntalam that Gothe, the great German poet studied the original text.

Kakatiyas were first Jains and afterwards embraced Saivism. The beautiful dance poses found in temples of Telengana especially those of Ramappa and Swayambhulingeswara temple bear testimony to the fact that the art of dance flourished. The Kakatiya period is remembered for the greatness of Nritta Ratnavali by Jayappa Senani. Machala Devi was the favourite courtesan of Pratapa rudra, well versed in dance and music. She became so famous that her life itself was staged as a drama in Warangal.

Art of dance like music and literature attracted the attention of Krishnadevaraya, the greatest of Vijayanagara monarchs. Abdul Razak, who witnessed the Maharnavami celebrations at Vijayanagar left his impressions as follows : "The part of musicians is generally filled by women. Some young girls with cheeks as full as the moon and with faces more lovely than spring clothed in magnificent dresses and showing features, which like the freshest rose, charmed every heart, were placed behind a pretty curtain opposite the king. On a sudden, the curtain was raised and again fell and the damsels arranged themselves for the dance, with a grace calculated to seduce every sense and capture every mind" (Major Abdul Razak—pages 36-37). Though the dancing saloon is not existing now even in ruins, thanks to the Portugese traveller, Domingo Paes, who visited Vijayanagar, who left a minute and meticulous description of this wonderful construction.

Andhras have a genius for tolerance and reconciliation, peace flourished during the Satavahana rulers. Megasthenese, a foreign traveller, who visited India at that time, said in his "Indica" that Andhras are a powerful race. In fact Satavahanas built the Andhra Empire, at a time, when Vedic Dharma was questioned and there was chaos and confusion in the minds of people between religious sentiments and practices. Santa Moola, the 1st Andhra king followed Hindu Dharma and his wife "Santi Sri" built Buddhist Chaityas and whereas another great task of Empire building was taken up by Andhras during the Vijayanagara period in the 13th century. Kakatiya kings and Reddy kings also saved Hindu dharma from the onslaughts of Muslims.

When we look into the prosperity of fine arts and literature besides religion, during the above periods, contribution of Nagarjuna is commendable. Kumarila Bhatta and Vallabhacharya also contributed their best to Vedic and Bhakti cults. Nagarjuna laid foundations for Bhakti cult. It is said that the great Sankaracharya the founder of Advaita philosophy learned his 'Maya Vada' from the well-established 'Sunyavada' of Acharya Nagarjuna.

Kumarila Bhatta lived in the 7th century and in fact restored Vedic religion to its ancient glory. He popularised study of Vedas among people and the practice of holy sacrifices and pujas in temples.

Gadha-Sapta-Sati of Satavahana monarch Hala, deserves mention. It is a collection of verses in Prakrit and contains poems of exquisite beauty replete with pathos, humour and descriptions of rural life. Life in Andhra Desa is well depicted in these verses and several of the poets in Gadha Sapta Sati appear to be Andhras.

Our Reddy kings—Kataya Vema, Kumaragiri Vema, Pedda Komati Vema and the great Velama king by name Singa Bhupala were all authoritative Sanskrit writers. Vidyanadha and Panditha raya Jagannadha were great writers on Sanskrit poetics. The great work by name 'Rasagangadharam' by Pandítharaya is very famous and he was patronised by Muslim emperors like Shah Jahan and Dara Shikoh.

In the field of art also Andhras have left their indelible mark and great monuments are left even today as great legacy. Architecture seems to be their pre-occupation, as solid rocks are available in plenty. During the Satavahana period Buddhism was the motive that inspired our architects. Kings and rich magnates vied with each other in excavating caves out of solid rock, thus beautifying them with the genius of man and presented them to Buddhist monks. The cave dwellings and chaityas of Karla and Kanheri are sights for angels. Sanchi Stupa in central India and Amaravati Stupa in Guntur district of Andhra Pradesh are a few of the great monuments which immortalise the skill of Andhra architects. The stupa at Bhathipvolu is a colossal brick structure Nagarjuna Konda in the Krishna valley contains innumerable gems of architecture. Kakatiya rulers were great builders in stone. The Swayambhu temple in Warangal fort, the thousand pillared temple at Hanumankonda, and the beautiful temple of Ramappa at Palampet, where the science of dance was engraved on the leaves of stone are a few monumental structures. The ruins of Hampi of Vijayanagara Empire are full of art in stone, especially the Lotus temple and Virupakshaswamy temple are living examples of the genius of Telugus.

In the divine arts of dance and music Andhras showed great originality and worth. The dance system in Andhra is based on Abhinaya Darpana of Nandikeswara. This rare work on dance is available in Telugu country only. The Tanjore Library (Saraswati Mahal) has a work called TALA LAKSHANAM, attributed to Nandikeswara. Most of the works attributed to him treat more of Natya than Sangita Nandikeswara is mentioned as the first writer on 'Rasa' (as per Raja Sekhara's account of Kavya Mimamsa, in his account of the origin of Sahitya Sastra). One of his major works was not available to Abhinavagupta. Abhinava, while quoting him says that he is reproducing Nandikeswara's views exactly as quoted by

Kirtidharacharya. Only on the authority of Kirtidhara and he himself never saw the work of Nandikeswara.

Nandikeswara's popular work Abhinava Darpana is available in print in Telugu by Nidla Mangalam Tiruvenakatachary and subsequently translated into English by A.K. Kumaraswamy and Duggarilal. The compilor of Bharatavasa prakarana printed along with it, was Sabhapati Ayyar, a Brahmin Bharatacharya of Tanjore court, a Bhagavathar, who finally settled at Mannargudi and taught his art to his students.

Chapter 13 of Abhinava Darpana deals with seven kinds of 'Lasya', which is a rare phenomenon.

Saraswati Mahal (Tanjore) gives some more information about the works of Telugu people.

Ajju tandava (Kannada), Kavitva Charitra by Bhagavathula Uma Maheswara Sarma, published by Andhra Vignana Samithi of Jamshedpur in one such. Another work by name "Samkeertana Lakshana Padhati" by Chinna Tirumalayya of Annamacharya's family is a rare collection, though not very popular. Prabodha Chandrodayam by Krishna Mishra in six parts was popular and a commentary was written on it by a Reddy king.

Chatur Lakshana Samkeertanacharya of Simhachalam wrote on Bhagavata Sampradaya and he is known to be the first person who coined the word "Bhagavtulu". Under the influence of Gita Govindam in the 12th century, Bhagavatha Sanghas were popular all over India, even at the time of the rule of Muslims and during 'Pothana's' time, when Veera Saivam was very popular.

During the Kakatiya period, Jayappa Senani, a commander of elephant forces of Ganapati Deva, composed a great manual on the divine art of dance by name "Nritta Ratnavali". Ramappa temple at Palampet is an illustration in stone of the theories of Jayappa. This art is kept alive and spread to the other countries of the world by the exponents of Kuchipudi style even today.

Kshetrayya wrote "Gopala-Padamulu", which are divine cups of melody and sweet thoughts. He belonged to Movva village in Krishna district and was a great devotee of Venugopala Swamy, a presiding deity of Movva village. Saint Tyagaraya poured out his heart in Krities and the Tarangas composed by Narayana Tirdha are very popular. After the fall of Vijayanagara Empire, these saints migrated to Tamil Nadu in search of Royal patronage.

During the Salankhayana period, Buddhism spread to the countries of the East and the Islands of Pacific with the revival of Hinduism in the Chalukyan age, Andhra missionaries and colonists spread the message of Trinity in the Eastern islands. Andhra culture sailed along with Andhra religion and commerce. Names like Trilinga, Amaravati, Kakulam, Simhapura and many others occuring in countries like Burma, Siam, Indo-China, Malaya, the Islands of Java, Sumitra, Borneo reveal the establishment of Andhra culture in these regions. The use of Sativahana era, which is peculiar to Andhra in the inscriptions of Java is another conclusive evidence of the spread of Andhra culture.

The art of Andhra and Sculpture, influenced the art of Java ultimately. The great stupa of Barobadur is modelled on the art of Sangharama at Amaravati.

In the words of Dr. Rayaprolu Subrahmanyam, the great historian "The colonial expansion of Andhra's civilised savage tribes in greater India, gave them a new religion, art and literature and created zest in them for a higher life".

Art of Amaravathi: Art of Amaravathi in depicting the female figures is simply superb and is world famous, with delicate caricatures of several poses. 'Pindibandhas', as per Bharata's Natya Sastra indicate that it is a separate school of thought. Most of these fine pieces can now be found in the British Museum, at London and in the State Museum at Madras. Experts express the opinion that nowhere such a tradition can be found. The depiction and treatment of female figures in the stupas is wonderful. It presents a departure from Amaravathi school and they seem to follow more the tradition of Sanchi and Madhura. They wear an Arthoruka above the knees and leave the upper part of the body without drapery. The abdomen and hands are unlike those of Amaravati school and suggest heftiness. Important motifs are creepers and garlands besides the characteristic makara torana. Salabhanjikas perforate jali work, Gajalakshmi and dancing Siva on the Lalata Bimba.

Lepakshi is a small village situated at a distance of 80 miles from Hindupur in Anantapur district of Andhra Pradesh. On a hillock known as Kurma Sila, there is a temple belonging to the early half of the 16th century. It is famous for its natural paintings which belong to the late Vijayanagara period. Seated in Padmasana, on a beautifully carved Padmapitha, Devi has two hands, the right arm holding a full blown lotus and the left hand gracefully bent downwards. She wears a close fitting choli in red colour with beautiful gold lace. Her figure is beautifully drawn with elongated eyes, delicate chin, narrow mouth, slender nose and nostrils. On the forehead are seen three lines of Vibhuti. The dancing pose of Parvati in the Natya Mantapa is marvellous. She stands left to Siva in tribhanga pose, holding a flower in each of the two arms. Her saree is striped and the waist cloth is of separate pattern, dark with black curls and big white spots. Ganga is shown as descending on the Jata of Siva like the curved hump of a cascade at the top, stretching wider as it proceeds down dense with fish, flowers and a snake.

Thus beautiful admixture of painting and sculpture can be seen in the carvings of Ajanta and Ellora caves, belonging to the period of Satavahana kings.

The dance poses of Ramappa temple reveal the new Karanas, charis and Sthanakas invented by Jayappa senani as explained by him in his Nrittaratnavali. These Sivapriya Nrittas were performed by men and wearing Rudrakshas and Vibhuthi on the forehead, chanting Rudra churnikas. They were playing in two rows or in circles with the sounds of Bheri, Mridanga, Hudukka, Samsya, Sankha in one method. In another method, men and women were separately playing in Lasya and Tandavad Puddati.

Chindu Nrityas: They were of 3 kinds—Suddha chindu, Tirumani and Kavadi chindu. Singing keertanas and laying steps in the 'Tala' men and women were delicately playing chindu Nritya gracefully. Jayappa mentions that Tamilians and Andhras were playing this Nritya Suddha chindu was played by Saivas, Tirumadi chindu Vaishnavas, Dravida Vaishnavas, Chittadi Vaishnavas, now called Satani Vaishnavas. These Nrittas were performed at the time of Mangala Gouri Vrata and in the month of Sravana in the early hours and during Sankrathi days by Vaishnavas.

Khandika Nritta was full of Hasyarasa. Some artists were playing 'Baharupi' not only in Andhra Pradesh and in other states also and were living on such performances. They were called 'Pagati Veshamulu'. Gollas, Yanadis, Lingabalgas were living on such performances.

Mode of worship of the rural folk is different from the civilised, sophisticated urban people. Village deities appear to be definitely asserted with vegetation. Villagers believe that if God is worshipped and if man offers God, what he has, he or she would be blessed with his boons. It is totally different from the ancient mode of worship. People in the early days prayed to Pancha Bhootas—the sky, the earth, air, water and fire and so God's image was not there. As times passed on, people learnt to mix up religion with worship, which took shape in different forms. Prayer was through singing, dancing individually or in groups.

Society learnt to live in harmony and to bring about integration, several stories were written and propagated. The stories of Ramayana and Mahabharata percolated into society and became very popular.

Sringara being a fine sentiment gained much more popularity. With the advent of Vaishnavism and the popularity of Jayadeva, Nayaka-Nayaki Bhavana gained momentum and Sringara rasa was much appreciated. Padmavathi, wife of Jayadeva was a Telugu girl and her birth place was Peruru village, a village in Nalgonda district.

There are "Sasanas" in Jagannadhaswamy temple at Poori that if at all it comes "Telugu people only should dance, and they should play Geeta Govindam". There was not only Vaishnavism there was Veeravaishnavism and Radha Madhava Pranaya was the main theme that touched the hearts of people.

Because of the influence of Geeta Govinda, Bhama Kalapam gained popularity in Telugu land.

Satyabhama is a Sringara Nayika. Her personality was developed in Hindu mythology as a Sweeya Nayak, Pragattha, daughter of such rich man like Satrajthu, Veera Nayika and one who could make the purana purusha Krishna surrender to her out of love. Satyabhama's character is unparalled and no other woman could have such individuality or assertion. Rukmini or any other woman had no such merit. That is why Bhamakalapa is evolved as a Sringara Drisya Prabandha.

Mixing up the philosophical and cultural and artistic ideas, Kuchipudi people are exhibiting it as a Kalapa and as a Nritya rupaka. Bhama kalapa has gained popularity all over the world as the best item of Kuchipudi reportoire and solos are performed by women.

From centuries, this item of Bhamakalapa had been presented by many and Vedantam Satyanarayana Sarma, being a man, had played the Bhama Kalapa with great skill and gained utmost publicity not only for himself but also for the Kuchipudi style for ever. This item is supposed to be popular from 20th century. The ragas exhibited by the Nayaki and when exhibited with Bhava, sppura Raga and Laya by the Kuchipudi Bhagavathars, it is simple display of Navarasasand Charturvidha Abhinayas, which pleases everyone.

Kuchipudi Bhagavathars consider Venugopala as "Akhilandakoti Brahmanda Nayaka" and sing as "Raja Gopalam Bhajemama Jeevavam Radha Lolam Bhaje" and also "Jaya Kuchilapurivasa Jaya Natya Kala Vilasa" with Nityopachara and also during Ekantaseva. This 'Madhura Bhavana' and 'Madhura Bhakti" of Satyabhama is taken by Sidhendrayogi as 'Virahakalapa' and after experiencing the Nayika Bhava, by himself expresses how intense his feeling is for Gopala in Neevele Vacheun Neebela Poyeva, rammanave varni vega rainmanave (ask him to come early) in Arabhi raga.

I wanted to bring out to lime light the contribution of Andhras to the great art of dance and dance-drama in different periods. Vijaya Raghava Maheejani was an expert in the art of dance. He gave place in his durbar to perini, Desi, Jakkini, Danda Lasyamu, Kanduka kreeda, chindu *etc.* and they were all considered to be followed from previous times.

Banasura Kadha, Samudra Madhanam were popular Yakshaganas, wherein women's role was not there. According to Saiva Sampradaya, Rama Kadha, Ravana Kadha, Ravanura Kadha and Tripuranta Kadha were much patronised and titles also indicated male characters and Bhakti culture. It is only after the introduction of Vaishnava culture, that female characters were introduced and so they got prominence.

Dance-drama form gives all the navarasas because the Pada Sahityas are in Kaisiki Vrithi, a soft feeling is created. That is why people appreciated these dance-dramas. People were perhaps taken away from the mundane problems and were elevated to a state of sublime thought. When one saw the dancer performing dance on the stage, man was taken to a dreamy world, where he enjoyed the delicate inner feeling of softness and joy. As the themes also were nearer and dearer to the Indian mind-set, they were very much appreciated.

That is why dance and dance-dramas written in simple language could win the hearts of people and move them. Class, creed differences were forgotten and fine art like dance worked as a linking force and paved the way for cultural synthesis.

Dr. Raghavan says that there was Kuchipudi tradition in Andhra Desa and there was Bhagavata Mela tradition in Tamil Nadu on the lines of Kadhakali. When we critically study some Ananda ragas Raga Lakshanas and some Apurva Ragas, there are some subtle differences between Geeta bhinayam and Yakshagana.

There was a time when Geeta was sung as Alapana. Harikadha is one of such styles Telaja Maharaja compared certain Raga Lakshanas with the style of Yakshaganas.

The dance-drama of Andhra Pradesh Kuchipudi is thus related to Bhagavata Mela, though the authors and compositions are different from each other. The original source of inspiration for the dance and music style of Bhagavata Mela is said to be Kuchipudi and this seems to be born out from the historical movement of the troupes from

Andhra Pradesh to Tanjore and another evidence is found in the lyric, which is in pure Telugu.

On a careful study of the epigraphical records of Andhra Pradesh, one can conclude that a place of pride was given to this composite art of dance in the cultural and aesthetic life of the people of Andhra. A special feature to be noted is the development of the fine art and its close ties with the temple and temple activities. Dance is considered to be one of the 'Shodashopa' (16) chara pujas offered to God. Badami Chalukyas, Cholas, Hoysalas, Kakatiyas, Pallavas, Vijayanagara monarchs, Kalyana Chalukyas have richly contributed to the development of dance. The evidences that they have left to future generations as legacy are many in the form of stone inscriptions.

Sata Vahana emperors of the second century BC were the pioneers and people later on carried innovations. Findings of the excavation of the Archaeological Deptt. reveal that there were two schools of dance.

(1) Devadasi (2) Kelika.

Before the onset of the influence of Buddhism, an exclusive style consisting of Devadasis and Kelikas existed.

Nritta Ratnavali is a great contribution of Andhras to this fine art of dance and Jayappa Senani a commander of the Kakatiya Elephant forces wrote this wonderful treatise on dance, depicting Desi and Margi traditions of Andhras. It is a master piece on dance.

The earliest dance sculpture in Andhra, dates back to 2nd century BC and is found in Amaravathi. This sculpture consisting of four dancers shows 'Pindivandhas', later on explained by Bharata in his Natya Sastra. Another beautiful description instone is now preserved in British Museum.

It is a dance scene with a dancer accompanied by two women one playing of flute and the other on Vina. From the ruins of Nagarjuna Konda, an amphitheatre is found out. It is a sculpture depicting a dance scene by three dancers and the seal of a lady by name SARASIKA.

Perini is one of the classical dances of Andhra. It has a Saivite religious origin. Jayappa describes a perini dancer as a man of attractive personality, of good pedigree, a man of taste, master of music and the instruments, endowed with excellent voice, an expert in language ready listted, eloquent and acquainted with both Tandava and Lasya. Main constituents of Perini dance are mainly five—Nrutta, Kaivara, Charghava, Vikata and Gita. The credit of culling out this form of dance goes to the famous Natyacharya, Sri Nataraja Ramakrishna.

Andhra Natyam is an old female dance tradition of Andhra Pradesh. Dr. Nataraja Ramakrishna the pioneer of Andhra Natyam defines Andhra Natyam thus "Andhra Natyam is a Lasya dance tradition performed by the cultured female dance artistes of the country in the temples, in the courts and at public places". At present, the three traditions mentioned above are brought under a repertire by an expert committee of Nritya academy and propagated by Dr. Nataraja Ramakrishna.

To maintain the balance in society with the faith in religion, and to preserve cultural heritage, the temple was used as the mainstream. For this, the temples, the shrines and the sanctuaries in India were used not only as places of worship but also as seats of learning.

Aryans were performing Aradhana Nrityam as an expression of their gratitude to Gods.

All arts have their origin and development in the temple. Sculpture, poetry, dance, painting, music *etc.* all have their roots in the temple. It plays a great role in the socio-economic conditions of society.

Most of the temples in South India have Deva nartaki, musicians and others for the service of God. In Andhra Pradesh, there are several inscriptions, which speak of this sort of worship and the donations made by royalty as well as empinent people of society.

So, in view of the above birds eye-view of past history of art in Andhra Pradesh, it developed to a great extent by the patronage of the community and to some extent, in some periods by the royalty.

But it is very unfortunate to find out that the divine art of dance, which was once practised in the corridors of temples by the Devanartakis, came down to the level of common people without any culture or taste and became unpopular as 'Bhogammelam' 'Samitta' or 'Mujinami'. After a period, it was shunned by the society and was abolished by the Govt. as per the Devadasi abolition Act. The woman, who is an artiste became a victim of the whole game.

For a revival of this fine art, a sincere effort is made by all concerned to lift it again to greater heights with nobler ideals. Though, Aradhana Nritya in temples disappeared, this divine art is getting good recognition.

In ancient India, there is a reference to "Somayagam" in Rigveda and at that time women do dancing holding pots on their heads and waists and also during ritual performance. There is no direct reference to idol or temple worship in Rigveda. Aryans gave preference to Yagnas, Homas, and worshipping the celestial fire. Their main conviction was to offer sacrifices. Agni, Indra, Varuna, Mitra and others were the Adhidevatas for the five elements. In Rigveda, it appears that our ancient Rishis considered beauty of nature and wealthy things as divine personalities. All the above Adhi devatas are now being worshipped in temples as Asta-Dik-Palakas at the time of routine daily worship and also in other religious functions.

The ancient dance which was popular as Aradhana Nrityam was developed during the time of Aryans. Aryans were performing Aradhana Nrityam as an expression of gratitude to Gods. There was music and dance. Henry white head in his "village gods of south India" says that worship of gods in South India, is the most ancient form of Indian religion. "Before the invasion of Aryans, which probably took place in the 2nd millennium BC, the native inhabitants of India, who are called Dravidians, were a dark skinned race with religious beliefs and customs that probably did not greatly differ from those of primitive races. They believed the world to be peopled by a multitude of spirits, good and bad who were the cause of unusual events, specially of diseases and disasters... probably village deities came into being when people began to settle down as agricultural communities. There was no philosophic thought. But old Dravidian cults were influenced by the superior religion of Aryans and Dravidians strongly reacted on them. Early Indian philosophical systems arose in the 6th century BC, it appears primitive forms of Dravidian religion were modified by Brahmin influence.

Greatness of Natya Kala Vaibhava of Andhras

Andhra Rajya was established by Vishnu Vardhana. Its capital was Srikakulam village in Divi Taluq of Krishna district. This was nearer to Kuchipudi of Bhagavatacharyas, and Movva village of Kshetrayya, the great Padakavita Pitamaha. After Bindusara conquered Andhra Desa, Ghanta Sala, Gudivada, Jaggayyapet, Amaravathi were selected for construction of Buddha Aramas. Famous among the rulers was one Kuntala Sata Karni, a Satavahana king and with him started the Salivahana Saka. It was at this time that dance and music of Andhras flourished. These Satavahana rulers ruled the country for 459 years and Andhras had good trade relations with Burma, Java, Malaya, and they carried their Hindu culture, as well as their fine arts.

Eastern Chalukyas (615-1127) ruled for nearly three hundred years upto Kanjeepuram and spread Andhra culture and arts.

Raja Raja Narendra of Rajahnmdry, patronised arts of Andhras and ruled for 30 years. During his son Kulothunga Cholas time, Vegi country merged with Chola Rajya and it was at that time that dance and other fine arts of Andhra began to spread to Tamil Nadu.

From Kalyana Chalukyas (975-1190), one Someswara, the 5th generation king, made Kalyani in Nizam area, as capital and ruled for sixty two years and among the Rashtra Kutas, one Govinda, Amoghavarsha were responsible in popularising Andhra's fine arts in Telengana area. Vallabha Chalukyas ruled Gujarat at that time. One famous book called Bharatarnava was written in the time of Chalukyas. Descendants of this Chalukyan dynasty ruled the North and South parts of the country and honoured poets, artists and their Bharatarnava with four thousand slokas is found in different forms. Tandava, Lasya poses described in this book are to be found in Andhra, Telengana, Tamil Nadu and in Gujarat in the sculptures of the temples and dance traditions of Kuchipudi also.

From Nataraja Tandava according to Bharatarnava written by Nandikiswara and Nagarajasuta Lasya, certain sthanaka Bhedas are invented in Andhra dance tradition, in accordance with Bharateeya dance form.

They are (1) Aaitamu (2) Avahithamu (3) Aswakrantamu (4) Motithamu (5) Vinivrithamu (6) Indramu (7) Chandikamu (8) Vaishnavamu (Apara) (9) Mandalamu (10) Samapadakamu (11) Vaisakhamu (12) Aaleedhamu (13) Pratyaleedhamu (14) Samhitamu (15) Swastikamu (16) Vardhamana (17) Parsnipeeda (18) Chaturasra (19) Ekaparsva (20) Ekajanu (21) Nandyakartha (22) Ekapada (23) Prushnothana (24) Brahma (25) Saiva (26) Vaishnava (27) Kurmasana (28) Samasuchi (29) Vishama Suchi (30) Kurm asanama (31) Nagabandha (32) Khanda Suchi.

These sthanakas are 'Bhangimas' (poses) upto the feet from underneath the waist. These 32 sthanakas can be seen in the temples of Andhra, Tamil Nadu, Mysore and Abu hills. But the sthanakas presented in Andhra tradition are not being exhibited in any other style.

The employees of a temple were of 4 kinds *viz.* Sthanapathis, Manulu, Sanulu and Usbandhakaras in the ancient period.

The satuluru epigraph of velaneti chief, Gonka district AD 1135 mentions about these kinds of employees. (V.V.P. Sastry—the Kakatityas p. 97). A similar statement of Sthanapathis, Sri-Karanam, Sani, Munnurukapu and Nibandhakaras occurs in a record in the temple at Juttiga dated AD 1221 (Ibid-268).

The series of the temples in those days were peculiar class of woman who were donated to the temples by the devotees for the purpose of dance during the time of daily Ranga Bhoga performed in the Ranga Mantapa.

An epigraph of Velpuru village in Guntur district, states that Mahamandeleswara Kota Ganapathi Deva donated Bhandaru Akkamma as 'Sani' to the God Rameswara and granted some land and house site for her because Nritya and Gita are included in the puja.

The Durgi inscription of the reign of Gandapathi Deva dated AD 1269 mentions about not less than 20 employees of Rangabhoga alone. They are Maddelakandru Avaja-Kadu, Kala-Kadu, Vasa-Kadu, tu-kadu, Bharata Kadu, Ratnalu, Padeti Varu, Siya Netalu (ladies) Katigapu—banesa grade guvadu, Amaruka Survasthu *etc.* The plural forms of some of the items indicate,. more than one employee of the job.

"Although the recorded history of ancient India begins before the Christian era, the earliest sculptural remains date from about the 3rd century BC. Thus our knowledge of the workmanship of stone masons, clay-modellers and other craftsmen is limited. The chowice-bearer from Didarganj, now-available in Patna Museum is a unique example of feminine grace conceived by a master sculptor, who might have been a contemporary to Ashoka" says Sri C. Sivarama Murthy.

Mouryas are succeeded by Satavahanas in the South.

Texts from the Jatakas and the master's life are incised as legends, which indicate the theme of the panels. For example, the panel showing the mansion of Indra, where the turban of Siddhardha was worshipped by Gods has an explanatory legend. And there is mention by name of the famous celestial dancers like Urvasi Padmavathi and others and of the Yakshas Yakshis and Nagas like Supavasa Yakshi, Chakravaka Naga, Sirama Devata, and Kubera Yaksha. The beliefs and rituals of the day—the worship of the tree spirit, Nagas, river gods and goddesses and of the celestials like Indra—are all tellingly expressed at Bharhut.

The great and steep descent from heaven to earth is indicated in a naive manner—a foot is carved at the top of the ladder and another at the bottom (page 154-155—The art of India).

Among the recently discovered Bharhut sculpture which are now in the National Museum at Delhi, there are many interesting pieces including a medalion depicting the division of the relics.

This anticipates similar work at Amaravati 3 centuries later and is a most interesting representation of an important episode in Buddha's life. The musical scene is similar to the orchestra and dancers shown adoring Siddhartha's turban in a work in the Indian museum.

Satavahanas known as Andhras also, had a vast empire in the Deccan and they had the resources to create monuments that still amaze lovers of art. Among their works are Sanchistupa, with its marvellous toranas, rock cut caves in western India and monuments, in the south including a stupa near Amaravati, the eastern capital in Krishna Valley.

The surviving paintings of the 2nd century BC are those from caves 9 and 10 at Ajanta.

School of Amaravati: The first and 2nd centuries AD saw the finest flowering of Art in Satavahana's Art in the Deccan. The great collections in the Madras Museum and in the British Museum are rich store houses of the most glorious artifacts of the Satavahana Civilisation.

There are important narrative representations of Jatakas and scenes from the life of Buddha that are no where else depicted. These sculptures are the only evidence of earlier texts, although now lost were preserved in medieval libraries such as Avadanakalpalata of Kshemandra and the Jataka mala of Arya Sura.

Carvings from Amaravti offer excellent examples of aesthetic principles.

Nagarjuna Konda has also yeilded excellent examples of Amaravati Art. The numerous Midhuna figures at Nagarjuna Konda are outstanding examples of this art form, particularly, the one in which the lover gazes at his beloved's reflection in a mirror.

During the Vijayanagara period, mantapas were very popular particularly the Kalyana Mantapas and the hundred—thousand pillared halls. Vithala Swamy temple at Hampi is one of the greatest achievements of Vijayanagar art and literature.

"That year, during the month of Rajab, on the day of full moon (1444 BC-Asweeyuja) on a spacious background Raya laid tents and has his durbar. At the time fixed by him, all the Pradhans, Mandaleswaras, Dalavayees, Brahmins, Pandits, Poets were seated appropriately before the raya—the gathering of the people was huge and the elephants and multi-coloured flags and horses luminating a huge ocean of colours.

(Basavaraju Venkata Narasimha Rao Garu—Foreign travellers—Pracheena Andhra Desam pp. 188-190).

There are 5 storied buildings and in them photos and paintings of various colours were hanging. They are all full of artistic excellence. Some are having Panchalikaya Matra and so are rotating. For every rotation, they take a peculiar shape exhibit here and there beyond description in words.

Opposite to the ground there was a mantapa built on pillars with a stair case. It has 9 storeys which are very vast and Raya had his durbar on the 9th floor. I was given a comfortable seat on the 7th storey and I was sitting with my staff and bosom friends. In the vacant land in between the mantapa and other build. Some wonderful things are shown to the audience. There were some musicians, singers, of heroic stories among them. From among the singers, there were beautiful damsels, whose cheeks were heckling the beauty and grace of the moon. Their faces brimmed with youth and were like red lotus flowers which were blossoming on the advent of spring fully with several types of jewellery. They were singing and dancing and their beauty, grace and their very looks were touching our hearts like roses. They were seated opposite to Raya, behind a beautiful curtain which was removed from both the ends. Then they started dancing. What a wonderful dance. They can move even the hearts of saints. Their bodily movements their bhavabhinaya, their side glances, were really beautiful. Our hearts rejoiced with joy. We forgot ourselves. (Bhavaraju Venkata Narasimha Rao foreign travellers—Pracheena Andhra Desa pp. 188-190).

Such was the wonderful description of Abdul Razak, after seeing the dance performance in Vijayanagar.

From the reports of foreign travellers like Abdul Razak barbosa, poes and the sculptures, it can be deduced that several courtesans were patronised by the king and they were very rich and maintained good relations with others. They gave good performances also.

(Forgotten empire by Sewell pp. 288-89) description of Natya mantapa by pars still interesting. "Thence we went up by a little staircase and entered by a little door into a building, which is in this manner. This hall is where the king sends his women to be taught dance. It is a long hall and not very wide, all of stone sculpture on pillars, which are at a distance of quite an arms length from the wall. Between one and another is an arms length and a half, perhaps a little more. These pillars stand in that manner all around the building. They are half pillars made with other hollows all gilt. In the supports (pedestals) on the top are many great beasts like elephants and of other shapes. It is open.

Art and Heritage of Vijayanagar Period: Soolai Bazaar or dancing girls street—at the foot of the pictureqe Matanga Parvatam is a lavishly built street in the ruins with about half a mile long row of pillared mandapam on one side. Though it must have been a fine royal thorough fare in its palmy days. This street is now under cultivation. We have to visualise from the description of the foreign travellers that both sides of the street precious stones and fruits of varied here were spread up in heaps for sale. At the north-western side, is a tank or wall with a ruined pavilion in its centre. The custom duties of 600 Varahas or Rs. 21,000 per day, got from the dancing girls were sufficient to meet the expense of maintaining 12,000 city guards or policemen. The capital was a grreat centre of courtesans. Abdul Razak describes the splendour of their houses, the beauty of the heart-ravishers their blandishments and agles.

Devadasis supported themselves by the practice of singing and dancing, which they raised to a level of excellence. Their affluences is inferred from their liberal charitable gifts. The fine costly "Soolai Bhavi" constructed near the present Malaponagudi on the way to Hampi.

Brahmins, as well as the Artisan classes joined together to make provision for the dancing girls attached to the temples and they were very much honoured and esteemed and were classed among those honoured ones, enjoying great priveleges in the court of Vijayanagara monarchs as per the version of the Portugese traveller of 1522, Domingo Paes.

This Bazaar bears testimony to the importance of the dancing girl-class in the polity of Vijayanagara Empire. The splendour Abdul Razak refers to concerns the diamond set pillows on which the dancing girls were reclining.

Abdul Razak, the Persian ambassador describes the magnificent festival of Maharnavami thus. Against the gates, there were two circles with many jewels of gold and diamonds and many pearls. Opposite the gate, which is on east side of the front of the open space, there are two buildings of the same sort as the house of victory known as "Vijaya Bhavan". Such was the grandeur and glory of Vijayanagara Empire as per the records.

Of course this art and style had to face some criticism also at certain times. After passing through a golden age, it had to undergo some rigorous opposition.

But there were people who gave patronage to this art in the good old days. As early as 1942 one Maringarti Seshacharyulu was a medical practitioner in Masulipatnam, a congress leader and a lover of arts. His wife Seetammagaru, was a great singer and a good house wife. His two daughters, Rangamani and Kanchanamala were taught dance by Sri Vedantam Lakshmi Narayana Sastrygaru. Later on M/s Kanchanamala was appointed as dance teacher in Tirupathi music college and Ranga Mani was practicing medicine. Bhairvabhatla Subba Rao was running a music school at Masula. VAK Ranga Rao prepared HMT records on Aradhana Nritya (72 mm records. CR Acharya wrote articles on Andhra Art in between 1958-60 in Krishna Patrika. Sri PR Ramachandra Rao, a lawyer, wrote on "art of Nagarjuna Sagar"' KM Munshi in his "Indian History Volumes (Part IV) wrote about Dance and Sri Maremanda Rama Rao, the famous historian wrote on the art of Iksvaku rulers. One Krishna Murthy a lecturer in Tirupathi SR College wrote on the "temples of Andhra". Dr. Syama could write on "dances in Royalaseema".

Lakshmi Narayana Sastry Garu taught 'Rama Sabdam' and later on "Krishna Sabdam". "Sata Koti Manmadhakara", "Ambujasanu Ranee, Amba 6 Jagadamba" were two popular Sabdams. Balasaraswati, the famous dancer of Tamil Nadu said "the first question he asked, the day he first came was "can you write the horoscope for Varnam" what he meant was a systematic classification of all aspects of each varnam as a way of understanding it thoroughly. This remarkable man shared his immense knowledge with me generously and without holding anything back. He gave me confidence to attempt those things that I am doing today.

Natya Sadassu of Delhi, after three years of its establishment declared Kadhakali, Manipuri, Kadhak and Bharata Natyam on a different par and classified Kuchipudi and Odyssy on another par. Dr. Vissa Appa Rao after coming to know about it spoke as follows. Kanchana Mala gave demonstration of "Vinayaka Kavatamu".

It is classical in style. In spite of all this it is strange that it is considered only as a tradition, whereas the secular solo dances, Bharata Natya and Kathak are mentioned as important classical styles... I don't know why the dance-dramas played by the Brahmana Melas of Kuchipudi and Malathur are not recognised as classical. I am glad tht at least Kadhakali the dance-drama of Kerala is mentioned as a classical type.

Steps have to be taken to spend the amount according to plan under the auspices of the Andhra Pradesh Sangeet Natak Academy—the technique and art of the surviving veterans has to be preserved by filming and tape-recording. I hope that immediate and active steps will be initiated for the revival and development of the dance-drama of Kuchipudi by the Sangeet Natak academy.

Smt. Rukmini Arundab, Sri PV Ratamannar, Sri Raghavan have accepted that Kuchipudi style is a classical style. Some of its features are as follows:

(1) **Sabda Vritha**—Pure dance of Kuchipudi style like Simhanandini.

(2) **Sabda**—Manduka Sabda, Prahlada Sabda, Dasavatara Sabda, Kasinadha Sabda, Rama Pallabhisheka Sabda are popular in Kuchipudi tradition.

(3) **Alarimpu**—This has no similarity with Tanjore Sabdam. It cannot be also said that this is a very ancient tradition in Kuchipudi style. Brahmasri Vedantam Lakshmi Narayana Sastry had carved it recently this is a new creation of Tanjore tradition and a special addition. In Sarabhendra Bhoopala Asthana, Vadivelu had introduced an item called Anga Vinyasa and this is known as Alarimpu.

(4) **Jati Swaram**—This can also be said as Jatiswaram. In Nritta Vinyasa, depending in the changes a Tala, Padabhedas can be exhibited by this method. It is of two kinds—(1) changing swara into Jati rupa (2) Mixing Jati and swara. Both these methods are available in Kuchipudi style.

In Tanjore tradition, only Kalyani Chakravaka are the two Jathis that are exhibited mixing up Jati & Swara.

(5) **Varnam, Padam**—Both these are exhibited in Kuchipudi and Tanjore styles. In Kuchipudi style, "churnikas", "koustubhas" are exhibited as special items.

Kuchipudi style starts with "prardhana" (prayer) and ends with Mangalam. But Tanjore tradition starts with Alarimpu, Jathi Swaram, Sabdam as a sequence and finally ends with Abhinaya of a sloka followed by Mangala harati. Saint Tyagaraja, Kshetrayya, Teerdha Narayana Swamy have richly contributed to this Tanjore tradition with their music and blessings.

Depending on the social, political and cultural transformation of society in Andhra Pradesh, dance forms evolved in course of time in different modes of presentation. Once rulers patronised and dance was performed in royal palaces. Aradhana Nritya in temples also could not keep up the standard of performance.

Several themes, were written switching from mere prayer to Rasabhinaya, from Aradhana Nritya to sentimental display of feelings through Nayaka—Nayaki Bhavana. People also appreciated the themes. Dance which originates from the desire of man to express himself, became a favourite past time of the elite of society. Several dance schools were started and it became a matter of honour to learn and perform dance on the stage in modern times. Girls of high class families also began to learn this supreme art of dance as a status symbol.

Thus, several popular dance forms in Telugu land, were evolved on basis of Vachikabhinaya with special emphasis on presentation of Sancharibhavas alongwith foot work as Sri V. Patanjali says. It can also be said that Kshetrayya's Padabhinaya tradition has been perfected by Kuchipudi performers. Many talented artists have developed this Rasabhinaya tradition very interestingly. In spite of several ups and downs, the dance forms in Andhra could preserve the rich traditions of this divine art.

This book is aimed at creating a deeper understanding and appreciation of the various dance forms of Andhra Pradesh. It is meant for the general reader interested in dance, a dancer and commoner interested in the art and dance traditions of Andhra Desa, where several regional forms of dance, dance dramas, folk dances, classical dances and various other forms existed for centuries as an essential part of sacred rites and festivals patronised by the royalty practised by the artists and appreciated by the elite of society.

My aim is to present the history, origin, technique and basic principles underlying the dance forms. A study of the art, architecture and literature through the ages reveals that the art of dance flourished and occupied a special place in the evolution of Andhra culture. "Andhni" style referred to by Bharata relates to Telugu land only. Popularity of compositions of Kshetrayya, Narayana Teerdha and others richly contributed to the enrichment of the various styles.

Madhura Bhakti of Atma was a popular theme in the remote past, and was replaced by Sringara rasa later on through the popularity of Satyabhama and Nayaka—Nayaki Bhavana. Now, there is world-wide interest on account of the Lasya and Abhinaya of these forms.

I began to study mechanics of dancing with all the intricacies. I met famous Natyacharyas and performing artists and several others and tried to know from them about the factors that contributed to popularising this fine art, unravelling a thousand mysteries. I wanted to write this book to satisfy myself and to many like me. I wanted to speak in a language in which a total stranger can also adore and understand this great art.

This humble book of mine is an attempt to share my ideas with my readers and I also wanted it to be a simple narration, to be understood by a layman also very easily. By all means, it is not a text, but, I hope it will be useful to students performers, general public, who may probably learn something from it.

I dedicate my offering with great respect to the soul of Andhras and to Sri Chintalapati—Murhy Raju Garu, a great lover of art, freedom fighter and an ex-Minister of Religions Endowments, Govt. of Andhra Pradesh, a noted Dana-Karna and a patron of several organisations in Andhra.

Pillar sculpture, Palampet

Acknowledgements

I made a serious attempt to study development of our dance traditions in the light of archaeological literary and sculptual evidences of Andhra Pradesh and tried to present the information gathered in a systematic way highlighting the contribution of Andhras. I took up this great task out of my interest in fine arts and out of divine inspiration of Devi, the Goddess of deity of Kanaka Gurga at Vijayawada.

I could make out an academic career due to the affectionate upbringing and encouragement of my parents, Late Sri Buchirajugaru and Smt. Rajyalakshmamma, a very sensitive and highly inteligent Indian woman, though not endowed with degrees and her sister, my maternal aunt, Smt. Lakshmi Narasamma, who was with me through my educational career. Though I was born and brought up in highly conservative traditions and values, I was given encouragement by my brother Sri Veerabhadra Rao a veteran journalist and a freedom fighter and his wife Rajyalakshnamma also was a force driving me to take the career of a writer. My five loving sisters Smt. Lakshmi Kanthamma, Mahalakshmimma, Hanumayamma Annapurna and Anasuya and their children gave me all the affection and emotional strength needed in times of my travelling and tire someness and in writing script.

My gratitude to MB RK Rao, my brother's son and his wife Smt. Vijayalakshmi, who made my stay in Delhi very comfortable and their two loving, beautiful daughters Sagarika and Pravallika who always stood by me and gave me encouragement to withstand the difficulties in the preparation of this book. I deem it to be God given privilege to have the blessings of all my Gurus and I always consider their moral support as a treasure .

My embounded thanks and gratitude to many and critics who guided me to take up the work.

My heart felt and heart rendering thanks to the authorities of Telugu University, Hyderabad, Central University, Hyderabad, Afzul Gunj Central Library, Osmania University, Saraswati Mahal, Tanjore Indira Gandhi Institute of Fine Arts, New Delhi, Bhandarkar Oriental Institute, Pune, Central Sahitya Academy, Information Centre (AP), New Delhi.

This book took the present form as a result of the extraordinary help and guidance of famous Natya charyas like vempati china satyam, Dr. Nataraja Ramakrishna and many others.

It is necessary that our dance items are propagated in the villages and avoid the evil effects of the western culture which is entering into our fine arts.

During the time of my study for five long years, I visited several libraries and institutes. I would like to thank the authorities of those libraries, State Archives, Hyderabad, Telugu University Library, Madras University Library, Saraswati Mahal, Tanjore, Osmania University Library, Bhandarkar Oriental Institute, Pune, Saraswati

Grandhalayam, Vetapalem, Siddhendra Kala Kshetram Library, Kuchipudi, Sundarayya Vignana Kendram, Hyderabad and several other such libraries. I thank whole heartedly all of them for the kind cooperation, they extended.

I thank Sri Seela Veerraju Garu, a famous artist who gave all his line drawings of Lepakshi and Ramappa temples, Sri G.N. Bhushanamgaru, a still photographer who had taken nice photos of Amaravathi sculptures in the State Museum and Sri Rangachari Garu, Asstt. Director of Govt. Museum, Hyderabad and his staff. I heart fully thank M/s Kala Jyothi (Pvt.) Ltd., especially Bapanna Chowdhary Garu, its Managing Director and his team.

My sincere thanks to Tirupathi Tirumala Devasthanam, Central Bank, Hyderabad, Subba Rao of Aswini Hair Oil. My special gratitude to Sadguru Sivananda Murthy Guru for his blessings.

Varalakshmi Janapathy

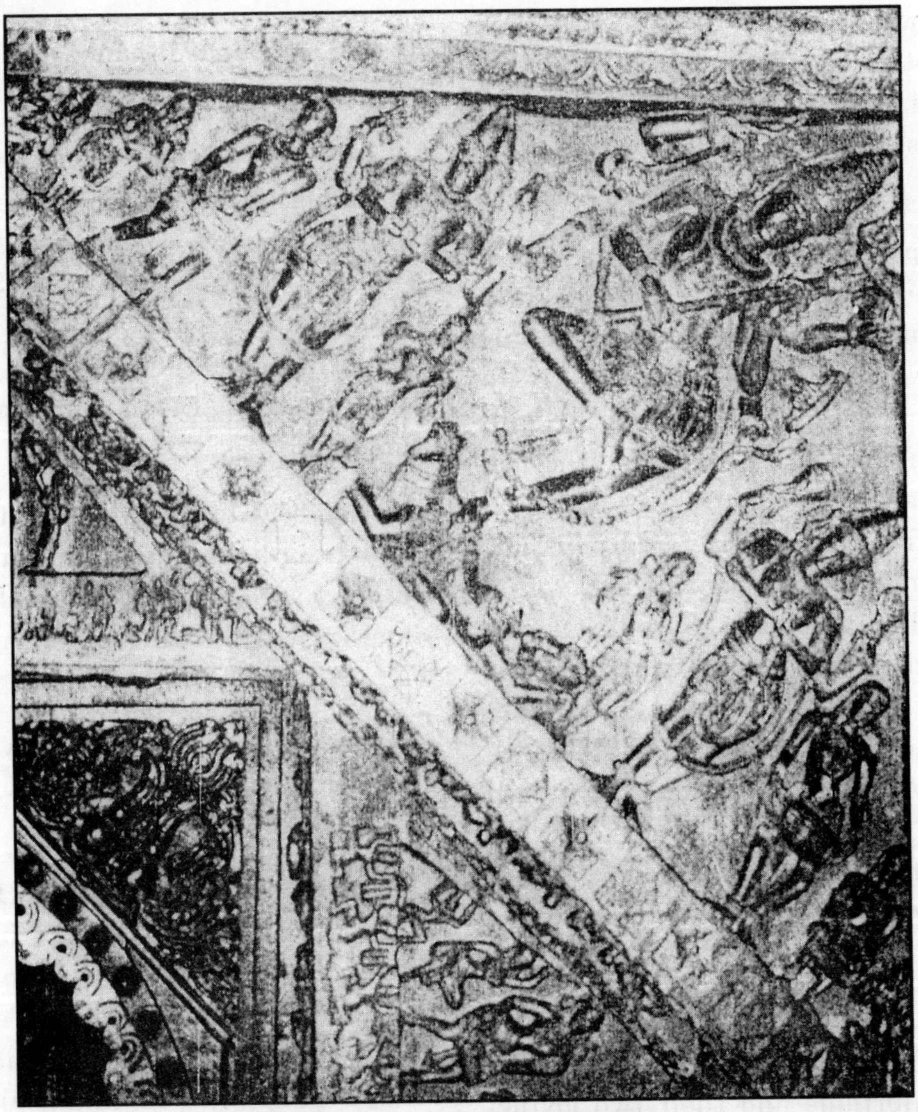

Ceiling corner slab, Nagulapadu

PART-I
CREATIVE GENIUS OF OUR ANCESTORS

1

Introduction

"Angikam Bhuvanam Yasya
Vachikam Sarva Vangmayam
Aharyam Chandra Taradi
Tam Vande Satvikam Sivam"

—**Abhinaya Darpanam**

The instinct to make 'Dhwani' (sound) was there, even before man developed into the shape of a man. Every bird, every animal and even a small insect makes noise and gestures. The whole universe, runs as per an order, a Laya, a Tala. The cosmic dance of 'Shiva' the Laya Murthy is a great phenomenon. The art of gesticulation perhaps developed an instinct to dance and when man felt happy to see the skies and the mountains and the seeds germinating after rainfall, he began to express his joy in mime and in course of time, this progressed into orderly steps and into an art, a science or a sastra.

When viewed critically, it appears that although, the instinct for dancing is universal, the development of dance as a fine art, had not been uniform in all countries. It developed according to the culture and the genius of the people living in a country. There had been remarkable developments in ancient cultures like Greece, Egypt and India and some other East Asiatic countries like Java and Bali Islands. In India this art developed and attained technical perfection and classified excellence.

Indian dance has a language and a grammar of its own, unlike the dance forms of the west. No other country could attain this level. It remains unique and pre-eminent even to this day.

When they did not know much about the mysteries of the Universe, people prayed to the fire, the rain, the wind and all the other five elements of the Universe.

Look into this lovely poem praying to Ushas (Dawn) to shower mercy on them:

"Dawn on us with prosperity

O Ushas, daughter of the sky

Dawn with great glory goddess, lady of the light,

Dawn thou with riches, bounteous one.[1]

Thus, it is evident that down through the ages, people learnt to express their feelings through gestures. They danced in prayer, in temples before idols, seeking blessings.

Kaushitaki Brahmana, an ancient text, says that goddess Saraswati, so loved the rhythm of the chanting that she would dance to the tala of the recitation and it was from this that Brahma discovered the metrical system.[2]

A Historical Perspective

In India, history of dance is the history of the soul of India–It is the concept of purusha and prakriti, an expression of the evolution of movements. This embodiment of sound and rhythm, which creates spiritual expression is dance or Nritya; we cannot separate it from religion or philosophy. Art together with religion and philosophy pertains to the spirit of the soul, which is indivisible and obtainable to the sage and the saint as well. Divine bliss or Ananda is attained which evolves round divinity.

The oldest available text on Hindu dramaturgy is the *Natya Sastra* attributed to the 3rd Century AD. The sage who composed it, by name Bharata, as known by all, states in the text that 'The art of natya' was revealed to him by Brahma, the creator, "giving a review of all arts and crafts". From Rig Veda hymns, Brahma drew forth, poetry, from the Sama Veda of chants and meters, music from Yajur Veda of rituals, gestures from the Adharvana of incantations and spells and sentiments. Thus, Natya Sastra defines same, as comprising of speech, Mime dance and music and contains instructions drawn from ancient sources of knowledge.

With the Buddhists of India, our poetic imagery and its mythology travelled to Japan and China, already culturally rich. The celestial nymphs of the heaven of Indra, Krishna and Brahma appear in a new but only slightly changed form. All Asia had taken India's gift and added to it, its own treasures.

If we go still further, we see, that the influence of India was known in Babylonia, in Egypt and that it even reached the Sumerians. The Athenian Greeks knew about it very well, wrote about it and even borrowed new ideas from its aesthetics. Alexander the great knew its music, called for its tunes and borrowed them.[3] This mysterious influence, this gift from India to the world, was a concept of the "Wholeness of life of civilization, in which art is inseparable from living".[4]

It is to be observed that arts and traditions of India that existed for centuries as an essential part of sacred rites and festivals and as classical arts patronized by the royalty and practiced by the artists, for the sake of the common folk, have a distinct vision, a clear perception and eloquent expression.

Of course, Greek drama and its influence was there but the tragic elements were not there. Indian concept of drama aimed at repose and not at tragedy. Even in the tragic themes of Bhasa namely Charubhanga and Kanthabharana, the ideal of a warrior is mentioned as attainment of heavenly abode if killed in the fighting, Drama was meant to evoke "Rasa".

Art and Dance Interwoven

When we trace the evolution of different traditions of India, we find, that art and dance were interwoven and were one with the religious fervour also, to make man enriched with greater ecstasies of joy. This is a very rare combination. In fact the survival of culture is the real life of a nation, it is the living arts that give life to forces, which survive through centuries.

There is a beautiful story depicting the creation of dance. According to the Hindu Mythology, the world came into existence, when Lord Shiva, the creator began to dance. The beautiful goddess Parvati also danced with him and from them came all the dancing in the world with its varied forms.

Religion was a difficult subject that a few learned men could understand and practice. So, the ordinary men and women prayed to Brahma for help to teach them an easier way to understand about God and the truth of the Universe.

Brahma created 'Natyaveda' to show them, the 'right way of living' through dance, music and drama.

Temples were the homes of all arts and every temple had Natya Sabha, where dancers, dramatists, musicians and poets gathered to demonstrate their talent. There was an ancient festival called 'Dola Utsava' or the swinging festival. Devadasis used to dance in temples known as Aradhana Nritya in temples.

Vishnu Dharmottara Purana has several verses which show how one kind of art depended on the other. The conversation between King Vajra and the learned Markandeya is very interesting.

Dharma means code and Natyadharma and Lokadharma are the principal codes of Indian dance–drama. As we have observed previously Natya Sastra is the oldest available treatise on India's classical dance compiled by the sage

Bharata though scholars disagree but place Bharata somewhere between 3rd century BC and 2nd century AD. The great sage set down the artistic and spiritual canons of this composite art of dance, with highly codified and specific rules.

Literary Perspective

Kalidasa, the great poet-dramatist of India, who lived in Ujjain during the reign of the Great Emperor Samudra Gupta (376–434 AD) reveals the high status of the arts in his plays. A contest between two rival dance masters of the royal court, is the theme of a court scene in Kalidasa's famous play 'Malavikagni Mitram'. The heroine, princess Malavika, the accomplished pupil of Ganadasa, "exhibits her art so faultlessly and quickly reproduces so perfectly that she seems to teach it again to me". She used to perform a special type of dance called "Chalitha".[5]

In the fanciful descriptive poem of Meghasandesam, Kalidasa describes the dances in the Mahakaleswar temple in Ujjain as follows:

"The women there, whose girdles long have tinkled in answer to the dance, whose hands yet cease and wave their fans with lustrous gems besprinkled".

Here the temple maids or Devadasis, who serve the gods are described perhaps, it is clear indication of an established religious custom in Kalidasa's time.

From the above discussion, it is evident that the Vedic culture of Aryans flowed southward from very early times and carried the Brahmanic rituals, the arts and the great epics. It is also a fact that Aryans enriched spiritual concept with fine arts, which is undoubtedly the specialty of Indians.

A magnificent symbol of the great synthesis of two different cultures–namely, Dravidian and Aryan–is that of Shiva, the Nataraja, the Lord of the cosmic dance. His mystic dance is the "embodiment and manifestation of eternal energy".

The cult of Shiva gave a new creative impulse to the arts of the temple architecture, sculpture and

the dance, under the patronage of rulers of South India mostly. The Mahenjodaro and Harappa Civilisation, dating back to 3,000 BC were characterized by a high degree of perfection in this art form. Whether dance in those days had religious significance or not is debatable but after the discovery of a fine statue of dancing girl at Mahenjodaro, it is definitely concluded by several scholars that dancing reached a high degree of sophistication by that time. Historians have proved, beyond doubt, that there was a fine civilization that existed even before the oncoming of Aryans. Call it Dravidian or native, it is definitely Indian. Ancient texts like *Silpadhikaram* are bearing clear testimony to this culture. Of course, Aryans brought their own ideas and more refined sentiments.

Description of Indian Dance

'Natya' includes Nritta (pure dance), Gita (song), Vachika (Speech) and Vadya (accompaniment of musical instruments).

Abhinaya is the term for all techniques of expression of body, face and eyes. It also includes the language of the body which the dancer makes. The audience feel the "Rasa".

Bharata's description of dance and Rasa:-

In the eye of Bharata, Rasa is nothing but dance form

"Natyancha Rasa Eketyukta Prayam"

Dwanyalokam[6]

Bharata further says "Vibha-vanu bhava Vyabha Charisam

Yogadrasa Nishpathi"

Bharata[7]

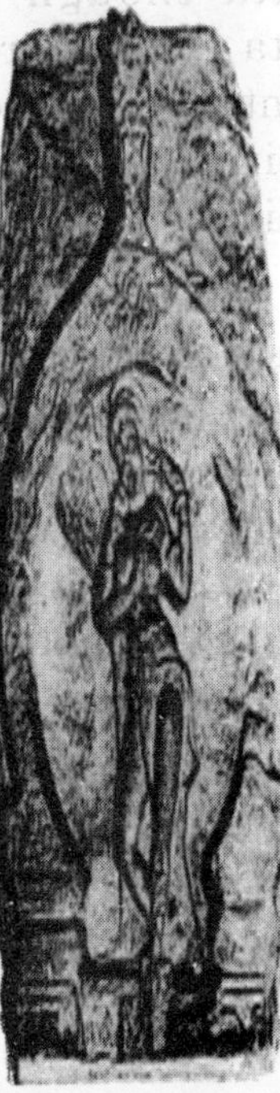

Bulusu Venkata Ramanayya says in "Andhra Parishat Patrika"[8] that Bharata's Natya Sastra defines Swarupa and so, his text is supposed to be the first treatise on aesthetics of Indian Philosophy. For the traditional Indian artist, artistic creation was the Supreme means of realizing the universal being. Art was a discipline (Sadhana), a Yoga and a sacrifice (Yagna).

The theory of Rasa as conceived by Hindu Aestheticians has two clear aspects–the first is the evoked state (Rasavastha) and the second the transitory state, which was the object of presentation.

"Dukhartanam Sramartanam
Sokartanam Tapaswinam
Visranthi Janana Kale
Natyame Tad Bhivshyathi".
Bharata[9]

Bharata means to say that for a man distressed, tired and for a man deeply engrossed Natya gives solace and pleasure.

"Nava Bhavopa Sampannam
Nanavasthantha rathnakam
Loka vrithanukaranam
Natyame Tanmaya Krutham".

Bharata also tells that 'Natya' is replete with display of different stages of human nature.

It is the crux of all arts. It is full of expressions

"Natat Jnanam Natat Chilpam
Nasavidya Nasakala
Naseyogo natatkarma
Natyesmin Yanna Drisyanthe"

Means there is no knowledge, art or yoga or karma, which is not found in 'Natya', Natya is full of all other arts.

"Yo yam swaphavo Lokaysa
Sukha Dukha Samanvithah"

Natya Mityabhi Dheeyate:—Bharata also tells that this world which is full of happiness and misery is worth depicting in the form of dance, with

Anga and Pratyanga and Upangas and is suitable for Abhinaya.

Mythological View of Art

What is 'Rasa' and what is Rasasvadana and Beauty and aesthetic emotion?–

(It is discussed by Viswanadha in his *Sahitya Darpana*).

Religion and art are thus names for one and the same experience–an institution of reality and of identity.

Agni purana says, 'Rasa is the life'. 'Vritta'–'prakritha', are intimately related as Shakespeare also says, "Apparel oft proclaims the man". As Vishnudharmottara purana says, "Prakritis are 'name Rayah'. Aharya which is dress is Prakrithi–Veshavinyasa. These three, 'Riti', 'Vritti' and Pravritthi' (speech, action and dress) are all Anubhavas (chapter XVIII of his Sringara Prakasa.) Singabhupala also followed 3 joja and said in his Text."[10]

References

1. Rigveda, mandal, Sukta 48.

   "They, bringing seeds and king, boon givers of all weather

   Have oft sped forth to lighten us,

   O Ushas, waken up for me the sounds of joy

   Send us the riches of the great".
2. Kaushitaki Brahamana PP.
3. The Living Art of Asia–by Martha Graham
4. *Ibid.*
5. P.S.R. Appa Rao in Introduction to Nritta Ratnavali.
6. Dwanyalokam, p. 182.
7. Bharata 6th chapter.
8. Andhra Paristhat patrika, 1934, Vol. 1, p. 23.
9. Bharata–1st Chapter–114 sloka.
10. Some concepts of Alankara sastra, p. 175 by Dr. Raghavan.

A Graceful Posture Ahobilam

2

Origin of Indian Dance

Shiva is believed to have danced to create the World. He gave regular rhythms to the Universe. The movement of the Sun, the Moon and the stars and circulation of the seasons. He created these new rhythms by his body movement. His dancing symbolized the creation, preservation and destruction (*Sristi, sthithi, laya*).

Shiva, the king of dance, Nataraja and his consort Parvati are thought of as pioneers of dances in India. Parvati danced the feminine dance form called lasya and that is why she is worshipped as lasyapriya.

Masculine dance is called 'Tandava' and danced with angels. There is a story that says when Shiva was explaining dance intricacies to Tandu, Brahma appeared and taught three dances, *i.e.*, Nrittha, Natya and Nritya to Bharata and asked him to extend them.

There is another tale that when Shiva was performing his dance in heaven, devils were against gods. Brahma suggested setting up a fence as a protection from devils. He declared that dancing was not only for pleasure but also for education and creativity. This idea suggests the high cultural value of Indian dancing.

There goes another anecdote. A king of the Jambudweepa by name Nahus, requested Indra to send Bharata to spread dancing on the earth. Indra accepted the offer. But in fact Bharata did not go to the earth. He sent his disciples by name Kahala and Sandilya who taught dance to the people with the help of the scripture of Bharata's, the Natya Sastra.

In another myth, God of wealth Kubera ordered the beautiful dancer *Urvasi* of heaven to hold a dancing concert for Gods. She danced splendidly. She received applause and good admiration from all. On her way home, a devil attracted by her charm attacked her. When a king of the earth Pururava heard about the attack, he went to fight with the devil and to help Urvasi. Urvasi appreciated the bravery and courage of Pururava. They fell in love but ultimately had to part with their union and Urvasi went back, as she was an angel. King Pururava dreamed of his happy time with Urvasi and she was also loving him immensely but she devoted herself to the practice of dancing.

There is another story depicting the origin of dance in India during the reign of Vaivaswata Manu, in the Tretayuga. Bharata says, people became prey to seasonal pleasure and therefore to evil emotions. Thus happiness in life came to be mixed with much sorrow and distress. All Jambudweepa, led by Indra the king of Gods went in a delegation to Brahma and explained the state of affairs, they said O ! Ancestor of Gods! We want some form of entertainment. Something that can be seen and heard. Something that all classes of people, even the Sudras who are barred from hearing the Veda may enjoy.[1]

Dwadasahasta Nataraja Murthy

Rising up from his meditation Brahma created the Natya Sastra from the four Vedas and summoned to get it enacted. But Indra pleaded his inability, and requested Brahma that this job of enacting, should be entrusted to the sages. When Brahma commanded Bharata, to stage the dance drama. Bharata with his hundred sons got ready to give performance on the day of Indra Dwajotsava (the banner festival of Indra) it was celebrated to mark the memory of the success of Gods over Asuras and the subjugation of evil spirits. Asuras, filled with envy and insult, paralysed all activity on the stage. But Brahma could beat them to pulp, and the drama could go on smoothly, perhaps, on account of this the flag staff called "Jarjara" is to be worshipped before enacting a drama or giving a dance performance even today.

Nandikeswara tells us that mainly Bharata was responsible for spreading dance among mortals. When he and his grand troupe of Gandharvas and Apsaras performed before Shiva and Parvati, the lord remembered his own cosmic dance and commanded the 'Ganas' to teach the metrical form to it. This became "Tandava".[2]

The story further tells us that Parvati, taught the gentle "Lasya" dance to Usha, the daughter of king Bana. She spread it among the women of[3]

"Dwaraka". The Gopis in return taught "Lasya" to the women of Sourastra who finally spread to the world.

Cave Temples of Undavathi

Thus in India, dance and drama commenced as plays or acts of god and continued to be so, from several centuries. The audience were presented with high and noble ideals and themes, which presented to them the fear of god and to the elevation of spirit, which in turn used them to perform their duty (Dharma) with warmth and dedication, thus leading a more useful and purposeful life.

Siva, Brahma, and Vishnu dancing From Warangal. Kakatiya, twelfth century A.D. National Museum, New Delhi.

Thus, the body is made use of for display of thoughts about divinity.

Perhaps the Natasutras of Silalin were the original sources of material to Bharata's Natya Sastra (the Nata Sutras of Silalin and Krivasva—Panini the famous grammarian mention Silalin V. (3, 110-11) as the author of Natasutras (Indian as known to Panini—his students forming the Vedic school of dancing designated as "Saila linah Natah (IV, (3-110).

The Sailalakas were originally a Rigvedic charana with their Brahmana cited as Sailaka Brahmana in the Apastamba-Srauta-Sutra (Keith—Apastamba Bahuriha Brahmana (J.R. A.S. 1915 p. (498) Katyayana also knows of the students of the Vedic school as 'Sailalah' (VI. (4. 144). It will be seen that the students of dramaturgy were called "Sailalinah". The growth of a secular text known as 'Nata-Sutra' under the auspices of a Vedic school, itself shows the scope that Vedic literature gave to knew intellectual development not directly connected with religion.

Look into the sutra of Panini.

(4-3-110-4th chapter of Panini). Amarakosa says (: which indicates that men were acting as women).

In all ages and among all peoples, dancing a significant part in the fined spheres of life. Religious folk dances with their simplicity and sentiment, are clear representation of the pattern of life of a people, rather than written volumes of books.

Thus Indian dancing is attracting the attention of people of the world, with its charm and beauty of human movements and varied expressions. Since times immemorial, sacramental view of life has percolated into all forms of art. In fact creative nature is the force of God.

Indian art, in its true origin, is the mere consciousness of the Aryan worship, which, in course of time evolved itself into a rare experience

Cosmic Dance of Siva

and became an open expression of life. From an object, which is 'Murtha' (visible), Indians could think of or imagine an 'Amurtha' (invisible) and that is the greatness of our Indian philosophy. They could also express 'Bhava' and view feelings with higher sentiments about the supreme being and attainment of bliss.

The cult of worship of objects or phenomena had been one of the traits of mankind from very remote times. The early forms of such practices has come down to us, in course of centuries, in the form of literary evidences, traditions and material relics. Having heard about the enquiry relating to the story of Natyaveda, from the ascetics, sage Bharata replied "After having purified yourselves and concentrated your mind you may listen to the origin of Natya Veda. After the passing of the age of Svayambhuvamanu and the lapse of Krtayuga of Vaivasvatamanu, the Tretayuga arrived. People began to indulge in base activities prompted by last experiencing happiness and misery deluded by wrath and jealousy. Devas, Danavas, Gandharvas, Yakshas, Rakshasas and Nagas beseiged Jambudvipa, well protected by the lords of the quarters. Then Pitamaha (the Creator—Brahma) was requested by Mahendra and other Gods "We would live to have a past time which is at once visible and audible". The conventional Vedas could not be spoken within the earshot of Sudras. So, kindly evolve a fifth Veda which could be of benefit to all castes. According to their request, he said "I shall promulgate a (5th Veda called Natyaveda which exemplifies righteousness, brings prosperity, causes fame, contains instruction, and comprehends all activities forming a guide to the future generations as well. It would be replete with the essence of all scientific ideas and demonstrative of all arts and crafts besides embracing episodes. Having resolved thus, he gave shape to a fifth Veda called Natyaveda out of the auxiliaries of the four Vedas.

He took the text for recitation from the Rigveda, singing from Samaveda, the gestural representations from Yajurveda and the aesthetic emotions from the Atharvaveda. Thus the omnicient god created Natyaveda, which should be devolved among those, 'who are proficient, wise, eloquent and indefatigable'. Having heard the command of Brahma, Sakra the lord of gods bowed to him and replied "O noble one, the gods are unfit for the art of theatrical presentation since they cannot easily understand meditate, comprehend or put it into practice. But these sages who have the knowledge of the inner secret of the Vedas and fulfilled their vows are fit to comprehend the art and perform it only. "After hearing the words of Sukra Brahma said "you along with your sons be the agent to produce this performing art. Thus being ordered, I studied the Natyaveda from Brahma and taught my sons with its mode of presentation. As ordained by Brahma the hundred and odd sons were trained to the roles suited to them.

They are (1) Sandilya (2) Vatsya (3) Kohala (4) Dattila (5) Jatila (6) Ambastaka (7) Tandu (8) Agnisikha (9) Saindhava (10) Paloman (11) Sadvali (12) Vipula (13) Kapaijala (14) Badira (15) Yama (16) Dhumrayana (17) Jambudhwaja (18) Kakajangha (19) Svarnaka (20) Tapasa (21) Kaidasi (22) Salikarna (23) Dirghagatra (24) Salika (25) Kantsa (26) Tandayani (27) Paigala (28) Citraka (29) Bandhula (30) Bhallaka (31) Mustika (32) Saindhavayana (33) Taitila (34) Bhargava (35) Suci (36) Babula (37) Abudha (38) Budhasena (39) Pandu Karna (40) Kerala (41) Rjuka (42) Mandaka (43) Sambara (44) Vanenla (45) Magadha (46) Sarala (47) Karta (48) Ugra (49) Tusara (50) Parsada (51) Gautama (52) Badarayana (53) Visala (54) Sabala (55) Sunabha (56) Mesa (57) Kaliya (58) Buramara (59) Pithamukha (60) Muni (61) Nakhakutta (62) Asmakutta (63) Satpada (64) Uttama (65) Paduka (66) Upanaha (67) Sruti (68) Casasvara (69) Agnikunda (70) Ajyakunda (71) Vitandya (72) Tandya (73) Kartaraksa (74) Hiranyaksha (75) Kusala (76) Duhsaha (77) Laja (78) Bhayanaka (79) Bibhatsa (80) Vicaksana (81) Pundraksa (82) Pundranasa (83) Asita (84) Sita (85) Vidyujjiva (86) Mahajihva (87) Salankayana (88) Syamayana (89) Madhara (90) Lohitanga (91) Samvartaka (92)

Pancha Sikha (93) Trisikka (94) Sikha (95) Sankhavarnamukha (96) Sanda (97) Sankukarna (98) Sakranemi (99) Gabhasti (100) Amsumalin (101) Satha (102) Vidyut (103) Satajangha (104) Randra and (105) Vira.

It is to be noted that the usage 'Sagram Putra Satam' justifing the enumeration of 105 sons. He who was suitable for a particular act was enjoined to do it. The dramatic performance has as its basis on the (3 vrithis literary styles, respectively known as Bharati verbal utterance sattvati (grand conception of the mind) and Arabhati (the violent one connected with physical activity.

He also enjoined to make use of kaisikivrithi also. It is characterised by a simple and charming dress and women are suitable since it could be represented only by women.

In the world of humans, worship should be ordained without such a worship, no performance should be initiated. The worship of the gods on the stage is equivalent to a sacrifice. Hence by all means, one should perform the worship on the stage. He who causes such a worship will reap good consequences and will attain the world of heaven. Thus Brahma ordained along with gods and instructed to perform the worship on the stage.

References

1. Bharata Natya Sastra, pp. 11-22.
2. Bharatarnava by Nandikeswara.
3. Sarangadhara Deva–VII, 1231-34.
4. The Buddha Charita or Acts of Buddha Part I—Sanskrit Text (Prakrit).
5. Gadha Sapta Sati (compiled by Satavahana king Hala edited with introduction and translation in English by Radha Govinda Basak (The Asiatic Society 1971).
6. India as known to Panini (a study of the cultural material in the Astadhyayi. V.S. Agrawala M.A. PHD; D.Litt. (Superintendent and head of the Museums branch, Deptt. of Archaeology New Delhi. (1953-University of Lucknow).

3

Aesthetics of Indian Dance

Rasa Tatwa

We learn from the renowned texts or Alankara Sastras "that beauty is of two kinds—organic and inorganic. For beauty to create Rasanubhuti, external thing of beauty and also the internal chaitanya is required. This in sastraic language is called Uddapana (stimulus) and Pratispandana (response)". This truth of mental science had been recognized by Greek aestheticians as well as Indian Sastrakaras. Through their texts, Socrates, Plato, Aristotle of ancient Greece also have enunciated certain fundamental rules as regards this 'Rasa Tatwa'.

As early as in the 3rd century, Bharata, in India, gave to the world his Rasa theory and codified certain rules. After him, in the 9th century, Acharya Anandavardhana, who was the State Pandit in the court of Ananta Varma of Kashmir, Abhinava Gupta, another Kashmiri pandit of the 10th century who wrote Dwanya Lokam, are the two great theoreticians in aesthetics. Acharya Anandavardhana wrote a wonderful commentary on Dwanyaloka, called 'Lochava' and on Bharata's Natya Sastra another commentary called "Abhinava Bharati", which brought him immortal fame.

Bharata mentioned about 'Vibhava', 'Anubhava' and 'Sancharee Bhava'. These lead to 'Sthayee Bhava', required for man as the main Rasa. Modern theoreticians like Kant, Hegel, Jean Paul satre have given new thrust and meaning to this Rasatatwa.[1] The theory of Rasa, as conceived by Hindu aestheticians has two aspects–the first is the evoked state (Rasavastha) and the second is the sentiments, the moods, the permanent and the transitory states which are the object of presentation.

Thus, for the Indian artist, artistic creation is the supreme means of realizing universal being. It is a discipline (sadhana). A yoga and a sacrifice (Yagna).

"Theatre is eternal, temporal, concrete and abstract set within the periphery of a circumference and with a boundary. This paradox is the secret of its surveillance, tenacity to nurture and individuality within a mosaic. Its 'Margi' and 'Desi', its Natyadharmi and Lokadharmi are the two sides of the same coin. The centre is Indianness which holds them totally together".

Very true a sort of cordial synthesis is achieved by the theatre. All the hierarchies and inequalities are forgotten during the hours of performance, all the members in the audience feel a sense of unity, and cohesiveness, with the ideals preached.

Bharata says in the beginning of his work "There is no wise maxim, no learning, no art or craft, no device, no action, that is not found in Natya, that ultimately it will be conducive to duty to dharma". It is also called Natya Vedam, (offshoot of Vedam).

There is not only lasyam but "Tandavam" the "Karanas" constitute an innovation and offering to the gods as well as a pictorial treat to the audiences. When the love situations are interpreted by the deity 'Lasya' condescences, which include 'Abhinaya', accompanied by music there is tremendous impact on the viewer. The delicate beatings of the drum also add rhythm, as Abhinava Gupta says in his Natya Darpanam.

As we have observed earlier, the function of all art and therefore of dance is to evoke 'Rasa' in the audience, because Rasa is Brahman.

Indian dancing has survived the changing times, century after century. Having had its birth in religion, it continues to stir and exalt the spirit even today.

"In thy dance, Divine Dancer,
Freedom finds its image
And dreams the forms
Its cadence weaves the threads of things
And unwinds them for Ages
Charms the atoms rebellion into beauty
Gives rhythm to the symphony of starts;
Thrills life with pain and churns up existence,
Into surging joys and sorrows".

-says, Rabindranath Tagore

Dance traditions developed in course of time.

Most wonderful thing is what was creative in man, he offered in worship to the creator of all mankind. The very concept is fine. It is against this background that dance traditions of India developed.

Temples were made as places of human congregation and women were to learn dance and music and to exhibit refined and subtle ideas, before the audiences, who gathered.

India and Egypt are the two countries which have an unbroken dance tradition for the past 5 thousand years. As dancing is as old as mankind, we are told that sacred stories were danced in the temples and queens and princesses took part in the orchestras that accompanied.

There is what is known as ritual dancing. It is interesting to note that Egypt also still retains its traditions, technique and skill in dancing. That influenced even the South East Asian countries. That is why Havelock Ellis says, "dancing belongs to the village, the temple, the church and most recently the state".

The light of Asia by Sir Edwin Arnold gives a vivid pen picture of the scenes during the birth day celebrations of Buddha in 563 B.C.

"The nautch girls in their sparkled shirts and bells, that chime light laughter sound their restless fett". Prof. Heinrich Zimmer in his "Myths and Symbols in Indian art and Civilisation" also tells about the traditional concepts of Indian dancing.[2]

The gods are supreme artists. To make them tangible to mankind, the sculptor took his chisel. The beauty he created can be seen in the myriad forms that adorn the walls of the temples in India.

Tradition, environment and spiritual inspiration gave each style a particular form of its own.

The harmonious blending of art, religion and philosophy comprised the sacred tradition of Indian culture and gave man the sense of the totality of the universe. The dance in India depicts the profound teachings of Hindu Metaphysics and presents in the simplest form the understanding of the unsophisticated. The cultural heritage continued in a remarkable way. In search of the highest wisdom to reach God, dance was invented.

The ritual is combined with prayer and inspiration. The sacred dance is performed in the precincts of the temples, not only to please the gods but to give enlightenment to the mankind.

It was also used as unifying force by the rulers. It is very interesting to note that man constructed temple or the abode of God, to serve several sociological functions and also to instill, a sense of honesty, truthfullness and integrity among the human beings. The Sumerians built a house for Gods, for the first time in human history. Aryans also built temples.

Temples and Sumerians

Known to history for the first time Sumerian script is from 6th millennium BC. That was

Bharata Muni

Hindocliff, "Babylon" (Revised Edition by Joan Oates), Published by Thames and Hudson. She says "In Mesopotamia, as we have seen, both the temple and Palace functioned as 'households'. Both played an important economic role and at an early period the temple seems also to have assumed certain social responsibilities, particularly, in connection with correcting the grievances of the economically underprivileged".[3]

People in Mesopotamia believed that man was created in order to serve the gods. This was interpreted literally and the deity, like the kings, was cared for, fed, clothed, and so forth. The temple staff included not only the 'SANGA' or Chief Priest who was in fact as much an administrator as a priest, various types of exorcist, the 'NARU' or singers and the 'KALU' whose duties included calming the god by music, but also such persons as scribes and the haridas who ran the temple businesses".[4]

"Central idea in official Babylonian religion, was the image of god itself. The deity was considered present in its image".[5]

"Temple and court ritual were closely related. We read for example of the God 'Nabu' going into the game park like the king to hunt".[6]

In India there is also a wonderful practice of taking of gods in the chariot for "Parveta" during the Dasara Festival. All the acts done by man are also performed by god funnily. Agama Sastras, speak of the several 'Sevas' (Services) done to god, from morning to night. God is woken up from sleep early in the morning by singing 'Suprabhatam' and after so much of routine, again god is put to sleep by 'Pavalimpuseva' in the end of the day. He is put in the cradle and 'Dolotsava' is performed by singing lullabies.

Thus, man takes solace in the service of god. He expects that god would shower his mercy on him, if he prays and serves him.

It is an unending question to answer, whether Man created God, for his living or God created Man, to lead a chaste life in the world. Man and the God are one and the same and are thus inseparable. Man tries to attain divinity or divine 'Ananda' through higher ideals of life–through fine arts.

Encyclopedia Britannica says, "The art of dancing is the art of using the body in a rhythmical way, usually to music, to express an emotion or idea, to narrate a story, or simply to take delight in the movement itself. The dance impulse seems, so far as is known, for there is no concrete evidence to date from the very beginning of Man's existence on Earth and to begin with his own life. Dance even had been the finest means of communication".[7]

References

1. The dance of Life of Havelock Ellis.
2. Prof. Heinrich Zimmer–*Myths and Symbols in Indian Art and Civilisation*, 1946, p.169.
3. *Babylon*–Revised Edition by Joan Oates, published by Thames and Hudson, pp. 174–175.
4. *Ibid.*
5. *Ibid.*
6. Mallowan M.E.N.–1947–Excavations at Brack and Chargar Bazar Iraq–Oates. D excavations at Tell Brak Iraq 39.
7. Encyclopedia Britannica, Vol. 5, p. 451.

4

Origin and Functions of Dance in Different Ancient Cultures

It is not known how primitives danced, but it can be deduced from the behaviour of primitive tribes living even today that the rhythms that the dancer adopts are taken from the best of their traditions like stamping of feet upon the ground. The earliest dance form might have been simple expression of pleasure or acts related to courtship, we know birds and animals, even spiders, dance to attract and impress a mate. However, dance was used for purposes of affecting a whole tribe. These were surely dances of thanksgiving for harvests, for good weather and for wanted rain.

Emergence of Religious Motivations for Dance

In early times the beginning of the religious aspect of dancing, has been used throughout history, not only for clarification but also before written books, as a means of communication between religious leaders and the people. Dances of worship continue even today in every part of the world. In the East, temple dancers preserve something of the style and traditions of ancient cultures. In the West, the most sophisticated of professional dancers put their art at the service of religion. Indeed, so far as anthropologists can establish dancing, has played an important role in the social life of all ancient civilizations. For example, classical forms of dance in Greece played a major role.

Dance in Classical Greece

Many Egyptian influences can be found in the Greek dance. Some came by way of creation, others through the Greek Philosophers, who went to Egypt to study, Plot (C 428–348 / 47 BC) was one among them and he became an influential theoretician. He distinguished the dances, that enhanced the beauty of the body from awkward movements.

It was the diplomatic Dionysian culture that brought about Greek Drama.

The Birth of Ballet

It was at this stage that the ballet was formed. Dance became the subject of serious studies in France. A group of writers aimed at a revival of the theatre of Greeks, with its music, song and dance. Florentina, wife of Henry II, with the help of the Italian dance masters, offered dances with allegorical and symbolical subjects. But the 'Ballet' comique 'Dala Reine' staged by Beaujoyeulux in 1581, told the story of the legendary Sorcare Circle and her evil deeds. The performers, recruited from the nobility, moved on the floor like animated costumes than individual distinct political moral also under kings Louis XV all the arts flourished. After 1700, ballet and social dance took separate paths. English poet and essayist, Soame Jeyus (1704–87) (in his lines in Le Bowseois Gentil Homme 1670) states "This is nothing so necessary to human beings as the dance without the dance, a man would not be

able to do anything. All the misfortunes of man, all the fateful reverses with which histories are filled, the blunders of politicians and failures of great leaders, all this is the result of not knowing how to dance".[1]

Poet Sophocles gave profound form to complex dilemmas of experience in the 5th century BC and wrote about 123 Greek tragedies. His main subject was crisis–calamity, pain, and misery.

12) Le Bowseios Gentil Homme (1670) by Soame Jeeyus.

Deaths are never accidental. They produce transformation from a spurious to a more authentic life. All these tragedies were written for Dionesian Festivals. It was for this perfection of form that the great philosopher Aristotle (in his poetics 335 BC) praised Sophocles above others singling out 'Oedipurs Rex' as his masterpiece.

In 438 B.C., Plato the Athenian Philosopher, propounded through his famous dialogues, that beauty in all bodies is one and the same. It is eternal and indestructable. There is in man a desire for immortality. The beauty is love and the human soul is always in love with beauty; that means the intelligible, changeless realities, which are nothing but ideas. So also ancient Hindus paid an equally important attention to art–sensuous and aesthetic, emotional and intellectual forms. Drama and dancing are considered to be imitative of life.

The ancient Greeks, applied music and dance in the worship of various deities. It was, in fact, the Greeks, who introduced classical dancing all over the continent of Europe, just contrary to the Romans, who flourished much later than Greeks, the Hellenic people have brought dance to bear on every day life, the fruits of good morals and high order of culture. The religion of the Greeks was not a mere religion of sheer ethics or dry theology but a religion of the whole man, not divested of his five senses.

In ancient Egypt, the dancing girls held their daily display of dance and music at every temple. Hilarious processions formed an important feature of the Egyptian ritual.

Likewise the origin of Hindu dance is quite ancient and romantic as well. As per some beliefs it flourished in heaven and has come down to earth. In very ancient days, king of the gods, requested Brahma to produce such a thing as would provide entertainment to his overworked and weary mind. Brahma produced fifth Veda called the Gandharva Veda which he learnt from Siva. Inspired by the different moods of nature, ancient man expressed his joy, through footsteps and by symbols.

"The Grey Entwined Looks fiercely fly

The double drum din its

Maddening sound,

The martial horn blows

Its terrible tone

The agile feet of Lord dance

To a rhythm"

This is Siva's Dance

R.B. Pinglary from

Probodha Bharata

Abhinaya Darpanam says, "we bow to the supreme divinity who reveals himself through the visible world, the audible music and the ennobled imagination".[2] At its origin, dance had been a visible manifestation of inspired devotion and worship. So, it was made an important item of entertainment, in the royal courts, in the temple yards and a popular rendezvous as time passed on.

Aestheticism, according to Kant, means beauty which in its subjective form pleases, without intellectual, moral and practical advantages or that, in its objective form is a thing or an action perceived.

Dance was, hence, considered to be a poetic expression of life which speaks through manifold rhythmic patterns, melodic gestures, and subtle facial expressions.

That is why dances in India, have had a high place in society, with all the religious sanctity. Shiva is known as Nataraja, symbolizing dance.

Together with dance and its varied expressions, so much of literature developed side by side. The princes of Dasakumara Charita are described to have learnt to play on veena *etc.*, some of them were proficient in vocal music.

Tikkana mentions different styles of dance like Dandalasaka, Kundali, Prenkanam and Peranam and their performance to the accompaniment of music both vocal and instrumental. He mentions a variety of instruments of music like, Sankha, Bheri, Mridanga, Dumdubhi, Missanna, Panana, Kanala, Chindanu, Gomukha, Damara, Shanta *etc.*, Buddareddy in his Ranga Nadha Ramayana describes a dance performance like this "Dressed in golden sarees, women grouped together—played Kolatas, performed Perani dances. They danced in Gola, Charini, Sradhri, Gurjara and Desi styles in different groups. Buddha refers to dancing girls as experts in music and dancers who would dance in Sudha Marga, singing Samagana and to a dance by some women, according to their Talagati, while their anklets, bracelets and beeds produced fittings somads and while some played, Mridanga, and others sang, still others played on the Veena".[3]

The temple, in India, continued to be the main prop of dance, music and song. Provision was made, in addition to worship for Gita, Nritya and Natya in every temple. Musicians who were proficient in vocal and musical instruments, drummers of different categories. According to one inscription, a whole row of house was given away to the dancers, drummers and other members of troupe. A certain feudatory of court consisted of actors, dancers, musicians, jesters, voice-entertainers, debaters, orators, poets and art critics. Besides, there were folk arts like collective dances on festive occasions, ballad singing, story telling, pantomimes, puppet shows *etc.*

Every temple also displayed sculptures representing gods, goddesses and saints together with puranas and epic stories.

13) The History of Andhra Country–Subsidiary Dynasties by V. Yashoda Devi, pp. 51-56.

Artistic excellence is sought to be achieved by 'Rasa Tatwa'. The aesthetic content is expected to be achieved through human body—gestures, movements, rhythms and sentimental expressions. In the human body no single part is left of according to all ancient treatises.

All important treatises gave 14 gestures of the head, 24 single handed and 30 combined, 5 movements of the bosom, 5 of the sides, 5 of the waist, 5 of the shoulders, 9 of the neck, 16 of the arrows, 4 of the belly, 5 of the shoulders, 9 of the forelegs, 7 of the knee, 5 of the wrist, and 13 of the feet, 50 for ancestors thought minute and accurate in the analysis of the expressive powers of the human body.

Besides, the above 12 varieties of the pratyangas, 36 rasa dristi Bhedas, 7 of the eye–from movements, 6 of in eyelids, 9 of the eyeballs, 6 of the neck, 19 arising of breathing 10 lip movements, 8 of the teeth, 6 of the tongue, 5 of the ankle, 8 heel movements, 7 finger movements, 5 toe movements *etc.* are also described in detail not to mention about numerous poses, posters, mobile patterns, revolutions and spinning *etc.*

13) Abhinaya Darpanam.

References

1. *Pilgrimage Centres of India* by B.N. Chaturvedi.
2. *Temple of South India* by K.R. Srinivasan.
3. *Temples of India–Myths and Legends* by Madhuram Bhootha Lingam.
4. *Delaware Temples*–Publications Division, Govt. of India.
5. *Ancient India*–An architectural album.
6. *Architecture for all* by Rev. Br. Gian Davide.
7. *Saga of Indian Sculpture* by K.M. Munshi. Purana by P.V. Parabrahma Sastry.
8. *Puranas* by P.V. Parabrahma Sastry.

5

Creative Genius of Our Ancestors

B. Venkata Ramanayya in *Andhra Parishat Patrika* says that Bharata's Natya Sastra defines Rasa Swarupa and so his text is supposed to be the first treatise on aesthetics of Indian philosophy. For the traditional Indian artist, artistic creation was the supreme means of realizing the universal being.

The cult of Siva gave a new creative impetus to arts of temple architecture, sculpture and the dance under the patronage of the rulers of South India.

The Mahenjodaro and Harappa civilization dating back to 3000 BC was characterized by a high degree of perfection. Whether dance in those days, had religious significance or not is debatable. But, after the discovery of a fine statue of a dancing girl at Mahenjodaro, it is definitely concluded by several scholars that dancing reached a high degree of perfection even by that time.

In a descriptive poem "Meghasandesam"

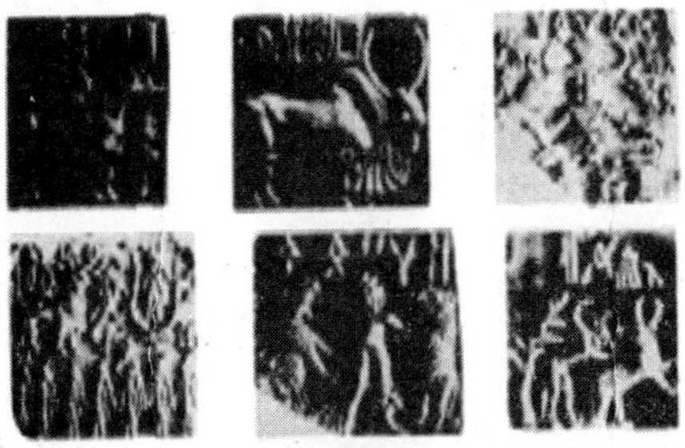

Kalidasa describes the dancers in the Mahakaleswar temple in Ujjain in these terms.

"The women there, whose girdles long have tinkled in answer to the dance, whose hands yet cease and wave their fans with lustrous gems be sprinkled".

Gods were described in Rigveda as kicking up the dust of the atoms that formed the earth, while clasping each other in the dance. Devotees were said to be dancing in the same way. Among the craftsmen and artists required for purushamedha rite a symbolic vedic sacrifice of primieval male called Purusha or Prajapathi, (Lord of creation).

The Sailusha (actor-dancer) is mentioned in the scriptures (Vajasaneya, Samhitha and Yajurveda) as dancing in the breast plates and women were dancing robed in garments fair as heaven. They were described in beautiful words and their creative genius is to be appreciated.

The great God Indra was involved in the Mahavratha sacrifice. To bring rains priests enchanted prayers and made offers while maidens danced with pots of water on their heads around the sacred fire.

Indra, overlord of the lords, was also a divine patron of arts. There were celestial singers (Gandharvas), musicians (Kinneras) and dancing nymphs (Apsaras) to entertain god, the Apsaras are described as 'Broad hipped', slender waisted, and graceful as panthers. They were accomplished dancers and divine courtesans.

Exploits of gods and their heroic deeds often were told in poetic story form by the Nata (Actor-dancer) who made use of gestures, song and music in his story telling. Nata is described as changing his costume and painting himself (Maitreyopanishad).

The art of dramatic representation has as its originator Brahma and Bharata was his first disciple, as we have known earlier. The art of pure dance was originated by Shiva and Tandu and Nandikeswara is his first disciple. So, we have the work Bharatarnava by Nandikeswara on Nritta or pure dance. This work is said to consist 11,000 verses, though we have only 1200 verses available now.

The ruins of rock–cut cave theatre of the 3rd century BC in Bihar bears witness to inscriptions naming an actress by name Sutanika and an actor Devadatta as the reputed artists of that period.

Ramayana and Mahabharata disclose a rich panorama of civilization and cultural life that existed in ancient India.

Vidwa-rupa

Many passages in Ramayana refer to music and dance. The epic states that Dasaradha invited all the community of dancing girls to his Aswamedha Yaga.

Mahabharata tells about Arjuna, who described himself as a dance master and taught the art of dancing to princess Uttara, and other girls in the court of Virata raja.

The popularity of these two great epics in folk plays and festivals in drama and dance and song proclaims the deep devotion of Indians to the heroes of India.

When the religious cult and also the arts spread to South–East Asia, from the 7th century, Ramayana and Mahabharata took deep roots in Java, Bali islands and in Thailand where they were staged as dance dramas and shadow plays.

In course of time, the tilt was towards Gita Govinda of Jayadeva, who sought to spread Vaishnavism. Simple narration of the story attracted the attention of one and all, high and the low. It could take the people to ecstasies of joy while telling universal truths and aim of life. People's life is thus interwoven with thoughts of dance and fine sentiments, from very ancient times.

References

1. *Indian Sculpture Today*, Jhangir Art Gallery Publication.
2. *The Hindu Temple* (Parts I & II) by Stella Kramsisch.
3. *Epic Scenes in Indian Plastic Art* by Jayantika Kala.
4. Classical Indian Dance in literature and the Arts. By Kapila Vatsayan Rhythm in Joy Classical Indian Dance Tradition Text by Leela Samson, Photographs by Avinash Pasricha.

Padmavati Sreenivasam, a Kuchipudi dance-drama by Guru Vempati Chinna Satyam's troupe

6

Ancient Texts and Commentaries

There is a rich contribution of literature in Sanskrit, as well as in other regional languages, by eminent scholars. Several writers wrote on the classical features of dances and music prevalent in their times and in addition there came several commentaries on the well known texts by later writers in course of time.

Let us know about some ancient texts and treatises.

Vidyaranya's Sangita Sara (1320–1350 AD) is written by Vidyaranya, a well-known figure in Sanskrit literature in south India. He was living in the kingdom of Vijayanagara, as per historical anecdotes. From the references in the Sangitha Sudha of Govinda Dikshita (p. 442-Adyar Ms notes) it is evident that Vidyaranya has written a text on music. But unfortunately this work is lost.

Sangitharatnakara of Sarangadeva is another famous text. Sarangadeva belongs to 1230. He came from Kashmir. His father and forefather came to south India, seeking patronage of Yadava kings. This is considered to be a standard work on swara, raga, prakarana, tala, vadya and Nritya. There are several commentaries on this great work and the most important of all of them is that of vittala in Telugu, Singabhupala, kesana, kalinadha, also wrote commentaries on this important text.

Sangita Chudamani is by Jayadeva Malla Pratapa Chakravarthy. He is the son of Someswara also known as Bhulokamalla, who lived in between 1134-43. In the 5th chapter, details about dance are given and the text called "SARA" now prevalent in Kerala, is a changed text of this Chudamani, with some alterations.

Rasa Gangadharam by Jagannadha Panditaraya is a well known text on Rasa. He is a Telugu man belonging to Kuchipudi village and was an Asthan vidwan of Shahjahan's court. Lavangi was a beautiful courtesan living in Shahjahan's court and it seems Jagannadha wrote on Rasa depicting her performances.

Abhilashitardha Chintamani was the author of this text. He belongs to the 12th century. It is like an encyclopedia and deals with several details about sastra. It is also called 'Manasollasamu'. He is the son of Tribhuvana Malla Vikramaditya who was the sovereign ruler of Kalyani chalukyas. He was an expert on several arts and sciences. There are several chapters on Geetha, Vadya and Nrutya.

Abhinaya Darpanam by Nandikeswara

An important early work on dance called Abhinaya Darpanam by Nandikeswara, which can be dated to 5th century AD, deals with an elaborate description of Hasta Mudra, music and drama with a number of actors.

There are evidences to show that Nandikeshwara was a Telugu man and his Abhinaya Darpanam is in Telugu. Even the manuscript available in Viswa Bharati in Bengal is in Telugu language only.

He also wrote another text by name Bharatarnava which was not so popular when compared to Abhinaya Darpanam. A copy of it had been personally handed over to me by Dr. Vedantam Satyanarayana Sarma, the famous exponent of Satyabhama character, when I had visited Siddhendra Kalakshetram of Kuchipudi.

Nandikeswara tells us that mainly Bharata was responsible for spreading dance among mortals. When he and his grand group of Gandharvas performed before Shiva and Parvathi, Lord remembered his own cosmic dance and commanded the Ganas to teach the metrical form to Bharatha.

Bharatarnava by Nandikeswara is said to consist 4,000 verses though we have now only 1200 verses available in all the oriental libraries.

(Vasudevara Sastri–research pandit Saraswathi Mahal Tangore, p. 13)

This work contains Chapters 1-9 giving details about several movements and poses for Nritta much of it is common ground with Natya Sastra but the padabhedas, sthanakas and charis are more numerous. Chapters 10-15 is the main body of the work and it deals with Nritta of various kinds. A notable feature in the Nritta in Bharatarnava is that Nadikeswara predicts that there is a particular Rasa in each item of pure dance as we have it in Abhinaya. Although the mudras in pure dance are intended for only to add grace to the movements of the feet and other parts of the body and do not convey any idea, the total effect of the movements of the features and the expression in the eyes can be ordered as to produce an approval to a particular Rasa. After postulating this aspect of pure dance, Nandikeswara proceeds to instruct the student of the art by a series of items.

First is given as 27 elementary pieces, each consisting of a pose, a step and a look intended evidently to serve as an alphabet of pure dance with rasa.

Each rasa has 2,3,4 or 5 forms all the nine making up to 27, these 27 simple pieces are curiously enough called by the name *Ankahara* which is used in a different sense by Bharata. It is one of 32 finished pieces in the dance of Shiva, each consisting of 10 karanas.

Nandikeswara's Ankahara is therefore different from the well known Ankahara.

After the simple pieces, combined pieces are dealt with next in the subsequent chapter in a series.

There are altogether 55 items in this book. All these have now gone out of use, but as per the instructions given in the text these items can be revised and taught to students.

After these two standard treatises we don't have any further details in the later works of Dattila and Kohala pertaining to dance but some of the extracts of Bharatarnava are to be found in the commentaries of Sangita Ratnakara, we have some compilations from classical authorities that cover the whole field of dance. Most notable among them are Nrityadhyaya Sringara Prakasa of Bhallata and Nritta Ratnavali of Jayappa Senani written about 13th century.

There has been an attempt to bring about some reform and systematisation about **1750** AD in Tanjore, during the time of Pratapa Simharaja. This movement was finished by the time of Serfoji of Tanjore. A number of dance masters have taken part in this work of systematisation and the present compilation of Utakad Govindachary is one of the bigger contributions towards this end. This work, as it is preserved in Saraswathi Mahal contains the full compilation in Marathi, with the originals in Sanskrit in some cases. The author has drawn from Sangita Ratnakara the well known classical compilation of Sarangadeva in 1200.

Sangita Muktavali and **Sangita Makaranda** are also from Bharatarnava of Nandikeswara which is the authoritative text for Nritta. The 1st volume deals completely with Angas, upangas, and Pratyangas. The 2nd volume deals with *sthanakas* and *charis* in full. The 3rd volume deals with *Karanas, ankaharas* and dance items that have survived at the time of the author.

The Tanjore library has a work called **Talalakshana** attributed to **Nandikeshwara**. Most of the works attributed to him treat more of

'Natya'. He is referred to as the 1st writer on Rasa (as per Mr. Rajasekhara's account of Kavya Mimamsa. One of his major works was not available to Abhinava Gupta).

Abhinava Gupta, while quoting him says that he is reproducing Nandikeswara's views as quoted by Kirti Dhara Charya only on the authority of Kirti Dhara Charya. He also says that he himself never saw the work of Nandikeshwara. Thus, Abhinava gives from Kirtidhara's large prose extract from Nandikeshwara (on pp. 51-54 on the prayog of Mani sakit dances in the Purva Ranga).

Abhinava Darpanam by Nandikeshwara is available in print in Telugu by Nidla Mangalam Tiruvenkatachari and subsequently translated into English by A.K.Kumara Swamy and Duggarilal.

The compiler of the Bharata Rasa Prakarana printed along with it was Sabhapti Iyer, a Bramhin Bhattacharya of Tanjore court, a Bhagavathar who finally settled at Mannargudi and taught his art to him.

Chapter 13 deals with 7 kinds of lasya.

Sangitha Ratnavali was written by Soma Bhupala who belonged to 1180. It has nine chapters. Last chapter deals with dance. He is the son of Jayadeva who was a guard in Ajayapala Maharaja's rule. He started his chapter on dance with the following lines. "Vitanvane .... Sivah Karyanilayam Suravara Chamatkara Chathuram".

Natya Chudamani is a text by **Somanarya** and he might have belonged to the time of Achyutaraya. There is a good commentary on this in Telugu. He also wrote another text on music by name Sarvaraga Sudha Rasa.

Sangitha Chintamani is by Vemabhupala. He is one of the Reddy kings of Kondaveedu. He was a great scholar and won laurels as the writer of commentaries on Amaruka and Gadhasapthasati. Sangitha Chintamani is full of details of Vadya, Nritta and Geetha styles. Only 6,000 slokas on Vadya and Nritta are available. Unfortunately, the last chapter on geetha is missing.

Abhinaya Bhushanamu is by **Sringara Sekhara**, who belonged to Warangal. His guru was Veerabhallata. They were two important personalities among the panditas that adorned the Asthana of Prataparudra of Kakatiya dynasty. He has dealt with the Pratyangas of human body in 1000 slokas. Because it was very popular in Tamilnadu, there appeared a commentary on this text in Tamil language.

Bhartardha Chandrika is by one **Parvathi**. Her time is not known, she has given description of various Mudras and this is evident from the Bharatarnava of Nadikeswara.

Sahitya Darpana is by **Viswanadha** the later works of Dattila and Kohala are not available some of the extracts of the second are to be found in the commentaries of Sangitha Ratnakara. From his commentary on the last chapter of Sangita Ratnakara his knowledge and efficiency is to be found.

The Hindu Grammarian **Panini** (500 BC) mentioned about a treatise called **Nata–Sutras** composed by two experts by name Silalin and Krisasva that contained rules and principles of dance, for the guidance of "Nata" (sutra means string).

Between the 6th and 10th century AD, unfortunately, no single treatise on dance survived.

A brother of Saluva Timmaraju and a Dwara Palaka during Devaraya–II by name **Gopendra Tipparaju** wrote **Tala Deepika**, a famous text on tala lakshana and also another text on dance out of dedication to Lord Shiva. During the time of Mallikarjuna Devaraya (1446-1465 BC) Chatura Kallinadha wrote Kalanidhi, a commentary on Sangita Ratnakara and it is one of the well–known writings of Vijayanagara empire. This text is known to be more famous than the one written by Sarvagna Singa Bhupala.

In India, so to say dance and drama commenced as plays or acts of god and continued to be so. Audiences were presented with high and noble ideals and themes which provoked them to the fear of god.

The body is used for display of noble thoughts about divinity.

An important treatise on the subject gives, 14 gestures of the head, 24 single handed and 30 combined 5 moments of the bosom, 5 of the sides, 5 of the waist, 5 of the shoulders, 9 of the neck, 16 of the arms, 4 of the belly, 5 of the thighs, 10 of the forelegs, 7 of the knees, 5 of the wrist, 13 of the feet. So minute and accurate is the analysis of the expressive powers of the human body.

The aesthetic value or artistic content is sought to be achieved through the human body and gestures, movements rhythms and sentimental expressions. In ancient treatises on dance, no single part of the body is left off.

As early as in 3rd century Bharata gave to the world his rasa theory. In the 9th century Acharya Anandavardhana, who was the state pandit in the court of Anantavarma of Kashmir, Abhinavagupta another Kashmir Pandit of the 10 century who wrote Dwanyalokam are the two scholars and theoreticians who promulgated aesthetics of Indian Dance.

Acharya Anandavardhana wrote a beautiful commentary on Dwanyalokam called 'Lochava' and another commentary on Bharata's Natya Sastra called 'Abhinava Bharati' which brought him immortal fame.

Sangita Muktavali

Belonging to Vijayanagar period, we have two works by authors having same name, one dealing more fully with theory, and the other with practice. The works are called by the name Sangita Muktavali and the authors are called by the name Devendracharya.

Sangita Makaranda: By Vedasuri

A good account of all surviving items in tradition are contained in Sangita Makaranda of Vedasuri a court dance master of Shahji, the father of Shivaji, these great compilations follow the standard treatises that already existed in Nrtya and Nrtta and describe the tradition as they existed at the time of the authors. Among these standard treatises there is Nrtya Sastra which contains 36 chapters and rules our 6000 verses in addition to prose passages.

The earliest tradition is preserved in the text by name Adi Bharatha said to have been described by Parama Siva to Parvati. We have five recessions of this work consisting of 200 to 300 slokas. Preserved in the Saraswati Mahal Library, Tanjore with Telugu explanations of a lengthy chapter they must be assigned to the period of our cultural renaissance under the Nayaks of Vijayanagar.

Hala's Gadha Saptasati : Description of all classical dances of Andhra Pradesh is found in Hala's Saptasati. It is believed to have been written somewhere between 200 BC and 200 AD.

Palkuriki's Panditharadhya Charitra and Basavapuranam : We find many references to dance and some belonging to the 12th Century in the above two texts.

Nritha Ratnavali of Jayappa Senani, is regarded as another authoritative work on dancing, which is a rich contribution of Andhra's to this great art. He is credited to have brought out an equally authoritative text on music by name Sangita Ratnavali but unfortunately, it is found missing.

Palnati Vira Charitra-Srinadha

This describes about 'Kanjalochana' a courtesan in the Royal Court of Nalagamaraja. Our other historical works are full with references to dance halls, dancers like Lakuma Devi of Kondavidu, and Machala Devi of Warangal.

Kridabhiramam : This first literary work in Telugu mentions about several types of dances.

Between the 11th and 14th Century AD a number of Andhra commentators added to the wealth of literature on dance and these included Nanyadeva, Bhoolokamalla, Kumaragiri Reddy, Pedakomati Vema Reddy, Lollu Bhattu, Singabhupala and Mallinadha.

(Kuchipudi Classical Dance by M.A. Naidu, p. 2)

Rasamanjari by **Bhanudatta Misra** deals with Sringara Rasa and this is also very popular in Andhra Desa. That is why Lasya which is graceful dance, is the main characteristic of Kuchipudi style.

The Natya Sastra written about, 3000 years ago or even earlier by **Adi Bharata**, also known as **Sada Siva Bharata**, contained 36,000 slokas. This ancient treatise also the later abridged edition of 17,000 slokas known as Brahma Bharata are unfortunately not available. (Sri. Vissa Appa Rao–Kuchipudi Natya Sadassu Utsava Sanchika 1959.)

Rasarnava Sudhakara of Singabhupala is an important work on Dramaturgy produced in Andhra. Later writers refined, classified and added some more ideas, to the traditionally handed down from Bharata.

Sringara Rasamanjari is an unpublished Telugu manuscript containing 100 Movva Gopala padas composed by **Kshetragna**, Prof. Vissa Appa Rao says as follows on this script.

"The name of the work is not mentioned in the manuscript. Sri Prabhakara Sastry told me that the MSS was one among those obtained from Venkatagiri Samsthanam.

The MSS is a Lakhsana Grandha on Alankara. It is a free and correct translation into colloquial Telugu prose of Kaviratna Bhanudatta Misra's Rasamanjari, a well known standard work on alankara written about 1560 AD. I compared the original Sanskrit text; 'Rasamanjari' with commentary called 'Vyaavardha Kaumudi' written by Ananta Bhatta–upto a third of the book line by line and the rest of it here and there. I find it to be a correct translation of text. It also brings out the important points discussed in the commentary.

Sanskrit text gives the Lakshanas of Nayakas and Nayakis in great detail and illustrates each Lakhshana by a sloka. The Telugu manuscript does not illustrate the lakshanas by translating the slokas. Instead, Movva Gopala is quoted under each lakshana as Lakshyas. There are nearly 160 Lakshanas in all and 230 padams as lakshyas. A few of them are padams of Sarangapani.

His patron is Kattamuri Bussa Nripala, who encouraged the author to translate Bharata's Sastra into Telugu and it has the honour of being the first in the field. The book is in Telugu verse (Prose) and is dedicated to Sri. Ramachandra, the presiding deity of Kasaluru.

Prof. Appa Rao says "I have not yet been able to locate Kasaluru, nor been able to identify Kattamuri Bussa Appa Rao".

An unpublished MSS was drawn by Sri Veturi Prabhakara Sastry and I had a copy made of it at Tirupati, from the Madras Govt. Oriental MSS library. I also understand that there is also another MSS in Tanjore palace MSS library.

Subba Rama Dikshitar mentions about **'Raga Tala Chintamani'** as a standard work on music, as found in the preface to Sangita Sampradaya Pradarsini, the MSS is divided into 5 chapters. The style is elegant and attractive. The MSS with the elements of important topics of Bharata Sastra, mainly of music. All the standard treatises on Bharata Sastra are in Sanskrit and hence not easily understood by the non-professionals interested in music. This Raga Tala Chintamani, will be very useful as an introduction to the study of music, to all general readers who can understand the language. It is highly desirable to publish their work.

Padas of Kshetragna

Kshetragna is reputed to have written 4,100 Padams. Out of them, 2000 were composed in the court of Tirumalendra of Madhura, 1000 in the court of Achutha Vijaya Raghava of Tanjore and 1100 in the court of Golconda Padusha by name Abdulla Kutubsha. Most of them are not available only a few with Achutha Raghava are to be found. He seems to have composed some on Tipaki Krishna, Commander under Abdulla Kutubsha. But the padas most famous are those dedicated to Gopaladeva of Movva, a small village in Challapalli

Samsthanam of Krishna District. They are called Movva Gopala Padas.

200 of these Padas were published by Vavilla Ramaswamy Sastri & Sons. Another printed book published nearly 50 years back, contains 20 more Movva Gopala Padas. The MSS Sringara "Rasamanjari" quotes 100 more padas with Movva Gopala Mudra. This makes up to a total of 320 only.

It is very interesting to note that Kshetragna's Padams illustrate exactly all the lakshanas of various types of Nayakis, detailed by Bhanudatta Misra. This cannot be mere accident. This must have been well designed and composed with a specific purpose of illustrating Bhanudatta Misra's Theory.

So, the MSS, Sringara Rasamanjari throws flood light on the important aspect of Kshetragna's eminent place in Telugu land on Alankara. His padas have literary merit of a high standard.

There is another text called **"Dakshayaga Bharani"** of 12th century belonging to the time of Kulothunga. It is a dance drama which starts with Sourashtra raga. It can be presumed that in those days, they followed only one style throughout south India, to bring about integration and cultural synthesis. The play ended with "Mangalam Maha Sri Sri".

Sugreeva Vijayamu by **Gunarudrakavi** is another drama available. It also ends with "Mangalam Maha Sri Sri", for which Sri Veturi Prabhakara Sastry garu, wrote foreword.

There is another palm leaf text by name **"Garuda Chala Vilasam"** a **yakshagana** by **Obayya Manthri**. It also starts with Sourastra Ragam, Aditalam.

"Patita Jagada dhara–aganita Bhavadura

Narahari chatura daitya vidara

Garudachala vihara"

The stanza speaks of the style of those days.

Original texts like Vasanthika Parinayam and Koravanji Natakam were written to preach religious sentiments.

There is a palm leaf text in Saraswati Mahal, Tanjore by **Ramakanta Sastry**, who wrote **Sita Kalyanam** in Prakrit. It was at the time of Pratapa Simha. The written script is in Telugu. Some details about characters and those who enacted are given as follows.

1. Chikkaji Nayaka -Ahobilam Sundaram
2. Dasaradha Maharaja -Rangayya
3. Sumanta -Seshudu
4. Lakshmana Vesham -Kannayya
5. Rama Vesham -Venkatachalam
6. Kousalya -Subba Rayalu
7. Sakhi Vesham -Peddi Vaiddi
8. Narada -Seshachalam Subbaiah.

I could come across a book edited by the Telugu pandit of Saraswati Mahal Tanjore, titled "Sabdam alias Tala Solkattu of Bharatam Kasinadhuni Kavi, King Shahaji and Naromakavi.

Mannaru Dasa Vilasamu is a great composition by a woman called **Rangajamma** and Vijaya Raghava arranged Kanakabhishekam in her honour.

The celebrated poem **"Sri Krishnamrutha"** was written by the poet Leela Suka. Krishna Leela Tarangini was a dance drama written in Sanskrit by **"Tirdha Narayana Yathi"**.

Parijathapaharanam of Siddhendrayogi who was a great scholar in Sanskrit and Telugu besides his expertise in dance and music, there seems to be some difference between steps and Jativinyasa.

Thus, dance was considered to be a good poetic expression of life's several moods. It speaks through many rythmic patterns, melodious gestures and facial expressions, that is why, all forms of dance are highly placed in society, with all the religious sanctity.

The princes of Dasakumara charita are described to have learnt playing on Veena. Some of them were even proficient in vocal music.

Gona Buddareddy in his **Ranganadha Ramayana** describes a dance performance in the following words : "Dressed in golden sarees, women grouped together, played kolatas, performed perani dances. They danced in *Golal, Charini, Sradhri, Gurjara,* and *Desi* styles in different groups. Buddha refers to dancing girls as experts in music and dances, who could dance in Sudha Marga, singing *Sama Gana* and to a dance by some women, according to their Talagati, while their anklets, bracelets and beads produced fitting sound while some played mridanga while some others sang, still others played on the Veena" (History of Andhra Country–Subsidiary Dynasties by V. Yasoda Devi, pp. 51-56).

There are descriptions in **Kreedabhiramam**, which is supposed to be the first known text in Telugu. Gollasudulu, Tandavapadas, Devara Vandra Kadhas, Parasuramuni Kadhas stand in support of the statement that people were singing Tandava Janapadas, Veerabhatas singing Srungara Nadas and playing.

Treatises like Abhilashitardhachintamani of Somasekhara II, Nritta Ratnavali of Jayappa Senani, Vasantha Rajeeyamu of Kumaragiri Reddy and Sangita Chintamani of Pedakomati Vema Reddy bear testimony to the many forms of music and dance which were prevalent in Telugu land under the distinguished guidance of many Brahmin Natyacharyas.

Kreedabhiramam mentions about several types of dances.

Lola Lakshmidhara, who luckily got the royal patronage of Krishna Devaraya and also of Veera Rudra Gajapathi of Orissa, wrote a commentary on **Soundarya Lahari** and in the long 'Gadya' he mentions about his ancestor by name Virinchi Misra, who wrote a great text on dramaturgy by name **Bharatarnava Kapotha**.

Dr. Bhandarkar, in his "Early History of Deccan" says that the reason why the result of the Aryan irruption was so different in south India from what it was in north, appears to be that when the Aryans penetrated to the south, there existed already well organized communities and Kingdoms.

Sir Henry Johnston in his "Living Races of Mankind" tells that even uncultured Dravidians like Todas and Kurumbas have got their own songs and dances and that the interest was not created newly.

Among the Reddy rulers of Kondaveedu, there are many authors, who wrote treatises on dance. The foremost among them is king **Kumara Giri Reddy** (1386–1402 AD) who wrote a valuable Natyasastra called **"Vasantha Rajeeyamu"** on his own alias name Vasantaraja, no manuscript in the art of dance can be understood. At the time of Sri Krishna Devaraya (1509–1530) a Natyacharya by name **Banda Lakshmi Narayana Pandit**, taught dance to the women of Royal palace and he wrote **"Sangita Suryodaya"**. There is a chapter on dance and he makes several references to Saranga Deva and Kohala and their writings. Kataya Vema his brother-in-law, who is also a commentator on Kalidas's commentary on Prabodha Chandrodaya Mallindadha on Magha and his son Kumara Swami on the Pratapa Rudriya made references to the famous work.

Kumaragiri's Successors, Pedakomati Vema wrote Sangita Chudamani

Most distinguished among Recharla Kings was Simha Bhupala, who gave us not only Rasarnava Sudhakara, on Rasa and Dance but also Sangita Sudhakara, a commentary on Sangita Ratnakara.

The first Telugu poet Nannechoda, in his Kumara Sambhava, describes Vasantotsava and the items exhibited. Nannechoda described Nritya of Rambha and also lasya Nritya of Rati Leela Vijaya.

Chetura Damodara who wrote **Sangita Darpana** also seems to be a Telugu Pandit. In one of the chapters, he mentioned about Nritya and in the last chapter, he tells about Nritta in detail.

There is another famous text called, **Sangita Muktavali** by **Devandra**. This is another great work on dramaturgy in Telugu land.

Raghunadhaabhyudayam printed in the Model Printing Press and by Andhra Sahitya Parishad and carrying a foreword by Sri Mallampalli Somasekhara Sharma, a well-known historian is found in the Saraswati Mahal and it is dated 22nd December 1932.

In the Rajya Sabha of Vijaya Raghava, Nattuva Roudra (Courtesans) were exhibiting their Natyavidya Vaidushya and it is evident from Rajagopala Vilasam of Kalakavi. They were all experts in Natya and Abhinaya.

Towards the end of 17th Century, **Parijatha Yakshagana Prabandha of Purijala Lakshmi Narayana Kavi**, speaks of men enacting women characters. There is a discussion between Satya and Sakhi about this proposal whether men can act as women characters. Why he spoke about this is not known but it may be presumed that perhaps it was a topic for discussion in those days.

But Cheru Belagallu inscription of 1514 talks about 'patni' daughter of Timmayya in Tanjikonda Nataka. Some also draw conclusions from the writings of Sreenadha about "Bhagothula Buchigadu" *Pendyala Nagi* and *Gangi* that there might have been some human participants in the troupe of 'Bhagothula Buchigadu' but there is a controversy about it. The above description is of Rama Kavi of the 18th century but not of Sreenadha (Preface to Kreedabhiramam by Sri Veturi Prabhakara Sastry, pp. 68-69).

Kuchi Manchi Jagga Kavi of 18th Century in his **Rekhavilasam** describes about "Bhagavathulu" from the description of "Adu Bhagavathuni Jada, Gaddamu, Muthi Nunnaga Gori Ginchu Kunnadu" it may be concluded that men were enacting the characters of women.

But there is evidence to show, that in the 19th century, women were participating in Veedhinatakas (Street Plays). "District Gazetteers" Visakhapatnam (page 130) says "Janaranjaka Natakamulo Streelupurushulu Veshamulu Vesukoni Vinikidi Chesedivaru" (women and men used to attire and used to give performance to the appreciation of all).

In the first half of the 19th Century a village officer (Grama Karanam) of Pedakandla Village of Atmakur Taluq, Nellore Dist., by name Swamy Raja Kavi used to invite 'Natamelas' and to provide suitable conditions for their happy living and give dresses and training to give performances of his Yakshaganas and out of them "Gonudinne Buggasani" used to act as Nayika (heroine) on his order.

Prof. Gulam Yazdani in his masterly survey of Deccan Art (10 to 13 AD) observes "Grace of poise, suppleness of limbs, sense of movement, the elegance of minute ornamentation are the salient features of the sculptors of this period."

The thousand pillared temple at Hanuma Konda is another great architectural triumph of Kakatiya period. It has been constructed by King Rudra Deva (12th Century) situated in spacious grounds with amazing skill and mastery. Rudreswara temple has various poses of dances and musical instruments.

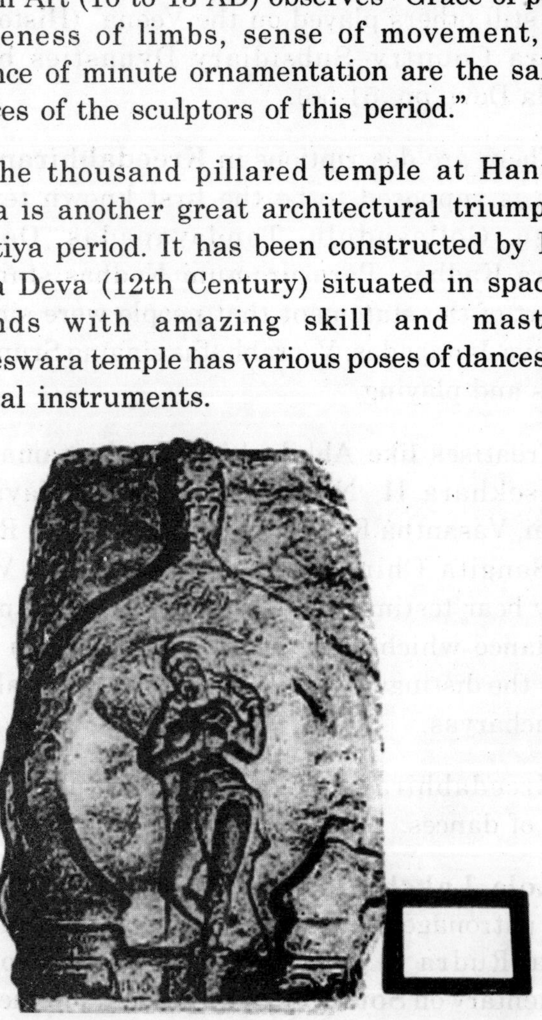

Marco Polo, an Italian traveller, visited Andhra at the time of Rudramamba and wrote an excellent account of what all he saw in Andhra.

Bracket figures on Ramappa temple are gracefully carved and marvelously chiselled. These figures represent dancing artists in different postures.

Thus, every temple, and every text, and every sculptural pose of dancers speak of the genius of our people and the creativity and their imagination.

Commentaries

The following are the best known commentators on Natya Sastra-Lollata, Udbhata, Sankuka, and the most famous of the Abhinavagupta. There is mention of a Bhashya and a Vartika, besides a Natya Sastra. This system of assigning sutras, Bhashyas and vartikas is common to all systems of Indian Philosophy. Hence the same has been introduced in the Natyadarsana also. Unfortunately our knowledge about these works except that of Abhinavagupta is very scanty.

Commentators

(a) *Nanyadeva.* He is reputed to be the Bhasyakara in this system. He has been quoted by Abhinavagupta and other early commentors.

(b) *Bhatta Lollata.* He lived in the 8th Century. (Abhinava Gupta has quoted him often).

(c) *Sankuka.* This commentator also has been quoted by Abhinava Gupta many times. He has been identified as the author of the poem Bhuvanabhyudaya. He flourished in the period of the Kashmirian king Ajitapida who ruled during 813-815 A.D.

(d) *Udbhata.* Abhinava has referred to his opinions a few times, possibly he is identical with the Alamkarika of the same name.

(e) *Bhattanayaka.* He is the author of Hridaya Darpana a work on the Dhvani theory and can be placed between 9th and 10th centuries. Abhinava Gupta makes respectful mention of this commentator.

(f) *Bhattayantra.* He has been mentioned by Abhinava Gupta. Nothing more is known about this author too.

(g) *Acharya Kirtidhara.* He probably flourished in the sixth century. He might have been a very early commentator. He is respectfully remembered by Abhinava Gupta.

(h) *Abhinavagupta.* He seems to be the same person as the celebrated author of the learned treatise on Kashmirian Saivism; and also the commentary on dhwanyaloka. His age is established in between 10th and 11th centuries. He is also known as Nrisimhagupta too. Inspite of some weak points such as faulty explanations here and there, this commentary has some additional value. It has got many quotations from a vast number of dramatic and other works. Serious students of Indian poetics, aesthetics and dramaturgy are sure to be profited by the thorough perusal of this commentary. Philosophical topics have given to the work a peculiar charm.

The Text of Natya Sastra

The work available now under the name of Natya Sastra of Bharata Muni contains about five thousand and six hundred verses. There is a shorter version with a reduction of nearly two hundred verses. Both the recensions possess great antiquity; which one is the earlier we cannot say. The problem of the relationship between different recensions of all ancient works cannot be solved this way or that way in an off hand manner. The very fact that the longer recension has more verses may be intentional or unintentional; scribes must have blundered by omitting verses here and there. Use of different meters *etc.* cannot be adduced as reasons for priority or posteriority.

Bharata is reputed to be the author of this work. Originally the word Bharata was used in the sense of an actor in a drama. The treatise dealing with the activities of Bharata are intended as a guide to him and this came to be called Bharatasastra. Later on the compound word began to signify the sastra propounded by Bharata. Bhavabhuti the dramatist is probably the first man to mention about Bharata Muni as the author and he calls him Tauryatrikasutrakara.

Contents

A mere perusal of the contents of the work will convince anyone for the variety of the topics discussed in it. Its principal theme is the dramatic art. It concerns the producers of the plays and also those who compose them, but Bharata wants the plays to be a Drusya kavya that can be successfully and profitably represented on the stage. This vital relationship between the literary and the technical aspects of a play has been analysed by him and justice has been done to both. The dramatic theory as well as practice has been elaborately dealt with. Hence manual gestures, facial expressions, poetics music, with all ramifications whether vocal or instrumental, prosody some points of grammar, costumes, ornaments, setting up of the scenes with proper background *etc.* have been thoroughly dealt with.

Style

The style of the author is simple but sometimes the technical details cannot be easily understood without a commentary or the exposition of an experienced sponsor of plays. In the main the work is in small Anustup slokas and some in Arya Meter. There are prose passages also. The author has treated the subject matter very analytically and not to hesitate to repeat the things mentioned earlier in order to be more specific. A technical treatise aiming at meticulous completeness can avoid diffuseness only at the sacrifice of clarity. The traditional practitioners of dance, music, drama etc have preserved the rules successively handed down from teacher to the pupil.

Cultural Projection

In addition to the topics relevant for the dramatic art, many other things to understand the various landmarks in the cultural history of India are found included in Natya Sastra :

(i) ***Linguistic:*** Prakrita and allied native languages are thoroughly dealt with by means of examples. References have been made to the languages of ancient tribes such as Barbaras, Kiratas, Andhras, Dravidas, Sabaras, Candalar *etc.*

(ii) ***Literary:*** Beautiful verses of very fine literacy excellence have been given by way of examples, while dealing with Dhruva songs, meters *etc.* In many of these verses we find the innate charm divested of all the artifices and linguistic thickeries of the later classical age. Rasas, Bhavas, Alankaras *etc.* are portrayed well.

(iii) ***Arts and Crafts:*** Dance is inseparable from drama. Bharata has done full justice to it. The various Abhinayas mentioned herein have been portrayed by mural paintings, sculpture, architecture *etc.* in our temples. Various crafts are brought into play to create a suitable background on the stage in different scenes.

(iv) ***Costumes and Ornaments:*** Chapter 23 gives detailed directions about the dressing material, modes of wearing the garments and jewellery, articles to be used by the different characters in a play in accordance with their social status, profession, the cult practiced *etc.* Naturally this has great significance in the understanding of the social life in those distant times.

(v) ***Mythological and Legendary Figures:*** Natya Sastra mentions mythological figures starting from the lowest stratum such as the Uragas, Patangas, Bhutas, Rakshasas, Asuras *etc.* and ending with the gods and goddesses of the Hindu Pantheon; the Daityas, Danavas, Guhyakas, Astadikpalakas, Gandharvas, Apsaras, Asvins, Manmatha, Rudra, Visvadevas, Brihaspati, Narada, Tumburu, Rishis Mantradrastas, Brahma, Vishnu, Shiva, Lakshmi, Chandika, Saraswati *etc.*

A prominent omission is of Ganesha and Avatars of Vishnu.

(vi) ***Geographical Details:*** In the chapters 14, 18 and 23 there are references to cities and rural regions such as Anga, Antagiri, Andhra, Avanta, Kharta, Anarta, Usinara, Odra, Kalinga, Kashmira, Kosala, Tamralipta, Tosala, Tripura, Dakshinapatha, Dravida, Nepala, Brahmottara, Magadha, Madraka, Maharashtra, Malava, Mahendra, Mosala, Vanga, Vatsa, Vartika, Vahlika, Videha, Surasean, Salaka etc, rivers and mountains such as Sindhu, Ganga, Carmavati, Mahendra, Malaya, Sahya, Himalaya, Vindhya *etc.*

(vii) ***Erotical, Psychological and Economical Sciences*** ***etc.:*** The necessity of learning the different sciences has been stressed in the Natya Sastra. The qualities mentioned to Sabhasatras (the members of the court hall) are exhaustive. (Readiness to work always, alertness, absence of indolence, affectionate feelings, forbearance, modesty, impartiality, training in polity, good manners and customs *etc.* (Ch. 34) It was also mentioned that knowledge of Psychology is essential for the successful portrayal of various emotions like Rasa, Bhavas *etc.*

Early Writers on Indian Drama and Dance

Panini the celebrated grammarian of the sixth century BC in his Astadhyayi (IV/3/110-111) mentions the Natasutras of Silalin and Krsasva. It is a pity that we do not possess the manuscript of these sutras. They may be manuals to the actors (Natas or perhaps sets of rules for dancers and pantomimists).

The sons of Bharata: In chapters 1-26 to 39 Natya Sastra there is an enumeration of the hundred sons of Bharata. Some of these could have been authors of works on dramaturgy, histrionics, dance, music and other allied topics. The following viz: Kohala, Dattila, Salikarna, Badarayana, Nakhakutta, Asmakutta and a few others have been quoted by later writers as their predecessors in the field of dramaturgy and histrionics. Unluckily these references alone are our source of knowledge of these writers.

(a) ***Kohala:*** In chapters 36-38 of Natya Sastra it is mentioned that Kohala in his Uttara Tantra (later Compendium). A commentary of Abhinavagupta and in the Bhavaprakasam of Saradatanaya there are references to the effect that Kohala wrote on dance, dramaturgy, histrionics and music.

(b) ***Dattila (Dantila, Dhurtila)*** is quoted by Abhinava Gupta. He was an author on histrionics and music.

(c) ***Sandilya and Vatsya (NS 36/75)*** are referred to herein as successors of Bharata for the propagation of the art of dramatic performance. If at all they had written any treatise it is lost to us.

(d) ***Satakarni (Salikarna):*** A reference to him is found in the Natakaratna–kota of Sagaranadin. Hence he might have been a writer on dramaturgy. It is possible that he is the king Satakarni mentioned in some inscriptions around the last years of B.C. and early period of AD. Kings and persons of royal descent were interested in fine arts, many had written works on dance and dramaturgy *etc.*

(e) ***Asmakutta and Nakhakutta:*** These two writers have been quoted by Sagaranandin and Visvanatha the author of Sahityadarpana. Bahurupa a commentator on Dasarupaka mentions about Nakhakutta. They were probably writers on dramaturgy.

(f) ***Badarayana:*** He is quoted by Sagaranandin. Further, another mentioned by him as Badari may be the same. These two are reputed writers on Vedanta philosophy too.

(g) ***Sangrahakara:*** In Natya Sastra VI/10 a Natyavedasangraha is referred to,

Abhinava Gupta and mentions a Sangrahakara. This treatise might have dealt with dramaturgy and histrionics.

Later Writers

Agnipurana and Vishnudharmottara: These two works contain elaborate explanations of various topics connected with Natya, Nritya, Rasa, Abhinaya *etc.*, they are not early works as the name Purana may lead us to suppose. Much of what is contained in Natya Sastra are reproduced therein.

Later Original Writings on Drama: It will not be out of place hereto mention briefly some writers who have acknowledged their indebtedness to Bharata but were not commentators. They are Dhananjaya, Ramachandra, Gunachandra, Ruyyaka, Saradatanaya, Kaviratna and Singhabhupala.

Dhananjaya: He is known to have flourished in the last years of 10th century A.D. during the reign of Vakatairaja of Malava. More than half of the chapter 20 of Natya Sastra deals with his work. Dhananjaya in his Dasarupaka elaborates on this topic. Of course some relevant connected topics too are dealt with. A noteworthy feature is his omission of histrionics and similar technical aspects of dramatic performance. He lays emphasis on the literary aspect of the drama. What we can conclude from this is that by his time the popularity of Sanskrit dramas had dwindled and only scholars took special interest therein, more as literary pieces than Drisya the playright and producer of plays was forgotten by Dhanjaya though his veneration for Bharata is eulogistically acknowledged. As far as dramaturgy is concerned Dasarupa seems to have superseded even Natya Sastra later on. It supplanted all other works on dramaturgy in due course of time. Later writers like the author of Sahityadarpana, *i.e.* Visvanatha Kaviraja benefited by the explanations in this work.

Sagaranandin: He is the author of Natakalalaksana ratnakosa, the manuscript of which was first discovered in 1922 in Nepal by Sylvian Levi. Later in 1937, M. Dhillion edited it and published it from London. Besides dramaturgy, histrionics and allied topics are dealt with. In the course of his work he acknowledges his indebtedness to many of the earlier writers on the dramatic art, especially Natya Sastra which he quotes verbatim or paraphrases.

Ramachandra and Gunachandra: They are collaborators of the work named Natyadarpana. Both of them were the disciples of the celebrated rhetorician Ramachandra. They lived between 1100 and 1178. Natya Sastra consists of four chapters in Anustup couplets. They themselves have written a Vitti (gloss) in prose elucidating difficult passages. Dasarupaka is subjected to serve as criticism which is its unique value bordering on superiority over Dasarupaka.

Ruyyaka: He is otherwise known as Ruchaka. He was a Kashmirian Pandit of the 12th Century. Various aspects of poetics have been elaborated by him in his works, the chief of which is the commentary on the Vyaktiviveka of Mahimabhatta. In this later work he mentions that he was the author of Natakamimamsa, a work on dramaturgy which has so far not been discovered.

Saradatanaya was a Daksinatya scholar who flourished in the 12th century. His Bhavaprakasana is Illuminator of Bhavas (mental emotions and fervour) is a more detailed work on dramaturgy than Dasarupaka and Natyadarpana. His preceptor Divakara is mentioned as the Director of a theatre. Hence the practical aspects of dramatic performances as obtaining during his days have been expatiated in this work. Despite his indebtedness to the earlier writers his approach to the topics can be said to be very original in shedding light from fresher angles of vision. To be brief, it can be said that Saradatanaya's treatment of the subject is more comprehensive than that of the Dasarupaka, Natakalasana, and Natyadarpana. He mentions many of the earlier writers both as authorities for his views as well as the objects of his critical remarks.

Visvanatha Kaviraja: He flourished in the 13th century. His Sahityadarpana deals with all branches of literature. The sixth chapter deals with drama. He has drawn materials from Natya Sastra–Dasarupaka and its commentary Avaloka.

Singhabhupala: His Natakaparibhasa is known only by name. But Rasarnavasudhakara treats of drama in the closing sections.

References

1. Dance Dramas of India and The Past by Bharata Iyer.
2. Bhavam, Ragam, Talam, Natyam by Ravindra-nath.
3. Dance as Text Ideologis of the Barotve body by Marco Franco.
4. G.K. Bhat (Bhandarker Oriental Research Institute, Pune (1983) Hindu dances 1983 (Nrityanjali) by Sri Ragini–Smit Publications.

Donor couple (dampati) at the right of the left-hand entrance of the facade of the chaitya at Karla. Satavahana, first century A.D.

7

Dance in Ancient India

During the Vedic age, dance became a part of the rituals, to win the favours of God. The apsaras, the Gandharvas, were treated as masters of dance and music. The Vedic references of dance clarify the glaring fact that dance existed even before drama.

The earliest reference to dance appears in Rigveda, while describing *Ushas* (Dawn) as revealing beauty like a dancer, removing the garment in the form of darkness. Here Ushas is compared to a 'danceuse'. Thus in the Vedic literature, the combination of vocal music, instrumental music and dance was known as 'Silpaka'. (Trividho Silpam Natyam Gitam Vaditrayam Ca).

'Nrityamano *Amratah*' is found as a reference for describing gods in Rigveda. In the Atharva Veda the word 'Nrt' is found (Yasyam Gayanti Nrityanti Bhumyam Mastyam" (Pridhvi Sukta 12-1-41) the words "Nritta", "Gita" are used often as "Nritya Sutam Gitaya Sailusam" (Vajasaneya Samhita XXXV).

The ritual dance of "Taittariya Samhita" is found again in other parts such as "Tandya Brahmana (V. 6) Aitareya Aranyaka, Boudhayana, Srautasutra, Apastambha Srautasutra. Minimum number of dancers were three and in some cases there were six or eight. Many carried pots on their heads and tapped right thighs and recited: "Ehavya, ehavya, ehavya Idam Madhuma Idam Madhu" (Aitareya Aranyaka) (>A).

Natya Veda

The origin of Indian dance is ascribed to Vedas and is known as *panchamaveda.* Natyaveda or the science of dramaturgy. God Brahma, the creator, selected speech and lyrical matter such as hymns, and prayers, dialogues between the Gods. The histrionic expressions of gestures known as *Abhinaya* from Yajurveda, musical part from Samaveda and the aesthetic *flavour* or *Rasa,* which contains emotional element from the Atharvaveda. Brahma, thus mixing up all the above four factors formed *Natya* or Arama and attached to it, the dignity, purity and sanctity of the other four Vedas. And elevated it to the high status of science.

"The art and religious thought seek the same end and the Hindu allegorical concept of divine aspects of dance really represent the manifold activities of God". (Eanakshi Bhavanani-the dance in India, p. 5).

The Dance

Thus in India, all forms of art have a sacred origin and the inner experience of the soul found its highest expression in music and dance. The Hindu attitude towards art as an expression of inner beauty or that which is divine in man, brought it into close connection with religion.

The Aryans who were warriors, herdsman have sacred scriptures in holy form–Vedas said to be divine spiritual knowledge derived from the supreme, the self-existing god, orally transmitted by holy sages through constant repetition and later on committed to writing.

Though Vedic references are fragmentary, they shed light on the role of the dance in the daily life of Ancient Aryans.

The gods were described in Rig Veda as kicking up the dust of the atoms that formed the earth, while clasping each other in the dance. Devotees were said to be dancing in the same way. Among the craftsmen and artists required for Purushamedha rite (a symbolic vedic sacrifice of the primieval male called Purusha or Prajapati, Lord of creatures), the Sailusha (Actor–dancer) is mentioned in the scriptures (Vajasaneya Samhita, Yajur–Veda) were dances of men with breast plates and women dancing "robed in garments fair as heaven" are described.

Some Mythological Legends

The great god, Indra, was invoked in the Mahavratha sacrifice to bring down the rains.

Priests enchanted prayers and made offerings, while maidens danced with pots of water on their heads, encircling the sacred fire. An ancient myth relates the serpent–dragon Vritha coiled around the mountain peaks, held the heavenly waters captive in his belly. Indra hurled his thunder bolt and destroyed Vritha, releasing the pent-up waters that streamed down the mountains to nourish the earth.

Indra, overlord of the gods, was also the divine patron of arts. There were celestial singers (Gandharvas), musicians (Kinneras) and dancing nymphs (Apsaras) to entertain god, in heavenly court. The Apsaras are described as "Broad Hipped" slender–waisted, and graceful as "panthers". They were accomplished dancers, and divine courtesans.

One of the secular hymns of Rig Veda is a dialogue between the heavenly nymph 'Urvasi' and Prince Puruvavas. Urvasi lived with the prince for some time on earth and left him heartlessly. In the mythological legends, the Apsaras are the accomplices of the gods in bringing about the destruction of evil titans by dubious means.

Exploits of the gods and heroic deeds of men were told in poetic story form by the Nata (Actor–dancer) who made use of gestures, song and dance in his art of story telling. The Nata is described in the Vedas as changing his costume and painting himself.[1] Theatrical costumes and ornaments for male or female artists are also mentioned.

Thus dance is evolved as an activity of man. Facial expressions, hand gestures, movements of various limbs, were used as a means of expression even before the formation of language. Through singing and dancing expressed their happiness collectively.

Dance, in India, definitely has a specific sentimental background. The different dance styles practised today in different regions of India are different from one another in their exposition but they have a common origin. Of course, pre-historic dance was primitive. Rural India developed folk arts, that were exhibited during harvests and ceremonies but the fine arts in the classifical form are mainly due to the common objective and they are mainly contribution of Hindu religion. The subjects they deal with are supported by Hindu thought, philosophy and mythology.

To please nature, various modes of worship came into existence. Vedas prescribed particular spirits to denote specific directions and purposes. The worship of dikpalakas, concept of heaven, the emergence of trimurthis of *srusti, stithi* and *laya,* all induced men, to express their thoughts in a very aesthetic manner. Thus literature, dance, music and drama became synthesizing factors which are inseparable from one another.

Ancient Indian dance was not only an expression of intoxicated energy or as an entertainment but as an image of activity of God. Our artists have identified beauty with the infinite glory of God and so the expression of beauty has been religious in nature. Dance was part of the worship of duty.

In *Shiva Manasa Puja,* we come across a Sloka "Oh Lord! Please accept my Pooja which I am offering to you with great determination and with an umbrella, with the waving of the two chamaras, from each side, *Pure Naivedya veena bheri* (a kind of flute) mrudanga song and dance, with praises by bowing down prostrate in front of you".

Temples became elaborate structures with a "*Nata Mantapa*" as an integral part. A temple without its group of dancers and musicians was inconceivable. The dancers were mainly Devadasis or maidens dedicated to the service of God. Temple sculptures testify to this practice. References are also found in Sanskrit dramas and kavyas about temple dancers.

In the *Meghadootam* Kalidasa describes the dances in Mahakaleswar Temple at Ujjain as follows, "It is said that the teachers of these Devadasis were a class of Brahmins who were expert musicians and dancers attached to the temples. They were also excellent narrators and story tellers and used to interpret the incidents of Ramayana, Mahabharata and the Puranas with gestures and music".

The art of dance has developed and flourished over the centuries primarily because apart from its aesthetic appeal, it had been a creative endeavour, which has not only sustained itself but which has also been a source of inspiration for other arts like literature, painting and sculpture.

Panini, in his work called *Astadhyayi,* (5th Century BC), Patanjali in his *Mahabhasya* specify the fact that dance and drama flourished during this period. Two other authors Silali and Krisala have elaborately discussed about the principles for the actors, known as *Natasutras,* unfortunately this work is not available now.

The earliest systematic work on the subject is Bharata's Natya Sastra, though we hear some names like Silali, Krisasya, Tandu, Brahma, Vasuki, Narada, Vyasa and Anjaneya.

The oldest Natyasastra, according to the work "*Yamalastaka Tantra*" is reported to have contained 36,000 stanzas. Sarada Tanaya, in his *Bhava Prakasana* (13th Century AD) mentions that a Natya Sastra containing 12,000 stanzas had been abridged by Bharata to 6,000 stanzas, for the convenience of study (P.S.R. Appa Rao–A Monograph on Bharatas Natya Sastra, p. 4).

Abhinavagupta treated SadaSiva Brahma and Bharata as the earliest dramatologist, their treatise contained 36,000, 12,000 and 6,000 stanzas respectively. According to some critics, the treatise containing 12,000 stanzas was the contribution of one sage called *Adibharata*. In the subsequent period of Bharata the work of dramatology was taken up by writers like Dattila, Kohala, Silikarna and Badarayana. Dattila was the disciple and one of the hundred sons of Bharata and he is supposed to have written a more comprehensive work on music (4th Century AD). Works of those writers are not available. Only their names and some of their views are mentioned in later works.

Next to Bharata's Natyasastra, the credit of writing on dramatology goes to Nandikeswara (5th Century AD). His two works *Abhinayadarpana* and *Bharatarnava* are of great importance. It is believed that Lord Siva taught Natyasastra, *i.e.*, pure dance containing Karanas and Angaharas with great tempo to Tandu to spread pure dance on earth. Tandu taught this dance to Bharata and he made this style of dance popular.

There were other renowned dramatologists such as Kirtidhara and Matragupta whose original works are yet to be traced (P.S.R. Appa Rao–Monograph on Bharatas Natya Sastra, p. 4).

In course of time, many commentaries were written by various writers like Bhatta Lollata, Udbhata, Sankuka, Bhattanayaka, Utpala, Tutabhatta, Bhatenduraja and Abhinava Gupta (P.S.R. Appa Rao, p. 4). Abhinava Bharatarnava by Abhinavagupta (10th Century A.D.) is the only work available, in all these works, dance is treated on par with drama and music.

The works like Vishnu Dharmottara Purana and Agnipurana compiled in 7th and 8th century A.D. contain chapters on dancing. Someshwara's Manasollasa is great contribution of Karnataka–Sangita Ratnakara of Sarangadeva assigned to 13th century is a monumental treatise on music and dance (7th chapter on dance) Lasyaranjana by Simhabhupala, Sangita Chudamani are worth mentioning.

Origin of Dramatic Representation

The art of dramatic representation has as its originator Brahma and Bharata was his first disciple. The art of pure dance was originated by Lord Shiva and Tandu. Nandikeswara is his first disciple. So we have the work Bharatarnava[2] by Nandikeswara on Nritta or pure dance. This work is said to consist 11000 verses; though we have only 1200 verses available in all the oriental libraries.[3] This work contains chapters 1 to 9 and tells about several movements and poses for Nritta. Much of it is common ground with Natya Sastra. But the Pada Bhedas, Sthanakas and Charis are more numerous. Chapters 10-15 are the main body of the work and it deals with Nritta of various kinds. A notable feature in Nritta treated in Bharatarnava is that Nandikeshwara who predicts that there is a particular 'Rasa' in each item of pure dance as we have it in Abhinaya. Although the mudras in pure dance are intended only to add grace to the movements of the feet, and other parts of the body, and do not carry any idea, the total effect of the movements of the features and the expression in the eyes can be ordered as to produce an appeal to a particular Rasa. After postulating this aspect of pure dance, Nandikeswara proceeds to instruct the student of the art by a graduated series of items. First is given 27 elementary pieces, each consisting of a pose, a step and a look intended evidently to serve as an alphabet of pure dance with a Rasa.

Each Rasa has 2, 3, 4, or 5 forms, all the nine making up 27. These 27 simple pieces are curiously called by the name Ankahara which is used in a different sense by Bharata, namely, one of 32 finished pieces in the dance of Lord Siva, each consisting of 10 Karanas. Nandikeswar's Angahara is therefore different from the well-known 'Angahara'. After the simple pieces, combined

Srinivasa Kalyanam—by Sobha Naidu Troupe

pieces are next dealt with, in the subsequent chapters in a series. There are altogether some 55 items in the book. All these have gone out of use now.

After these two standard treatises, we do not have at present the later works of Dattila and Kohala pertaining to dance, though some extracts of the second are to be found in the commentaries of Sangita Ratnakara. We have however compilations from classical authorities that cover the whole ground of Dance. The most notable are Nrityadhyaya of Sangita Ratnakara, Nritta Ratnavali of Jayappa Senapati and Sringara Prakasa of Bhallata, all written about the 12th century.

There has been an attempt for a thorough systematization and reform about 1750 A.D. in Tanjore during the time of Pratapa Simha Raja. This movement appears to have been brought to a finished form during the time of Raja Serfoji of Tanjore. A number of dance masters appear to have taken part in this work of systematisation and the present compilation by Utake Govindachary is one of the bigger contributions towards that end. This compilation in Marathi is very useful to the students of dance.

References

1. Maitreyopanishad.
2. Bharatarnava by Nandikeshwara.
3. K.Vasudeva Sastry, Research pandit, Saraswati Mahal, Tanjore (p. 13).

8

Dance and Drama in Telugu Land

Let us now confine to the study of Andhra Desa as it will be a very big task to study entire Indian dance. "What can be called Kuchipudi, was connected with both literary writings of the medieval period, called the *Desi* (italics) form and the pure dance forms, which are closely associated with temple ritual and about which, there are ample literary, inscriptional and archaeological evidences. While the Devadasis performed in temples, the Kuchipudi Brahmin boys formed itinerant troupes in village courtyards. In the beginning, their stories revolved around Saiva puranas and after the great wave of Vaishnavism, the popular stories of Bhagawata Purana were given prominence. The performers were called Bhagavathulu".[1]

Mention of the classical dances of Andhra Pradesh, may be found in Hala's 'Gadha Sapta Sati', *i.e.*, before Christ. It is believed to have been written somewhere between 200 B.C. and 200 A.D.

In Palkuriki Somanadha's Panditharadhya Charitra and Basavapuranam, we find many references to dance, and drama. They are supposed to belong to 6th century.

Later on, Nritta Ratnavali of Jayappa Senani is regarded as an authoritative work on dancing and a rich contribution of Andhras, to this art. Jayappa Senani is credited with having brought out an equally authoritative text on music entitled Sangita Ratnavali but unfortunately, it is found missing. '*Palnati Veera Charitra*' by Srinadha describes about 'Kanjalochana' a courtesan, in the royal court of Nalagamaraja. Besides, our historical works are replete with references to dance halls, dances and dancers like Lakuma Devi off Kondavidu and Machala Devi of Warangal.

Kreedabhiramam mentions about several types of such dances.

Between the 11th and 14th century AD, a host of Andhra Pradesh commentators added to the wealth of already existing texts on dance and these included Nanyadeva, Bhoolakamalla, Kumaragiri Reddy, Pedakomati Vema Reddy, Lollu Bhattu, Singa Bhupala and Mallinadha.[2]

On the Pillars of Amaravathi and Nagarjuna Konda, on the temples of Bikkavolu, Palampet and Draksharamam and in the caves of Undavalli near

Vijayawada, are etched dance poses which are as ancient as they are exquisite.[3]

The classical dances of Andhra Pradesh at least as much as those of any other part of the country to Bharata's Natya Sastra. Andhra Classical dance also follows the four kinds of Abhinaya–Angika (Movement of the limbs), Vachika (Speech), Aaharya (Costume) and Satvika (emotions and facial expressions) laid down by Bharata.[4]

Abhinaya Darpana by Nandikeswara deals with Angikabhinaya. Rasamanjari by Bhanudatta Misra, which deals with Sringara rasa is also very popular in Andhra Pradesh. That is why 'Lasya; which means graceful dance, is the main characteristic of Kuchipudi style and other styles.

One school of thought believes that Indian dance began to lose its spiritual impact, long before the dawn of 1000 A.D. Eminent scholars concerned over this trend, according to this school, launched a movement to stem the root and that Kuchipudi was one of the centres where the movement was organized.[5]

Another school of thought holds the view that Kuchipudi was the starting point of a movement to restore 'Vachikabhinaya' to its due importance. This Abhinaya had increasingly been relegated to the background in the various dances of India. The latter view is reinforced by the fact that in Kuchipudi dance, the dancer renders in Vachikabhinaya while in other forms of Indian dance, it is the background.[6]

Long before Kuchipudi Brahmins adopted dance–drama and dance Solo as their profession, there existed dance–drama in folklore and classical dance as Nattavamela.[7]

Devadasis were performing 'Puja Nritya' on the Balipitham of temples.

Kuchipudi Bhagavatars refined and lifted the dance drama from folk to classical level and

dedicated themselves to the propagation of Madhura Bhakti, devotional love of God.[8]

It is a misnomer that is spread that Bharata spoke about Bharatanatyam only. The sacred sage spoke about all forms of classical dances prevalent in his times and codified only, in a systematic way, all the dance forms that existed then.

The only version is Bharata's Natya Sastra containing 6000 slokas. (Research scholars have assigned this sastra to the 3rd century BC).

"Coming to the present context in Bharata's Natya Sastra, the name 'Andhri' is mentioned as one of the regions of south India. A particular type of dance was being practiced and Bharata comments the kaisikivritti" delicate and graceful movement in the dance of this region. Geographically, the boundaries of Andhra are mentioned as the Venna river, the present Krishna and the Penna river, now in Nellore district. A particular raga, by name "Andhri" was the contribution of this race of people, to the music of India. Thus, we see that the Andhras developed even in the 3rd century BC, an individual idiom in dance and music".

We have further information, authentic and historical from various sources, about the dance tradition in Andhra Pradesh. The ancient temples of Andhra Pradesh, and the Buddhist ruins excavated at Nagarjuna Konda, Amaravati, Ghantasala, Jaggayyapeta and Bhattiprolu are the main sources, which were carved during the reign of Satavahana rulers of Andhra they also bear ample evidence of these; (2nd century BC) Amaravathi stupa relics are the most ancient.

Among the sculptural remains, safely preserved, I had the proud privilege of visiting Siddhendra Kalakshetra of Kuchipudi, which is on the way to Challapalli and 125 kms from Vijayawada.

"Further a critical examination of the elaborate description of the various types of dances given by Palkuriki Somanadha in Panditharadhya Charitra" show that an indigenous system of the art was prevalent in Andhra country during the Kakatiya period–the 12th and 13th centuries.

Evolution of Dance Tradition in Andhra
(Sculptural and Literary Evidences)

The history or antiquity of dancing in Andhra goes back to very early times. The dances of Amaravati, Nagarjuna Konda, are the testimonials to the 'Pindibandhas' or a group of dances mentioned by Bharata or elaborated by Abhinaya Gupta. The dancing figure of Nataraja at Mogala Rajapuram near Vijayawada is probably one of the earliest representations in south India. The verbal descriptions in the Sanskrit texts become concrete in the beautiful depictions in stone such as in Amaravati scene.

The forms of Nritya or Nritta can be dated to 3rd century AD. The early Chalukyan temples at Alampur, Satyavolu and Kalyana Chalukya temples at Nandikonda represent the great heritage of the dancing god Nataraja.

Besides the sculptural representations mentioned above the early literary works like *gadha sapta sati of Hala* (a Satavahana King) has many references to the art of dancing. In a verse, it is said "it is pleasant to spend the night with a gazette–eyed damsel, who is tired after a dance performance".

The important early work on dance, Abhinaya darpana, by Nandikeswara which can be dated to 5th century AD, deals with an elaborate description of Hasta Mudras, music and drama with a number of actors.

Between 6th century and 10th century AD, unfortunately no single treatise on dance survived. In the Virata Parva (11th century AD) of Andhra Mahabharata by Tikkana, there is a reference to some forms like Dandarasaka, Gundalini, Prenkhana, Prerana as practiced by Arjuna during his childhood days. In another extract in the same text Arjuna mentions to king Virata thus "I can teach your daughter the art of dancing. I am an expert in the dance form of Dandalasaka or (Dandarasaka), Kundalini, Prenkhana or (Prenkhana) and Perani. I can play several musical instruments. I know songs, srutis, Gatis and Abhinaya". Bruhannala taught Uttara, dance subsequently, and it is a well known story to all of us.

The period between the 12th and 13th centuries can be taken as the golden era in the history of dance, drama and music in Andhra Desa. The writers who dealt with the subject of dance are Palkuriki Somanadha, Srinadha, Jayappa, *etc.*, and their works set a standard to this divine art.

In Basava Purana and Panditharadhya Charitra of Palkuriki Somanadha, there are several references to music, dance and drama. The story of Mugdha Sangayya, who was an innocent devotee is interesting. He visits the house of a dancing girl, also a devotee who entertains him with a variety of dances performed by her maids. Another devotee called Natya Namuttanda misconstrues the dance posture of Nataraja to be a deformity of the limbs and tries to straighten them in vain. He then prays to the lord who teaches him the Tandava form of dance.

Somanadha in the same work refers to dance forms like Kolatta, Dandarasaka, Patra, of which we hear for the first time. There might have been some popular forms which found place in the above texts.

References

1. Andhra Sculptures–By Sri O.C. Ganguly (Calcutta).
2. Andhra Pradesh archeology-A review 1987-2001–By Deptt.–A & M, GM of AP, Hyderabad.
3. Sculptural Art of Andhra, By Dr. M.L. Nigam.
4. Sculptures from Amaravati (in the British Museum) by Doglas Barrett.
5. Yasstilaka and Indian Culture by K.K. Handiqi (No. 2 Raja Jina Samskriti Samrakshana Sangha, Sholapur.
6. A.L. Basham–The wonder that was India (New York, 1954).
7. Albert Grumwedd–Buddhist Art in India (London, 1901).
8. Stella Kram risch–Indian Sculpture (Calcutta, 1993).
9. Area–south Indian Buddhist–Antiquities. (Survey of India new imperial, service XV, Madras 1894).

Group of donors, Panel of bluish schist, Second or third century A.D. National Museum, Karachi The panel represents three men and three women offering flowers to the Buddha, Dressed in rich clothes, they must be of princely rank. The panel is one of the best of its kind. The type of costumes, reminiscent of Iran both in the cut and in the drapery, makes the second century the more likely date.

PART-II
CLASSICAL DANCE FORMS OF ANDHRA PRADESH

9

A Study of Epigraphical and Sculptural Wealth in Andhra

On a careful examination of epigraphical records from South India, we can conclude that a place of pride was given to the composite art of dance in the cultural life of people. A special feature in the development of this fine art is its close liaison with the temple and temple activities.

Ramappa Temple, Warangal

The references found from all over South India, spread over almost ten centuries, provide references to dancing girls and dancing masters, Satavahanas, Ikhvakus, Badami Chalukyas, Cholas, Hoyasalas, Kakatiyas, Pallavas, Vijayanagara monarchs, Kalyana Chalukyas, have richly contributed to the development and pursuation of the art of dance. The evidence they have left to posterity in the form of stone in sculpture leads to the fact that dance developed under the able guidance of rulers. A study of the epigraphical records would reveal that this art formed an integral part of the religious scope of people, thus adding new dimensions to this wonderful art. This art form, which is a celebration of man's creative genius and his priceless gift to future generations, is a treasure trove, stored and preserved as a jewel.

The epigraphical record also reveals that the grants given for the service of the gods called *Rangabhoga* included money, land and even entire villages. This service was a special one among other temple rituals. Even the smallest of the shrines in remote villages have records, which register grants for the service of Rangabhoga. Since it was performed in the temples, with all the religious fervour and sanctity, it was acceptable to the society.

Of course, today, the Rangamantapas in the temples are rarely used for a total form of representation of dance. But development of this divine art of dance is a clear testimony to temple activity and rituals and helps to substantiate a vital fact that it was an absolute artistic pursuit blended with religious faith and this practice was sustained through some centuries under the royal patronage, in all times.

The practice of performing dance in the temples existed till the end of the nineteenth century. Construction of Rangamantapas also appears to have been an essential part of the south Indian temple architecture. There were occasions, when a dancing hall had been constructed in a

Hampi

temple, specially for dances and some of the inscriptions indicate that this portion of the temple was earmarked for the performance of dance as part of the temple rituals.

The term *Angabhoga* referred to such activities like Abhisheka, Alankara *etc.*

The temple being the epicentre, Rangabhoga service became significant, because it implied a superior quality of the art, its technique and presentation. The service was considered to be very special and so much privileged one that girls were dedicated to temples for this purpose.

Entire staff of dancing girls, dancing masters and musicians were maintained by the temple authorities solely for the purpose of Rangabhoga.

Some inscriptions record that Rangabhoga was performed as a routine and there are instances to show it was performed as a special service at the time of festivals or utsavas.

References to Rangabhoga are available as early as tenth century AD.

Flourishing of Performing Arts in Andhra

During the 12th century, at the time of Kakatiya rulers, dance flourished and the temples of Ramappa and Ghanapur stand good testimony of their excellence.

The period of half a millennium from 1000 AD, constitutes the most creative epoch in the history of Andhras. Political security, peace and prosperity prevailed under Chalukya, Cholas, Reddis, Velamas and the kings of Vijayanagar during the 14th and 15th centuries and they were responsible perhaps for the tremendous activity in literature, art, architecture, sculpture, dance, drama, music and learning.

The existence of musicians and dancers in the courts of Gonas and Malayalas, is attested by records. Buddha mentions that music and dance concerts were held in most auspicious fashion, while each performance has to the accompaniment of many musical instruments. In his Ramayana, Buddha describes a dance performance dressed in golden sarees, women grouped together to sing and play. While some were singing songs about Raghava, they in the presence of Bharata, showing their expert knowledge in Bharatasastra and instinct adherence to the specified Talas, played kolatas, performed perani dances and danced in gola, charni sindhu, gujjaru and desi style in different groups. Rudra refers to dancing girls who were experts in music and dance and who could dance in Suddhamarga, singing and to dance by some women according to talagati while their anklets, bracelets and beeds produced fitting sounds and while some played Mridanga and some sang while others played on Vina.

The court of Rama is said to have included musicians–vocal and instrumental, dancers, poets, jesters, experts in arts, puranas, sastras and vedas and dancing girls with sweet faces, playing on musical instruments and singing pleasant songs. The instrument nissana (glid) was used to announce the beginning of war.

Hampi : Vijayanagar times

Near singarutla agrahara, there is a stone carved with the figure of Durga, sitting on the conquested Mahishasura. At Durgi, near a mantapam in the temple in the lower half, the figure of Saraswati is on a swan. At Veldurti, a vinayaka is an armed soldier and dancing to attack with sword and shield in defence of a woman.

In many of the temples in Palnad Taluq of Guntur district, there are representations of Gajalakshmi on the doorways.

Kridabhiramam describes the Abhinaya dance performed by men and women at Warangal, showing the valour of the heroes while women were singing about the heroes of Palnad. Thus the ballad of the heroes of Palnad was the subject of dance performances in the 13th century AD, to the accompaniment of music, and to the delight of vast audiences.

The importance attached to music and dance in the courts of Nalagama and Mallideva at Gurazala and Macherla is seen from Palnati viracharitha by Srinadha. Srinadha describes a music and dance concert that took place in the court of Nalagama the vocal musicians in a striking fashion took the vinas, tightened the wires, tuned them and played in such a marvellous way that the swara saptahas, the different Arohanas and Avarohanas were tuned.

An inscription at the time of Krishnadevaraya on a pillar in the Kesavaswami temple, Cheruru, Bolagallu, Kurnool district is dated 1514 AD. It records that Basavesvara made a gift of a plot of land to the actor, Vagayya, whose father Chagayya, had become famous in the drama called Tayikunda Nataka and to the actress and dancer, daughter of the Vathura Timmayya of Potavar. The gift was made in the presence of God Jalasingadeva for the merit of the king. It appears that this grant was made in appreciation of the drama and the hero and heroine of the drama receiving the best actor and best actress award.

An inscription of 1538 AD referring to the reign of Achutaraya, on the southern wall of the prakara of Lakshmidevi temple at Gurupalli Hindupur Taluq of Anantapur district. It records that Virana Nayaka received a gift made by the toll and the revenue raised in the fair held on every Friday at Lakshmipura by the settis and patnaswamies for the service of Goddess Mahalakshmidevi of Haru Lakshmipura. This gift was made for presenting dance and music in the temple every Friday.

Vijayanagar Empire

The courtesan women played a very important role in society. They were regarded as respectable community by the people. So much is evident from the place which the poets assigned to them in the social order described in their poems. According to Prabandhas, they were required to give an account of their activities.

The courtesans were divided into two classes:

1. Those who were attached to the temples.
2. Those who lived independently of them.

These Nagins exhibit different poses of dance and Prof. Raghavan made a deep study of these figures.

Lapakshi

During the Vijayanagara period, an employee by name Virupanna constructed a temple on a hillock, which is in a small village called Lapakshi in Anantapur district, and it has tremendous poses of sculptural wealth, which speaks of the grandeur of Andhra Desa.

SHIVA IN THE FORM OF BHIKSHATANA MURTHY

PARVATHI GIVING THE BOWL

PARVATHI

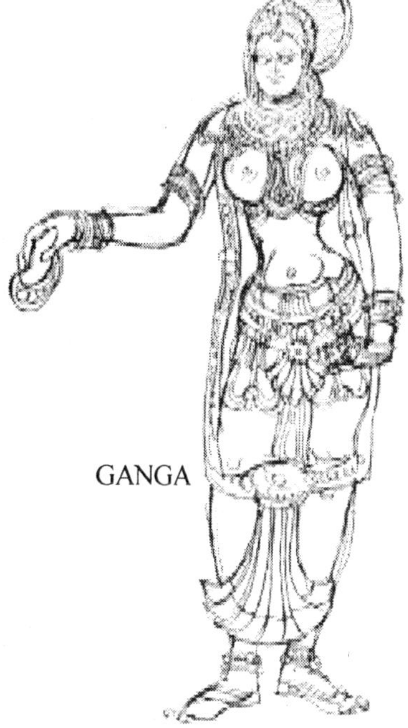

GANGA

DWARAPALIKA

LADY ATTENDENT

DWARAPALIKA

GRACE OF
A GODDESS

PARVATHI

PARVATHI
IN DETAIL

She did not suffer from any social disabilities.

(FE p. 242) They are very much esteemed and classed among those honoured ones who were the mistresses of rulers and elites. Respectable man may go to their houses, without any blame attached to them.

The most important lesson which the courtesan girls had to learn was to evoke love in their customers without loving any of them in return. (Barbosa, p. 22).

She was supposed to be a learned scholar, a skilful musician, a clever gambler and a brilliant conversationalist.

Sculptural Wealth in Andhra

The courts at Gurazala and Macherla had many poets and dancers. Srinadha gives a fine description of Nalagamas court. At Karempudi, a curious mantapa known as Nayudu mantapa has five flower sculptures. A slab has two figures:

1. Hanuman standing in front of a figure riding on the horse back.
2. Panel beneath this represents two women sitting with a pot between them.

It is said that they possibly represent "Silambika" or "Nayakuralu".

Near Singarutla Agrahara, there is a stone carved with the figure of Durga, sitting on Mahishasura–Bull. At Durgi, near a mandapam in the temple in the lower half of the figure of Saraswati on a swan. Rati, wife of Kamadeva is recognized by her parrot, Parvati by her bull, Saraswati by her swan, Sachidevi, wife of Indra by her elephant, Lakshmi by Garuda.

Dachepalli in Palnad Taluka of Guntur district has some very interesting sculptures. In Nageswara Swami temple. A woman with uplifted hand holding branches with two attendants. The grace and symmetry of the figure is very striking.

The sculptures in the Nayakuralu temple are fresh even now. One sculpture represents a queen

probably Nayakuralu with attendants worshipping the lingam. Another shows a King and a Queen–probably Narasimha and Nayakuralu according to Sewell. Another stone has a Durga on Mahishasura, she has eight arms, holding the chowk, seapture, sword, spear, discus, bow, shield and the kay of the buffalo monster. In many of the temples in Palnad, there are representations of Gajalakshmi on the doorways. At Veldurti, in the temple of Durga, is a representation of a group of players, two on drums, one flute and a monkey on the bagpipe.

Kridabhiramam describes that Abhinaya dance was performed by men and women at Warangal, showing the valour of the heroes and simply the kavya with symbols. (History of Andhra Country by Yasodha Devi). Thus the ballad of heroes of Palnad was the subject of dance performances in the 13th century AD to the accompaniment of music–vocal and instrumental, to the delight of vast audiences.

Srinadha describes Nalagama's court as follows :

The great dancer named Kanjalochana, majestic in gait, sweet in speech, learned in the several ragas in Bharatasastra came and stood, where all were waiting with eager expectation. She bowed to the dance master, took the bells given by him, tied them to her feet, with devotion repeating sacred hymns. With side glances at the King, taking the initial step with her feet, samapada, bowed to the gods, gave puspanjali, and began the dance to the musical accompaniments. In highly technical style, she danced "kaikolu" and "vidudala", *i.e.*, releasing and receiving (with her arms) and shared by her gestures–kaimudi and kalna (used for keeping time). Next, she and kalna (used for keeping time). Next, she performed the bhuchari dance of 9 kinds and then showed gatichari differences. After these poses, she demonstrated pani bhedas differences by clever and expert gestures, by combing Sthauka, Samchaya and Samyukta. She danced wonderfully the Sapta Tandavas–Prerani, Desini, Prenkhana, Suddha, danka, kundali and bahuchari, to the great astonishment of the assembly. Then with several women assistants on both sides, she performed Samyuta, Asamyuta, Chalna–manifesting Santuchita–intimate and several gestures of arms expressions of thoughts–nanardha karamulu and Natyahastamulu–postures of hands appropriate in a dance. Then making use of the eighteen angas–the six angas, six upangas and pratiangas–namely head, eyes, cheeks, eyebrows, teeth, lips, neck, chin, focal expression, chest and so forth. They danced the several gitas in Andhra and Sanskrit, in praise of god Macherla Chenna, demonstrating most effectively the meaning of those songs. All were astonished at this grand performance. The king presented them with several clothes and ornaments. Of the Sapta Tandavas, 'Kundaki' is the dance performed in a circular form.

Several musical instruments also are mentioned by Srinadha. When Mallideva started for war, the following instruments were sounded–Damayi, muraja, bura, bheni, potudhara, kasala, vankini, kalikanni, couch, sannayi, dollu, murali, mukhavina, naraga, tappeta, dolu, tamma tamme, viraramu, heavy runja, kamakatappeta, cheyanta and cherngunta, ranabheri, dhakka, dhanamika, dangura, patcha were also sounded of these, damang is a leather instrument. Potudhara means huge coach, dangura and viranna are identical.

Kavyalankara Chudamani is the oldest of Telugu works on alankaras, *i.e.*, sahitya sastra, the 2nd being Narasabhupaliya by Bhattumurthi in the 16th century AD. It is summary of the works on alankara in Sanskrit with some additions. Peddana followed prataparudra yasobhushana in his cantos four and five, except the sections on Gunalankaras and Dandin's kavyadarsa in the position on gunariti and alankaras in cantos four and five. In his Prabhandaraja Venkateswara Vilasa, Ganaparam Venkatakavi mentions the lahshanas of pedalana.

Panels from pillar (J) in (From a water colour drawing)

The earliest dance sculpture in Andhra dates back to 2nd century BC and is found in Amaravati. This sculpture, consisting of four dancers, shows 'Pindibandhas', later on explained by Bharata as such. Another beautiful description in stone is now preserved in British museum. It is a dance scene with a dancer accompanied by two women, one playing on flute and the other on the vina. A sculpture at Goli in Guntur district shows a lady playing on the harp. Another sculpture at Nagarjunakonda shows a lady playing on the vina.

From the ruins of Nagarjunakonda, an amphitheatre was found out. It is a sculpture depicting a dance scene by three dancers, and a seal of a lady by name *sarasika*. The dancing ladies in the sculpture are shown as wearing *Ardhorukas*, of course, a type of costume not advocated by Bharata in his Natyasastra. Even in the 12th century, during the Kakatiya period, we find such costume in the dance sculptures of Ramappa temple at Palampet. This leads to a conclusion that there were some types of indigenous dances in Andhra for a long time, along with those, that were recognized by Bharata.

References

1. History of Andhra Country by Yashoda Devi.
2. Palnati Veera Charita by Srinadha.
3. Nritha Ratravali by Jayappa Senani.
4. Kavyalankara Chudamani.

Ceiling panel (a), Palampet

Ceiling panel (b), Palampet

10

Some Prevalent Desi Dance Forms in Andhra Pradesh in the Past

History tells us that certain communities like "Erukalu", "Koyalu", "Maastulu", "Pamulavandru", "Pambalavandru", "Devaravandru" have various forms of dance, on happy occasions and also on unhappy occasions. That means, a man not endowed with education or literary knowledge, also could show interest in arts, dance and music and put in practice certain artistic ideas, so as to add entertainment and refinement to life.

The following verse of Vallabhacharya of 1420 speaks of Nagaswara, which is the sole monopoly of uncivilized Andhras :

"Pootkara Ravamulu poorinchu pukkillu,

Musidipandula thoda muddu guriya

Sandati sanku poosalasaddu katu dumbi

Nadaswarojrumbhana mula nadapa

Nedu raudrhammula nirekela vrellanu

Vikkanu sabdamul chokkatamuga

"Naga-Sindhu pradesa na-nanarata

Raga gandharva laharika–rambhanamulu

Mihi padambula bamula mengabunde

Bhojirajulu narthimpa–Nagasaramu"

Aryans, the so called civilized people, with all their fine sentiments migrated from North India and found the lower castes living in South India, practicing dance and music and there was a sort of cultural synthesis achieved miraculously in course of time.

Dr. Bhandarker in his "Early History of Daccan" says "the reason why the result of the Aryan irruption was so different in southern India from what it was in the north, appears to be that, when the Aryans penetrated to the south, there existed already well organized communities and kingdoms".

Sir Henry Johnston in his "Living Races of Mankind" tells that even uncultured Dravidians like Todas, and Kurumbas, have got their own songs

and dances and that the interest was not created newly.

There are descriptions in Kreedabhiramam, which is supposed to be the first known text in Telugu.

"Hara Hara yinta yoppune Maharabhatin Gaja

Jhankruta swara

Murali vimisritankara va murchala jithamulubhi

Yikkalem

Ndvarn nade yadajochiri Kadungadu Vedka Samunnva

Tpayo

Dhara yugabhara bheerutama Tandava Lagramulaine Nruthyamul".

.... (Kreedabhiramam)

Just like this, those who sang "Tandava Janapadas" (repeating the same verse) Veerabhatas singing srunga Nadas and playing are also depicted.

"Veera Mylara Devera Veerabhatulu

Gondhi yadinchu chunnaru gorige paduchu

Nadu chunnadi chudu Mardabhinayamu

Taru vithi Kasilanta gami ledu".

Gollasuddulu, tandava Padas, Devara Vandra Kadhas, parasuramuni kadhas clearly stand in support of the above statement.

The women who work in the fields sang songs in the form of a dialogue with question and reply, this speaks of the artistic fervour of Andhras. There are Bhajana Melas also among these lower castes. There is dance and drama in their singing, even to this day in the form of chorus. When we think of chorus, ancient Greece seems to have had similar troupes, who lived on singing and dancing and toured from place to place.

In Greece, in the name of chorus, there were, songs by drama troupes. There were not less than 50 people, who gathered and danced, in one troupe. Our Bhajan troupes are also on the same lines and there is prose narration also, in between.

Whether song and drama entered into the lives of people before their learning to read or write or after, is a question to be studied. But it can be said vociferously that they entered people, who could not read or write. The stories are all about Ramayana and Mahabharata and so there is a doubt expressed that they were enacted after the advent of Aryans or before.

When we make a comparative study, it appears that there were Bhajan troupes in India, Greece and Egypt also at the same time. But it can't be said who copied whom. Col. Todd in his 'History of Rajastanas' says that our Balarama has gone to Greece and taught them civilization.

Our texts inform us that there were 'sani–troupes', 'bhogam troupes' and 'jakkula troupes' from very early times. Some of them are known as Devadasis (dedicated to god) and they lived on the lands gifted to them by the temples.

The point of controversy is whether this sort of ritual in temples was in practice even before

Aryans came or after the coming of the Aryans. It can be well said that this practice is not that of Anaryans. Before the coming of Aryans, there was worship but it was not refined. Jataras and worship of grama devatas is a reminiscent of the old practices of Anaryans. But, Aryans with their civilized notions and sentiments introduced this temple worship and along with it, dancing as a form of worship and women performing it as a mark of dedication was introduced. All the devadasis belonged to temples, which could afford to give them land (manyam). So, it can be concluded that the dance and music in the temples started only after the synthesis of the Aryans and Dravidians.

'Bhagavatam', 'Tolubommalata' and 'Pagati Veshamu' seem to be the three types of entertainment prevalent. There are some communities which lived on entirely performances of these arts as a profession. But to say precisely, which is the first and which is the next, there are no basic evidences. Kolachalam Srinivasa Rao, in his 'Dramatic History of the World' (English) tells that in islands like Java and Sumatra, there were plays of wooden toys since very ancient times and imitating them, our people in India started performing shadow plays with puppets. There is also another school of thought which says that from India, the above art was taken to these islands. As regards street plays (Veedhi Natakas) from the following verses, it can be said that in Telugu land, from the time of Pingali Surana and Ramaraja Bhushana, street plays were performed.

"Jadanidhi Yanu Teramaru gatu

Vedali Nilichinatti Yataveladia pollen"
(Prabhavati pradyumnamu)

"Haridambhoruhalcochanan gagana Raga Bhoga Rangathamo

Bhara Nedaphyamu Noyya Sadalimpan Rathiri Sailushikin

Varusan mouktika pattayaun Nitalamun Vaktrabum Dochena

Harinamkakriti Bolcherekay, Sagambye, Bimbamai Toorupunan" (Vasucharitra).

"Avishnu Lokemunakana, Ma Vahini

Vinayayamama Manitha Moksha

Srivarna raga Bhagava, Tavali Subhalagna samaya

Yavanika Polen"

(Kalapoornodaya)

From the above descriptions it is evident that the present Satyabhama's description is there.

Sreenadha also described about Veedhinatakas in his writings and gave the opinion that men were acting as women and that this practice was there since a long time.

"Bhutalamandu Dhataku Sapnjyata Kalgenu

Rentapoota Bhagothula Buchiganikini".

Sreenadha lived one and half centuries before Suranarya and belonged to the 15th century. From his writings it can be presumed that 'Bhagavatas' were there even before and the 'Surname or family name of 'Bhagothula' came in to existence, even before that time.

It can be said from the following stanza of Suranarya that 'Pagativeshamulu' and 'Natakas' (dramas) were displayed during day time only.

"Nanu Nelokonumanayam, bunu mee yugigamu chittambuna kekkagane

Nonaru Neti aminu, Manamuna Nentayau nidukoni Manmimpa dagun".

(Suranarya)

"eppuduvachu contudinu Deppudu grukunatanchu Natmalo Muppnrigonna Raga sa-matakatamya kanudoyi kubhaga Doppaga Doguchudkaniva–Dhamani Sareku Jndaga Juni Ippaluponde Needadava–Helikramamuna Dalche Raktimen".

(Prabhavatee Pradyumanam)

'Netitami' here means today's night. Another is the description of the sunset. From the above works it can be presumed that these plays were depicted during day–time and not during nights.

Not only in our country in ancient Greece also, the plays were during daytime only.

Mr. Lee Banon Hubner further in his "Ramble Round the World" tells that in Japan the plays were shown from sunrise to sunset. Perhaps, the plays originally displayed during the daytime switched on to night time in course of time and only the entertainment and jugglery remained for day time.

It can also be presumed that these plays and the Bhagavathas and Veedhinatakas (street plays) have all originated from the same source.

"Manamula Nitrabhuchunu Nata Veshmabu Dharinchi Tamakunu deginayati vara seemanthinu vathambu Goluva, vaivika vainakika, Mourajaka, Janadi natya Samagri"–from the above stanza from Prabhavati Pradyumnam, it can be said that men and women participated in the performances and there were men and women also among the audience.

There are great literary works, produced by eminent writers like Palkuriki Somanadha, Srinadha and Jayappa. Panditaradhya charitra refers to certain popular Desi types of folk dances which were played on Sivarathri day in the famous Mallikarjuna temple of Srisailam. More popular Desi dances described in this work are "Vedayata", "Kodangiyata", "Perini", "Bahurupa", "Veddanga" (which is full of karanas) and varied gatis in imitation of celestial and semi-celestial damsels, bird dance' walking on top of bamboos, shadow plays showing Mahabharata and other episodes, puppet shows and fancy dress also were popular.

Lastly somanadha has a very interesting list of gaits in peacock, elephant, bull, monkey, goat and serpent.

In *Palnativira charitra of Srinadha* also there are references to these desi dances. The author gives a detailed description as to how the musicians and dancers in the royal court of Palnad entertained the rulers. The description is as follows :

"The musicians held the vinas and the strings are tuned up for the singing concert and ready for the Aroha and Avaroha (crescendo and decrescendo) and to play several melodies and tunes.

Then the players entered the scene after making obeisance to the king Nalagama. The drummer took his place to the right of the stage and the musician to the left to keep time beats (Kaimudi). The place of Mukhavina stood there and the accompanying singers at the rear–end. The lotus eyed "prima donna" entered majestically as the queen of cupid. She had a sweet voice and was an expert in Bharata's Natya Sastra. She wore anklet bells and dressed in colourful costumes. Timing was tuned to the beat of the drum. She stood in Samapada Sthanaka (firm foot placement) and glanced at the Sabhapati (the lord presiding) she prayed to the gods and offered flowers in obeisance. The Chorus girls began singing from behind, then the dancer commenced the nine buchari movements (around Moves) than the sixteen Akasa charis (moves above ground) followed. In succession, anga haras (limb movements) were displayed, Bhramara rounds were pivoted brightfully, attitudes in candences of hands and feet flowed out. She played dance varieties of Perini, Desi, Prenkhana, Suddadandaka, Kundalini, Bhuchari and the seven kinds of vigorous Tandava dance were exhibited. She posed the patterned single and double hands communicating a variety of meaning, combined with the actions of the hand, glances, cheeks, eye-brows, teeth, neck, chin, face and chest.

Six actions of limbs, six of the sub-limbs, and other subsidiary limbs were cogently practiced to heighten the excellence of the dance play.

In addition there is a beautiful description of the durbar of Nalagama as a kalabhavan and of the dance performance of a nartaki called Kanja lochana as follows:

"Kanjalochana yanu ghanamynapatya
madanu pattapudanti Manjula vani

Bharata Sastrochita pranamul Padiya

Kaligina Yakkanta Kantubanambu

Vale vachi sabhavaru varnichi chudu

chuchi Rambhadulu chodyambu Nadi

Sirasulu Vanchiyu siggunu chedi".

.... **"Palnati veera charitra"**

Like any other woman, she has no five senses, but ten senses. Bharata mentioned that there are ten parts of Lasya and so this woman dancer, an expert in the exposition of Lasya is described to be having ten senses by Srinadha. While entering the stage she looked from the corners of her eyes at Nalagamaraja and danced as follows in 'Ghanakala Saili':

"samapadayutamyna sthanka stithini

Ahila devatalaku Alarulu Toda

Pushpanjali yousufga Pooni natyambu[1]

She mixed 'Margi' 'desi' styles. As per Srinadha:

"Venalnyanga Tommidi Vidhamulynatti

Bhuchari Natyambu ponduga salpi

Padaharu vidhmula Barigina yarti

Akaschriyn Namarangandi

Angaharyahyache Namaru Batyambu

Viditame tommidi Vidhamula nadi".[2]

"Gatichari bhedamul Ganupadinatilu

Bharamana samyata Deepti patima feeranga

pani Bhedambulu padahedamulunu

sthanika sanchaya samyakta lamara".[3]

Kanjalochana exhibited her knowledge of the various 'Charis and Srinadha praises her excellence in several words.

He further says :

"Perini Deini prenkhana sudha Dadika-mandalataga Bahuchari

sapta tandavamulu salpa, chitramuga

sabhavara lascharya samyutalure".

Kanjalochana gracefully exhibited some desi nritya Ritis also. In fact, she appears to be the make of Srinadha's mind and that she is no parallel in satvikabhinaya to none else. Even Rambha, the Apsara, is stunned to see her dancing.

Vallabhacharya, the creator of Kreedahiramam describes dances performed while worshipping Veerambika, the goddess. There is some controversy about the name, though the common version is vallabhacharya is none else than Srinadha. He has highlighted "Pamulata" wherein Nagavarali Raga in Nagaswara is depicted.

"Pootkara Ravamulu poorinchu pukkillu

Musidipandula Toda Muddu guriya

Pamula Vengadusda, Bhejirajulu vartimpa Nagasorarnu

Nagasorarnu"[4]

So, in Vallabhacharya's poetry, there is happy blending of desi and margi styles.

Dance under Kakatiya Dynasty

For dance traditions in Andhra, the period of Kakatiya rulers can be described as a golden age. A more detailed account of dance form, is found in Nrutta Ratnavali of Jayappa, a commander-in-chief under Kakatiya Ganapatideva. He was well versed in Sanskrit, music and dance. He himself mentioned that he had composed two other treatises on music entitled Geeta Ratnavali and Vadya Ratnavali which are now not to be found. He has also written 'Atmacharitra'.[5]

Nrutta Ratnavali, the great work of Jayappa is in eight chapters. Judged from any angle it is a rich contribution of Andhras to the art of dance.

Chapter one contains the definition of Natya and its four constituents, the four Abhinayas, Nritya and Nrutta, Marga (Classical) and Desi, Tandava and Lasya. The four important Abhinayas are dealt with in the second chapter, which included the Angika Abhinaya (Angas, Pratyangas and Upangas). Chapter three takes up the initial movements of the legs called charis. The poses of the legs called sthanas (postures which included different and reclining postures). Then follows the description of sequences of Charis called mandalas. Chapter four describes the hundred and eight poses of the feet and hands called Karanas, the Angaharas which are composed of two or more karanas and the movements of the feet, hands *etc.* called Rechakas, which are involved in these Karanas. Chapter five is devoted to those Desi traditions of Sthanas, Karanas and Bhramaras or wheeling movements. Chapter six describes the Desi Lasyam in which finer and technical points and elements of grace of dance are included. Chapter seven deals with such general topics. Such as times suitable for beginning lessons in dance, the stage, preliminary practice, exercises, costumes *etc.* The second part of the same chapter gives a description of several interesting popular dance forms, Desi Nruttas as follows: Perini, Prenkhana, Sudha narthana Rasaka, Charchari, Natya Rasaka, Sivapriya,Gentu Kandukanartana, Bhadika–Nritta, Ghatasani, Charana Nrutta, Bahurupa, Kolatta and Gondali. The concluding part of this chapter describes the theatre and its types. In chapter eight, the general suggestions pertaining to the time for presentation of a dance recital, arrival of the chief guest *etc.* are dealt with.

The basic and foremost authority on which Jayappa based his findings was (as per his own version) of Bharata's Natya Sastra. Next to him, he cited Kohala, Matanaga, Bat-ttandu, Kirtidhara charya, Sankuka, Abhinaya Gupta, Someswara *etc.*

As already pointed out, Nrutta Ratnavali is noteworthy for its mentioning several regional forms of dance. In the first four chapters, the work deals with the classical forms as handed down from Bharata. In chapter five he describes the Desi styles as prevalent in his time like Perini, Bahurupa, Gondali *etc.* Now, I would like to briefly describe them.

Gondali

Gondali may be identified with Kundalini Nritya played in both Marga and Desi Styles by Young women and girls arranging themselves in Circles.[6]

The earliest references to this type of dance is found in Manasollasa of Someswara. In a festival, king Someswara witnessed a huntress, singing and dancing. Being captivated by her performance, he organized it into a regular dance sequence. Later on, it became popular as Gondalividhi.[7]

Perani

The dance Perani has a Saivite religious origin. The name Perani is also known as Prerani. The Perani dancer is most striking by equipment, as well as by dress. Jayappa describes Perani dancer as a man of attractive personality, of good pedigree, a man of taste, master of music and the instruments, endowed with excellent voice, adept in languages, ready witted, eloquent and acquainted with both Tandava and Lasya. The main constituents of Perani dance are five–Nrutta, Kaivara, Charghana, Vikata and Gita.

Prerana or Prenkhana

It is mentioned along with Perana by Jayappa. He describes the general nature of the dance Prenkhana. It consists of Utpluti–karanas, Bhramaris and charis and Mandalas, Prenkhana seems to be forceful dance, specialising in jumps and wheeling movements.[8]

Rasaka

This is a group dance of ladies numbering sixteen, twelve or eight presenting different women by the members of the group. These patterns are called pindibandhas, which came down from the time of Bharata.

Pindi might have been down from Pindana. It is also known as Srinkhalika (Chain like formation). Jayappa speaks of expert male dancers and dress of dancers also saree, shorts, cotton wear of the body, hair in a bunch or plait, or dress according to the region.

The method of the entry of the dancers on the stage is described as follows : "As the instruments are being played, the dancers, executing the same charis, enter in pairs from either side. In Rasaka, the dancing ladies are compared to Gopis thereby indicating a relation to the rasa dance of Gopis with Krishna".[9]

Charchari

When the dancers enter singing charchari songs, it becomes charchari. Charchari songs comprise of Sringara or Vira Rasa, describing the seasons and the qualities of the patron–kings.[10]

Natya Rasaka

Jayappa mentioned it as a Desi form different from Rasaka and Charchari. The season for this also is Vasantha. The style of dance is Padabhinaya and he mentions songs in Hindola raga.[11]

Danda Lasaka

This is the next dance described by Jayappa in the rasaka series. This should be played with short sticks in the hands which the dancers strike to keep rhythm. The sticks or dandas used are short, coloured, made of Arjuna wood instead of two dandas, a fly-whisk or a dagger along with one stick. On the mode of entry 8 of the dancers may first enter and gradually by the addition of batches of four, the number may raise to sixty-four, formed in two rows.[12]

Siva–Priya

This dance was performed by Saivite devotees during the festivals. Trumpets, drums, eyeballs, and kirikiti are usually played in it. The Kirikiti instruments, looking like serpents with spread out hoods are held by the dancers in one hand with the playing konas on the other. The dancers are dressed like Saivite devotees with holy ash and Rudraksha Malas and comprise of men and women. The songs are in praise of Siva and the movements are in two rows, facing each other or in a circle.[13]

Chintu (Chindu)

Chintu is a mode of play, chindu, being a type of song. The noteworthy characteristic of chindu is the rhythmic swaying by the dancing women of their breasts, arms and hops which is the Desi Lasyanga called Killu. Chindu is practiced till recent times in Andhra desa by village communities as part of the festivals (Jataras) of village deities.[14]

Kanduka Nrutta

The ball game has been systematized into a dance. In this the ball was sent up in every direction and while doing so the dancer moves about in a variety of poses of legs, hands (karanas) which are pleasing to look at. Because of the speed at which the ball was being hit on all sides, the female dancer had to step in fast, round and round, executing Mandalas appearing to create a cage around her. The other terms used for her movements are Panchabindu Prasarata and Gomutrika. According to Jayappa, the Kanduka Nrutta is a group dance performed by several women. The balls might be of metal or wood with small round pieces in size to make them resonant like rattles during play. The throwing and catching of the balls involve movements and while moving the charis, gatis and the lasyangas are to be displayed and it is this that lifts up the game of the ball into a dance form.[15]

Bhandika Nritta

This is a dance of clowns or Bhandas who shout and cry and make all sorts of noises of birds and animals like ass, dog, *etc.* and execute movements imitative of the lame and stunted, the children and the animals like monkeys. They indulge in unbecoming words and acts, dwarf their limbs in their movements and themselves laugh. As the instruments are played, they keep the rhythm by uttering the rhythmic syllables by mouth or by clap of palms. This dance is intended to be comic and divert the king from monotony.[16]

Ghatisa or Stri Nritta

It is a desi dance described by Jayappa as Ghatisani. Ghatisani or 'Ghatisi' may mean the women with Ghatisa. The woman who is the dancer here is a chandali and a sweet voiced singer, reciting songs of philosophical import. The subject of the songs is the god of hunters–Siva in the form of a Virata–*etc.* she herself carries on her shoulder, the Hudukka which she keeps on playing and is surrounded by male and female singers, flutists, drummers and beaters of cymbals. Here the drum is known as kantal. The dance movements should be soft and graceful. This is mainly a female dance but a male may also perform it.[17]

Charana Nritta

This is a dance mode from Gujarat, which men and women of ministerial class perform. The main characteristic is the circular movement, mandalvritti. Women throw over their heads on the ends off their garments like a veil. The characteristic song of this dance is Dohaka derived from dohakametre. Besides the group moves in a circle, there are also individual Bhramaris along with hand movements steppings are to be forceful, though on the whole the style should be lalitodhatta partly soft and partly forceful.[18]

Bahurupa

This dance is described in several works. It derives its name from the fact that it depicts a variety of characters of the world. The main Bahurupa player is to be quick, versatile, and capable of speaking different languages. The Bahurupa troupes, are prone to present lower types of dancers, involving unbecoming actions and speeches.[19]

Kolatta Nartana

This is an acrobatic feat which involves walking on high rope, poising, swinging or wheeling around on a high pole, escaping unhurt, through sharp swords brandished about, lifting heavy weights and executing high jumps. These feats are accompanied by a large variety of drums, trumpets and cymbals. These acrobatic dancers with swords etc used to be exhibited till recently in south India. The dance on pole and rope is still practiced by dommaras who are particularly adept in such type of feats.[20]

According to Jayappa, it appears that before the actual dance starts, the dancer stands on a raised platform with a canopy above, on the stage. In front of the dancer thus standing, there are to be three curtains or sometimes more. These curtains richly embroidered and measured eight cubits by four in dimensions. They are held at their ends by pairs of beautiful ladies. The dancer is to wear a close Artoruka or half drawer so that the thighs are to be seen for correctness of the poses in charis, karanas *etc.* The Arthoruka is covered by a transparent apparel. The close pyjama and the saree worn over it down to a little below the knees is intended to provide a clear view of leg poses, which later developed as the traditional costume of the nautch dancers. Pearl garlands and other ornaments, which do not closely attach to the limbs should not be used as they would interfere with the free movements of the limbs.[21]

The chief court dancer was a highly respected person and she was entitled to come to the hall in a gilded palanquin attended by women, who carry parasol, fly whisks *etc.*[22]

Dance performances were arranged and presented for the sake of one's prosperity and welfare on the occasion of marriage celebration, the birth of a son, performance of Vratas, pilgrimage, entry into a new city or a house, or appointment, 'Mahadana' or victory *etc.*[23]

In addition to these literary works, there is great sculptural wealth. (Please refer to the chapter on Sculptural wealth in Andhra Pradesh).

Now, let us study in detail the sculptural wealth of Warangal fort and Ramappa temple which throw light on the then prevalent dance styles. The exquisite sculptures at Palampet, Ghanpur, Nagulapad, Nandikonda, Pillalamarri, Bejjanki, Dharmapuri, Kothapalli, and the sculptured fragments lying in the Warangal fort and other temples at Warangal, which contain delicately carved statues in charming and graceful dance poses amply testify the great level to which the art of dance had reached during Kakatiya period.

The beautiful representations of a dancer carved on brackets at the main Palampet temple are very noteworthy. These figures are said to have been carved according to the poses mentioned in the Nrutta Ratnavali. There are large sized brackets of figures of dancers in the Ramappa temple. By examining them in the light of the texts and illustrations relating to the karanas reviewed above, it is clear that they do not illustrate the karanas or of Desi Karanas.

Kakatiya dance sculptures can be broadly classified into 3 varieties: (1) Dancers, (2) Gods and goddesses in dancing postures, (3) Miscellaneous figures in Desi forms of dance.

We find relics of dancers in almost all the temple sculptures. In the Warangal fort, we come across beautiful dancers that appear in different postures. Many dancing women are represented inside beautifully carved Makara Toranas which may be indicative of the figures of court or temple dancers. A panel on a bracket at the Palampet temple with a figure of dancer may be cited here. Her head is gracefully bent in Nata Pose, the waist is split and the right hand is elegantly raised with the palm being in a tripataka pose.

Her right hip is curved and the right leg is in Udghatita or firmly placed on the ground. The left knee is in swastika (crossed) while the toes are in Agratala Sanchara or pointing to the ground. The other two small dancing figures are carved relatively in tiny propositions moving round the main dancer. Scholars feel that these are the reproduction of the text of Nritya Ratnavali by Jayappa Senani (Dr. V. Raghavan, p. 115). Nagini and other dancers these two figures are represented on a door joint at Palampet temple. The third figure is that of a Nagini. She is shown holding a serpent in her left hand. The left foot is well set on the ground. The waist is gracefully bent to the right. The hands are raised over the head.

The central figure and the first one on the right one well costumed and the forearms are damaged. The figure is firmly but the left hip is raised to give grace to the feminine standing posture. The right leg is raised above the head while the left is bent at the elbow. The forearms cover the belly. In the first figure, the same posture is sculptured, but the right knee is bent to cross over the left foreleg which is damaged.

Another bracket figure of a dancer found in Palampet temple has her head in Adhootam posture (slant) indicating inner desire. The eyes are fully open, not out of fear or excitement but of fullness of amiable feelings. The chin is in samabhaga (Normal). The mouth is in udvaha pose (closed lips), neck is in tryasra mudra (side movement). The left hand is in Arala Pose (curved). The right hand is in Uttara Mudra (lifting up). The left up palm is kartari mukha (scissor faced). The right palm is Tryasva Mudra (Triangular). The right knee is Avartita (Circling) in nata (bent) and in Parivruta poses (rounding). The right foot is in Agratala sanchara (moving on the tops of the foot). The left foot is in samabhanga (Leveled) pose.

Another figure of a lady is shown standing in Dvibhanga posture by poising her entire weight on the right leg while the left one is raised and bent at the knee. Her half opened mouth suggests that the lady is singing. The combination of singing and dancing is admirably shown in this figure. The graceful fold on the stomach, the amazing expression in her eyes are very attractive. Two drummers are shown in miniature size on either side of the central figure.

A figure of lady is shown standing and exhibiting Abhinaya. Her hands are raised above her head, but forearms are badly damaged. Her slender waist is bent to right. Her fully opened eyes are looking upwards. On either side, of the central figure, drummers are shown in rhythmic movements.

Another panel representing a Nartaki in Bhujanga trasa pose, poising her weight on her left leg while the right is raised and bent at the knee point, to suggest that she is giving a dance performance on the stage.

Nagins of Ramappa Temple—Palampet

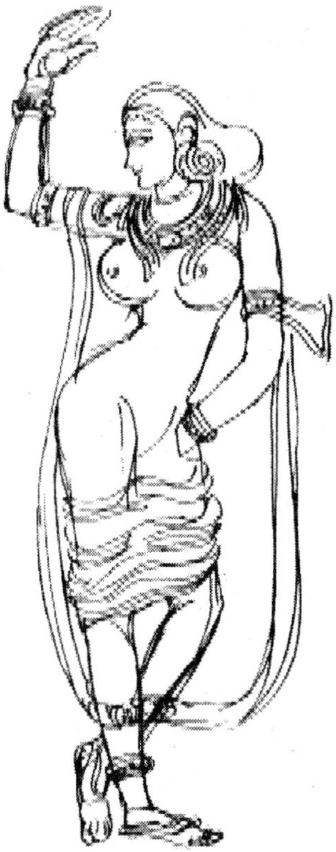

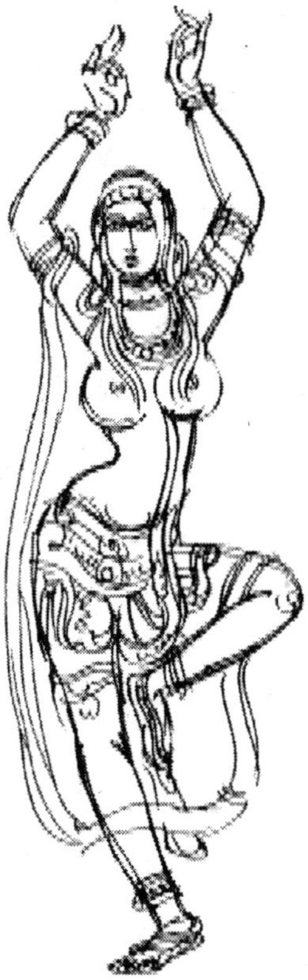

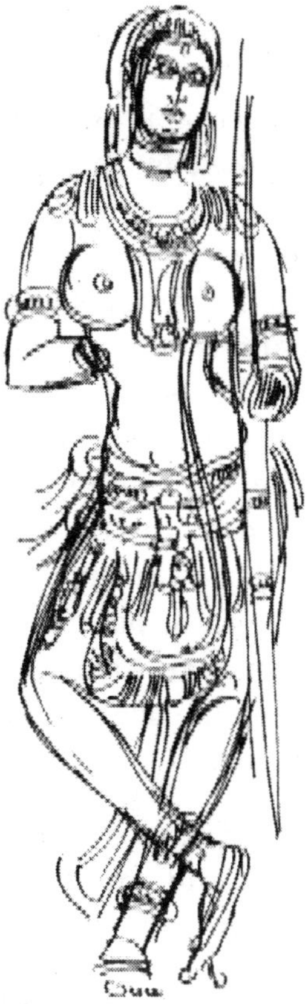

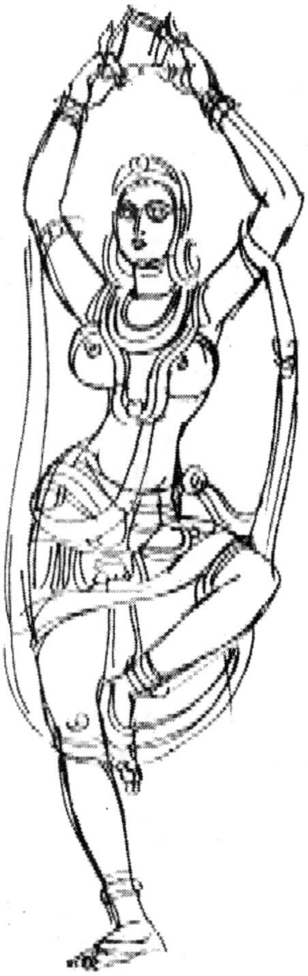

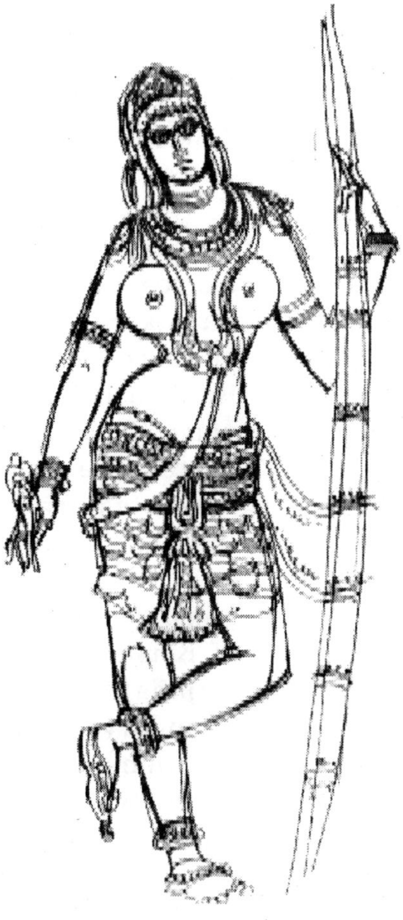

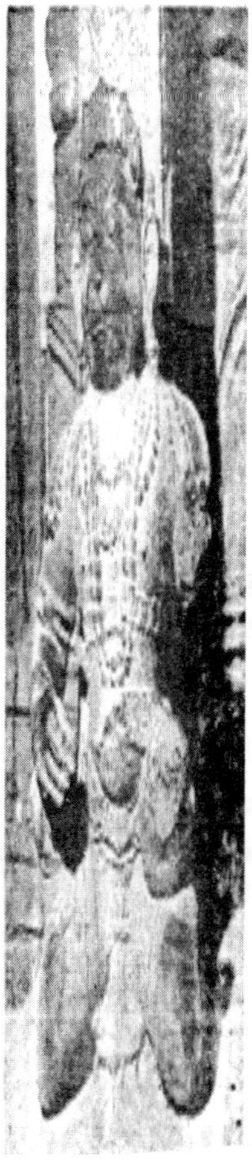

The window front of the main temple, depicts a lady dancer in different postures. The whole depiction is shown in six rows. The dancer is shown flanked by male and female drummers. They are also seen dancing in tune with the rhythm, while playing the drums. In the first row, the dancer is seen bending her right leg at the knee point. Her palm is in Suchi Mudra (pointed upward) and Arala Mudra is depicted by the raised right hand. In the second, she is shown standing in the Abhanga Pose and right palm in Varada and left in Mruga Hasta Mudra. In the third row, she is seen bending her right leg at knee point, raising the hands upwards. The right palm is stretched to a side, while the left arm is in Mruga hasta. And in the sixth row, she kept her right arm to a side and left in Mukulita Mudra.

The most exquisite dance form of Nataraja Siva is found on a wall sculpture in the temple of Someswara at Panagal.

Dancing Ganesha which is a rare pose is carved on a pillar in the temple at Palampet. The panel represents, a dance concert of Ganesha with other instrumentalists. Ganesha is seen with drummers on either side. Two more dancers are at either end.

The ceiling of the dilapidated mantapa in Warangal fort, is fully carved with figures of dancers and Goddesses. Goddess Saraswati is mounted on her vehicle Hamsa and the four sets of hands are seen holding a series of weapons besides a vina. The waist is beautifully bent towards the right, while the right foot is a Agratala sanchara posture and the toe pointing to the ground, while the figure is standing on the outstretched left leg.

On the pillars of Navaranga Mantapa and Ranga Mantapa of the Palampet temple, we find panels of dancers. These panels are identified as Perini, by a famous Natya Charya Nataraja Ramakrishna. The central figure appears to be legless and it is to be understood as standing knee to knee while the side figures are bent and appear shorter than the central figure. The dancers are surrounded by drummers, instrumentalists and cymbal players.

Dance under the Vijayanagara Kings

Dance and music flourished well under the Vijayanagar kings, in addition to literature. Vidyaranya who established the Vijayanagara Empire is said to have written "Sangeeta sara" and mention is made about it in the "Sangeeta Sudha" written by Raghunadha Nayaka of Tanjore. During the rule of Deva Raya II, a Parsee traveller by name Abdul Razak visited Vijayanagara and described about the Dasara celebrations. Maharnavami was performed with great pomp and excitement, he mentions and writes that excellent dance performances were given at that time by courtesans.

Let us have a look into the literature available. In between 1433–34 BC, a Devadasi in Agneeswara temple of Nadamaru Village called, Aramvalatha nachiyar, visited Devaraya II and took donation for a temple. A brother of Saluva Timmaraju and Durga–Palaka (Guard of the palace) during Devaraya II, by name Gopendra Tipparaju wrote "Tala deepika" a famous text on Tala Laksana and also another text on dance out of dedication to Lord Siva. During the time of Mallikarjuna Devaraya (1446–1465 BC), Chatura Kallinadha wrote 'Kalanidhi', a commentary on Sangeeta Ratnakara and it is one of the well known writings of Vijayanagara empire. This text is known to be more famous than the one written by Singabhupala. From his commentary on the last chapter of Sangeeta Ratnakara, his knowledge and efficiency in the art of dance can be understood. At the time of Sri Krishna Devaraya (1509–1530) Natya Charya by name Bandaru Lakshminarayana Pandit, taught dance to the women of the royal palace and he wrote Sangeeta Suryodaya'. There is a chapter on dance. In it, he makes several references to Saranga Deva and Kohala and their writings. Lolla Lakshmidhara, who luckily got the royal patronage of Krishna devaraya and also of Veera Rudra Gajapathi of Orissa, wrote a commentary on Soundarya Lahari, and in the long 'Gadya' he mentions about his ancestor by name Virinchi Misra, who wrote a great text on dramaturgy by name "Bharatararnava kapota'.

Apart from the above literary works, there is ample evidence to show from the reports of foreign travellers like Barbosa, Paes and from the sculptures of those times. From the reports of these travellers, it is known that several courtesans were patronized by the kings and they were very fabulously rich and maintained very good relations with them. The description of Paes of the Natya Mantopa is noteworthy.

Robert swell in his "A forgotten empire Vijayanagar 1900" says "The fighting kings of Vijayanagar became the saviors of the south for two and a half centuries. The early members of this dynasty were Saivites in faith, but there is no record of the workings of the reformed religion, which has spread southwards before Vijayanagar became a power.[24]

"It is said that there were 64 institutions of dance at Srisailam, which is one of the most important Siva temples of Andhra Pradesh. During the period of Kakatiyas, Saivism was the state religion. So all the dances were in praise of Lord Siva. Siva Tandava was very popular in those days and was moulded into different styles. 'Ganapthi Kautham', 'Siva–Tandava' are prominent Saiva dances, whereas, Bhujanga, Bujanga trasa, Sudha Kaustubha, Puspanjali are recognized as Vaishnava dances. Slokas or kouthams are explained through "Abhinaya". As there is recorded evidence to show how devadasis performed dances in temples. From this the amount of respect and recognition that the dance and music, commanded in those days can be assessed.

If only this Natya mandapa was intact, it would have been a treasure trove, which would have revealed many more details about dance and music of Vijayanagar kings. It would have had a place among the sculptures of Chidambaram and Tanjore. But unfortunately it is ruined and there are no traces of its past glory. There is a general impression that Vijayanagar kings patronized literature more, rather than the other art forms like dance and music. But, it does not seem to be correct to say so. The dance poses on the temple of Tadipatri in Anantapur district, which are of the same time, are very fine pieces and are replicas of the art that prevailed at that time. Nadendla Gopanna, an employee of Krishna Devaraya, wrote 'Prabodha chandrodaya' and tells about singanacharya in his commentary. This singanacharya may be the singanabhattu of the court of Pedakomati Vemareddy, who wrote a Telugu commentary on Sangeeta Ratnakara.

"Chatura Damodara, who wrote Sangeeta Darpana also seems to be a Telugu Pandit. In one of his chapters he mentions about Nritya and in the sixth and last chapter he tells about Nritta in detail. In this chapter, he gives details of Nritya Prabandhas of the south.

There is another famous text called Sangeeta Muktavali by Devendra. This is another great work on dramaturgy in Telugu Land.

Later on, Tanjore kings like Raghunadha Nayaka and Vijaya Raghava Nayaka patronized dance and music.[25]

Dance under the Reddy Kings

There are several writers on Natya Sastra among Reddy Kings of Kondaveedu. The first one being Kumaragiri Reddy (1386–1402). He has another name "Vasantharaju". 'Vasantha Rajeeyamu' is his masterly work, but is not to be traced till today. But his Prime Minister, his brother-in-law and writer of a commentary on Kalidasa, by name Kataya Vema Reddy, Mallinadha, a commentator on Maghapurana, his son and commentator on Pratapa Rudra, Nadendla Gopa Pradhani, a commentator on Probodha Chandradoya have all references about this Vasantha Rajeeyamu.

The well-known writer of those times, Sri Srinadha, describes in his "Kasikhanda", that several dance forms prevailed and one Karpooratilaka, a courtesan danced very gracefully before Ratneswara in Kasinagara.

The famous king among Racharla dynasty is Singabhoopala known as 'Sarvagna'. His works with titles as 'Rasarnava Sudhakaramu" on dance and "Sangeeta Sudarnava" a commentary on Sangeeta Ratnakara are famous and it was at his time that Yakshaganas were very popular.

Inscriptions of Andhra Pradesh

Several inscriptions of Andhra Desa speak of devadasis having landed property. In an introduction given by Sri Veturi Prabhakara Sastry Garu to Kreedabhiramam, he mentions about the inscriptions of Machala Devi, a courtesan, who lived at the time of Sreenadha. One such inscription can be found in the ruined temple of Chennakesava Swamy in a village called Gudimetta, which is 4 miles away on the south to Somidevipalli railway station of Kurnool District.[26]

There is also a version that she had several other inscriptions to her credit. An inscription No. 989 (ARNO 164 of 1893) on a pillar in the Mantapa near the Gopalpura.[27]

"Swasthisree–Sree Narendra Mahadavaraku

Sandhya deepamunaku sanivadavalaya *etc.*"

and another inscription No. 996 (Arno 171 of 1893) on the same pillar states.

"Swastisree poushya Pancha Dasiyu

Sri Manmaha Mandaleswara Kulothuga Choda *etc.*"

and yet another inscription (in South Indian Inscriptions Vol. VI on a Chebrolu inscription), speaks of "Three hundred Sanis and three hundred Brahmins can rule" stand proof that 'Sanis' were given lands for their maintenance.[28]

So, it can be concluded that the classical dance of Andhra (in addition to folk forms), as evidenced in sculpture, literature and other forms, took different shapes in course of time and was exhibited in temples by Devadasis and by Raja Nartakis in durbars and also by Bhagavathullu, who toured and gave performances entertaining the people.

Some popular styles of Desi Nrityas are as follows:

Vedayata : (Vikata Nartana).

Chindu : (Kodangi Ata–May be similar to Wanandika Nritya described by Jayappa–This is by a hasyakara).

Perini : This is also found in Jayappa's text, there are some acts of pramadha ganas.

Bahunatakas : Also mentioned by Jayappa.

Veddangamu : Nrityamkaranas of Amara gandharvanganas, plays of birds, Gadatalu (Domaratalu) Pagativeshamulu.

Perini is mentioned as 'panchansi' by Somanadha. In Natya Sastra, five parts are included by him namely Nrittamu,Karivaramu, ghargaram, vikatamu, Geethamu–said Jayappa.

Those dances performed in front of the temples are mentioned by Somanadha. He stated these Nrityas with the description of the jewellary of the dancers and their dresses while dancing, they were wearing 'Ardorukas' (Langotas). As soon as dancers entered the stage, singing and dancing started. He also mentioned about Brahmani Nritya. Though this has not completely disappeared in the modern times, its performance is rare.

Somanadha described several 'Angas'. Some do not find place in Jayappa's Sarangdevas Parsvadevas, Vemabhupalas writings. So, Somanadha's descriptions are very helpful to know about dance techniques of his times.

Later he gave a list of Abhinayas, some are facial (4), eyebrows (7), eyes (26), nose (5), ears (10), neck (9), chest (3), feet (5), thighs (5). In addition he gave 22 sthanakas, 34 drishtis, hands 64, charis 32, Bhramaras 7, 108 karanas, 100 Alankaranas, 13 sirobhinayas, 32 dandanas.

He also gave a list of Hansa, Nemali, Snake, Elephant, Bull, Monkey, Lamb, he says it is essential to compare one with the other.

After Somanadha, there are descriptions of dance is Basavapurana. At the time of Basava, he mentioned about Kolatam or Dandarasakamu (there is no such description anywhere else) Gondli, Perini are also mentioned. Ananda geetas, Sankara geetas are mentioned. Poorva sangeetha, Desi lasyangamu, Mukhanasamu, Soushtavamu, Lali, Bhavamu, Dhookali, Jhankali, Theva, Vibhranamu, Ackha are mentioned. Afterwards, there is a list of technical words in connection with Desi sangita relationship.

In Kridabhiramam, there is description of Machaladevi, a dancer in Prataparudra's court and her story was staged as a drama. Among the Reddy kings of Kondaveedu, there are several drama writers. The 1st among them is Kumaragiri Reddy (1386–1403). He has another name Vasanta Raju. He wrote a Natya Sastra called Vasanta Rajuyamu. This is not to be found even now. But, the prime minister of Kumaragiri, sister's husband and commentator on Kalidasa by name Kataya Vema Reddy, Mallinadha, his son, Kumaraswami, the commentator on Prabodha Chandrodaya Vadendla Gopavardhana have mentioned in their writings about V. Raju. The then kavisarvabhouma Srinadha, in his Kasikhanda mentioned about the dances of his time. One Karpura tilaka of Benaras is described in his writing. She performed Kundali Nrutya, Charika Karana Angahara Rechaka, Bhramika dance and impressed Siva and Parvati, parents of Lasya Nritya.

Among the Recharla kings, one *Sarvagna Singa Bhupala* wrote *Rasarnava Sudhakara*, and also Sangita Ratnakara. It is at this time that Yakshagana (Nritya Natika style) took shape.

During the Vijayanagara kings also dance and music flourished.

During the pre-Chalukyan rule, to give a gift of Agrahara to Siva temple was considered to be one of the advantages like "Tala", "Ghana", "Sishira", "Anaddha", Vadya, Vadaka, Gayaka, Natyaka-charya, Vilasini Jana's patronage (Tala, Ghana, Sishira, Anaddha are four kinds of instruments).

Near Akkanna, Madanna caves in Vijayawada, on the wall pillars of Jammidoddl, bars of the roof, there are some dance poses, which belong to pre-Chalukyan tradition that flourished in 8th and 9th centuries. From these dance poses, we can find out the people's appreciation of dance. Towards the end of this era, appreciation of dance even increased and importance of temple increased, Anga ranga Bhogas became a daily routine to swami, so, 'Gayaka', 'Mardangika', 'Nartakijana' got more importance and for their maintenance either salaries or lands were given and thus the art of dance gained much popularity.

Construction of a Natya mandapa in every temple became customary and during Archana (worship) of swami, chanting of Siva Kadhas in Saiva temples and Vishnu kadhas in Vishnu temples became a routine to sing and dance about the Lord. On account of this custom, during pre-medieval times, there was no single temple, which has no natya mantapa or dancers.

During Kakatiya period, that dance was very popular, can be established by the writings and sculptures and literature of that period.

Recheruvula Vani Reddy gifts of houses to singers, musicians, and dancers for the sake of temple service is evident from Pillalamarri inscription.

Mylamba gave gifts (as per Panagal inscription) to singers and dancers. Dharma sagara inscription, stands as evidence that some nivarthanas of land was gifted away to singers and musicians.

As per Kakati Ganapatideva and Jayappa, (Chebrolu inscription) gifts were given to ten dancers.

In 1183 Kakatiya Maharani, Rudrama gave gifts for (Mandana-modern mandada village) gave gifts for construction of temple built by Golakimatha vidyasthana in the temple for 10 dancers, one musician and fourteen musicians and they patronized dance and music as per Malnapura sagana.

In addition to these inscriptions Kakatiya rulers built temples and the sculptures in these temples speak volumes about dance traditions and about their linkage with religion may be found in Hala's Gadha Saptha, *i.e.*, before Christ. It is believed to have been written somewhere between 200 BC and 200 AD.

In Palkuriki Somanadha's *Panditaradhya Charitha* and *Basavapuranam* we find many references to dance and music. They are supposed to belong to the 12th century.

Palnati veeracharithra by Srinadha describes about a courtesan by name 'Kanjalochana' who was in the royal court of Nalagama Raja. The historical work is full with descriptions of dance halls, dances and dancers like Lakuma Devi of Kondavidu and Machala Devi of Warangal.

In between 11th and 14th century AD, a host of Andhra commentators added to the wealth of literature on dance already existing. They included Nanyadeva, Bhuloka Malla, Kumaragiri Reddy, Pedakomati Vema Reddy, Lollu Bhattu, Singabhupala and Mallinadha.

Andhra classical dance developed in its own way and has been divided by scholars into two different categories, namely 'Natya Mela' and 'Nattuvamela'. The first one consists of dance drama and the second one as pure dance. Devadasis and Raja Nartakis were exponents of the latter category. Devadasis were performing Puja Nritya on the Balipithas of temples.

Banda Kanaka Lingeswara Rao, a lover of fine arts and a producer of dance dramas in AIR, Vijayawada, mentioned as follows :

"Coming to the present context, in Bharata's Natya Sastra, the name 'Andhra' is mentioned as one of the regions of South India. A particular type of dance was being practised and Bharata commends the 'Kaisikivrithi' a delicate and graceful movement in the dance of this region.

Geographically the boundaries of Andhra are mentioned as the Venna river, the present Krishna and Penna rivers. A particular raga, by name 'Andhri' was the contribution of the people to the music of India.

Thus, we see that the Andhras developed their dance form even in the 3rd century BC.

The art of the Ajanta and Ellora caves, which was carved during the reign of Satavahana rulers of Andhra, also bears ample evidence. Of these, the Amaravathi stupa relics are the most ancient (2nd century BC).

"Further, a critical examination of the elaborate description of the various types of dances given by Palkuriki Somanadha in his panditharadhya charithra shows that an indigenous system of the art was prevalent in Andhra country during the Kakatiya period in between the 12th and 13th centuries.

(Sri Vissa Appa Rao–Kuchipudi Natya Sadassu utsava sanchika, 1959).

It can therefore be safely assumed that a tradition of classical dance flourished at Kuchipudi during this period (Vissa Appa Rao).

"After the fall of Vijayanagara Empire, some of the Natyacharyas and artists of Kuchipudi migrated to Tanjore. They are patronized by Achutappa Nayak and established themselves at Achutapuram the modern Melattur".

(Dr. Vissa Appa Rao)

Sculptural evidences of Amaravati speak of the grace and beauty of the dance poses. We can see a group dance of four dan senses (drawing 10, plate XIII–Amaravati sculptures in the Govt. Museum, Madras which is very remarkable for its composition, balance and grace. In the Amaravathi sculptures preserved in the British Museum (Kingston Museum) which I had the proud privilege to see during my visit to London in 1982, there is beautiful dance scene well depicted, with a dancer, accompanied by two ladies playing on the flute and the vina. The sculpture of Goli in Guntur district shows a lady playing on the harp (Plate VI Fig.1 Madras Museum bulleton on Buddhist sculptures from a stupa near Goli).

Amaravati 2nd Century A.D. Male Fly Dancers

Procession of Male Dancers and Musicians (Amaravati)

Apsaras
Palampet : 12-13th Century

In Nagarjunakonda also, we have not only a similar sculpture of a lady playing on veena (pl. XLIV (a) Longhurst, the Buddhist antiquities of Nagarjunakonda, memories of the Archalogical Survey of India) There is also a scene of a group dance by these dansenses (IHQ-Calcutta XXVIII No. 2 June 1952-T.N. Ramachandran–Excavation at Nagarjunakonda–plate 10, facing page 118) which, though less beautiful and striking can be studied along with the group dance in Amaravathi sculptures referred to above.

Pillalamarri inscription of Receruvula Nami Reddy (corpus of Indus No. 37) records the gift of houses to musicians, drummers and dancers, attached to the temples.

Along with these epigraphs, the sculptural wealth found in the various temples built by the Kakatiya kings confirm, the continuity of dance traditions and their association with the religious traditions and the temples.

Most noteworthy among them, belonging to the Kakatiya period, are the dance-sculptures of the famous Ramappa temple. They acquire their additional significance because they were done during the rule of Ganapatideva under whose patronage Jayappa wrote his Nritta Ratnavali.

In the annual report of the Arch. Deptt. of H.E.H. Nizams Dominions (1915-16, 1917) we have description in plate VII, pillars, and doorways of the great temple of Palampet carved with dancing figures.

Pl IX shows the interior of the temple at the eastern end of the Ramappa Tank Bund, Palampet (Warangal) with dancing figures in different poses, accompanied by lady drummers on doorways from the western end. The report for 1934-35 (1938) pl.vi (a) shows door lintel from Warangal fort carrying similar dance-carvings. The Swayambhu Lingeswara in the Warangal fort has miniature representations of the dance of Shiva (see Mallampalli Somasekhara Sarma—History of Reddy kingdoms, p. 428).

On the literary side, we have Sanskrit and Telugu works, bearing witness to the extensive range of dance in their age. On the Sanskrit side, we have Nritta Ratnavali itself. On the side of Telugu works, we have substantial information and material pertaining to this art.

Panditharadhya Charitha, the great work of Palkuriki Somanadha (Andhra Grandhamala) 30– see also M.S. Sarma–History of Reddy kingdoms– pp. 425, in the Parvata Prakarana of this text not only a resume of the technical terms of dance but a description of folk dances is given. This work confirms the dual association of dance and temple and of dance and for the work describes these dances, as part of Maha Sivarathri celebration at the Srisailam shrine.

The more popular Desi dances described in this text are "Vedayata" which is Nataka Nartana (chindu) dealt with by Jayappa also, 'kondangiyata', which is clown dance and can be compared with the Bhandika-Nartnan in Jayappa's work, 'Perani' found in Jayappa also, plays depicting the acts of pramadha-ganas (Bahu-Natakamulu), 'Bahurupa', which is described by Jaya also, 'veddanga', which is full of karanas and varied Gatis but is obscure imitation of celestial and semi-celestial dances, bird-dance, dance on top of bamboos (vamsa nartana) by Dommaras, shadow plays showing Bharata and other stories, puppet shows and fancy dress (Pagati veshalu).

Srinadha in the Bhimeswara khanda describes the dance of courtesans, which he has actually seen in Draksharamam as follows :

1. "Gandharvopanisha drehasyamulu vakka-nintuvaa.......................

   Gandharvapsarasal puropovamika kalpa-druma chayalan"

2. Manitulokoti komala Janathasamulu ravali mattela yagalimpa

3. Virula Dandala Todi venika Bharambu ponkambu pirudula Borani yadasani Esaiyei Mahotsavamu nandu Galanava chandra kantapu ginnepuni veedhi Bhikshatana monarehu velajeyu marala nrityambu jagamula marulu kolupu"

(Bhima Khandam 1–105)

Srinadha, after seeing the dance of the courtesan feels that it is the "Easani Lasya". He felt that the sounds made by the gingling bells worn on her feet to be like that of "Gandharupasa Rasas", who are adepts in dance and music.

Even the instruments used by the courtesans of Draksharama are of high order, in the eye of Srinadha. He describes them as 'Pasidi kinnera veenalu', 'Hemakahalas'.

'Kridabhiramam', a work by Srinadha, throws more significant light on a courtesan dancer of high repute by name Machala Devi, who was a friend of Pratapa Rudra and her life was dramatized and enacted.

Basavapurana, another great work by Palkuriki Somanadha gives description of dance. He refers to 'kolatta', 'dandarasika', 'patna', 'Gondali' and 'Perani' (Andhra Patrika Edition, p. 62).

Perani is mentioned and said it was done, according to the dance masters of Sowrashtra.

On Magha, and his son Kumaraswamy on Pratapa Rudriya (*Journal of the Madras Music Academy*, Vol. IV. pp. 24, 50) made references to their famous work.

In Kasikhanda of Srinadha, the great Telugu poet of his time, there are references to dance.

Srinadha speaks of a dancing girl of Banaras by name Karpura Tilaka, who danced in front of Ratnesa, while describing her dance, he speaks of Kundali Nritta and different views on dance, promulgated by Kohala and other Acharyas. The distinction between 'Desi' and 'Margi', the Chari, the Karana, Angahara, Rechaka, Bhrarika, and the tradition of Siva and Parvati is brought out finely and described Siva and Parvati as promulgators of Tandava and Lasya.

Most distinguished among Racharla kings was Simha Bhupala. This was the period when a peculiar type of dance drama called 'Yakshagana' developed.

For glimpses into dance, during the period of Devaraya II, we have the following evidences. A Parsee traveller by name Abdul Razak travelled Vijayanagara and described about the Dasara celebrations. Maharnavami was performed with great pomp and excitement. He mentions as follows that excellent dance performances were given by courtesans.

That year, during the month of Rajab on the day of full moon (1444 BC–Asweeyuja) on a spacious background Raya laid tents and had his durbar. At the time fixed by him, all the Pradhans, Mandaleswaras, Dalavayees, Brahmins, Pandits, Poets were seated appropriately before the Raya. The gathering of the people was huge and the elephants and multi-coloured flags and horses were luminating a huge ocean of colours.

(Bhavaraju Venkata Narasimha Rao Garu–Foreign Travellers–Pracheena Andhra Desam, pp. 188-190).

There were 5 storied buildings and in them photos and paintings of various colours were hanging. In these paintings, there are images of birds, animals, men and women. They are all full of artistic excellence. Some are having panchalikavya matra and so are rotating. For every rotation, they take a peculiar shape exhibit 'hue here and there' beyond description in words.

Opposite to the ground, there was a Mantapa built on pillars with a staircase. It has nine storeys which are very vast and Raya had his durbar on the 9th floor. I was given a comfortable seat on the 7th storey and I was sitting with my staff and our friends. In the vacant land in between this mantapa and other buildings, some wonderful things are shown to the audience. There were some musicians, singers of heroic stories among them. From among the singers, there were beautiful dancers, whose cheeks were heckling in beauty and grace of the moon. Their faces brimming with youth, were like Lotus flowers, which were blossoming on the advent of spring, decorated fully with several types of jewellary, they were singing and dancing and their beauty, grace and their very looks were touching our hearts like roses. They were seated opposite to Raya, behind a beautiful curtain, which was removed from both the ends. Then they started dancing. What a wonderful dance ! They can move even the hearts of saints ! Their bodily movements, their bhavabhinaya, their side glances, were really beautiful. Our hearts rejoiced with joy. We forgot ourselves"

(Bhavaraju Venkata Narasimha Rao Garu–Foreign travellers–Pracheena Andhra Desam, pp. 188–190).

Such was the wonderful description of Abdul Razak–after seeing the dance performance in Vijayanagar.

Two important observations made by Razak can be taken note of :

1. One is that the dancers were singing while dancing. This kind of singing while dancing is peculiar to Telugu Land and this tradition can be noticed, even now among the Kuchipudi exponents.
2. The second is, before the dancer starts dancing, the curtain is raised to both the ends. Even now, Satyabhama puts her plaint on the curtain, as it is a tradition carried on through centuries.

From the reports of the foreign travellers like Barbosa, Poes and the sculptures, it can be deduced that several courtesans were patronized by the kings and they were very rich and maintained very good relations with others. They gave good performances also. (Forgotten Empire by Sewell, pp. 288-89).

The description of the Natya Mantapa by Paes is very interesting.

"Thence we went up by a title staircase and entered by a little door into a building, which is in this manner. This hall is where the king sends his women to be taught dance. It is a long hall and not very wide, all of stone sculpture on pillars, which are at a distance of quite on arms length from the wall. Between one and another is an arms length and a half, perhaps a little more. These pillars stand in that manner, all around the building; they are half pillars made with other hollows; all gilt, in the supports (pedestals) on the top are many great beasts like elephants and of other shapes. It is open".

There is a beautiful description of the durbar of Nalagamaraja as a kalabhavan and of the dance performance of a Nartaki called kanjalochana by Srinadha in his Palnativira Charithra as follows:

"kanjalochana yanu Ghanamyna patra
medanu pattapudanti manjula vani
Bharata sastrochita pranamul padiyu
Kalinga yakkanta kantika nambumlu
Vale vachi sabhavaru varninchi chuda
Chichi Rambhadulu chodyambu nandi
Sirasilu vanchiyu siggunu chendi"

(Palanati Veera Charithra)

He further says like any other woman she has no five sense but ten senses. Bharata mentioned that there are ten parts of Lasya and so this woman, as an expert in the exposition of Lasya is described to be having ten senses by Srinadha.

While entering the stage, she looked from the corners of her eyes Nalagamaraja and danced as follows in 'Ghana kala saili'.

"Samapadayuta myna sthanaka sthithine

Akhila Devatalaku alarula thoda

Pushpanjali yosanga pooni natyamulu

Samakathi vadyambu savhayella gramma"

She mixed 'margi' and Desi' styles as per Srinadha

"Velayanga Tommidi vidhemulynatti

Bhuchars Natyambu ponduga salpi

Padaharu sudhamula berigira yatti

Akasachariyu namaranga nadi

Anga jaryakhyache namarn natyamulu

Viditame tommidi vedhamula nadi

(Dr. Budaraju Venkata Sarada–The musical status of ancient poets, pp. 38-50, PHD thesis).

Gatichari Bhedamul Ganupadu nattu

Bhramana Samyukta Deepti patima meeranga

Padi bhedambulu padabheda mulunu

Sthanika sanchaya samyukta lamara"

(pa.vir.charithra 769–779)

Kanjalochana exhibited her knowledge of the various charis and Srinadha praises her excellence in several words.

He further says,

"perini desini prenkhana sudha

dandika mandala taga bahuchari

sapta tandavamulu salpa chitramuga

sabhavaralascharya samyukulya"

Thus, Kanjalochana gracefully exhibited some Desi Nritya rites also. In fact, Kanjalochana appears to be the make of Srinadha's mind and she is no parallel in Satvikabhinaya.

Even Rambha, the apsara is stunned to see her dancing.

Vallabhacharya, (some say that he is none other than Srinadha) the creator of Kreedabhiramam described the dances performed while worshipping Veerambika, the Goddess. He has highlighted "pamulata", wherein Nagavali raga in Nageswara.

"Pootkara pavanambu poorinchu pukkillu

musidi panduula toda muddu guriya

pamula vengadade, bhogirajulu

vartimpa nagasaramu
(kreedabhiramam-pamulata)

So, in Vallabhacharya's poetry there is happy blending of desi and margi styles.

Dance and music under the Vijayanagara kings :

Dance and music flourished well under the Vijayanagar kings in addition to literature.

In between 1433–34 BC, a devadasi in Agneeswara temple of Madamianu village called Anamvalatha Nachiyar, during Deyaraya II, took donation for a temple. A brother of Saluva Timmaraju and a Dwarapalaka (guard of the palace) during Deva Raya II, by name Gopundra Tspparaju wrote Tala-Deepika, a famous text on tala lakshana and another text on dance out of dedication to Lord Shiva.

R. Sewell in his "Forgotten Empire" Vijayanagara 1900 says "the fighting kings of Vijayanagar became the saviours of the south for two and a half centuries. The early members of this dynasty were in faith, but there is no record of the workings of the reformed religion, which had spread southwards before Vijayanagar became a power".

"It is said that there were 64 institutions of dance at Srisailam, which is one of the most important Saiva temples of Andhra Pradesh. During the period of Kakatiyas, Saivism was the state religion. So, all the dances were in praise of Lord Siva. Siva Tandava was very popular in those days and was moulded into different styles. (Banda Kanaka Lingeswara Rao)

"Ganapathi koutham", Siva-tandava "are prominent Saiva dances, whereas bhujanga, trasa, suddha kaustubha, puspanjali were recognised as Vaishnava dances. Slokas and kouthams are explained through Abhinaya. There is recorded evidence to show how devadasis performed dances in temples". From this account, it can be assumed how much of respect and recognition dance and music commanded.

If only the Natya Mantapa described by Paes would have been intact, it would have been a treasure and would have revealed many details about dance and music of Vijayanagara kings.

But unfortunately, it is ruined and there are no traces of its past glory. The general impression is that Vijayanagar kings patronized literature more rather than the art forms like dance and music. But it does not seem to be apt to say so. The dance poses on the temple of Tadipatri in Anantapur district which are of the same time, are very fine pieces and are replicas of the art that prevailed at that time.

In an introduction to Kreedabhiramam, Sri Veturi Prabhakara Sastry Garu mentions about the inscription of Machaladevi, a courtesan, who lived at the time of Srinadha. One such inscription can be found in the ruined temple of Chennakesava Swamy in a village called Gudimetta, which is 4 miles away on the south, to Somidevipalli Railway Station in Kurnool district. (Pendyala Venkata Subrahmanya Sastry–Andhra Sahitya Parishat Patrika. Easwaranama Samvatsara Samputa).

There is also a version that she has several other inscriptions to her credit.

An inscription No. 989 (A R No.164 of 1893 on a pillared mantapa near the Gopulara.

(New Imperial series Vol. XVI–south Indian inscriptions Text, Vol. IV).

"Swasthisree–Sri Narendra Mahadevaraku

Sandhya Depamunaku Saninda velayu etc

And

Another insciption No. 996 (AR No. 171 of 1893) on the same pillar

"Swasthisri poushya suddha panchadasiyu

Sriman Maha Mandaleswara kulothunga choda *etc.*

And yet another inscription in south Indian inscription Vol. VI, a Chebrolu inscription which speaks of "three hundred sanis and three hundred Brahmins can rule" stand proof that 'Sanis' were given lands for their maintenance.

(Andhra Sahitya Parishat Patrika–Manmagonda Gopaladeva's Sila Sasanam, p. 772 Jayanthi Ramayya Pantulu)

So, it can be concluded that the classical dance of Andhra, as evidenced in sculpture, literature and other forms took different shapes and was exhibited in temples by Devadasis and by Raja Nartakis in durbars and also by Bhagavathulu who toured and gave programmes, entertaining the people.

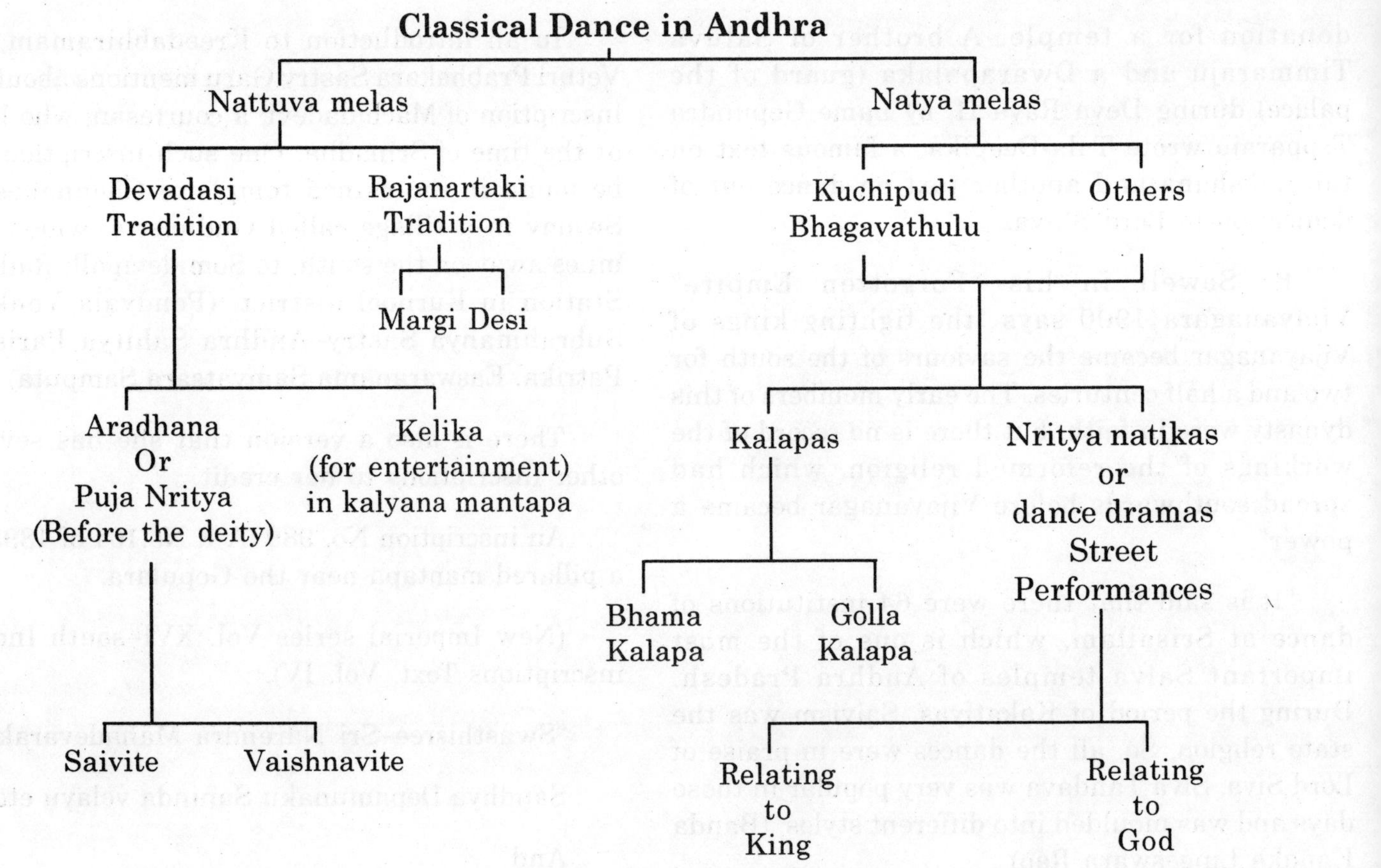

References

1. Palnati Veera Charitra.
2. Dr. Budaraju Venkata Sarada–The Musical Status of Ancient Poets–Ph.D Thesis, pp. 38-50.
3. Palnati Veera Charitra, pp. 769-779.
4. Kreedabhiramam–Pamulata, p. 224.
5. P.S.R. Appa Rao–Introduction to Nritta Ratnavali as per the guess of Sri Manapalli Rama Krishna Kavi.
6. Nritya Ratnavali by Dr. V. Raghavan, p. 134.
7. *Ibid.*
8. Nritya Ratnavali by Dr. V. Raghavan, p. 145.
9. *Ibid.*
10. Nritya Ratnavali by Dr. V. Raghavan, p. 145.
11. *Ibid.*, p. 146.
12. *Ibid.*, pp. 146-47.
13. *Ibid.*, p. 147.
14. *Ibid.*, p. 148.
15. Nritya Ratnavali by Dr. V. Raghavan, pp. 149-150.
16. *Ibid.*, p. 150-151.
17. Nritya Ratnavali by Dr. V. Raghavan, pp. 151-152.
18. *Ibid.*
19. *Ibid.*, p. 152.
20. Nritya Ratnavali by Dr. V. Raghavan, p. 153.
21. *Ibid.*, p. 154.
22. *Ibid.*, p. 161.
23. Manohar Ghosh (Ed.) 1934, Nandikeswara's Abhinaya Darpana.
24. Robert Swell–A forgotten Empire.
25. Sri P.S.R. Appa Rao–Andhrula Charitra Samskriti.
26. Pendyala Venkata Subrahmanya Sastry–Andhra Sahitya Parishatpatrika–Easwaranama Samvatsara–Samputa.
27. New Imperial Series Vol. XZ, IV South Indian Inscriptions Texts, Volume IV.
28. Andhra Sahitya Parishat Patrika–Manmogonda Gopala Deva's Silasanam, p. 112, Jayanthi Ramayya Pantulu.

11

Nritta Ratnavali—Definitions of Certain Terms

The literary monuments of ancient India are so vast and scattered and also the sculptures and paintings are beyond the capability of scrutiny and survey for a single mind, the method used in the treatment of the subject, is to give what are considered as the most popular and authentic representatives of the finest specimens and then if there is any theoretic background, to examine it, in relation to these specimens and finally to connect the whole review with the ideals of Indian art and beauty, in general and of dancing in particular.

Mr. C. Sivarama Murthi, in his Chitra-Sutra of the Vishnudharmottara wrote that the attitude of the painter in offering his paintings as a mode of worship is also reflected in the divine origin of the art itself narrated in the Vishnu dharmottara. To Vishnu itself attributed the exposition of the art of painting as he evolved the Angaharas in Natya. The Mahabharata attributes all forms of knowledge including those of the fine art to Vishnu.

We get traces of the dance art of the Apsaras from the earliest scripture Rig Veda. In Sayana's commentary of the Rig Veda, we find renderings—

"Nritya Maneo Amritah"

For dancing Apsaras Jagama Nrityatey—bodily movements in order to dance, Nritya Nrityanta for when dancing mention of the dance art of Apsaras is in galore in the ancient texts.

The puranas mention about the ritualistic dances, by the Apsaras in the Maha Vrata ceremony. They danced round the fire having pitchers full of water on their heads and pour it on the sacrificed fire. The stotra is being sung. This signifies that the sloka is an invocation to Rain God and desired richness in milk and crops. At the end of the Aswamedha Yagna, the Apsaras danced round the sacrificial fire to endow the sacrificers with might, they gave beating with their feet on the ground and sing "This is honey" (Idi Amritam).

The dance art of the Apsaras has been elaborately explained in Vikramaditya charitam.

The fable goes on to narrate that once Indra pleased Shiva by severe penance and Shiva, as a reward gave him an exquisite throne. Indra treasured the throne and decided never to part with it except to more wordhy of it than him.

In those days, Shiva's consort—Parvati had for her close companions thirty two Apsaras from Indra's court. One day, Shiva appeared before them and admired their beauty and each of them in their turn wished him to be her lord. Parvati saw Shiva's admiring looks and was full of anger. She cursed the Apsaras to become lifeless statues and adorn the throne of Indra. She blurted out to them "there in Indra's court, you will get all the admiration you came for".

The Apsaras were aghast on hearing the curse and prayed to Parvati to release them from this curse. Parvati relented and said to them that this throne would earth the each in the reign of Vikramaditya centuries later it would be found by Raja Bhoja. When he would try to mount on it, they would stop him and ask him to tell stories from the life of Vikramaditya. If he be enough to bear all of them out, then the Apsaras would be free from the curse.

It is well known that the art of dancing practised by the Devadasis is the origin of all the classical dances of India—Bharata Natyam, Manipuri Kadhak *etc.*

When the temple of Jagannath was completed, Jagannath, his brother Balabhadra and his sister Subhadra were carried in three chariots called Taladwaja, Devadalana and Nandighosha. Heavenly singers sang while Urvashi and Rambha danced. Here begins the tradition of dancing in the temple.

The Maharis of Orissa trace their origin to these heavenly dancers and have been continuing the tradition since then.

We have three stages in the institution of Devadasis. The first one is when the Devadasis were regarded consorts of the deity of the temple. They used to please the presiding deity with their art of dance and music. They were not meant for the enjoyment of human beings. A very high place was given to them at this stage. She was next to God. Such devadasis were classed as the Daivik group.

The second stage came, when she was dedicated for the enjoyment of the priest alone, the highest and the noblest of all human beings the third stage is her worst condition when she is dragged down from a high pedestal to the level of giving physical enjoyment to the common man. She became a courtesan at this stage.

"Geeta Vadyadi Militam

Laya Sutra Samanasrayam

Anga Vikshapanam Nrittam

Bhavedabhinayognitam"

(Nritta Ratnavali—p. 16)

Song mixed with the round of instrument with Laya and exhibiting Abhinaya is Nrityam, Karana mixed with Angahara is Nrittam. This never conveys any meaning. It is only mixed with Avayava Vinyasa or movement of limbs.

"Yago dwaha Mahabhisheka Nagaree

Versa pravesodhaka

Kreedanu priya sangama

Vrata Mahodanatma Jotmathishu

Yatra parva pareeksha notsava Jayananda

Pratishthe hita

Prapitshya bhyuda yaya Nritta muchitam

Sya adheva puja dishu"

(Nritta Ratnavali—p. 2)

Yagnam, marriage, coronation, entry into the city, Jalakreeda, Priya Sangamam, Vratam, Mahadanam, Putra Jananam, festival gaiety, utsavam, vijayanandam, Devalaya Pratishtha, Ishtardha Siddhi, Devapuja are the occassions, when Nrittam is exhibited for progress.

"Gatra Vikshepanardhatwat Nritta

Baheela Mangikam

Vividhena Vilasena Kshepo Vikshepa Ishyate"

(Nritta Ratnavali—p. 8-9).

To stretch the body is the benefit of it, there will be more of Angikabhinaya in Nrittam. To exhibit various kinds of beautiful poses with the help of the bodily limbs is Vikshepanam.

When "Nrit" is added to 'Kyap', the word Nrityam is formed. Nrityam is added to 'Bhava'.

After 'Nrittam', Natyam was born. Mixtures of these two is 'Nrityam'. But Bharata never called it Nrityam. Vipradasa of the 15th century, in his 'Sangeeta Chandra' has used the word 'Natyam' as a 'paryaya pada' to Nritya. Amara Simha of 4th century BC mentioned that Tandava, 'Natana', 'Natya', 'Lasya', 'Nritya', 'Nartana' are synonimous words. That means, Nritya was in good publicity by 4th century itself.

In Abhinaya Darpana, it is mentioned as follows as to how Nrityam (Lasyam) appeared on the land.

Brahma gave Natya Vedam to Bharata. He exhibited Natya-Nritta-Nritya before Siva, the Laya Murthy. Siva taught his Uddhata Nritya to Bharata through Tandu. That dance which Tandu taught to Bharata was taught to mortals by our sages. Parvati taught Bana's daughter Usha, 'Lasya' and this was learnt by Gopikas of Dwaravati. From these Gopikas, Yashitas of Sourashtra learnt Nrityam and from them, women of different countries learnt and that got established as Nritya.

Thus, Bharata, out of his adoration to 'Siva' the creator of Natya, speaks of his Natya Sastra as Brahma Proktam (given by Brahma). He added divinity to Natya Sastra.

"Pranamya Sirasa Deve

Pitamaha Maheswara

Natya Sastram Pravakshyami

Brahmana Yadu Dahitam"

So, Nrittam, Nartanam, Nartaki and Nartaka are words born out of 'Nrit'.

Relationship between Nritta, Natya and Nritya

It was Nandikeswara who defined the above three words comparatively for the first time.

"Natyam Tannatakam Chaiva

Pujyam purva kadha yutam

Bhavabhinaya Heenanthu

Nritta Mityabhi Dheeyate

Rasa bhava vyanjanadi yuktam

Nrittya Miteeryathe".

That which is "heena" or less of Bhavbhinaya is Nritta. That which is mixed with "rasa" "bhava" "vyanjanadi" is Nritya.

After him, Dhananjaya, who is the writer of Dasarupaka and Dhanika, commentator of this have discussed in detail the 'Swarupa' of the above three.

(Telugu Nataka Vikasamu—1967, pp. 11-13).

Later on Sarangdeva of Sangeeta Ratnakara, Jayana of Nritta Ratnavali have defined their 'Swarupa' in a subtle manner, as Nandikeswara did. But all these four have not agreed with Nandikeswara as regards 'Nritya'. Nandikeswara said 'Nritya' is 'rasa-Bhava vyanjanadi yukta but the other four have said that have not included, rather discarded the word "rasa". So, in their view, Nritya is not 'rasa vyanjana'. But, afterwards, Natyadarpana Karthas like Ramachandra Gemachandra (12th century) said that 'Nritya' is rasa-Bhava-Vyanjanadi yukta. Like 'Natya', Nritya is also 'rasasphoraka' *i.e.*, it is responsible for creating rasa.

Telugu poet, Nannechoda (12th century) agreed or recognised the above fact.

(Kumara Sambhava—9th chapter—p. 38)

So, it is clear Rambha Natya Varnava Nritya like Natya is 'rasa vyangara'. Nrittam is minus Bhavabhinaya. That is why it depends on Tala—Layasraya. Nrityam is full of Abhinaya. In this sense, Nritya is synonymous with Abhinaya, in the colloqual sense.

In Nritya, Sahitya (Geyas *etc.*) is mixed up. In Abhinaya, Nritya-Natya are equal. But Nritya is primarily dependent on Angikabhinaya, whereas Natya is primarily Satwikabhinaya. So, Sastrakaras have decided that 'Nritya' is prati padardhabhinaya' and Natya is Vakyardhabhinaya. So, because of these differences between, Natya-Nritya-Nritta, Nartana is of three kinds and because of the difference between Tandava and Lasya, Nritta and Nritya are of two kinds according to Sarngya Deva.

So, it can be said that Jayana's definition of Nritta, Nritya and Natya was in accordance with the ancient Sastra Karas only.

"Song, instruments mixed with Laya, performing of Abhinaya or moving limbs is Nritta (1-58).

"Mixed with Bhava, doing abhinaya is Nritya (1-50).

"Natya full of Satwika bhava, and mixed with rasa, doing abhinaya with Vakyardha is 'Natya' (1-25).

In spite of such clear definitions, in the colloqual world, Natya is used as Nritya (Malavikagni Mitram).

Till 15th century, this uncertainity continued. But Jayana's Nritta Ratnavali says more of Angikabhinaya.

Development of Art of Dance of Andhras—Literary Wealth

Dance is one of the sixty four arts enunciated by Vatsayana. Even before Bharata spoke of his Natya Sastra, dance was shining as a great art in India. In Andhra Pradesh, such a dance flourished even during the period of Satavahanas and our ancient texts and sculptures are great evidence to the progress of this art.

From the Buddhist sculptures it is evident, that our dance form was in great heights. Ajanta, Ellora paintings speak of our ancient Nritya paddhati our ancient temple sculptures, 'Aga Mokta' process are good evidences of our dance forms and their progress.

From Nannechoda's Kumara Sambhava, dance forms of Andhras are evident. Abhinaya Darpana and Bharatarnava are the two great works by Nandikeswara, a great Telugu scholar. Tikkana's description of Brihannala in Mahabharata speaks of the dance traditions of Andhra Pradesh. Nritta Ratnavali of Jayappa Senani of Kakatiya times is great evidence of dance and "Sangeeta Chintamani" of Pedakomati Vemareddy and Vasanta Rajeeyamu of Komaragiri Prabhu speak of the traditions of their times. Lakuma Devi Asthana Nartaki of Reddy king was a great exponent of our dance forms and Machala Devi of Pratapa Rudra, another Asthana Nartaki.

Palkuriki Somanadhas Panditaradhya charitra, Srinadha's, Bhimakhanda and Palnati Veeracharitra tell about the Veedhi Natakas and Yakshaganas that were in great publicity in those times.

Kandukuri Rudrakavi of Krishna Devaraya's Astadiggajas wrote Sugriva Vijayam, a popular yakshagana.

Rangajamma was a great scholar in Sanskrit and Telugu and she could gain popularity.

Kuchipudi village is the birth place of the Kuchipudi dance style of Andhras.

By 1502, itself this Kuchipudi style could get recognition by Veera Nrisimha Raya. Kuchipudi Bhagavatars could exhibit the evil deeds of Sammeta Guravaraju, a zamindar before Nrisimha raya. They could also impress Achutappa Naik and get Melathur village as a gift.

Padabhinaya of Kuchipudi Style

Late Sri Vedantam Lakshmi Narayana Sastry could give training to dancers like Indrani Rehman, Korada, Yamini Krishna Murthy, Sudha Doraiswamy, Raja Sulochana and could give performance in the International dance festival in 1951 at Paris by Mrinalini Sarabhai. Usha Parinayam, Prahlada Charitra and Kshetrayya Padas could gain utmost popularity because of their new techniques and some innovative ideas.

Some popular items of Kuchipudi, Padabhinaya of Kuchipudi style is to be mentioned specially. In an 'Astapadi' like "Dheera Sameere Yamuna Teere"—Yamuna river, Malayanila, flower gardens, drizzling of water, are to be played and situation like sunrise and sunset, plays of fish, Vihara of Gopikas, sports of Brindavana are to be shown with Padabhinaya and hava-bhavas.

Chandra Rekha was Asthana Nartaki of Vijaya Raghava. She was a great expert in Abhinaya. She could exhibit Kshetrayyas' Padams with ease and efficiency. It was during Kshetrayya's time that the method of Abhinaya could get great recognition.

Abhinaya of Astavidha Nayikas like Swadheena Patika, Proshita Priya, Uspralabdha, Virehotkanthitha, Vasaka Sajjika, Khanditha, Kalahantarita, Abhisarika is a special feature of Kuchipudi style. The Nayika has to exhibit doubt, enthusiasm, sadness, laziness in addition to feelings of love and grace, out of thirty two Sanchari Bhavas, Late Sri Chinta Venkataramayya and Sri

Vedantam Lakshmi Narayanasastry could exhibit such Vyabhichari Bhavas and could get international name and fame to their Kuchipudi style.

To show several poses of Natya Paddhati for one pada is no where found in the world except in Kuchipudi style. For this sort of process, specially, Tallapaka Varu, Ghattupallivaru, Ponangi Varu, Muvvanalluri Varu, Kasalapuri Varu, Agiripalli Varu, Sobhanagiri Varu, Kommipuramu Varu, Dharmapuri Varu—all Vaggaya Karas could write Padams.

Several of them were honoured with awards not only for writing but also for Natyabhinaya. Several of them dedicated their lives.

One Muvvaluri Sabhapathaiah did Abhinaya of "Tamara Sakshapada" in Sarabhog Asthana (durbar) so excellently that the king was very much impressed and asked him "what do you want". Then Sabhapathaiah asked for Krishna Vigraha which the king was daily worshipping. The king tried to convince him to ask for land, house, or anyother thing other than his Krishna Vigraha but Sabhapathaiah was very particular of Krishna Vigraha because he was very much impressed with it.

Veera Narasimha raya of Chandragiri invited Annamacharya in a Palanquin and asked him to write about him. But Annamacharya refused saying with a tongue, which used for singing about Venkateswara I cannot write Padams about a man. Then the king got him arrested. But when Annamacharya sang and requested Venkateswara to remove him from the tyranny of the king, with his song, his fetters disappeared. Enemies captured Chandragiri, when the king was immersed in dance and music. After realising that all this havoc and chaos is caused because of Annamayya, the king requested him to pardon him. Enemies left Chandragiri immediately and Annamacharya was honoured with all royal honours.

In some Padams of Annamacharya Sringara is depicted and in some, the secrets of life, the relationship of Atma with Paramatma is depicted.

While exhibiting Abhinaya, without having any thing in mind one has to show the feelings of having all of them like birds, flowers, flies, parrots that is why Abhinaya darpana, Bharata Rasa Prakarana are the books that are considered to be standard works on Abhinaya.

In Kuchipudi style, Adhyatma Ramayana is dedicated to Venkata Chala, Geetopadesa, Churnikas are very important.

While exhibiting Arjunas Vishada yoga, showing trembling, swelling, shivering, shedding tears is necessary, while doing Abhinaya, for Annamacharya's padams, it is good to exhibit the inner meaning of his words.

In Kuchipudi style, of Natya it is essential to exhibit Rasanubhuti (feeling of one's own experience of love, tiresomeness *etc.*)

Rama exhibits sringara while moving with Sita, Veerarasa while breaking the Siva dhanus, Hasya while talking to Surpanakha, Roudra while killing Ravana, Santa rasa while saving the sages.

Ancient Dance forms in Andhra Pradesh

From Hala's Saptasathi, it can be presumed that dance-dramas were in great publicity in Andhra Pradesh. There are stories of several poets that lived on the soil of Telugus. On account of the word "Andhri", it is evident that by the 1st century itself, Andhras developed their fine arts *(Chalukyan age—Saiva poets).*

"Gunaga Vijayaditya (848-92) had a title by name 'Gandharva—Vidya Praveena". He donated some land of Attili village to one devangana called "chellavva". IInd Ammaraju (945-70) with the encouragement of Chamekamba, a Jain, donated Kanchumarri village. She was an expert in dance and was instrumental in constructing several dance schools in Andhra and Karnataka and also Natya mantapas in temples.

In the 9th chapter of Kumara Sambhava of Nannechoda, there are references of Natya Salas. In the writings of Palkuriki Somanadha (12th century), there are many references to dance, music and dance-dramas. Sangayya's Kadha is a good evidence to their statement as Sangayya went to a ganika and she arranged a dance with her Vilasini Jana. In the Parvata Prakarana of Panditaradhya

Charitra, Somana described the dance and music programmes conducted on Sivarathri day.

Pradhama Prataparudra (1158-1195) was winner of a title called "Vidyabhushana". Somanadha might have been a contemporary to him. Ganapathi deva of Kakatiya dynasty ruled for 60 years and gave encouragement to art and architecture. Jayappa, his brother-in-law wrote Nritta Ratnavali, a great text on dramaturgy and a great contribution of Andhras to the art of dance.

Machala Devi of 2nd Prataparudra's time was a great dancer. In Kreedabhinamam, there are descriptions about her, her daughter Madana Rekha and Kama Manjari and Madhumavatti. They were also dancers perhaps. Sarada Tanaya, who wrote "Bhava-Prakasa", also belonged to this period. From the writing of Pedakomati Vema Bhupala by name "Sangeeta Chintamani", it can be presumed that Telugu Land was the origin where from dance and music spread.

During the reign of Reddy kings Yerrapragada wrote 'Harivamsa', in which there is description of sunset and holding of a red curtain before the entrance of a dancer.

The poet that was famous during this period was Srinadha (1402-1420). He was Kavi Sarva Bhowma and introduced himself as one who can recite "Sangita Sahitya Chaturya Kavitha".

Krishna Deva Raya and His Times

Krishna devaraya was not only a lover of literature but arts also. After his Vidwat Goshti, he was witnessing dance. The leader of such Nritya Mela was "Srirangaraju". His daughter was "Kuppayi" or "Kuppa Sani". Srirangaraju was recipient of a title called "Vidwat Sabha raya Ranjika". His daughter also received this title. So, "Ranjakam", became their family name or Surname. Kuppayi had two daughters—Tirumalamma and Muddu Kuppayi. Muddu Kuppayi was Raja Nartaki in the durbar of Achuta raya. From the inscription of 6.6.1531, it is evident that Achuta raya appointed her as a devadasi in Govindarajaswamy temple of Tirupathi. Another inscription tells that Tiruvenkata Manikyam, daughter of Tipp asani was given a palanquin as a matter of honour. It appears that dancers donated lands to temples, according to some inscriptions. (Most of them are in Tamil language). Resident of Belgula, Charukeerti Panditanadhyanis student by name "Mangayi" had a title like "Rayapatna Chudamani" (E.C. Vol. 341).

Ranjakam Srirangaraju and his daughter Kuppayi were exhibiting their dances in the 'Nritya Sala' of raya. In that dance school, even women of Antahpura were learning dance.

Paes, a foreign traveller, described this dance school in detail, saying that every pillar had a Nritya bhangima (dance pose) but he never mentioned the name of that 'Sala'. From the inscription of 1599 (E.C. XII Kg. 29. p. 36) it is evident that Immadi Hari Kempaya Gowda, king of Elahanka had a state dancing saloon by name 'Pattada—Nataka Sala". It may be guessed that this Sala of Krishna Devaraya, also might have had such a name.

Grand father of Jagannadha Pandita raya by name Kesavabhattu, was an expert in Kuchipudi dance and after impressing Krishnaraya by his performance, he received "Munganda Agraharam" as a gift. An inscription district. 25.11.1518, which is in Brahmeswara Alaya says that Krishnaraya gave bhudana to a Natyacharya (Rangacharya Toplist-11-1223). Krishnaraya built a 'Ranga Mantapa' in the premises of Virupakshaswamy on the day of his coronation (Introductory remarks of Vedam to Amukta Malyada—p. 147).

The interest of Krishnadevaraya in the fine arts can be seen in his literature also. In Allasani Peddana's Manucharitra (V-63) Rama Raja Bhushana's Vasucharitra (1-108) Tallapaka Tirumalayya's Vairagya Vachana Geetas there is mention of Natya Salas. Praise about several dramas can be found in his kavyas. There is detailed description of display of a drama in pingali Surana's prabhavati pradyumnam.

Rama rayala's brother Tirumala raya, received dedication of Ramaraja Bhushana's Vasucharitra and while doing so, Ramaraja Bhushana introduced himself as "Sangeeta Kala Rahasya Nidhi" (1-16). Experts among Veena players say that the poems in Vasucharitra can be played on Veena very well as ragas. Ramaraja Bhushana described an ideal Sangeeta Sala and laid down rules how it should be (111. 34). Then Krishnadevaraya's Sangeeta Sala also might have been similar. Recipient of the Kavya 'Kalapurnodayam' of Pingali' Surana by name Nandyala Krishna Vibhudu was praised as "Samsthavyana Veenagana Sarasatwa Mahatwa Marutta maajudu" (Kala purnodayam V. 227). Kakutsa Vijaya Kartha, Sri Matla Ananta Bhupala was "Sangeeta Ani Keerti" and he was also called "Vainikagresaru Swani" (p. 1-94, 29).

Konamanthri, Nritipati of Panduranga Mahatmya was known as "Gana Kala Tumburudu" (p. 1-47). So, it is clear that several experts in dance and music were adorning the Sabhas of several kings in those times.

Like Reddy rajas, who were performing Vasantotsavas, Vijayanagara kings were conducting Maharnavami Utsavas. They were conducted for nine days in the month of Asveeyuja. In addition to the remarks of Rajat, Paes also described these Utsavas in detail. In these Utsavas, there was more stress on heroic performances. There were three kinds of dancers among women—Raja Nartakis, Devadasis and Waranganas of the city. Dancers dedicated to temples were leading pious lives. Dancers of those days commanded more respect and they were chewing betel leaves in front of the king (Amukta Malyada 1-60). From the money received from these women—2000 Panas, the security guards of the city were paid. The times of Naik kings (18th and 19th centuries).

Chevvappa Naik became the ruler of Tanjore in 1550. After the war of Tallikota and after the fall of Vijayanagara empire, this Naik king became a Sovereign. Achutappa Naik was his son and ruled from 1586-1614. His son Raghunadha Rayalu (1614-1631) became the ruler. The son of Raghunadha Naik is Vijaya Raghava Nayaka (1633-73).

Raghunadha and His Contribution

Like Krishnadeva raya to Vijayanagar empire, Raghunadharaya was a Sahiti Samarangana Chakravarti to Tanjore. Raghunadha and Vijaya Raghava both were writers of many books and they encouraged writings of several writers.

The most important thing that is to be noted during their rule is encouragement to poetesses. The 2nd one is to encourage Yakshaganas and Veedhi Natakas and it was considered to be a golden age.

A great scholar like Govinda Deekashita was Prime Minister to Raghunadha Nayaka. It was he who wrote 'Sangeeta Sudha' and named it as the work of Raghunadha Nayaka, says the 2nd son of Govinda Deekshita by name Venkata Makha Chaturdandi.

But Raghunadha himself was a great scholar and expert in music and dance. Yagna Narayana Deekshita's 'Sahitya Ratnakara' (VI-1-39) gives a description of the Veena performance given by Raghunadha Nayaka for the first time.

From the slokas of Sangeeta Sudha, it is evident that Raghunadha invented ragas like 'Jayanta Sena' and talas like Ramananda, and so as to facilitate singing of all ragas on Veena, in his name, he invented ragamela. "Yakshagha Geeta Mapi gana Sailam"—a padam in Yakshagana was first defined in Sangeeta Sudha.

It can be said that Raghunadha encouraged Desi Nrityas. In his Valmiki-Charitra (III. p. 42) perini, Danda lasyamu, Bekkani, Kundali are four kinds of Nritya. From the Kavyas of Vijaya raghava and Rajagopala Vilasamu of Changalva Kalakari, it can be said he patronised many female dancers. Their names and the names of their dances are also given.

Kalakari has described 'Chandra Rekha' mostly. She was mentioned as 'Muddu Chandra Rekha'. She had many titles given by pridhvi Mahendra. She was also described as the lover of Vijaya Raghava. The list of female dancers and the names of their dances are given as follows:

Muddu Chandra Rekha—Perini

Rupavathi–Padacholi (Chowpada Kalika)

Sasi Rekha—Jakkimi (Desi lykalakani)

Loka Nayika—Durupada Kelika (Navapadashy Kalakari)

Keera Vani—Durasaina Kopu

Champaka—Sabda Chudamani

Murthy Vadhuti—Jakkini

Komalavalli—Koravu (Kopu)

Ratnagiri—Darupadamulu

Bhagiradhi—Perani

Apart from these dances like Koravanj, Sivaleela, Gujarati Desi were performed by some others.

All these female dancers are described by Chemakura Venkata Kavi as follows:

"Chelagi Impuga, Jada Cheppa Jaduva Valana, Valapimpa Nirchina Yalaru Bondlu; Vipula Bharata Kala Sastra Nipurulaina Biruda Patrulu". (Vijaya Vilasam 1-80).

From the text of Vijaya Vilasam, it is also evident that there were several 'Natya Salas'. In the city of Raghunadha itself, there was "Navaratnamaya Mantapa" (embedded with Navaratnas—Vijaya Vilasamu—p. 1).

Not only in the city. In Sringatakas also, there were Natyasalas. (Raghunadha bhudaya Yakshagana p. 13).

In Kaemarasu Venkatapathi Somayaji's "Vijaya Raghava Chandrika Vihara" there is mention of "Byte Nataka Sala Paduchu". We do not know how many such women were there. From this, it is evident that there were innumerable female dancers. That is why Chemakura Venkata Kavi described Raghunadha rayalu as follows—"Bharata Vidya durandharudyna Rangasthalambu Ramalankruthamu chesenu" (Vijaya Vilasamu-1-21). Raghunadha raya patronised not only Asthana Nrityas but also temple Nrityas. He gave donations to Ranga Pati Alaya for the sake of 'Natyas'. (Rajagopala Vilasamu—1-45).

Vijaya Raghava's Times

Vijaya Raghava wrote several yakshaganas and made them exhibited. A vaggeyakara—kshetrayya (1600-1680) visited Vijaya Raghava's Ashtana and coined padams on him. Narayana Teerdha of Krishna Leela Tarangini was a contemporary to him and the story of his 'parijatapa harana' only, was translated into Telugu as 'Nritya Natika'.

Vijaya Raghava's Dharmapatni Rangajamma wrote a street play by name "Mannarudasa Vilasamu". It is said that Asthana Kavayithri Vijaya Raghava by name Krishna mamba (Krishnagi) was an expert in dance (Natya Praveena). She was the daughter of Ravinuthala Tirumalayya, who migrated from Guntur. Display of Yakshaganas was at its zenith during Vijaya Raghava's times. Like Vijaya Raghava, Maharastra kings who ruled Tanjore, also wrote several Yakshaganas in Telugu and got them exhibited.

Naik Kings : Yakshaganas

Like the Naik kings and Maharastra kings, Naik kings who ruled Madhura and those Tondamandaru kings of Pudukkottai were themselves poets and encouraged artists well versed in dance, music and literature.

There was a Sangeeta Kalanidhi by name Tiruvengalacharya during the time of Vijaya ranga Chokkanadha. He was a great expert in playing Veena.

Satyabhama Bhama Santwana Kriti Karta by name Lingana Mahi Kameswari Kavi told about himself that he was "Vallaki Vadana Dhureena" and "Varna Geetadi Gandharva Swara Kalpana Praveena".

Copies of these Yakshaganas are available in Saraswati Mahal, Tanjore. But it appears that women never participated in dramas. They were dancers only. Kantheranarajn of Mysore (1701-13) wrote 'Natya Vidya Vilasa', mixing Sanskrit with Telugu. Female dancers spoke about their efficiency in dance. He wrote several Yakshaganas in Telugu.

Lingamugunta Matru bhutayya Kavi wrote a prabandha with three Aswasas by name "Abhinaya Darpana". Though Nandikeswara's Abhinaya darpana, was the basis for this book, there are several differences of Sampradaya at several places.

Chillakura Divakara Kavi wrote "Bharata Sara Sangraha". This was a summary of all Natya Sastra grandhas beginning from Bharata Muni's Natyasastra to Sangeeta Ratnakara. In those

Bharatas mostly, with Telugu summing up, they are available in Saraswati Mahal, Tanjore.

It is said, that Damarajn Somayya wrote a Bharatam, according to prabandha Ratnavali of Redapati Jagannadha Kavi. Somayya might have belonged to 16th century. Shahaj Maharaj's (1687-1711) Asthana Kavi by name Giriraja Kavi had a brother by name Venkatagiri (Kamigiri) who translated Abhinaya Darpana and dedicated it to Khandojiraya who was a relative of Shahaji.

Times of Nawabs of Golconda

Like the kings of the south, the Nawabs of Golconda also patronised dance, music and literature. Abdulla Kutub Shaw (1620-72) patronised Kshetrayya. There was a Vaggeyakara by name Tulasi Murthy in his Asthana. Abul Hassan Kutub Shaw (1673-1687) much impressed with the performance of Kuchipudi Bhagavatavs, gave a gift of Kuchipudi village as Agrahara.

During the period of these Nawabs, Akbar Shaw (Bade Saheb) wrote in Telugu "Sringara Manjari", that explains the differences of Nayak with Nayika. But this book is not available. Imitating this Telugu text, he himself wrote in Sanskrit another Sringara Manjari. Mentioned as the basics for his Sanskrit Sringara Manjari, there is Narasa Bhupaleeyam by Bhattu Murthy.

In Maharastra Raja—the 2nd Sarabhoji's (1798-1832) Asthana, there was Maharaja Annami Subbaraya Nathiva Varu and he was a great expert in music and dance. Her sons Chinnaya, Ponnayya, Vadivelu and Sivanandam were adepts in the art of dance. Vadivelu among them was an outstanding personality out of them. He was a close associate of Sri Tyagaraja (1767-1847).

These four brothers were the people who gave a shape to modern Bharata Natyam. They laid down basics for Alarippu, Jatiswaramu, Sabdamu, Varnemu, Padamu, Tillana and Slokabhinaya. Alaripu, Jati Swaramu, Tillana are in accordance with Nritya and Pada, sloka and sabha are relating to Nritya. Solotype of dance of Bharatanatya is extended to three hours and is mainly belonging to females.

Pallavi Rajagopalayya, who belongs to the family of Venkatrama Sastry (1st part of 19th century) has written twelve Yakshaganas in Telugu. They are being exhibited even now.

In 19th and 20th centuries, several people have written rupakas in Sanskrit and several sastric versions. Malukumalli Nrisimha Kavi wrote texts of "Bharata Sastra Sarvasvamu" and 'Sangeeta Saramu' and also a drama entitled "Jala Kreeda Vilasa Natakamu". He might have been a Natya charya. His wife Janakamma was a great poetess. Vehigoti Sarvagna Kumara Yachendra Bahadur wrote 'Nritya Ganabhinaya Sastra'. Lepakshi Venkata Narayana Kavi wrote in 1890 "Natya Pradeepana", which was a Bharata Sastra. This was mostly unpublished and only a small part is available. In this 32 Adavus were defined. He wrote several Yakshaganas and got them exhibited.

Narayana Teerdha : Krishna Leela Tarangini: The study of Lord Krishna is depicted by several parts in several ways.

"Kalaya Yaso devata Balam

Khala balaka khalana lolam

Padhi Padhihinthina dadibhadam

Pavati Mirasata Marthandam".

In these words, Narayana Teerdha speaks of his Advaita Drishti. Though he was born in Telugu land, he migrated to Tamil Nadu and settled there. But he never forgot the lifestyle or sentiments of Telugus. While writing about Rukmini Kalyanam, he gave in detail the description of a Telugu marriage and made Rukmini and Krishna, an ideal Telugu couple.

"Hema Mukta Mani chatram
Chamarasya Jana Vrutam
Kamakoti Sama Gatram
Syama Sundaram Pavitram
Heera Vatra Kati Sutram
Sardindu Vaktram
Kanakangadadi Vichitram
Sarana Gatodhara Gotram".

He talks of the Gotra—name of Krishna.

Narayana Teerdha's incomplete 'parijatha kadha' is still available in Saraswati Mahal, Tanjore.

Siddhendrayogi is considered to be his disciple and that he came back to Kuchipudi and taught his Natya Vidya to Brahmin boys there.

In addition to Krishna Leela Tarangiri, he wrote Sikyotsana, Parijatha Kadha, Varahapuri, Venkateswara Sri Varada Venkateswara Mahima Stotra, consisting of 125 slokas. He also wrote Haribhakti Sudharnavam, Bhaktyadhivarama Mala, Sandilya Bhakti Sutra Vyakhya, Sureswara-chariyula Sanchukarana, Bhattabhasha Vikasamu, Nyaya-Muktavalee Teeka, Yoga Sutra Vyakhya.

The Taranga gana Sampradaya, which Narayana Teerdha started, mixed with Sanskrit should be kept alive and the tradition should continue as Bhakti Sangeet.

Kshetrayya—His Padams

Some consider Kshetrayya's Padams as samples for Madhura Bhakti. A human being is Jeevatma whereas Krishna is Paramatma. Union of these two forces is Madhura Bhakti. But some considered his padams full with Sringara. The Padams which are now available and are within our reach reveal thoughts of very high standard. Such thoughts are considered to be jewels in any literature.

Such padams should be played by dancers for the pleasure of humanity. Not only that, literary geniouses should bring out the flavour of such tolerance and should write comments and spread them throughout the country.

Kshetrayya's birth place is Movva village in Krishna district, near Kuchipudi village. With a view to teach Padabhinaya to the students, a training institute was started by the Andhra Pradesh Sangeet Natak Academy and it was inaugurated on 14th August 1974. The academy came forward to pay for the dance teacher at Movva. It also took responsibility to run the training centre on systematic lines, so that his Sringara Padams are spread throughout the country and people get the benefit of enjoying 'Rasa', on account of these padams.

Nandikeswara tells in Abhinaya Darpana "Subhardhi bhih Prayoktavyam Mangalyam Sarvakarmasu"—which means Nritya pradarna during auspicious occassions is Mangalapradam. The dance which is performed for pleasing Gods is pious. So, it was improving, progressing and shining since Vedic times.

Kuchipudi School

This well-known school flourished from the 14th century onwards and was initiated by one Siddendrayogi. The school flourished in Krishna district at Kuchipudi. This school is primarily the Bhagavatha Kadha dance and the peculiarity is that it is practised by Brahmins. This school is the only one that attracted outside scholars, interested in music and dance and it therefore finds a place in works of dances of India, on account of its Lasya or fine display of sentiment.

A note is appended here from local records regarding the performance of this Kuchipudi school in the time of Vira Narasimha raya (1486-1509).

May we hope that in the present days, when the art of dance is receiving the utmost consideration from the cultural side, the dance in the Telugu country, will once again revive in all its prestige glory as many of the religious and philosophical truths had been preserved and inculcated mainly through the medium of the twin arts of music and dance.

References

1. Viswakosha
2. Dictionary of Vedic language—Max Muller
3. Classical dictionary of India—(PUO) Jorn Garnell
4. Satapatha Brahmana
5. Srimad Bhagavatam (Astamaskanda) 8th Chapter
6. Chitnadutna of the Vishnu Dharmottara (p. 3).

12

Kuchipudi Style

The Kuchipudi style of dance is an outstanding contribution of Andhras, to the enrichment of Indian culture. This variety of classical Indian dance was developed and preserved by male members of Brahmin families familiarly called Bhagavathulu of Kuchipudi or Kuchelapuram.

Sri Arudra, a well known poet, writer, and critic after his research study pointed out that the Kuchipudi mentioned in Machepalli Kaiflat belongs to Vinukonda revenue division of Guntur district, with a curious mind, I went to Kuichinapalli village (Kuchipudi is not there in Vinukonda division (Guntur District) and I had the opportunity of meeting Sri Subba Rao, the village Karnam and other elders of the village and an old Harikadha exponent of 92 years.

I was told that never such an art existed in their village and their fathers and forefathers never told about any performances from their village. Nobody is practicing such an art form now. So, it can be safely concluded that the Kuchipudi of Divi Taluq, where the reminiscences of such dance, form, are existing even now, can be taken as the Kuchipudi mentioned in the Kaiflat. The recipients of the land might have migrated to Kuchipudi from Vinukonda revenue division initially and later on settled at Kuchipudi.

Even before these Bhagavathulu could take up public performances, Devadasis, dedicated to god, were performing Aradhana Nritya in temples. May be solo performances or in groups. An inscription in the temple of Srikakuleswara or Maha Vishnu temple at Srikakulam of Divi Taluq, Krishna District, speaks of 300 Devadasis. It is a well known fact that Srikakulam was the capital of Satavahana kings and that they patronized dance and other fine arts.

Natya charyas, with their original ideas might have given a different shape and the performers, depending on the patronage they received, might have given solo performances or group performances. So, it can be also concluded that the elite and the royal hierarchy, only were concerned more, with the performances and patronage, though the audiences consisted of the high and the low.

As the forms of performances were on popular themes, known even to the uneducated, they were witnessed and appreciated by one and all. It is interesting to note that the dance practiced by the temple dancers, was slowly handed over to the elite, who in their turn, taught to their future generations with utmost dedication and fervour.

The earliest reference in history to the Bhagavathulu of Kuchipudi is in the Machepalli Kaifilat written in 1502 AD (Dr. Vissa Appa Rao). We gather from the Kaifiat that a party of Bhagavathulu went to Vijayanagar during the reign of Vir Narasimharaya. The king, who had already heard of their name and fame, ordered for a performance, which he attended along with his queen and other members of the royal family. The artists enacted a play, exposing the misrule of Sammeta Gurava Raju of Siddhavatam. As a result, immediate steps to replace Gurava Raju were taken by the king, to the surprise of one and all.

Their prayer song:

"Angikam Bhuvanam Yasya
Vachikam Sarva Vangmayam
Aharyam Chandra Tararkam".

Indicates that, in the initial stages, they were enacting a variety of Siva Lila Natya and also during the Kakatiya period.

But with the advent of Vaishnavism and under the influence of Jaya Deva, they probably began representing popular stories of Bhagawata purana and this must have given them the name 'Bhagavathulu'.

Inscriptions of 8th, 9th 10th centuries show the existence of another group of artists known as 'Nattuva' Melas', in Kashmir, Andhra, Tamilnadu and Karnataka. In these Nattuva melas, the importance of women artists was deteriorating gradually and men, with an intention to preserve the quality and pristine purity, organized Bhagavata Melas with men only. They were receiving education in Sanskrit and Telugu and were proficient in Natya Sastra, Nandikeswara's Abhinaya Darpanam, and Alankara sastra and under went a well disciplined and rigorous training in Nritta, abhinaya and music.

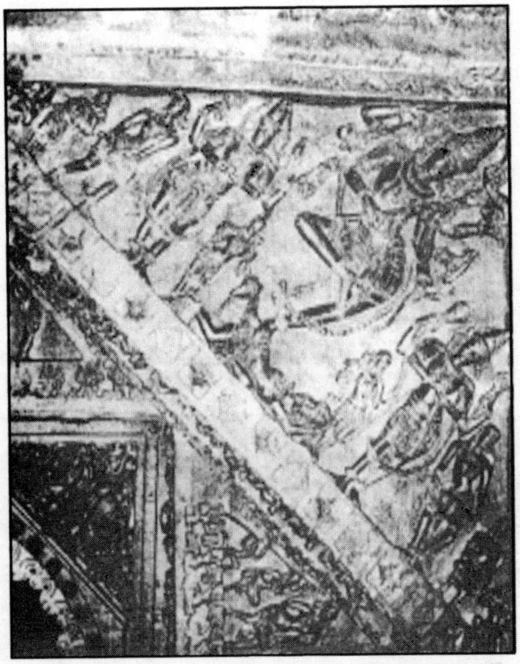

With the fall of the Vijayanagara empire, these artists migrated to Tanjore and they were patronized by the Nayak Kings. King Achutappa Nayak, who ruled from 1561 to 1614 AD, granted an agraharm to 500 Brahmin families, with a land of 5 acres, a house and a cow for each in order to encourage and develop the art of dance. This village known as Achutapuram originally became popular as Melattur or Melaputuru which is 8 kilometres away from Tanjore. The court language was Telugu in those days and so dance dramas written in Telugu were enacted. One Melattur Venkatrama Sastry, who was working as Vidwan in Pudukkottai, migrated to Melattur and wrote fourteen dance dramas, like Prahlada Charitam, Harischandra, Rukmini Kalyanam. He was contemporary to the great music composer, Sri Tyagaraja and there is evidence to show that Tyagaraja visited him.

Even today, in the villages like Melattur, Sulamangalam, performances are given by local artists, who migrated to live in different places, in search of employment. They gather for Nrisimha Jayanthi now with their families and give performances to keep up the tradition of their ancestors. They are all highly educated some are bank employees, income tax officers and only some are teachers. Their old people live with the property left off in the village.

I had the proud privilege of witnessing some of the performances by them during May 1987 and so, I would like to give in detail some of my personal observations. (see Chapter on Bhagavata Mela)

The religious fervour and the dignity with which the performances are given, is really very interesting and though there is not much of patronage from any corner, they are carrying on their humble effort with utmost sincerity and dedication. These youngsters, though not strictly professionals, give performances, after a few rehearsals. The original text, which was written in Telugu, is now rendered by them in Tamil.

For instance, to provide continuity, the linkage is given as follows. "Kadha kramamabethi danina" This is rendered in Tamil. Among the audiences many are Tamilians only. But they are able to follow and enjoy the performance. That is the beauty of it. So, for a cultural synthesis, language never stands as a barrier even before or now.

One Subba Iyer, an old man of nearly 70 years, has got a metallic and melodious voice and he sings continuously for all the 7 hours, *i.e.*, throughout the play, which starts roughly at 8 PM, and goes on upto 3 AM. Mention should be made of two important characters—the hero and the heroine. The hero is a teacher who works in Tiruchinapalli and the heroine is a local boy, a village karnam. His father, a landlord, was receiving guests and feeding them in their house, thinking that it is a ceremonial duty. My personal acquaintance, with all of them and their affection and intimacy is an unforgettable experience for me.

It is not known why 'Vira' Rasa was given so much of importance. Might be to rejuvenate people or might be due to the influence of Bhajana Sampradaya which was the origin once.

It is interesting to note that the dance dramas of Kuchipudi and Melattur have common characteristics. For instance the Pravesa Daruvu which introduces the characters on the open stage, in front of the temple, torch lights, the bag–pipe called the drone, the mridangam and the back-ground music are the same.

It has to be concluded that the solo performances given by the temple dancers, took a different shape in course of time and the rulers encouraged raja–Nartakis, who also followed the same rules of dance. This is now what is being called Andhra

Natyam by Sri Nataraja Ramakrishna Garu. I had an elaborate discussion with Sri Vempati China Satyam Garu, who is the doyen among the contemporary dance teachers of 'Kuchipudi'. He explained to me at length the rules or code of conduct, followed by his ancestors, especially his father, who fasted for the whole day of performance and performed pooja around the stage with a religious fervour and pristine purity. Probably, this goes to say that the Bhagavatha sampradaya, followed by the Kuchipudi is of high standard and in devotion to god.

The original dance form must have taken different forms as times went on and Natya Charyas, with their new innovative ideas, might have invented new techniques and methods to give performances. But so long they followed the rules prescribed by Bharata and others, it is nothing but classical. It is a wonder why this form of dance was not included in the list of classical dances. Morever, it was also considered to be folk type by some. Andhras, being what they are, might have not gone to far off places or might have taken care to see that the other man does not get name and fame, though it is not beneficial to himself. Anyway, it is all a past story. Now that this type of dance is getting, glory all over the globe, one need not feel pessimistic.

Epigraphical evidences of the plates in different temples show that there were several women, dedicated to god. For instance, Chebrolu Sasanum tells us of 300 'Sanus' (Devadasis) (Epic indice Voi Vi-Andhra Sahitya Parishat Patrika–by Jayanthi Ramayya Panthulu.)

This Art, which was once a monopoly of Devadasis came ino the hands of the elite in course of time. When we make a comparative study of Bhagavatamela traditions of Kuchipudi and Tanjore, it is clear that the Bhagavata mela of Kuchipudi is synonymous with that of Tanjore especially Melatur.

Kshetrayya wrote 'padams' about Movva Gopala, and with the introduction of Movva Gopala padams, which are classical models of lasya in addition to the art of abhinaya, there was further development of Kuchipudi style. These padas deal with Nayaka and Nayika bhavas and stand out as masterpieces of erotic psychology. Kshetrayya, was a master musician and dancer and hailed from Movva, a tiny village near Kuchipudi. He was also patronized by Vijaya Raghava Nayaka of Tanjore. Kuchipudi artists specialized in the abhinaya of the padas of Kshetrayya and these padas because of the main stay of Rasabhinaya and Satvikabhinaya and elevated the art to a high degree of excellence.

A New Technique : Bhamakalapam—Solo Type

Siddhendra yogi, a disciple of sant Narayana Teerdha wrote Bhamakalapam, which came to lime light in course of time. The story goes that Narayana Teerdha, also a contemporary of Tyagaraja wrote Krishna leela Tarangini and several Adhyatma Ramayana Keertanas. Being a blind man, he could not see Krishna dancing on his chest, while he was singing. But Siddhendra yogi could see Krishna and out of that experience and immense inspiration he wrote Bhamakalapam. It is the story of satyabhama. Who is full of pride and who requests celestial Lord Krishna to get the celestial Parijata tree to her garden. It is not known where from this yogi hailed and what were his other works. But he belonged to the seventeenth century. He took an oath from the residents of Kuchipudi, that every boy born on the soil should give performance and when villagers promised to do so; he came to Kuchipudi, after taking jalasanyasa. It is said that he belonged to Kuchipudi and when he wanted to come back to meet his wife, there were floods in Krishna river and he took sanyasa in the midst of the river in spate. But there are no authoritative evidences to show what is what. Nothing is known about his parentage or nativity also.

Several artists participated in this dance–drama which gives scope for the exhibition of sringara, karuna, Hasya, Vira and other Rasas. But only one gifted artist renders padabhinaya in a single rasa generally vipralambha sringara and develops bhavabhinaya to its highest experience elevates the artist prominently to heights. This is the speciality of Kuchipudi and out of this, a solo form is culled out in the modern times.

Abdul Hasan Kutub Shah, Nawab of Golconda (AD 1672–1687) who gave away the village of Kuchipudi as agraharam to the families of Brahmins who dedicated their lives to this great art, issued a copper plate to this effect. The oath taken by the Brahmins was honoured and the art was handed over from generation to generation and the great heritage is preserved even today.

Narayana Teerdha who was also a 'Yati' lived in between 1680 to 1690 AD and he composed and sang several sabdas or sollukattu, at the end of some of the songs indicate that the 'yati' was very familiar with natya and he intended his composition to be put to dance. Kuchipudi artists incorporated his 'tarangas' also into their art and improved the quality of its Nritya. Jayadeva's Astapadas also were rendered by these artists with efficiency and perfection.

Golla kalapam is another philosophical dialogue between a Brahmin and a milk–maid and this was a new addition to the reportiere of Kuchipudi school of dance during the latter half of the 19th century. Annamacharya's samkeertanas of Lord Venkateswara are another addition by the modern artists.

Dasavatara, depicting the ten Avataras of Lord Vishnu is yet another interesting item of Kuchipudi style.

Nearly 200 years ago, a family of Kuchipudi dancers were induced to migrate and settle in the village of Kappurralla near Alampur (Mahabubnagar) by the Nawab of Banganappali, who granted them a piece of land as Inam. To this day, we find their successors performing Bhamakalapam but their style is slightly different from Kuchipudi style.

Bhagavathulu of Pothakamarri were experts even earlier to Bhagavathulu of Kuchipudi, in giving performances of Bharatam and Bhagavatham. They were giving 'Natya–seva' before Narasimhaswamy of Ahobilam in Kurnool district. Challa Muddukrishna, Challa Kalattayya, Challa Mohanakrishna were eminent experts of this Bhagavata tradition. They took the prestige of this style to Maharashtra. It seems that every male child was taken to the temple of Kalattayya and swinging bells were tied down to his feet and thus he was given the first lesson in dancing. The Nawab of Banaganapalli gave this village of Kapatrala as an inam to this artist.

"Sri Velayapala Varidhi Pavvalinchi jo" was a lullaby written by these Bhagavathulu. Tallapaka Annamcharya has mentioned about them and so their expertise in song and dance can be judged. Nidadavoluvenkata Rao Garu, an eminent researcher and scholar, while writing introduction to "Arts and origin" by a poet by name 'ellora' has mentioned that they belong to 1280 roughly. So it is evident that in Rayalaseema region also, there were Bhagavathalu since several centuries though now they are missing.

Roughly in between 1700-1750 AD, the Nawab of Banaganapally brought some artists from Kuchipudi and gave them lands not only near Kapatrala and Kotakonda area. Most popular among them is the 'Challa' family Bhagavatham Dasu Bhotlu is the first among them and Bhagavatham is their prestige name, it seems.

Parijathapaharanam, of Siddhendra Yogi was displayed with devotion, by this Challa family. Late Shri Bharata Sastry is the ninth inheritor of Sri Narayana Sastry and he was an expert in displaying Bhamakalapam. Gollakalapam, and the padas of Keshetrayya. He was giving Astapadas of Jaya Deva, with Sanskrit commentary with great skill, since he was a scholar in Telugu and Sanskrit, besides his expertise in dance and music. There seems to be some difference in their style of steps and Jativinyasa from that of Kuchipudi and this was pointed out in the Natya Sadassu, conducted by A.P. Sangeeta Nataka Academy. Some parts of their kalapam were tape recorded. When the Academy was making serious attempt to study the origin and details of their tradition, he passed away unfortunately and so, there was no opportunity for future generations to know about their tradition.

What is now known as Tanjore style of Bharata Natyam with Alarippu, Jatiswaram, Sabdam *etc.* is of a recent origin, being less than 150 years old. It developed as an elegant style from Sadir Nrityam, which was practiced by devadasis and courtesans. Dr. Padma Subrahmanyam, who did research on Bharata's Natya Sastra says that the present Bharat Natyam is a Natya prescribed by Bharata Muni.

Smt. Chitra Visweswaran, another exponent of Bharata Natyam, is of the view that Bharata

Natyam was there from the time of Silpadhikaram a famous dance drama of Tamilnadu.

The solo type of Natya that was exhibited in temples and Durbars of the ruling classes was the original form and from this, the latter poses came. Raga Alapana and singing of padas in Bharata Natyam were greatly influenced by the Katcheri Music during the last 100 years. The Kuchipudi style resembled the music of pre-Tyagaraya days, not only in singing but in Nritta and Nritya, sabda muktayimpu and tirmanam. This Bhagavata kattu or bani is of historical importance.

In Kuchipudi style, what is termed as lasya is more and certain fine sentiments are evoked by the display of certain Mudras and facial expressions. Let us now study in detail the classical features of Kuchipudi style in the light of the guidelines given by sastrakaras.

There is a world of difference between the two terms viz classical and popular. Any classical form is of high order, having association with chaster, highly intellectual and stiff forms of expression and also expressed in Sanskrit language which is the mother of all languages. Popular version gives an air of a natural, facile and easily understood mode of presentation.

Yamini Krishna Murthy

Speaking of gestures, A.K. Coomaraswamy the famous art critic says "as the musician has neither the liberty nor the necessity of inventing new notes of haphazardly applying the existing ones, so the nata or the dancer has no room for being original by inventing gestures *etc.* for that is the business of the masters of the art, Acharyas, who know the theory and its practice thoroughly well".

The ten vital necessities of a dancer are described by Nandikeswara as 'agility', 'Steadiness' (Sthiratwam), a sence of delineation or straight position of all the limbs (Rekha), practice in the Bhramara Movements, expressive glance (dristi), endurance (as namah) intelligence (Medha), devotion of the art (Sraddha), articulate verbal expression (Vacaka) and ability to sing (gitam). Finally the achievement of Rasa is mentioned, which is the ultimate aim of dance.

References

1. The Art and Architecture of India (2nd edition London, 1956) Buddhist remains in Andhra.
2. K.R. Subramanyam–(Bet 225–610 AD) Madras (1932).
3. Yasastilaka–Soma Devasuri.
4. Amarakosam.
5. Abhilashi Tartha Chintamani.
6. India in Panini's time–Gold Stacture (German).
7. Dasarupaka.
8. Sarasika–K.K. Krishna Murthy.
9. Cave Sculpture of AP—by Chandra Mouli.
10. Rayavachakam.

The cave Temples of India–(London 1880) J. Fergusson and J. Burgess and RP Spiars.

13

Kuchipudi Style–Its Classical Form and Features

Kuchipudi dance is not only ancient but also perfect from historical and literary perspective in its technique. The evolution and development of this art is very interesting.

Kuchipudi style is a unique combination of Lalita and Uddhata types and it is a fusion of pure dance, music and Abhinaya. Another significant feature of the mode of dance is that the dancer renders vachikabhinaya also.

The items that formed the repertoire of Kuchipudi school of dance are Bhamakalapam, Golla kalapam, Vidhinataka, Yakshaganas and also Dasavatharas of Sri Mahavishnu, Astapadas of Jayadeva, Tarangas of Narayan Teerdha and padams of kshetrayya.

Kuchipudi style of dance. In accordance with comprehensive principles and techniques of the classical dance as enunciated in Natyasastra by Bharata Muni, has highly developed its classical features has come down to posterity in a dance-drama form. Under royal patronage, arts and crafts in AP flourished through centuries and they represented stories, with high ethical talent, reflecting various artistic trends of the people of different times.

Very fine and delicate dance sculptures of dances of apsaras, gods and goddesses with the accompaniment of musical instruments decorate the temples of Amaravathi, Ramappa temples at Palampet (Warangal), cave temples of Bhairavanikonda in Nellore district and other ruined temples of Hampi.

Recent excavations conducted by the Archaeological Department of Government of India in Andhra Pradesh reveal that rich traditions existed in the art of dance since the times of Satavahana emperors of the second century BC. The sculptures reveal that there were two schools of dance (1) devadasi (2) Kelika existing under the patronage of temples and rulers of the country. It is said that there were three hundred families of devadasis at SKLM, the original capital of the Satavahana Empire. At Ghantasala, before the onset of the influence of Buddhism, an exclusive street consisting of the families of devadasis and kelikas existed.

In the Amaravathi sculptures, there are four dancers and the central figure suggests a pose, which is similar to modern Harappa of Bharata Natyam. The movement made by the Narthaki. Just after she enters the stage she stands in *vaisakha* basic attitude (sthana) and sways her limbs in all the prescribed monuments (recitas or rewcakas p.187 iv 281-282 commentary) she carries a pushpanjali or a handful of flowers (Bharata's great commentator Abhinavagupta describes the karana for this as talapushpapuja and after offering them all around to the Gods, she begins to dance. This excellent pose suits the dancer for a graceful feminine dance.

In the drawing of mack enzie published by Fergusson (pl. IXXIII–fig. 1) six dancers are entertaining a king by their art. The central one among the three is more in Vaisakha than in the Mandala sthana and her hands are on the waist. The karana here appears to be 'chinna' with suggestion of valitorn and apaviddha. The dancer has raised her leg in the *'Bhajanganita fashion'*. Her left hand is in the 'Recita' attitude and the right in the 'pataka hasta' near shoulder.

To the front, there are three dancers in a row. The first one stands in 'Sampada sthana'. The dancer to her right is in karana known as latavrscika, her left hand and leg being in the 'tala' and vrisehika postures respectively. The pose descent from heaven. She is balanced on the other side by another dancer in similar pose.

The other scene is in a harem, where a dancer shows her skill with her feet and moves in 'Atikranta karana' which is suggestive of valour. She answers the description of a perfect dance sense, who while marking the tala, with her feet, uses the art of gesture with her eye movements and symbolic postures of the hand, to express the emotions of the song, poured out by her sweet voice (Abhinaya Darpana, Text 36 p. 5).

One of the sculptures first dug out from Amaravati by Col. Mackenzi and sent to the Asiatic Society of Bengal, is now preserved in the Indian Museum at Calcutta. It shows some of the Devas dancing merrily, while some others play on musical instruments, as the Boddisatwa descends to the earth in a beautiful pavilion from the Tushita heaven for birth in the royal palace of Suddhodana. A deva towards the extreme right top behind the pavilion is dancing in the famous karanas known as Vridhvajana.

Thus Amaravati sculptures include all the four elements of Abhinaya, angika, vachika, charyika and satvika. Angikabhinaya is seen in various hastas, karanas and stanas. Vachikabhinaya is suggested by the musical instruments which accompany the music of the dancer. Even Aharyabhinaya, the dress, suggestive of the theme, can be seen in the dress and ornamentation used for the figures.

The Natya poses, described by Bharata and Abhinavagupta as pindi Bhandas, are found in the Amaravathi sculptures. These dance poses described by the authoritative texts in words, have taken beautiful shape in Amaravathi sculptures. One such beautiful picture is found in Amaravathi (group of dancers) where four women dancers dance as a group. The grace and the beauty is praiseworthy. Among the rare postures preserved in the British museum, there is another beautiful dance pose. While a woman is playing on the flute, another woman plays on veena. Another woman dances in sequence. In Guntur district, in a place called 'Goli', there is a beautiful sculpture, where a woman is playing on veena. In Nagarjuna Konda, a woman plays on vipanchi, and three women dance as a group.

Of all the dance and sculptural poses, of the Kakatiya period, those of Ramappa temple are really praiseworthy.

Those Andhra writers who wrote about the history of dance and music opined that Kakatiya dance and sculptural wealth are clear examples of the descriptions of Nritta Ratnavali.

On the big temple of Palampet, on the pillars of Dwarabandhas, there are dance poses carved on stone. Inside, there are several dance poses. On the east side of Ramappa tank, on the edge of the tank there is a big temple, there are figures of women drummers and dancers in several poses. So also, on the western side there are sculptures of women drummers in several poses on the fort of Warangal, there are such poses carved out even on the circular umbrella type plank. On Swayambhu Lingeswara temple in the Warangal fort, there is a dance pose of Sivatandavam.

Even the Sanskrit and Telugu scripts produced during Kakatiya period, say that the art of dance was very popular. Jayappa's Nritta Ratnavali, which is the best of the dance texts produced in Andhra. Jayappa tells that he wrote this great text in between 1253–54.

Vema Bhoopala in his "Sangita charitam" kumbakarna in 'Sangita raja' made use of the Nritta Ratnavali. It is a sangraha Rachana of Bharata's Natya Sastra and mentions about the then prevalent Desi Nrityas also. It is a valuable text as it describes the Margi Nrityas mentioned by the great sage and Abhinava gupta. It also speaks of the comments made by Keertidhara and Bhattatandu. When viewed from the rare texts of these great writers their basics are found in south India.

In the chapters on Desi Nritya, Jayapa's Perini, Prenkhanamu, Dandarasakamu, Sivapriyamu, Chindu, Kandukamu Bhandika mu, Ghantasari, Charanamu, Bahirupam, Kolatamu *etc.* are mentioned as Janapadas and regional techniques of dances. Those styles which are not found in contemporary Yadava kings productions of Sangeetaratnakara, are found in these chapters.

In the Telugu writings of those days, not only suggestions are found, some more traits of art of dance are found. In the Panditharadhya Charita of Somanadha, in the Parvata Prakarana, in addition to the technical terms description of the Janapada Nrityas mentioned in Nritta Ratnavali are found. The great text established good relationship between dance and Saivism and described the grandeur of Maha Sivarathri utsava in Srisailam.

Jayappa Senani

Bhama Kalapam

It is musical prabandha in Telugu which rotates to Bhagavatha tradition and was written by Siddhendrayogi. The story is depicting the pranaya kalaha of Lord Krishna and Satyabhama. The way the story is depicted and the style in which Abhinaya was done is very beautiful, attractive and could attract the attention of one and all and it could achieve special laurels for Andhra's artistic fervour.

Yati Narayana Teerdha had described Krishna in his Krishna Leela Tarangini as Jagannadha, as a great lover of Radha and their pranaya Kalaha is a beautiful episode, written in Sanskrit. Siddhendra, with a view to bring Krishna Kadha to the level of common people, has mixed up Nrittam, Nrityam and Abhinaya in such an exemplary way that an experiment was made in Telugu when he wrote Bhama Kalapam.

This story could gain such great publicity among people that many tried it in many ways and several poets wrote it in many ways and it was danced and patronised by many and is still being appreciated by all

The Kalapa nartana Reeti (the method of presentation) of Bhamakalapam could win the hearts of people and all artists from Barampuram to Kurnool could play the Bhama Kalapam even in remote places, to which there were no living roads even.

The original story of Siddhendra was adopted by several writers like Nethimarla, Nagarikanti, Duvva, Chintalapati, Narasingapalli, Kesavapuri, Venkayala, Sri Dasu Sriramulu *etc.* Kuchipudi Bhagavatars are playing Siddhendra yogi's script as well those of Dasu Sriramulu and Nagarikanti and Kesavapuri.

Devadasis of West Godavari district are playing scripts of Nullimarla, Duvva, Narasingapally, Kesavapuri in addition to Siddhendra yogis writing.

East Bhagavatars and artists of Srikakulam and Vizag districts are playing scripts of Vankayalavaru, Chintalapati Varu, Narasingapalli Varu in addition to Siddhendra yogis writing.

Kotakonda Bhagavathars of Kotakonda and of Royalaseema are playing Siddhendrayogis story as well as the writings of Nagarikanti Varu, Kesavapuri Varu.

In Telengana region, Yakshagana's are in good publicity but Bhama Kalapam is not being played by Bhagavatars.

Except in Devadasi style, only men are playing as women.

In Andhra Desa, women have learnt this Bhagavatha style and are exhibiting Bhama Kalapam with great talent and this is a matter of pride.

Siddhendra Yogi taught Bhama Kalapam to Kuchipudi Bhagavatars and exhibited before Padusha of Golconda and Kuchipudi was granted as gift to the artists as we read earlier.

Nawab of Banaganapalli incited some Bhagavatars to Rayalaseema and gave Kotakonda, Kapatrala villages as gifts and popularised their great art in Rayalseema.

Zamindars of East Godavari, educated Agra have Kulu patronised Devadasis. The zamindar of Pithapuram Sri Gangadhara Rama Rao made a special writing of this Kalapa and gave training to a family and that is Nellimarla's Kalapam.

In addition to patronising artists, some of East Godavari learnt this Kalapa by themselves and exhibited Vankayala Balarama Murthy wrote this Kalapam and freely taught to artists and propagated it. Chintalapativarn were Kshatriyas. They made a special Kalapa and propagated it. Narasingapalli Venku Naidu got a special Kalapam in dedication to Venugopala Swamy of their village and patronised publicity of it. Thus, the small seed sown by Suddhindra could develop into a mighty tree and could develop into several branches.

Some famous artists of this Kalapa:

Sri Chinta Venkatanamayya, Sri Venpati Venkata Narayana Garu and Vedantam Lakshmi Narayana are very famous artists.

After Kuchipudi, Mandapeta of East Godavari is famous for this Kalapa. One Duggirala

Manikyamba was very popular. She taught this art to many. Mandapeta had sixteen Kalapa players, still there are some old artists in Mandapet. Pandir Venkata Ratnam Nayudu Satyam, Pendyala Satyabhama of Pithapuram Kunti Madhavaswamy Smt. Kone Chottiraju, Aunabullula Venkataratnam of Mummadivaram are some famous dancers of this tradition.

The style of East Godavari is called 'Bobbilo Bani'. A great expert in this style is Sri Nandivarana Venkayya Sri Varada Adinarayana, Sri Dudala Sankarayya, Sri Jontalapati Jagannadham are very famous exponents of this style.

Out of Kotakonda artists, challa Bharata Sastram Lakshmi Narayana is very popular.

Artists of East Godavari are good singers and are popular with their singing. The rest exhibit their play and Abhinaya.

With this Kalapa, the great picture of Bhagavatha art in Andhra can be judged.

Alekhya

Jonnalagadda Anuradha, a famous exponent of Kuchipudi (Dean, Hyderabad Central University, Dance Deptt.)

Some Luminaries of Kuchipudi Style

Vedantam Lakshmi Narayana Sastry of today's Kuchipudi dance was a legend in his life time. He was creator of a new tradition, which was responsible for the quick rejuvenation of Kuchipudi art form. The three stalwarts—Sri Chinta Venkata Namaiah, Sri Kumpati Venkatanarayana and Vedantam Lakshmi Narayana Sastry emerged as the leading spirits of the destiny of Kuchipudi art. The eldest among the three was Chinta who found an alternative to the Kalapam tradition. Chinta Venkata Namaiah's (1860-1949) experiment was a success because he carefully modelled it on the classical framework of Bhama Kalapam. He took up Yakshaganas of mythical importance and also obtained the assistance of actor-disciples like Hari Chalapati, Vedantam Chalapati, Vedantam Janardanaiah, Vedantam Ramayya, Vedantam Ramakrishnayya, Vedantam Raghavayya, P.V.G. Krishna Sarma. Venkatarama Natya Mandali founded in 1875 was true repertoire of the best type. The 2nd one was Vempati Venkata Narayana (1871-1935) who became famous as Kalapam specialist gaining such title as "Kaliyuga Satya Bhama" for his excellence in Bhamakalapam which emphasised Satvikabhinaya. He was proficient in Vachika Angika and Satvika. The third in order was Vedantam Lakshmi Narayan Sastry (1880-1957) whose solo dance turned out to be a boon to himself and Kuchipudi art itself. The Abhinaya of Devadasis attracted him. He was more akin to lasya style.

The most fascinating part of Vedantam Lakshmi Narayan Sastry's artistic splendour was

Smt. Alehhya

Km. Pavani

his astonishing consolidation of different compositions quite dissimilar from each other. It included Puja Nrityam, Pada Varnam, Varnam Swara Pallavi, Jati Swaram, Javali into a repertoire, which could be followed by himself, and also his students for generations. Sloka and Tyagaraja Keertana, Adhyatma Ramayana Keertana Tarangam and Astapadi also found place. There were Sanskrit, Telugu, Tamil, Hindi and even Marathi songs.

Vedantam Lakshmi Narayana Sastry was a genius and a giant and was a great visionary. Not only of Kshetrayya's Padams, but also of a number of others (over 150 items) were choreographed by him and he built up Jatis based on emotional and rhythmic components. Two important aspects engaged his attention—Abhinaya and writing performance manuals for Abhinaya.

Abhinaya

Vedantam Lakshmi Narayana Sastry's attitude towards Abhinaya, specially of Padams depended on a combination of Angika and Sattvika thus giving a secondary place to vachika. He was an expert in showing a Bhava and employing several Mudras in quick succession to suit the Bhava.

Pada-Abhinaya relates to a Nayika pining for love. If this is enacted by a male performer, he can only creat an imaginative reality. If the heroine is shown as pining for Movva Gopala—her agony is narrated in the text. Mukhajabhinaya establishes it. This can be shown in thirty different Mudras, each time evoking a different image, each relating to Gopala. The text is only two lines in script. But this can be elaborated in Abhinaya by any amount of time.

In a note on Balasaraswati learning Abhinaya from Vedantam Lakshmi Narayana Sastry, Sri N. Pattabhiraman quotes a conversation between Lakshmi Narayana Sastry and Balasaraswati as follows (Sangeet Natak 72-73, April-September 1974, p. 27).

She (Balasaraswati) studied with Vedantam Lakshmi Narayana Sastry to gain new insights into Abhinaya. Sastry was an expert in the interpretation of Padams. He spoke his own idiom. He would ask Bala "can you do this varnam? How could you cast its horoscope?" Tiruppamburam Swami Nadha Pillai was not greatly impressed with Sastri's musical attitudes, but Bala was quick to appreciate his creative imagination. She tells us how Sastry commanded her to "cast the horoscope" of a Todi Varnam one day. "I did it without any repetitions. He responded by asking me to give it up and stick to Padams! "They are your family's heritage" he said and "with some one like your mother singing Padams, you can have the whole world in your hands".

Thus Vedantam Lakshmi Narayana Sastry was credited with supplying a performance manual for each one of the compositions he set for choreography. He called it as 'Jaatakam' (horoscope) of the song. The Jaatakam contained thorough description of the type of heroine chosen, the basic rasas, the avasthas, the Vibhavas and Anubhavas. This was almost a word-to-word description of the imagined performance. He taught his students in this method. This helped all his disciples to become able teachers.

The above method is not entirely new. In our Sastraic models, we have a sloka or a poem being commented up on with a word-to-word meaning (ardham) followed by a tatparya.

In dance also, Abhinaya is embedded in several layers of expression—like Padabhinaya, ardhabhinaya, Vakyabhinaya, bhavabhinaya, Sareerabhinaya and finally Sampurnabhinaya. At a time when these in-depths practices died away, Vedantam Lakshmi Narayana Sastry had revoked them.

His contribution to Kuchipudi art is both intensive and extensive. He introduced the practice of presenting individual items in a systematic way and also built a huge repository of items. They are very rich in Sahitya and so varied in their emotional content. He introduced girls into dance and became the visionary leader of Kuchipudi dance world. He also designed the costume of a female Kuchipudi dancer.

Kuchipudi owes its national fame to him. By constantly touring, demostrating, performing and teaching Kuchipudi art, he kept the flag very high. He was a rare creative genius. He will be remembered as long as solo dance tradition of Kuchipudi continues to be a prominent mode of dance recital.

As a man, he was very simple and innocent. His needs were very few. He was a good teacher. As a performer, he was excellent. His Abhinaya new no comparison. His Jati elaborations were full of laya and bhava.

His disciple, M/s Kanchanamala gave a wonderful description of Lakshmi Narayana Sastry, who as Bhama was looking very elegant and in one hour a 65 year old man was looking as a 25 year old Bhama after his make-up and was walking proudly.

Kanchanamala, who was a dance teacher of Bharata Natyam at Tirupati and her sister Rangamani, who later became a professional medical doctor were daughters of Dr. Maringanti Seshacharyulu, a practicising doctor with a liberal mind and Smt. Seetamma, his wife who was endowed with an artistic temperament and a good singer living at Machilipatnam, their house was a cultural centre in those days. Both of the girls became Vedantam Lakshmi Narayana Sastry's disciples. He taught them for several years.

When girls from respectable familes were learning dance, more women came forward to learn Padabhinaya or solo dance than men. Lakshmi Narayana Sastry went to all places in Andhra—to Eluru, Gudivada, Rajahmundry and Tenali, keeping his base at Machilipatnam. Jagannadha Sarma, Sastry's son took his place in school. Sastry Garu was consolidating all his findings into 'course work' and taught to Kachnanamala and to Akhileswari, to Sakuntala at Gudivada, to Andhra sisters at Machilipatnam, to Sry Rajyalakshmi at the same place and Manorama and others at Rajahmundry.

Andhra Nataka Kala Parishad honoured him in 1945 for his artistic contributions. Madras government and the citizens of Madras honoured him with a Simha Talatam and title "Kuchipudi Natya Kala Nidhi" in 1948. He was honoured at Vijayawada, at Vizag, and at Movva village. In April 1951, the Kshetrayya festival at Movva was a very big memorable event because, very distinguished scholars, poets, researchers and performers saw his demonstration of 'Pada Abhinaya' with veneration. So also in a function at Madras in 1948, P.V. Raja Mannar, E. Krishna Ayyar, Prof. P. Samba Murthy, Balasaraswati and others were awe struck with appreciation.

On the invitation of Srivissa Appa Rao Garu, the famous researcher, Sri Sastry went to Visakhapatnam to demonstrate Pada Abhinaya and explained the intricacies in them.

The last days of Lakshmi Narayana Sastry were not very happy. He continued to stay at Machilipatnam and to teach Akhileswari, the daughter of CVR Prasad, a man with a fine artistic sensibility and with a background of Santiniketan. The family looked after him as an "innocent old man" of the household.

Akhila was his last student. He went to Madras when Akhila went to Madras. While in Madras, several luminaries in the field of dance learnt from him. The famous dancer Balasarswati acknowledged openly her indebtedness to him. Ramayya Pillai, Gauri Ammal, Ramayya Pillai's son Chamaraj and many others were benefited by the expertise of Lakshmi Narayana Sastry Garu. He joined Akhila in Hyderabad when her family was shifted to Hyderabad and within fifteen days of his arrival, Sastry Garu breathed his last on 13th July, 1957.

Bharatacharya, Andhra Natya Kala Pitamaha, Kuchipudi Natya Kalanidhi Sri Vedantam Lakshmi Narayana Sastry was born in 1880 in Kuchipudi village and could win laurels from several samsthanas and could spread his name and fame throughout the country. He could set standard to the famous items like Bhama Kalapam, Gollakalapam. He could sing and dance a single Daruvu of Bhama for five to six hours. He was recognised by Vanaparthi, Jataprolu, Gadvala, Challapalli, Vuyyur Raja durbars.

With a view to have honours from Mysore, Sri Sastry approached Sangeet Kalanidhi Sri Rachappa could sing letters like 1, 2, 3, 4, 5, 6, 7, 8, 9, 10 for 5 hours and Lakshmi Narayana Sastry could show Abhinaya for all the five hours including Vedantardha and Sangitardha and could move the audience.

In between 19-20 century, Sastry could travel through the North to South of India and could spread the greatness of Kuchipudi dance form, which is the pride of Andhras.

After witnessing, the Padabhinaya of Hyderabad as 'bhama', world famous dancer Udaya Shanker, took his feet and said "Guruji, please come to Almora and kindly teach your Natya Sampradaya."

In 1948, composite Madras State Govt. honoured him with a Golden Simha Talata Kankaram and with a title of "Kuchipudi Natya Kala Nidhi" under the auspices of Dr. Bizawada Gopala Reddy and justice PV Rajamannar. The present famous Natyacharyas like Rama Pillai, Vedantam Raghvaiah, Jagannadha Sarma Vempati Satyam, Tandava Krishna were all his disciples. Famous dancers of Kena Seema like Anna Bathula Chitti, Pushpavathi grand daughter of Veena Dhanam and famous dancer Bala Saraswati, Duggirala Jagadamba of Manda Peta, Sri Virajitham learnt dance from him.

He made tireless efforts to lift the art of Kuchipudi dance to greater heights by introducing new trends. He prepared a systematic action plan to teach the art and he wanted to start a "Kuchipudi Natya Kala Samstha" at Hyderabad and with this view he arrived to the city on 29th June 1957, after consulting the then President of Central Music and dance academy and passed away within fifteen days.

There is no Tarangam in Bharata Natyam style "Neela Megha Sareera" is a prominent Kuchipudi item—very popular and very much appreciated.

Vedantam Lakshmi Narayana Sastry first taught Abhinayam. He was an expert in Abhinaya. He used to say that he was "Satbharatacharya" Satbharata Sastra Nipunudu. He went to Kumbha konam on tour and had his stay in a hotel managed by a Devadasi. There is a wonderful story in this context. One day, this Devadasis had the habit of giving Dakshina of one rupee to every Brahmin who had his meal there. He was neglected because he did not have pierced nose string. Then she asked him whether he knew dance when he was invited to her house and after learning about his efficiency, she learnt dance under him. He taught in Mysore samsthanam also for some time. Balasaraswati, the famous exponent in Tamil Nadu learnt from him Pada Abhinaya after she saw him after his Sanmanam in Madras by PV Rajamannar, EV Krishna Aiyar and Vedantam Raghavayya.

Kuchipudi exponents were scholars, experts in Pancha kavyas and probably they taught Abhinaya to Devadasis.

He learnt the tradition from one Venkata Narayana. Kuchipudi got popularity in Madras because of him (in 1955). Kuchipudi and Bharata Natyam are from the same source, *i.e.*, Natya Sastra, he used to say. Nritta from Tanjore side. He was teaching Padas, Sabdas, Tarangas, Varnas, Swarajathis, Swara Pallavi and Tillanas and Adhyatma Ramayana Keertanas, Astapadhis, Javalees, some special talas like Vinayaka Talam, Simha Nandini Talam out of 108 Talams. He taught Sapta Talas Nritta after Dasanatara Sabda. The speciality of it is to show the angas with the leg movement. He used to teach dance on the tray with water with a tumbler full of water on head.

He used to teach "Marathi Song"—Radhika Ramana—Madhura Nagarilo—and other songs also. Balasaraswati used to say :

"When I was a already in my thirties, Vedantam Lakshmi Narayana Sastri opened great new vistas for me, especially in Varnam improvisation. He once said "If I had a singer like your mother, with her music, I could have taken my art throuout the world." He felt that no one understood the values of what he did and told me "I had better learn it." He spent many hours with me in my house, although he was very orthodox.

Lakshmi Narayan Shastri

Narayana Tirdha is hailed as the South Indian Jayadeva. There are several theories about his birth place and the year of his birth. But many scholars prefer Kaza village near Guntur as his birth place. His family name Talla Vajjula. It is said that he mastered Sanskrit, carnatic music and Bharata Sastra very early in his life. He was ordained as a Sanyasin by Sivarama Tirdha to whom he pays obeisance in his work. When he was on his way to Tanjavur district, he was afflicted with severe stomach pain and he prayed to Lord Venkateswara for relief. A divine voice told him to follow the first object he saw the next morning. This object happened to be a boar which led him to Varahur (Bhupathi rajapuram). So tirdha settled down in that village and rendered yeoman service to Carnatic music.

His Krishna leela Tarangini is a lengthy music play in Sanskrit and comprises 12 Taranganas, which contain 147 Kirtanas, 267 slokas, 30 gadyams, 50 darus and link passages. He signed his songs as Vara Narayana tirdha 'Siva Narayana Tirdha' and 'Yati Narayana Tirdha'.

'Jaya Jaya Gokula Bala' is the most popular song from Tarangini. Its original raga was

Santi Vedantam

Km. Kollapalli Padma

Kuravanji but it was later converted into a raga malika. 'Vikshche Kada' in Ahiri is a song full of pathos, which Rukmini sang, when she learnt about his marriage with Sisupala. Rukmini's message was represented in moving verses in Bhagavatam commencing with the words 'Srutva Guman Bhavana Sundara and tirdha condensed them in the form of beautiful Gadya.

It is believed that Narayana Tirdha was closely associated with the Bhagwata Mela tradition of Melattur. I met a gentleman of Kaza village in a train journey and he told me that they are planning to have a statue for him in their village.

His Leela Tarangini is a treasure, which can be preserved by dancers and musicians for centuries to come.

Kshetrayya's Padams

Kshetrayya's Padams might have dominated the dance dramas in the past. Otherwise, they would not have survived to our times with such pristine purity.

Let us see a few gems of Kshetrayya. "Evvade Vadu Nenu Pavvalinchina Vela Puvvu Bana Mesi Ravva Chesi Poye". How nicely Sankarabharana Raga shows dignity in this Padam.

What frustration we find in "Emo Raadamma indhundi Poyi Jaamaayenamme."

What pathos "Mukhari" brings in this padam yeaning for his beloved, the Nayaki cries out "Giri Varada". Only Kshetrayya's Nayaki can have the audacity of addressing Movva Gopala as "Giri".

We can see in "Manasu Ninnedabayadu Pranesa", how Kshetrayya used such a serious raga as Sri Raga for such a Sukumara Sringararasa.

Kshetrayya used freely Srirangararasa for Bhaktinasa. When Krishna admonished the Gopikas to go back to their homes and serve their husbands, Gopikas retorted Krishna that while

Natya—Mela of Kuchipudi

they were serving the universal soul itself at Brindavan, they were serving the individual souls in their homes.

Dance Dramas of Kuchipudi

Dance dramas of Kuchipudi are a night long affair. They are performed in the open. A stage is arranged temporarily and the audience sit on the ground. Before the dance drama actually begins, a prayer in praise of Amba—Amba Paraku—Devi Paraku—Mammelu Maa Jagadamba Paraku" is recited. Then a boy enters the stage, who circles round the holding a flag staff, the Jarjara Dhwaja of Indra, as referred in the Natya Sastra. Then follows the lamp and dhupa (incense) and the dancer offers pushpanjali (flowers) then the Sutradhara enters with his Kuthilaka (crooked stick) and conducts the performance. He announces the title of the play and keeps the tala with the cymbals and takes his seat among the musicians on the stage.

Before the actual dance-drama begins, two people, holding a curtain and behind the curtain, a dancer with the mark of a Ganapati shuffles his feet. The curtain is then removed and the dancer performs as the elephant headed God, Vigneswara is worshipped to avoid any obstacles. Then enters Satyabhama, from behind the curtain. In Kuchipudi style, it is known as Patra Pravesha daru, it introduces the character. The dancer-cum-actor establishes the character by singing and introducing herself or himself either in first person or third person. It gives him an opportunity to display the full gamut of his talents. The Sutradhara gets up and impersonates the role of Madhuri Satyabhama and the Sutradhara converse and Satyabhama tells about her plight and she rebukes Manmadha (cupid) and the moon for torturing her. The unfolding of the dance-drama continues with dialogues in Telugu, with humour, songs and dance. The literary devices are used Vachanams, risardhams, Kandams and Kandardhuns. Nritta, Abhinaya, dialogues and songs follow carrying the story and the action together.

The dance-dramas favoured by the audience are Prahlada charitam, Usha parinayam, Sasirekha parinayam, Rukmini kalyanam, Golla kalapam *etc.* A very interesting feature of these dance-dramas is inclusion of Tarangams from Krishna Leela Tarangini of Narayana Teerdha and also sabdams, Abhisvekams, Padams, Javalis. The dancer sometimes balances a water tumbler on the head and sometimes plays Abhinaya on a brass plate and executes complex talas.

Another interesting feature is drawing a picture on the floor while dancing to a specific tala. A drawing of Ganapati is executed during such renderings of Vinayaka Kavutam, of a pea-cock in Mayura Kavitam, a lion with Simhanandinitala and so on. Singers also use different Jatis in different speeds, while directing intricate and lively dance patterns.

So far Aharya is concerned, the costumes and the make-up of the characters will be in accordance with the traditional, mythological personnel. Music will be in carnatic bani and the instruments used are usually Mridangam, violin, flute, cymbals and harmonium. During the festival of Gokulastami dance dramas are staged at Kuchipudi village.

Vedantam Satyanarayana Sarma shows his talent as Satyabhama and he outshines all other characters. The principles enunciated by Bharata in his Natya Sastra for the Nayikas are utilised in his performances. He was trained by Chinta Krishna Murthy and Prahlad Sarma. He is the head of a Natya Mandali called Venkatrama Natya Mandali which tours in Andhra Pradesh as well as in all other parts of India. He is also associated with Siddhendra Kalakshetra of Kuchipudi in his native place.

Pranaya Varudhini

Sri Krishna Parijatham

Krishna Parijatha

Padmavathi Srinivasam

Nritya Chuda Mani—Sobha Naidu

Natya Leela

Satya—Krishna

Bhakta Prahlada

Sharma also played female roles and gave solo performances.

Vempati Chinna Satyam migrated from Kuchipudi to Madras and for some time joined films, but soon gave it up and established the Kuchipudi Art Academy to train young dancers in Kuchipudi. He brought in a big measure of sophistication and created interesting dance movements maintaining the spirit of the Kuchipudi dance and lent a stature to the form with a sizeable repertoire, which has come to stay. On the contemporary scene he has put his signature as is seen in the case of Birju Maharaj in Kathak and Guru Kelucharan Mahapatra in Odissi. He has studied the *Natyashastra* thoroughly and correlated the various movements to the basic tenets, emphasizing the classical nature of the dance form, placing it on par with other forms like Bharat Natyam, Kathak, Manipuri, Odissi, Kathakali and Mohiniattam. Kuchipudi has established itself as one of the major neo-classical dance forms with a number of gifted solo exponents, most of them Vempati's disciples. He has devised a course, a training methodology and series of dance units on the lines of the *adavus* of Bharat Natyam. The movements are scintillating and have a quicksilver quality. They are rounded, have a hobbing up and down quality distinct from Bharat Natyam. Whereas Bharat Natyam movements are geometric, with straight lines, circles, and triangles, in Kuchipudi the movements are, as observed, rounded with an forgiveness and sends it with Madhavi to him. Krishna relents and returns to Satyabhama's palace. After an interesting inrerlude of repartee, the two are united again.

The principles laid down in the *Natyashastra*[17] regarding the expression of *Vipralambha shringara* and *Sambhoga shringara* are beautifully

Kalyana Srinivasam

Menaka Viswamitra

portrayed in the play: Satyabhama is separated from Krishna and in the end is united with him. In particular, the *Vipralambha shringara* offers scope to the artiste to display his histrionic talent and suggest the pangs of separation. In a variety of ways the *nayika* depicts the pangs. Her confidante tries to engage her into various diversions, but nothing makes the *nayika* happy. The separation as per the *Natyashastra* is depicted by anxiety, weariness of the body, gazing vacantly at the sky, lassitude, sighs and so on.

Ardhanareswaram—Reflecting the Uniqueness of Kuchipudi Form

Kuchipudi dance academy presented a dance-drama staged at Thyagaraya Gana Sabha as a part of the recently concluded Kinnera Art theatres Nrityotsava, which I could witness. It is a ballet coming from Sri Vempati Chinna Satyam. Its smooth flow of narrative, the logical interpretation to ancient mythology credible costumes, excellent stage adoptability a live and faultless accompaniment are the important features of this wonderful ballet.

'Ardhanareeswaram' one of the old dance-dramas of Kuchipudi received its best treatment in the hands of Sri Ravi Shanker, son of Sri Vempati, who carried the ballet, single-handed.

Ravi as Shiva was impeccable both in 'Acharya', 'Abhinaya' and 'Nritya'. He made an excellent entry to the stage with a series of Jatis. His footwork though not complex, was very brisk and balanced. His steps in the dance with the Rishis were excellent. Capturing of Ganga in his locks, the pining for his consort Gowri pacifying an ennoyed consort were like testimonials to Ravi's emotive ease of expression. His artistry reached its peak as he donned the Ardhanareeswara garb (fusion of male and female)—an original concept of our mythology like God dividing himself into two—the right side that of Lord Shiva and the left side as Sakti. The entry of Ardhanareeswara in the typical

Kaushalya Reddy demonstrates the simha mukha hasta, the left hand depicting a lion's face. Here the middle and ring fingers are bentforward to touch the thumb in Pataka Hasta to suggest a deer, cow, bull, throne, yagna and of course the lion. The right hand is in the Tripataka Mudra and conveys the sun, the seasons, crow, light, trees, fire.

Popular film actress and now Kuchipudi soloist, Meenakshi Sheshadri

Kuchipudi style was very impressive and a powerful portrayal followed. The 'Abhinaya' the footwork was excellent and the attention paid to minor choreographic details was noteworthy. Music had an enhanting effect on the ballet. Melodic vocal recital was an asset. Accompaniments like veena, flute, violin and mridangam were also upto the mark.

So, it can be concluded that the Kuchipudi dance-drama is a piece of 'Rasa'. It is a full Kavya depicted through dance and acting. It is not simply a display of physical experiences. The spectators react to the sentiments displayed as the subject matter is mythological.

The veterans of Kuchipudi art have subsequently added Nritya items to their repertiere. These are known as 'Sabdams'. They are compositions of a rhythmic character around a piece of lyric.

Raja and Radha Reddy. This duo have done pioneering work is not just the promotion of Kuchipudi, in India and abroad, but also in imparting to the style a much needed elegance and sophistication.

Two dancers—Deccan, Hyderabad-18th Century

Some are in the praise of patrons and some are recitals of a story or a particular incident from the puranas. Some are compositions playing upon words by poets. The following are some typical examples.

The 'Dasavatara Sabdam' depicting the ten incarnations of Lord Vishnu, composed by Siddha Bhattula Rangadas of Peda Pulivarru village. The text is intermixed with 'Jatis'.

The 'Manduka Sabdam' (frog dance) a composition by Melattur Kasinadhayya. It is a piece of word-jugglery, the text representing the sounds made by frogs in a pool on a rainy day. In the end, it depicts the incident of Gajendra Moksham from 'Mahabhagavatam'. The artist sits like a frog and dances.

The 'Prahlada Sabdam', composed by Melattur Venkatarama Sastry relates to the story of Prahlada from the Mahabhagavatam.

The 'Sri Rama Pattabhishekam', recounts the coronation of Sri Rama, on his return from Sri Lanka, after the death of Ravana.

The 'Tuljaji' is composed by an unknown Kuchipudi scholar on Tuljaji alias Tukoji, a Tanjore ruler of 18th century.

The 'Sivaji Sabdam' is on the Maharatta ruler who ruled Tanjore.

The 'Thaddi Sabdam' was composed in praise of one of the Rajas of Kalahasti.

There are some 10 such Sabdams in the Kuchipudi Repertoire. In addition to this fact, the Kuchipudi artists are experts in Jatis, which are introduced in a dance drama, whenever the play is felt to be dull. They have about 100 such in their repertoire and compose new ones whenever the need arises.

In addition to the dance-dramas and Sabdams mentioned above, the Kuchipudi artists dance to the songs of Jayadeva's Gita Govinda, to the 'tarangams' of Narayana Tirdha and to the 'Padams' of Kshetragna.

They also perform 'Abhinaya' to the 'Slokas' to Lilasuka's Sri Krishna 'Karna Mrita'. There are dances also, involving high virtuosity.

When a dancer performs the 'Balagopala Trangam' from the Krishnalila Tarangini, the artist executes his steps with a pail of water on his head, on the sharp edges of a brass tray. He also dances on the spherical surface of an earthen pot. And while he performs, he is able to draw pictures on the floor with the toes of his dancing feet. There are a few examples of the virtues as skill.

Another popular diversion offered by the Kuchipudi artistes is the imperonation of stock characters to the accompaniment of humourous discourses. In the off-season, some of the Kuchipudi artists visit the villages by day, with impersonations of this kind and entertain the villagers with their humour. In this role, they are known as 'Pagati Veshalu'.

The play begins with the recital of extracts from the four Vedas. According to tradition, as we noticed earlier, the Natya Sastra is the fifth Veda composed by Brahma taking Patya (text) from the Rigveda, Abhinaya from the Yajur Veda, vocal music from the Sama Veda and the sentiment or Rasa from the Atharvana Veda. Thus the four opening extracts from the Vedas symbolise the composition of the Natya Veda. Next, the stage is consecrated by the sprinkling of holy water. This is known as 'punyaha vachana' is performed by a dancer and is followed by Rangalankarana, the decoration of the stage with coloured powders. Incense is offered by another artist. A bunch of 58 lights is offered to the Ranga Adhi Deva—the deity of the stage. Flowers are offered to the audience by way of invoking their blessings.

Afterwards, the flag staff of Indra is set upon the stage. There is an episode in the Natya Sastra in this connection. The sage, Bharata was asked to produce a play, 'Amritha-Madhava' by Indra. This is perhaps to be regarded as the first dance-drama. During the course of the play, the Asuras felt humiliated and attacked the Devas with black magic. Bharata could not speak a word. Indra scented the evil doings of Asuras and destroyed them with his flag-staff. Hence, Indra's flag staff was known as Jarjara. He gave it to Bharata asking him to plant it on the stage in the beginning of every play. It was a terror to the Asuras.

Since then, it had been the practice to plant Indra's flag staff on the stage at the beginning of every drama. After this, the lord Ganesa appears and blesses the artists, so that there may be any kind of obstruction to the performance. The traditional 'Amba Bardhana' and 'Guru Bardhana' are then sung by the sutradhara with two or three colleagues. The Nandi stotra then follows.

The Sutradhara stands up with his curved stick. This stick was presented to Bharata by the lord Brahma, as mentioned in the Natya Sastra.

It is known by the name of Kutilaha. He offers prayers to his Guru and welcomes the audience. He narrates the story to the audience and explains its implications. Thus the drama starts. He also plays the part of Vidushaka in the play. The Sutradhara is an adept in humour. By gestures and dialogue, he gives relief to the audience.

Some of the veterans of this art form deserve mention outstanding during the preceeding century were (1) Vedantam Samhayya (2) Hari Chalapathi (3) Bhagavanthula Ramayya, hwo recast the Golla Kalapam with ingenious interpretations and compositions (4) Bhagavatula Dasaratdhana-mayya (5) Bhagavathula Rama Das (6) Nagalin-gayya (7) Subrahmanyam (8) Vissayya (9) Bokka Parvateesam and several others. During the early part of the 20th century Vempati Venkata Narayana was famous and the elders hold his talent in high esteem still.

Vedantam Lakshmi Narayana Sastry formed more than a score of students. It was he who initiated Miss Yamini Krishna Murthy and others into this art. Distinguished artists of North Indian schools Uday Shanker, Ragini Devi and others were stunned to see his performance even in his seventies. The late Chinta Venkataramayya, founder of Venkatarama Natya Mandali, was a typical Guru and Sutradhara. He was a very great scholar and trained as many as 50 or 60 students, who are still maintaining the torch of Kuchipudi. Among them Vedantam Raghavayya Vempati Satyam and Pasumati Venugopala Krishna Sarma deservè particular mention. Chinta Krishna Murthi, the director of Venkatanama Natya mandali is his son. He was responsible for propagation of his art against many considerable odds. It was he who trained presidential award-winner Sri Vedantam Satyanarayana Sarma for heroine's roles.

Of late, there is a craze for Kuchipudi style and it has become a necessary item in the programme by the artists all over India and also abroad.

An institute had been started at Kuchipudi to train dancers under training by experts in this art. There are hostel facilities also attached to the institute. An auditorium is also being constructed. The institution is being aided by the Central Sangeet Natak Academy as well as the Andhra Pradesh Government.

Some famous Natya Charyas of Kuchipudi Style

Sri Vedantam Raghavayya was a famous exponent of Kuchipudi style as a woman. He was born on 8th June 1919 to Ramayya and Annapurna. His Guru was his own father and his maternal grand father Chinta Venkataramayya who evolved him into a great actor. Nice body, good facial features, nice voice, his adoptability to Nritya Bhangimas, expertise in Abhinaya are his great assets and people were coming in large numbers to witness his Nayika performance.

His 'Usha' in Usha Parinayam was in great demand in his early days.

In 1934, one Vimalendu Bosu, who came from Bengal gave performances of Siva Tandavam, Indra Nrityam in the town hall of Machilipatnam Sri Mutnuru Krishna Rao, editor, Krishna patrika was commentator for those plays. It was Raghavayya who brought into lime light the dance of Balagopala Tarangam having a tumbler on the head. He was living in Usha Kanya and Sasi Rekha with his sweet voice and his roles as Harishchandra and Lakshmana were also very popular. The talent he showed in the cinema field and his Devadas in Telugu was very popular rather than in Bengali or Hindi.

He was honoured in Masula by the AP Natakakala Parishat and he was made responsible by the AP Sangeet Natak Academy to conduct national dance performances. He was awarded with "Bharata Kala Prapoorna" title.

In 1938, during the Navya Sahitya Conference held in Bandar, the famous art critic, Sri K.V. Ramachandran, who came from Madras, to witness Raghavayya's "Usha" wrote in "Triveni" as follows:

"Vedantam Raghavayya claims the honours as the best exponent of this Kuchipudi school by his amazing recording record in speedy execution".

Vempati China Satyam

Born (1929) during the resurgence of nationalist fervour, when the traditional art forms of India were revived and brought again to the main stream of the national art scenario, Guru Vempati China Satyam breathed a new life into the form. He was born to Smt. Varalakshmamma and Sri Chalamayya in Kuchipudi village. Vempati had his earlier training under Sri Tadepally Perayya and Pasumarthi Kondala rayudu. He learnt the finer aspects of the art from a celebrity like Sri Vedantam Lakshmi Narayana Sastry.

His Mahaprasthana from Kuchipudi village to a city like Madras (Chennai) in search of a career, turned out to be an opportunity to bring out his inner artistic talent and to start the Kuchipudi dance academy in 1963, which turned out to be a centre to train several young aspirants in Kuchipudi style.

Dr. Vempati produced many marvels like Padmavathi Srinivasa Kalyanam, Vipranarayana Charitam, Menaka Viswamitra Sakuntalam, Bhama Kalapam, Chandalika, Rukmini Kalyanam, Hara Vilasam, Siva Dhanurbhangam and Ardha Nareeswara. He has also composed Kumara Sambhavam Padmavathi Tirumanam and Sri Krishna Parijatha in Tamil. His latest production is Sripada Parijatha (Annamayya) and Kiratarjuneeyam).

Notable among the numerous awards, honours and citations conferred on him are "Padma Bhushan" by Govt. of India, "Fellow" by Sangeet Nataka Academy, New Delhi, "Kalaprapoorna" from Andhra University, Kuchipudi Nritya Pramukh by Sangeet Natak Academy (New Delhi) Honorary doctorate (D. Litt.) by Sri Venkateswara University (Tirupathi) Asthana Vidwan by Sri Venkateswara temple (Pittsburgh) TTK Memorial Award by the Madras Music Academy, Kalidas puraskar by Govt. of Madhya Pradesh, Kalai Mamani by Govt. of Tamil Nadu.

The Mayor of Miami presented the Golden Key Award in 1984, the Mayor of Dayton, Ghio, declared September 25, 1994 as Vempati China Satyam Day and the Mayor of Atlanta declared 3rd December, 1994 as Kuchipudi Dance Drama Day and the Mayor of Ghana (Ghio) declared April 27, 1984 as classical Indian Kuchipudi Ballet Dance Drama Day. The Mayor of Cleveland conferred honorary citizenship on Dr. Vempati. The Mayor of Memphis declared September 24, 1994 as "Ramayana Day"

and key to the city was awarded to him. Gold Medal was presented to him by the President of Tunisia at the Cartage festival. Citations and honours were conferred at the Avignon festival, France in 1995.

Dr. Vempati is not a natracharya in the world of dance but an outstanding personality endowed with noble human qualities like commitment to his art, his love for his disciples, single minded devotion to Kuchipudi art form.

'Padmabhushan' Yamini Krishna Murthy

She is one of the famous exponents of the classical dance forms of India. Yamini Krishna Murthy has emerged as a major figure in the post-independence cultural renaissance. She was trained originally in Bharata Natyam but soon attained expertise in Kuchipudi and Odissi also and has been hailed as one of the best interpreters of India's temple nurtured classical dance forms. Yamini has been unique for her remarkable communicative power and she possesses a lively dramatic manner.

Yamini gave performances both in India and abroad and had the priviledge of presenting her art to several world luminaries including the British queen. Being a magnificently expressive artist, Yamin has been hailed for her unique creativity and for "the fantastically subtle and precise insignia for her fingers and hands, the tireless calliography of her movements", which were "matched by the animation voiced through her eyes".

Yamini was the youngest of the Padma Shri award winners when she was honoured with the title. She could win the Sangeet Natak Academy Award (1977) and was presented the freedom of the city of Cleveland (Ghio) in the US. She received the Kalaparishad Award and the Nritya Chudamani Award as well. Yamini was appointed as 'Asthana Nartaki' of the Lord Venkateswara temple, Tirupathi and was awarded the honorary degree of D.Litt. by Sri Venkateswara University, Tirupathi.

Yamini established an institution by name Nritya Kaustubha at Delhi in which she gives training in Bharata Natyam.

For her contribution to the rejuvenation of the classical dance forms of India, she was awarded the 'Padma Bhushan Award' by the Govt. of India in 2001.

Sobha Naidu—Padmasri

Smt. Sobha Naidu is one of the outstanding exponents of Kuchipudi Dance today. She is known for her dedication to the exacting nuances of dance and for her imaginative exposition of it without losing its classical purity.

She was a disciple of Guru Vempati China Satyam. She achieved several laurels in the field. She led a delegation to West Indies, Mexico, Venezuela, Texas and Cuba as early as in 1973. In 1974, she visited the Eastern countries. In 1983 she toured USA with an eighteen member team and gave several performances. In 1988, her tour of USSR inspired the dance lovers so much that a couple of students came all the way to India, to learn Kuchipudi dance style. In 1996, she led a team to UK.

She established Kuchipudi Art Academy at Hyderabad in 1980 and had been teaching students since then as its director. She could train several disciples who are most promising in the field.

In the realm of dance-dramas, Sobha is the Prima Donna. As Satyabhama in Bhama Kalapam and Krishna Parijatham's Chandalika, as Devadevi in Vipranarayana, as Padmavathi in Kalyana Srinivasam, her performance is excellent. Her recent productions, Sri Krishna Saranam Mama and Vijaysthute both choreographed by her, have received unprecedented laurels both from the public and the scholars. She also appeared as Vivekananda clad in a silken role and turban, attempting to say about the philosophy of Vivekananda.

Sobha Naidu has received the coveted title of 'Nritya Chudamani' from Sri Krishna Gana Sabha, Madras and the prestigious Sangeet Natak Academy Award in 1991. She is also the recipient of the titles 'Nrityavihar', Nritya Kala Siromani and Nritya Kala Sagara by well known cultural bodies.

Sobha Naidu had been honoured by the Government of India with Padma Sri and with the 'Hamsa' Award by Govt. of Andhra Pradesh.

Padmasri Dr. Sunil Kothari

Dr. Sunil Kothari is a renowned dance scholar, author, historian and critic. He earned his doctorate for his research work on "the dance drama tradition of Kuchipudi, Bhagawata Mela Nataka and Kuravanji, with special reference to Rasa theory as expounded in Bharata's Natya Sastra submitted to the M.S. University, Baroda.

After retiring from Ravindra Bharati University, Calcutta, where he worked as head of the Department of dance, he settled down at New Delhi.

Dr. Kothari had the unique opportunity of meeting several maestros in the field of dance, including Uday Shankar, Balasaraswati and Rukmini Devi Arundale and documenting their work. He travelled from Manipur to Tanjore, from Ahmedabad to Calcutta and gained expertise on all the classical dance styles of India.

Dr. Kothari has several commendable works to his credit. His books include—Bharata Natyam, Indian Classical Dance Art (1982), Kathak Classical Dance Art (1988), Odissi : Indian Classical Dance Art (1990) and Kuchipudi Indian Classical Dance Art (2000).

Dr. Kothari was awarded by the Central Sangeet Natak Academy (1995) Gujarat state.

Sangeet Natak Academy (1998) and has been honoured by Govt. of India with 'Padma Sri', in 2001 for his efforts in promoting Indian Dance.

Abhinaya Tapasvini—Alekhya

Alekhya, described once as a jewel in the world of dance is one of the foremost as well as top ranking exponents in both the Kuchipudi and Bharatanatyam styles of dance.

A recipient of the prestigious Ugadi Visist puraskar for the year 2002 by the Government of Andhra Pradesh as well as the highly coveted Hamsa award, for her service and commitment to Dance,, Alekhya started dancing since a very tender age under the tutelage of Late Shri Dayal Sharan, continuing with Dr. Uma Rama Rao and is an artist to reckon, with over three decades of work in these two styles.

Her performances, rendered at the highest level in India and abroad, include all the prestigious and sought after dance festivals conducted in various parts of the country, as well as all over the world, including The United States of America, The United Kingdom, Syria, Abu Dhabi, Dubai, Muscat, Qatar, Lebanon, Bahrain and Cyprus, Mauritius, Poland, Turkey and Bulgaria both through the Indian Council of Cultural Relations, as well as on invitation through organizations there, were highly appreciated and still remembered as a renditions of the highest class. It is a tribute to her expertise of highest quality that her artistry was highly appreciated in these areas, in spite of the extreme differences in cultures.

Alekhya had the honour of performing at the prestigious Khajuraho fèstival which conducts annual performances by artists of the highest level. Her other highly appreciated and cherished performances were at the prestigious Haridas Samaroh, Kalidas Samaroh, Kuchipudi Mahotsav, Soorya and Konark, Nishagandhi, Natyanjali, Siddendra Yogi, Parangat and Kalakshetra art festivals, to name a few, as well as several important festivals organized by Central Sangeeta Nataka Academy. Apart from the above solo performances, she has brought to life many mythological heroines like Alamelu Manga, Gouri, Parvathi, Thilla Kali, Mandakini Durga, Sasirekha, Andal and Draupadi in several dance ballets which have brought her lot of laurels and appreciation both from critics and connoisseurs alike.

Her traditional and innovative repertoire in solo technique, her portrayals as mythological heroines in various dance ballets, as also her subtle presentation of Satvika Abhinaya have become her hallmark through which she has carved a special niche for herself and is recognized as one of the rare artists from the younger generation to carry out the legacy of Kuchipudi greats like Padmashri Vedantam Sathyanarayana Sharma and Pasumarthi Krishnamurthy.

Alekhya's scholarly demonstrations on various subjects like the compositions of Annamacharya, Kshettraya, Jayadeva, Sarangapani and the technique of Kuchipudi at different institutions, universities both in India as well as abroad while participating in several seminars and conferences, the most recent one being the Natyakala conference held by Krishna gana sabha, Chennai, have won wide acclaim from great Kuchipudi masters scholars and rasikas.

Alekhya is a top-ranking artist of Doordarshan Kendra in both Bharatanatyam and Kuchipudi. She has also been honoured by several cultural and literary organizations for her dedication and contribution to the field of dance.

Alekhya is a graduate in English literature, psychology and philosophy and also holds a bachelor's degree in dance (Bharata Natyam) Osmania University. She holds a postgraduate degree in ancient Indian history, culture and archaeology. Alekhya is at present doing her PhD in the 'Padams of Kshetrayya' and his contribution to Telugu culture.

Apart from achieving fame through her on-stage performances and the above mentioned academic pursuits, Alekhya has been actively involved in teaching and propagating dance. She is presently teaching dance in P.S. University.

14

Perini Siva Tandavam

Perini Sivatandavam

Splendour of the Classical dances of Andhra Pradesh is noteworthy and remarkable.

Perini is a classical male art form of Andhra and is one of the graceful rhythmic dance styles among the South Indian classical forms and it exhibits mainly Veerarasa.

Perini Sivatandavam is a male dance of the 10th century AD in Andhra Pradesh.

Mahashiva is a Layakara as we know. His dance is cosmic and is of 12 varieties.

(1) Ananda Tandava

(2) Sandhya Tandava

(3) Kalika Tandava

(4) Vijaya Tandava

(5) Oordhva Tandava

(6) Uma Tandava

(7) Samhara Tandava

(8) Muni Tandava

(9) Ugra Tandava

(10) Bhoota Tandava

(11) Bhujanga Tandava

(12) Pralaya Tandava

Looking into the created world, he does Ananda Tandava expressing his joy.

His 'Damaru' creates a sound (Nada) which is responsible for his creativity. From his left hand, Agni is created to put an end to the forces that obstruct the well-being of society.

From the third hand, he gives Abhaya to the people who sacrificed their lives for the welfare of the world. His fourth hand 'Pathaka Hastha' indicating success. His Angikabhinaya is the movement of the living creatures of the world. His vachikabhinaya is all the source by the nature. His Alankaras are one Chandra and the Stars in the Sky. His Satvikabhinaya is the mental balance of man living in the world.

(Nataraja Ramakrishna-Page No. 51, 52, 53 of Natyakalacharitra of Dakshinatyas)

Kalika Tandavam— Shiva

Sandhya Tandava

Looking at the creation, developing and continuing, Siva, out of joy performs Sandhya Tandava.

Kalika Tandava

Kalika Tandava is nothing but the glowing of the eternal logent, which takes away ignorance of the world.

Vijaya Tandava

Vijaya Tandava is assassination of Gajasura. When Shiva was doing this Tandava, Devatas were glad to see him dance.

Oordhwa Tandava is the union of the spirit and mother.

Sandhya Tandava was performed by Siva to win over Uma and succeeded in his attempts. To see the quarrel between Uma and Sankara, Yakshas, Gandharvas, Kinneras and Kimpurushas gathered and witnessed the whole scene.

Samhara Tandava of Shiva

Muni Tandava : This is a dance performed according to the rhymic feet movements of Patanjali at Chidambaram. This is the 'Lasya Natyam'.

Ugrava Tandava : This is performed by Shiva to protect his devotees and for the sake of Gajasura. This is found in Rajya Natyam.

Bhoota Tandava : Shiva performed this dance after he removed his clothes and wore animal skins. This we can see in "Pattasa Natyam".

Pralaya Tandava : This is performed by Shiva during Pralaya Kala.

Bhujanga Tandava : During the time of 'Amritha Madhana' this is performed by Shiva after drinking the poison. This is in Pitha Natyam.

Suddha Tandava : This is performed by Shiva in the presence of Rishis. This is found in Padachari Natyam.

Uma Tandava Shiva

Perini consists of 5 Angas.

(1) Gargharamu, (2) Vishamamu, (3) Bhavasrayamu, (4) Kvi Varakamu and (5) Geetamu.

The most rewarding description of Siva Leela dances is given in panditharadhya Charita of Palkuriki Somanadha, who belonged to the 13th century. These were performed by groups of devout Saiva Bhaktas.

The earliest form of stylized dance with Uma was Jarshgana. This perhaps had its roots in tribal usage, but in course of time, it matured into a theatre art, involving dancing, acting, singing also thus carrying a blend of the folk and the classical styles. The first Yahshagana by name Sugriva Vijayam was written in 1570 describing this Tandava.

Sudha Tandavam of Shiva

Aesthetics of this type of dance is described in detail by Palkuriki Somanadha. The significance of the rituals conducted at the time of Maha Sivaratri is well portrayed by his writings. Kakatiya rulers being Saivites encouraged this dance form.

Detailed treatment is given to the dress, Jewellery, hairdo and the facial make-up of the dance in Nritta Ratnavali.

Future of this form depends on the research being done in view of the legendary, literary and historical sources. It has to find a rightful place among the established classical dances at national level.

It appears to be less arithmetic, more equated with Hasta Mudras and intricate foot work, suitable for strong bodied men.

Kakatiya rulers, who ruled Warangal and some parts of Telangana 600-700 years ago, encouraged this perini dance and these poses can be found on the thousand pillared temple of Warangal.

Kakatiya rulers were followers of Veera Saivism. Jaya Senapathi's dance treatise is full of the norms of a base line type of dance. It is a highly spirited dance, with heroic movements, rigour and masculine footwork.

There is an interesting story about Jayappa's dedication of his wonderful treatise to Ganapati Deva. Accordingly, Jayappa Senani trained some youth who trusted this Veera Nritya (heroic dance), much to the delight of the princess and her father was very much pleased by his rich performance. Ganapati Deva ordered that this type of dance should spread out through the length and breadth of the entire Kakatiya Kingdom. It was also patronised by the successive rulers with great respect to Jayappa.

With the decline of the Kakatiya dynasty, this dance form also went into oblivion.

The famous Natya charya Nataraja Ramakrishna could revive this dance form again and bring it to lime light after 600 years.

Sudha Tandavam of Shiva

Performed in solo and in groups also, this has simple costume—a Vesti or a dhoti tied above the knees. So as to actuate quick and vigorous movement, with a few ornaments or armlets, resembling the armour of a warrior of the past years, this dance is performed. Its footwork, Nattuvangam is also very powerful. Its facial expression is full with neck, eye movement and gestures. Mainly providing difficult footwork is the high-tech of this ancient art.

The mythological Shiva Tandava, as we have studied at the beginning of this book, is similar to this form in a way. It immortalises the spirit of creation of mankind.

Kala Krishna, a disciple of Sri Ramakrishna, is an adept in this art form and has given some thousands of performances, both in India and abroad and won laurels. He could find a special place for himself and a great name and fame to this form of dance.

Perini Siva Tandavam, totally a warrior dance and a male dance, falls in the parameters of Natya Sastra. It is one of the classical dances prevalent in Andhra Pradesh-Kuchipudi, Perini and Andhra Natyam and Vilasimi Nratyam.

Tandavam is essentially a rigorous masculine dance that originated from Lord Nataraja. It is a Telugu version of the Sanskrit word prename (inspiration).

This dance form conforms to the detailed description of Bharata's dance drama, depending on the social, political and cultural history of Andhra Pradesh. It was evolved in a mode according to the traditions prevalent in Andhra Desa.

Kala Krishna also is a great Natyacharya and a great dance artist of this marvelous style. He is winner of a prestigious title as "Abhinava Satyabhama' and his display of the character of Satyabhama is splendid. He was recently awarded a gold medal by the famous cine-actor Sri A.K. Kineni Nageswara Rao in Hyderabad. His body is suited to the character of Satyabhama judged from any angle and he almost lives in this wonderful character of Satyabhama through his Mudras.

He is a great and dedicated disciple of Sri Nataraja Ramakrishna.

Nritta Ratnavali of Jayappa Senani in the 7th chapter tells about perini. After listening to the sound of the instrument, called Samhas hasta, it should be started with Regavani, padamu and pysaramu—the three yaties. Afterwards, with Upasamana first dancer offering should enter and dance. He should make 'Kaivara', the circle.

He should move the foot without the gingling bells and at the 2nd stage, he should play with Margaand Desi Gates and finally with 'Eka', 'Antari' Kriyas he should make praharanas. In Lagna Praharana, with Bhramareenarana he should dance with the music of all the instruments. Afterwards, he should perform Vispama Tandava.

He should, with a view to please the audience, do Raagalapana. He should then sing first Prabandha and also play on the instrument. He should increase sound two three times higher and mix with it the sound of the bells. Extending Abhoga either with yati or praharana, he should dance along with other colleagues.

Karitamu, Uttavani, Khanayati, Avechhedekamu should be mixed with Righoni with Vikalpa. Afterwards, the dancer should enter the Ranga mantapa.

Afterwards he should run the Mukhava which is called by desi experts.

With his entrance on the stage the pushpanjali should be made. There may be instruments like "Hudukki", 'Karata', 'Desipata hami' also. To make the sound more musical and pleasing, cymbals should be played.

In Righoni Ekatal, Addatal Nissakukamu may be used. According to the player, there may be some more, some more talas may be used.

Brisk movement is the speciality of this dance, Saiva Agamas speak of Navarasas. But Veera rasa is given more importance in this dance form so as to inculcate in people a sense of valour.

This is performed in solo as well as in groups. Jayappa describes perini dancer as a man of attractive personality, a man of taste, master of music, endowed with good voice and acquainted with both Tandava and Lasya types of dances. He also tells us that the main parts of perini are five in number, namely Nrutta, Kaivara, Charghana, Viviata and Gita.

'Perini Tandavam'

Courtesy: Dr. Nataraj Ramakrishna

Palampet, where the Ramappa temple is located, is about 40 miles from the ancient Kakateeya capital Warangal. On the pillars, doors, panels and freezes of the temple are sculptured unique poses of.dance based on Nritta Ratnavali. Nritta Ratnavali which is an elaborate treatise on the dance forms prevalent in those days was written by Jayasenani, a feudatory and general of the elephant hordes of the Kakateeya king Ganapathi Deva. The Kakateeyas were mighty rulers from the 10th to the 13th centuries A.D. Jayapa was the desciple of Gundayamatya, a great teacher of dance.

The revival of this form which has been now taken up is based on-Nritta Ratnavali of Jayasenani and the sculptures that were shaped at Palampet after the tradition described in this treatise. Besides, the other works consulted are "Bharatarnva" of Nandikeswara, 'Sabha Ranjani' of Sarvagna Kumara Yachendra; and for Jatis 'Nandeeswara Bharatam' originating in Bobbili. The tradition followed is 'Saiva Aagama' of Srikalahasti.

It was a time when the art of dance in India was developing into two different styles—South Indian and North Indian. Sarangadeva who belonged to the Devagiri court, wrote ' Sangeeta Ratnakara' during this period. The style followed in playing the drum and composition of the jatis is mainly of Druvapad Reeti. This is an ancient style which is still practised in remote parts of Andhra Pradesh in Srikakulam and Visakhapatnam Districts.

The Kakateeyas were Saivites and Veera Saiva-Pasupathi Sampradaya, a sort of extreme Saivism gained popularity during their regime. Pasupatis, Mahesas, Veeras and Mailaradevas who are all Saivites belonging to this extremist cult worshipped Siva with dancing rituals six times a day. This led to the popularisation of dances dedicated to Siva.

Siva Tandava is of two types consisting of seven variations in each type. The first one consists of Ananda, Sandhya, Kalika, Urdhva, Uma, Gouri and Samhara; and the second of Suddha, Desi Perini, Prenkhana, Kundali, Dandika, and Kalasa. The later ones are called Desi Tandavas. Jayapa described these forms elaborately in his treatise. Of these Perini is an important dance performed in those days. It has five parts having 125 Vinyasas.

Perini Tandavam
(two types)

Performed by men | Performed by women

The men who perform these ritual dances in Saiva temples are Veerulu, Mahesulu, Pasupathulu and Mailardcvulu. The women perform them as Kelika (entertainment) at the Kalyanamandapams of the temples when the Gods have their durbars. The temple ritual dances are a pure form of dance-Nrittain various Talas. In the Tandava of the virile type Abhinaya or Nritya does not have any place. Only some verses arc recited in praise of Siva. It is composed of Nritta only and of 125 vinyasas.

Kelika is an entertaining performance and has Nritta, Nritya and Abhinaya. The performance starts with Nritta and ends with Abhinaya. This is a classical performance meant for the learned scholars and the initiated. Many scholars in these parts opine that the present day classical style of Bharatanatyam evolved as a Katcheri in the courts of Zamindars in the South was evolved from Perini of old.

The Katcheri performances of the Rajanartakis of the following courts indicate this :

Tanjore (Tamilnadu)

Karvetinagaram (Chittoor District)

Kalahasti (Chittoor District)

Venkatagiri (Nellore District)

Banganapalli (Kurnool District)

Proddatur (Cuddapah District)

Gadwal, Kollapuram, Wanaparthi (Mahaboobnagar District)

Bobbili (Srikakulam District)

Vijayanagaram (Visakhapatnam District)

Madugula (Visakhapatnam District)

Tuni, Pithapuram, Peddapuram (East Godavary District)

The forms developed in all these courts were the same except for a few variations in items. Nearly a hundred years ago Sarvagna Kumara Yachendra, ruler of the Venkatagiri Estate, held a conference of scholars in music and dance from all over India. After this conference he wrote the book 'Sabha Ranjani' in Telugu. In this book he discussed in detail the various forms prevalent in the Zamindaris. He also discussed in detail the original form of Perini.

Smt. Kalahasti Rajamma, a great scholar in Sanskrit and Telugu; Abhinaya, Bharata, and Agama Sastras; a temple artiste of Shri Kalahasti, attended the conference. She taught me Agama Nritya, Abhinaya and Bharatam.

Ritual dances were popular during the regime of the Kakateeyas. They were followers of Pasupati Sampradaya of the Saiva cult. The Pasupathis worshipped Siva with dance and music. The music and dance were followed certain rules depending on the time of the day, *i.e.* morning, highnoon, evening, night *etc*. There were Bali peethams inside the temples facing the main deity. The ritual dances were performed there.

Perini is a very important and difficult dance to perform. Even in recent times 40 years ago some of the Desini dances in their original form were performed in the Shri Kalahasti temple by the male dancers of my Gurus family. Particularly Urdhva Tandava on the night of Sivarathri at midnight. which is Lingodbhava time. The Panchamukha Vadya, Surya Mandala, Chandramandala, Dhavala Sankha, Mahamaddela and Nandi Maddela were played as accompaniments. In Saiva Agama Nartana I learned the various Jatis and Perini Paddhati from my guru Smt. Rajamma.

Today only some portions of these great dances are being performed by the Vira Musti Community in the Worship of Virabhadra.

Mythologically it is said that on the dawn of civilization Siva performed the Desini Tandava to please Parvathion mount Kailasa during the Vasanta Festival.

A word about Shrikalahasti and Bobbili:

Shri Kalahasti is in Chittoor District, the Southern end and Bobbili is at the eastern end of Andhra Pradesh. Though they are thus located apart there are reasons for the uniformity of art development throughout Andhra. There are four major communities which ruled the land-Kshatriyas, Velamas, Reddis and Kammas. The rulers of Karvetinagaram, Tuni, Peddapuram and Vijayanagaram are Kshatriyas. The rulers of Bobbili, Pithapuram, Nuzvid, Shri Kalahasti and Venkatagiri are Velamas. These Zamindars were closely related and the Natyacharyas of one estate used to frequently visit the other. The famous Natyacharya at Bobbili Bhugata Ramayya was a great scholar in Natya Sastra and Mridanga player. He followed the ancient Drupad Bani. My Gurus ancestors were court artistes of Shri Kalahasti. Both these artiste families used to meet frequently and there was great similarity in the development of art-forms in these courts.

Nandiswarabharatam is a book of practical jatis performed by these artistes. They were taught to me by my Guru and I am using them in this dance composition.

In Andhra there was great rivalry between the followers of Vira Saivas and Vira Vaishnawas. Frequently there were disturbances. In order to bring unity between these two sects Brahmanayaka of Palnadu and Tikkana, the great poet started a new movement known as Harihara cult. In this Siva and Vishnu cults were amalgamated. There is a temple for Chennakesava at Macherla and in the same compound is a temple of Virabhadra. Here Perini used to be performed in both the Siva and Vishnu temples. Now during the Sivaratri festival a few jatis from this dance are performed at

Kotappakonda by Viramustis. At Karamchedu, now a village near Macherla, there are temples for Virulu (heroes fallen in the battle of Palnadu). Every year there is a jatra here when some jatis are performed as invocation to these heroes. But for these, the form is almost dead now. And I have reconstructed this form with the aid of all the material available and taught it to one of my disciples Chy. K. Sudarshan. Financial assistance has been provided by the Andhra Pradesh Sangeeta Nataka Akademi, Hyderabad for the project. Two drummers from Srikakulam District, who play the Maha Maddela and Druvapada Bani have taken part as accompanists. Besides Maha Maddela and a wind instrument Mukha Veena used to accompany for the songs. Now it is difficult to get Mukha Veena Players so also the rare instrumentalists of Panchamukha Vadya, Suryamandala, Chandra Mandala *etc.*

The Technicalities of Perini

Perini consists of 5 parts and is performed in 25 talas. The popular Adi Tala and 24 other talas from the 101 talas are used. Some verses in Telugu, Ravana's stotras and Tripura Samhara stotras are recited. Kaivarams to the five lingas : 1. Prithvi linga 2. Jala linga 3. Tejo linga, 4. Vayu linga and 5. Akasa linga are recited. In the end a Kaivaram from Sukrachary's Virabhadra Kavacham is recited followed by a Thirmanam.

The dance begins with Ambara vinyas (Alapa) in Nata Raga and ends with Surati Raga. Traditionally besides Nata and Surati, Kalyani, Mohana, Aarabhi, Sankarabharana, Anandabhairavi, Bhairavi, Hindola, Kedaraganla, Nilambari, Kapi, Shanmukhapriya, Madhyamavati and Devagandhari are also sung.

The whole dance runs in Samagati Vinyasa. The following talas are used in the dance: Adi, Brahma, Vinayaka, Matya, Jampa, Mallikamoda, Hamsanada, Dwitiya, Purna Kankala, Abhanga, Simhavikrama, Udgata, Sarabhlila and Kokila priya.

In the invocation dance of EKADASARUDRA (NARTANA) the following 11 talas are used : 1. Rajavidyadhara, 2. Kuruttaka, 3. Makaranda, 4. Prati, 5. Turangalila, 6. Sama, 7. Laghusekhara, 8. Gajalila, 9. Simhalila, 10. Ratilila, 11. Garuda.

Jatis pertaining to these talas are danced. The five yatis are : 1. Sama, 2. Vishama, 3. Damaruka, 4. Mridanga, 5. Pipilaka.

The five Bandas are : 1. Padma, 2. Naga, 3. Chatra, 4. Khadga, 5. Chakra.

The gati Vinyasas are as follows :

Mayura, Marala, Mattebha, Hasina, Sukha.

Jatis are five :

3, 4, 5, 7, 9 letter-metres.

Bhramaras are twentyfive :

1. Dakshina, 2. Vama, 3. Sama, 4. Bhujanga, 5. Lata, 6. Lila, 7. Vidyuta, 8. Chakra, 9. Chatra, 10. Kuchita, 11. Anga, 12. Thirada, 13. Antarbhamara, 14. Bahya, 15. Ootha, 16. Padma, 17. Bhoobhrama, 18. Urdhva, 19. Vayu, 20. Parswa, 21. Dola, 22. Suchi, 23. Chitra, 24. Sankima, 25. Samputi (kuta).

There are nine varieties of Sringaranartana.

Talas specified for each item are :

Pushpanjali-Matya Tala

Vinayaka Kautham Vinayaka Talam

Devi Kaivaram-Bhrama Tala and Adi Tala

Vinayaka Kautham consists of five parts :

1. Sulu Vinyasa 2. Tatkarami 3. Thana jati 4. Kautam 5. Five thirmana jatis.

The five Angas of Perini are as follows :

1. Gargara, 2. Vishama, 3. Kavivaraka, 4. Gita, 5. Vikata, (also called Bhavasraya). In some traditions the order of performance of these Angas may vary.

The Performance

Ambara (Alapam) in Nataraga on flute or Mukha Veena. The Ayitham is sung followed by the invocation verse to Vinayaka and Siva. The performance begins with a Mukhtayi. After Mukhtayi Malaprapti is performed in Matya Tala. This is followed by Pushpanjali in Tahana Vinyasa. Then the first part of Perini follows thus :

The gargara vinyasas are six : Pata vata, Patava, Lakadima, Sirabira, Kuluhula, halabida.

In this the various types of pada vinyasas are demonstrated in 5 yatis Mridangam, Damarukam *etc.*

After these five varieties in foot work the invocation to Mahasena (Kumara swami), Vinayaka Kautam and a Kaivaram to parvathi take place.

Then follows Sringanartana of nine varieties—in this nine jatis and bhangimas are performed.

Part II consists of the following :

25 varieties of Bhramaras with 125 circular movements in Vishama is performed. This ends with a Samputi Karana jati.

Part III and IV have Kavivaraka and stotra gitams are sung in praise of the five lingas and different instruments played. Then 11 talas (jatis) are danced for the Ekadasa rudras.

Part V is vikata or Bhavasraya; dance to 'Panchamukha Sabdas' is performed.

Before the finale (Tirmanam) Virabhadra Kavacham of Sukracharya is recited.

SRINGANARTANA is a Nritta Unit. It is composed of two charis and one Angahara and ends with a sthanaka. Sringa is of 9 varieties. It starts with an Akasachari and ends with a Bhuchari. In between comes Angahara. In this the Bhangimas from Ramappa temple are demonstrated. For the charis and Padabheda jayapa has given full details. While demonstrating the jatis in Sringa the tala is Adi. We have 9 jatis with 9 different gati prastaras, taken from the 101 talas. Some of the jatis are from Saiva Agama and some from Nandiswara Bharatam.

In Vikata or Bhavasraya the movements imitating birds, animals and Kanduka krida (ball-game) are some times performed.

Panchamukha Sabdas : From the five faces of Siva. In this various syllables (Patava Aksharas) are sung which form part of the Mridanga jatis of rare beauty. The jatis composed with these sabdas are danced in Bhavasraya.

The specific character of the tirmanams in this is that while generally a tirmanam is played three times it is played five times in Perini.

It took two years to compose this dance and since one year two Drummers and one aritste practised this dance.

In some traditions NAVA RASA ANGAHARA NRITYA is performed in Bhavasraya.

Perini Siva Tandava Performed in Andhra

In honour of the chairman of the Netherlands Foundation Sri V.G.M. Marijnev and the ambassador Sri T.J. Amurs, Andhra Pradesh Sangeet Natak Academy arranged Perini Siva Tandava performance on 6th November 1974.

The audience very well appreciated the performer Sri K. Sudarsan and his Guru Sri Nataraja Ramakrishna and the academy for having arranged such a programme and forgiving them an opportunity to witness the best Nritya Kala rupas of Andhra Pradesh.

When Rashtrapathiji, Sri Fakruddin Ali Ahamed came to Hyderabad, in his honour another performance by Sri K. Sudarsan on 2nd November by the Information and Broadcasting Department of Andhra Pradesh and everyone appreciated such good performance of Perini Siva Tandavam.

Indian Herald patrika wrote about that day's performance as follows :

"Magnificent is the work to describe the dance of K. Sudarsan, who performed at the cultural performance arranged in honour of the President Fakruddin Ali Ahmed and Mrs. Abid Ahmed by the Government, at Ravindra Bharati here this evening.

For a moment, it was as if a temple sculpture had come to life and tempted the cymbals to play for its dancing feet. The dance was "Perini", a sequence of intricate footwork and rhythm consisting of 25 "talas" based on the temple sculpture of the Kakatiya period, found in Warangal district. The dance, the drums and other accompaniments were equally good.

A classically handsome face and well maintained body adds to Sudarsan who is a Sangeeta Nataka Academy scholar".

On 24th November, another performance was arranged by the President of Hungary in Rashtrapati Nolayam.

On 30th November Perini Siva Tandavam was arranged in the palace of Nizam Nawab and it also received applause by all.

On 3rd and 4th of December in Ravindra Bharati, another performance of Perini Tandavam was arranged before Yugoslavians Folk artists and

A Profile of Dr. Nataraja Ramakrishna (in Telugu)

పేరిణి తాండవ పునరుద్ధారకి నటరాజ రామకృష్ణ

నటరాజ రామకృష్ణగారి జననము బలిద్వీపంలో. మీనాక్షి సుందరంపిళ్లైగారివద్ద భరతనాట్యం, కాళహస్తి రాజమ్మగారి వద్ద అభినయం, ఆగమనర్తనం, భరతశాస్త్రం, అలంకారశాస్త్రం అభ్యసించారు. ఉత్తర హిందూస్థానం వెళ్లి కథక్, మణిపూరి నృత్యాలను నేర్చుకొన్నారు కూచిపూడి నృత్యాన్ని వేదాంతం లక్ష్మీనారాయణ శాస్త్రిగారివద్ద, భామాకలాపాన్ని పెండెల సత్యభామగారి వద్ద అభ్యసించారు. ఈ వివిధ కళారీతుల ప్రాచుర్యం కొరకు హైద్రాబాద్‌లో 'నృత్య నికేతనం' స్థాపించి రెండు వేలకు పైగా విద్యార్థులకు శిక్షణనిచ్చారు. భండారా సంస్థాన నాట్యాచార్యులుగా ఎన్నుకోబడి "నటరాజ" బిరుదాన్ని పొందారు.

తమ 16వ ఏట 'నృత్యాంజలి' పేరుతో ప్రథమ రచన చేశారు. ఇంతవరకు నృత్యకళ గురించి 80 గ్రంథాలు వెలువరించి అనేక కేంద్ర, రాష్ట్ర ప్రభుత్వ బహుమతులు పొందారు.

నర్తకుడు, నాట్యాచార్యుడు, నృత్యకళా ప్రచారకుడు, రచయిత అయిన రామకృష్ణగారు మరుగునపడిన విశిష్టకళారీతులను వెలుగులోకి తీసుకొనివచ్చారు. అనేక నృత్యనాటికలను రూపొందించారు శ్రీ వేంకటేశ్వర కళ్యాణము, కుమారసంభవము, మేఘసందేశము, శ్రీకృష్ణలీలాతరంగిణి వానిలో ముఖ్యమైనవి. "కుమార సంభవం" సంస్కృత నృత్య నాటక ప్రదర్శనకు వీరికి ఉజ్జయిని కాళిదాస నాట్యసమారోహ్‌లో ప్రథమ బహుమతి లభించింది.

వీరి కళాసేవను గుర్తించి ఆంధ్రప్రదేశ్ సంగీత నాటక అకాడమీ వీరికి 'భరతకళాప్రపూర్ణ' బిరుదానిచ్చి సన్మానించింది. అంతే కాక శాతవాహనకాలం నుండి తెలుగునాట విలసిల్లిన నృత్యకళను గురించి వీరు రచించిన బృహత్తర గ్రంథాన్ని అకాడమీ ప్రచురిస్తున్నది.

A Profile of Sri Sudarsan

పేరిణి సుదర్శన్

చిరంజీవి సుదర్శన్ స్వస్థలం కాకినాడ. జన్మ స్థలం ఔరంగాబాదు. ఇతని తల్లిదండ్రులు శ్రీమతి కమలాదేవి, శ్రీ కె. నరసింహారావు. వయస్సు 17 సంవత్సరాలు.

బాల్యము నుండి శాస్త్రీయ నృత్యకళ యందు ఉత్సాహముండినను కాకినాడలో అభ్యసించే అవకాశములేక, అభివృద్ధి గాంచలేక పోయెను.

మూడు సంవత్సరాలుగా శ్రీ నటరాజ రామకృష్ణగారివద్ద వుండి భరతవిద్యలో ప్రత్యేక శిక్షణ పొందుచున్నాడు.

ప్రారంభములో యితనికి ఆర్థికసహాకారం చేసి ప్రోత్సహించిన కళాహృదయులు శ్రీ ఎల్. మాలకొండయ్య I. A. S., శ్రీ గ్రంథి వేంకటరమణ (కాకినాడ)

1978 లో సంగీతనాటక అకాడమీ వారు శ్రీ నటరాజుగారి దర్శకత్వంలో ఏర్పాటు చేసిన అభినయస్కూలులో శిక్షణ పొందినాడు.

ఒక సంవత్సరంగా అకాడమీ వారి ప్రోత్సాహంతో స్కాలర్‌షిప్పుతో, శ్రీ నటరాజ రామకృష్ణ గారు "పేరిణి తాండవము"లో ప్రత్యేక శిక్షణ నిస్తున్నారు.

the special officer explained the unique features of the dance poses of Andhra Pradesh and their speciality.

Perini Performed—Laurels won

On the 9th December 1925, Andhra Pradesh Sangeet Natak Academy arranged Perini Tandava Nrityam in Warangal. Bharata Kala Propoorna Sri Nataraja Ramakrishna could arrange several such programmes previously and could win the appreciation of people.

Janadharna, a weekly of Warangal commented as follows:

"The dance programme of Perini, arranged on 6/12/1974 started at 7 p.m. and went upto 8O'clock. The audience consisting of more than six thousand people were immensely moved with the performance. The efficiency shown by Sri K. Sudarsan and the laya Vinyara exhibited by the Mardangikas (drummers) was apprreciated with constant shouts and Harshadwana.

After the performance, the district collector of Warangal, Sri M.B. Balaraj IAS spoke that "the great art form of Perini exhibited belonged to Warangal and it is a matter of pride" he said. He appreciated the effort put up by Sri Nataraja

Ramakrishna and garlanded Sri Sudarsan, the artist and also the drummer.

'Link' magazine of Delhi, reviewing the performance dated 29th December, wrote as follows :

"The Andhra Pradesh Sangeeta Nataka Academy, with the expert help of Ramakrishna has a research project on that dance form. Also a regular training school for talented dancers is run in Hyderabad. K. Sudarsan, 18, known as Perini Sudarsan, has already given many performances of Perini dance. In Warangal, he danced recently on the occasion of the All India Telugu Cultural Festival before an audience estimated about 6,000. Suryalingam on Mrudangam gave excellent support".

Perini Tandava school was started at Hyderabad on 8th April 1974 and its special officer Sri J. Bapu Reddy IAS, explained the efforts put up by AP Government to lift the arts remaining in the dark. Education and Cultural Affairs Minister of AP Govt., Sri M.V. Krishna Rao promised to give financial assistance to run the school for 5 years.

On 12th April, the performance of Perini Siva Tandava was arranged on the day of the inauguration of the World Telugu Conference.

Perini Siva Tandavam

15

Andhra Natyam

Andhra Natyam

Dr. Nataraja Ramakrishna, a famous Natyacharya is the architect of Andhra Natya, the most ancient classical dance performed by artists of Andhra Pradesh in temples. He culled out this type of dance from the Aradhana Nritya of ancient Deva Nartakis, who dedicated their lives to the service of God.

Aradhana Nritya : Deva Nartaki, it is difficult to say how this Aradhana Nritya gained publicity from, when and by whom but it could get due recognition from Puja Nritya as a part of temple worship.

Deva Nartaki

So long this Aradhana Nritya was confined to the temples only, they could stick on to 'Sastra' and 'Sampradaya' and they kept their sanctity. But once they started to give performances in the streets along with the Saiva Murtis of temples, it turned out to be an art for pleasing the people and standard thus lowered down.

Pushpanjali Samarpana—Near Dhwaja Stambha

Thus a pious art form entered into Raja Durbars in the form of Raja Nartakis, who lived under the patronage of kings. Though these Raja Nartakis followed Sastra conventions in their performances, the original sanctity of the ancient Aradhana Nritya was lost. Devadasis commanded more respect in society because they lived on the income of or the property given to them by temple authorities. They never depended on individuals their efficiency in the art of dance, their selfless-ness, dedication to higher values of philosophy and to God was much appreciated by one and all in society. But, in course of time, they turned out to be performers for seeking patronage or wealth in course of time and society, was also responsible for this downfall, so to say.

The sculptures of ancient temples still stand as a witness to these Deva Nartakis.

A girl dedicated to God as Deva Nartaki was done so in a traditional way and she was given training in fine arts from her childhood. This training was started from the age of 5 years.

On festival days, taking a round to the temple, worshipping Asta Dikpalakas was a custom in every temple and Deva Nartakis were performing 'Nava Sandhi' or 'Baliharana' Nritya to please God.

After offering flowers to the God, near the Dhwaja Stambha, dance was performed with Indra's Aradhana, with special ragas and eight purva Talas. These dances were performed.

Deva Nartakis offering flowers do standing on the Stanaka.

At 10 O'clock, in the night Deva Nartaki was performing Kelika Nritya when the Swami returns from his journey through the streets this Nritya was 'Kelika' because she does it to please God. There was a good gathering of great pandits, efficient dancers and lovers of fine arts in the temple. Nartaki was dancing by her talent. Art lovers from them were questioning her on so many issues concerning her performances. It was a test for her talent, she was not only serving entertainment to the audience, starting from Alarimpu, she was displaying sarva palli Sabda, Varna, Sloka, Padas and Javalis and was concluding with Abhinaya. This Kelika was meant for entertainment.

The Nrityas exhibited before the main deity in Saiva temples are different from Vaishnava paddhati.

After Pavalimpu Seva only the temple doors were closed. Dolotsava was performed thus putting God to sleep. So, starting from 'Melukolpu, she was worshipping God in the day. On all situations the Deva Nartaki gave performances even at the time of 'Aragimpu' at the time of offering of Naivedya to God.

In the ancient days, it was the temple culture, that was considered to be instrumental to the prosperity of the country and by the spread of time presence of Deva Nartaki, as she has no widowhood was considered to be auspicious at the time of marriages *etc.* and Deva Nartakis of Andhra followed Abhinaya (tradition).

At Suchindram temple, in South, it was considered, marriage of Devadasi to the idol was symbolic of the marriage of Parvati to Shiva. The priest recited the Mantras and tied the Tali round the neck of the girl.

There are two descriptions of the dancing girls (Deva Nartakis) in the Kingdom of Vijayanagar.

The first one is by Domingo Paes, who was a member of the Portugese embassy. He talks about the idol which has the body of a man and the head of an elephant (May be Ganesha). This idol was attended by girls, who fed it and danced before it and also dedicated their daughters to it. He says "who can describe the treasure these women carry on their persons. Collars of gold Tickly set with diamonds, rubies and pearls, bracelets also on their arms, jewelled girls and anklets on their feet. There are some among them who have had lands presented to them and so they were main servants to God. One woman is said to have in this city possessed 1,00,000 pagodas about £ 25,000 and I can believe this from what I have seen". His description is authenticated by Fernao Numiz a countryman of Poes, who gives similar description. They were highly educated, and polished in their manners and were able to provide their patrons with their talent.

Ananda Kumaraswamy rightly says "As soon as beauty is sought not for religion and love but for pleasure, it degrades the seeker and the sought". These women who were once masters of their art lived in obscurity due to fear of ridicule by society in course of time as the Deva Dasi system was abolished by Government and lands given to these Devadasis were taken back by the authority".

Andhra Natyam exhibits the same "Adavus" as enunciated by Bharata in his Natya Sastra.

A sincere effort was made by Sri Ramakrishna, the famous Natyacharya, to lift this art from the image attached to it. When girls from respected families also began to learn this art and began to give stage performances, in public, it could regain its importance as dominant. Dance schools have been started in every city and many performing artists have come up in life as efficient performers.

This art form has a chair in the central university. Hyderabad and in the potti Sriramulu Telugu university in Hyderabad and several students are learning and giving performances on the stage.

Eminent Natyacharyas are teaching this style of dance and doing research and encouraging new forms and talent.

As in the other classical dances of India, Andhra Natyam also consists of Nritha, Nritya and Abhinaya. The Nritha part, considered as the most important aspect of any classical dance, is practiced in the initial stage of training to any student.

Ashta Dik Palaka Radhana—Deva Nartaki (Vaishnavo)

Though the three aspects Nritha, Nrithya and Abhinaya are given equal importance in exhibiting padams, poems, Javalies and Daruvus, Satwikabhinaya dominantes.

There are many different patterns of 'ADAVUS' in Andhra Natyam.

The basic position is 'Sama'. From, here body is made to move. It is also known as 'Santavam'. Holding two Ardha Chandra Hastas, on the Waist, standing in a straight line with feet in 'equal level' is called 'Sthayaka of Natya Sastra' says Dr. Nataraja Ramakrishna, the pioneer of Andhra Natyam.

Nritha aspect has to be understood as a technique of body movement. Mrs. Kapila Vatsayan explains that the Indian dancer is not concerned with masculature of the human form, but rather like the sculptor, takes the joints and fundamental, anatomical bone structure of the human form as the base. From such a base the dancer strikes to achieve.

A rich and complex subject as Indian dancing has several aspects. That which was sacred to the Gods and danced for them was 'Margi' and that which was meant for pleasure of human beings is Desi.

It was further divided into Tandava and Lasya.

Tandava was first danced by God Shiva, who conveyed this art to mortals through his disciple Tandu. Shiva the symbol of procreation and so Tandav is regarded as male dance. Tandava covers all dance forms, which express actions and feelings with strength and vigour. When it is danced with facial expression, it is called Prakashani Tandava and when it is without facial expression, it is Bahurupa Tandava, these are given accepted types of this Tandava, said to have been danced by Shiva.

The Images of Shiva are divided into four classes. (1) Samhara Murthy, (2) Dakshina Murthy, (3) Anugraha Murthy (boon giving aspect) and (4) Nritha Murthy (dancing aspect).

Nava Janardana Parijatham

The main guru of Vempati Chinna Satyam, has also trained C.R. Acharyulu, who became the Kuchipudi Guru for Mrinalini Sarabhai's Darpana Academy at Ahmedabad. Lakshmi Narayana also trained Nataraja Ramakrishna who reconstructed some old performance traditions of Devadasis, like Nava Janardana Parijatham categorised under Andhra Natyam.

Nataraja Ramakrishna in his revived Navajanardana Parijatham, a tradition of the old pendyala Devadasi family of Pithapuram, has trained Kalakrishna for performing Satyabhama's role—though the dance comes under Andhra Natyam. Pasumarthy and Ekswarapu Srinivasan are among the males doing female roles. Nataraja Ramakrishna insists on Satwika Abhinaya.

References

1. Indian dances: Their history and growth by Rina Singha and Reginald Massey.
2. Creations by Mrinalini Sarabhai.
3. Indian performing art by Banerjee.
4. The splendous of Indian dance by Mohan Khokar.
5. Kuchipudi Natya Manjari by M. Sanka Siva.
6. Art of Indian dancing by Brojesh Banerjee.
7. Speaking of dance the Indian by Monadakranta Bose.
8. Dances of the Golden Hall Ashok Chatterje—by Geer, N. Delhi.
9. Indra standing Kuchipudi by C. R. Acharya Malloka Sarabhai.
10. Bharata Natyam (in cultural prospective) doted by George Kliger.
11. The symbolics of and gestures – By Tara Michael.
12. Siva in Dance, myth and iconography – By Anne-Marie G Aston.
13. New directions in Indian dance Edited by Sunil Kothari.

Andhra Natyam Ancient Temple dance of Andhra Pradesh

16

History of Andhra Natyam

In the cultural history of a place, classified arts are important. In the history of Andhras, a prominent place was given as the inscriptions, literature and sculptures available in Andhra.

Andhras have a great history from the time of Satavahanas upto the British period. It is not easy to come to a general conclusion, about the cultural development of such area.

There are people of many races many religions and communities living in Andhra Desa. Satavahana administration was stable and there was great prosperity and so it was described as the golden age of the country. Satavahanas followed Vedic rituals, even though Buddhism flourished alongwith Brahaminism. Satavahanas were great patrons of fine arts. After them Ikshakas ruled and they helped the foundation of Buddhist University, the biggest in the South at Nagarjuna Konda. It was a very big religious and educational institution and also a centre of arts and culture. After them, Salankhayanas ruled the country and Vishnukundins followed them. Chalukyas ruled for four hundred years. During the time of Eastern Chalukyas there was construction of numerous temples and the organisations of dancers and musicians were attached to the Pallava dynasty grew impower by the end of the 6th century. The era of Eastern Chalukyas is important in the history of Andhras not only for its long rule, but also for its achievement in literary and cultural fields. Chalukyas laid the basis for Telugu literature to grow by their patronage and developed all fine arts. Saivism and Vaishnavism were popular in the region. Kakatiyas who were the feudatories of Western Chalukyas became independent. Jayappa Senani wrote Nritta Ratnavali, Vadya ratnavali and Githa ratnavali. Ramappa temple and the pillared temples were famous constructions of the period.

Velama kings rose to power, after them and established Vijayanagar empire in the South Western Region. After a long ruling period of three hundred and forty years of Vijayanagar empire collapsed, though Krishna devaraya whose name was written in golden letters, was known as a gallant warrior, accomplished writer, a shrewd statesman and a noble king and was patron of arts and literature.

It is a wonderful point to be noted that all the above dynasties that ruled encouraged building of temples and development of various arts of different religions.

Evidence of Dance

In the Telugu literature, there are thousands of descriptions of dances performed by the Deva Raja Nartakis and the folk artists.

Once temple dancers were believed to be Nitya Sumangalis and were invited to the marriage ceremonies of high families. They used to sing Mangalaharatis and used to give black beeds to the bride who would be blessed by God as a 'Sumangali'.

Vedic tradition helped to transmit culture and endured continuity of civilisation. Such culture was preserved predominantly in the temples of India.

Devanartaki the temple dancer is not a "Bhagini". There are some inscriptions in

Tripurantaka temple and Bezwada Kanaka Durga Malleswaralaya in which "Sani" is mentioned as a suffix to the names of some women donors or to the wives of the donors.

In Natyasastra, Bharata Muni mentioned about 'Abhyantana Parivaram", in which he mentioned about seven classes of women, who were performing different duties in a place. He described them as follows :

1.	Mahadevi	The queen (Chief)
2.	Devis	Queens
3.	Swaminulu	Daughters of Generals and Ministers
4.	Sthapita	Ordinary Wife
5.	Bhoginulu	Royal concubines or inferior wives of a king
6.	Natakiya	Actress
7.	Nartaki	Dancer

As per the above description, a nartaki is not a bhogini but a bhogini can be a nartaki. There are some incription in which the word 'sani' is added to the names of the wives of the kings. In the inscription of Mukhalinga Kshetra there is mention of the above fact. These are some other inscriptions in Tripurantaka temple.

According to a commentary on Kanika Agama, there are three types of Deva ganikas.

(1) Rudra Ganika, (2) Rudra Kanyaka, (3) Rudra Dasi.

Above three types of dancers had different dance forms. Suddha Nrityam was performed by Rudra Ganika infront of Sivalinga. Misra Nartanam was performed by Rudra Kanyaka which consists of puranas added to Nritam and Kevala Nartanam which was performed by Rudra Dasis which consisted of secular version. Rudra Ganika had to complete the 'Nityapuja' (daily worship in the temple) at a scheduled time in daily worship and also on festival days. There are several terms to denote the temple dancer.

Temple dancers were of several types. They are :

1.	Datta	One who of her own accord offered herself as a gift.
2.	Vikrita	One who was sold to the temple.
3.	Bhritya	One who offered herself as a servant of the temple for its prosperity.
4.	Bhakta	One who dedicated herself to the temple out of devotion.
5.	Alankrita	One who was well trained in the profession and was presented to the temple by the king or a noble after decoration with ornaments.
6.	Harita	One who was enticed and gifted to the temple
7.	Rudra Ganika	One who was employed by the temple to dance or gopika and sing at regular hours on payment of wages.

"Temple dance is a spiritual art. To dance in temple or to witness it is a spiritual experience. Andhra Natyam is a temple dance form of Andhra Pradesh. It was performed by cultured lady artists, who were well-versed in music, dance, and particularly in Agama Sastras.

"......... the temple dance form of Andhra Pradesh *i.e.*, Lasya is independent from that of Kuchipudi....... Kuchipudi had its birth in 17th century and it is a Natyamala tradition. But the temple dance of Andhra Pradesh is of purely Nattuva mela tradition. It had its origin 2000 years back when the temples were built for the Gods. An expert lady artiste, who had complete knowledge about the temple rituals, was allowed tooffer Kumbha harati to the presiding deity. Such artists were highly respected in society."

—says Padmasri Nataraja Ramakrishna

The definition of Rudra Ganika gives us a clear idea that a temple dancer was appointed in the temple for singing and dancing. There are several inscriptions about Deva ganikas who donated various things and constructed various wells and lakes. As regards artists of Andhra Natyam, there are stories and historical evidences. In the temple of Draksharama in East Godavari district. There was a Deva nartaki by name Maniyamba, who dedicated her life to perform dance and finally unified herself with the Lord Bhimeswara, the presiding deity. The inscriptions of A.D. 1535 I and A.D. 1545 II reveal that the dancers Chikkayasani, Govinda Sani Bejji Hanuma Sani and Linga Sani dedicated their lives for the temple rituals.

There are many inscriptions describing donations of Devanartakis or Sanis, who played important roles in temple rituals. There were Sanis who accepted donations given by others and who gave donations such as lands and other assets to the Lord to whom they dedicated their lives.

Sri B.N. Sastry, a great research scholar and historian has given a list of 72 Niyogas, who were associated with all the important temples of Andhra Pradesh in the old days. They took care to see that the daily ritual offerings of the deity and also the Rangabhogaa *i.e.*, worship through dance and music, were regularly carried on.

This tradition was carried on till recently *i.e.*, till the Endowment Act was passed. Now, Govt. employees, the Executive officers are managing the affairs of the temples. Most of the temples are having all the heriditary rituals and festivals. Some of the Sanis are performing Nritya Seva also in the festivals of some temples.

Kalyan Mahotsavam is celebrated every year in a grand traditional environmentin every temple.

Andhra Natyam—The Lasya Dance Tradition of Andhras

Temple as the cradle of Hindu culture preserved religion and culture is a culmination of different fine arts like poetry, sculpture painting, dance and also music including several other arts. Our ancestors preserved our cultural heritage with great faith in religion and the temple was used as the mainstream. Temple in India, was used as a place of worship and also as a centre of learning and a guide to spiritual life. Sagunopasana is a method by which idol worship is used to attain Moksha (Salvation of the human soul) Nirgunopasana is a procedure where idol is not required.

All the rituals performed in the temples depend on our Agama Sastras, which are of three types, *viz.*, Saiva, Vaishnava and Sakteya. Dance was a part of the temple rituals and was one of the shodasopachara pujas.

Deva Nartaki played a major role in the preservation of Lasya Nartanam of the temple tradition. She had to present different types of dance items in the morning worship, evening worship, night worship and also in festival worship as prescribed in Agama Sastras. Dance was performed in three places of themple—at Balipeetham or infront of the sanctum sanctoram in Kalyana Mandapam where marriage of the deity was performed and also outside the temple precincts. They are known in different names as follows :

(1) Agama Nartanam—Ritual dance for spiritualisation at Balipeetham.

(2) Aasthana Nartanam (or Kelika)—For intellectual community at Kalyana Mandapam.

(3) Prabandha Nartanam—A Parijata performance for the common people outside the temple.

Kelika in a king's court is also a similar performance and is known as Kachcheri, Nartanam, Darbaru etc.

Rudra Ganika had to complete the Nitya Puja at a cheduled time in daily worship and on festivals.

Temple dancer had a good place and also respectable place in society. Raja nartaki had a honourable place. Before they were appointed as temple or court dancers, they had to face several examinations both practical and theoretical and examined by scholars. "A Sani is a perfect artist who has mastered the Sangita Sastra in the seven swaras, SA, Ri, Ga, Ma, Pa Da, Ni *i.e.* SA to Ni who has passed all the tests and mastered Bharata Sastra, Rasa Sastra and epics etc. Therefore the word 'Sani' denotes an artist who has complete knowledge of Sangita Sastra in the combination of vocal and instrumental music and dance". "Gita Vaditya Nrityanam Trayam Sangita Nrityu Chyate."

In the ancient times, the dancers sincerely dedicated their lives to the world of art. She had to lead a pious life as mentioned in the scriptures. So, they were living as Tapaswinis. Later on, as times passed on, due to some social, political and economic influences, their life style changed and they were tempted to have heridiatry rights to perform temple duties. They could enjoy temple lands and so they adopted their relatives, children and dedicate them to temple service. This situation also changed. Instead of having relatives, children, they wanted to have their own children. Heads and chiefs of the villages took advantage of their situation and began to exploit them for their selfish ends. This caused gradual degradation of social status of these temple dancers. On account of this situation, a different life pattern developed and a separate class of dancers and this resulted in the fall of the art of dance particularly in the temples, in the eye of the public. So, the art of dance was driven out of the temples. In the beginning of the 20th century, because of the influence of Devadasi Act, dancers had to give up dance completely and search for other professions. Even they were identified as a separate class and called "Kalavantulu". The impact of the Devadasi Act was two fold. One was the art of dance lost its grandeur, greatness and prestige and other was to give a new life to the dancers, who were looked down upon.

Some elite of the society and art lovers like Sri C. Samba Murthy, Sri E. Krishna Iyer and Smt. Rukmini Devi, Arundale took revolutionary steps to promote the art of dance in Tamilnadu. They revived and developed 'Sadir' tradition the Devadasi dance tradition of Tamilnadu and gave it a new name Bharata Natyam. They worked hard to make people understand the richness of the art of dance and its sprituality and aesthecity.

Like Sri E. Krishna Iyer, Dr. Nataraja Ramakrishna is trying to promote the dance traditions of Andhra Pradesh.

Avoiding rigid items of Agama Nartana performance, some eminent artists made some changes in the repertoire of Andhra Natyam to suit to the modern stage. The whole night performance of 'Kalapam' had to be abridged to 2½ hours performance. So the wide repertoire of Andhra Natyam, which is a culmination of three traditions, has to be brought into a nutshell.

This dance tradition, which has sacrosanct qualities has to be developed on new innovations in accordance with the social changes that occur from time to time.

Origin and Development of Andhra Natyam

This distinct dance form called Andhra Natyam was mainly patronised propagated and developed by female artists of Andhra Pradesh. It had its special features. This dance form is as old as temples of Andhra Desa. Female artists of Andhra Pradesh, with the leadership of Annabathula Bulli Venkataratnam gave programme on 23rd August upto 12 o'clock and very eminent personalities, artists, scholars attended the conference.

All the artists accepted to develop the art form with a combination of Agama, Asthana and Bhagavatha traditions and named this dance tradition of Lasya as "Andhra Natyam". Abhinaya was its special feature and importance is given to singing.

Dr. Nataraja Ramakrishna convened a seminar of Lasya dance artistes in 1970 at Rajahmundry on behalf of A.P. Sangeeta Nataka Academy and the Abhinaya Sadassu christened the name "Andhra Natyam" to this Lasya dance tradition of female artists of Andhra Pradesh and also lead to the preparation of a syllabus. Later on, in the year 1982, the syllabus of Andhra Natyam, with some minor modifications was approved by the then Nritya Academy. The same syllabus, with an addition of perini Sivatandavam was reapproved by a committee of Potti Srinamulu Telugu University, Hyderabad in 1994. On 23rd January, 1995, the A.P. Govt. issued Go Moho 7, approving introduction of courses in Andhra Natyam at diploma and certificate levels in Sri Tyagaraja Govt. College of Music and Dance at Hyderabad.

This female dance tradition pertaining to Lasya style, which depended on Kaisiki Vrithi was developed as "Andhra Natyam" since two decades.

Andhra Natyam is now a stylised classical dance with naturai expression of Sattvikabhinaya.

This art performance of dance in the temple was a ritualistic sacred item in the temple and it was restricted to the precints of the temple only and the ritual dances were performed according to the Agamas only. But some eminent artists made changes in the repertoire of Andhra Natyam to suit to the modern stage. The whole night performance of Kalapam was abridged for 2½ hrs. performance. Modern artists can bring about any number of innovations in the traditional values of this tradition. Andhra Natyam, as a Lasya dance tradition has finally thus crossed many obstacles and has come to a stage of receiving recognition as an ancient temple ritual dance.

Books Referred :

(1) Nritya Academy Proceedings.

(2) Abhinaya Sadassu-1970-Rajamundry.

(3) Inscription.

(4) Articles on Andhra Natyam.

(5) Andhra Natyam-Syllabus Vivarana (1982).

(6) Dakshinatya Natyakala Charira by Dr. Nataraja Ramakrishna.

(7) National Seminar on Andhra Natyam—Sept. 1994.

In 1958, a conference was held by Sri R.B. Ramakrishna Raju, Raja of Karvetinagaram, who was President of Sangeet Nataka Academy of Andhra Pradesh and Dr. Nataraja Ramakrishna garu was the convenor. Chittajallu Vaidehi of Marempalli village, and Induvadana played Gollakalapam. Nirmala Joshi, Secretary of Central Academy, speaking in Sanskrit, appreciated the performance very much in the presence of Dr. Rajendra Prasad, the then President of India. She wanted to hold the performance at Delhi but unfortunately she resigned and the President died and the performance was not done.

Chinna Parankusam, Pedda Parankusam of Pithapuram were playing in temples in the year 1956. Rajeswari (also known as Ammam) was doing Kutcheri. Pendyala, Kone families were performing Kalapam. Satyabhama, Chittiraju were playing in three different banis (styles) in Vijayanagara Samsthanam they were famous in playing Bhamakalapam for 9 nights. Pendyala Gangadhara Rama Mohana Rao took, inspiration after witnessing Devva Rajeswaris excellent performance in 1948.

Annabathula Bulli Venkatanatnam was playing Kalapas, Bharata Kala Prapoorna Saride Manikyamma of Vijayanagaram Samsthanam was performing.

It was known as Bhogam Melam, Sani Ata, Mejuvani in those days.

One Cheyyuri Sarada, Chataparru Bala Samdari (Elur) and Jeevaratnamma were also playing Kalapas depending on all the traditions in Andhra *i.e.*, Vaishnavam, Nrityam and Saivam.

(Courtesy Dr. Nataraja Ramakrishna)

The two conferences in Navabharata Guru Kulam at Rajamahendravaram succeeded in bringing together many artists from various places of Andhra Pradesh. Demonstrations by artists and discussions after the meetings gave a rebirth to the Lasya tradition as "Andhra Natyam".

The reports of these two conferences were presented to the Government of Andhra Pradesh and the Sangeeta Nataka Academy. The inspiration of the first conference led to conduct Abhinaya classes at Ravindra Bharati from January 1973 to April, in Hyderabad. Smt. Annabathula Bulivenkata Ratnam, Smt. Saride Manikyamma, Smt. Duggirala Jagadamba and Dr. Nataraja Ramakrishna taught Lasya dance tradition to the students, who attended the classes from various states of our country and also from Germany and America.

Sri K.R. Parama hamsa, special officer of Sangeeta Nataka Academy took keen interest in these Abhinaya classes.

Students that attended were :

(1) Vijayadurga (Hyderabad)

(2) Usha Dathar (Bangalore)

(3) Vijayalakshmi (Hyderabad)

(4) Chandramukhi (Hyderabad)

(5) Subhashini (Hyderabad)

(6) Raksena (America)

(7) Haide Culao (Germany) and some others.

The second conference held in 1974 (February, 25-27) gave a shape and recognition to the Lasya dance tradition *viz.* "Andhra Natyam".

During the regime of Sri T. Anjayya as the Chief Minister, Andhra Pradesh, Sangeeta Nataka Academy was split into separate Academies for each art as Nritya Academy, Music Academy and Nataka Academy. In the year 1982, the member of Nritya Academy agreed to have a discussion about the syllabus. Bharata Kalaprapoorna Dr. Nataraja Ramakrishna who was the President of Nritya Academy at that time discussed with Bharatakala Prapoorna Sri Korada Narasimha Rao about various aspects of the Lasya Dance for 2 days from 6-7 July 1982.

Details of Discussions

Introduction : Tandava Riti and Lasya are the two main classical streams that flowed in Andhra Desa.

Tandava : This masculine dance was developed and performed by men mainly. It was developed as a dance drama and was called as Natya mela. Female characters in a dance drama were also performed by men only. Later on, it was called as Bhagavata mela. Suddha Tandava is an Eka-Patra-Kelika (solo dance performance). Another tradition of Tandava is also known as Natya mela. The performers used to travel from place to place in the country to educate the common people in religion, social customs and about cultural heritage.

Lasya : Lasya, mainly the female oriented dance performance was called as Nattuva mela. Sometimes the orchestra also comprised of females. This Lasya technique is a combination of Nritta, Nritya and Abhinaya. The performance of Satvi Kabhinaya is also known as Suddha Lasyam.

Lasya is of three kinds :

(a) Lasya performed during the rituals in a temple as an offering to God.

(b) Kelika which was performed in Kalyana Mantapam of a temple in the presence of several scholars, other artists and elite of society.

(c) Dance performance outside the temple, which was called 'Prabandha Nartanam'. It was for the entertainment of common people.

3rd Conference of Andhra Natyam : The 3rd Andhra Natyam conference was held on 17th July 1994 at Vijayawada. Smt. Sarada Ramakrishna, Principal of Ramakrishna Kala Kshetram and also an artist of Andhra Natyam conducted this conference successfully. Conference was inaugurated by Sri K. Sada Siva Rao, IAS, several eminent personalities like Dr. Mikkilineni Radhakrishna Murthy, Dr. Arudra, Dr. Viswanadha Satya Narayana, Sri Korada Narasimha Rao, students and teachers of various schools, journalists attended the conference.

Smt. Annabathula Satyabhama, Smt. Annabatha Mangatayaru, Annabathula Venkata Narayanamma, Annabathula Lila Sayi, Annbathula Surya Kantamma, Smt. Saride Manikyamma and Ku. N.V. Lakshmi Prasanna participated as demonstrators. Famous artist of Andhra Natyam Sri Kala Krishna introduced all the artists to the audience. Annabathula Manga Tayaru gave demonstration with her Abhinaya presentation to a sloka from "Pushpabana Vilasam" and all the other artists also gave performances.

Dr. Arudra, cleared doubts about Andhra Natyam. He said that the name 'Andhra Natyam' was chosen by the old artistes, who attended 1970's Abhinaya Sadassu at Rajamundry. He defined Andhra Natyam as the temple art of female artistes of Andhra. He mentioned about the importance of this dance and added that 'women' have the natural tendency to dancing and dance must be performed in the presence of the Lord of the Universe for the welfare of the country and people.

Journalists gave good coverage for the conference in all Telugu and English Newspapers.

The conference again confirmed Andhra Natyam as the classical Lasya dance tradition of Andhras.

Later, a National Seminar on Andhra Natyam was held at Hyderabad from 24-25th September 1994.

Several artists and eminent scholars of National level attended the conference. Research scholars from various universities, dance scholars, dance artistes of various traditions and lovers of dance attended the seminar.

In a way, the seminar was an important landmark in the history of Andhra Natyam.

All the artists gave demonstrations of various styles of ancient days.

Reacting to the demonstrations, Sri VAK Ranga Rao, said that he recollected the days when he learnt Javalis, Padams and other items from the dancers of Bobbili Samsthanam. He wished that the original style should be preserved.

The two day seminar brought to light some more forgotten talents of veteran dancers of yester years. Annabathula family said that Gollakalapam was to be encouraged as it went out of vogue. So also Suddha Nartanam of rare talas was presented by Gantur sisters. They wanted Panchamukha and other talas to be practised.

As a result of the struggle of Andhra Natyam artists for two decades, a Government order was issued on 23rd January, 1995 recognising Andhra Natyam as one of the dance disciplines.

Nava Janardhanam

17

A General Introduction to Lasya and Dance Traditions

(Dakshinatyas-Lasya and Lasyangas-according to different texts-regional dance styles and recognised classical dances *etc.*,)

Mahendro Malayah Sahyomekhalah palamanjarah!
Etheshu samsrita desasten jneya dakshinapathah!
Kausalasto salaschaiva Kalinga yavanah jhasah!
Dravidandhra Maharastra vainnavivanavasajah!
Dakshinasya samudrasya tatha vindhyasya chantare!
Yedesasteshuyumjeta Dakshinatyantu nityasah![1]*–Natyasastra*

Bharata mentioned in the 13th chapter of his Natyasastra that the pravritti or the regional identity was to be recognised through costume, dialect, habit, tradition, custom and occupation. Here it may be mentioned that there are innumerable variations in the factors that contribute to and establish regional identities. These, infact, vary even within a particular region.

However, for the sake of brevity, I may say that, Bharata classified some identities. They are Dakshinatya, Avanti, Odhramagadhi and Panhalamadhyama. Broadly speaking the classification of Bharata may be taken as of Southern, Western, Eastern and Northern regions of India respectively. Each of these regions consists of different tracts of land with separate identities. Bharata, the author of Natyasastra mentioned that the South Indians practised the Dakshinatya style of Kaisiki Vritti, *i.e.* the delicate and graceful dance with erotic sentiment.[2]

In Hindu mythology it is believed that Siva and Parvathi are the first divine couple (Husband and Wife–Adi Dampatulu) of the universe. Most of the dance treatises mentioned that Siva was the first dancer. There are mainly two types of dances in the world, namely one is feminine (dance) and the other is masculine (dance). The feminine dance is known as LASYA and the masculine dance is known as Tandava.

According to Abhinayadarpana, Sangitaratnakara and other medieval dance treatises, dance is divided into three distinct categories *viz.*, Natya, Nritya and Nritta. Here Natya corresponds to drama, Nritya to mime performed to a song or a poem and Nritta is pure dance where the movements of the body do not express any mood (Bhava) or meaning. These texts also characterised dancing either as masculine (Tandava) or feminine (Lasya).[3]

Lasya is not defined in Natyasastra. It gives a list of ten Lasyangas auxiliary to Bhana and discusses them. The Vishnu dharmottara Purana says that Lasya is a form of Nritta which can be performed either on a stage or elsewhere. In Natyasastra, Bharata mentioned "Sukumara Prayoga" merely as the essence of Lasya, being the main feature of the dance of Parvati, but the nature of the 'Sukumara Prayoga' was not elaborated.

While discussing the purvaranga, Bharata defines Chari and Mahachari as the movements for the expressions of Sringara and Vira Rasas respectively. The distinction between them is similar to that of Tandava and Lasya. This shows an awareness that Lasya type of dance requires graceful movements, and this perhaps led to the recognition of Lasya as a separate style. Natyasastra enumerates and defines Lasyangas while describing the Bhana type of drama and says that Lasyangas are to be presented by a single character as in the case of a Bhana and not by a group of characters. These Lasyangas are briefly described as below:

1. **Geyapada:** When a heroine performs a dance by singing a song directed towards the hero, with appropriate accompaniments and with or without histrionic expressions is called "Geyapada".

2. **Sthitapatya:** When dance is performed in which a (love-stricken) heroine renders a song in prakrit to create rasa is called as "Sthitapatya".

3. **Asina:** When a heroine sits in a depressed and ruminating mood unaccompanied by any music, it is called "Asina".

4. **Pushpagandhika:** When a dancer performs a dance in which a woman assumes the role of a man and renders a song with music and dance is called "Pushpagandhika".

5. **Prachchedaka:** In Prachchedaka the dancer dances like a heroine, who is in love, meets any unfaithful hero in the moonlight.

6. **Trimudhaka:** When a dance is performed by a dancer or a character in which the metre is even, employing words that are neither harsh nor severe and which is mainly natural, it is called Trimudhaka.

7. **Saindhavaka:** When a dance is performed employing Instrumental Music and diction in prakrit, it is called Saindhavaka.

8. **Dvimudhaka:** When a dance is performed in a circular movement accompanied by melodious vocal and instrumental music expressive of the inner feelings of the character through pretentious gestures it is called Dvimudhaka.

9. **Uttamottamaka:** When a dance is performed accompanied by a song and instrumental music and full of sportive and joyous movements, it is called Uttamottamaka.

10. **Uktapratyukta:** A dance performed by a dancer, wholly with coquetry and love dalliance accompanied by diction full of saccharine and satire is called Uktapratyukta or amoebacan song.

11. **Chitrapada:** When a dance is performed in which a love torn character amuses himself or herself by looking at the portrait of his or her opposite, it is called chitrapada.

12. **Bhavika:** When a dance is performed in which the heroine dreams about her lover and expresses diverse feelings wistfully, it is called Bhavika."[4]

The description of lasyangas in Bharata's Natyasastra constitutes Lasya. The Lasyangas which are defined in other texts like Nartana Darpana, Sangita damodara, and Nartana nirnaya are similar to Natyasastra, with some minute changes. Some of them have given extra notes and differences, but it appears in many aspects that all these texts have followed Natyasastra only. Abhinaya darpana mentions Lasya as a style of delicate dance of Parvathi. Manasollasa describes Lasya as a graceful style of expression consisting of Angaharas. Saradatanaya discussed Lasya in detail and defined it as a form of a delicate Karana and Angahara, accompanied by a song and that Kaisiki Vritti (graceful dance) was added to it. So, Lasya can be divided into four kinds *viz.*, 1. Srinkhala, 2. Lata, 3. Pindi and 4. Bhedyaka.

1. **Srinkhala:** It consists of ten types of Lasyangas. The Lasyangas referred to, are the same as mentioned in Natyasastra.

2. **Lata:** This is of three types, viz as Rasakas; Danda, Mandala and Natyarasaka.

3. **Pindi:** It seems to have no divisions and apparently it may be a Tandava dance, which has many divisions.

4. **Bhedyaka:** This again has ten Lasyangas, which are same as mentioned in Natyasastra.

In another context Bhava Prakasini refers to Bhana type of drama and says that it employs ten Lasyangas which are same as those mentioned in the notes on Srinkhala and Bhedyaka, *i.e.* the Lasyangas which are mentioned in Natyasastra.

Bhavaprakasini seems to mean that these Lasyangas constitute Lasya. It says once more that apart from these Lasyangas there are, according to some other writers, four Nrityabhedas. They are Gulma, Srinkhalita, Latabandha, and Bhedyaka.

1. **Gulma:** It is danced together by a group of dancers in a slow tempo.

2. **Srinkhalita:** It is danced in the form of a chain comparatively in a faster tempo.

3. **Latabandha:** It is danced to a tempo neither too slow nor too fast by the partners holding, each other.

4. **Bhedyaka:** Each dancer in a group of dancers, plays her own part to a fast tempo.[5]

The above pindibandhas which are mentioned as Nritya Bhedas in Bhavaprakasini, are having the same names *i.e.*, Srinkhala, Latabandha, Pindi and Bhedyaka that occur in Natyasastra. But Natyasastra considers them as varieties of Pindibandha, and says that Srinkhala is Gulma *i.e.* a group. It uses the terms Lata and Latabandha synonymously. Natyasastra does not describe these in detail but defines them. It states that the various Pindis are designed to please gods, and each bears the name of a god or a goddess.

Bhavaprakasini gives with its own interpretations to the views mentioned in Natyasastra on those movements that are graceful and delicate. It also considers the Lasyangas mentioned in Natyasastra as parts of Lasya, because they are delicate. But later Bhavaprakasini says that Lasya consists not only these but also of other types of movements, which are mentioned as Nrityabhedas.[6]

Sangitaratnakara defines Lasya as a dance of delicate movements which arouse erotic sentiment.

Sangita damodara says that Lasya is a division of Nritya, and considers it as a desi form of dance, performed by women. It gives two sub-dvisions to Lasya as churita and yauvata.

1. **Churita:** The hero and the heroine dance and act with embraces, kisses in the middle of an act.

2. **Yauvata:** The dance performed by the dancers with delicate movements and over-powering charms is known as Yauvata.

Jayappa in his treatise Nrittaratnavali defines Lasya thus:

Slokam:
Bhavah sthripunsayorlasaha
tadarthah (rtham) tatra sadhuva
Lasyam Manasijollasa hetu Mridangaharavat
Devyaidevopadisthatvat prayah sthribhihi prayujyate!!

(Nrittaratnavali : page 18 : sloka 57)

"The mutual understanding of thoughts between men and women is Lasa *i.e.*, Lasya which consists of delicate gestures-arouses erotic sentiment. Lord Siva taught this to His consort Parvati, and hence ladies are expected to exhibit it."[8]

Bharata and others mentioned Lasya and Lasyangas as parts of Natya. Saringa deva mentioned and described Lasya and Lasyangas as Desibhedas in his Sangitaratnakara. They are ten in number.

1. **Chali:** Chali is the simultaneous movement of the feet, hips, thighs and arms. It should be soft, graceful and attractive synchronising with the tala. It should neither be too fast nor too slow and is to be done obliquely.

2. **Chalibadha:** Chali which is done quickly with straight movements. is chalibadha.

3. **Ladhi:** It is soft and graceful and contains simultaneous oblique movements of the hips and the arms.

4. **Suka:** Suka is the rhythmic movement, either slow or quick and full of feminine charm (Hava), of the ears with beautiful (glittering) ornaments.

5. **Urongana:** The graceful oblique movement, slow or quick, of the breasts and the shoulders is called urngana by the experts.

6. **Dhasaka:** Dhasaka is the rhythmic bending down of the breasts with extreme grace.

7. **Angahara:** The gradual bending of the two halves of the body in the form of a bow, gracefully to time is Angahara. So says, Sarngadeva.

8. **Oyaraka:** Oyaraka is accepted to be the slightly oblique downward movement of the head.

9. **Vihasi:** Vihasi is the smile which is full of the sentiment of love, that which is different from the trained (smile) and which has an extremely subtle and novel charm.

10. **Mana:** Mana is accepted to be that which has the tempo of the sthayi belonging to songs *etc.*

Sangita Damodara discusses the ten Lasyangas used in Bhana in the following manner.

1. **Geyapada:** The heroine sings and is accompanied by instrumental music.

2. **Sthitapathya:** This agrees with the Natyasastra in prescribing charis and chachchatputa. This also suggests recitation and Panikala-*i.e.*, hand-gesture.

3. **Asinapatya:** The heroine sits and acts with graceful movements of the hands, feet and eyebrows.

4. **Vaimudhaka:** This is Lasya performed by men in women's attire.

5. **Pushpagandhika :** This Lasya is performed with various graceful movements or the heroine tries to understand the hero and in order to do so, she sings in various ways.

6. **Prachchedaka:** A woman, sings to the accompaniment of the vina in grieving over her separation from her husband who is in love with another woman or a woman who becomes jealous on seeing her husband attached to another woman.

7. **Uttarottaram:** The simple conversation of a woman with her lover whom she imagines to be by her side.

8. **Uktapratyukta:** The heroine abuses the hero.

9. **Vimudhaka:** The heroine sings and dances gracefully.

10. **Saindhava:** The dancer dances and sings songs which are appropriate to the Sindhu country. Sangitadamodara also describes Lasyangas as forms of Nritya, with their origin in Karnata and which are full of hand gestures and movements of the other parts of the body.[10]

The Lasyangas which are mentioned by all the above authors are used in all the Indian classical dances. The Desi Lasyangas which are mentioned in Sangitaratnakara, Sangitadamodara and in Nrittaratnavali are found in Lasya dance tradition of Andhra Pradesh. Many of the Lasyangas can be seen in the performance of padams, Javalis *etc.*

Mathanga, the author of the musical treatise called "Bruhaddesi", used the word Desi for the first time. The word 'Desi' was used by many other authors like Someswara in his Abhilashitartha Chintamani (or) Manasollasa, Sarngadeva in Sangitaratnakara, Parshvadeva in his 'Sangita samaya saram *etc.* They all described the Desi traditions or Desi styles.

Apart from the above texts, Jayapasenani's Nrittaratnavali deals in two categories with the Desi tradition in detail in four chapters. In the first part the Sthanakas, Utplutikaranas, Bhramaris, Pada, Pata, Chari, Lasyanga, Gatibhedas are mentioned as supplementary to Marga Bhedas. Perini, Rasakam, Charchari, Bahurupam, Bhandika, Kollatamu are the various varieties mentioned by Jayappa in the second part of Desi styles. Jayappasenani defines Lasya and Tandava as the two varieties of Nritta and Nritya. Lasya is a feminine dance style which arouses the erotic moods with its delicate and graceful movements. Siva taught this dance style to His consort Parvati.

Lasyangas mentioned by Jayappasernani in Nrittaratnavali are same as in Natyasastra, Jayappasenani also agrees with Bharata that the Angas are ten in number.

The authentic texts like Natyasastra, Abhinayadarpana, Nrittaratnavali, Sangitaratnakara define various technical terms of dance and dramatology. The two main categories of dance are Marga and Desi styles, which are again divided as Natyadharmi and Lokadharmi.

Nritta Technique

Saushtavam–A beginning Posture

Lalitham–A natural female Posture

Feet are in Sama Position

A starting Position of Didite–Adavu

Mandala Sthanakam in a Abhinaya Sequence

1. Natydharmi is conventional tradition. 2. Lokadharmi is realistic tradition.

Nrittaratnavali mentioned forty six Desi Lasyangas. They are:

1 . Saushtavam	2. Sthapana	3. Rekha
4. Dalam	5. Chali	6. Chalavali
7. Lali	8. Thrikani	9. Ullasam
10. Sukalasam	11. Uronganam	12. Bhavam
13. Dharaharam	14. Kittu	15. Desikaram
16. Nijapanam	17. Dillayi	18. Lavani
19. Gitavadyata	20. Abinayam	21. Laya
22. Komalika	23. Oyaram	24. Aniki
25. Angaharam	26. Manodharmam	
27. Angam	28. Anangam	
29. Vivartanam	30. Jhanka	
31. Mukharasam	32. Theva	33. Vihasi
34. Thasakam	35. Talam	36. Vitalam
37. Rasavritti	38. Masrunata	
39. Anumanam	40. Pramanam	
41. Langhitam	42. Amshagati	
43. Susandhi	44. Padapatam	
45. Gatistham	46. Chandanam	

They are described as Desi lasyangas in Nrittaratnavali, but they partially follow the Marga tradition. To make it clear, I have adopted Natyasastra and other tests in defining lasya. Coming to the subject. Lasya as defined by the traditional artistes, female artistes of Andhra Pradesh in particular, is different from that of the above texts. Though these artistes follow these texts they make regional changes in their performances.

The performance of a Padam, Varnam, Slokam *etc.*, in a sitting position is called Lasya in Konaseema of East Godavari district. While performing a Padavarnam the artistes depict histrionic expressions for the Sahitya *i.e.*, text part, and they sing the svaras. They do not stand and perform the Jatis for the svaras. They call this tradition as Lasya. When they perform pure dance *i.e.*, Nritta by standing for Svarapallavi, Dasavataras, Sabdapallavi *etc.*, they call it as Tandava. It means the performance of an abhinaya piece by sitting is called Lasya, and the pure dance or Nritta performed for the items by standing is called Tandava. {Informant : Dr. Nataraja Ramakrishna}.[11]

The artistes developed the Rasabhinaya tradition all over Andhra and in particular in East West Godavari districts. In this tradition they sit and sing and perform the abhinaya for a Padam, Padavarnam, Slokam, Poem, Javali *etc.* They exhibit histrionic expressions according to the texts like Bharatarasa Prakaranam, Rasarnava sudhakaram *etc.*,. The Nayikabhinaya *i.e.*, developing the Nayikavasthas according to texts in Satvikabhinaya is a notable thing in this tradition of this region. This abhinaya is called as Suddhasatvika and is a very complicated one. The Lasya dance tradition can be divided into two types. The first type of the Lasya dance tradition is involved with festivals.

Batukamma, Gobbiata, Kolatam, Jadakolatam *etc.*

The second type of Lasya in the classical dance tradition, is performed by trained artistes.

The classical lasya dance tradition follows the Marga or Natyadharami with the regional changes. It is according to the texts. This classical dance can be classified into three parts (particularly in Andhra Pradesh):

1. Temple Dance	(Ritual & Spiritual)
2. Court Dance	(Intellectual)
3. Atabhagavatam	(Parijatams or Prabandha Nrityam) which has sahaja bhavas, hastas and karanas (natural expressions, hand-gestures and postures).

Again in temple dance there are three varieties.

Padaarthaabhinayam

Mundati

Vale

Napai

Nenarunnada

Nasami

Muchchatalu

Eka

Nelara

Temple Dances

(i) ***For Deities***-(Main deity, Asthadikpalakas *etc.*) As ritual duty, these types of dances are exhibited as a part of the rituals in special talas, special ragas and also on special occasions. Pure dance *i.e.*, Nritta is performed in these dances.

(ii) ***Asthana***-(Utsavam or Kelika) Generally there is a daily procession in the evening for Utsava vigrahas (Processional idols), the idols are brought to the Kalyana mandapa and a kelika is performed. This performance is for the presiding God and also for intellectuals who assemble there. Generally this performance is Nritya and Abhinaya oriented.

(iii) ***Prabandhanrityam***-A parijatam is performed only on the occasion of a temple festival. So it is an occasional performance for the common people as well as for the intellectuals. The purpose is to educate the masses about myth, epics, culture, customs *etc.* Parijatams are generally performed on the marriage day (Kalyanotsava) of the deity and also on several other important festivals.

Classical Lasya dance traditions follow Marga paddhati with Natyadharmi in relation to the regional changes. They can be recognised by their appearance, language, body kinetics, music (used for the dance) and customs which are followed by the dancers or the artistes.

Bharatanatyam, Odissi, Mohiniattam, Andhranatyam, Kuchipudi, Manipuri and Rasalila are the classical dance traditions of India.

Regional (Desi) Lasya dance traditions like Gobbiata, Batukammaata, Kollata Kopulu *etc.*, are in vogue in Andhra Pradesh. The following Desi dance styles are mentioned in Nrittaratnavali:

1. Rasakam, 2.Charchari, 3. Natya Rasakam, 4.Dandarasakam, 5. Sivapriyam, 6.Chintunrittam, 7. Kanduka Nrittam, 8. Ghatisani Nrittam, 9. Charana Nrittam, 10.Kollata Nartanam.[12]

These Desi dances were used to be performed by both male and female artistes in the past. Some of these dances are still in vogue. Desi styles mentioned in Nrittaratnavali are Perini, Prenkhana, Rendu Tegala suda *etc.*

People in India perform dance on various occasions like feasts and festivals. One of their expressions of worship is Temple dance.

All arts have their origin within the human development. According to the cultural systems developed by the human being, the dances can be classified under five major categories.

1. Aradhana Nrityam—worship through dance which can also be called as spiritual dance or ritual dance.

2. Sastriya Nrityalu—Classical dances.

3. Prachara Nrityalu—Traditional and Popular dances.

4. Janapada Nrityalu—Folk dances.

5. Atavika Nrityalu—Tribal dances

1. **Ritual Dance:** Aradhana Nrityam:-The dance performed in various festivals like Devinavaratri *etc.*, can be called as Aradhana Nrityam. Such as:

Vira Natyam in Virabhadra festival, Garapalu in Devinavaratri festival.

The dance of Deva Ganika/Deva Nartaki in the temples, Agni aradhana of Maharastra, Lamas dance in Tibet, Parsachi dance in Srilanka, Kavidi Chindu of Tamilnadu, Rasalila and Laya haroba of Manipuri, Ankiyanat of Assam, Ramaleela of Uttar Pradesh, Karma dance of Gonds, Sarhal festival dances of Orissa come under Aradhana nrityalu (worship dances). Aradhana dances stayed with Natyadharmi and Lokadharmi in various places. Deva Ganika dances with regional changes, Sevakali, Layaharoba and Ankianat are some for example.

2. **Classical dances :** The dance style which mainly follow the Natyasastra, Abhinaya darpana, Bharatarnava, Hastalakshanadipika and other texts, with regional effects and the tastes of the rulers and the intellectuals of the region can be called as classical dance. Nritta, Nritya and Abhinaya, these three aspects are exhibited in equal proportions with the textual Sthanakas (stances) Rechakas, Utplavanas, Karanas, Angaharas are performed in combination with the Gati, Yati, Jati,

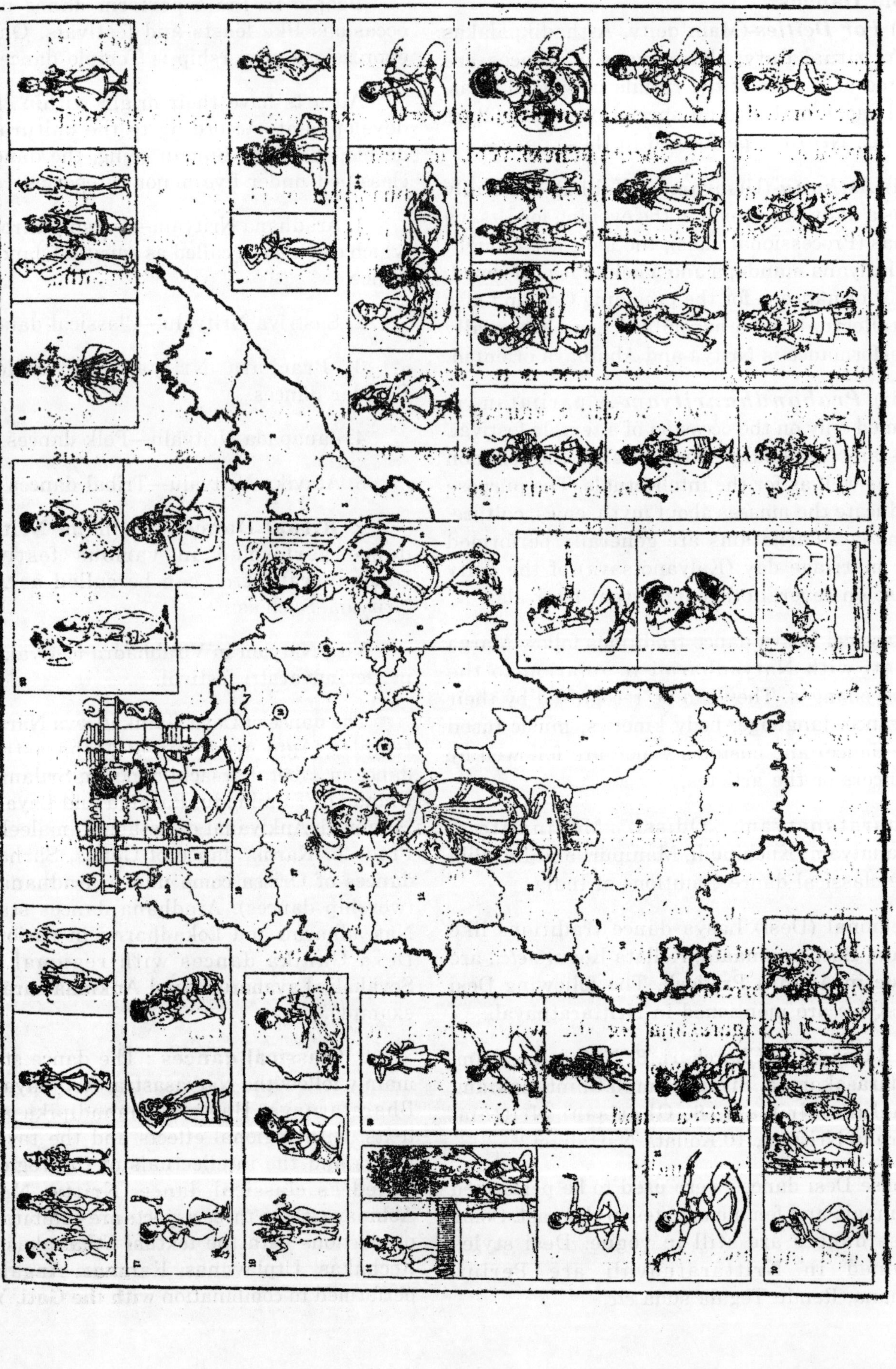

Dance Traditions of Andhra Pradesh

Bandha, in this classical dance. These classical dances are recognised for academic study by the provincial governments with regional identity. The following are the classical dances that are recognised by the concerned provincial governments:

1. Bharatanatyam	-	Tamilnadu
2. Mohiniattam	-	Kerala
3. Bharatanatyam of Mysore	-	Karnataka
4. Andhranatyam and Kuchipudi	-	Andhra Pradesh
5. Odissi	-	Orissa
6. Kathak	-	Uttar Pradesh
7. Manipuri	-	Manipur

that are celebrated by the people with regional variations. These dances are Gobbiata Batukammaata, pungidi, chemmachekka *etc.*, in Andhra Pradesh; Kummi, Kottayam *etc.*, in Tamilnadu; Kaikottukali in Kerala; Garbhanritya in Gujarat; Apart from the above there are Vrathachari, Puliata, Gurram Ata, Buttabommalata, Dasarla Nrityam, Palnatikatha, Jangamkatha, Katamarajukatha, Bobbilikatha, Voggukatha, Burrakatha *etc.*, are popular in Andhra Pradesh.

5. **Atavikula Nrityam:** Tribal dance is performed on every occasion like birth of a child, cradle ceremony, wedding, during the agricultural errands, at the harvest and even on the occasion of death of a person *etc.*, Savaras, Koyas, Chenchus, Baigas, Kurmas *etc.*, come under hill tribes. Dance is a part and parcel of their life and culture as a social activity.[13]

The development of dance can be again divided into three different types as under:

1. Dance for Gods	Ritual dances
2. Dance for Kings and Intellectuals	Court dance (Kelika)
3. Dance for common people	Open air performance like Parijatams.

The female artistes of the Lasya dance tradition of Andhra Pradesh used to perform the above three traditions in the temples, in the courts and at public places. I have given references regarding these from several books like Natyasastra, Abhinayadarpana, Sangitaratnakara, Nrittaratnavali, Bhava Prakashini *etc.* My object is to make a study of Lasya with the correlation of the above treatises and the different definitions given by the artistes of Sagarasima for the words Lasya and Tandava. Dance traditions are broadly divided into two categories:

1. Marga and 2. Desi

Again divided into two kinds:

1. Natyadharmi
2. Lokadharmi

Again divided into two varieties:

1. Tandava
2. Lasya

Again divided into five major types:

1. Worship dance
2. Classical dance
3. Popular dance
4. Folk dance
5. Tribal dance

Among all the above Andhranatyam is an old female dance tradition of Andhra Pradesh. Dr. Nataraja Ramakrishna, the pioneer of Andhranatyam defines Andhranatyam thus: "The Andhranatyam is a Lasya dance tradition performed by the cultured female dance artistes of the country in the temples, in the courts and at public places". At present the three traditions mentioned above are brought under a repertoire by an expert committee of Nritya Akademi and propagated by the eminent guru Dr. Nataraja Ramakrishna by teaching it to his students. My subject for the present thesis is "Andhranatyam—The Lasya dance tradition of Andhras", with special reference to Smt. Saride Manikyamma, a former temple dancer of West Godavari Distt., and an eminent guru who participated in every event of Andhranatyam and an awardee of the Central Sangeeta Nataka Akademi for her sincere efforts and specialisation of Adhyatma Ramayana Kirthana Abhinayam. I do cover other aspects like the historical background of Andhranatyam, its resurrection, its present technique and repertoire as a recognised classical dance tradition of Andhra Pradesh.

The dance tradition of Devaganikas developed in three streams.

1. **Ritual Dance** which is purely **Spiritual** performance done on the Balipitha or infront of the Garbhagriha. It is called as 'Agama Nartanam', (the dance performed according to Agama Sastras during rituals.)

2. **Intellectual Dance** which is performed at the Kalyana Mantapa during 'Asthanotsavam'. This is also called as Asthana nartanam, Kelika, Darbaru, Kachcheri or Karnatakam.

3. **Prabandha Nartanam or Parijatham** is performed to educate the common people about our culture, religious values, epics, and their moral duties *etc.*

Above three traditions were performed by different types of devanartakis, dedicated to the temple. Their performance technique was in three types as Nritta, Nritya and Abhinaya. They follow the treatise Bharatarnava. Abhinaya darpana which is a special treatise for Angikabhinaya and an abridgement of Bharataŕanava was also followed by them.

Devanartakis perform two types of dance *i.e.*, Lasya and Tandava (dealt before). Lasya consists of delicate and beautiful expressions with graceful bodily movements with Kaisikivritti.

Tandavam consists of profound expressions with valour and majestic movements, with Arabhati vritti.

The devanartakis of Andhra Pradesh in ancient times had different understanding about Lasya. According to them, a performance of Abhinaya in a sitting position was Lasya and doing Nritta for pallavis, sabdams, svarajathis was Tandava.

Technique and Items of Temple Ritual Dance

Temple dancer
Devanartaki (or)Devaganika (or) Gudisani

Vaishnava Temple dancer | Saiva Temple dancer

1. Agamanartanam

2. Asthana or Kelika Nartanam

3. Prabandha Nartanam

I. Modes of presentation–(Dharmis)
Natyadharmi and Lokadharmi

II. Styles or Vrittis :

(a) Kaisiki (graceful) main Vritti

(b) Arabhati (energetic)

(c) Satvati (grand)

(d) Bharati (verbal)

Dance Technique

Nritta | Nritya | Abhinava

To depict the meaning of a song dancer uses different hand gestures called 'hastas'. They are of three types.

1. Asamyuta hastas—Single hand gestures.

2. Samyuta hastas—Double hand gestures,

3. Nritta hastas—Which are used to perform pure dance.

'Mudra' is the hand gesture used during ritual performance. Hasta is used in dance terminology.

ASAMYUTA HASTAS : 30

1. aka	2. Tripataka
3.Arthapataka	4. Kartarimukha
5. Mayura	6. Ardhachandra
7. Arala	8. Sukatunda

9. Musthi
10. Sikhara
11. Kapitha
12. Katakamukha
13. Suchi
14. Chandrakala
15. Padmakosha
16. Sarpasirsha
17. Mrigasirsha
18. Simhamukha
19. Langula
20. Alapadma
21. Chatura
22. Bhramara
23. Hamsasya
24. Hamsapaksha
25. Sandamsa
26. Mukula
27. Tamrachuda
28. Trisula
29. Urnanabha
30. Bana.

SAMYUTA HASTAS (24)

1. Anjali
2. Kapotha
3. Karkata
4. Svastika
5. Dola
6. Pushpaputa
7. Utsanga
8. Sivalinga
9. Katakavardhana
10. Kartarisvastika
11. Sakata
12. Sankha
13. Chakra
14. Samputa
15. Pasa
16. Kilaka
17. Matsya
18. Kurma
19. Varaha
20. Garuda
21. Nagabandha
22. Khatva
23. Bherunda
24. Avahitta

NRITTA HASTAS 33

1. Gajadanta
2. Talamukha
3. Viprakirna
4. Suchividda
5. Nalini Saroja Kosha
6. Makara
7. Jnana
8. Pallava
9. Ardharechita
10. Keshabandha
11. Kapota
12. Parshvamandala
13. Tripataka Pakshavanchita
14. Karihasta
15. Urdhvamandala
16. Mushti
17. Svasthika
18. Udhvritta
19. Puromandala
20. Nitamba
21. Ulbana
22. Prayuktaala Pallava
23. Lathakara
24. Suchikasya Urahparshvamandala
25. Dandapaksha
26. Paksha Prathyotita
27. Mukula svastika
28. Rechita
29. Avitta vaktra
30. Aralakatakamukha
31. Mudra
32. Garuda Pakshi
33. Varadabhayam

Beyond the above, there is a regular use of Pataka, Tripataka, Sikhara, Alapallava, Katakamukha and Pasha can be seen in the'performance of Nritta.

GRIVABHEDAS (NECK MOVEMENTS):

While performing the Nritta, Nirtya, Abhinaya the neck is made to move sideways, (to and fro), front side and back side, in a half moon shape and like a peacock. Grivabhedas are 19 :

1. Dhuta
2. Vidhuta
3. Adhuta
4. Avadhuta
5. Kampita
6. Akampita
7. Udvahita
8. Parivahita
9. Anchita
10. Nihanchita
11. Paravrittam
12. Utkshiptam
13. Adhomukham
14. Lolita
15. Tiryannatonnata
16. Skandhanata
17. Aratrika
18. Sama
19. Parshvabhimukha

4. DRISHTI (EYE MOVEMENT)

There are three types of eye movements to express the emotions (Bhdvas).

1. Rasa dristhi
2. Sthayibhava dristhi
3. Vyabhicharibhava dristhi

(A) Rasa Drishti:

1. Kantha	2. Hasya	3. Karuna
4. Raudra	5. Vira	6. Bhayanaka
7. Bhibatsa	8. Adbhuta	

(B) Sthayibhava Drishti (8):

1. Snigdha	2. Hrishta	3. Dina
4. Kriddha	5. Dripta	6. Bhayanvita
7. Jugupsa	8. Vismita	

(C) Vyabhicharibhava Drishti (20):

1. Sunya	2. Malina	3. Sranta
4. Lajjita	5. Sankita	6. Mukula
7. Ardhamukula	8. Glana	9. Jihva
10. Kunchita	11. Vitarkita	12. Abhitapta
13. Vishanna	14. Lalitha	15. Akhekara
16. Vikosha	17. Vibhranta	18. Vipluta
19. Trasta	20. Madira	

5. PADAVINYASAM (FEET MOVEMENT)

Movements of feet are of thirty two kinds. They are:

1. Chalanamu, 2. Sankramanamu, 3. Saranamu, 4. Kuttanamu, 5. Lunthitamu, 6. Lolanamu, 6. Vishama, 7. Sancharamu, 8. Anchita, 9. Kunchita, 10. Suchi, 11. Agratala Sanchara, 12. Udghattita, 13. Sama, 14. Sarika, 15. Ardhapurathika, 16. Svastika, 17. Sphurika, 18. Nikuttaka, 19. Talotsepa, 20. Pushpotsepa, 21. Veshtana, 22. Ardhaskhalitaka, 23. Kuttha, 24. Purathika, 25. Pravritha, 26. Ullola, 27. Samasakalathika, 28. Lathakshepa, 29. Prenkhana, 30. Samotsaritha, 31. Mandala and 32. Lalita.

6. STHANAKAS: (STANDING POSITIONS)

At the commencement and at the end of a dance there must be a particular stance which is known as Sthanaka. There are (32) Thirty two types of sthanakas.

They are:

1. Ayatha, 2. Avahitta, 3. Ashvakrantha, 4. Mothitha, 5. Vinivritha, 6. Ayindra, 7. Chandrika, 8. Samapada, 9. Vaisakha, 10. Mandala, 11. Alidha, 12. Pratyalidha, 13. Swasthika, 14. Vardhamana, 15. Nandyavartha, 16. Chaturasra, 17. Parnipida, 18. Ekaparshava, 19. Ekajanu, 20. Parivritta, 21. Prishtothana, 22. Ekapada, 23. Brahma, 24. Vaishnava, 25. Saiva, 26. Garuda, 27. Samasuchi, 28. Vishamasuchi, 29. Khandasuchi, 30. Kurmasana 31. Nagabandha and 32. Sahaja.

7. CHARI:

Chari is combined movement of feet, knees, thighs and waist. They are (25) twenty five which are divided into two types :

1. Akasa Chari—Airely movement (Movement above the Floor)

2. Bhu Chari—Earthily movement (Movement on the Floor)

Akasa Chari: is the movement of the body without touching the floor in a standing posture.

Bhaumi Chari: is the movement of the body in a sitting position *i.e.*, on the floor *i.e.*, performing the mande, *i.e.*, sitting on toes on the floor and the knees are placed side ways.

8. KARANAS: Karanas are 108. All the Karanas are not used in dancing. Atikrantas Sakatasya, Mayura, Lalita, Gangavatarana, Lalatatilaka, Talapushpaputa, Bhujangatrasa, Talasampodita, Lalita, Dandapada *etc.*, are used.

9. TALAS: There are 108 talas like Vinayaka tala, Rudra, Lakshmi, Gajalila, Viravikrama, Raja Chudamani, Simhanandana, Turangalila, Rangapradipa, Hamsanada, Vijaya, Makaranda, Malla, Sama, Purna Kankala, Lila, Bramaha *etc.* All the 108 talas are not in use.

10. ANGAHARA: The combination of several Karanas is known as Angahara. Each karana is performed in a special tala and in a particular gati. Angaharas are performed in different styles and in different varieties of movements.

Karana is a movement, it is also a synonym for adavu. Adavu is the unit which emerges as a coordinated pattern of movement of the feet, thighs, torso, arms, hands, neck, head and the eyes.

Example: *(Teyyam datta–Teyya tai).*

Angahara is a complete movement with a finish. A jati consists of various adavu patterns and angaharas, and ends with a tirmanam. Jati may be considered as an angahara also according to old tradition.

For example:

Teyyam datta-Teyyattey

Tiku danaku janu Ta-ditei,

It is performed on both the sides (Right and left) and ends with a tirmanam thus:

Tei Tei diditei-Tei!

Tei Tei diditei-Tei!

Tei Tei diditei-Tei diditei

Tei diditei! Tei!!

There are nine angaharas known as Navarasa Angaharas.

1. Lalita	2. Vikrama	3. Karunika
4. Vichitra	5. Vikala	6. Bhima
7. Vikrita	8. Ugratara	9. Santija

Generally it is said that karanas and angaharas are to be used in pure dance which does not express any mood. But some scholars developed Nava Rasa Angaharas to depict the mood or sentiment in Nritta (pattern) in relation to the song or an item.

Rasabhinaya is of two types. One is the abhinaya performed for a song in accordance with the predominence of Ragabhava. The other is to depict the sentiment with a combination of talas, jatis and swarakalpanas with orchestra. This type of dance was used to be performed in the temple rituals during Asthadikpala aaradhana. Both peddamelamu and chinnamelamu (both groups) were maintained in every temple in ancient days. Peddamelam was the name given to a mangalavadya consisting of a sannayi, dolu, sriti, talam *etc.* Chinnamelam was the name given to dance group consisting of a devanartaki, nattuva, mridangist, mukhavina, sriti *etc.* (Asthadikpala aradhana will be described later).

The special dance items which were performed in the temple during morning, evening and in the festival rituals were very different from the modern classical dance items. The construction and Choreography of these items were according to the special talas mentioned in the Agama sastra and the melodies and rhythms were specially set in Sabda, Jati Githams or Stotrams. Prayers were in different talas. Apart from Dhruva, Matya, Rupaka, Triputa, Jhampe, Ata and Eka there were 108 different talas used for these items.

Panchamukha talas: 1. Chaachatputa; 2. Chachchatputa; 3. Shatpita putrika; 4. Sampakveshtaka and 5. Udghatta were also very famous.

Repertoire of Temple dances can be divided into three types.

I. SPIRITUAL DANCES or RITUAL DANCES, which were purely Nritta oriented and were set in typical talas and typical movements.

(a) Pushpanjali-Additachari vinyasam

(b) Kautham

(c) Kaivaram

(d) Asthadikpala Aradhana Nrityam

(e) Sabdam

(f) Saptalasyams

II. KELIKA:

(A) PALLAVI:

1. Svarapallavi
2. Sabda Pallavi

Prabandha Nartanam
Navajanardana Parijatam

Asthananartanam

3. Sahitya Pallavi

(B) Sabdam

(C) Varnam

(D) Padam

(E) Kirtana

(F) Javali

(G) Ashtapadi

(H) Tarangam

(I) Padyam

(J) Jakkinidaruvu *etc.*

III. PRABANDHA NARTANAM

(a) Parijatam or Bhamakalapam

(b) Gollakalapam

(c) Radhamadhavam

(d) Kshirasagara Madhanam

Other Vabandhams which also may be choreographed into dance.[40]

I. SPIRITUAL DANCE (Agamanartanam):

The pure dance items were used to be performed for the ritual purposes. So they were very spiritual. The offering of dance in ritual at Balipitham or in front of the garbhagriha was to make the environment spiritual. So they were rigid in composition and ritualistic in performance.

Devanartaki used to wear white saree, to indicate purity. Kumbhaharati–the sacred lamp was the identity for the tradition. Devanartaki who was dedicated to the deity had to maintain physical and mental balance with sacred thoughts. It was a yogic process for her to attain the real bliss by performing dance as an offering, as if she were one with the Lord. The ancient devanartakis used to attain that level. So the tradition was alive intact as long as there was dance worship.

Devanartaki used to be present in the temple during these rituals as she herself was an offering to the deity.

Kumbhaharati offering

Pushpanjali-Ahobilam

During the ritual Devanartaki had to stand in front of the garbhagudi. After the rituals, like abhisheka (Sacred bath), vastradharana (clothing), alankarana (decoration) and naivedya (offering food) the curtain used to be removed and the deity's "Sarva Mangala Vigraham, the most auspicious idol of the Lord with all the decoration could be witnessed by the devotees. Then the Kumbha harati was handed over to Devanartaki by the priest. Peddamelam used to play the Mangala Harati and other musicians used to play their instruments like Baka, Nagara, Shankha, Dhakka, Suryachandra Mandala Vadya, Suddha Maddela and Panchamukha Vadyarn while the devanartaki offered the Kumbha harati, (the Sacred lamp) to the Lord. Kumbhaharati was to remove the dristhi dosha to the Lord.

Then the Natyacharya (Dance Master) used to lead the instrumentalists and make them stand in a particular order behind the devanartaki. Devanartaki used to stand in the middle and the dance master who played Nattuvangam and a Taladhari who played cymbals and showed the talangas with two Mridangists on either side or a Mridangist on one side, the other musicians used to stand in their respective positions. This process in total was called as 'Kutupa Vinyasam'.

After offering of the Kumbha harati the dancer used to stand in 'Talapushpaputa' karana holding some flowers in her hands, and recite a churnika. like, *"Srimat Samasta Sadguna Nayavinaya viveka vitarana vichakshana daksha, Gudhartha nirnaya nissandeha niraghata niravandya gadya padya vachana suvachana"-Tarka vedanta mimamsa vyakarana sankhya yogadi sastra parina sangita sahitya sakalakala pravina sarvesham! Bhajat-vam pushpatvaka Vandanam!!*

Then orchestra used to play the Muktayi :

"Dhittalangu takatalangu takadhiki tam ditei ditam ditei ditam ditei".

Then dancer used to offer the traditional vandanam. In olden days the wind instruments like flute, mukhavina and sruti were operated or played after the churnika as a lead for the dance performance. This is called as 'Ambaram'. After Ambaram, Ayatta was performed. Ayatta means to play some patavaksharas (Mridanga Sabdas) very melodiously with soft sounds.

Mridangist had to play the following sounds:

Tvaaham tehiyam datvaham

Tehi Tehiyam datvaaham

Tateihi Tehiyam Datvaaham

Dinakita Tam! Dinakita Tei! Dinakita Tam!!

After performing the Ayatta the dancer used to perform Alapam or Addimohara or Addita chari vinyasam which was known as Addika. This item was set to Jhampe tala and Nataraga.

'Addika' consists the words like-

"Tat-Jagadatta" Todigidam
To digi
dam dam-dam:

and its finish is called 'Mohara'.

Addika

Tam ta tei tei-Tei jagadattam,

To digidam to digi dam dam daam

Dam dam dam damdam dam!

Dam dam takadhiki-taka tadigina tom!!

To digi dheem! To digi dim dim dheem

Dheem dim dim! dim dim-dheem

dim dim takadiki-taka tadigina Tom!!

To digidham Todigi-dam dam dam

Todigidheem Todigi-dhim dhim dheem

Todigi dam dam ! Todhigi Dheem Dheem

Todigi dam! Todigi Dheem

Dam Dam-taka diki taka

Tatomta doddo,

Dam dam daam-Takadiki taka

Tatomta doddo

Dam dam daam-Takadiki taka

Dam dam daam-Taka diki taka

Tungaku–Takadhiki

Tongutaka–dadiginathom

MOHARA:

Tititi tei-kitataka Titi Ti tei

To digi dam dam-takadhiki taka

Tungaku taka tom

Taka tom diki tunga

digi digi taka tunga

FAST TEMPO :

Taka taka tunga! taka taka

Tunga Tunga!

Tom Tom Tunga! tom tom

Tunga Tunga!

First Speed :

TAKKATO! DIMI DIMI DIMI DHEEM DODDODDO!

TODIKATOM! DIMI DIMI DIMI DHEEM DODDODDO!

TAKKATO DIMI DIMI DIMI

TADIKATO DIMI DIMI DIMI

DAM-GINADHEEM

DAM DAM-GINADHEEM

DA DIDDA DIDDA DITRANGA

TOM DIGI DHAM-DAM DAM

TI TI TI TEI-KITATAKA TI TI TI TEI

TIRIKA (ENDING):

TOM DIGI DIM DAM

TAKADIKITAKA! TUNGAKU DADIGINA-TOM

After Addika performance Nandi or Sabdam was used to be performed by Devanartaki Sabdam was commenced with mridanga jatis and had the sthotra gitam (prayer) and then Thirmanam. It was divided into three parts. Prarambha Jati, (Starting Jati), Joharu gitam or prayer and ending.

Sabdams were of two types viz :

1. Bhujangatrasa Nrittam performed in Siva temples

2. Bhramari Nrittam performed in Vaishnava temples.

In both pure dance pieces were performed in Brahma tala. This item was continued with the Bhramara Nritta in Brahmatala then the sabdam used to commence in other talas like Adi, Ata, Rupaka *etc.*

Nandi

Tadhee, Kritakajham–Tadhimita kitataka jham

Takkita Taka—dhikkitataka–Tomgitattaka

Nangitataka-Nam Nam Kitataka

Ta tei tei dattatam–Kitataka

Atei tei dattatam!!

Sabdam: (Aditalam)

Jamtaari Kitataka dhaa

dharikita dhaa-jeki taka

dharikitataka-dhim kitataka

dhi dhitalangu taka–kitataka

dhaanu dhanaa dhanamtha-Jhenu dhimita

dhimi gadhita

tatomtaka takudhikukku ritha kita

jenu thaka kitataka dha,

Bhramara Nrittam-Brahma talam–Angas :

Brahma talam consists of 28 letters:

+		0		+				0		+					
1	2	3	4	5	6	7	8	9	10	11	12	13	14	15	16
0		+								0					
17	18	19	20	21	22	23	24	25	26	27	28				

kinadana-jenu dhimi-gadi!!

Taari taari kitatraka!

Takuku jhekuku! Rita kukundaree

Tattha dhinku! Taddhim dhimku!

Tajhommitam gadhee taari kuntaa!

Jhamtari kitataka, takkudu

Tom Tom gida taka!

Tom Tom nam nam gidataka

Tongudu kitataka! taka thadiginatom!!

Muktayi:

Jham tarikitataka! takkudu Tidimgitataka

To dom nam nam gidataka! tongu 'kitataka

Ta tadiginatom!!3 times!!

Tei datta tam!!

Sreela! Neela satee Manolola!

Kukshistha Charaa chara jaala!

Sadbhakta janaavana pala

Narasingapalli pura khela

venkunayakadi paripala

Joharu venugopala-3 times.

Tirmanam:

Kidatakakidataka! dharikita taka!

Jhemkidataka! dharikita taka!

dhim kitataka! Kitataka Kitataka!!

diddhit! talaangu taka! talaangu talaangu taka!

Talaangu taka! Tadigina tom! !!3 times!!

Taddhanat! tajjhenata! tadhimita

Gadhita takita dadiginata!!3 times!!.

After Nandi and Sabdam another pure dance item 'Vinayaka Kautham or Kausthubham used to be performed by the devanartaki. (Kautham will be described in the later chapter VI, Technique of Ardhranatyam).

Above items were a part of the ritual offerings and they were performed for spiritualization. During the Sangita Seva the temple area used to revibrate with all instrumental music and dance bells and the recitation of vedamantras. It was a wonderful feast for spectators who witnessed the whole process of this ritual performance.

After performing the Kautham, devanartakis used to perform 'Sapta Lasya' and finish the ritual in complete spiritual atmosphere infront of the main deity.

Sapta lasyas were also in vogue in the Telugu country. The description of Sapta Lasyas is mentioned in Nrittaratnavali of Jayapasenani. Some poets, like Srinatha, Palkuriki Somanatha also described them in their works.

SAPTA LASYAS:

1. Suddhanatyam 2. Desi Natyam 3. Perini Natyam 4. Prenkhana 5. Dandalasya 6. Kundali 7. Kalasa

To perform Sapta Lasyas following Gatis, Karanas and Talas are to be used.

I. For the Suddhanatyam

(a) Bhramaries

1. Dakshina Bhramana
2. Vama Bhramana
3. Lila Bhramana
4. Bhujanga Bhramana
5. Vidyut Bhramana
6. Lata Bhramana
7. Urdhva Tandava

(b) Gathis:

1. Mayuragati 2. Maralagati
3. Turanga gati 4. Gaja gati
5. Simhagati 6. Suka gati

(c) Karanas:

1. Mayura lalita 2. Gangavatarana
3. Karihasta 4. Simha vikridita
5. Kira bhushana

(d) Charis:

1. Sthitavartha 2. Urudhrutha
3. Vakthrabandha 4. Syandhitha
5. Upasyandhitha

Above charis were performed in 12 talas *i.e.*, Bhucharis in 6 talas and Akasa charis in 6 talas.

(e) Talas:

1.	Mallikamoda	2 Laghus ; 4 Dhrutas
2.	Hamsanada	-1 Laghu; 1 Plutham; 2 Dhrutas
3.	Jampetala	-Dhrutam; Dhrita virama; 1 Laghu; 2 ½ Matras
4.	Dvithiya tala	-2 Dhrutas; 1 Laghu

5.	Purna Kankala	-4 Dhrutams; 1 Guruvu; 1 Laghu
6.	Udghatta	-3 Gurus
7.	Abhangatala	-1 Laghu; 1 Plutam
8.	Simha Vikrama	-3 Gurus; 1 Laghu; 1 Plutam; 1 Laghu; 1 Guru; and 1 Plutam
9.	Sarabha Leela	-2 Laghus; 4 Dhrutams; 2 Laghus
10.	Jampe	-Dhrutam; Dhruta virama; 1 Laghu; 2 ½ Matras
11.	Kokilapriya	-1 Guru; 1 Laghu; 1 Plutam
12.	Jampe	-Dhrutam-Dhrutha virama; 1 Laghu; 2 ½ Matras

Above 12 talas were used and Karanas, charis were set to the above gatis. This was called as Suddhanatyam.

II. Desi :

1. Manmadha Karana
2. Saundara Karana
3. Varuna Karana
4. Gajavikridita Karana
5. Chandra Karana

Above five Karanas

1. Chashagati Chari
2. Vichyava Chari
3. Addita Chari
4. Janita Chari
5. Sakatasya Chari

Above five charis

1. Nikunchita gathi
2. Kunchita gati
3. Akunchitha gathi
4. Parshva Kunchita gathi
5. Ardha Kunchita gathi

Above five gati bhedas and Purna Kankala tala are used in Desinatya of Sapta Lasyas.

III. Perini:

Perini has five (Angas) parts.

1. Gargharam; 2. Vishamam; 3. Bhavasrayam; 4. Kaivarakam; 5. Githam

Gargharam: It is of (6) six varieties.

1. Patavatam; 2. Patavam; 3. Surivattemu;

4. Lakadimi 5. Siribiram 6. Halabidam

IV. Prenkhana: It has the valour and profound expression and consists of different karana vinyasas, chari bhedas and ends with circular (Bhramaries) movements. Sanka Karanam, Samotsaritha Mathali chari and other movements are used for Prenkhana.

A tala called Rajavidyadhara which consists of 1 laghu, 1 guru and 2 Dhruthams is used in Prenkhana.

V. Dandika Lasyam (Kolatam): It is famous as a group dance. Generally it starts with vinayaka talam. It has six varieties of postures and various gati vinyasams. Dancers hold two sticks called 'Kolalu' in both hands. Vishnukrantha Karanam-Adyarthi Chari. Vijayananda tala which consists of 2 laghus, 3 gurus and has the (8) eight letters time are used in dance.

VI. Kalasa: To perform Kalasa Lasyam Garudapluta karana, Edaka kridita chari and Jayamangala talam which consists of 2 Laghus, 1 Guru, 2 Laghus, 1 Guruvu and has the eight letters (matras) are used.

VII. Kundali: To perform Kundali Lasya nrityam Narayana Karana and Mattallika chari are used. Lakshmisha tam which consists 1 laghu, 1 dhrutam and 1 laghu in 2 1/2 letters time are used.

Above seven Lasya Nrityams were very famous in ancient times. Though we cannot witness their technique, we are fortunate enough that Dr.

Nataraja Ramakrishna has preserved them in his "Dakshnatyula Natya Kala Charitra" a complete work on South Indian dance traditions. It has the complete description of the dances that were performed in the temples, with practical notes. But one must be trained under this great guru who learnt these dances from a temple ritual dancer. Dr. Nataraja Ramakrishna had his initial training in temple dance from two great gurus who were dedicated to the temples. He learnt Saivagama temple dance from Smt. Rajamma who was a devaganika in Sri Kalahastiswara Swamy Temple and he studied Vaishnava temple dances from Smt. Pedda Parankusam, who was a devanartaki in Kunthimadhava Swamy Temple in Pithapuram. He has the Sampradaya Vyakhyanam of Sri Kalahasti temple dance tradition.

Another important Aradhana Nritya (Dance worship) was the Dikpala Aradhana. During daily worship the Peddamelam and the singers used to follow the priest to offer Bali to the eight guardians of a temple. There used to be Hechcharikas for handing over the temple to the Astadikpalakas of the temple in the night. During festival days, particularly in the Kalyanamahotsavam (marriage ceremony) of the deity there used to be grand celebrations in temples all over South India. On those holy days Asthadikpalakas were invited by the priests with Vedamantras and Shodasopacharas and were entertained with music and dance. Devanartaki the main entertainer used to follow the Agamic tradition and performed dances that were mentioned in the Agama sastras. These dances are prescribed in Churnikas and Gadyams. This dance was called 'Navasandhi'.

After the completion of ritual dance worship to the main deity with pushpanjali, Addika, Bhramara (or Bhujangatrasa in Siva temple) Nrityam, Ganapathi Kautam and Suddha natyam, the priests used to worship the Asthadikpalakas. They used to perform rituals to Indra first. After the ritual performance they used to recite the gadya of each god. The devanartaki had to perform whatever the priest recited in the gadya.

WORSHIP PROCESS AND PERFORMANCE

1. INDRA: He dwells in the East. His vehicle is the elephant (Airavatam). His wife is Sachidevi. His capital city is Amaravati. His weapon is Vajrayudham. He likes Deva Gandhari Ragam and Lalita Nrityam. Nadanama Kriya raga may also be used for this purpose. He likes the Meghanada Vadya. Standing posture for the dancer is Sama. Standing in Sama posture, dancer should hold the Arala hasta with the left hand and Tripataka with right hand at her forehead.

After the completion of circumambulation with mangala vadyam the priest had to perform the rituals to the demi gods who rule each art in the compass. Chinnamelam *i.e.* Devanartaki, Natyacharya and other musicians follow him. Priest recites the prayers.

According to Vaikhanasa Agama Brahma and Garuda then Indra, Agni, Yama, Niruti, Varuna, Vayu, Kubera and Isanya are worshipped in a prescribed order on the festival days. To invite all these gods to the Lord's marriage ceremony an elaborate ritual process has to be followed by the temple priest.

Nowadays dance is not performed during this process, but the priest recites veda mantras according to the Agama sastras and offers some 'Akshantalu'-made of rice, turmaric and kumkum. The Asthadikpala Aradhana or Navasandhi is an elaborate ritual performance. Dr. Nataraja Ramakrishna, who learnt the temple dance tradition is the only person who can teach this particular aspect. Smt. Saride Manikyamma used to perform the pure dance at Navasandhi. Now she remembers only some Pallavis and Kautham but not all the items that were performed during Navasandhi as she has become very old.

I mention here the worship of Indra during Navasandhi as explained by Dr. Nataraja Ramakrishna in "Devanartaki-Alaya Nrityamulu" and as described by him during my research.

Sarvavadya Aradhana: Sarvavadya Aradhana was used to be performed in temples after Shodasopacharas. All types of musical instruments like Mukhavina, Murali, 'Sannayi, Dhavalasankhu and other wind instruments; String instruments like Vina, 'Gotu Vadyam, Violin *etc.* and, Percussion instruments like Dolu, Mridangam, Nagara, Suddhamardalam, Dhamarukam, Suryamandalam,

Chandramandalam and Panchamukhi were used for this Aradhana.

Though it was called as Sarvavadya Aradhana it used to commence with Nrityam. This may be considered as a special feature. Every instrument was played separately one after another and then all were played combinedly. Afterwards diparadhana and a dance recital were performed by the temple dancer.

II. Kelika:

Kelika, Karnatakam, Darbaru ata, Kachcheri ata are the synonyms for the Asthananartanam. Asthanam means an assembly or a court. These dances were of two types,the one that was performed in the temple at the kalyana mandapam after the evening rituals and before the night rituals by the devanartakis in the presence of the Utsava vigrahas. The other one that was performed in the court of a king. Both the performances were intellectual feasts.

The oldest term used for these dance performances seems to be 'Kelika'. Darbaru and Kachcheri were borrowed from Hindi. Dance performed during rituals was considered as an offering. In Asthananartana the dancer had freedom to exhibit her scholarship in Nritta,Nritya and Abhinaya. Here the dancer had to face scholars,as scholars in Tarkam (the science of reasoning: logic) Vedantam (the theological part of the vedas) Vyakaranam (the grammar), Jyotishyam (astrology), Mimamsa (theological criticism) poets, artistes and others were used to be invited for the Asthanostavam. They had liberty to question the artistes about the theoritical part of the dance and music *etc.* It was a test for the Uevanartaki or Rajanartaki and an entertainment to the audience as well as to the presiding God or

Sl. No.	*Gods Name*	*Name of the Dance*	*Raga*	*Tala*	*Vadya Instrument*
1.	Vishnu	Bhramara	Malahara	Brahma, Adi	Yudhanada
2.	Siva	Bhujangatrasa	Sankarabharana	Adi, Rudra	Matrukananda
3.	Indra	Lalitha	Devagandhari Nadanamakrya	Sama, Gajalila	Meghanada
4.	Agni	Kalinga	Nata, Lalita	Adhyapana viravikrama	Simhanada
5.	Yama	Kartari	Malahari/ Kaisika	Bhrungini/ Rajachudamani	Saudananda
6.	Nairuti	Vidhrutha	Kaisika Bhairavi	Malla,	Vijayananda Ranga Pradipa
7.	Varuna	Utsanga	Megharanjani Sriraga	Bhrungari	Mangala Makaranda
8.	Vayu	Suvyapaka bhairavi	Gaula, Vasanta.	Tankari Vijayatala	Gambhirananda
9.	Kubera	Sankirna	Nata, Sriraga	Babhru Turanga Lila	Susampata
10.	Isanya	Dandapada	Hindola Sankarabharana	Vrisha Nandalila	Matrukananda

the King. Eventhough dancer had the freedom to perform dance of her choice, she had to create the spirituality in the audience and thus lead them towards the spiritualization.

Generally in South Indian temples the performance of the Kelika used to begin with Melaprapti and then the dancer used to offer kumbhaharati to the Utsava vigrahas and then the regular dance item *Alarimpu.*

Alarimpu is the name given to a pure dance defining the movements of the dancer's body as a flower blossoms gradually.

Alarimpu consists of Mridanga *Patavaksharas* which are generally sung in Nataraga. It is performed in 5 (five) *jaati*, in Tisra, Misra, Khanda, Chaturasra and Sankirna. It is also performed as 'panchamukhi' with a combination of 5 *jaatis.* The movements are set to the prescribed tala and it starts with Samasthanaka.

This first item of a dance recital gives an enchanting feeling to the audience as if a statue in the temple is reacting to the Nadam and to the cymbal sounds and to the instrumental music with its gradual development of the (Anga, Upanga, Pratyanga) bodily movement. Though it is a pure dance item without any Bhava or emotion it creates different pictures and colours and joyness in the minds of the audience.

Some of the temple dancers used to commence their recital with pallavi which is of three kinds.

1. Svara pallavi, 2. Sabda pallavi and 3. Sahitya pallavi.

Pallavi: This is also known as jatisvaram. This is a pure dance to a composition of jati's set in order of the svaras to a tala (Adi, Rupaka *etc.*). This pallavi contains only svaras and jatis.

1. Swara Pallavi: This is performed to the svaras which are set to a tala. It is a pure dance item.

2. Sabda Pallavi: It is a composition of mridanga aksharas like, "Tam Dhitam, Taka dhim, Jhanutham' *etc.*, in a raga and set to a tila. A pure dance is performed for this.

Smt. Saride Manikyamma (a Temple dancer), Smt. Nagasani, (a court dancer of Gadwal) and Smt. Annabattula Satyabhama and Mangatayaru (famous dancers of Mummidivaram) told me that they used to perform Sabda Pallavi in the Kachcheri dance performances.

3. Sahitya Pallavi: It has sahityam (literary content poetry or lyrics) in praise of God Siva or Vishnu or in praise of a king. The basic movements are set in an order to perform Nritta.

4. Sabdam: This is a descriptive composition which consists of mridanga sabdas (Patavaksharas) along with the lyrics. It is choreographed to a mimetic dance *i.e.* Angikabhinaya. This may appear like Kautam, but it is composed either in praise of God or a king. Kauthams were composed in special talas in olden days. Sabdams are generally composed in Kambhoji Raga and set to Misrachapu tala.

5. Varnam: Varnam is of two types *i.e.*, Padavarnam and Tana varnam. Tana varnam is meant only for music. It is rendered to expose the Ragabhava only. Padavarnam, is used in dance recitals as a prominent item. The performance of a padavarnam is a challenge to the dancer, as it contains Pallavi, Anupallavi, Muktayi, Svaramu and Charanamulu. It is a complete item in which Nritta, Nritya and Abhinaya can be exhibited in equal proportions.

6. After the performance of padavarnam pure abhinaya-oriented items such as Slokas from Krishna Karnamritam, Megha Sandesam. Malavikagnimitram and Kumarasambhavam *etc.*, were used to be performed.

7.Padam: This is famous for its erotic sentiment. An elaborate description of the nayika (Heroine) can be expressed with the help of Satvika Sanchari bhavas. It is a melodious musical composition in slow tempo (Vilambita laya).

8. Kirtana: This is a devotional song. It is generally in praise of God Vishnu in particular. This is a descriptive one. It is performed descriptively, interpretatively or narratively.

Annamayya, Tyagayya/Munipalle Subrahmanya kavi and some other poets composed kirtanas and they are now used in dance recitals.

9. Tarangam: Yati Narayana Tirtha wrote 'Sirikrishna Leela Tarangini' in a narrative and descriptive poetry with musical melody. These are famous for vocal music. Some selected tarangams are choreographed for dancing. They became very famous for tala, laya and nritya vinyasa as they are like waves in an ocean.

10. Jakkini: This is a musical composition consisting of Jatis and Sahitya (Poetry). Generally Jati vinyasam *i.e.*, the pure dance part is elaborate and the sahitya has less importance in Jakkini.

Generally Kelika of a devanartaki used to end with an elaborate performance of Abhinaya. All the items were not performed in one day, because they had to be performed daily as the duty in the temple, according to the ritual timings. She had to present the items to the audience with due consideration of the performance. Performance used to begin with a Nritta piece and end with an abhinaya piece.

III. Prabandhanartanam :

Parijatams are known as prabandhas. The story of Lord Krishna and Satyabhama, which is also known as Sri Krishna Parijatam and Bhamakalapam is a famous prabandha in Telugu.

Prabandham has two Avartanams:

1. Talavartanam-The ending of a complete talangas.

2. Githavartanam-The lyrical part of the song ends from where it starts.

Generally prabandham means a literary poetical composition. Here parijatham is a Sringara Drisya, Sravana audio-vidio prabandham, as it contains the erotic sentiment it can be enjoyed by witnessing it or hearing it.

Parijatham was usually performed by the dance artistes on the festival days outside the precincts of a temple. It was also performed in dedication to the Lord of the temple by only the artistes attached to the temple. This performance was meant for the common people to know about our religion, culture, cults, spiritualism, social aspects *etc.* It was an education through entertainment for the people.

Source for temple dance items:

Ref: Devanartaki Alaya Nrityalu, Dakshinatyula Natya Kalacharitra

-By Dr Nataraja Ramakrishna.

Informants: Eminent gurus-Dr. Nataraja Ramakrishna

Smt. *Saride Manikyamma*

Smt. *Annabattula Satyabhama*

Smt. *Nagasani*

(Courtesy—Dr. Suvarchala Suresh)

Tirupathi Venkatakavulu used to visit this court which they described thus:

"Saamanta raajanya sanghambulokavanka

nokavanka Raja bandhutkarambu

tulaleni Manchi yudyogasthulokavanka

Nokavanka divya vainika ganambu

Sastra maryaada visaaradulokavanka

nokavanka Gaandharva yuvati chayanu

Nindu perolagammuna nundi koluva melugaa

nelukonuchu Gadvala (Bhupa) puramu!!"

Sri Sitaramabhupati was praised by these poets as "Andhrabhoja" and Gadwala Samsthanam as "Vidvadgadwala". This smasthanam patronised several poets, singers and dancers both local and outsiders. All of them used to receive 'Tambulam' and Dakshina from this court according to their scholarship.[20]

20th century dancers of Andhranatyam

1. Cheyyuru Sarada:-was associated with Sundareswara temple of Cheyyuru, Chengalpat district which is at present situated in Tamilnadu.

2. Madhurantakam Radha and Andal :-were associated with the temple of Lord Sri Rama at Madhurantakam. This temple is situated in Chengalpat district, Tamilnadu.

3. Karimbidu Ammani :-Originally she belonged to Karimbidu of Chengalput district but later she migrated to Karvetinagara samsthanam as a court dancer.

4. Tiruttani Ranganayaki :-a reputed danseuse at the temple of Subrahmanya Swamy at Tiruttani. She was a Telugu artiste. She had many disciples.

5. Kaluvayi Saraswati was the temple dancer of Narasimhaswamy temple at Penchalakona.

6. Macherla Radha and Chandramukhi :-Both hail from Macherla of Guntur district, Chandramukhi's dance was so famous that it was considered that the pilgrimage to Chennakesava temple with which she was associated was incomplete if her performace was not witnessed.

7. Pula Mahalakshmi, Narsaraopet :-A popular artiste herself, Mahalakshmi was an adept of Vedic knowledge. With her shrewdness she used to keep the scholars who indulged in scholarly deliberation with her in awe. Her demise at an early age was an irrecoverable loss to the art world.

8. Sabharanjani, Jaggayyapet :-She was an expert in the performance of Kelika. She belonged to Jaggayyapeta in Krishna District.

9. Meduri Rattalu :-Hailing from Meduru of Krishna District; Rattalu specialised in the presentation of Kelika.

10. Sriranjani :-She belonged to Murikipadu village of Guntur district. She was not only a wellknown dancer but also a popular cine artiste. She was reputed for her mythological roles.

11. Rangapushpa Chitra :-Hailing from Tenali of Guntur District, Chitra was known for introducing modern techniques such acrobatics as balancing pots and bottles on her head *etc.*, which is considered as Menaka tradition. She was honoured with the title 'Rangapushpa' by the Nizam of Hyderabad.

12. Chadalavada Samrajyam :-Samrajyam, who was a Kelika performer, hails from Eluru. She was a reputed dance teacher. She had many disciples.

13. Kandikattu Manikyam :-A wellknown guru of Kelika tradition. Manikyam was honoured at her young age with a gold medal at Guntur for her excellent dance performances. She trained many students at Eluru.

14. Chataparru Balatripurasundari :-She was known as the most beautiful lady of her time, She specialised in abhinaya. She was a native of Eluru.

15. Chataparru Valmiki Chudamani:-She was a reputed performer and guru of Kelika tradition. She belonged to Eluru.

16. Puvvula Papachalam :-Papachalam specialised the Bhagavata tradition. She also hails from Eluru.

17. Marampalli Peda Venkataratnam and China Venkataratnam:-Both these sisters practised parijatams. They were well known as kalapam artists. They were reputed scholars in Sanskrit. They belonged to Marampalli village of West Godavari District.

18. Marampalli Vaidehi and Induvadana :-Experts in Kalapams. They were the nieces of Pedavenkataratnam of Marampalli. Their performance in the national level got recognition to the Kuchipudi dance as a classical art. They were scholars in Sanskrit and Telugu. They used to perform Gollakalapam in Sanskrit, with commentary in Sanskrit.

19. Eluru Ranganayaki :-She was a performing artiste and teacher of Kelika tradition. She belonged to Eluru and had many students of calibre.

20. Bandi Srivirajitam :-She followed the Kachcheri tradition. She belonged to Eluru and she was a dedicated teacher and performer.

21. Bandi Gangaram :-An expert in abhinaya. She was also a popular teacher. She belonged to Rajahmundry of East Godavari district.

22. Maddula Varahalu :-Varahalu was reputed for abhinaya as she specialised in performing Javalis. She belonged to Manepalli village of Kona seema region of East Godavari district.

23. Annabattula Reddy Sastry :-Reddamma was an expert in Sanskrit, and acquired great knowledge in Vedas and various Sastras besides Bharatasastra. She was honoured with the title 'Sastry' for her excellence in Vedic knowledge and so she came to be known as "Reddy sastri".

24. Annabattula Bulivenkataratnamma:-A scholarly artiste of Mummadivaram of East Godavari District. Bulivenkataratnam was the only lasya nartaki who received the honour of 'Bharatakala Prapoorna' from Andhra Pradesh Sangeet Natak Akademy. She was the chief artiste for the revival of the lasya nartana and to name it as 'Andhranatyam' at the seminar held at Rajahmundry In 1970.

25. Chinta Virabhadram :-A reputed performer of Parijatams and abhinaya. She was a native of Ramachandrapuram in East Godavari District.

26. Chinta Chinaganiraju :-She was the niece of Chinta Virabhadram. She was well versed in abhinaya and parijatam performances. She belonged to Ramachandrapuram of East Godavari District.

27. Chinta Ammasani: She was the grand mother of Chinagani Raju. She practised prabandha Nartana tradition. She was a great artiste of Ramachandrapuram of East Godavari district.

28. Bade Venkataratnam, Srikurmam :-She associated as a Devanartaki with Lord Vishnu's temple of Srikurmam in Srikakulam district. She was a follower of Vaikhanasa Agama tradition.

29. Duggirala Srivirajitam :-Srivirajitam was a popular performer of parijatam and abhinaya. She was the native of Mandapeta of East Godavari District.

30. Nayudu Pedasatyam :-Naidu Pedasatyam was wellknown for her Abhinaya and was equally reputed for Parijata performances. She also belonged to Mandapeta of East Godavari District.

31. Tuni Chandravadana :-She performed dance both in temples and courts. She was reputed for her beauty and artistry. She belonged to Tuni of East Godavari District.

32. Podugu Ammani :-She was an Asthana Nartaki of Viziaanagaram samsthanam. She was reputed for her Kelikas.

33. Duvva Ammani and Suryakantam, Pithapuram :-Both were court dancers in Pithapuram Zamindari of East Godavari District. They used to perform Kelikas.

34. Kone Chittiraju and Udayachalam :-Both these artistes belonged to Pithapuram. They were reputed for their Parijatam performances.

35. Gandham Lakshmikantam, Madugula :-She lived under the patronage of Sri Sri Vikrama deva Varma of Jaipur Estate, now situated in Orissa State. Formerly it was in erstwhile Madras province and after formation of Orissa province she migrated to Madugula in Visakhapatnam district. She was famous for her Kelika performances.

36. Yandamuri Ramaratnam :-She was noted for Abhinaya. She also performed Kelikas. She belonged to Kakinada situated in East Godavari District.

37. Yandamuri Peda Parankusam and China Parankusam :-Both of them were the Devanartakis of Kuntimadhava temple of Pithapuram. They used to follow vaikhanasa agama.

38. Jakkula Nukaraju :-She was a popular Kelika and abhinaya performer and she was equally reputed as a musician. She was a disciple of Late Sri Veena Sangameswara Sastry and Sri Vemanadora.

39. Kotipalli Sanyasamma :-She was a wellknown guru of Kelika tradition. She was in Vizianagaram samsthanam.

40. Maddela Ramudu and Appadu :-Both of them were the asthana nartakis of Vizianagaram estate. Later they settled at Vizianagaram as gurus and produced many artistes of repute.

41. Kalavar ringu (Lakshminarasamma) :-She was a popular philanthropist and Kelika artist of Vizianagaram. She was, infact the first person to recognise the talents of Sri. Ghantasala Venkateswara Rao, the renowned cine playback singer. She encouraged him by presenting a tambura.

42. Challenge Maddaguru Apparao :-A performer and guru of Kelika tradition. She lived in Vizianagaram.

43. Jampa Muthyam :-She was a court dancer of Vizianagara estate. She was well known for her Kelika performances.

44. Armuru Girasani :-She was a native of Armuru situated in Nizamabad district. She specialised in performing abhinaya to compositions of various languages Sanskrit, Telugu, Persian and Urdu and was popularly known for her beauty.

45. Vellala Lakshmikantamma :-She was an extremely beautiful danseusc of Proddutur. She was a Kelika performer and was well known for her charitable disposition.

46. Kale Kamakshi :-She was a noted performer of Parijatams. She belonged to East Godavari District.

47. Gaddibhukta Chiranjivi, Sanjivi, Suvarna and Jivaratnam :-All these, who belonged to one family, were well known as court dancers of Bobbili estate.

48. Kotipalli Madhuram and Pichchayi :-Both of them were experts in abhinaya and parijatam performance. They lived in Kotipalli, East Godavari District.

49. Jakkula Navanitam :-She practised abhinaya and Karnatakam, Navanitam was the mother of Nookaraju of Pithapuram, East Godavari District.

50. Valmiki Parijata Pushpavati :-She was a well known Parijatham and abhinaya artiste. She hailed from Amalapuram of East Godavari District.

51. Allu Mahalakshmi and Pallavapani:-They were mother and daughter respectively. They were popular for the abhinaya. They belonged to Vadapalli village of East Godavari District.

52. Kotipalli Subrahmanyam and Sitamma :-Both these artistes hail from Mummidivaram, East Godavari District. Subrahmanyam was reputed for her abhinaya and Sitamma was famous for rendering songs for dance.

53. Alwal Venkatamma :-She was the devanartaki of Lord Venkateswara temple situated in Alwal, Secunderabad. She used to follow Vaikhanasa agama.

54. Maddela Suryakantam, Chiranjivi and Kotapalepu Sattiraju :-All these three were exponents in Kelika. they were in the court of Maharaja of Vizianagaram.

55. Mannarupoluru Subbaratnam :-She was a devanartaki in the temple of Lord Ranganayaka of Mannarupoluru, situated near Sullurupeta in Nellore district.

56. Venkatagiri Navaratnam :-She was a popular performer of Kelika and Abhinava. She was under the patronage of Venkatagiri estate.

57. Vizianagaram Sitanagaratnam, Maddela Paidiraju, Rajeswaramma and Jarajapu Sanyasamma :-These artistes who flourished under the patronage of Vizianagaram estate, practised the Kelika tradition.

58. Sangitha Saraswati Duggirala Manikyam:-Manikyam was an exponent of Navajanardana parijatam. She was the head of a dance troupe consisting of nine artistes at Mandapeta.

59. Annabattula Venkata Vijaya Gopalaratnam :-She was a well known artiste of Parijatam and abhinaya. She belonged to Mummidivaram of East Godavari District.

60. Saride Seshamma, Venkataratnam and Mahalakhsmi :-These three were the nartakis of the Madana Gopalaswami temple situated in Ballipadu of West Godavari District. Seshamma was the grand mother of Smt. Saride Manikyamma, with whose reference I have written this thesis.

61. Nangigadda Krishnaveni and Srihari :-Both of them were popular Kelika artistes. They were from Nangigadda of Krishna district.

62. Vijayavilasam:-She was a devanartaki of Srikakuleswara temple situated Srikakulam in Krishna District.

63. Mula Chittemma :-She was a wellknown Kelika performer of Bhimavaram situated in West Godavari District.

64. Madala Srihari :-She was a native of Madala village near Sattenapalli of Guntur district. She was well versed in both temple and court traditions.

65. Rangasani :-She was a devanartaki associated with the temple of Lord Suryanarayana of Arasavilli situated near Srikakulam.

66. Bandi Satyabhama :-Satyabhama specialised in performing Parijatam. She belonged to Bikkavolu of East Godavari district.

67. Pullampeta Mahalakshmi :-She perfected the art of Abhinaya and Kachcheri. She was a native of Pullampeta situated in Cuddapah district.

68. Nagaraja Kumari :-She was well versed in Abhinaya and Kelika. She was a native of Ongole.

69. Sanku Papayi and Pandiri Venkataratnamma :-Both of them were reputed Parijata performers of Mandapeta situated in East Godavari District.

70. Ammula Venkataratnam :-She was a Kachcheri artiste. She was a native of Nangigadda in Krishna District.

71. Ammula Venkatagiri and Srikrishna :-Both of them were Kachcheri artistes of Nangigadda.

72. Puvvula Lakhmikantamma :-She was a disciple of Kandikattu Manikyamma. She was trained in Kachcheri tradition. Later she became a stage, and cine artiste. She belongs to Eluru.

73. Jampa Subhadram, Kanta Bhuktam, Manemma and Maddela Potayyagari Suryanarayana :-All of them were wellknown Kelika artistes of Vizianagaram Samsthanam.

75. Dasari Anjamma and Koteswari:-They were well versed in Karnatic music and abhinava. They belonged to Guntur district. Anjamma specialised in Javalis, padas and Adhyatma Ramayana. She belonged to the fourth generation of Dasari family who were great dance artistes.

76. Radhamma :-She was a court dancer of Gopalapeta Samsthanam of Mahaboobnagar District. She is an expert in dance, music and Sanskrit.

77. Chintagunta Ramamani :-She belongs to Vargal village of Medak district. She was associated with Venugopala temple of Vargal as devanartaki. This tradition came to an end with her.

78. Annabattula Satyabhama :-Annabattula family was dedicated for generations to the worship of Lord Siva at Visweswara agrahara in East Godavari district. Satyabhama, daughter of Bulivenkataratnam is a reputed teacher. She specialised in Nattuvangam and she used to accompany her mother Late Buli Venkataratnamma to sing, and play Nattuvangam.

79. Annabattula Alimelu Mangatayaru :-She is an exponent of Abhinaya for were reputed Slokas, Javali, Padam, Varnams and also a reputed Kelika artiste. She learned Bhamakalapam and Golla Kalapam from her grand mother late Bulivenkataratnamma. She is now running a dance school in memory of her grand mother at Mummadivaram. She also learned Harikatha.

80. Annabattula Venkatanarayanamma :-This 90 years old lady is an expert in performing Javalis. She is elder maternal aunt of Satyabhama.

81. Annabattula Lilasai :-She is a performing artiste of the same Annabattula family. She performs Sabda Pallavis and other classical dance items.

83. Gudigunta Nagamanamma :-She was a devanartaki dedicated to Penchalakona Nrisimha Swami temple in Nellore district. She was a disciple of Smt. Nayudupeta Rajamma of Kalahasti. After returning from the duties in the temple she went and lived with her daughter in Nellore where she trained many students. She participated in Abhinaya classes and trained students in 1972 at Hyderabad on an invitation from A.P. Sangeeta Nataka Akademi. She was also honoured with a title 'Kalapravina'. She loved dance, so she helped Dr. Nataraja Ramakrishna in conducting dance classes when he went to Russia for the comparative study of dance traditions.

84. Smt. **Chadalawada Samrajyamma :-**She was a great scholar of dance art. She was requested by Sangita Nataka Akademi, A.P. to accept th honour, but she rejected it. She once told Dr Nataraja Ramakrishna that their practice and training was different and hard when compared to the present day training. She used to say that their body itself speaks when the dance.

85. Smt. **Pullasani and** Smt. **Lakshmasani :-** Both were the court dancers of Gadwala samsthanam. Raja Ram Bhopala Deva honoured them by providing them with 'Jodu Kagadalu' and palanquin which was a rare honour.[19]

Above artistes were well-versed in their respective traditions and were recognised by the people as eminent artists, but the Devadasi Act compelled them to stop the rhythemic sounds of their ankle bells. Gradually they learned to live without dancing and went behind the screen. Now some of them who are alive do not like to be identified as dance artistes.

Different Lasya Dance Traditions of Andhra Pradesh: Basic Training System

Basic Training in dance is called as "Adavusamu". *i.e.* Training the body for flexible movements and for keeping the body under self control and also for physical endurance during the performance.

The "adavu" system of Karvetinagaram, Kalahasti and Bobbili traditions were similar. Bobbili was famous for its "Jaru' Advu and 'Usi' laya. Artistes of Bobbili had fascination to perform varnams with Jaru adavu. Late Jivaratnamma trained some of the old students of Nrityaniketan at Hyderabad. Mrs. Raghava Kumari is one of the old students of Dr. Nataraja Rama Krishna who learnt the Sankarabharana varnam "Manavi Chekonara" from Smt. Jivaratnamma. Mrs. Raghava Kumari demonstrated this Varnam in the third conference of Andhranatyam held at Hyderabad in 1994.

Sri Kalahasti Tradition

Both Late Smt. Gudigunta Nagamanamma and Dr. Nataraja Ramakrishna were the disciples of Smt. Nayudupeta Rajamma, who was a devanartaki at Kalahasti.

In my field work I visited Nellore where Smt. Nagamanamma lived and trained her grand daughters. I met Kum. Lakshmiprasanna one of her grand daughers to know about their tradition. I learned some of the basics and preserved them in drawings. Smt. Padma, elder sister of Lakshmi who is a very good dancer and a winner of many prizes, taught me these basics.[22]

Adavus

Before practising the Adavus, I was taught ardhamandali. Standing in Ardhamandali with stretched hands on both sides I had to count I to 150. First day I counted 1 to 25, then next day 1 to 50, and gradually developed the time up to 150 counts. Ardhamandali is called as 'Mallam'. Chikkulu, Moggalu were also taught to me as a part of samu.

I. Adavu:

1. *'Tei'* Adavu:

   A. *Teyya tei* (with Pataka hasta)

   B. *Teyya tehi* (with pataka hasta)

   C. *Teyya tei! Teyya tei!!*

Above units are to be practised in four varieties in three tempos—Vilambita, Madhya and Dhruta layas.

II. Pakkadavu:

This adavu is performed with stretching a leg to one side while standing in Ardhamandali. Movements are to be changed alternatively, first right then left with Katakamukha and Padmakosa hastas respectively.

1. *Teyya tei*
2. *Teyyo tei-A tei*
3. *Teyya tehi-Teyya tehi*
4. *Teyya tehi-Teyya tehi*
5. *Teyya tehi-Tei Tei diti tei* (with Tripatlika hastas.)
6. *Teyya Teyi, Teyya Teyi tei tei dititei* (with Tripataka hastas)

7. *Teyya Teyi, Teyya Teyi Teyya Teyi! Tei Tei dititei.*

(Katakamukha and Padmakosa hastas)

8. *Teyya Teyi! Teyya Teyi! Teyya teyi!!*

III. Tattai Adavu:

1. *Tattai tam! diteitam* (Sikhara and Pataka hastas)

2. *Tattai tam! dittai tam* (in mande Katakamukha and Padmakosa hastas)

3. *Tattai tam! dittai tam* (Mande)

4. *Tattai tam! dittai tam* (Mande in side ways.)

IV. Teyyam dattam

I. *Teyyam dattam! Teyyam Taha* (Padmakosa and Katakamukha)

2. *Teyyam dattam! Teyyam Taha*

(Kapittha, Pataka hastas and also tripataka and pataka hastas)

3. *Takita! Takita! Takita! Takita!* (Tripataka and Pataka hastas)

V. "Nettu Adavu" or "Kundu Adavu":

1. *Teyyam datta! Teyyataha*

(Ardhachandra hastas and crossed Padmakosa hastas)

2. It is done in various kinds of hand movements.

3. *Taditditei, Taditteyya*-stepping must be on toes and it is used to go around the stage in a circular path Ardhachandra, Padmakosa and Katakamukha hastas are used for this adavu. The adavu can be performed with the plain movements of the toes or by jumps. One type of doing this adavu is plain movement on toes and the other is practised with jumps.

***VI. Mande adavu** (it is to be done in Tisram):*

Teitta teitain teitta tei, these are of six varieties.

VII. Nadakalu (Gaits) :

(a) Ubuku adavu-	Teyya a tei (4 types)
(b) Jaru adavu-	Teyya tei! Teyya tei (2 types plain and usi)
(c) Pollu adavu-	Detitei-ditei (2 types)

VIII. Muktayi:

Lakshmi prasanna calls them as Diditei adavulu and Ginatom adavu-lu which are of two types.

(a) Ginatom Adavu:

(a) Ginatom with Tripataka hasta also with Pataka.

(b) Tei ginatom with Tripataka

(c) Tei tei ginatom with Tripataka

(d) Tei Tei Tei ginatom with Tripataka

(e) Tadi Tadi Tei ginatom with Tripataka

(f) Tadi tadi tei ginatom (by sitting) in mande it must end with a circular movement.

(b) Dititei advu:

(a) Dititei! Aditei-Ardhapataka (Katakamukha and Padmakosa)

(b) Tei dititei-Katakamukha, Padmakosa

(c) Tei Tei dititei-Katakamukha, Padmakosa

(d) Tei Tei adittei

(e) Teihatta! teihatta! Tei Tei diditei!

Vizianagara Sampradayam (Tradition)

ADAVUS:

1. *Tei Tei ta*-one hand is Sikhara and the other Pataka, this adavu is done in Samapadam.

2. *Ditteyistata Kitataka ditte hi stata*-Sikara and Pataka

3. *Tehidatta tejam Tehidatta tehi* (three types)-Holding Pataka hastas.

4. *Tehista Tajam! Tehista tai!*-It is practised in Tisram. and performed in three varieties. Chandra kala and Mukula, little finger extended in Mukula. Banahastam,

5. *Tehista Tehista Tehista Tajjam! Tehista Tehista Tehista tei!!*

Two types- 1. Holding Tripataka,

2. Holding Ardhapataka

6. Teyyum datta ! Tejjam

Teyyum datta! Tehi-Holding Pataka in one hand and the other with little finger extended Mukula. This adavu is performed in six varieties. (Banahastam)

7. *Dititei! dititei!*-Three types, Pataka and Sikhara

8. *Taditditei! Taditditei!*-Sikhara and Pataka

9. *Didititei! didititei*-Holding Sikhara hastas on shoulders

10. *Tadjte! Kitataka! Teji tehi!*-Holding Pataka hastas is one type, and holding Ardhachandra hastas is second type.

11. *Datta hatta hatta dhim! Datta hatta hatta dhim!*-Holding Pataka hastas, this adavu is practised in many ways. After the completion of Adavu training 10 Sabdams are taught to the students.[23]

3. Fundamental units of the Karnatakam and Bhagavata traditions of East and West Godavari Districts.

Samu is common for all artistes. Doing Pradakshina adavu,

Diteihita ta, Diteihita ta, Diteihita Ta.

digi digi tei! digi digi tei! digi digi tei!

Artiste pays obeisance with folded hands to Gurupitham-Nattuvangam stick and to the guru.

1. ADAVU:

1. Tei! Tei! Tei! Tei!

This is practised in sama pada position in two varieties with Ardhacandra and Sikhara hastas.

2. Vishama-Tisranadaka: Teyyatta! Teyyam! Teyyatta ! Tei!

-Starting with Pataka; ending with Katakamukha, two types.

3. Tei! Tei! Ta Kitataka! Tei! Tei! Ta

-One hand Katakamukha and the other Pataka.

4. (a) Diteihita! Ta! Kitataka! Diteihita! Ta!!

(b) Diteihita! Diteihita! Diteihita! Ta!! Holding Sikhara hastas in the beginning and Pataka hastas at the end. Two varieties of this adavu are to be practiced :

(i) The movement of Pataka hastas is in front side and then side ways.

(ii) Katakamukha hastas are also used.

5. Tei ditite!! Tei! dititei!

-2 Types of movements with Pataka and Tripataka.

6. Usi Adavu, and Samam:

(a) Ajam Ajam Ajam taka jam (usi)

(b) Jam S Taka jam !!Samam! with Pataka hastas.

7. Takajam! Takajam! Takajam!

-with Pataka hastas; ending with muktayi-Taka tadi ginatom!!

8. Dititei! ditei S

-Two types holding Pataka and Kataka-mukha for each.

Tadi ditaihi dititeihi

-two types holding Pataka and Katakamukha for each.

9. The hands are to be kept on waist while practising these adavus.

-1. Di dinna Kitataka! Dadi Dinna Kitataka

-2. Digi digi tei! Digi Digi tei! Digi digi tei!!

-3. Tehi hi dattam Tehi hi tei tei-two types.

-4. Tei hihi! dattam Ta tei hi tei! hita tam-3 types.

10. Ditei teyya!, Tei teiyya (mande tisram) Tam tatta dinda! Tam tatta dinda

11. Using Pataka, Katakamukha, Solapadmam, Sarpasirsha and Tripataka.

Tehita tehita tehita tei are practised.

12. Ta kitataka jam Ta ta kitataka jam!! Ata! Ata! atakkitataka jam

13. Mande Adavu Teerika (ending)

-(a) Takkitatakajam tatakkitatakajam Taka tadiginata Taka Tadiginata! Tak Dadiginata,

-(b) Kitatakajam! Kitataka jam Taka tadiginatom-two times ditta tadiginatom! Ditta Tadiginatom! ditta tadiginatom!!

Above adavus are practised by the Konaseema artists of East and West Godavari Districts for Karnataka Sampradaya nritya performance. Some of them are used in Kalapam performances also. Other adavus used in Bragavata tradition are of various types of gaits (types of walking in daruvus) and according to the daruvu they use the following adavus.

1. Ditta! Tahata! Ditta! Tahata! ditta!

-6 Varieties of movements are performed for the above sollukattu.

2. Dititei! dititei—4 varities

3. Gutthi varusa Ditei

4. Pandrayittu-Tam Tam Takkitataka Tatom tom takitataka

5. Tirika : tei! tei! tei! ta ta.

In the traditions of Sagaraseema *i.e.*, coastal districts of Andhra Pradesh, Kamatakam and Bhagavatam artists end with their presentation of Javali and daruvu with a 'Gaptu adavu'. It is a Manodharma performance and it is performed on all the four sides of the stage. The reason for this is to cover all the audience on all the four sides, as the stage is an open one.[24]

NARASARAOPETA TRADITION

According to Smt. Nagamanamma, her guru Smt. Puvvula Mahalakhsmi was a great scholar in dance and Sanskrit. Smt. Mahalakhsmi once visited Gadwala Samsthanam and presented abhiyana for Sanskrit slokams which were composed by the asthana poets on the spot. She did not teach Sanskrit as special subject to her students but she taught them the Sanskrit slokas, Tarangams, Asthapadis. She used to teach the word to word meaning and the bhava while she taught abhinaya. She also taught singing, nattuvangam and trained how to maintain accompanists for performance.

According to Nagamanamma the basic training for the tradition of Narasaraopeta is as follows:

The training system:

1. Dandalu & Moggalu-Daily between 4.00 a.m. to 6.00 a.m.

2. Basic steps (Adugulu Practice) Morning 7 to 10 o' clock

3. Adugulu, hastas, Medamayamu (neck movements) between 1 p.m. to 3 p.m.

4. Adugulu, hastas, neck movements and eyebrow's *etc.*, between 4.p.m. to 7.p.m.

Mandigam-sitting mandalam and standing are to be practiced in three speeds. Mandalam is also called as mandigam. Dandalu, a type of exercise holding a stick.

Chikkulu tiyuta-moggavaluta are practised in 5 Jatis.

1. Chaturasram-Tom Tei. Tom tei-4 speeds

2. Tisram-Tadhit tei tadhit tei

3. Misram-Tadit dittei tadit dithei

4. Khandam-Tadhit dhitei tadhit dhitei

5. Sankirnam-Tadhit ditteitei Tadhit ditteitei

Eye brow movements are also practised in the same way.

Basic foot work-Adugulu:

1. Chaturasram-Patakahastas

Te chcha tei kitataka

Te chcha tei kitataka

2. Three Aksharas-Pataka hastas:

Techcha techcha tei

Techcha techcha tei

3. Chaturasram-Pataka hastas:

Techcha techcha techcha tei

Techcha techcha techcha tei

4. Chaturasram-Pataka hastas:

Techcha techcha tei tei dham

Techcha techcha tei tei dham.

5. Chatarasram-Tripatakahastas

Tei hita tei dam tei hita tei hi-8 varieties

6. Chatursram-Sandainsa hastas:

Ta dit tei ta dit tei hi

7. Chaturasram-Alapallava and mrigasirsa:

Teyyam datta tei datta teyyam dattat tei datta.

8. Chaturasram-

Alapallavam, Hamsa paksha lifting ankles and standing on toes and then come to the normal position.

E dattam tehi E dattam tehi E dattam tehi.

9. Chaturasram

ddittitei, diteihi-only in speed.

10.Chaturasram-

Tripataka hasta: *Tei Tei diditei-Tei Tei diditei*

11. Tisram

Sandamsa, Alapallava and Hamsapaksha.

Tam tei dat Tam tei dat

12. Misram-Samdamsa hasta

1	2	3	4	5	6	7
Tam		*Ta*	*Tei*	-	*da*	*tta*

13. Chaturasram

Tripataka hasta Tei dha-Tattei dha-tei dha tattei dha

14. Chaturasram-speed (Quick Temp)

Tajjenu-Tajjenu-Tajjena-Tajjenu.

15. Chatursram-Circular movement on toes,-speed

Jhenu, Jhenu Jhenu Jhenu Jhenu Jhent Jhenu Jhenu

16. Chaturasram:

Ta tei data teida teida teida data teida teida

17. Chaturasram:

Tatei, Tatei, Tatei, Tatei, Tatei, tatei, tatei, tatei

Tadiginata-Tadiginata-Tadiginata

Music is also practised along with dance'. All items were clearly explained and taught by gurus. They used to perform Alarimpu, Swarajati and Padavarnam. Adhyatma Ramayana Kirtanas, Tarangams, Asthapadis, Padams, Javalis and at the end of the programme 'Mangala Harati. Hindi songs and Urdu songs were also in reputation but Smt. Nagamanamma did not practise them.[25]

I collected different basics from traditional artistes. I attended two conferences of Andhranatyam which were held at Vijayawada and Hyderabad, where I could meet several artistes from various districts. I tried to find out the differences in their respective traditions. I saw similarities in their abhinaya, and also in fundamental training. All of them were trained in the same manner but sources of the adavus were different. I discussed about practical part of each tradition with my guide Dr. Nataraja Ramakrishna who is the only authority of Andhras dance traditions. He told me that all classical dance traditions had same basics but the social, economical, geographical and political influences made them differ in some aspects, and the artistes developed their own traditions according to the tastes of their patrons. The three regions of Andhra Pradesh-Telangana, Rayalaseema and Sagaraseema were once under different rulers and some of the artistes migrated from one region to other regions. Ritual dance which was performed for its spiritual value is maintained and followed under the 'Marga' tradition, but kelika had different quality of performance in various places. Repertoire was also composed according to the taste of their patrons. Due to this reason only the dancers of Bobbili and some other samsthanams, used to start their performance with a sabdam, in praise of their patron. In some places the performances used to commence with sabda pallavi or svarapallavis and at some other places alarimpu, kautam or kausthubham was the first item. Whatever may be starting of the items and whatever may be the continuity of programme the basics for all these are the same.

(Courtesy—Dr. Suvarchala Suresh).

Technique of Andhranatyam

Numerous descriptions are found in ancient Telugu Literature about Nritta, Nritva and Natya and about the Natyasalas and Nrityasalas. Almost all the Telugu poets described dance styles that were in vogue in their times."

According to Abhinayadarpana, Sangita ratnakara and other medieval dance treatises dance is divided into three distinct categories *viz.*, Natya, Nritya and Nritta. Here Natya corresponds to drama and Nritya to gesticulations when it is performed to the words in a song. Nritta corresponds to pure dance in which the movements of the body do not express any meaning or bhava. The above three divisions are again subdivided as Tandava and lasya. According to Abhinaya darpana the sweet and graceful dance is lasya, the majestic dance is tandava. Nritta consists of the movements of body-limbs and the performance of exhibiting the meaning of a son—is nrityam. Performance of natakam (Drama) or dance drama is natyam. Pure dance *i.e.* nritta is known as the rasabhavahina by ancient scholars. Nandikesa and others mentioned nritya as 'Rasavyanjakam'. The Nritta' also is explained as Rasavyanjaka by contemporaries. Hence the technique of classlcal Indian dancing can be classified either under Nritya, Nritta, Natya, Tandava or Lasya *i.e.* Sukumara. The terms are also prevalent among practising dancers of North and South and from East to West. We find that dancers speak an identical language of basic technique, even though there are significant variations in interpretation.

The term 'Technique' can be explained as the method of doing or performing especially the arts, (Oxford advanced learner's dictionary of current English-A.S. Hornby, Bombay 1991 page 1319). Technique means method, skill, artistry, procedure, usage *etc.* The method or the procedure followed by the artistes of dance can be called as dance technique.

Dance is an imitation of nature. So several technical aspects like hastas, charis, gatis are named by the authors of dance treatises after certain animals or things around us. For example, Padmakosa hasta, Simhamukha, Ardhachandra hasta *etc.* Mayuragati, Maralagati, Vyaghra gati depict the gaits of animals.

The nritta technique of Indian dance is according to the law and methodology of human movements. The sculpturesque quality of Indian dance does not need any emphasis, but it must be understood that the pose or stance in the dance is the most important.

As in the other classical dances of India Andhranatyam also consists of nritta, nritya and abhinaya. The nritta part which is considered as the most important aspect of any classical dance, is practised in the initial training as adavus, adugus, jatis and in later items like Vinayaka Kautam, Additachari Vinyasam. Though the three aspects nritta, nritya and abhinaya are given equal importance in exhibiting padams, javalis, poems and the daruvus of Navajanardana parijatam the satvikabhinaya dominates. Nowadays the dance training commences with adavus. Previously the samu was a necessity, I started my dance practice with samu and moggalu *etc.* under Smt. Saride Manikyamma. My classes early in the morning were for the practice of samu, moggalu and adavus and also to learn music. In the evening, I used to practice dance items. But at present the adavus are taught to the students directly. There are many different patterns of adavus in Andhranatyam. The basic position is sama. From here the body is made to move. It is also known as Sausthavam. Holding two Ardhachandra hastas on the waist standing in a straight line with feet in equal level is called 'Sthanaka mandala' by Nandikesa and it is synonymous to Samapada Sthanaka of Natyasastra.

The Nrittaratnavali dealt with 'Sausthava'. The body is to be kept in straight line without bending, stretching too much or trembling. All the limbs are to be kept in normal position or relaxed slightly. There can be a slight movement in the feet. The raised chest, neck, waist, head, elbows and shoulders are to be kept in a straight line." Jayapa says that 'Sausthava' must be practised during exercise and that without 'Sausthava' an artiste cannot appear gorgeous.

Nritta is the main aspect to construct the technique of any Indian classical dance. The Nritta aspect has to be understood as a technique of human body movement. According to Natyasastra terminology one may say that all the major limbs (angas) and minor (upangas) limbs are utilised in Nritta. Chapter VIII and IX of Natyasastra contain detailed analysis of the movements of major and minor limbs (the Angas and Upangas). This is followed by a discussion on basic stances *i.e.*, the sthanakas, the combination of the primary movements, such as charis, mandalas, karanas *etc.*, The classification of the head, hands, breast or chest, sides (waist) hips and feet constitute the major limbs (angas). The shoulders, arms, back, belly, thighs, the calves, wrists, knees, elbows are pratyangas and the eyes, eyebrows, eyeballs, eyelids, cheeks, nose, jaws, lips, teeth, tongue, chin and face, ankles, fingers. palms *etc.*, are upangas. The angas and the upangas are utilised in both Nritta and Abhinaya technique. Nritta hastas are also mentioned in Natyasastra, Abhinayadarpana *etc.* The performance of Nritta, Nritya which consists of adavus and adugus, jatis tirmanas. These are executed in five varieties of geometrical movements of the body and hastas. These movements are invariably in 45, 90, 180 and 360 degrees. (Pictures are showing the possibility). The movements of the body are in triangles, circles and half circles. Mrs. Kapila Vatsyayan explains this thus, "The Indian dancer is not concerned with musculature of the human form, but rather like the sculptor, takes the joints and fundamental anatomical bone structure of the human form as its basis. From such abasis the dancer strives to achieve absolute form, since the muscles cannot suggest absolute form and create abstract geometrical patterns easily. The different parts of the body and their respective movements have been analysed from this point of view. It is from the key joint of knee, hip and shoulder that a movement emerges in both the lower and upper limbs; the neck joint is the pivot for movements of the head and face". The dance technique which has three aspects as Nritta, Nritya and Natya is with its divisions of Tandava and Lasya developed under Natyadharmi, where we can witness the predominance of graceful gesticulation and it can also be known as suggestive dance or stylised dance. Where an attempt to exhibit the emotions in a natural, graceful manner is Lokadharmi. The dance technique follows the Natyadharmi and Lokadharmi. The distinctivity will be in the training system, Nritta technique and they vary with regional influences.

The basic adavus in Andhranatyam are called as 'Tattu-Adavu', Natu-Adavu, Kundu-Adavu, Jaru-Adavu *etc.* As I mentioned earlier about the Sausthava and that Samapada is the first stance, the second position is known as 'Ardhamandali' or Ara-mandi. In this position the knees and feet are out turned with well balanced body by bending it suitably. "The movements of angas, upangas and pratyanas comprise of various body movements and various adavus are devised depending on these movements. Adavu is a fundamental dance unit where hands, feet, head, eyes and other parts of the body move in a co-ordinated manner. Adavu is a generic term used for any body movement. The dance movement using both hands and feet is called karana. Karana also represents a combination of various sthanakas, charis and nritta hastas. Therefore karana also becomes the basis for adavu. In order to achieve anga suddhi *i.e.*, perfection in movement, an adavu has to contain four lakshanas viz: Sthanaka (stance assumed at the beginning and ending of an adavu), Nritta hasta (hands used in the performance), Chari and rechaka (Movements of feet and hands) and Hasta kshetra (position of hands) throughout the performance.

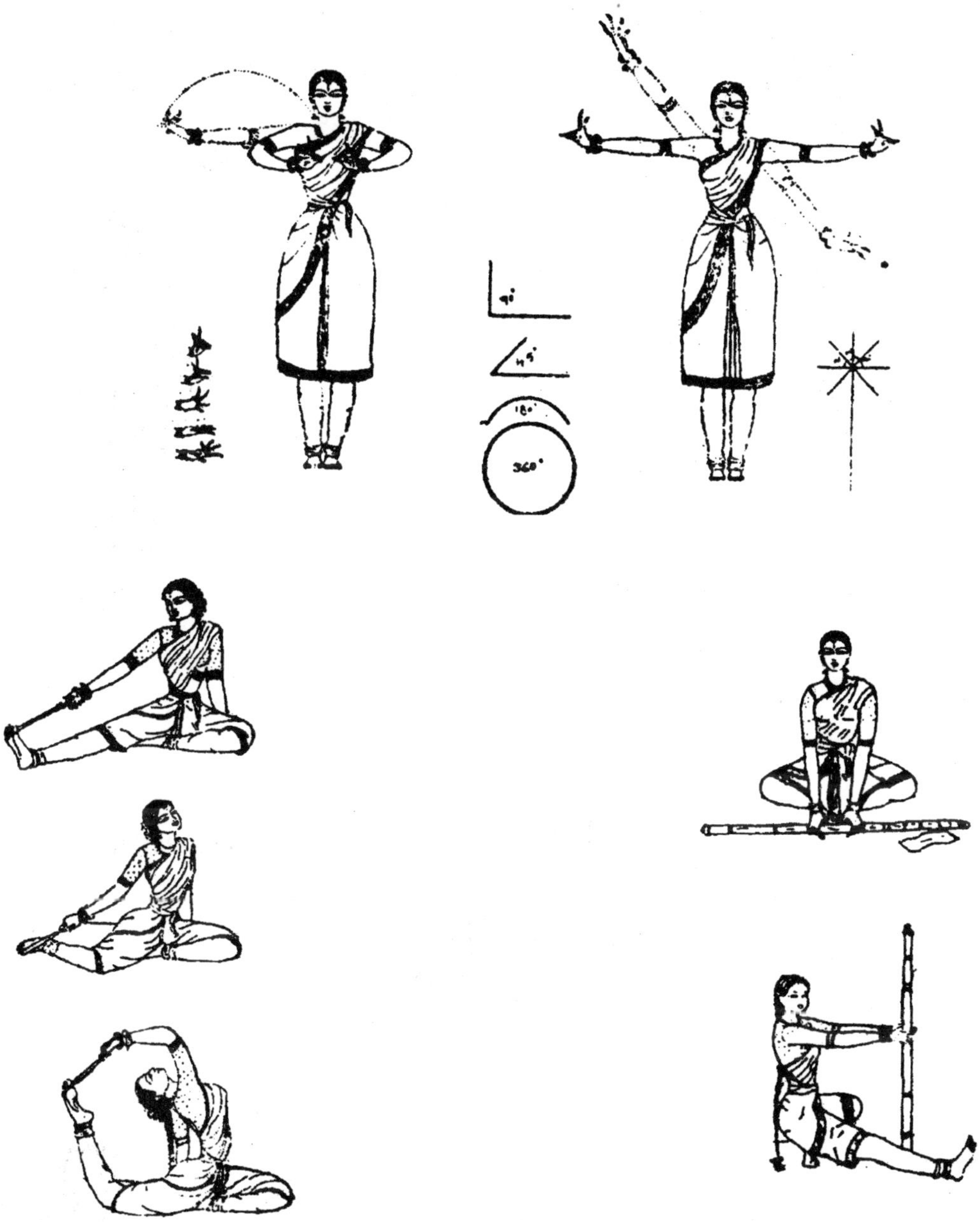

Some of the 'Samu' Postures

Cheti Chikkulu Exercises

Karra Samu-Exercises

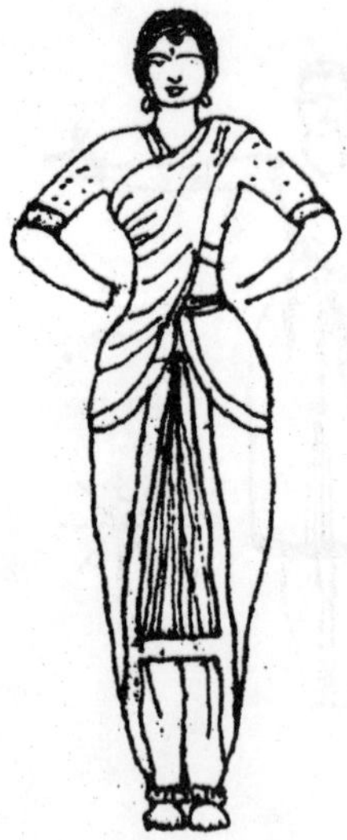

Samam

Valitam

Mandala

STHANAKAS

Ayitam

Gatanugatam

ADAVUS of Andhranatyam:

At the beginning of the practice of adavus an artiste has to learn the 'vandanam'. Namaskaram (vandanam) to Lord Sivaby reciting "Angikam bhuvanamyasya", Namaskaram to guru by reciting "Gururbrahma-Guruh Vishnuh" and namaskaram to the earth Bhuvandanam by reciting 'Samudra Vasane devi:-after the recitation of above three slokas moving the hands around the shoulders and above the head traditional namaskaram is taught to the students which depicts the meaning thus: "making my body a flower I offer this dance to the gods and I pray to the gods, the guru and the audience" (Dr. Nataraja).

1. Tattu-Adavu: Standing in Ardhamandali position both feet (Right and left) are alternatively lifted and stamped on the floor. This adavu gives strong base to continue in Ardhamandali position where the knees and feet turned outside by lowering the body height. It also makes the legs strong. First it is to be performed by holding the ardhachandra hastas on the waist and then with extended arms with pataka hastas. These are also practised in Jatis, with Tisra, Misra, Chaturasra, Khanda and Sankirna rhythms.

1. Ta-Right foot stamping, Tei-Left foot stamping

2. Ta-Ta-Two beats with each foot Tei-Tei

3. Ta-Ta-Ta-Three beats with each foot. Tei-Tei-Tei

4. Ta-Ta-Ta-Ta-Four beats with each foot. Tei-Tei-Tei-Tei

5. Ta-Ta-Ta-Ta-Ta-Five beats with each foot. Tei-Tei-Tei-Tei-Tei

6. Ta Ta Ta / Ta Ta Ta/ Tei Tei-Tei /Tei tei Tei-The third beat is absent here

7. Ta-Ta-Ta-Ta/Ta Ta Ta / Tei Tei Tel-Tel/Tel Tei Tel-First four beats are in slow speed and other three are in double the speed.

8. Ta-Ta-Ta-Ta-Ta-Ta-Ta-Ta-Ta /Tei-Tei-Tei-Tei-Tel–Tel-Tei-Tei-Tei

Stamping the right and left alternatively; with nine beats

Tattuta means to beat. In Bharatasaram 'Tadita padam' is equivalence to this. "*Padadvaye neikhada chettadyate taaditam bhavet.* Beating the floor with the feet is known as Taditam." It is also mentioned in Natyapradipa, Bharatasastra text verse by Sri Lepakshi Venkatanarayana Kavi. In this he mentioned 32 varieties of advavu persons which were in vogue in his time (1900). Some of these adavus, with variation of hand gestures are similar to the adavus of Andhranatyam. Tattu adavu is similar to 'Tattu-Jaggadavu' of Natyapradipa. "Tattu Jaggadavu" is defined as the beating of the feet by bending the knees side ways and keeping the feet apart at a distance of a 'jana' or span.

This aduvu is also similar to the padalakshana "Talahati" as mentioned by Jayapa in his Nrittaratnavali. The 'Tattu adavu' is the basic unit for the other adavus which start with the Ardhamandali position and stamping of feet to create various patterns.

II. NATU-ADAVU

A. In Telugu 'Natu' means to plant, or to pierce. The word depicts that the heel of the feet is to be stamped like planting. This aduvu is done with lifting the leg from Aramandi stamping with the heel in an extension and the other leg is bent with flat foot and the extended leg is again brought to the same place and the same movement is to be repeated with the other leg. Then the first (Right) leg is shifted to the back side of the other leg and the beat is with toes and then placed with a stamp at the native place. The movements are repeated with the other leg. This has rhythmic syllables as "Teyyam datta-teyyam-taha".

B. There is another 'Natu-Adavu'. In this movement, the legs are in crossed position. It is nearer to the desi sthanaka mentioned as Paravrittam by Jayapasenani in his Nrittaratnavali. The feet are crossed one heel facing the big toe of the other and the other heel facing the little toe.

The second part of the Adavu in which the foot is placed crossing the other behind it, facing the big toe, towards little toe and the two heels touching each other. The Natu-adavu is practised in various patterns; *i.e.*, side ways front side, *etc.* These are used in Nritta and Nritya items.

III. DIDITEI-ADVU:

This is a common step and used in almost all Indian classical dances with slight variations. In Andhranatyam technique these are practised with two legs and also with one leg and feet. In the constructive Nritta pattern it is practised with both legs thus; the leg extended sideways and stamping with the heel for the syllable 'Di' and the other is 'Di' stamped with the flat foot and the extended foot is brought to the original position by a stamp on 'Tei'. This adavu pattern is practised in various types with several combinations of hand gestures and various positions of the feet. These are also used with other patterns.

(a) This adavu in Bhamakalapam is to be done with one foot-3 beats di, di tei with one foot, the foot extended and the 'di' stamped with heel and with a movement to the back another 'di' is stamped and the foot placed at with a stamp in the beginning position.

(b) This adavu is also done by crossing the feet front side and back side of each other.

(c) Tei diditei-tei is a stamp with flat foot, crossed foot *etc.* (Front and back sides).

(d) Plain stamping combined with diditei (side ways diditei).

(e) Crosed foot front side and the side ways diditei.

(f) Back-crossed foot with the combination of and the sideways diditei.

(g) Leg lifted and crossed at the knee of the other leg and the beat will be with flat foot and diditei is done with the lifted leg. This can be done with a jump or without a jump.

(h) Other one is with a silent lift of the leg for 'Tei' and 'did-itei' is same.

(i) Tei-Tei-diditei: All above mentioned varieties are practised with two beats.

(j) Tei-Tei-Tei-diditei: same as above. The hastas like Tripataka, Pataka, Alapallava, Katakamukha *etc.* are used in basic training.

IV. DITTEI-DITTEI-KUNDU ADAVU OR KUPPI

This is a distinctive adavu pattern with a slight jump on both toes followed by stamping of both feet together. There are a number of ways to execute this adavu. Padmakosa, Katakamukha, Ardhachandra and Tripataka hastas are used while this beautiful movement is executed in Ardhamandali with extended arms and bent arms close to the chest.

Another type of this adavu is to be practised with crossed legs and feet.

This is used in Dasavatarams and also in the Navajanardana Parijatam.

1. Dittei-Dittei
2. Dittei-Diditei
3. Dittei-Dittei-diditei
4. Dittei-Dittei-Dittei-Diditei.

Dittei adavu is similar to the description of 'Desipadam'-(Kramataditam) in Nrittaratnavali. By standing on the both toes of the feet and stamping by making sound with the sole of the feet is called Kramataditam.

V. TATTEI-TAHA-DITTO TAHA ADAVU:

The Tattei taha adavu is to be performed with a stamping of the right foot and then the left foot followed by a jump on the toes and stamping of both the feet together. The alternate beginning of the adavu brings a good balance in exhibiting the different complex rhythmical structures of the extended arms with pataka, 'sikhara, kapitha, tripataka and katakamukha hastas. This adds grace and beauty to the performance.

VI. JARU ADAVU: (Gliding or skating movements):

'Ta-dit-dittei, Ta-dit-tteyya' are the syllables for this adavu. It is used in both nritta and nritya. This adavu begins in Ardhamandali position with stamping of the flat foot and the leg moves to a side with a gliding movement and rest there for one beat then the other leg corresponding to the first leg crossed back and stamped with toes and then first foot is stamped, then the same movement is to be continued with other foot. This adavu is done to make circular movements and to cover the whole stage. But the basic training of the adavu is given at one place. This Jaru adavu is performed with the help of Pataka, Ardhachandra, Katakamukha and Padmakosa hastas with extended and circular movements of the arms.

Other types of Jaru Adavu is to glide with the feet towards front and side ways, another one is to make the foot to glide side ways and the other foot also moves correspondingly to it. The Jaggu Jaru adavu which is defined by Lepakshi Venkatanarayana Kavi in his Natyapradipam is similar to this Jaaru adavu. It is defined thus "holding a hand above the head with a beautiful movement of the neck-and both feet moved at a time is Jaggu Jaradava. These gliding movements are practised and performed in several varieties. Predominently, these graceful movements are used in nritya.

VII. MANDE-ADAVU:

Mande means to kneeling down. The Mande adavus are practised in mandala sthanaka. The adavu begins from mandala sthanakam. These mande adavus practised in several varieties with different movements of legs and arms. At the beginning of this mande adavu a slight jump on the toes is necessary and then sitting on the heels for the other following movements of the legs and arms.

1. Complete sitting position, Tehista, Tehista, Tehista, Tehista

2. To start with sitting position then legs and arms extended adavu. Tehista Tajham-Tehista-Tei.

3. To start with sitting position then making circular movements are the varieties in mande-adavu. These are generally practised in Tisram and Misram. Tehista-Tajhem-Tei-Tirugudu tei.

VIII. JATI-ADAVU

1. Takita-Tirsam-3 beats

2. Taka-Takita-5 beats

3. Takadhimi Takajhanu–Chaturasram-4 or 8 beats.

4. Takita-Takadhimi-Misram-7 beats

5. Takadhimi-Taka-Takita-Sankirnam-9 beats.

IX. UTPLAVANAS-JUMPINGS:

(a) Utplavanas or jumps are practised with a lifting of both feet backside and making a jump by touching the hips with the heels.

(b) These jumps are practised by jumping on both the sides with stamping a foot and bringing other foot up with a jump and crossing the first.

(c) The combination of utplavanas, mande adavus and the bhramaries create several types of these adavu patterns.

X. USI ADAVU:

Stamping the foot against the beat is Usi. These adavus are used in nritta, nritya and to move to front, back and side ways in presenting Tillana and Varnams.

XI. MUKTAYI ADAVUS AND TIRMANAM ADAVUS:

Muktayi leads a dance item and tirmanam indicates its finish. Muktayi is used while starting a nritta piece and tirmanam is performed at the end of an item.

A. Muktayi Adavuly:

1. Ginatom
2. Tei ginatom
3. Tei Tei ginatom
4. Kitataka tei
5. Tei tei ginatom
6. Tadi Tadi tei ginatom *etc.*

B . Tirmanam adavulu:

1. Kitataka tarikitatom-3 times

2. Tadhim ginatom-3 times

3. Tadiginatom–Takatadiginatom-3 times

Takadhiki tadiginatom

These tirmanams are practised in angular movements of arms, circular movements of arms and circular movements of the body.

XII. The last adavus are practised in three types, in sama position and aramandi position.

1. Taka Taka Taka Taka-stamping the feet alternatively in Sama position.

2. Dhigi Dhigi Dhigi Dhigi-stamping the feet with toes alternatively in Ardhamandali position.

3. Dhrugu Dhrugu Dhrugu Dhrugu-Stamping the heels alternatively in same position by raising the fore part of the feet. As explained above there are 12 patterns of adavus in Andhranatyam at present. Some of the adavus are also used as adugulu. The difference between adavu and adugu is simple. The adavu in nritta patterns is followed by the nritta hastas and is very systematic in presentation. Adugu is used in nritya where the feet follow the tala, laya and the hastas depict the meaning of the words of the song. The adugu means a natural step. According to Dr. Nataraja Ramakrishna, adugu is normal walk or natural step, generally used in nritya to depict some meaning and the Adavu is a complete scientific movement in a combination of chari, rechaka nritta hasta, used in pure dance items. Basic training of foot work in accompaniment of arms and other body limbs is necessary for learning the items of Andhranatyam.

REPERTOIRE OF ANDHRANATYAM

Repertoire which has to be pronounced as repertwa(r) which means a stock of pieces, plays, Operas *etc.* Andhranatyam is a female oriented Lasya dance tradition containing three traditions *viz.* Agamanartanam, Asthananartanam and Parijata Prabandhanartanam. In olden days the order of performance used to commence with a Kutupam. The orchestra artistes used to enter the stage and stand in an order which was called Kutupam. Then the members of the orchestra used to set their instruments in a 'Sruti'. All the instruments in harmony with each other was called as melaprapti, melavimpu or milanam *i.e.* to unite the sounds of various instruments. After the melaprapti the dancers used to enter the stage. Then a *raga* (melody) used to be played on a mukhavina or a flute or any other wind instrument. It was called 'Ambaram'. Then the singers or Nattuvaralu used to sing some mridanga jatis in samagati which was called as 'Ayattam'. Then the churnikas were used to be sung by the artistes. Then the dancer had to submit Pushpanjali (offering of flowers) then sabhavandanam, then only the dancer used to tie her ankle bells, after that she never paid the sabhdvandanam. This process of kutupam, melaprapti, ambaram and ayattam were observed upto the early 20th century. The above process was strictly followed and it depicts the discipline of the artistes of those times. Any dance performance in the above process creates a 'Rasanubhuti' says Dr. Nataraja Ramakrishna." All the classical dance artistes of India follow a similar invocation that is the above kutupavinyasam.

The distinctivity of Andhranatyam is the process which depicts the old tradition to suit the modern stage. With the harmonious base of the orchestra the sinorer today sings Ganesastuti and a Narayana Tirtha's Tarangam. "Puraya Mamagamam". Then the dancer enters the stage with kumbhaharati in her hands while the singer chants the 'ayattam' (mridanga jatis) and the dancer offers kumbhaharati to the gods. This is followed by a churnika and pushpanjali, Bhuvandanam and then an invocatory item Addi Mohara or Additacharivinyasam, which is also known as alarimpu performed in khandam, rendered in Nataraga. Kumbhaharati is an identity of Andhranatyam. Alarimpu or alarinchu means to please, Alaru in Telugu is to shine, blossoming of a flower *etc.* This item consists of various patterns of adavus and is performed to please God and the audience. This is a suddha nritta item (Pure-dance) depicting the blossoming of the artiste for future items. It does not contain any rasa or bhuva but pleases the audience with its distinct quality of performance by the movements of the dancer. The first part of the item leads with a muktayi.

MUKTAYI:

Tadhit Jham Tarita

dhit Jham Tarita

Jham tarita

Takadhit Jham tarita

dhit Jham tarita

Jham tarita

Tadhit Jhamtari tam!

Takadhit Jhamtari tei!

Tadhit Jhamtari-Takadhit Jhamtari

Takanaka Jhanu

Takadhiki Tadiginata Taka tadiginata

Tadiginata diginata ginatom

Second part of the item is known as 'Addi' or Auditachari vinyasam.

1. *Tam ta tei tei–tei jugadattam*

Todigidam todigi dam dam dam

dam dam dam dam dam dam!

Dam dam takadhikitaka tadhiginatom!!

Todigidhim-todigi dim dim dim

dhim dim dim dim dim dhim!

dhim dhim takadhikitaka tadiginatom!!

2. *Tain ta tei tei-Tei jaga dattam !!*

Todigi dam todigi dam dam dam

Todigi dhim todigi dhim, dhim dhim

Todigi dam dam todigi dam dam

Todigi dam-todigi dhim!!

dam dam takadhiki taka tattomta doddo

dham dham dham takadhikitaka tattomta doddo

dam dam takadhiki taka

dham dham dam takadhiki taka

Tungaku takadhiki tongutaka tadhiginatom!!

Tam ta tei tei teijagadattam.

MOHARA:

Titittitei-Kitataka tittittitei

Todigi dam dam-takadhiki taka

Tungaku takatom-Taka tom

dhigitunga, dhigidhigi taka tunga taka taka tunga!

taka taka tunga tunga tom tom tunga!

tom tom tunga tunga-3rd speed

takkattom-dhimi dhimi dhimi dhim doddoddo!

Tadiddo-dhimi dhimi dhimi dhimi doddoddo!!

Takato dhimi dhimi dhimi

Todigi to dhimi dhimi dhimi

Dam ginatom-dam dam ginadhim

Takato dhimi dhimi dhimi todigito dhimi dhimi dhimi

Dam ginatom-dam dam ginadhim!!

Dadiddha didda dhittanga

todigidham-dam dam ......

Titittittei Kitataka tittittittei!

TIRMANA:

Jham Jham dhirgudu dhinna dhinna kitataka dhinna dhinna dhinna

kitataka kitataka kitataka Dhinna kitataka

dhirgudu dhirgudu dhirguud dhim,

Ta-Jham-Tajham

takadhiki tadiginata,

taka tadiginata

tadiginata

diginata

ginatom

Tajham, takadhiki, tadiginata, taka

tadiginata, tadiginata, diginata, ginatom-2

Tajham-ditittei, dititei, dititei, dititei-3 times

tei tei dititeitei! tei tei dititei tei! tei tei dititei tei!

dhrgudu tei!

Tam ta tei tei tei jagadattam!

Addimohara is the warming up dance item for the performance. This is a worship of the stage, a kind of Rangapuja, while pushpanjali is the offering of flowers to God. The basic attitude of these items is obeisance to God and they used to be performed in a temple. The second item in the repertoire is Vinayaka Kautam is also known as Kausthubham. It consists of mridanga jatis to a musical notation. Kautams are written in praise of Vinayaka, Siva, Vishnu and Lakshmi or any other God or Goddess. These are composed in special talas like Vinayaka. Rudra, Lakshmi, Simhanandana. Garuda *etc.* The Nritta is composed to the guru, laghu and plutha of the particular tala. Vinayaka Kautam is given more prominence in Kautams. Vinayaka, the Lord of obstacles, who protects us from all obstructions in our endeavour.

The Vinayaka Kautam composed in Vinayaka tala has the 72 matras. The talangas are Ga, Ga, Ga, La, La, Pa, Ga, La, La, Pa, "Ga is the Guruvu of 8 matras, La is the Laghuvu is of 4 matras and the Pa is the plutam containing 12 matras. *i.e.,*

Ga,	Ga,	Ga,	La,	La,	Pa,	Ga,	La,	La,	Pa
8+	8+	8+	4+	4+	12+	8+	4+	4+	12 = 72

Total tala letters are 72. The present day Vinayaka Kautam is rendered in Sankarabharana ragam. Every Kautam had five Angas. 1. Sulu vinyasam, 2. Tatkaram, 3. Tahanajati, 4. Kautam (Main part) and 5. Tirmanams.

SULU VINYASAM

The dancer's body should move at the beginning lightly like a flame of lamp which flickers when there is a gentle breeze. Then the eyes, neck are to be moved to depict the Sulu vinyasam. The mridanga notation is used for the Sulu vinyasam is, thus,

1. Titittei kitataka tittittei

Dittei Dittadu-dattat ttaham!!

Tattanutakita kitataka

Tari Tari kunda kuku

dhittimta diginatom

dhigi dhigi dhigi dhigi.

dhi teyya tei!

2. Tatkaram:

Ta tata tatta-Tajham tatta

Ta ta dhi dhi-tom tom nanna

Ta dhi kitataka-Takkita taka

Dhikkitataka-tom kitataka

nam kitataka-too dhim!!

3. Tahanajati: If sounds of a mridangam are produced with musical notations on a Vina they are called as Tahanajati.

Tahana Jati:

Tadhim datari tadana jhanumtari

darehi namtari rehina namtari

namtari kumtari humtari kumtari

Tadana dhanam jhanutam dhimitam jhanu

tahata natadhimi jaganaga

namta kumta rumtahata renkina

dhittalangu takaham tadhiginatom

tadhiginatom, taka tadhiginatom

tattalangu tadhiginatom

Muktayi: *Teyyam detta teyyam taha*

Teyyam datta tei hattei

After performing the above three parts the next part which is known as 'KAUTAM' is to be presented by tirmanas.

Vinayaka Kautam, Vinayaka tala-composed in 72 matras

G(S) *Takkitataka tei; Ditittei dittei dittadu datta taham*

G(S) *Dattanutakita kinatonga dhekkutam tonga, nangita kitataka, nangita kitataka nangitakitataka*

G(S) *Dhimi tam nutakita kinatunga dhekkutam tonga-Ta tangi tangi Kitataka*

L(1) *Dhikkitom-dottam dirgudu tom tom*

L(1) *Dikkumtari-dhikkita kitataka Dhikkitonga-Hari hara*

P(1) *Karimukha Vighna Vinayaka*
Venakati(ta) Harulava Ganapati
Je je jekkita notariki dhem
jeje jekkita

G(S) *Notariki dhem, kinnam tadhikku*

todhikku anam gautari
tongita kitataka

L(l) *Tongutaka devara Ganapati dhikkita kitataka*

L(1) *Dikkutonaa Ganapati kautam gaddari*

P(S) *Vinayara (Vinayaka) tarugudu tam*

Dhirgudu dhim takku

Dhikku takkita tongita kitataka

Dheyam tangi kitataka dikkitom

Muktayi: *Dattam todigi dam todigidhim*

Tatom tongutaka, tongutaka

Todhiginatom!!

Teyyam datta Teyyam taha

Teyyam datta teyya tei

Kautam consists some literature in praise of God (Devara Ganapati, Hari hara Karimukha *etc.*), but the dance is performed in pure nritta, the Sahitya is not presented with Angikabhinaya, *i.e.*, mimetic action. The tirmana jatis are performed in Aditala *i.e.*, in Samam. Five jatis were performed previously, but presently three or two tirmana jatis are performed.

The third item is Kaivaram which is also an applause in praise of Lord Siva or Vishnu. This consists of nritta and nritya. The mimetic actions depicting the bhava of the stotras are introduced in this item. Generally these stotras are written in the praise of gods and also of kings. Asthadikpala Kaivaram was also composed by Dr. Nataraja Ramakrishna. The performance structure of the Kaivaram is stotra which is followed by a jati and at the end by a tirmanajati. Now, Andhranatyam dancers perform two Kaivarams, Siva Kaivaram and Vishnu Kaivaram. These compositions are similar to Kautams. The difference is the stotra in Kaivaram is exhibitted with mimetic actions in devotional emotion, but in Kautams pure nritta patterns are executed. These are temple ritual items which are performed in great dedication and devotion.

To please the gods Hindus recite Bijaksharas like Aum, Aim, Hrim, Srim. When the Bijaksharas are rendered in a special manner a divine power is generated. In the same manner the mridanga notations are set in a Kautam to please the Gods. To depict the five elements, the panchaksharis, the pancha pranas the Additachari is composed in khanda gati *i.e.*, in five angas. The three items of the first part of Andhranatyam repertoire pertain to Agamanartana Sampradaya. These items are the special compositions and were performed in temple rituals only.

The second part of the repertoire is the Asthana Sampradaya. In this, the selected items like Adhyatma Ramayana kirtanas, tarangams, padavarnams, padams, javalis, salamjatis, slokas, sabdams and tillanas *etc.*, are performed. Kelika, Asthana nrityam, Karnatakam, Kachcheri, Darbaru are the synonyms used for the performance in the kalyanamantapa of a temple or in the court of king. The performance is similar but the basic attitude is different. Asthana kelika in a temple is different. Asthana kelika in a temple was of a devotional content which leads the people towards spiritualism. It was also an intellectual feast for the elite and the artistes. Darbaru ata, or kelika in the court of a king was to entertain the king and the scholars and the intellectuals, the ministers and others.

1. Padavarnam: This is a musical composition containing sahitya (poetry) to portray the nritta, nritya and atbhinaya. The Bhavas (emotions) are exhibitted with elaboration of angikabhinaya and Satvikabhinayam. The Padavarnams are compositions in erotic sentiment or expression in praise of God. In varnam abhinaya skills reach their pinnacles and the dancer shows her mastery in nritta and nritya. Examples: 'Manavi Chekonarada' in Sankarabharana raga-Aditala and 'Danike tagu janara'-Todiraga set to Rupaka tala.

2. Dasavataramulu: Ten incarnations of Lord Vishnu. This famous composition which was choreographed and practised by the famous Andhranatyam artistes Smt. Induvadana and Vaidehi of Marampalli is now performed as one of the items in Andhranatyam. This is a beautiful and unique composition of peculiar and distinct quality of Andhranatyam. The jatis are choreographed in different talas and gatis, lyrics are rendered in Mohanaragam.

3. Tarangam: Tarangam literally means a wave. Sri Narayanatirtha's Krishnaleela Tarangini is famous for its devotional content and scholarship. Tarangams are the great compositions in which the aspect of nritya is extensively, elaborately performed. They are rich in ragabhava, talabhava and layavinyasa says Dr. Nataraja. This is the most useful item for showing the skill of the artiste in laya vinyasam with various patterns of adugulu.

4. Sabdam–Salamjati: The descriptive compositions of Bharata, Ramayana and Bhagavata are known as Sabdams and they are also composed in praise of Kings. Many Salamjatis were composed by Sri Kasinathayya kavi. Sabdams and Salam jatis are similar compositions. These are chchandorachanas (composed in prosody) consisting of yati, prasa, yamakas and gamakas.

Example: Salamjati: Dharani rathamai deva janu landaru Janambirugadala nagada! Aruduga Sankaruna kitavai Ajudu Sarathiganu pogada!! Sabdams are generally composed in Kambhoji raga set to Misrachaputala.

5. Padam: Abhinayam (Histrionic Expression) in Andhranatyam:

Abhinaya is of four kinds. They are :

1. Angikam, 2. Vachikam, 3. Aharyam and 4. Satvikam.

(i) Angikabhinaya is to express the meaning of a song or a poem through various gesturcs and hastas.

(ii) Vachikabhinaya is to sing, a song or poem melodiously and express the bhava of the song or the poem.

(iii) Aharyabhinava is the decoration and ornamentation, make-up to depict a character.

(iv) Satvikabhinaya is the histrionic express to portray the rasabhava. Satvikabhinaya is superior to the other three abhinayas. Bharatamuni mentions that the abhinaya which consists of more Satvika is the superior one, abhinaya which consists satvika in equal proportion to the other three is mediocre and the abhinaya which consists less of Satvika is the inferior.

Satvikabhinaya was well developed by the Andhranatyam artistes since ancient times through their performance of Padams, Javalis, asthapadis of Jayadeva and Amaruka slokas *etc.* The extensive expression of sthayibhava (static emotion) sanchari bhava (voluntary emotions) and satvikabhava (histrionic expression) for the representation of a nayika or nayaka with less hand gestures and more elaborate emotional expressions through facial expressions in a natural way (Sahajabhinaya) is known as 'Suddha Satvikabhinaya'. Abhinaya can be performed in two ways *viz.* Natyadharmi and Lokadharmi. The scientific approach with naturality is natyadharmi, it is known as stylised expression where as the lokadharmi is the scientific approach with regional variation containing naturality. Padam is the best suited item for the presentation of Satvikabhinaya.

Padam means a word in general in Telugu. But!as a musical melody it was defined as a musical composition pertaining to the nayaka and nayika lakshnas relating to erotic sentiment. These are composed in the form of a song which contains Pallavi, Anupallavi and Charanams. Padams are useful to perform satvika and sanchari bhavas. These are mostly sung in slow tempo (vilambita laya) and are the compositions with a splendid Ianguage containing scholarship in philosophy and spirituality. Thc symbolic the allegorical content of these padams is to be traced to the Bhakti Cult. Where the human being is the lady-love waiting for union with the Divine who is Visualised its the lover. Generally Kshetrayya padams are performed by the Andhra artistes.

A rare padam *i.e.*, 'Vennelapadam' of Yuvaranga is also practised by the Andhranatyam artistes. The materials for the performance of a padam are the nayikas (sviya, parakiya and samanya) the different categories in above three, and the ten states of mind-(Dasavasthas), eight varieties of their stages. The eight nayikas, sthayi bhavas, sancharibhavas and satvikabhavas. To develop the satvikabhinaya through the angika, vachikabhinayas one should study deeply the vyaparas and chestas of the nayika portrayed in the padam.

Abhinayam to a padam is composed and performed with an extensive guidance of veteran gurus who can teach not only the padarthabhinaya *i.e.*, expression to word meaning but also the depth of the bhava of the song. Mrs. Kapilavatsyayan says that the literary imagery is so rich and full of traditional allusions that a dancer without adequate background and training tends to execute padam only superficially. In the training of a Bharatanatyam (even in Andhranatyam) dancer of this particular area is not taught until she has attained a certain maturity both in technique and understanding. They seem easy pieces, but when one begins to explore their depths, one realises that they should not be touched by those with insufficient knowledge or by those who are uninitiated.

Satvikabhinaya mainly depends on the emotional expression of the theme by sanchari bhavas and satvikabhavas. Relating to satvika, Andhranatyam dancers developed a tradition to present the abhinaya in sitting position. The padam presentation thus has four stages: Padarthabhinaya, Vakyarthabhinaya, Bhavabhinaya and Rasabhinaya.

1. ***Padarthabhinayam:*** word to word meaning.

Example: Mundati vale napai nenarunnada swamy depicting the meaning of the words by hastas.

Mundati: Past-depiction by using the pataka, ardachandra or suchi hastas.

Vale: Like-hamsasya hasta

Napai: Keeping pataka on chest

Nenaru: Love-hamsasya at the chest

Unnada: (do you) have-pataka hasta

Swami: Sikhara hasta to depict the husband.

2. ***Vakyarthabhinaya:*** The whole meaning of the sentence corresponds to the bhava of the sentence with Angika.

"Mundati vale napai nenarunnada swami"

Do you love me now like past days?

Bhava with facial expressions corresponding to the gesticulation.

3. ***Bhavabhinaya:*** The presentation of the whole pallavi depends on the understanding of the emotional content of the theme. Here sanchari bhavas are included and elaborately presented.

The nature of the Nayika *i.e.*, Sviya, Parakiya or Samanya[37] and the action and reaction due to the experience of love union or separation, the eight avasthas like Proshitabhartruka, Abhigarika, Khandita, Vipralabdha, Kalahantarita, Svadhinapatika, Vasakasajjika and Virahotkanthita are to be exhibited. The various voluntary and involuntary (sanchari vyabhichari) bhavas relating to the dominent emotion result as responsive emotions. So for this reason only Bharata says that the configuration of determinent (Vibhava) consequent (Anubhava) and transidary (Vyabhicari) emotions give rise to rasa. (Vibhava Anubhaua Vyabhichari samyogat Rasanishpattihi-

Natyasastra-VI Chapter-196 Telugu PSR Apparao). The bhavabhinaya leads to rasabhinaya.

In ancient days the audience used to sit at the same height of the artiste so they could see and enjoy the abhinaya. Now the modern stage is widened and auditorium is big, abhinaya is stylised and presented to communicate the bhava by gesticulation and movements are widened to cover the entire stage.

Rasabhinaya includes the Vachika (voice modulation in singing according to the Bhava). Nowadays the dancer is depending on play-back singer and so all repetitions are already set-up to the given time. But in olden days the dancers had to know how to sing the raga to enlighten the bhava, the tala system and rasa-sastra. So they used to perform a padam with raga bhava, tala bhava rasabhava to take the audience to reach the bliss or the rasananda. The padams like 'Nene-jana, ne china dana'; Evade vadu are taught to the students of Andhranatyam now.

Padabhinayam: (Example) : Padam 'Mundati vale'

Poet	:	Khsetrayya
Nayika	:	Sviya, Khandita, Madhyadhiradhira
Nayakudu-Shathudu	:	Ayoga Vipralambha Sringaram
Rasam	:	Raudram
Ragam	:	Bhairavi
Tala	:	Triputa

Pallavi :

Mundati vale napai nenarunnada?

Nasami muchchatalika nelara?

Anupallavi :

Enduku Mogamichchakapu mata ladevu

Era ma Muvva Gopala meragadura!!

(i) Stanza *Piluvanampina ravu pilichinanu gaikou*

Palumaru vedina palukavu

Valapu nilupa 1eka cheluvuda vani ninne

Talachi talachi chala talladillute gani!!

(ii) Stanza *Chinnanati nundi cherina denchaka*

nannu chauka jesedi nyayama?

Vanne kada nidu vanchena lerugana

ninnana baniledu nejesina pujaku!!

(iii) Stanza *Kaluvala redanchu (kalatha lemiyuleka) kanchivarada ninna*

Lalana inta duramu ranichchena

Alaru Viltuni keli nalamu konuchu nannu

Kalisina papaniki kannulajuda vachchitivo!!

Pallavi *Mundari vale napa*

expressed proudly with anger Nenarunnada-nasami

Vitarkam-deliberation

Sanka-apprehension

Dainyam-depression caused by humbleness (humility)

Muchchata lika nelara?

Chinta-Anxiety, painful reflection

Vitarkam-descrimination

Vishadam-grief, despair, loss of energy

Enduku mogamichchakapu mataladevu

Depression *(Dainyam)* expressed in a culmination of Vitarkam and Vishddam.

Era (ma) Muvva Gopala meragadura

Vishadam in combination of vitarkam and dainyam

Vitarkam and *Sanka* and *Vitarkam.*

1. Piluva nampina ravu pilichinanu gaikovu

Sancharis: *Autsukyam* combined with vishadam,

Vitarkam Vishadam, Vitarkam combined with *Avegam;*

confused and quickened action.

Autsukyam means impatience, not able to bare the suspense.

Santapam-nisvasa, chinta grief

Palumaru vedina palukavu

Dhruti (contentement) with dainyam (depression) and vishadam (despair) dainyam and vishadam

Valapu nilupaleka-cheluvada vani ninne

Autsukyam-impatience, *Harsham*-exaltation, *Dhruti*-contentment;

Nirvedam-discouragement, *Mati*-assurance.

Talachi talachi chala talla dillute gani

Adhyanam-Nitturpu = deep sighing and depression due to not obtaining the loved one.

Arti: Satvikabhavas: Sthambanam, loss of energy, trembling, paleness of the face are the result of the separation and the reaction is rashness with pride.

Alasycini: Indolence, drowsiness, twisting the eyes *etc.*

Unmadam: Delirium, insanity, laugh without any apparent cause, walking sitting and crying or to do some unrelated things.

2. Chinnanatinundi–cherina denchaka

Smruti and mati: recollection, feeling happy by recollecting the past happy experiences and sadness due to the present situation.

Dhruti: Hero neglects her even though she recollects her past experience.

Vitarkam: deliberation, descrimination.

Harsham: Joyful, exaltation.

Nannu chauka jesedi nyayama ?

Vrida, nirvedam, dainyam with *vishadam.*

Vrida can be performed by vitarkam, sanka, nirvedam, lajja, siggu by turning the face away covering the face, turning the face to the floor, nipping the nails.

Nirvedam: Sorrowful face, tears, deep sighing and beseeching *etc.*

Vannekada nidu-vanchana lerugana:

Autsukyam with *Vishadam*

Smruti, Avahitta (dissimulation–pretention)

Paschattapam: Compassion due to trust in him.

Ninnana baniledu–nejesina pujaku!!

Proudness with anger, Nirvedam, Vishadam dainyam *etc.*

Stanza III. Kaluvala redanchu (Kalathalemiyuleka)-Kanchi varada ninna

Harsham-exaltation; Dhruti–satisfaction

Mati-realisation; *Asuya*-Jealousy

Lalana Inta duramu-ranichchena

Vitarkam, Sanka

Proudness with anger,

Alaru viltuni keli-nalamu konuchu nannu

Srama. Supti, Harsham; Kamukeli; Arthi, Alaru viltunikeli–Erotic movements. Srama: perspiration, half closed eyes, a deep sighing *etc.*

Supti: Closing the eyes, hard breathing *etc.*

Arti: bristling, trembling of the body, *etc.*

Kalisina papaniki-kannulajuda vachchitivo

Vitarkam and Smruti, Sanka, Vishadam, Asuya, Vitarkam, Sanka etc.

Padam can be elaborately presented with all the sancharibhavas in culmination of satvika bhavas. But the sanchari bhavas are selected and presented according to the status and situation of the heroine. It is not necessary to use all the bhavas prescribed by the authors for elaboration. The sanchari bhavas move like waves in an ocean and they are not to be static. So the related sancharis are combinedly performed to enhance the bhava. The condensation of erotic depiction in the performance of a padam is visible to day so some of the decent padams are taught to the students of Andhranatyam.

The third part of the repertoire is Navajanardana Parijatam: Two nrityarupakas are famous. They are Jayadeva's Gita Govindam (in Sanskrit) and Bhamakalapam (in Telugu.) Parijatam is a synonym to Kampam. Turpu Bhamakalapam is performed by the male artistes of Eastern region of Andhra Country, which includes Ganjam, Srikakulam, Vizayanagaram and Visakha districts. It belongs to the ancient drupadabani. The second tradition is Kuchipudi Bhamakalapam which is performed by the Bhagavata artistes of Kuchipudi. This is also a male oriented one. The third tradition is the Navajanardana Parijatam mainly performed and practised by the female artistes of East and West Godavari Districts. The fourth one is the Parijatam performed by the Rayalaseema artistes. Now it is completely vanished.

The third part of the Andhranatyam. *i.e.*, Navajanardana Parijatam is a special subject which is included in the repertoire by the eminent artistes who participated in preparing the syllabus for Andhranatyam. This Navajanardana parijatam is distinctive in nature from the other two. It was performed in dedication to Lord Kuntimadhava (who incarnated at Pithapuram) by the artistes of Pendyela family for nearly 400 years. The last artiste of the family was Late Smt. Pendyela Satyabhama from whom Dr. Nataraja Ramakrishna learnt this great drisya prabandha. The same style and tradition are followed by the young artistes who are his disciples.

"Bhamakrodha" means a woman in anger. Here Bhama means Satyabhama (abbrivated from Satyabhama). Kalapam means an angry discourse or to explain in detail. Bhamakalapam is the detailed description of Satyabhama's pranaya kalaham with Lord Krishna. Navajanardana Parijatam is a madhura lasya prabandham.

"Nava Janardana parijatam is a Sringara Divya Drisya Sravya Prabandham" says Dr. Nataraja. Prabandham literally means a musical composition."[40] Navajanardana Parijatam was previously performed on nine consecutive nights at Kunti Madhava temple by Late Smt. Pendyela Satyabhama and the artistes of same family of Pithapuram. It used to end with a recitation of tenth chanto of Mahabhagavata on the tenth night. This was performed by the nine dancers at a time and it was performed under the direction of Sangeeta Saraswati Late Smt. Duggirala Manikyam. The nine troupes', performance was conducted twice with their accompaniments. If it were performed thrice it would have been a *yajna* according to their belief. There are nine Janardana temples on the Northern bank of Godavari river in East Godavari District. It is believed that the idols in these nine temples were installed by Sage Narada. This Parijatam was being performed in these temples. So it was named as Nava (nine) Janardana Parijatam. The nine temples of Janardanaswami are situated in Mandapeta, Dhavaleswaram, Madiki, Jonnada, Alamuru, Kapileshwarapuram, Korumalli, Kotipalli and Macherla, where the Navajanardanam was performed. The another sceintific reason is the performance of nine states of the Nayika *i.e.*, Chakshupriti, Chinta, Samsruti, Gunakirtana, Arti, Tapam, Lajja, Tyagam, Gamanam are used to perform in nine days performance. The word 'Nava' also means New. Navajanardana Parijatam performed in neoteric way at present with a culmination of Gita, Vadya, Nritya and Abhinaya. So also it can be called as Navajanardana parijatam. Navajanardana Parijatam is a collection of texts written by various poets in dedication to their native gods at Nellimarla, Korukonla, Dvarakatirumala, Keshavapuri, Rangapuri, Ryali, Kodavalluru, and Duvva *etc.* As mentioned earlier this parijatam is a Sringara Divya, Drisya, Sravya prabandham. It is a story of Pranaya kalaham of Lord Sri Krishna and His consort Satyabhama. The story is based on an incident that occured during a conversation between Satya and Krishna. Satyabhama offended Krishna with an injudicious remark about her own superiority in beauty. Krishna walks-out from her in a huff. At first Satyabhama maintains her stiff attitude, but as time passes on emotion gives place to practical logic. Satyabhama starts getting agitated (virahotkanthita), later she becomes sober and goes in search of her Lord (Abhisaarika) and later she becomes desperate and severely criticises Krishna for his supposed lack of understanding (Khandita). She passes the succeeding inexorable phases and ultimately becomes happy when she hears Krishna's divine flute, suggesting that after all he is on his way to make up peace with Satyabhama. The legend of Navajanardana Parijatam has 150 daruvus each of which depicts one or the other moods or plights which Satyabhama undergoes from the time she realises her folly till she once again becomes her usual happyself with the knowledge that her Lord is coming back to her. Each 'Daruvu' represents one or the other 'Nayikas' *i.e.*, Virahotkanthita or Abhisarika and so on as the main Nayika, there being one or two other 'Nayikas' as upanayikas (subordinate heroines). Again each Daruvu has its 'Rasa' (mood or sentiment) either Sringara (Erotic) as the main mood 'Karuna' (pathos) or Hasya (humour) as the subordinate moods."'

Divyaprabandha-The heroine Satyabhama and hero Krishna are divine couple who are believed to be the incarnations of Lord Vishnu and Bhudevi. Though the story is simple incident its content is elaborately performed to the spiritual experience to educate the common people and to lead them towards madhura bhakti tatva that is the union of Atma with Paramatma. It is performed through four abhinayas and can be enjoyed by listening to musical melody and the simple common Telugu language in Daruvus. Karnataka Ragas Nata, Regupti, Asaveri, Ahiri, Kambhoji, Yadukula Kambhoji, Saveri, Saranga, Bilahari Kedaragaula, Kalyani, Ananda bhairavi, Bhairavi, Todi, Saurashtra, Sankarabharanam, Bhupala, Madhyamavati, Mohana, Abheri, Kanada *etc.*, are used for various daruvus. The nritya aspect is very rich in execution of Daruvus. They are mainly executed in Sama (equal) and Vishama (unequal) gatis. All the Sapta talas, Adi, Ata, Triputa, Rupaka, Jhampe and Misrachapu are used. The peculiar adugus in the execution of Daruvus are Sama-Adugu, Usi-adugu, Dampa-adugu, Kattera-adugu, Uma-adugu, Valu-adugu, Vidambapuadugu, Vishama-adugu, Halaya-adugu, Nitu-adugu, Teta-adugu, Jaru-adugu, Anda-adugu and Puliteti-adugu. Nritta is executed in jati performance.

"There will be nothing to learn in Bharatabhinaya Sastras if one learns this Parijatam completely"-says Dr. Nataraja Ramakrishna. This is a complete composition having the Nirtta, Nritya and Abhinaya. Siddhendra said that, Abhyudaya Paramparabhi, Vriddhiga naa yonarpambunina parijata prabandhambunaku, Sringara Kavyambunaku, Natakalankarambunaku, Bhava Jnanambunaku, Raga jnanambunaku Talajnanmbunaku, Sri Krishna Chidvilasambunaku Katha kramambettidanina"–above prose describes the qualities of Parijata Prabhanda. The Bhamakalapam of Siddhendra which is performed by the Bhagavata artistes of those times influenced lasya nartakis of nattuvamelam. So they collected various daruvus written by numerous poets and made it a great composition as Navajanardana Parijatam. The slokas from Krishna Karnamritam, Ramakarnamritam and Tarangams of Sri Krishna Leela Tarangini were also used in between daruvus to elaborate the performance and to enhance abhinaya.

The Daruvus are composed as dhruvaganas like Jayadeva Asthapadis. In dhruvagana the Sahitya in songs are written to a particular tala. There is gati prastara in it. Sahitya can be sung in different gatis for elaboration of Bhava. The Telugu term for dhruvaganam is Daruvu. Daruvus are the musical compositions are of six kinds.

1. Vinikidi daruvu: This is an introductory daruvu played behind the curtain. "Bhamayani pilature–Vayyari Styabhama yani Talature ...

2. Pravesha Daruvu: This is sung at the time when an important character enters the stage. It depicts also the mood of the nayika (heroine). "Dadhimadana–neevu ravayya madana mohana

3. Abhinaya daruvu: Abhinaya is dominently executed in this daruvu. In Andhranatyam the abhinaya obtains importance and Satvikabhinaya is the dominent one.

4. Samvada daruvu: Conversation or dialogues in between two characters.

5. Sampurna daruvu, Bhavavikasa daruvu or Nayika Nayaka daruvu: The tala vinyasam, layavinyasam, all are executed in various bhangimas (postures) with bhava and abhinaya.

6. Manovega daruvu: The mental state of the nayika is executed in this.

Present performance of Navajanardana Parijatam is a dignified characterisation of Satyabhama which expounds the royal dignity as a queen and a courageous lady (Veeravanita). The speciality of the character Satyabhama is Sviya (a married wife), Svadhina Patika (one who is in full control of her loving husband), Saundarya garvita (very proud of her beauty), Pragalbha (who boasts about herself, her beauty, her riches and most of all her being in complete possession of her husband's love and affection.)

The present text followed by the Andhranatyam artistes is the text learnt by Dr. Nataraja Ramakrishna from Late Smt. Pendyela

Satyabhama. This Navajanardana parijatam was patronised by the Zamindars of Pithapuram. Sri Rao Mahipati Gangadhara Rama Rao was the last patron of this Parijatam.

Present performance contains some of the selected daruvus from this Parijatam. Vinikidi daruvu is used as playback song behind the curtain, the dancer enters with a jati and performs the daruvu 'Dadhimadana nivu navayya, Madana". This is taught to the students in the beginning. The daruvu contains a pallavi, anupallavi, charanam, dvipada. Previously, "Adugo Chandrudu udaymbayenu" was the first daruvu performed for the entrance of Satyabhama. The other daruvus like "Siggayenoyamma" followed by a padyam, "Indranilaputalu" and another daruvu "Alanatinundi" which is followed by the kalaha karanam padyam. "Okanokanadu". It also contains ardha chandrikas, vennela daruvus and chandamma daruvus. Chandamama daruvu is very important in Pithapuram style in which the boyhood of Lord Sri Krishna is described is nine stanzas.

The revised style of Pendyela Satyabhama is the absence of Krishna's Character in Bhama Kalapam and another revision of this, made by Dr. Nataraja Ramakrishna is avoiding all the comedy, which disgraces the character of Satyabhama and the character Madhavi (Vidushaka or Hasyakadu). Only Satyabhama, the main character, performs the daruvus in connection to the legend, the commentary follows.[47] The dignity of the Royal Lady is maintained. The daughter of Satrajittu one of the richest kings who had the Samantakamani and a wedded wife of Krishna is meticulously maintained, never allowing any cheapness for attracting the gallery.

Though the Andhranatyam is a female oriented dance, for the propagation of Andhranatyam, Dr. Nataraja Ramakrishna had to train some of the male dancers. The first male performer of Navajanardanam with feminine grace is Sri Kalakrishna who has been propagating the dance style since two decades. The titles like "Abhinava Satyabhama", "Madhura Lasya Kalanidhi" are the awards for his excellency in portraying the Satyabhama character.

(Courtesy—Dr. Suvarchala Suresh)

Dr. Nataraja Ramakrishna—The Pioneer of Andhra Natyam

Geetam Nrittam tatha Vadyam prastaragamana kriya!
Etani pancha yo vetti sa acharyah prakirtitah!
Uhapohan matischaiva smritirmedha tathaivacha!
Sishya nishpadanam chaiva shadacharya gunah smritah!

—Natyasastra - Chapter-26

According to Natyasastra of Bharatamuni, an Acharaya must possess the qualities of having complete knowledge of Music (Svarajnana) Nritta, the movements called angaharas etc. Instrumental music (Chaturvidha Atodyamulu) the tala system and playing the tala according to the character in different gatis and he must also possess the visualisation of the poetry and story. He must possess great retentiveness and scholarship to grasp the subject and he has to enlighten the intellectual qualities of the students by his great intellectual ability."

Smt. Suvarchala showing the present technique of Andhranatyam in National Seminar at Hyderabad-1994.

As mentioned above all the characteristics can be seen in Padmasree Dr. Nataraja Ramakrishna of A.P. who is the pioneer of Andhra classical dances. Twenty five years back 'Kuchipudi dance was not considered as a classical art form by the Central Sangeeta Nataka Akademi. Then Dr. Nataraja Ramakrishna, as the convenor, conducted a seminar under the auspices of State Sangeeta Nataka Akademi and got it approved as a classical one. He gave several suggestions and methods for its development and propagation.

Nataraja was born in the Dream Island 'Bali' of Indonesia in 1933 in a noble family of Andhras. His forefathers were great patrons and promoters of fine arts. In his younger days learning the art of dance was a taboo amongst cultured society. Dr. Nataraja with deep urge for art of dance left the family and abandoned his rich share in the ancestral property and had to undergo troubles and turmoils due to poverty in' quest of this art. He spent his boyhood at Ramakrishna math at Madras, under the care of Swamy Saswathanandaji. Later on he went to Gandhiji's Ashram where he came into contact with great personalities like Asha devi, Arya nayakam, Deenabandhu Prabhakarji and others. They were his ideals in his later life. He got inspiration and encouragement in his boy-hood from his elder brother Syamasundar who taught him Sanskrit and Music.

During his search for fulfillment of his inner urge for dance he came across great gurus like Meenakshi Sundaram Pillai, Nayudupeta Rajamma, Vedantam Lakshminarayana Sastry and Pendyela Satyabhama under whom he learnt various forms of dance. He says that the four Gurus are like four vedas for him. Smt. Nayudupeta Rajamma, who was a devaganika of Sri Kalahasti temple was a great scholar of Agamanartanam and Satvikabhinayam. She was the guru who inspired him to learn Agama dance tradition with great exposer of Nada upasana, the relation between the sound and vibration, its impact on the human body, the dance movement, etc. He learnt Satvikabhinayam and Agama nartana Sampradayam from Smt. Rajamma.

Nataraja was introduced to Raja Ganapathi Rao Pandya of Bandaru Samsthanam by one Dr. Sonak, who was the family doctor of that royal family. After an extensive test he was appointed as a court dance artiste Asthana Natyacharya of Bandaru Samsthanam, near Nagpur. He had an opportunity to visit Tanjore, when he was in that samsthanam. He studied old manuscripts on dance and music in Saraswathi Mahal library at Tanjore.

Sri Kalakrishna's performance as Satyabhama of Navajanardana Parijatam.

Dr. Nataraja traversed in all the traditions of dance art in India, studied and practised them. After careful study of all the dance forms he came to the conclusion that the dance art of Andhra Pradesh was the richest of all. So he ultimately settled in Andhra Pradesh the native land of his ancestors.

His ceaseless efforts and urge to search and to prove the cultural heritage of Telugu people by the media of dance which is a powerful medium of expression became fruitful. As an investigator he succeeded in promoting the Kuchipudi as a classical dance tradition and as an innovator he recreated the Perini Siva Tandavam as one of the vigorous, majestic male dance by his extensive study and understanding of the 12th century dance treatise, the "Nrittaratnavali" of Jayasenapati. Nataraja says, "Pernini" is a derivative of the word prerana meaning invocation, is a dance dedicated to Lord Siva, who is the Supreme dancer. This is a group dance where the dancers moving according to the rhythm, go into a trance, and imbibe the power of Siva into their bodies. While invoking Lord Siva, a Perini dancer says, I give you my body, come into me, and dance through me".

Dr. Nataraja Ramakrishna encouraged the propagation of the folk arts like Chindu Yakshaganam, Turpu bhagavatam, Veeranatyam, Garagalu, Tappetagullu, Guravayyalu, Veeedhibhagavathulu, Urumulu etc., of the three regions of Andhra country. His services to Andhranatyam, the Lasya dance tradition, apart from other dance traditions in bringing into lime light of its splendour occupy first place. As a pioneer of Andhra classical dance he had to strive hard in contacting the female artistes of the yore, who were great scholars in Bharatam i.e., Nritta, Nritya, Abhinaya. With the help of Late Sint. Annabattula Bulivenkataratnamma he could bring together the artistes who were reluctant to participate in the seminar of Rajahmundry in 1970.

Nataraja has written many books in Telugu and English on Indian dance traditions. As a result of his research on Andhra classical dance forms he could write more than 50 books. Sonic of them are meant for children to enthuse them to learn the art of dance. Some of them are useful to the scholars and research students. Six of his books won the State and Central Government awards.

As a choreographer he was the first preceptor in A.P. to write and compose a ballet on Lord Venkateswara. In the ballet he introduced all the dance traditions and music traditions of ritual, classical, folk and tribal forms of A.P. This is the first of its kind in the cultural history of A.P. This was later translated into Hindi as 'Balaji'. He composed 'Kumarasambhavam' the immortal classical poem of Kalidas Mahakavi as ballet and presented it at Ujjain during Kalidasa Samaroh in 1962. It was adjudged its the best and all round best dance ballet ever presented at Ujjain. He got 'Swarna Kalasa' for the best production and the special Kalasa for all round best production i.e., presentation of music rendering of Sanskrit slokas, dress, presentation of the theme, dance and abhinaya. fie composed 'Meghasandesam' as a dance ballet for the same Samaroh (1963) but it wits treated as a special programme to give an opportunity to other troupes to (yet prizes.

Dr. Nataraja Ramakrishna visited USSR and France as research scholar sponsored by the Government of India in 1975 to propagate Indian dance art and to make a comparative study of Indian and Western classical dances and folk dances. He has written a book on this subject.

Due to his immense dedication towards dance art he never thought of his family life. Ratna Rao Sekhar in an article viz., "The architect of Andhranatyam" writes thus: Dr. Nataraja Ramakrishna lives, breathes and thinks dance. His whole body speaks of his love for the art" Yes, it's true. So many of the scholars who know him intimately say that he is the only person who spent his life to the service of dance traditions of Andhra country, without aspiring a return. He spent his wealth for promoting the lasya dance tradition i.e., the Andhranatyam and encouraging the young to learn dance. As a philanthropist he gave financial help to many old artistes who were in a poor condition. As an enthusiastic guru he taught dance free of cost to all those who could not afford to pay. He even gave free food and shelter to deserving disciples.

As a pioneer of Andhranatyam he participated in 1970 Abhinayasadassu as its convener in conducting discussions on several aspects of Lasya dance tradition.

Dr. Nataraja's services to the art of dance were well recognised. The most important honours conferred on him are:

1. Nataraja: Conferred by the ruler of Bandaru State Sri Raja Ganapati Pandya at his 18th year.

2. Bharatakaldprapoorna: By A.P. Sangeeta Nataka Akademy in 1968.

The Pioneer of Andhranatyam—Nataraja Ramakrishna

3. Bharatakalasavyasachi: By the Artistes Association of West Godavari in 1979.

4. Kalaprapoorna: An honorary Doctorate conferred by the Andhra University in 1981.

5. Kalasaraswathi: By Kalavedika of Hyderabad in 1982.

6. Best Natyacharya of South India: By Central Sangeeta Nataka Akademy in 1984.

7. Best Research scholar: By LVR Trust, Madras in 1986 for recreating 'Perini'.

8. Asthana Natyacharya of Srisailam Devasthanam 1980.

9. Asthana Natyacharya of A.P. 1980.

10. He was presented with a Gold crown by the art lovers of A.P. which no other artiste could get. It is a Rare Honour.

Nataraja Ramakrishna

11. Prestigious Awards: Rajalakshmi Award in 1991 and Rajiv Foundation Award.

12. Padmasree in 1994.

13. Best Natyacharya - Limca Award- 1995.

He writes in his book Ardha Sathabdi - Andhranatyam that: Since some years my friends admirers and others wanted me to write my biography. My travelling since 45 years to various places, states, countries and the meeting of several poets, authors, artistes scholars, scientists I learnt many things from them and my experiences, my knowledge obtained by observations and experiments all put together is the history of Andhranatyam. So the life history of 'Andharanatyam' is my biography.

Dr. Nataraja Ramakrishna revived and developed Andhranatyam and recreated Perini Sivatandavam and propagated them inspite of much criticism and obstacles during the last two decades. This Lasya dance tradition with its rich traditional and technical qualities is flourishing well as it has a great admiration of the people of India in general and Telugu in particular. He believes that seven crores of Andhras can make Andhranatyam. live forever. He is a Yogi (Hermit); a Tapasvi (an ascetic) of dance.

In his words Lord Nataraja has three eyes. The left eye is Andhranatyam, the right eye is Kuchipudi and the middle one is Perini Sivatandavam.

'Dancing is the expression of life's urge' said Projesh Benerji. But dancing is not merely an expression of one's emotions but a Yoga with splendid spiritualism according to Guru Dr. Nataraja Ramakrishna.

"Dr Nataraja Ramakrishna is a living encyclopedia of dance art and a University of Dance for the students" as scholars consider.

Courtesy : Dr. Suvarchala Suresh

Godfather of Andhra Dance Art—Nataraja Ramakrishna

18

Vilasini Nrityam

We have crossed several crucial cross roads in the long history of humanity. There were many transitions in the past such as—from the caves to forests, from agricultural, pre-industrial, post-industrial civilisations. We are now involved in a most crucial and important of all transitions, to a global society. A new consciousness, that would enlighten every individual is emerging in view of science and technology. All arts and sciences are undergoing a thorough change.

Today, we are in a new era. Dance which was a unifying factor like other fields has undergone several changes but is still surviving in all parts of India, so also in Andhra Pradesh because of the people's patronage. A very large majority of people, though deprived of the opportunities of modern life including access to media and education are respecting the basic values of life on the basis of religion, and culture. They are the commoners that are patronisers of all art forms, especially dance.

Devadasi tradition, which once had the royal patronage fell into bad days and was abolished by Governments. But, it is still surviving in some parts of Andhra Pradesh, especially in East Godavari district, in areas like pithapuram *etc.* Some seniors, who are experts in the Desi tradition are still alive. Swapna Sundari, a leading soloist has made a recent study in identifying such women. She learnt from them the intricacies of display of Sringara and dance techniques. She renamed her dance form as "Vilasini Nruthyam" (Bold words). This tradition had been kept alive by the Devadasis or Kalavanthulu of Andhra Pradesh even though the darkest period of early 20th century has thrown them into oblivion. This art form had been kept alive though their lives are shattered.

I had an occasion to see Swapna Sundari's performance of this style, in Sundarayya Vignana Kendram, Hyderabad recently. She gave a brief introduction of all her items in between her performance. Especially, her 'Javalis' were more interesting.

This feminine tradition of Andhra Pradesh was well appreciated by people of all categories in the rural community. I remember to have seen during my childhood days a very good performance of one "Manohari" living in our native place. I feel glad to see that this ancient art is still kept alive.

I tried to meet Swapna Sundari and know more details about this Vilasini Nrityam because I kept a separate chapter but it was not possible. There are no published books also in the market. So, I am not able to provide more information on this type of dance.

Swapna Sundari learnt the art of the Telugus Devadasis directly from several aged traditional dancers including the late Maddula Lakshmi Narayana. She revitalised the ancient dance system with the guidance of late poet and researcher, Dr. Arudra who named it as Vilasini Nrityam.

Vilasini Nrityam is the comprehensive representation of the temple court and theatrical dance traditions of Telugu Devadasis. This dance-style is distinguished by its unique Nrittha, typical Abhinaya and a distinct repertoire, which was evolved out of the various contexts in which the traditional female artists of the professional group of dancers called Kalavanthulu, performed.

This system of dance fell into disuse following the abolition of the dedication of devadasis to temples. In 1994-95, this dance form was rejuvenated as Vilasini Nrithyam. Today, it is being performed all over the country.

In the post-independence era of Indian dance, when the ancient temple dances were reapplied to their original ritualistic purpose, Swapna Sundari made an attempt and performed at the 400 year old Ranganadha Swamy temple in Rangbagh, Hyderabad. This practise is being continued and she is giving performance during the time of Brahmotsavam of the temple every year.

PART-III
TECHNIQUES OF INDIAN CLASSICAL DANCES

19

Techniques of Indian Classical Dances

Dance Techniques

Expression in dance is sought to be achieved through facial expressions, hand gestures and footwork. The expression of the face, head, eyes, eyebrows and the neck and the footwork, through timing, rhythm.

Bharata did not make any clear divisions in the Indian dance. But Nandikeswara and other medieval writers made a clear division. Bharatarnava and Abhinaya darpana are the authoritative treatises on dance.

After these works, many writers who wrote in Sanskrit and regional languages tried to make attempts to treat dance as an independent art. Later writers tried to include many new concepts that were practiced at their times, in addition to the ones already illustrated by Bharata.

Nritta, Nritya, Natya Tandava, Lasya, Margi, Desi, Abhinaya, *etc.* are the repertoire found in dance. Entire dance system is within the orbit of these fundamental concepts.

Treatises, such as Abhinaya Darpana, Sangita Ratnakara, Natya Sastra Sangraha, Bharatarnava have divided Indian dance into three different categories namely, Nritha, Nrtya and Natya.

Second classification done is known as *Tandava and Lasya.*

The third division according to time, Rhythm and tradition is known as Margi and Desi.

Nritta: Nritta is known as pure dance, which does not convey any sentiment, emotion of it is only an ornamental form of dance and at sings follows a particular rhythm. It does not convey any meaning based either on music or on the syllables of drums. The feet movements are coordinated with the rhythm of A *Vanadda.* In this types of dance, entire body is kept intact. Stamina is maintained by making maximum use of the feet and hastas in a limited space and time. The important aspects of dance movements depicted in this type of technique of dance are Charis, Karanas, Mandalas and Angaharas.

The Chari is the single write of movements which are numbered as 32 and divided into 16 Bhumicharis, *i.e.*, movements on the earth, Akasachari or the aerial movements, where the feet is lifted from the ground.

Next to chari the Karana and the Mandala occupy important position in describing Nritha aspect of dance.

The Angahara is the formation of number units movements or karanas.

Bharata has discussed about 32 Angaharas. Bharata has prescribed 30 Nritha hastas or hand gestures of Samyukta Hastas. Apart from these techniques circular movements thus the movements of major limbs (Angas) and minor limbs (Upangas) are employed as the elaborate intricacies of Nritha or pure dance.

Nritya

Though Bharata did not make a separate division of this type of dance, he discussed minute aspects of this technique of dance and named it as Angi Kabhinaya. This is commonly applicable to dance and also drama.

Nandi Keshwara, Sarangadeva and some others suggested that this type of dance should be performed on the basis of some basics. So, Natya involves a poetry, a lyric pertaining to some event or events and descriptions along with a mime. Hence in this type of technique, meaning is conveyed through the facial expressions and emotions.

The gesticulation of head, neck, eyes, eyebrows, chin, cheek, nose and lips when performed significantly express a particular movement.

When such movement is combined with emotions 'rasa' is evoked. The hastas namely, Asamyuta or single handed or Samyuta or double handed are in basic alphabets of Abhinaya or histronics.

There are some more terms used in pure dance like recika or circular movements, *i.e.*, Brahmaras turns the utsavas or leaps and jumps, and lastly the pindibandhas or group compositions. The Natya Sastra describes only some pindibandhas. Four varieties of Pindibandhas are mentioned in the following words.

1. Gulma–a collective dance (a group of dancers follow the entrance of main dancer).

2. Srunkhala–A chain formation–where the partner forms a chain by holding each other's hands.

3. Latabandha–Formation of a creeslive structure. The dancers put their arms around each other.

4. Bhadyaka–dance performed by a single dancer.

All these types of pindibandhas are suggested by Bharata in the beginning of the play to attract the attention of the audience.

Several types of Bhramaris and 5 types of utplavanas are described by Abhinaya Darpana and Sangita Ratnakara.

The Bhramara's of Abhinya Darpana, and receitas of Natya Sastra belong to the class of there, dancer has ample scope for imagination or real Natya. Five way of no pressing the lyric. Nine rasas and Nayika Bhavas can be amply performed 3rd category of dance is known as Natya, which is the combination of Nritha, the pure dance and Nritya, the historic dance based on a story and performed by various characters. Here, dancing and acting are combined to narrate a story.

The theory of Indian dancing has to be studied as the complex synthesis of the arts of literature, sculpture and music. That is why the writer of Natyasastra says "This art will be enriched by the teaching of all scriptures (Sastra) and will give a review of all arts and crafts" and further says "there is no wise maxim, no learning, no art or craft no device, no action that is not found in drama" and finally he asserts "Hence I have decised the drama in which all the departments of knowledge different arts and various actions". There are no limitations of theme or content in this art.

Later texts, which deal with dance as an independent art, consider these principles. Nandikeswara in his Abhinaya Darpana has treated dance from the point of view of principles. He is followed by some other writers of treatises on dance. Sarangadara and the authors of Vishnudharmothara Purana and the Natya Sastra Sangraha, all followed the analysis of Nandikiswara.

Different aspects of dramatology are shown in the following pages.

Classical Dance Poses of India

Samanakha

Lina

Vishkamba

Katichinna

Classical Dance Poses of India

Ardha Rechita

Ganda Suchi

20

Hand Gestures

Hand Gestures

The Natya Sastra and Abhinaya Darpana agree in classifying the hand gestures into three classes :

(a) single hand (Asamyuta hasta)

(b) combined hand (samyuta hasta)

(c) hand gestures for dance (nritha hasta)

These three classes possess many common names but, as regards the numbers of gestures in each class and their definition and application, they differ.

I. Single Hand Gestures

According to Natya Sastra, there are 24 gestures in this class, while in Abhinaya Darpana, there are twenty eight. In both the works, 22 gestures have common names, their description, hand application also, in both the works, has considerable agreement.

The 24 gestures are :

1. Pataka
2. Tripataka
3. Kartari Mukha
4. Ardhachandra
5. Arala
6. Shukatunda
7. Musthi
8. Shikara
9. Kapiththa
10. Kataka Mukha
11. Shuchi
12. Padmakosa
13. Sarpasirsha
14. Mrigasirsha
15. Kangrla
16. Alapadma
17. Chatnna
18. Bhramara
19. Hamsasya
20. Hambsabhaktra
21. Hampcksha
22. Sandansha
23. Mukula
24. Tamkachuda

1. The definition of the following thirteen gestures is similar in both the works.

1. Pataka

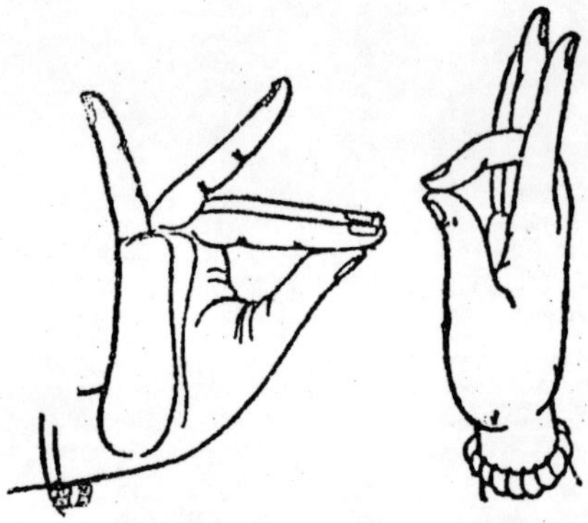

Left Right

Brahma

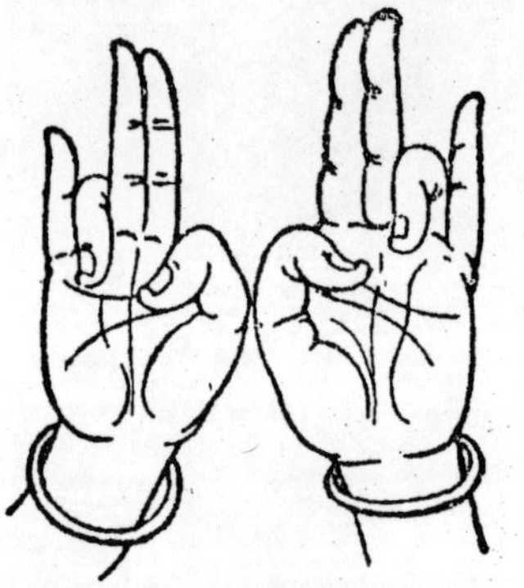

Vishnu

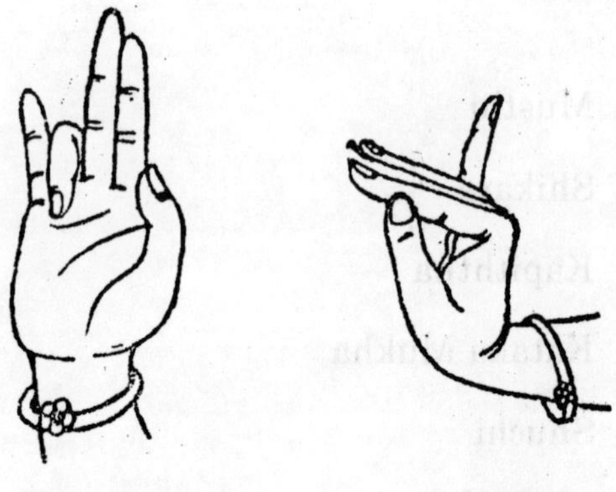

Right Left

Shiva

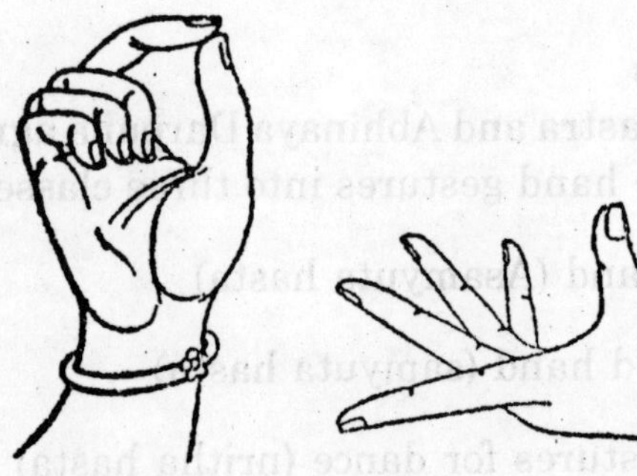

Right Left

Surya

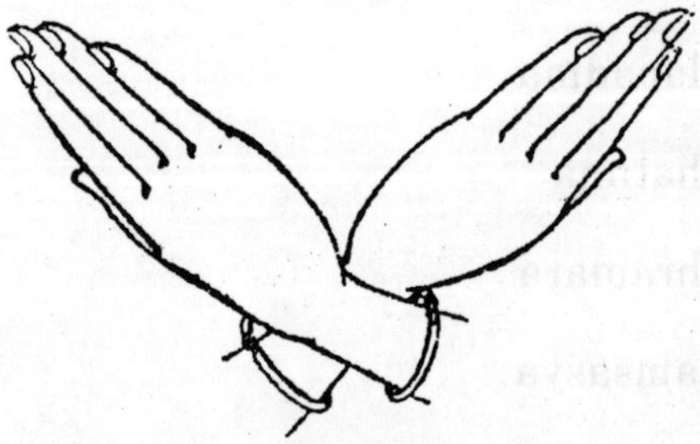

Trees

Woman

Peacock

Star

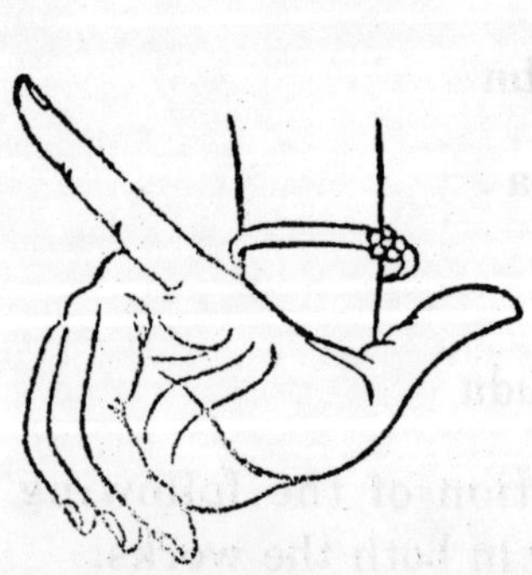

Moon

Is

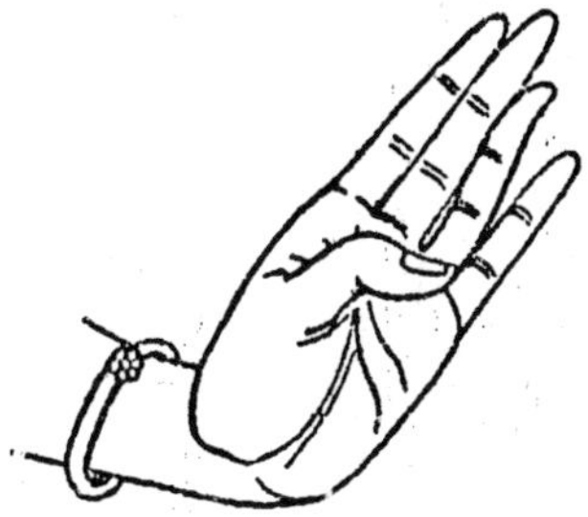

Am, Are

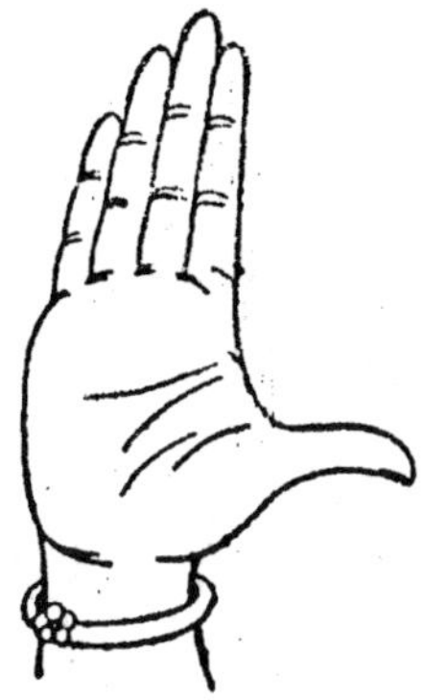

There

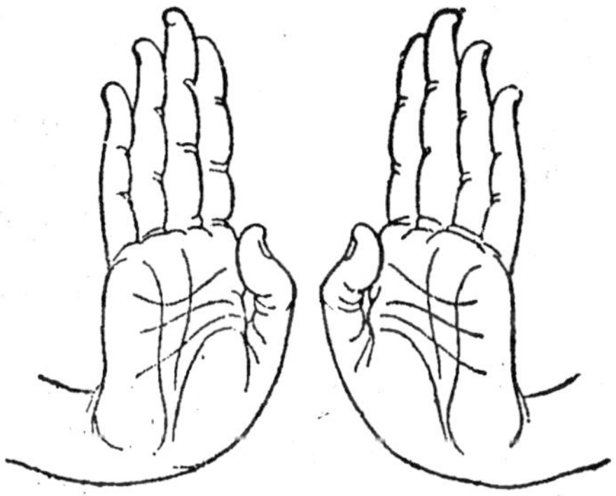

No, Not

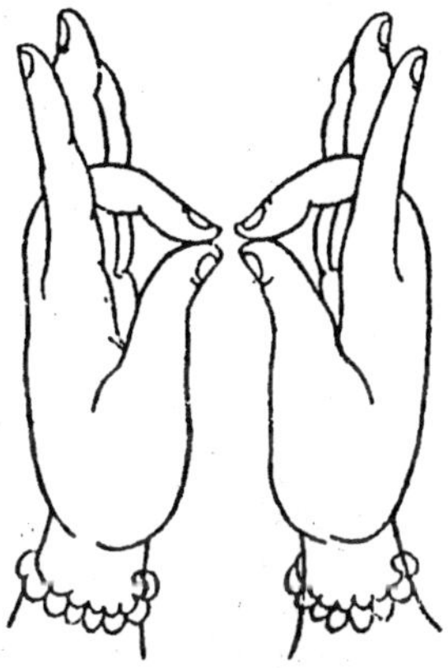

Walking

Give me

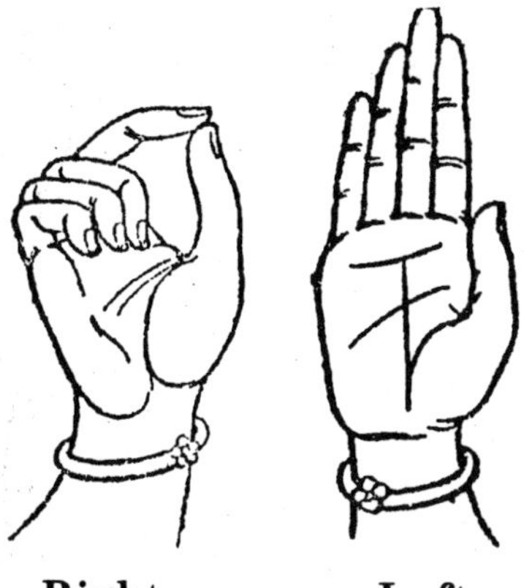

Right Left
Gold, Riches

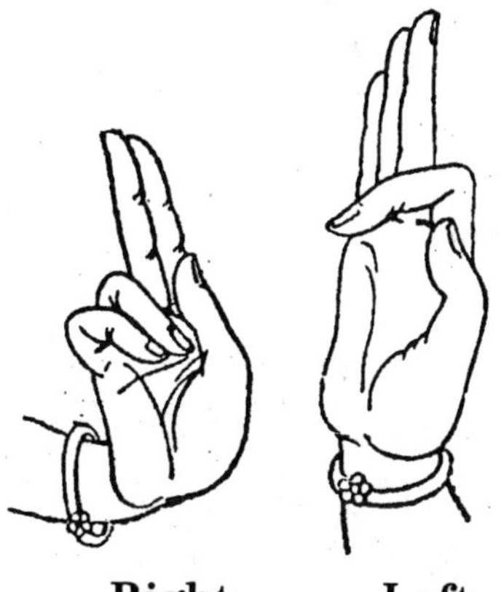

Right Left
Breeze

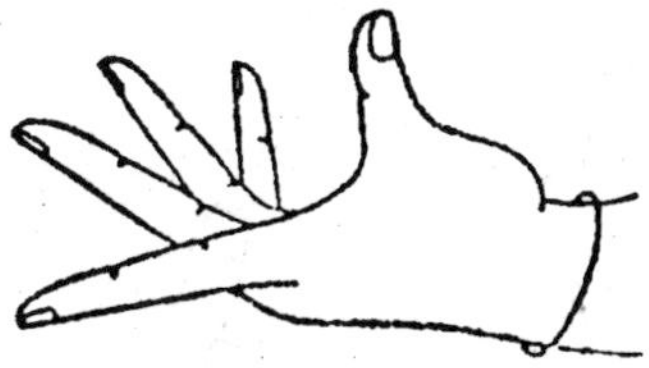

Good, Beautiful

A COMPARATIVE STUDY

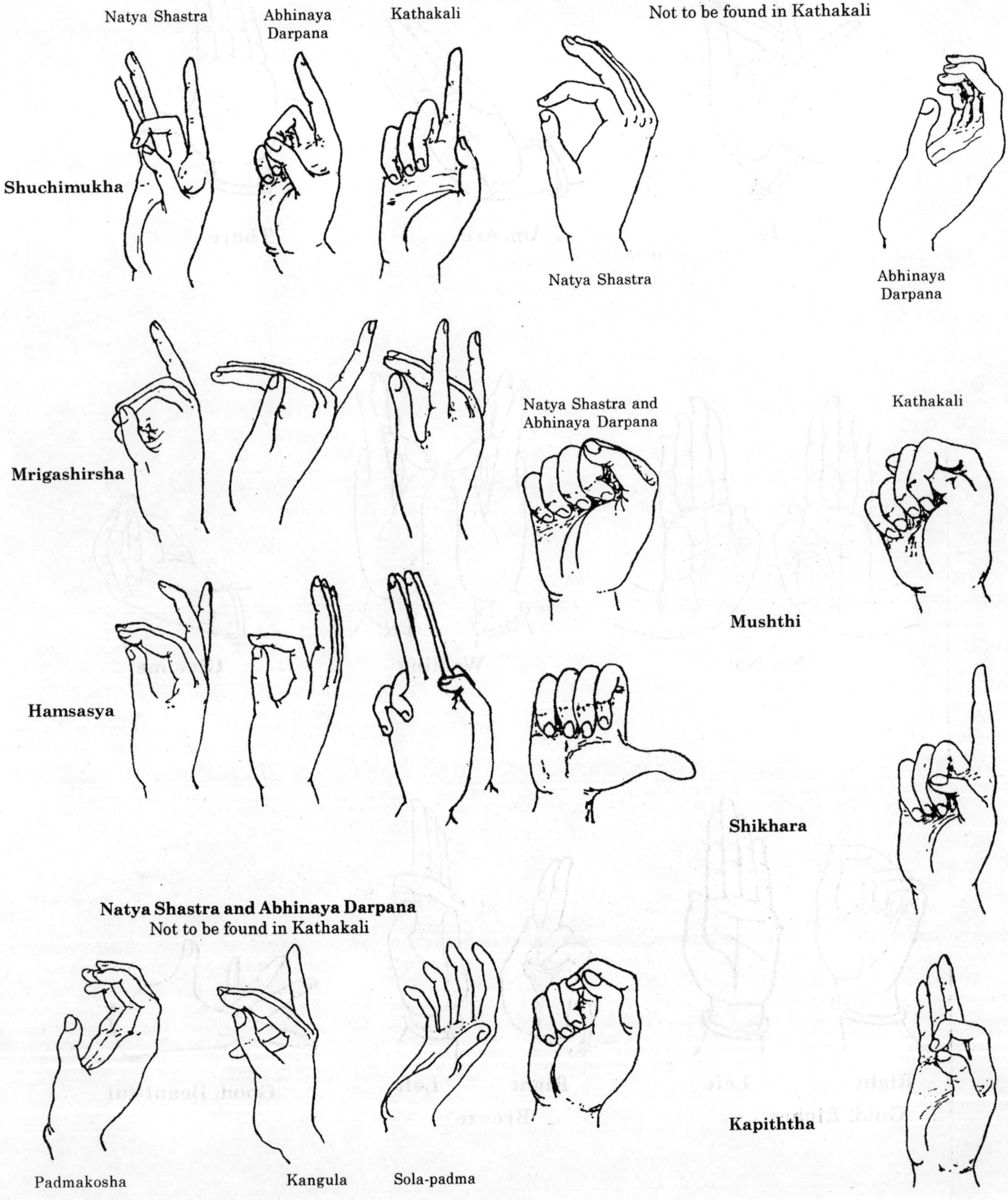

Same in the three Authorities

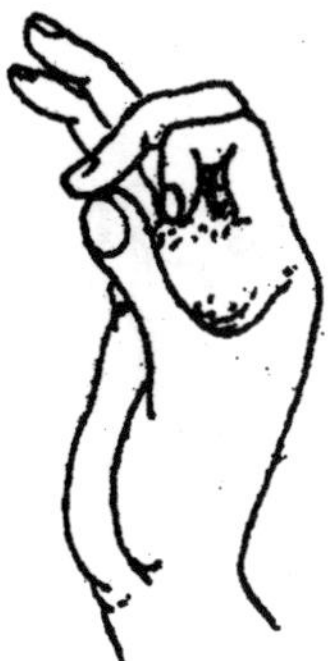

Natya Shastra and Abhinaya Darpana

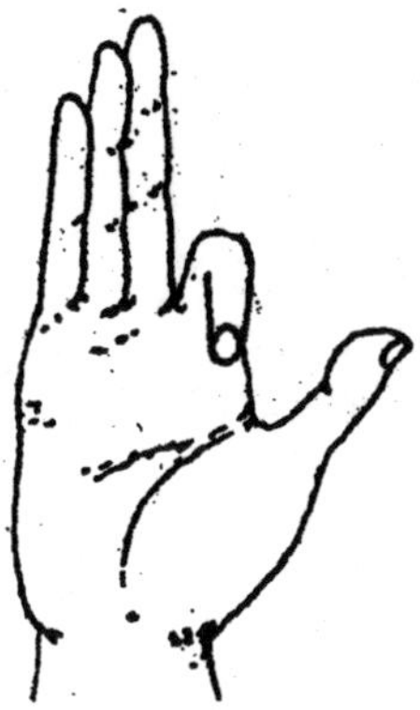

Kathakali

Bhramara

Katakamukha

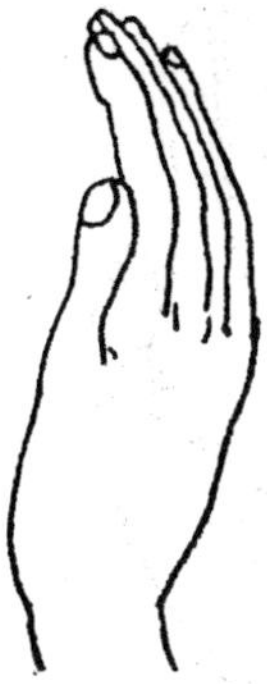

Sarpashirsha

Makula

Only in Kathakali

Mudra

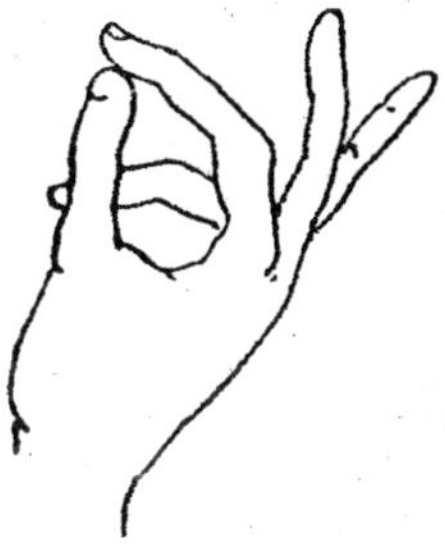

Makura

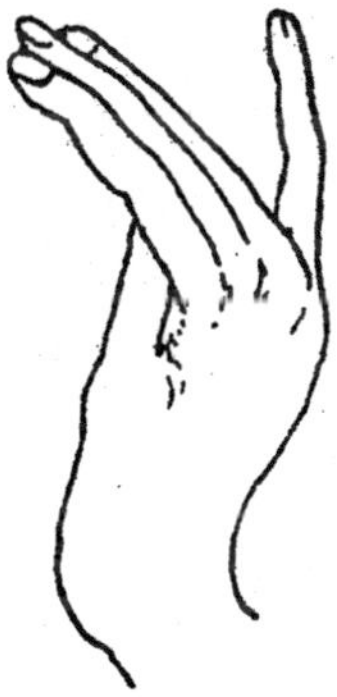

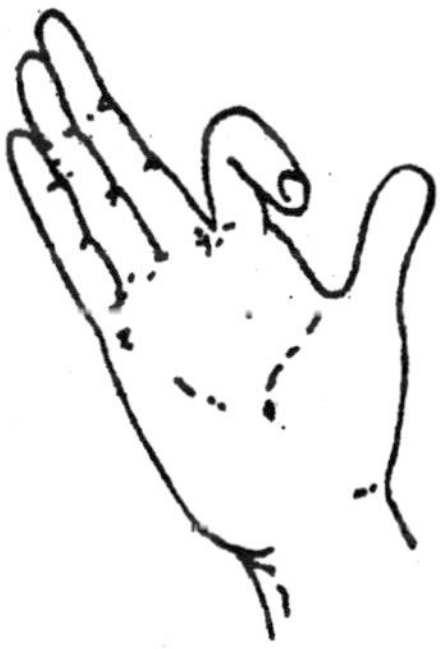

Hamsapaksha

Pallava

Only in Kathakali

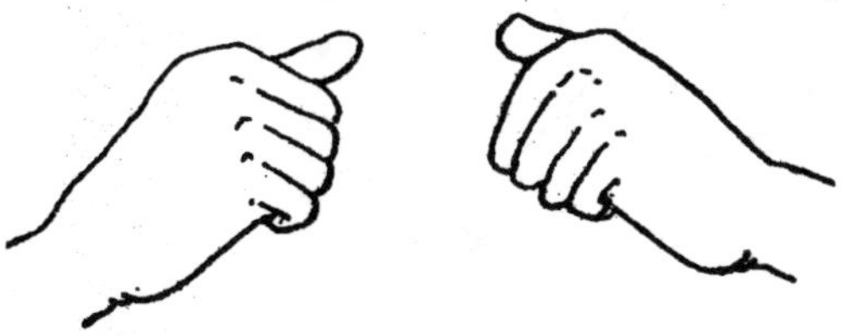

Vardhamana

Kataka

Not to be found in Kathakali

Natya Shastra

Kathakali

Urnanabha

Simha-Mukha

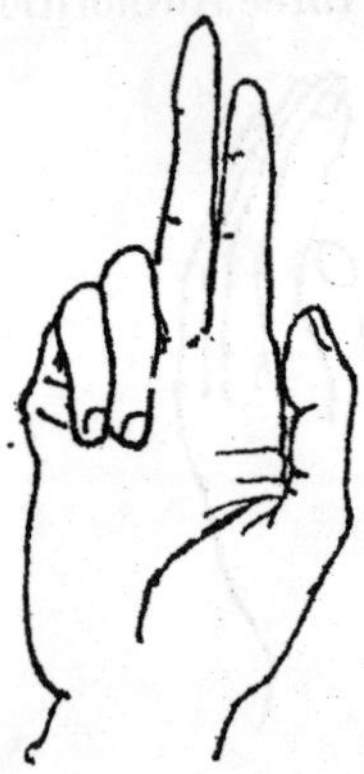

Ardhapataka

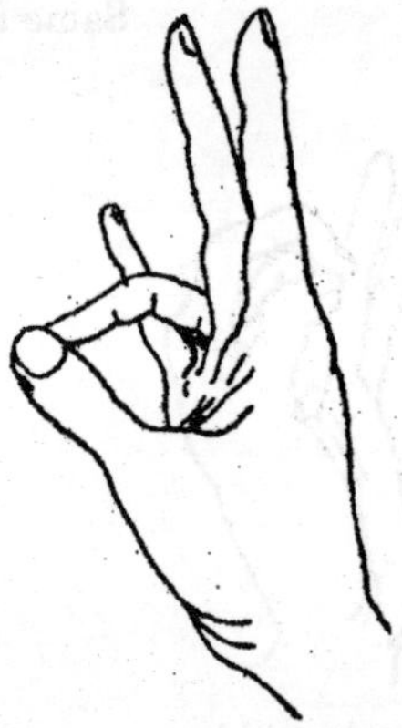

Mayura

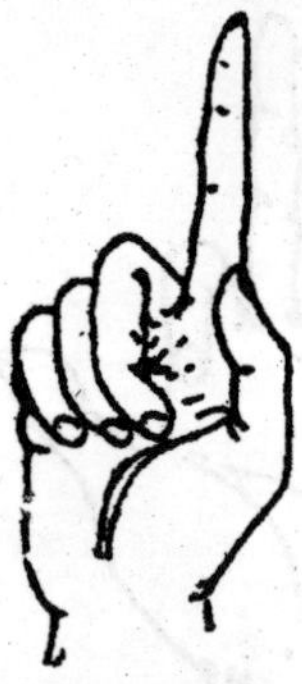

Ardhasuchi

Palli

Bana

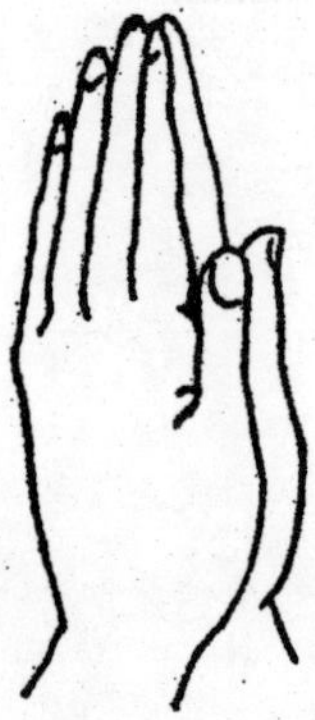

Anjali

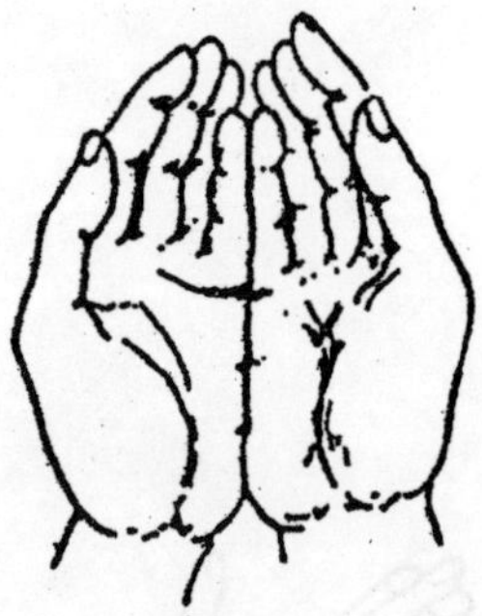

Kapota

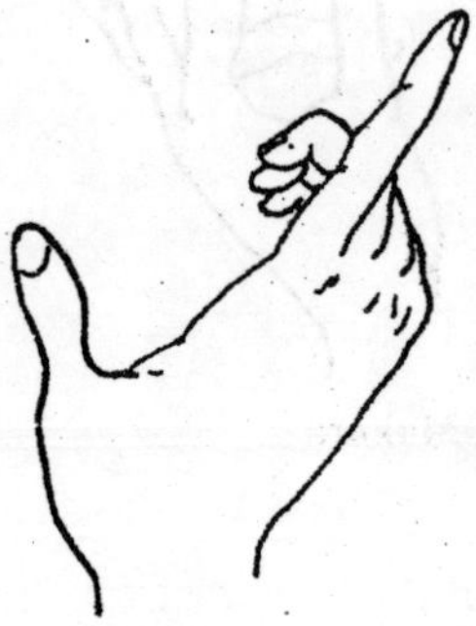

Chandrakala

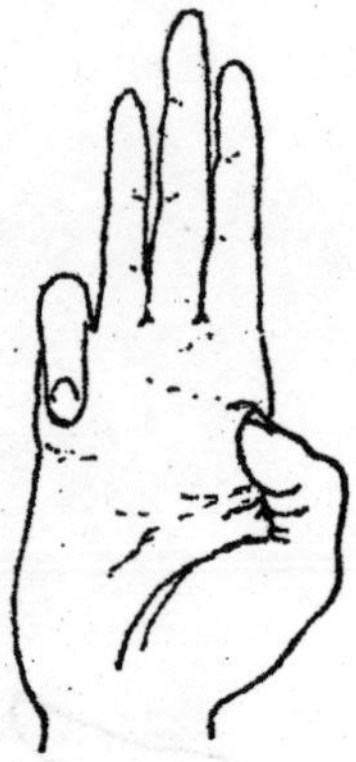

Trisula

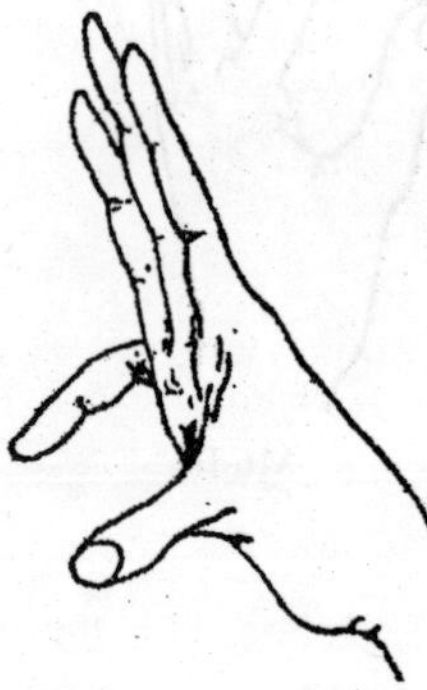

Vyaghra

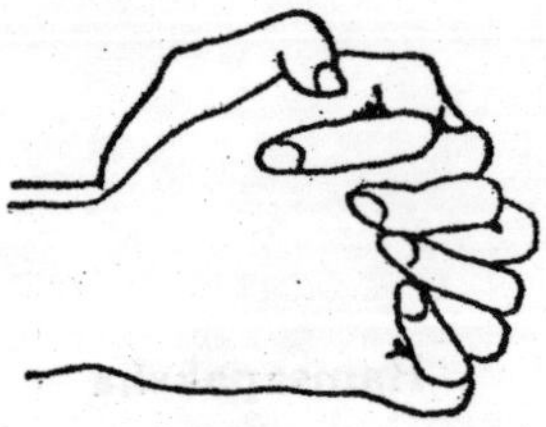

Karkata

Not to be found in Kathakali

Natya Shastra

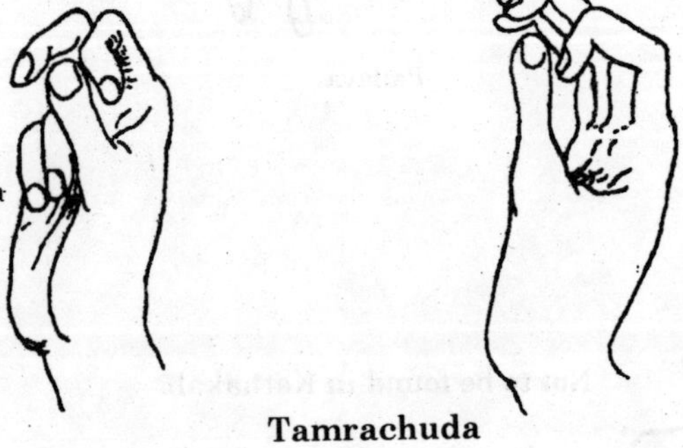

Abhinaya Darpana

Tamrachuda

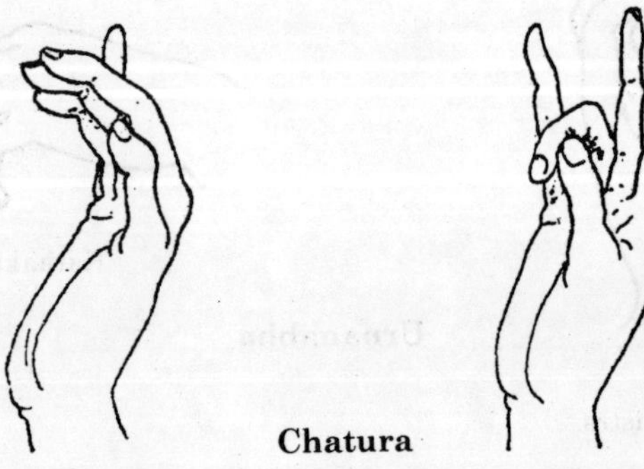

Chatura

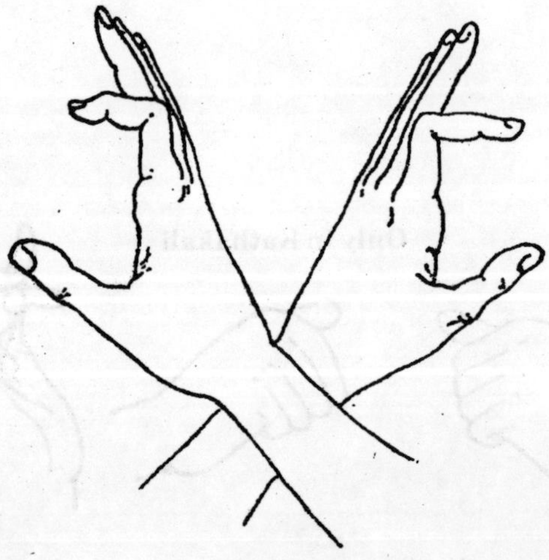

Shakata

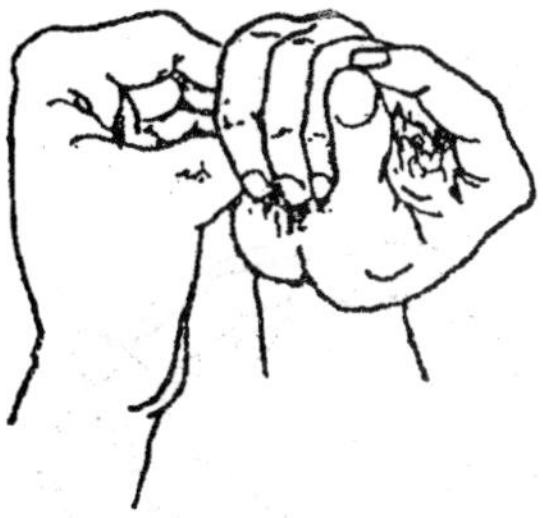

Nishedha

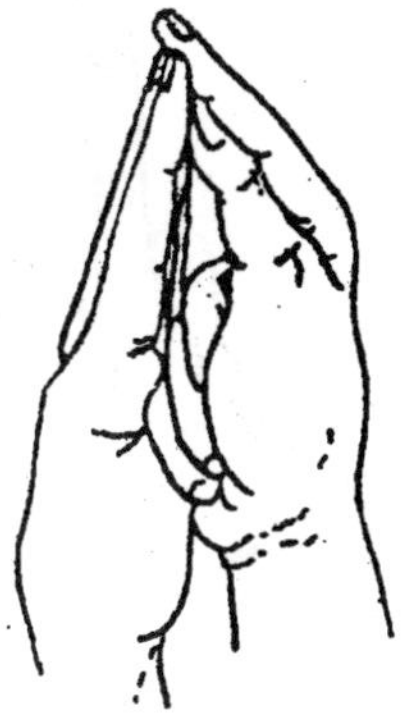

Shankha

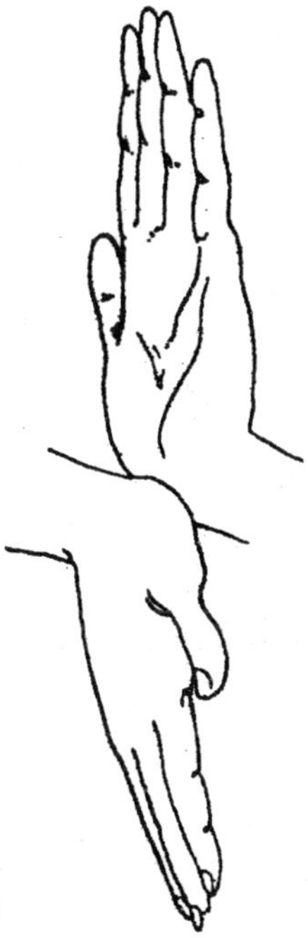

Swastika

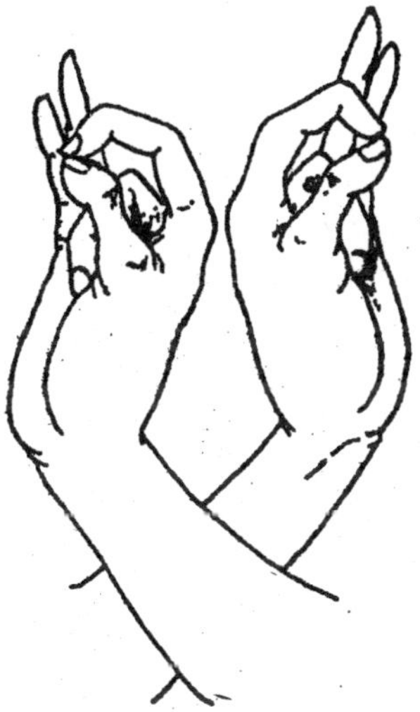

Katakavardhana

Pushpaputa

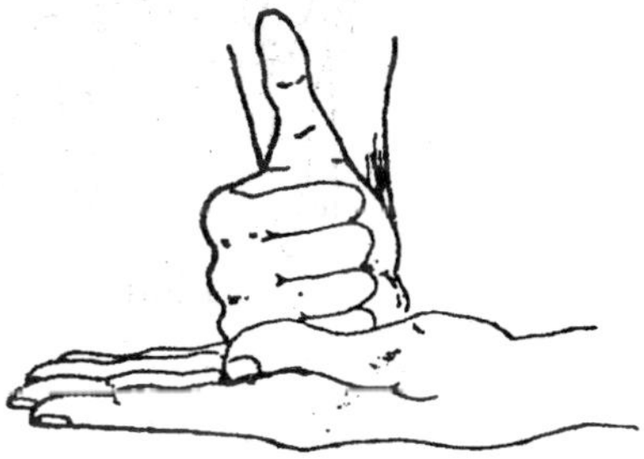

Shiva Linga

Kartari Swastika

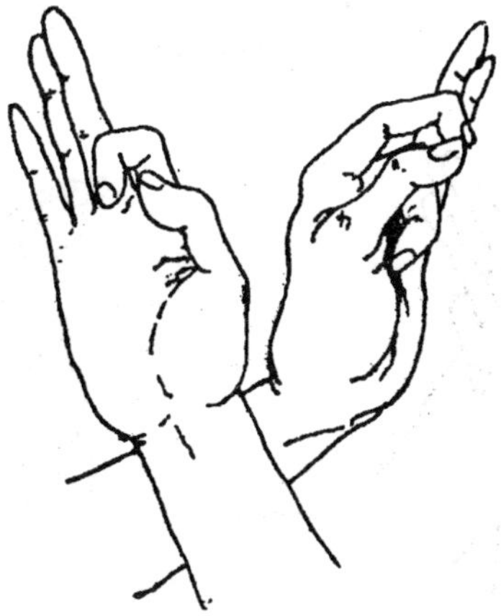

Arala Katakamukha

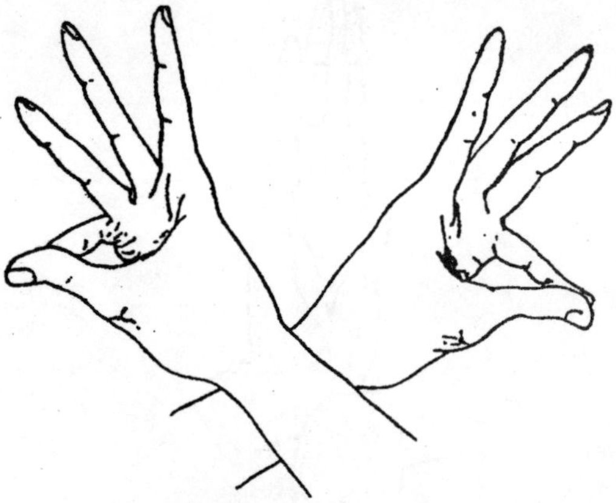

Nalini Padmakosha

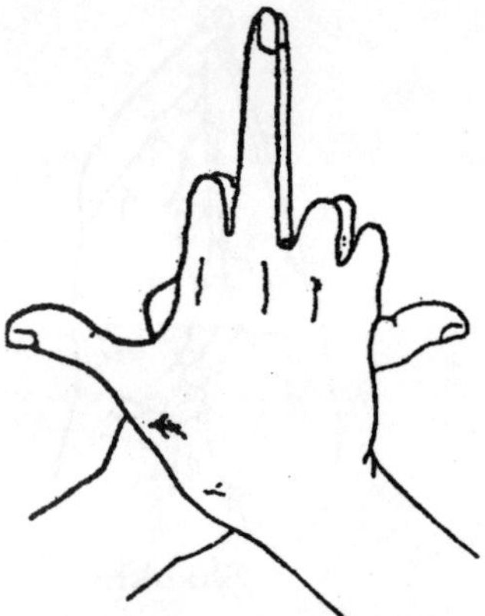

Makara

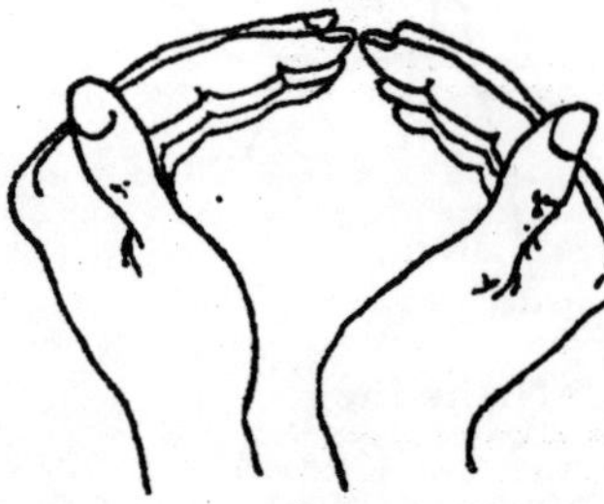

Kilaka

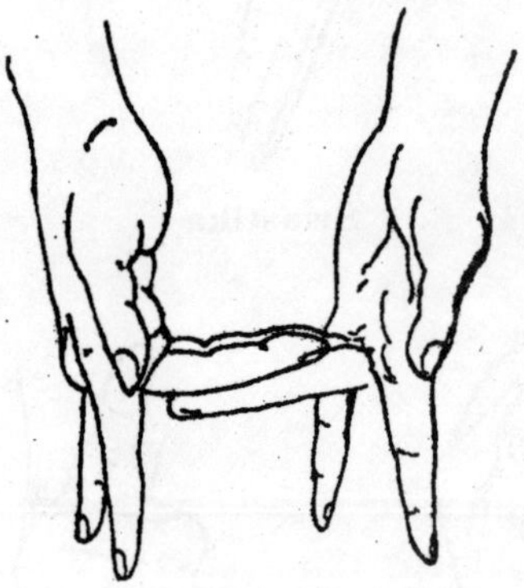

Khatwa

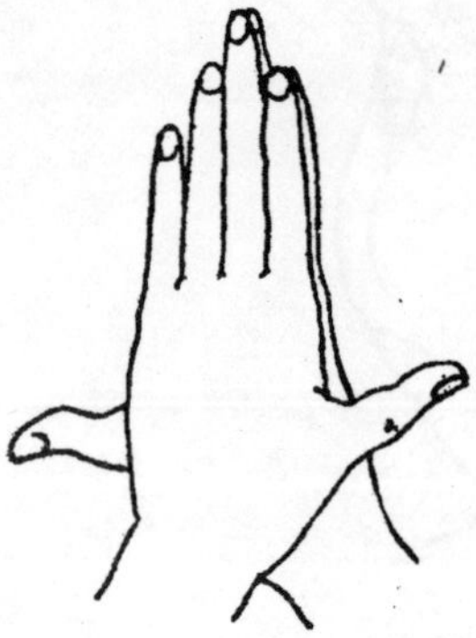

Matsa

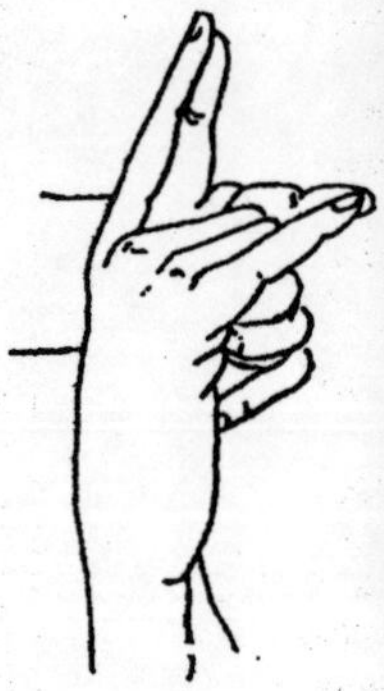

Kurma

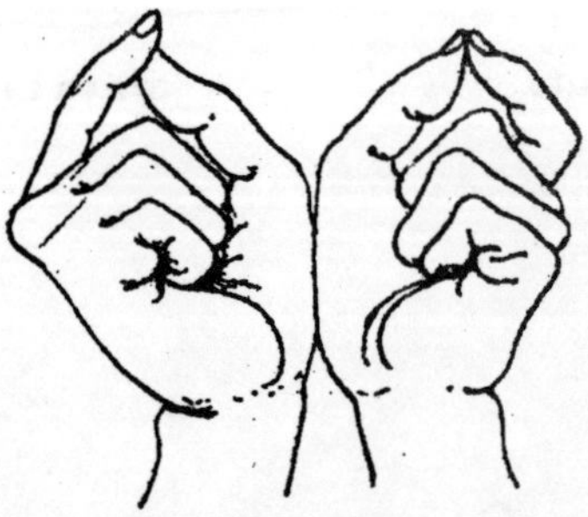

Bherunda

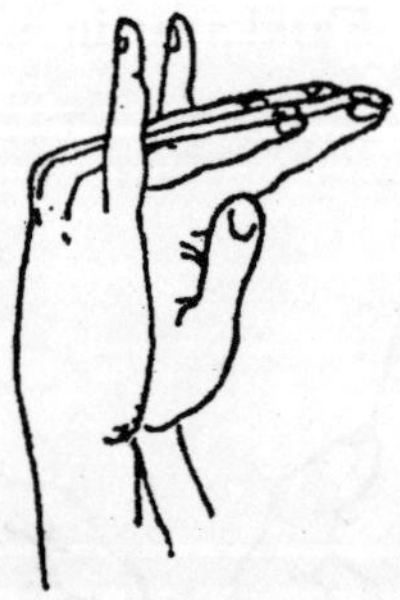

Varaha

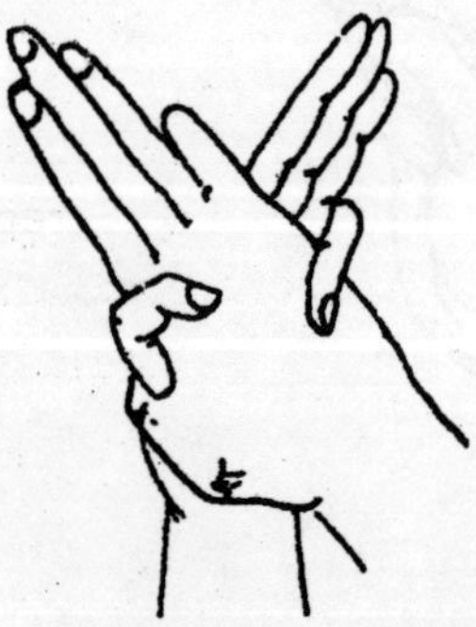

Chakra

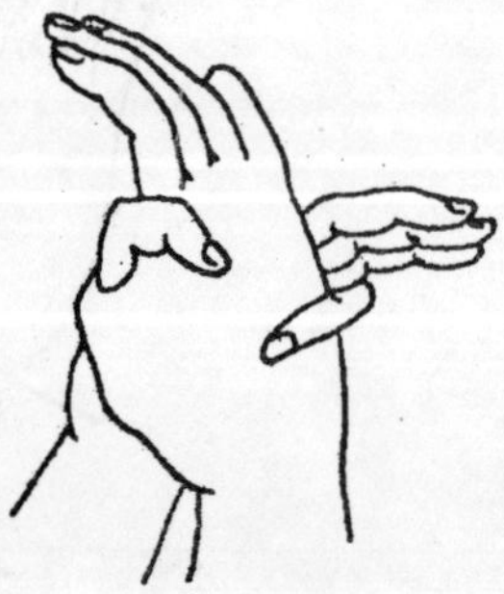

Gamputa

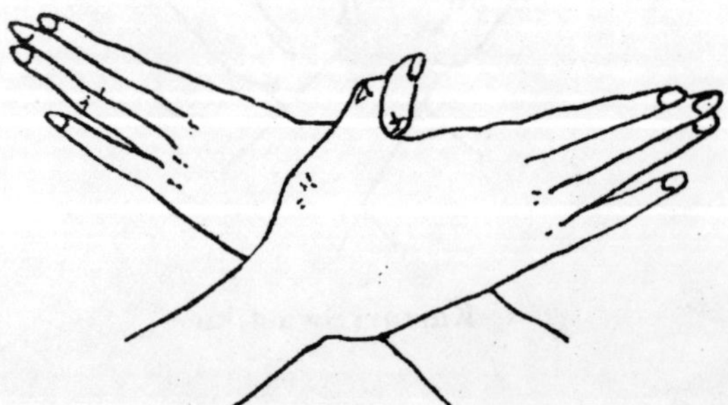

Garuda

2. Tripataka
3. Ardhachandra
4. Arala
5. Shukaturla
6. Mustha
7. Shikhara
8. Padmakosha
9. Sharpasirsha
10. Mrigasirsha
11. Chatura
12. Bhramara
13. Mukhla

2. The following gestures have some points of agreement as regards their application. They are :

1. Pataka
2. Tripataka
3. Ardhachandra
4. Mushti
5. Katakamukha
6. Padmakosha
7. Sarpasirsha
8. Mukula

3. The definition of the following gestures vary in both the works :

1. Kastrarimukha
2. Katakamukha
3. Kapritha
4. Shuchi
5. Kangrla
6. Alapadama
7. Alapallava
8. Hamsapaksha
9. Samdamsa
10. Tamrachuda

4. The following gestures of Natya Sastra have been sub-divided according to their usage and special instructions have been given as to how a gesture is to be used in different groups like Tripataka, Arala, Shuchimukha, Chatura and Samdamsa.

II. Combined Hand Gestures (Samyuta gestures)

Natya Sastra names 13 gestures of this class while Abhinaya Darpana gives twenty-three.

The two classification have eight common names they are :

1. Anjali
2. Kapota
3. Karkata
4. Swasthi
5. Dola
6. Pushpaputa
7. Ustranga
8. Vatakabardhara

As a result of the comparison of the combined gestures named similarly in both the works, we have the following facts.

The following gestures in both the works have the same definition and their application also agrees to a great extent. They are Anjali, Kapota, Karkata, Pushpaputa, the gesture named Pushpaputa is almost similarly defined in both the works.

The remaining three gestures are differently defined and applied in the two works.

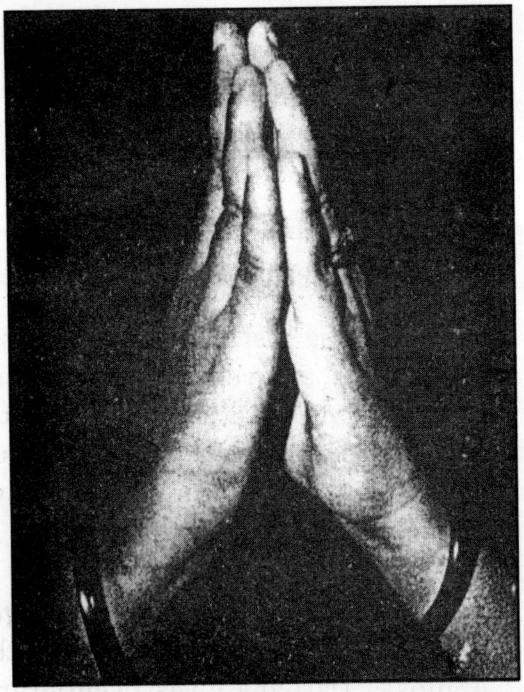

Anjali

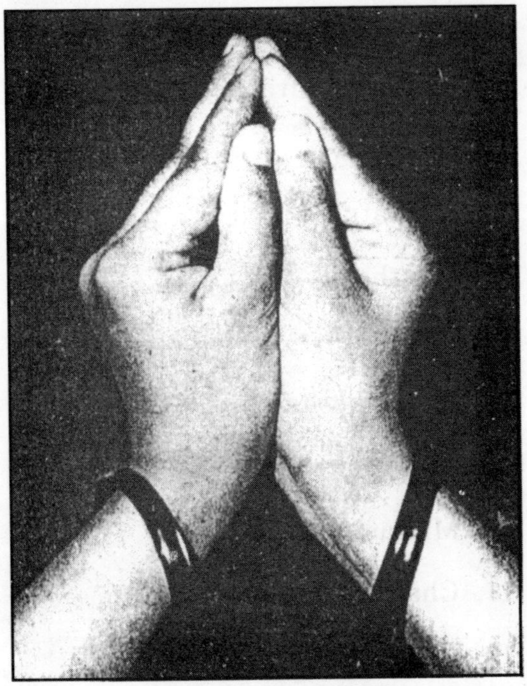

2. Kapota

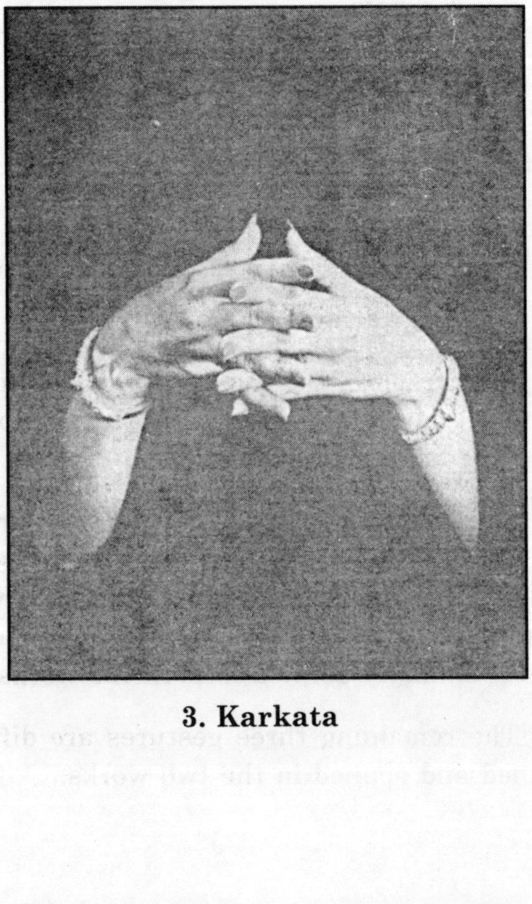

3. Karkata

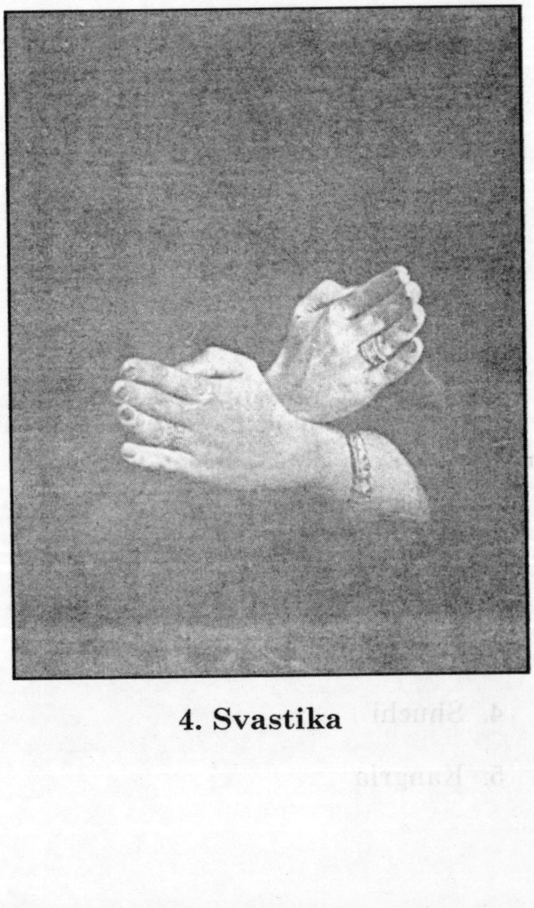

4. Svastika

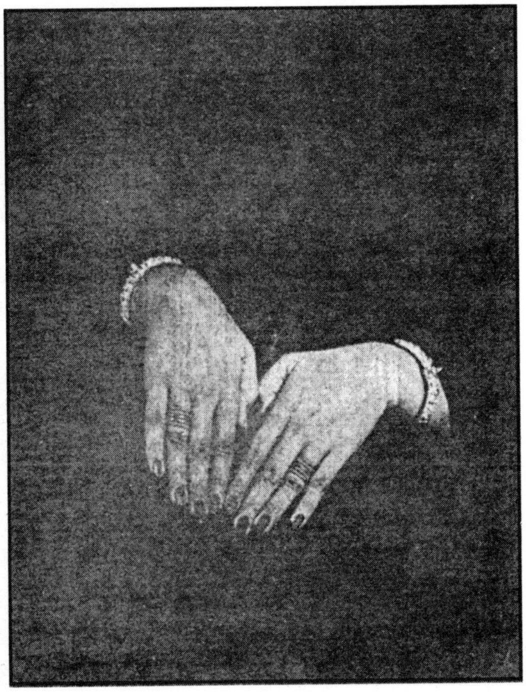

Dola

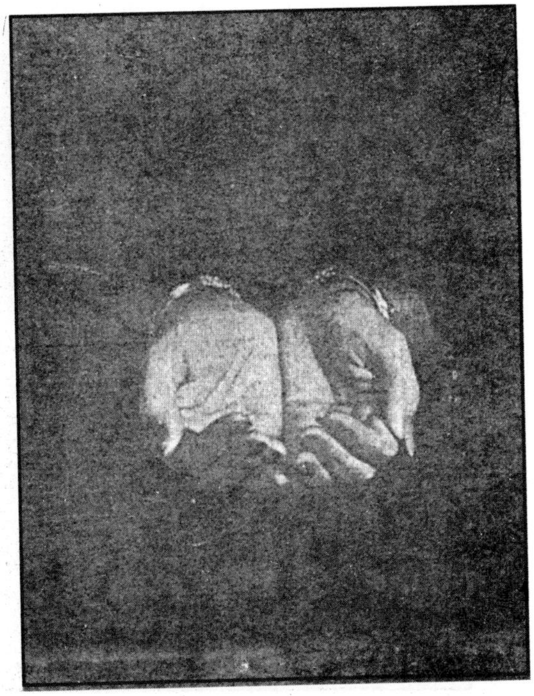

6. Utsanaga

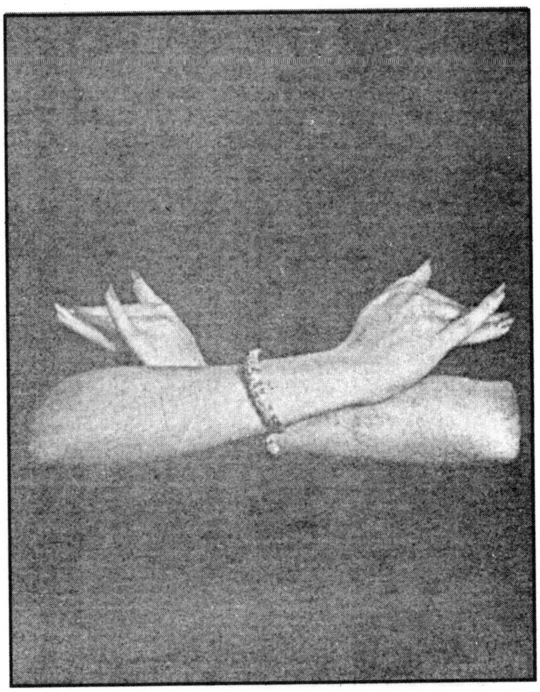

Utsanga

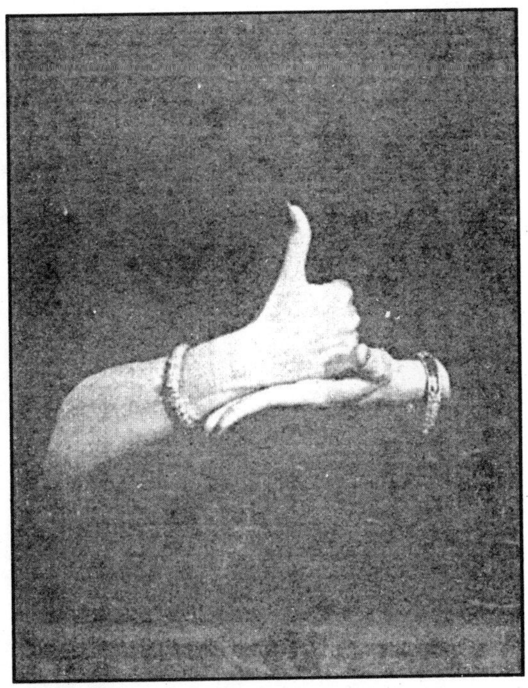

8. Dola

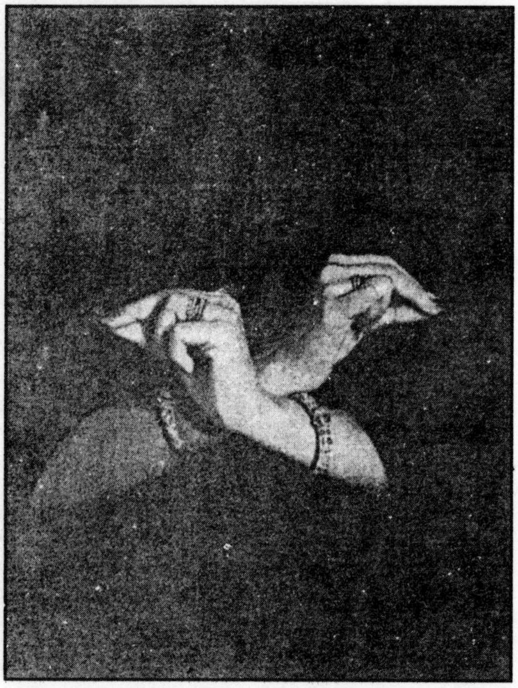

Kataka vardhana

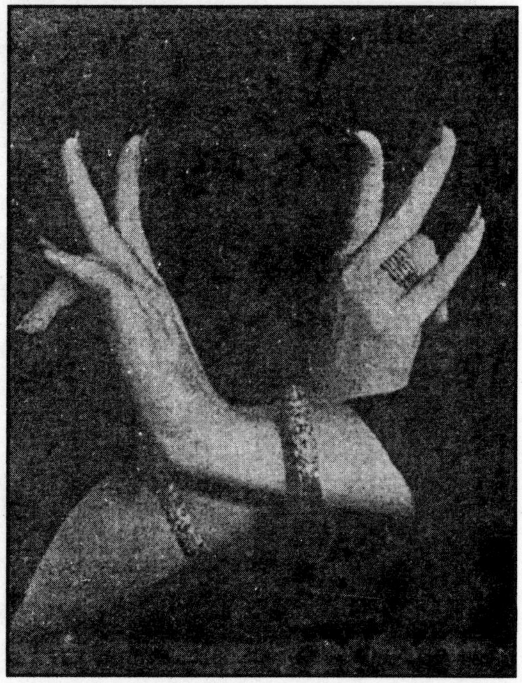

10. Makara

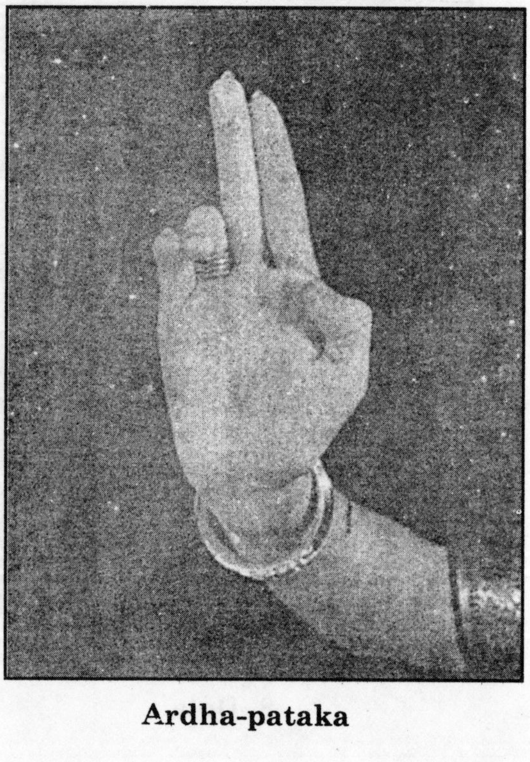

Ardha-pataka

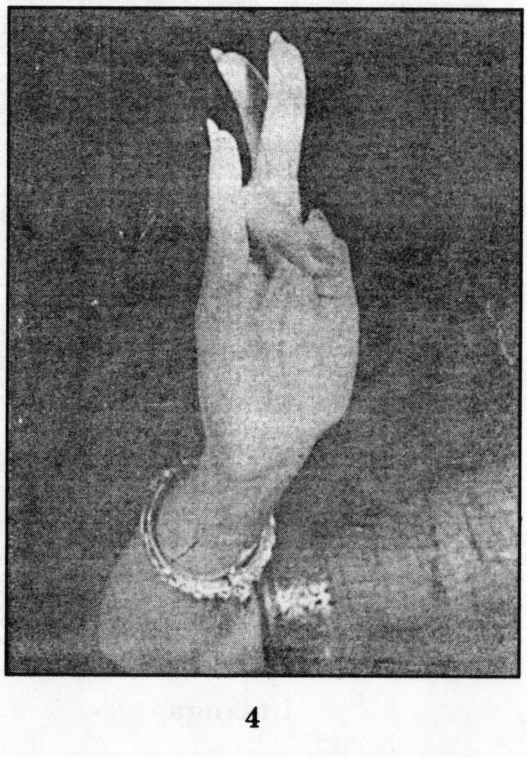

4

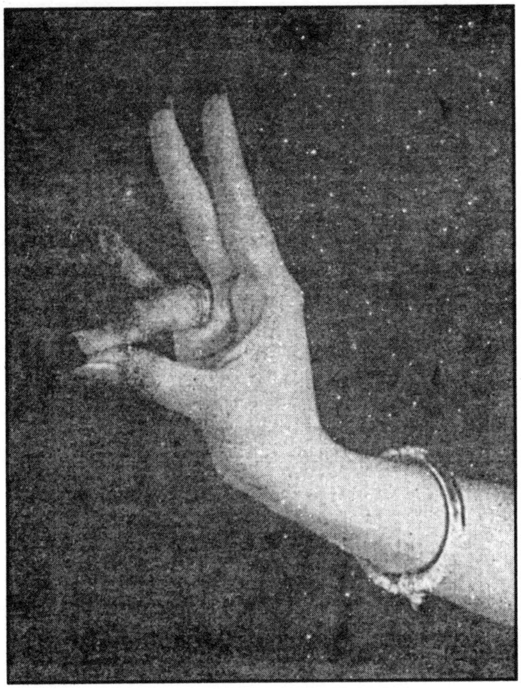

Mayura

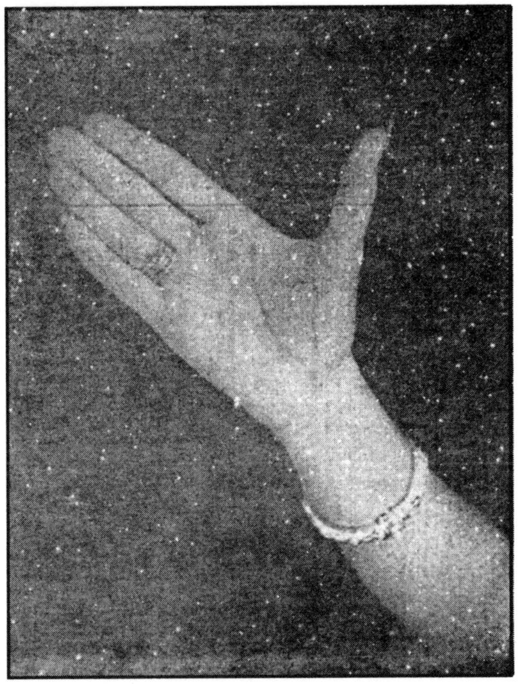

6

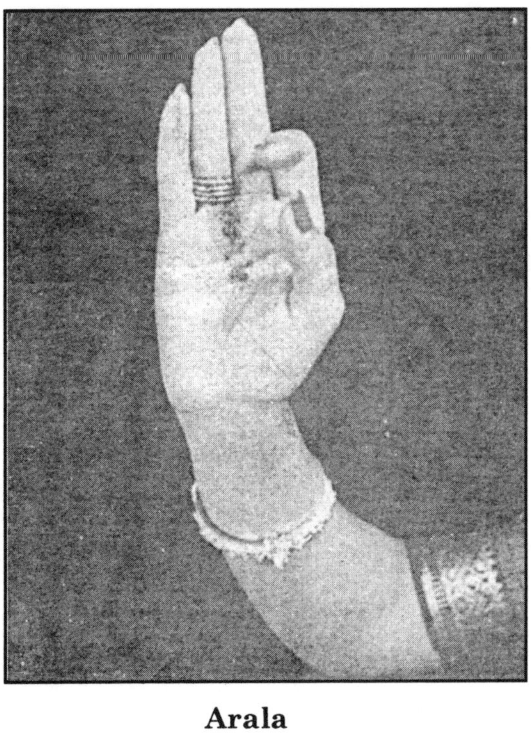

Arala

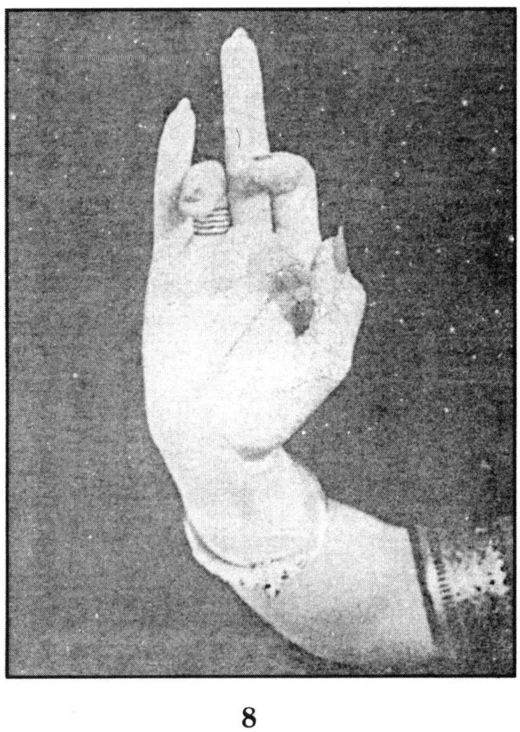

8

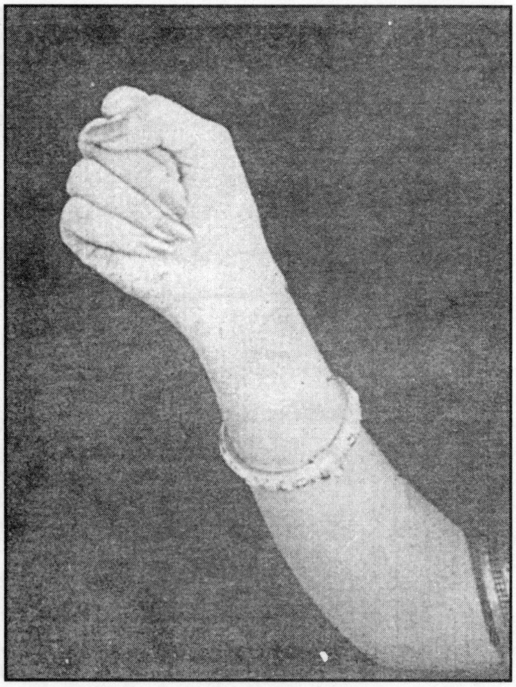

Mushti

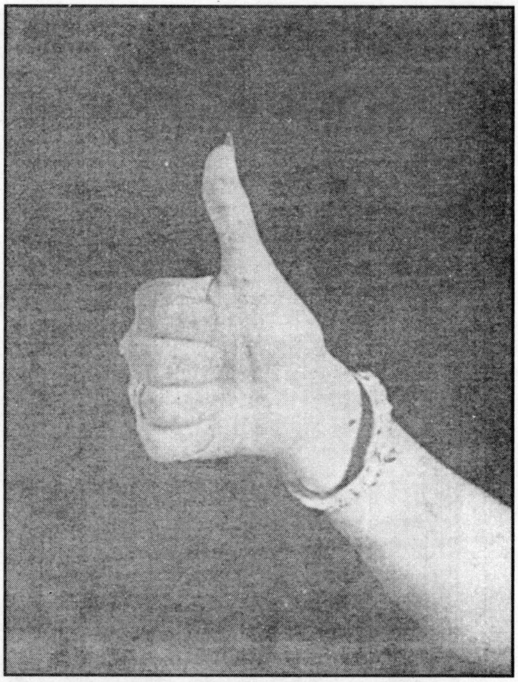

10

Kapittha

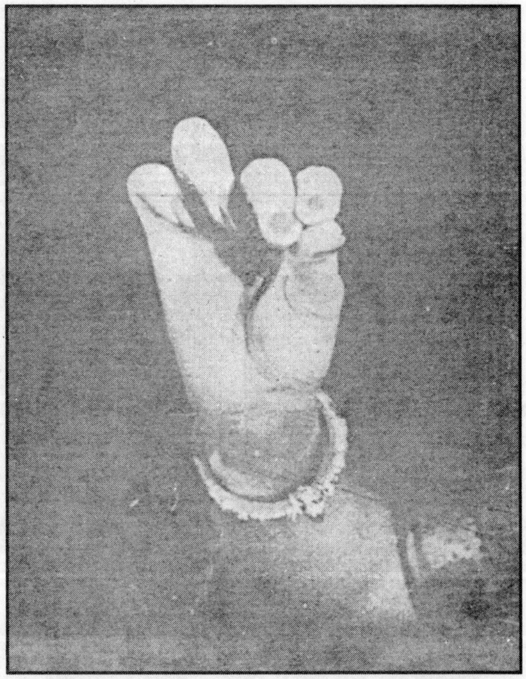

12

Suchi

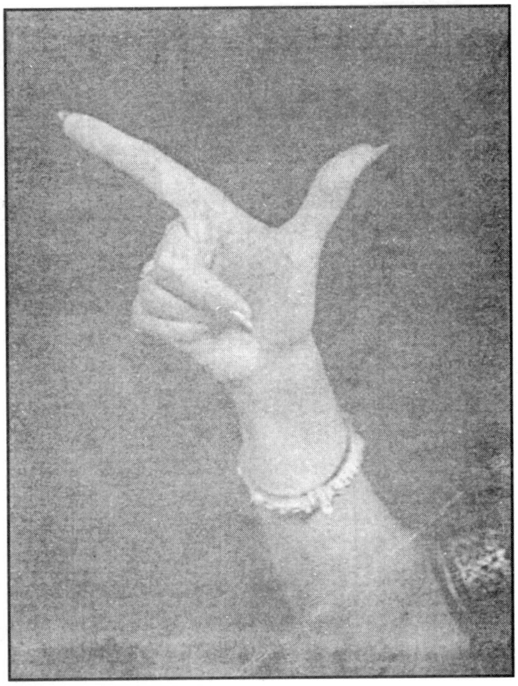

14

Shakata

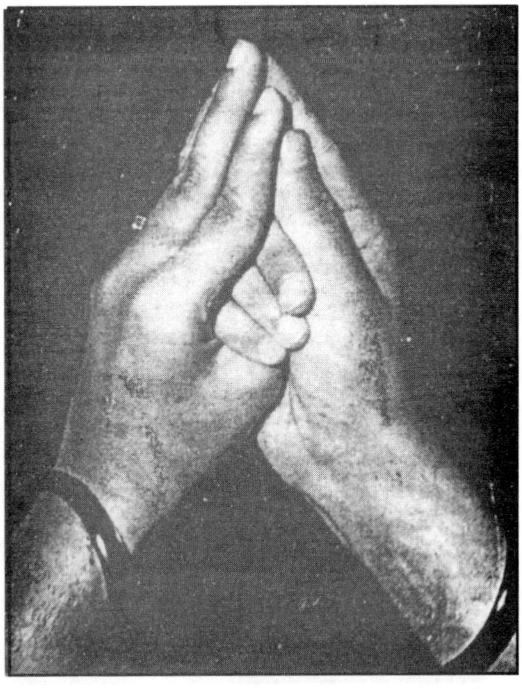

12

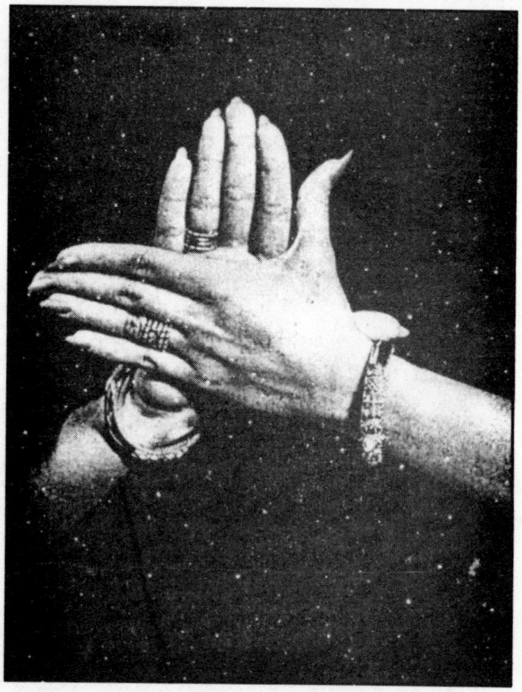

Chakra

Samputa

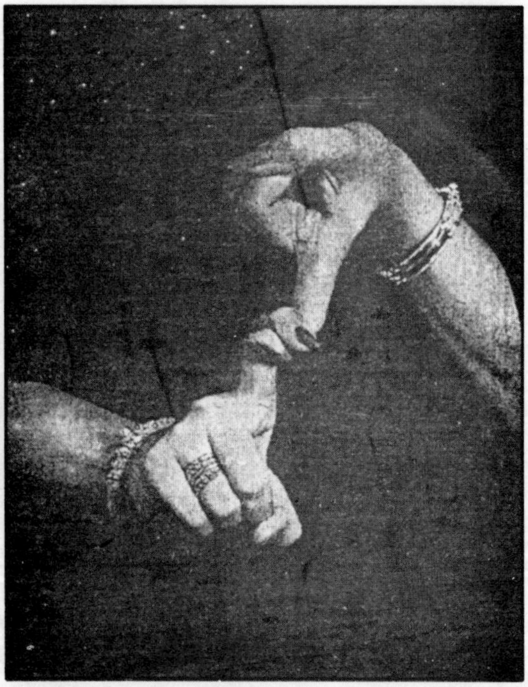

Pasha

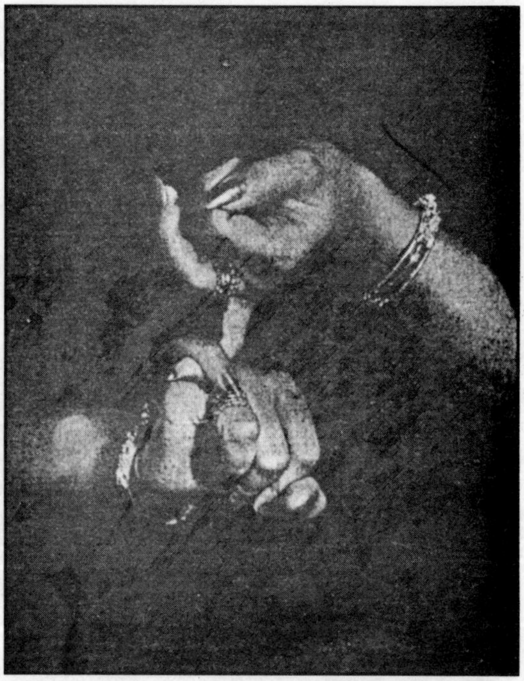

16

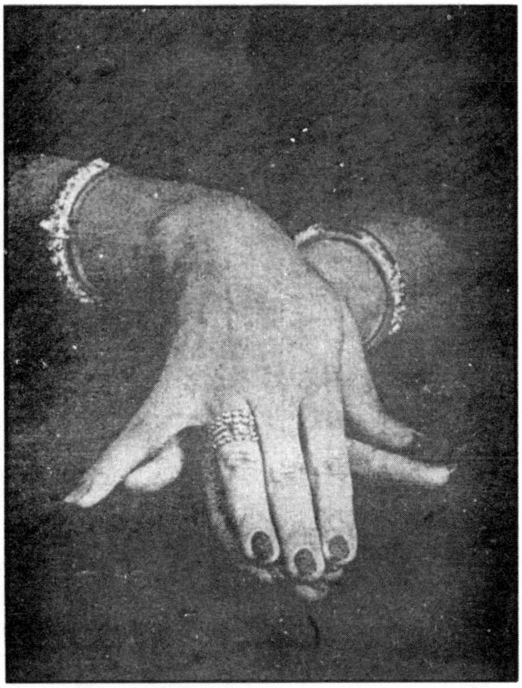

Matsya

18

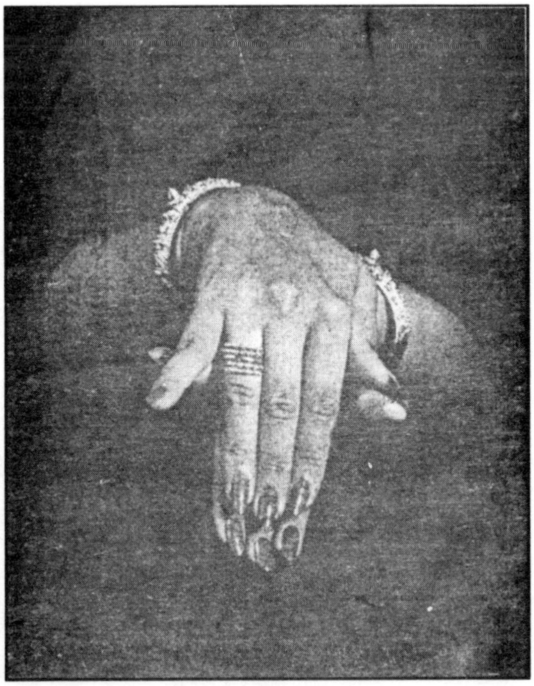

Varaha

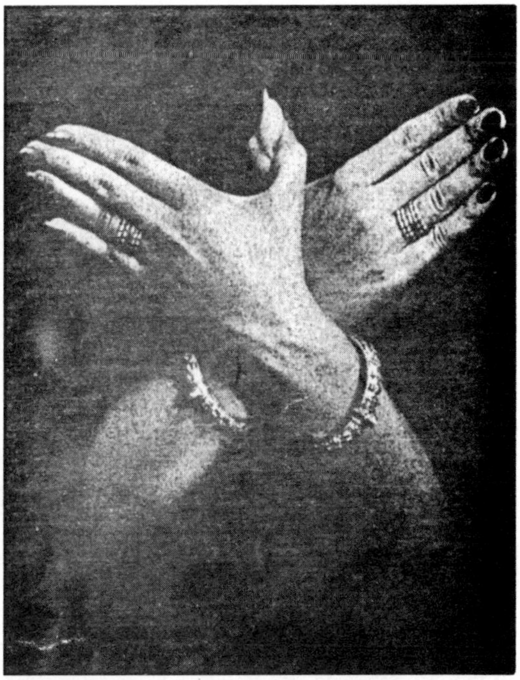

20

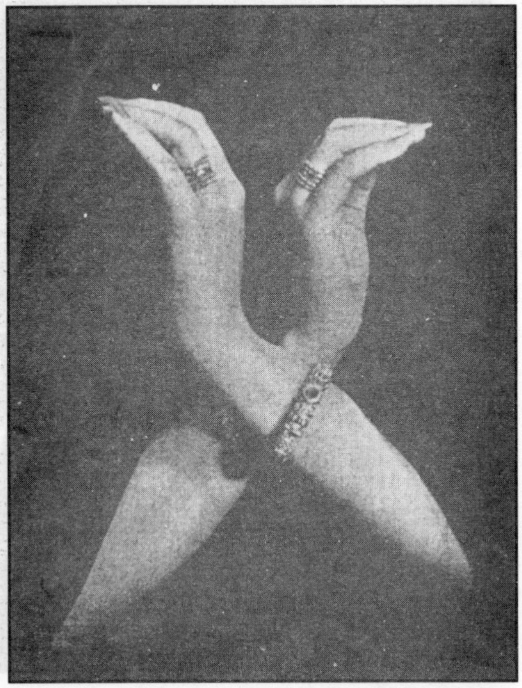

Naga-bandha

22

Mriga-shirsha

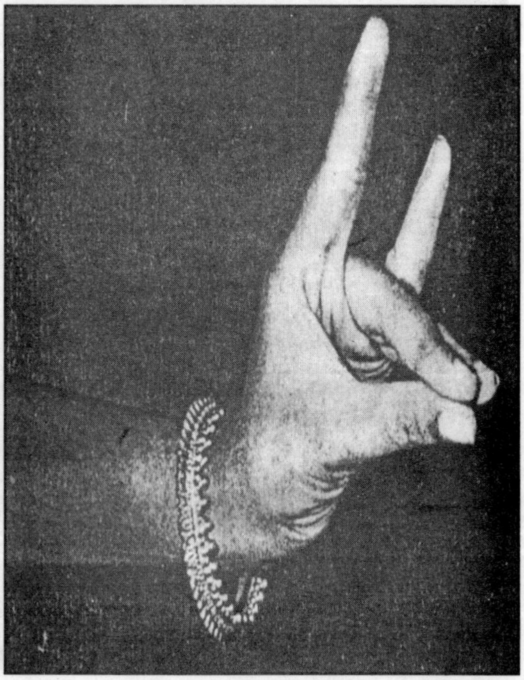

Simha-mukha

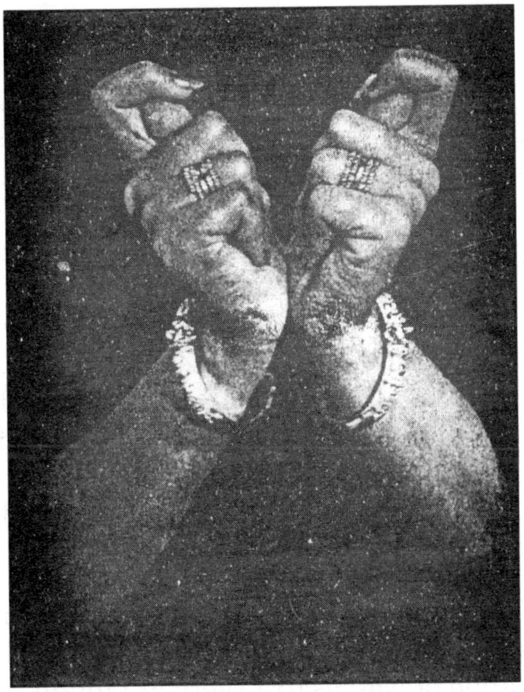

Bherunda

24

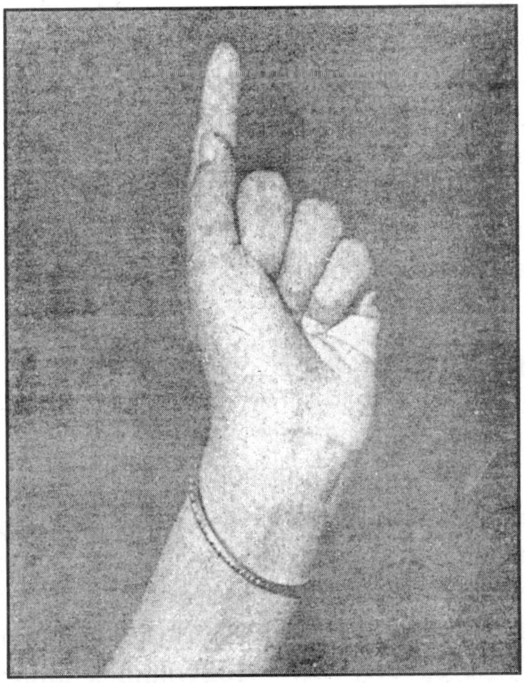

Ardha-suchika

III. Nritha Hastas

According to Natya Sastra, they are 27 in number and different from single hand and combined hand gestures.

Their number in Abhinaya Darpana is 13 and they are not different from the single and combined hand gestures. For 6 of them namely Pataka, Tripataka, Shikhara, Alapadma and Hamsasya are the same as single hand gestures of the same name and the remaining given namely, Anjali, Swastika, Dola, Vatkabardhna, Chakata, Pasha and Kilaka are the same as combined hand gestures of the same name.

Thus they are sixty-four according to Natya Sastra, Fifty-one according to Abhinaya Darpana.

Hastas—Movements of Hands

The gestures of the hands are the natural means of expressing emotions. They are so symbolic that they actually form the speech or language in dance, and convert the song-word to sign-word. The dancer weaves a tapestry, narrates a major event, conveys the meaning of the lyrics for which she is dancing through the various hastas or hand gestures. They are informative, expressive and interpretive aspects of dance. The graceful movement of hands blended aesthetically with music, literature and rhythm, brings out all the phases of life effectively. In Indian dance when the hand is moved, it moves and sticks to a position with a specific purpose. No gesture is made, without a definite meaning.

The dancer considers the palm of the hand as the most important centre of hand expression. Showing to the spectators in various disposals of the fingers is the characteristic of gesture language. The wrist becomes a pivot for the movement of the hand in any direction. The motions are further supplemented by expressive use of elbows. After learning the dance techniques thoroughly the dancer uses her hand so easily to specify the meaning as though it is spontaneous action. But the science of dance prescribes the position, the movements of hand with complexity and multiplicity of uses. Every hand gesture is significant and can be represented with various meanings. The language of hand gestures is not only used in dance or drama, but also in ritualistic worship and to represent the icons, since ancient times. There is a prevailing tendency to use the terms Hastas and Mudras in the same condition. But the Natyasastra does not tolerate this confusion. It is true that both Hasta and Mudra refer to features of hand, but the words belong to two entirely different universe of discourse. Hasta has a strictly aesthetic connotation. It is the only term to be used when a gesture of hand in dancing is to be indicated. Mudra on the other hand is used in iconography and in Buddhistic and Tantric theology.

The Samyuta and Asamyuta Hastas are used in expressive dance. In Manmohan Ghosh's translation of Natyasatra there are totally 67 hand gestures classified into 24 single handed, 13 double handed and 30 Nritta hastas. In the Baroda edition of Natyasastra only 29 Nritta hastas are mentioned. Sangitaratnakara listed 70 hand gestures adding three more gestures to the list of Natyasastra. They are Dvisikhara, Nikunchaka and Varadabhaya. Hastamuktavali gives 30 single hand gestures, out of which 25 gestures are as in Abhinayadarpana and the other 5 gestures are not found in any other dance treatise. They are Kadamba, Krishnasara, Mukha, Ghurnika, Anukusa and Tantramukha. Fourteen double hand gestures are mentioned in the same treatise.

In Bharatarnava twenty-seven single handed gestures, sixteen double handed gestures and twenty Nritta hastas are mentioned. Abhinayadarpana has given a list of 28 single handed gestures and 24 double handed gestures. Nritta hastas are not mentioned under a separate heading. But in Bharatarnava 27 gestures prescribed by Bhaspati and 21 additional hand gestures are given. Arnava manuscript known as Bharatasara Sangraha by Krshnabhupala mentions 402 complex hand gestures with their multiple uses. In Abhinayadarpana we find a detailed description of Deva hastas (Hastas signifying the deities), Dasavatara hastas (hastas denoting the incarnation of Mahavishnu), Navagraha hastas (hastas signifying 9 planets), Jati hastas (hastas showing creed and caste), Bandhu hastas (gestures interpreting the relation).

Whatever may be the classification of hand gestures explained by various writers from time to time it appears that they are all derived from the single one. Now, a brief description of them.

Arala Hasta: Bring the thumb in touch with the first finger in flat pose. It makes Arala Hasta.

Katakmukha: In this pose the last finger remains straight, the third half bent, second in touch with the palm and the first with thumb.

Mirg Sheersh: In this pose the second and the third fingers are brought in touch with the thumb and the first and the fourth are kept straight.

Sarp Mukha Back: In this pose the back side of the hand is brought under vision and the fingers are kept open and little bent.

Padam Kosh: In this pose the fingers remain open and scattered and bent towards the palm.

Mukul Hasta: If the tips of all fingers are brought in touch with each other it is called the Mukul Hasta.

Sarp Sheersh: If the fingers are bent followed from Pataka Hasta it is called the Sarp Sheersh.

Bhramar Hasta: In this pose the first and the other fingers are kept straight. It is called Bhramar Hasta.

Musthi: In Musthi pose all the four fingers are kept closed and the thumb over the first finger.

Mukul Mukh Musthi: If the tip of the thumb is brought out through the gap between the second and third finger it is called the Mukul Mukh Musthi.

Musthi second: If the fingers are kept closed and brought in touch with the palm pressed by thumb it is called the Musthi second.

Mayur Hasta of Both Hands: If the first and second fingers are kept straight and the third and fourth called the Mayur hasta of both hands.

Anjali: The two pataka hands united together make Anjali pose.

Poses of Hands

There are about 250 poses of hands but how many of them are used in dance depends upon the theme of the story for dance. Taking all the things together there are 67 essential poses–24 of the hand, 13 of both hands and 30 of dancing pose. Some important poses commonly used in dance are as follows :

1. ***Pataka***:-Spread all the fingers like a flag. It will show a Pataka pose.
2. ***Soochi Mukha***:-Keep the finger straight and other three bent. Bring the thumb in touch with straight finger. It is Soochi Mukha.
3. Bring the 3rd and 4th fingers in touch with the thumb and the other two straight. It is called the half flag pose.
4. ***Sandesh***:-Keep the first finger bent and the remaining fingers and the thumb straight. It is called Sandesh.
5. ***Mayur Hasta***: Keep the third finger in bent pose and the remaining fingers straight. It is called the Mayur Hasta or the pose of a peacock.
6. ***Shuktund***:-Bring the second, third and fourth fingers in touch with the thumb and the first finger in half bent pose.
7. ***Soochi Hasta***:-Bring the 2nd, 3rd and 4th fingers under the thumb and the first finger straight. It is called the Soochi Hasta second pose. This pose is nearly the same with a difference that in Soochi Mukha the thumb touches the first finger while in Soochi Hasta the finger remains under the thumb.

The hand gestures mentioned in Natyasastra and *Abhinayadarpana* are illustrated by the dance sculptures, paintings and the contemporary dancers. From time immemorial the Natyacharyas and the dance traditions or sampradaya made use of the hand gestures of the two texts and brought into practice the multiplicity and combination of hand movements. It is appropriate to discuss the categories of hastas presented in *Natyasastra* and *Abhinayadarpana*.

Asamyuta Hastas: Single hand gestures

The single hand gestures are the real essence of dance language. They are used to symbolize so many things, animals, animate and inanimate objects, gods, emotions *etc.* they are used according to the situation either holding up or inverting down or kept horizontally or vertically. The same gesture when used in different directions conveys altogether different meanings. They are used by both the hands but they are not combined like double hand gestures. When the hands are placed near different angas and upangas they imply different concepts and meanings. The following are the Asamyukta Hastas described in Natyasastra and Abhinaya-darpana.

1. Pataka (Flat)

The principle hand gesture used at the beginning of a dance, to denote clouds, a forest, bosom, might, peace, a river, heaven, moonlight, wave, an oath, sword, palm leaf, strength, sunlight, silence, entrance, great joy and saying 'I too' or 'We too'. While pointing downwards it represents anything that is closed, covered, protected or concealed. When the same gesture moves up and down for a number of times it signifies the speedy movements of waves, the breaking of the water against the shore and flood. The palms of both Pataka hands rubbing against each other shows that anything washed, pressed cleaned, pounded and holding the hill uprooting. The rechaka of this hand represents many things such as crowd, height, flight of birds, drum beating and other uses in practice.

2. Tripataka (Three parts of the flat)

This hand gesture is used to denote the holding of a trident, turning round, crown, flower, tree, light, invocation, stroking the hair, arrow, lamp, to bid goodbye, raising up, salutation, sipping the tears, arranging the tilaka, touching the hair, to cover the nose, mouth and ear.

3. Kartarimukha (Face of the arrow shaft)

This is used to express opposition, disagreement, separation of lovers, falling down, creeper, buffalo, deer, fly, elephant, hill top. While handling downwards the gesture in single hand or both the hands indicate decorating the feet, showing the way, arranging the tilaka. When the middle finger is bent backwards it indicates death, turning round, trust and guess.

4. Ardhachandra (Half moon)

It indicates a young tree, digit of the moon, holding a conch, jar bracelet, driving out by force, showing exertion, the thinness and fatness of the waist. Women by this hand should represent girdle, waist, hips, face talapatra (a type of ear-ring) and ear-rings, wearing bangles, holding mirror, ear of an elephant, *etc.*

5. Arala (Bent)

This hand gesture is used to show courage, pride, zeal, beauty, steadiness, heavenly objects, favourable states, to express nectar, drinking poison, dressing the hair and decorating the face. The two Arala hands represent the preliminaries of marriage. When Arala hands are held in Svastika position (Crossed) it indicates the circle, things arranged on the ground, the crowd, calling, asking not to come, smelling sweet, good things and removing sweat. Women can use Arala hand in place of Tripataka.

6. Sukatunda (Parrot's beak)

It is used to represent to signify 'Not I', 'Not you', 'Not to be done' *etc.*, invocation and farewell which held horizontally it expresses the sense of shooting an arrow, mystery, anger symbolically used by Brahma the creator, fighting and the row.

7. Musti (Fist)

It represents blows, exercise as in fights, exit pressing holding a sword, staff, spear, holding a book, Yama (the God of death) to express the justice, victory, valour and like emotions.

8. Sikhara (Spine)

It is used to denote holding of reins, whips, goad and bow, throwing a spike, applying colour to lower lip or showing the lips in amorous action raising up hair, showing pride, vigour, questioning, silence, sound by a bell, pillar, husband, saying no, embrace, hero, the number four, spire and intensity.

9. Kapitah (Elephant apple)

It is used to denote holding weapons like sword, bow, discus, javelin, spear, club, spike, thunderbolt, arrows, signifying true and wholesome deeds, holding cymbals, flowers, rope offering lights, milk, in gait of dance, winding, ponding seeds. To represent Lakshmi (the goddess of wealth) and Saraswathi.

10. Katakamukha (opening in a link)

This hand gesture is used to present sacrifice, umbrella, oblation, drawing up reins, fanning, holding a mirror, drawing decorative patterns powdering, holding long stick, arranging a pearl, a necklace, garlands holding the end of the cloth or garment, churning, drawing out arrows, plucking, holding and collecting flowers, drawing out goad, a whip and showing the sight of woman; applying scents, breaking a twig *etc.*

11. Sucimukha (Needle)

Sucimukha has the multiple use as Pataka when used in different directions and held in various levels. When holding upward, it represents, lighting, banner, blossoms, ear, ring, fish, young serpent, smoke, various creepers, falling down, life, solitude, stalk of a lotus, curve and roundness. When the fore-finger is raised, it indicates stars, nose, number one, stick, and club. When the fore-finger is stretched, shaken and moved up it indicates no or speak, this or that, up and down. When moved in a circular motion it shows the whip and disc of Lord Vishnu, world, umbrella, beating the drum showing the way, asking to get out. When both the fore-fingers of Sucimukha hands are united it indicates union. When separated it represents separation; when crossed it indicates quarrel; when pressed against each other it shows bondage, when faced to each other and held separately on the left side of it signifies close of the day; when held to girth side it represents right; when they are raised to forehead they represent the eyes of Hara and Sukra.

12. Padmakosa (Lotus bud)

It represents Kapitha and bilva fruits, the breasts of a woman, mango flowers, water lily, curve, bud, cluster of flowers, bell-shaped, charm, brilliance. When both the hands join near the wrist and fingers moving it signifies the full blown lotus, water lily; with the ends bent it signifies accepting fruits, offering worship to deities, offering first funeral casket, multitude of flowers *etc.*

13. Sarpasirsa (Snake head)

It is used to denote offering water, the gait of snake, sprinkling of water challenging for a duel in wrestling, patting the shoulders and thighs, stroking elephant's temple applying sandal paste, washing face, short man, image, slow, *etc.*

14. Mrgasirsa (Deer head)

This hand gesture is used to indicate 'here', now' it is today, splendour of power, throw of dice, wiping the sweat, pretending anger, express fear, the face of a deer, drawing lines on the brow and cheek, calling the beloved, showing respect, discussion, pressing the leg, holding umbrella, showing stairs, growth of child or women to draw patterns on the floor, mixing the things, applying the tilaka on forehead by men to show a lady *etc.*

15. Kangula (Tali)

This represents raw fruits, and small ones, angry words of women water, water lily, grapes, seeds, blue lotus coral, the breasts of the bride, the bird chakora and chataka, *etc.*

16. Alapallava (full–blown lotus)

It is used to denote feelings such as "whom do you belong to ?" it is not unmeaningful words, woman's illusion, full-blown lotus, anger, praise, full moon, round face, ball, beauty, vehicle, mirror, height, pond, place *etc.*

17. Chatura (semi–circle)

This hand gesture is used to represent policy, discipline, penance, clever girl, afflicted person, deceit, proper words, the sense of little, sorrow, playfulness, converse, sweetness, face, gold and metals, eyes, difference of varnas, slow pace of walking chopping the tings, oil *etc.*

18. Bhramara (the bee)

It represents the plucking of flowers with long stems bee earring, practicing yoga, parrot, birds, *etc.*

19. Hamsasya (swan face)

It is used to show beak, tying the thread of marriage, certainty, a drop of water, caressing the baby, jasmine.

20. Hamsapaksha (swan feather)

This gesture of hand indicates offering water and gifts, decoration of cheek, sipping water, accepting meals by Brahmins, embracing excessive paralysis, touch, horripilation, massaging, arranging things features, covering and number six.

21. Samdamsa (grasping)

This hand gesture has manifold uses according to the various sentiments and moods. When held in front it represents the plucking of flowers, arranging them, holding grass, leaves, hair, and thread, pulling out thorn. When held near mouth, it denotes completing decoration. When it is held to sides it represents delicacy, abuse and jealousy. It is also used in various activities such as colouring the eyes, deliberation, drawing designs by women, showing generosity worship offerings, the number five, small bud, gentle dances, eclipse, the garland, pointing, snow tying the marriage thread and advising.

22. Nukula (Bud)

It represents offerings to gods and deities, bud of lotus or water lily, flying kiss (by a vita) contempt, scattered objects, taking meals, gold, counting, narrowing of the mouth, quickness, gift, eating, banana flower, fruit and applying religious mark.

23. Urnanabha (Spider)

This gesture is used to indicate holding hair, stealing, scratching the head, skin–disease, lion's paws, tiger, taking up stone, head of a lion and spider.

24. Tamracuda (Cock)

It is used to show falling down with a sound, beating time, inspiring confidence, to express a cock, drawing or writing camel calf, number three, vidas leaf *etc.*

The twenty four hand gestures so far discussed are illustrated in Natyasastra giving scope for multitude uses and moving them freely to express human emotions. These are the basic gestures and form the dance alphabets. The combination of these single hand gestures weave a beautiful and vivid formula in dance. In Abhinaya Darpana Urnanbha with hasta of Natyasastra is not discussed. 23 hand gestures of Natyasastra are dealt within Abhinaya Darpana and 5 more hastas are discussed, namely Ardhapataka, Mayura, Candrakala, Simhamukha and Trisula. These five gestures given by Nandikeswara were in use at his time. They are very popular even today. We find the representation of these 5 gestures along with 24 gestures in the sculptures.

1. Ardhapataka (half–flag)

It is used to express two persons or both, horn, knife, flag, tower, spear, the bank of a river, saw, sword, *etc.*

2. Mayura (Peacock)

It represents peacock beak, wiping away something, wiping away tears, creeper, bird, vomiting setting the curls on forehead and tilaka.

3. Candrakala (Digit of the Moon)

This gesture is used to express the crescent moon, the face and the crown of Lord Siva.

4. Simhamukha (Lion head)

This denotes pearl, coral, listening, rabbit, elephant, vedic rituals, face of the lion and deer lotus garland, fragrance, stroking the hair *etc.*

5. Trisula (Trident)

It is used to express trident number three and the leaf of wood apple.

Samyukta Hastas (Gestures of Combined Hands)

In Natyasastra 13 gestures of combined hands are illustrated, whereas in Abhinayadarpana additional 14 hand gestures are illustrated. The following are the Samyuta Hastas.

1. Anjali (Salutation)

This gesture is used to offer salutation in case of God, to be held on the head, in case of elders near one's face and friends and spectators near the chest.

2. Kapota (Dove)

It is used to express the approach with modesty salutation conversation with elders taking an oath conversation receiving things casket nectar, plantain flower. When it is held near bosom by women it signifies cold and fear.

3. Karkata (crab)

This gesture is used to indicate massaging of the limbs in love condition yawning after awakening from sleep a big body holding a counch, supporting the chin, showing a crowd, bending the branch of a tree, a crab *etc.*

4. Svastika (Cross)

It indicates the quarters clouds, sky, ocean, forest, seasons, earth. When held in crossed position it expresses praise, timed speech, order, direction, svastika, crocodile, *etc.*

5. Kataka Vardhamanaka (Link of Increase)

Either held crossed or placed near wrist indicates love-making and salutation to express marriage, rituals, flowers, garlands, coronation, *etc.*

6. Utsanaga (Embrace)

It expresses touching the object beyond sight, act of anger, when pressed hard by women to show jealousy, embracing, shyness, showing the armlets, punishing the children *etc.*

7. Nishadha (Defence)

It is used to indicate correct understanding, acceptance, holding, speaking truth the purport. (This gesture is not mentioned in Abhinayadarpana).

8. Dola (Swing)

According to Natyasastra, dola hands are used to indicate hurry, dejection, fainting, intoxication, panic, excitement, state of illness and wound by weapon. According to Abhinayadarpana this is used in the beginning of dance, and wishing welcome.

9. Pushapauta

It indicates receiving and carrying of corn, fruits, flowers, carrying and removing water, offering of lights, performing vedic rites.

10. Makara (Fish)

It represents crocodile, shark fish, stone, lion, tiger *etc.*

11. Gajadanta (elephant tusk)

This gesture indicates carrying the bride and the bridegroom, excessive weight elapsing a pillar, uprooting a hill or a stone.

12. Avahitha (Eagerness)

It indicates weakness, pointing to one's body the thinness of one's body, and longing, amorous actions, holding ball, breasts, eagerness, interest and keenness.

13. Vardhamana (Stretched hands)

This is used to indicate opening of the latticed window.

14. Sivalinga

Lord Siva is represented symbolically by this gesture.

15. Kartari Swastika (Crossed arrow shafts)

This gesture is used to indicate trees, the summit of a hill, branches *etc.*

16. Sakata (Car)

This gesture is used to indicate the demons.

17. Sankha (Conch)

This represents conch shell.

18. Cakra (Discus)

This hand gesture is used to show the chakra of Mahavishnu.

19. Samputa (casket)

It is used to express a casket, concealing things and closing something or covering the things.

20. Pasa (Noose)

It is used to express a nose, emity and a chin.

21. Kilaka (Bond)

It is used to express affection, lovers talk, fondness and love.

22. Kurma (Tortoise)

This gesture is indicated to denote the tortoise.

23. Varaha

This gesture is to be used for representing the boar.

24. Garuda (A bird of Mythology)

It is to be used to interpret Garuda, the vehicle of Vishnu.

25. Nagabandha (serpent tie)

This is used to express pairs of hands, coil of a snake, spells, creeper, atharvana hymn *etc.*

26. Khatya Hasta

This hand is used to show the cot or bed.

27. Bherunda (Bird)

The couple of Bherunda birds are represented.

These single and double hand gestures have ample scope in dance presentation. In spite of these prescribed gestures and uses Bharata has given margin for conventions as they can be used according to situations and emotions. The experts are to use the hand gestures according to the popular practice (and in this matter) they should have an eye to their movement, object, sphere, quantity, appropriateness and mode.

III. Nritta Hastas: (hand gestures used in pure dance)

In Bharata's Natyasastra, Sangitha Ratnakara and Natya Sastra Sangraha, number of Nrittahastas are discussed. These hand gestures are used along with feet movements. They contribute to the formation of 108 Karanas and Angaharas.

These gestures are ornate ones and are employed mainly in pure dance.

1. Caturasra

On the level of shoulders, chest and elbows two Katakamukha hands are held forward eight talas apart.

2. Udvrtta or Talavrtta

The two Hamsapaksha hands are waved like a fan.

3. Talamukha

The two Kamsapsksha hands are danced each other in Casturasra Position.

4. Svastika

At the wrist level the Talamukha hands are crossed.

5. Vipra–Kirna

After holding in the Svastika position the Talamukha hands are released.

6. Aralakatakamukha

The two alapallava hands with the palms upwards are changed into padmakosa hands.

7. Aviddhavakrta

The two pataka hands touching the shoulder elbow and arm with palms facing downward forming a graceful movement.

8. Sucimukha

The two sarpa hands with their thumbs touching the middle finger.

9. Recita

The two Hamsapaksha hands move swiftly facing upwards.

10. Ardha Recita

The right hand as in Recita, (hansapaksha hand facing upwards) and the left hand katakamukha holding at different level of the body.

11. Vttana Vancita

The two Tripataka hands are moved at different levels of arms and elbow.

12. Pallava

The two pataka hands are joined at the wrist.

13. Nitamba

The two pataka hands are moved from shoulder to hip.

14. Kesabandha

The two hands (Gesture not specified) are moved from the hair knot and held on the sides.

15. Lata

The two hands are stretched sideways.

16. Karihasta

The lata hand is held in a waving movement and another hand held in Tripataka.

17. Pakshavancitaka

One Tripataka hand is placed on the waist and the other on the head.

18. Pakshapradvotaka

The Pakshavancitaka hands change the places.

19. Garudapaksha

The two Pataka hands pointing downwards move near hips and turning the palms quickly.

20. Dandapaksha

The two Kamsasksha hands are moved alternatively and stopping as a staff.

21. Urdhvamandalin

Near the appear part of the body the two hands moved in a circular movement.

22. Parsamandalin

When the circular movement is made on the one side.

23. Uromandalin

After the circular movement one hand is to be raised up and the other hanged down.

24. Urahaparsvardhasmandala

The Arala and Alpallava hands are moved by turns above the breast level and on the sides.

25. Mushtikasavastika

The two Katakamukha hands are bent at wrist and moved round.

26. Nalinipadmakosa

The Padmakosa hands are moved by turns with Vyavartita and Parivartita Karanas.

27. Apapallava

Moved sideways and circular movement.

28. Ulbana

The two Alpallava hands are to be stretched up and waved facing upwards.

29. Lalita

The two Alapallava hands are moved near the head.

30. Valita

The two lata hands are crossed near elbow.

Apart from the above three types of hand gestures Nandikeswara in his Abhinayadarpana has dealt with a variety of hand gestures. Bharata has left it to the discretion of experts in the field to make use of hand gestures according to the circumstances. Perhaps Nandikeswara summarized the gestures which were used by the dancers in his time to denote various situations and brought them in a framework which are also represented iconographically.

Four Karanas of hand gestures are mentioned which are the particular movements of the hands executing hand gestures expressing various ideas.

1. **Aveshtita:** The hand is turned inward towards the chest and movement starts with the first finger.

2. **Udvisita:** The movement begins with the first finger, the hand is turned outward away from the chest.

3. **Vyavartita:** The movement is same as in Avershtita, but it starts with the last finger.

4. **Parivartita:** The movement is same as in Udvisita, but starts with the last finger.

Lastly there are ten movements of arms involved with the four Karanas of hand gestures. They are:

1. Tiryak Gati—Oblique movement
2. Urdhva gati—Movement of the head
3. Adhomukha gati—Movement downward
4. Ancita gati—The movement starts at the chest
5. Apaviddha gati—Thrown off movement
6. Mandala gati—Circular movement
7. Svastika gati—Crossing the hands
8. Prshtanusarana—Turned to back
9. Udveshti gati—Movements of the fore-arms.
10. Prasarita gati—Extended movement of hands.

All the above hand gestures have their own movements. When they are moved in different directions they can not be used in varied situations. Hand gestures according to the theory of histrionic representation have three kinds of general movements, *viz.*, upwards or Utthana, sidewards or Parsva and Adhomukha or downwards.

Further discussing on the movements of arms Bharata specifies 20 types of actions which are used to produce various emotions in histrionic expressions.

They are :

1. Utkarsha - To pull up
2. Vikarshana - to drag
3. Vyakarshana - to pull out
4. Parigraha - to accept
5. Nigradha - to refuse
6. Avahana - to welcome
7. Tudana - to encourage
8. Samstesha - to join
9. Viyoga - to separate
10. Rakshana - to protect
11. Mokshana - to release
12. Vikshipta - to throw out
13. Dhunana - to push
14. Visarga - to leave out
15. Tarjana - to threaten
16. Chedana - to split
17. Bhedana - to break
18. Sphotana - to explode
19. Motana - to contract
20. Tadana - to beat

Bharata gives a key note for restricting the movements of arms to bring out the characterization effectively. When the superior types of objects or persons are to be indicated, the hand gestures should be limited and kept near the forehead. When the middle ones are represented the hand gestures are medium and held near breast portion. When depicting inferior objects or persons, the hand gestures are used abundantly and held below. In certain situations only facial expression is of more importance and hand gestures are strictly prohibited. In the situations such as sorrow, madness, helplessness, motionlessness, penance, floating in water, dreaming, confusion, depression *etc.*, it is the inner moods or the temperaments which are to be shown on the face naturally. When the hand gestures fail to press any idea, then the facial and bodily expressions are of more value than mere gestures.

Vaksha

The movements of the chest are mentioned as 5 in number. Sangita Ratnakara and Lasya Ranjana also described the same movements.

Parsva

There are 5 sideward movements which are explained in Natyasastra and in Sangitha Ratnakara and Lasya Ranjana.

Jathara

The movements of belly also contribute in expressing emotions symbolically, Bharata mentions three movements of belly as Kshama, Khalva and Purna. The later writers also mention similar movements.

Kati

The gestures of the waist are of 5 types. Sangita Ratnakara and Lasya Ranjana also deal with same types of the movements of waist of as Chinna, Nivritta, Recika, Prakampita (Kampita) and Udvahita.

Urus

Kampana, Valana, Stambhana, Udvartana and Vivartana are the 5 types of movements of thighs dealt in Natyasastra, Sangita Ratnakara and Natyasastra Sangraha. The movements of thighs are both in expressive dance and also in Nritta.

Janghas

The Natyasastra furnishes 5 moments of shanks, which is the joining limb to the thigh and feet. Sangitaratnakara and Lasya Ranjana mention 5 more movements of shank in addition to 5 movements of Natyasastra. They are considered as pratyangas, subsidiary limbs, nistra, paravrtta, tiraschina, bahirgata and kampita.

Padas

The combination of various movements of feet create the dance movements. According to Natyasastra there are 5 movements of feet namely, Udghattita, Sama, Agratalasankara, Ancita and Kuncita. Sangitaratnakara and Lasya Ranjana consider 7 more movements of feet which are in practice *viz.* Tadita, Gratitotsedha, Ghattita, Mardita, Agraga, Parsvige and Parsvaga.

A particular movement down the waist is intended when there is a synchronized movement of the limbs such as feet, thighs and shanks. The associated movements of these limbs along with the hastas or hand gestures bring out a specific karana. Bharata has not dealt separately with the minor limbs such as knee, ankle, toe, heel and sole and they are related to the movement of the feet. But the later writers specifically classified the movements of toes, knees, ankles, heels, fingers, soles, wrist, shoulders, arms and hips.

Head Gestures

According to Natya Shastra, there are thirteen gestures of the head, while Nandikeswara has only nine. Among them, 5 gestures have common names in both the works. In addition to these 5, 2 gestures agree partially, names of all these gestures are found in both the above works given below.

Abhinaya Darpana: Sama, Nedvahita, Adhomukha, Alolita, Bhuta, Kampita, Paravritha, Utkahipta, Parivahrita.

Natyasastra: Avampita, Vamprita, Bhuta, Bridhuta, Parivahita, Adhuta, Abadhuta, Archita, Nihanchita, Paravritha, Adhogata, Lolita.

Movements of Head

Movement of the head precedes action; the auspicious pose which precedes all performance.

(1) *Sama:* (Level), not moving, not bent, not raised. Usage—At the beginning of dancing, sitting for prayers, pride, authoritative speech, satisfaction, feigned anger of love, indifference and cessation from action.

(2) *Udahita:* (Raised) raising the head and keeping it still. Usage—flag, moon, firmament, mountain, flying things in the air, anything tall.

(3) *Adhomukah:* (Face inclined) the head is bent. Usage—modesty, sorrow, bowing,

regarding anything vile, fainting, things on the ground, bathing.

(4) *Alolita:* (Rolling), the head is moved in a circle. Usage—sleepiness, obsession, intoxication, faintness, dizziness, hesitation, uncontrolled laughter.

(5) *Dhuta:* (shaken), used by Bharata and others. The hand is turned from right to left and left to right. Usage—denial, looking repeatedly at things, condolence with others, astonishment, dismay, indifference, cold, fire, fear, fist moment of drinking liquor, preparing for battle, rejection impatience, glancing at one's own limbs, summoning from both sides.

(6) *Kampita:* (Nodding, shaking), shaking the head up and down. Usage—indignation, saying, "halt", enquiry summoning, threatening *etc.*

(7) *Paravritta*: (Turned round). When the face is turned round the head is called Paravritta. Usage—in denoting the command, 'It should be done', anger, shame, turning away the face slightly, hair of the head, a quiver.

(8) *Utkshipta*: (Thrown up). When the head is turned aside and then raised up it is called Utkshipta. Usage—can denote the command or request, "take this" or "come". The supporting of (something) and acceptance.

(9) *Parivahita*: (Widely moved). When the head is moved from side to side a Chauri, it is called Parivahita.

Eye Gestures

According to Natya Sastra, these are three classes of eye-gestures.

(a) Eyes for expressing 'Rasas'.

(b) Eyes for expressing 'Sthayi-Bhavas'.

(c) Eyes for expressing 'Samchari Bhavas'.

Each of the classes (a) and (b) in their turn have eight varieties and class (c) has 20 varieties.

Abhinaya Darpana is not so elaborate in its classification of these gestures. It enumerates only eight varieties.

Neck Gestures

The Natya Sastra mentions about nine kinds of these gestures. Abhinaya Darpana give, only four kinds of such gestures.

A sculpture of Vijayanagar

21

Karanas

Karana is defined as the simultaneous movement of hands and feet in dancing. Two Karanas in a dance constitute nritta matrika 2, 3 or 4 Nritta Matras makeup an Angahara. 3 Karanas comprise a Kalapaka. 4 of the Karanas constitute a Mandala whole cluster of 5 give shape to a Sanghataka. 6, 7 or 8 or 9 Karanas join together to form an Angahara on occasions.

The study of dance technique is incomplete without the discussion on the aspect of Karanas. The Karana is the source and origin of all the dance movements. Certain major and minor limbs with their movements form karana. It is the portion above the waist moved along with the Hastas and the portion below the waist moved along with the padas. All the major, minor and subsidiary limbs are associated with the movements of Hastas (Hands) and padas (feets). A simultaneous movement of the hands and feet a posture which need not be a static one but transitory and timed properly. Such postures are called Karanas which are single postures. Thus the combined movement of hands and feet form a posture which need not be a static one but transitory and timed properly. Such postures are called Karanas which are single postures. Thus the combined movement of hands and feet in dance is called the Karanas.

A Karana is coordinated with the prescribed position (Sthanaka) the gait (Cari and hand gestures Nrtta Hastas). The 6 Sthanakas, 32 Caris (Bhuma and Akasa) and 30 Nrtta Hastas are incorporated in forming 108 Karanas. There are infinite movements of the limbs of the body and it is neither possible nor necessary to enlist all these in any Sastra. So, the scholars have chosen only those movements that are charming and expressive. Bharata has taken up 108 of these important Karanas and defined them. Bharata describes Karana as a unit of movement, indeed a cadence of movement culminating in a pose. It has not been clearly understood that, when a unit of movement is broken up, into successive positions that constitute it, several poses can result at different points in time Karana is a final movement of the limbs moved in different directions and placed in a particular position. Karanas are derived from the characteristic movements of either pada or hasta, kati or griva (feet, or hands, waist or neck). While shifting from one Karana to the other any one of the above four limbs, is emphasized (moved) and comes to a final form or pose. The gap filing from one pose to the other is known as recakas. Recaka is displacing of a limb from a particular position, lifting it, rotating it and freely moving the particular limb.

Application of Nrtta Hastas which have been prescribed for dance is generally implied by Karanas. In the Karana the left hand should generally be held on the chest and the right hand is to follow the (right) foot. Though Bharata feels that these Karanas are to be used for pure dance, it is evident that they are also used in impressive dance. Some of the Karanas when combined with facial expression make great impact in conveying the meaning (This point is made clear while illustrating each sculpture taken for study). Karanas are used in dance, fight, personal combat, walking as well as movements in general. Foot movements which have been prescribed for exercise of Sthanas and Caris are applied to these Karanas also.

As mentioned by Lord Siva before teaching Karanas to Bharata, the dance was made beautiful by Angaharas consisting of different Karanas. They are the basic postures formed by varied movements which enhance the grace and beauty of dance. Sri Gopinath and S.V. Ramana Rao made an useful attempt in identifying the Karanas with sculptural representation of Karanas given in the Natyasastra and discussed their uses in the art of dance. Dr. Kapila Vatsyayan has made a critical and elaborate study in reclassifying the Karanas in terms of the distinctive features and also compared the Karanas represented on the gopurams of Chidambaram temple with the verses of Natyasastra. All these studies by eminent scholars are valuable to rectify the inaccuracies of the performers who do not have a thorough knowledge of the theoretical aspect of dance.

The combined movement of Hasta and Cari form a Karana. Two Karanas will make one Matrka and such two, three or four Matrkas constitute an Angahara. This Angahara is the coordinated unit number of Karanas or a continuous movement. The Angahara consists of six, seven, eight to nine Karanas. The combination of Angaharas create the beautiful and exquisite art of Hindu dance.

The Karanas are single postures, special gestures of them being that the left hand is generally put on the breast while the right hand follows the movements of the feet.

Bharata defines a 'karana' in the following manner. "Let it be understood that, in what is to be said here after the movements of the hand and foot should accord with those of the waist, side, chest, back and belly. Each unit of dance consists of certain positions, movements, and poses of the hands. A combination of these constitute a 'karana'.

Again in verse 172, he says "As a general rule, the left hand should be placed over the chest in producing the karanas, the foot and the right hand should accord with it" (The verse 172 is repetition of verse 57 and that is found in the Gwalior edition, which adds 4 more slokas in the end).

Bharata again states "O, Divijas, I shall describe the performance of these with the karanas and also tell the actors to combine the movements of the hands and feet in the several Angaharas and Karanas. Angaharas have their origin in Karanas. I shall describe these (karanas). A 'karana' in dance is the coordination of the movements of the hands and feet".

"There are one hundred and eight karanas enumerated by me".

One hundred and eight varieties of karanas have been mentioned by Bharata, but Abhinavagupta, the commentator of Natyasastra, states, in clear terms that the list is by no means exhaustive.

Angaharas arise out of a combination of either two, three, four of such karanas or single unit matrika.

Bharata illustrates thirty-two varieties of such Angaharas.

Abhinavagupta explained the meaning of the term 'Angahara' in two ways :

1. The movements of limbs in proper direction or
2. The movements of limbs as depicted by Shiva.

The sage mentions four types of rechakas which imply movements of the foot, the waist, the hand and the neck and pindibandas is the finished figure developing from particular poses of dance. He did not properly define and clearly explain the Angaharas, Rechakas and Pindibandhas.

Movements are again divided into 'Matrika', 'Kalapaka', 'Bhandaka' and 'Sanghataka'. A single unit (Matrika) of action consists of two karanas, three karanas make a 'Kalapaka' and four a Bhandaka. A combination of five karanas is called 'sanghataka'.

Bharata in another sloka (Version No. 173 Ch. iv) gives a contrary definition of Matrika. Here he says that Matrika as a primary unit is constituted by charis and nritha hastas.

If analyzed properly, it becomes obvious that a karana is the source and origin of all movements.

All the 108 karanas are cut on rocks at Chidambaram temple with appropriate verses from the Natyasastra and the most remarkable point to be noted is that all the postures are exhibited by female figures.

So, Karanas are obviously mixture of dance movements. But the sculptures depict a particular striking pose of the movements employed in a karana. In other words, a striking and artistic and dynamic movement in a karana, has been made static and afterwards has been inscribed in frame, carved out in the stone wall of the pillar on the Gopuram, on the courtyard of Chidambaram temple.

In this context it should be remembered that the familiar stature of Nataraja is also not in a static posture. It is also a striking movement, which might have attracted the sculptor out of many similar movements.

Another peculiar feature is that all such sculptures of karanas have no resemblance.

It appears that Bharata did not draw any line of distinction between a male and a female dancer. He attributes the whole chapter IV of his book as Tandava Lakshanam. Perhaps dance according to him is 'Tandava'. It does not necessarily mean that all the karanas or postures should be performed by females only.

Bharata seems to have trained his sons and disciples in the part for which he is fitted. He discovered that certain aspects of the dance could be performed only by women. With this idea in mind, he approached Brahma, who immediately created Apsaras (celestial nymphs), Kaisikivrithi (Graceful style) suited them, which is one of the four modes of dramatic style (Natyasastra Ch. I).

Three selected poses which are suitable to women are to be found in the sculptures of Chidambaram temple.

A karana termed as 'Arddha Rechita' or 'half–whirl' is in the Soochi pose, the hand is in 'Apaviddha' in the Soochi pose, the leg in 'Nikutta' and the side in 'Sanata'. Apavidha soochi hand is joining the tips of the middle finger and the thumb and the remaining fingers are curved. Sanata is well bent of the head on one side.

In Unmatha the legs are bent and the hands are in rechita. Rechita of the hands are lifting them up and throwing about moving round and round and drawing them back.

The left hand is placed on the chest. The right hand is in Proddhestita Tala. The legs are in Anchita, proddhestita tala occurs when the hand in Tripataka (the third finger is bent and all the other fingers are pointed upwards close to each other) is raised to the ears and put in uddhvestita pointing downward. Anchita of the legs occurs when all the toes are stretched out. This karana is termed as 'karihasta' (elephant truck) and seems to be the best in the postures meant for females.

The following karanas bear manly qualities and some of them possess virile sentiments they are–26, 42, 44, 46, 47, 50, 52, 53, 64, 66, 70, 75, 76, 80, 83, 84, 99, 100, 106, 107 and 108. The respective numbers of the verses are 87, 103, 105, 107, 108, 111, 113, 114, 125, 127, 131, 136, 137, 141, 144, 145, 160, 167, 168, 169. These karanas are twenty-one in number and the remaining eighty-seven karanas may be prescribed for both the sexes, but some of them seem to be for females only.

'Vrischika' occurs when the right leg is bent backwards at the tip of the nose with the left hand in a bending manner.

In Kunchita urdhvalata, which means bending the leg so as to expose the surface of the toes.

'Swastika' is crossing the wrists in the form of swastika.

All the Angaharas are evolved through Karanas and the names of these together with their actions shall be explained.

The simultaneous movements of hands and feet while dancing can be called Karana. Two Karanas constitute one Matrika, two, three or four Matrikas making up one angahara. A Kalapaka is evolved out of three Karapas, a Mandaka [Sandaka] out of four and a Samghataka out of five. There are well known Angaharas consisting of six, seven, eight or nine Karanas.

I shall now expatiate the movements of the hands and feet for the evolution of the Karanas.

The Karanas one hundred and eight in number are as follows:-

Talapuspaputa, Vartita, Valitoru, Apaviddha, Samanakha, Lina, Svaticarecita, Mandalasvastika, Nikuttaka, Ardhani-kuttaka, Katicchinna, Ardharecita, Vaksassvastika, Unmatta, Svastika, Prsthasvastika, Kiksvastika, Alata, Katisama, Aksiptarecita, Viksiptak sipta, Ardhasvastika, Ancita, Bhujanga Trasita, Urdhvajanu, Nikuncita, Matalli, Ardhamatalli, Recaka-nikuttita, Padapaviddhaka, Valita, Ghurnita, Lalita, Danda Paksa, Bhujanga Trastarecita, Nupura, Vaisakharecita, Bhrama-raka, Catura, Bhujangancitaka, Dandakarecita, Viscikakuttita, Katibhranta, Latavrsaika, Channa, Vrscika. Vrscika-vuamsita Lalantava, Krinuka, Keacrs, Cakramandala, Uromandala, Aksipta, Tajavilasita, Argala, Viksipta, Avrtta, Dolapada, Vivrtta, Vinivrtta, Parsvakranta, Nisumbhita, Vidyudbhranbata, Atikranata, Vivartitaka, Gajakridita, Talasamsphotita, Garudaplutaka, Gandasuci, Parivrtta, Parsvajanu, Grdhravalinaka, Sannata, Suci, Ardhasuci, Suci-viddha, Apakranta, Mayuralalita, Sarpita, Dandapada, Harina-pluta, Prenkholita, Nitamba, Skhalita, Karihasta, Prasarpita, Simhakridita, Simhakarsita, Udvrtta, Upasrta, Talasmghattita, Skhalita, Visnukranata, Sambhranta, Udvrtta,Upasrta, Talasamghattita, Skhalita, Vsnukranta, Sambhranata, Viskambha, Udhattita, Gangavatarana, Lotitaka, Nagapasarpita, Sakatasyam, and Gangavatarana, These Karanas are expected to be employed in the course of dance, fighting, indulging in personal combats, strolling and in all general movements.

Those movements of the feet allotted to the exercise of Sthanas and Caris must be considered the Karanas too. So also in the case of Nrittakastas. These Sthanakas, Caris and the Nrittahastas are called Matrikas. The variations thereof are known as Karanas.

I shall explain Caris pertaining to fight when discussing the details of Gati (movements). The dramatic preceptor shall make use of them in a manner befitting his histrionic skill. In the Karana holding of the left hand on the breast is recommended. The right hand is to follow the right foot. Now pay attention to the movements of hands and feet while dancing in their connection with the movements of hip, sides and thigh and also their relation to the breast, back and belly.

The Karanas Defined

Talapuspaputa—Hand is held on the left side the foot is in the position Agratalasancara and the side is Sannata (bent).

Vartita—Hands bent at the wrist and place these hands on the thighs.

Valioru—Hands in Vyanartita and Sarivartita form and thighs in Valita (moving and turning).

Apaviddha—The right hand in Sukatunda gesture falls on the thigh, the left hand kept to the breast.

Samanakha—The two feet touch each other with the nails symmetrical, two hands hand down, the body in natural position.

Lina—The two Pataka hands are held together in the Anjali position on the breast, the neck is held high and the shoulder is bent.

Svastikarecita—Two hands with Recita and Aviddha gesture held together in Svastika form then separated and held on the hips.

Mandalasvastika—Two hands kept in Svastika gesture-palms turned upwards the body in the Mandala Posture.

Nikuttaka—The hands moved up and down in turns between the head and another arm—legs moved similarly.

Ardhanikuttaka—Hands with Alapallava gesture bent towards shoulders—legs moved up and down.

Katichinna—The hip serially in the Chinna position—two pallava hands held alternately and repeatedly on the head.

Ardharecita—Hand with Sucimukha gesture moves freely, feet move up and down in turs-side in Sannata posture.

Vaksassvastika—Two legs on each other in Svastika form—two Recita hands joined together similarly on the breast kept bent.

Unmatta—Feet to be Ancita and hands—Recita.

Svastika—Hands and feet respectively held together in the Svastika form.

Prsthavastika—Two arms after being thrown up and down coming together as a Svastika with Apakranta and Ardhasuci Caris.

Diksvastika—Tuning sideways and towards the front in course of a connected movement thereby forming Svastika with hands and feet.

Alata—After making Alata Cari the hand is taken down from the level of the shoulder making Urdhvajanu Cari.

Katisama—Feet kent separated after Svastika Karana, one hand placed at the navel and the other at the hip—sides in the Udvahita pose.

Aksiptarecita—Left hand on the heart right hand Recita—thrown up and sideways—then both the hands Recita with Apaviddha gesture.

Viksiptaksiptaka—Head and feet thrown up then down.

Ardhasvastika—The two feet make Svastika, right had Karihasta gesture left one lying on the chest.

Ancita—In the Ardhasvastika the Karihasta alternately in Vyavartita and Paarivartita movement, then bent upon the tip of the nose.

Bhujanga Trasita—The kuncita feet thrown up—thighs have and oblique Nivartana movement—the same movement in the hip and the thigh.

Urdhvajanu—Akuncita foot is thrown up—knee stretched on a level with the breast—hands in harmony with the dance.

Nikuncita—Feet to be moved as in the Viscika Karana—Both hands bent at the sides, right hand held at the tip of the nose.

Matalli—Make a whirling movement while throwing the two feet back—move hands on the Udvestita and Apaviddha movements.

Ardhamatalli—Feet away from the position in the Skhalita, left hand Recita and later part on the hip.

Recitanikuttita—Right hand Recita left foot Udghattita, left hand Dola gesture.

Padaviddhaka—The katakamukha hands with backs against the navel and feet to be in Suci and then Apakranta Cari.

Valita—Hands to be Apaviddha, beet to be in Suci Cari—Trika turned round (lower part of the spine).

Ghurnita—Left hand in Valita and moved round—right hand with Dola gesture and the two feet to be drawn away from each other from the Svastika position.

Lalita—Left hand in Karihasta gesture—right turned aside (pavartita) two feet moved up and down.

Dandapaksa—Observe Urdhvajanu Cari, Lata hands to be placed on the knee.

Bhujanga Trastarecita—Feet in B.T. Cari hands Recita to be moved to the left.

Nupura—The lower spine gracefully turned round Bhramari Cari, hands showing Lata and Recita gestures and the feet the Nupura Pada Cari.

Vaisakharecita—Hands and feet to be Recita, the hip and the neck also and the whole body in Vaisakha Sthana.

Bhramaraka—Svastika feet in Aksipta Cari, hands in Udvestita. The sacrum turned round.

Catura—The left hand with Ancita gesture, right hand Catura gesture, right feet in Kuitita pose.

Bhujangancita—The feet in Bhujangatrasita Carik, right hand Recita, left hand Lata gesture.

Dandakarecita—Hands and feet freely thrown about all sides like a staff and then Recita.

Vrscikakuttita—Assume the Vrscika Karana and make the Nikuttita movement of the hands.

Katibhranti—The Suci Cari, Apaviddha gesture with the right hand, hip to be moved round.

Latavrscika—A foot to be Ancita and turned backwards, Lata gesture with the left hand—palm and fingers bent and turned upwards.

Chinna—The Alapadma hand to be held on the hip in china pose, body in the Vaisakha Sthana.

Vrscikarecita—Assume Vrscika Karapa—the two hands in Svastika form gradually becoming Recita to show Vipra-kirna gesture.

Vrscika—The two hands bent and held over the shoulders and a leg bent and turned towards the back.

Parsvanikuttaka—Svastika hands to be held on one side the feet Nikuttita.

Lalatatilaka—Assume the Vrscika Karana or mark is to be made on the forehead with the great toe.

Krantaka—Bending a Kuncita leg behind the back and the Atidranta Car—both the hands thrown down.

Kuncita—Leg in Ancita and left hand held on the left side with palm upwards.

Cakramandala—The inner Apaviddha (Addita Cari) with the body bent and held down between the two arms hanging straight.

Uromandala—Two feet drawn away from Swastika position and then hands on the chest. Feet in Apaviddha Cari.

Aksipta—Hands and feet thrown about swiftly.

Talavilasita—Foot with toe and sole turned upwards, held high on the side, palm of hands bent.

Argala—Feet stretched backwards and kept two Talas and a half apart. Hands moved in conformity.

Viksipta—Hands and feet thrown backwards or sideways in the same way.

Avarta—The Kuncita feet put forward—two hands moved swiftly to befit the dancing movement.

Dolapada—Kuncita foot thrown up two hands swinging from side to side in a manner befitting the dance.

Nivitta—Hands and feet thrown out—Trika to be turned round—hands to be Recita.

Parsvakranta—Observe the Cari of the name, throw out hands forward, then move them in a manner befitting the dance.

Vinibitta—Observe the Suci Cari Sacrum to be turned round, hands to Recita.

Nisumbhita—A foot bent towards the back, breast is raised high, hand held at the middle of the forehead.

Vidyudbhranata—Foot turned backwards and the hands in Mandalaviddha gesture stretched very close to the head.

Atikranta—Observe Atikranta Cari, stretch both the hands forward in a manner befitting dance.

Vivartitaka—Hands and feet thrown out Trika turned round, hands to be Recita.

Gajakridita—Lift hand bent and brought near the left ear, right hand in Lata gesture, feet Dolapada Cari.

Tala Samsphotita—Foot swiftly lifted up and placed forward, hands show Talasamsphotita gesture.

Garudaplutaka—Feet stretched backwards hands with Lata and Recita gestures breast raised.

Gandasuci—Feet in suci pose, side to be Unnata, one hand bent on the chest, other bent touching the check.

Parvitta—Hands raised in Apavestita gesture, feet in Suci position, Sacrum turned round in the Bharamari Cari.

Parsvajanu—One foot in Sama position and the opposite thigh is lifted up, one Musti (fist) hand on the chest.

Grdhravalinaka—One foot stretched backwards and one knee slightly bent, both the arms outstretched.

Sannata—Leap forward, then place the feet forward in Svastika form, showing sannata gesture with both the hands

Suci—Akuncita foot raised and placed ahead on the ground, two hands in harmony with the performance.

Ardhasuci—The Alapadma hands Is held on the head, right foot in Suci Karana.

Suci Viddha—One foot of the Suci Karana being put on the heel of the other, hands placed on the waist and chest respectively.

Apakranta—Make the Vilita thigh and perform Apakrata Cari both the hands to be moved in harmony.

Mayuralalita—Assume the Vrscika Karana, keep hands in Recita, turn the Trika (Sacrum).

Sarpita—both the feet to be moved from Ancita position, head is in Parivahita gesture, hands in Recita.

Danda Pada—After the Nupupa Cari observe Danda Pada Cari and Aviddha hand is shown quickly.

Harinapluta—Observe Atikranta Cari the dancer should jump and stop. He then bends the shanks and throws them up.

Prenkholitaka—After observing the Dola Pada Cari, jump and let the Trika turn round and settle down.

Nitamba—Arms at the outset are thrown up with fingers pointing upwards.Baddha Cari is to be observed.

Skhalita—Observe Dolapadacari and then turn round the hands with Recita gesture in harmony therewith.

Karihasta—Left hand is placed on the chest, the other hand is Prodvestitatala. The feet in Ancita.

Prasarpitaka—One hand in Recita and the other with Lata gesture, the feet in Samsarpitatala.

Simhavikridita—After observing the alata Cari, move swiftly making the hands to follow the feet.

Simhakarsta—On foot stretched backwards, hands to be bent and turned round in the front and again bent.

Udvitta—Hands, feet, whole body raised up, Udvitta Cari to be observed.

Upasrtaka—Employ Akshipta Cari and harmonize the hands therewith.

Talasamghattita—Employ Dolapadacari, clashing the palms together, left hand in Recita.

Janita—Keep one hand loose holding the other to the chest, employ Talagrasamstthita Cari.

Avahittahaka—After employing janit a Karapa raise the hands spreading out the fingers, let them fall slowly.

Nivesa—Both the hands kept on the chest that is in Nirbhugna state. The dances then assumes Mandala Sthana.

Elakakridita—Jump with Talasancara feet and come to the ground with the body bent and turned.

Urudvitta—A hand in Avrtta or Vyavartita state, keep the gourd with the body bent and turned.

Madaskhalitaka—Two hands kept hanging down, head in the parivahita gesture, feet turned round in Avidha Cari.

Visnukranta—One of the feet stretched forward and bent as though one is about to walk hands in Recita.

Sambhranta—One hand in the Vyavartita movement is kept on the thigh in Aviddha.

Viskambha—One of the hands to be Apaviddha Suci Cari, foot in Nikuttita state–Left hand on the chest.

Udghatta—Feet in the Udghattita movement, hands in Talasamghattita and then places on both sides.

Vrsabhakridita—Employ Alatacari both hands in Recita gradually taken to Kuncita and Ancita.

Lolita—Hands in Recita on both sides then in Ancita, head lolita and Vartita.

Nagapasarpita—Draw back feet from Svastika position, head in Parivahita and the hands in Recita.

Sakatasya—At the body is in rest. Then advance with a Talasancara foot–keep the chest Udvahita.

Gangavatarana—Foot with the toes and the sole turned upwards, hands show the Tripataka, fingers point downswards, hands show the Tripataka, Fingers point downwards, Head in Sannata state.

The eight sthayi bhavas or permanent moods corresponding to the eight sentiments are as Rati (love), Hasa (mirth), Soka (sorrow), Kridha (anger) Utsaha (courage), Bhaya (fear), Jugupsa (aversion) and Vismaya (wonder). The vyabhichari Bhavas (transitory moods) are enumerated as thirty three and they are named as follows. Niveda (self-disparagement), Glani (debility), Sanka (apprehension), Asuya (envy), Mada (intoxication), Srama (weariness), Alasya (indolence), Dainya (depression), Cinta (reflection), Moha (distraction), Smrithi (recollection), Dhrita (equanimity), Vrida (shame), Chapatals (unsteadiness), Harsha (joy), Avega (flurry), Jadata (stupe faction), Garva (arrogance), Visada (dispondency), Autsukya (longing), Nidra (drowsiness), Apasmara (dementedness), Supta (dreaming), Visbodha (awakening), Amarsa (impatience of opposition), Avahitha (dissembling), Ugrata (sternness), Mati (resolve), Vyadhi (sickness), Unmada (madness), Marana (death), Trasa (alarm), and Vistarka (doubt).

The sattvika Bhavas which can be taken generally as involuntary evidences of internal feeling are specified as eight in number. Stambha (stupor) Sveda (respiration Romance (horripilation) Svarabhanga (break of voice) Vepathu (trembling) Vaivarnya (change of colour) Asru (tears) and Pralaya (loss of consciousness).

The four kinds of Abhinayas (representations) pertaining to the drama are Angika (gestural conveyed by bodily actions) Vacika (vocal-conveyed by words) Aharya (extraneous conveyed by dress, ornaments, decoration *etc.*) and sattvika (internal conveyed by the manifestation of internal feelings such as perspiration throtting *etc.*)

The vrithis or styles of dramatic composition are four—*viz.* Bharati, Sattvati, Kaisiki and Arabhati which form the foundation of the piece.

There are four pravrithis or regional variations of dramatic performances called Avanti, Dakshinatya, Udramagadhi and Panchala madhyama.

Dharmis—the rules of dramatic representation are of two kinds—Lokadharmi (natural or realistic), representation as noticed in the world around, and Natyadharmi (theatrical performance based on certain conventions).

Abhinaya (representation) is based on real life and hence classification as Lokadharmi *etc.* is meaningful. Siddhi or achievement (the performance) is of two kinds as divine and human. The Svaras (musical notes) are seven and are of 2 kinds. Corporeal and those produced by instruments like vira, Atodya (musical instruments) belong to four kinds with their own characteristics.

They are 'Tata' (the stringed instrument) Avanaddha (drums) Ghana (used for beating time) and susira (having holes as in a flute).

There are 4 sentiments which are considered as basic. They are sringara (the erotic) Raudra (the furious) Vira (the heroic) and Bhibhatsa (the disgusting).

In the facial mode of representation of the different emotion and sentiments, the action of the head is presented. The actions of the head are of 13 kinds. (1) Akampitam (2) Kampitam (3) Dhutam (4) Vidhutam (5) Parivahitam (6) Adhutam (7) Avadhutam (8) Ancitam (9) Nihancitam (10) Paravrittam (11) Utksiptam (12) Adhogatam and (13) Lohitam.

The glances relating to Rasa or sentiments are 8 in number as follows—(1) Kanta (2) Bhayanaka (3) Hasya (4) Karuna (5) Adhbuta (6) Randri (7) Vira and (8) Bhibhatsa. The glances relating to Shajibhavas or permanent moods are also 8 in number. (9) Snigdha (10) Hrsta (11) Dina (12) Kruddha (13) Dripta (14) Bhayanista (15) Jugupsita (16) Puvismita. The twenty glances relating to Sancharibhavas or transitory feelings are given as—(17) Surya (18) Mahina (19) Sranta (20) Jajyanvita (21) Usglana (22) Sankita (23) Visanna (24) Mukula (25) Kunchita (26) Abhitapta (27) Jihma (28) Lalita (29) Vitarkita (30) Ardhamukula (31) Vibhranta (32) Vipluta (33) Akekara (34) Vikosa (35) Trasta (36) and Madira are the 36 types of glances on which the dramatic representation is based.

Action of the eyebrows is of 7 kinds as (1) Utksepa (lifting up) (2) Patana (taking down) (3) Bhrukuti (knitting) (4) Catura (beautiful) (5) Kuchita (contracted) (6) Recita (loosening) and (7) Sahaja (natural). Actions of the nose are of 6 types as—(1) Nata (depressed) (2) Manda (mild) (3) Vikrsta (expanded) (4) Socch vasa (having the respiration) (5) Vikunita (slanted) and svabhavika (normal or natural).

There are six kinds of Ganda (the movement of the cheek) *viz.* (1) Ksama (emanciated) (2) phulla (blown up) (3) purna (full) (4) kampita (shaken) (5) kunchita (contracted) (6) sama (level or even).

The activities of the lips are classified under six types as—1) Vivartana (rotling) (2) kampana (tremor) (3) visarga (spreading out) (4) viniguhana (concealing) (5) sandastaka (biting) and (6) samudga (closed up).

The gestures of the chin are 7 enumerated as—1) Kuttana (clashing) (2) Khandana (cutting) (3) Cchinna (closing) (4) Chakrita (separating) (5) Lehita (licking) (6) Sama (natural) (7) Dasta (biting).

The facial activities are of six kinds as—Dvinivritta (turned) (2) vidhuta (spreading) (3) Nirbhugna (lowering) (4) Bhigna (a little flat) (5) Vivrta (open) and Udvahi (turned upwards).

The colour of the face is enumerated as 4 types—(1) Svabhavika (natural) (2) Prasanna (pleased) (3) Rakta (reddish) and (4) Syama (dark or cloudy).

When things are to be represented in a natural way, the colour of the face should be Svabhavika. In the representation of sentiments like Adbhuta, vira and sringara, the expression should be prasanna. In the sentiments like vira, rudra and bhayanaka as also in the emotion of arrogance the rakta face should be employed. In the sentiments of bhayanaka and bhibhatsa, the face should be syama-dark and moody.

Thus in the representation of the theme delineating emotional moods and sentiments, appropriate facial colour should be employed.

The gestures of the limbs :

The gestures of the chest are enumerated as consisting of 5 types—1) Abhugna (slightly bent) (2) Virbhugna (not bent) raised (3) Prakampita (shaking) (4) Udvalita (lifted up) and (5) Sama (level or even).

Abhigna may be understood as that chest which is kept lowered the back is raised higher with the shoulders slightly bent and kept at ease. Its application may be used in situations of embarassment, worry swoon, sorrow, fear, disease, mental agony, cold, rain, and bashfulness. Nirbhugna is that chest with the back bent and shoulders raised and resulting in stiffness. Its application may be understood as in embarassment, arrogance, look of wonder, statement of truth, pride and courage.

In prakampita, the chest is heaved up and down almost incessantly—a feature to be recognised by the practitioners of drama. They should use this situations like laughter, weeping, fatigue, fear, cough, sigh, hiccup, sorrow *etc.*

Udvahita is the chest which is kept raised up and its application is in letting a deep breath, looking at an object kept in high place and in yawning. In samam, the chest is evenly placed and made attractive due to the symmetrical placement of all limbs.

Now gestures of the sides are of 5 types—(1) Nata (bent) (2) Samurrata (lifted up) (3) Prasarita (extended) (4) Vivartita (turned round) and (5) Apasrta (slightly withdrawn).

In Nata, the waist is slightly bent as also are sides and a shoulder is drawn away a little. In the unnata pose, as a result of one side becoming bent the waisty side and shoulder of the other side become raised up and result in the variety called unnata. In prasarita, both the sides are stretched out in their respective directions.

In vivartita, the sacrum is kept turned round. In apasrta, the side, which had turned back in the vivartita is brought back to the previous position by a turn.

While approaching some one nata should be employed and unnata, when one goes away. Prasavita is applied when one is delighted and vivartita when one is turning about. Apasta is used in the act of returning.

Gestures of the belly. They are of 3 types—(1) Ksama (slender or emanciated) (2) Khalla (depressed or hollowed) and (3) Purna (full or inflated).

The Ksama type of belly is employed in the deprection of laughter, cry, sighing, and yawning. The ksaka is used in showing disease, renance, fatigue or hunger. The purna variety is resorted to in gasping out stoutness, drapsy and excessive consumption of food.

Gestures of the hip: The gestures of the hip in dramatic performance and dance are of 5 kinds—(1) Cchinna (turned aside) (2) Nivrtta (turned up) (3) Recita (surrounded) (4) Kampita (shaken) and (5) Udvahita (raised).

Turning of the middle waist is called Cchinna, and turning to the front from a reverse position is termed Nivritta. In Recita, one turns about to different directions. Prakampita is that in which shivering in the hip occurs (as in the case of a hunch back). In Udvahita, the sides of the hip are raised slowly along with the whole waist. Cchinna is employed when one turns back to look at something in haste or in doing exercises. Nivritta is employed in the act of returning and Recita in turning a full circle. In the movements of a hunch back, dwarf, or a low type of persons, prakampita is made use of. In the gait of a stout person or women, the hip assumes the pose called Udvahita.

Gestures of the thighs: They are of five types. (1) Kampana (shivering) (2) Valana (turning round) (3) Stambhana (becoming stiff) (4) Udvartana (springing up) and (5) Vivartana (turning away).

Gestures of the feet: Gestures involving the feet are of 5 kinds. (1) Udghattita (with firm heel) (2) Sama (even palms) (3) Agratala sanchara (on tip toe) (4) Ancita (extended) and (5) Kuncita (bent).

In Udghattita, one stands on the forepart of the feet and then lets the heel touch the ground. This is to be employed in walking through an edge, in treading one's way on and in the action like jumping over to pass it.

There is a gait called sucipada, in which one stands on the big toe of the right foot keeping the heel raised. The left foot is placed in this in the normal position. In dance and in decorating the foot with anklet, this variety of foot is used.

The dancers should employ feet, shanks, thighs *etc.* at the same time for all action of the feet. In all the charis of the foot they must act together and at the same time.

The simultaneous movements of the limbs like feet, shanks, thighs and lips are technically referred to as cari. This is called vyayama (exercise). When the movements are governed by appropriate rules and the limbs are in concordance with each other in their activity. The movement involving a single foot is designated as cari and the movement of the two feet is called a karana.

A group of karanas form a khanda and three or four khandas make a Mandala. A dance is initiated by cari movements and all movements proceed from caris.

The natural placing of the feet on the ground is called SAMA and it is used to represent the natural disposition while representing the natural situation, the feet are held or placed firmly on the ground but they are often moved by the experts to show various Karanas involving Recita.

In Agratala Sanchara, the heel is raised, the big toe is stretched out and the other toes are bent. This should be made use in goading, knocking, standing, thrashing, kicking, turning, removing as also in various movements including the gait of the person whose heels are wounded.

In Ancita, the heels touch the ground, the fore part remains raised and toes are bent. This is to be employed in movements of persons, whose feet especially, foreparts are wounded and in turning round, striking of the foot on something and also in various Bhramari movements.

In Kuncita, the heels are raised, the fore part of the heel stressed on the ground with the toes bent. The centre part is also bent in the Kuncita type.

One of the shanks is raised with a slant with the turning of the heel onwards. In Addita, the front foot is placed forwards and backwards rubbing against the fore part or back of the other feet. In utspandita the foot moves gradually in and out in the manner of padarecaka. Hand is made into a fist and placed on the chest and the other hand in the same position is moved about. In this gait called Janita, the feet are kept in Talasanchara position (forepart firmly on the ground). In Syandita, one foot is put forward five talas away from the other foot. In Apasyandota, the other foot is also placed similarly (5 talas away). In Samotsarita Mattathi, the front foot is placed with a flourish with a circular movement. This is used in physical exercises. Mattathi is spoken of as that in which a backward step is made with feet with circular movement and the hands respectively assuming the poses of Udvestita and Apaviddha (entwining and separating).

Now I will say something about the aerial varieties of caris. In Atikranta, the foot is raised bent and stretched forward before placing it firmly on the ground with force. The foot is bent and raised with the thighs being twisted and turned. The foot is then set down sideways to form this Apakranta cari.

Raise the bent foot high so that the knee is placed on a level with the breast and then place it on the ground hitting the same with the heel to form parsva kranta.

Raise the bent feet high to place the knee on a level with breast. While keeping it like that emulates the same with the other foot to form Urdhna Janu.

One foot is bent and raised above the knee and stretched. Earthly cari movements are 16 in numbers—(1) Samapada (2) Sthitha varta (3) Sakatasya (4) Adhayardhika (5) Casagatih (6) Vicyava (7) Edaka kirdita (8) Baddha (9) Uurudvritta (10) Addita (11) Utspandita (12) Bavita (13) Syandita (14) Apasyandita (15) Samotsarita (16) Mattathi.

There are 16 aerial cari movements. They are—(1) Atikranta (2) Apakranta (3) Parsva kranta (4) Aksipta (5) Aviddha (6) Nupara padika (7) Dolapada (8) Avsipta (9) Aviddha (10) Udvritta (11) Vidyut bhranta (12) Alata (13) Bhujanga trasita (14) Mrgapluta (15) Danda (16) Bhramari.

In Samapada, both the feet are kept close with the nails placed in symmetry. This is used when the actor changes his stance.

In Sthitavarta, the front foot makes a circular movement inwards rubbing the ground before it is set. The same action is repeated by the other foot also.

In Sakatasya, the actor rests on a foot in a sitting position and the other foot is put forward keeping his chest in an erect position. The learned say that in Adhyardhika, the left foot is placed behind the right foot and then it is moved backwards further casagati is described as follows. The right foot is extended forward and placed firmly. The left foot is also similarly set on the ground away from the right foot.

Placing the place together and assuming the position of savapada when the right foot is used to pound the ground, its called vicyava. In Edakakridita, one jumps again keeping the forepart of the feet firmly on the ground. In Badtha, the shanks are held in a transposed position and turned about with the moving of the thighs. In Uruduritta are stands on Agratala Sancharapada firmly placing forepart of the foot on the ground.

Assume the Nupurapada and rule the back foot with the front foot and stretch it forward with a flourish to form Dandapada.

In Bhramari jump forward and hit the ground and turn round the sacrum. The other foot may be moved on its sole.

These charis of aerial basis employing the graceful movements of the limbs may be used in the discharge of bow and arrow, thunder bolt, sword *etc.* The actors should show poses of hand before or after or even along with the movements of the feet. The hands should move in tune with the feet as the actors deem it to be fit. The hands should move in tune with the feet and the hip should follow the course of the hands. After the setting of the feet, one should appropriately use one's eyes, brows and other limbs. As the feet resumes its former position in the ground after the dancing steps, the hands should take natural rest on the hips after performing their actions.

Karana is defined as the simultaneous movement of hands and feet in dancing. Two karanas in a dance constitute Nritta Matrika. 2, 3 or 4 Nritta Matrikas make up an Angahara. 3 karanas comprise a kalapaka. 4 of the karanas constitute a Mandaka while a cluster of 5 give shape to a Sanghataka. 6, 7, or 8 or 9 karanas join together to form an Angahara on occasions forward to place it on the ground with a thud by force to form the cari called suchi.

Fix the heel on the ground and raise the forepart and then hit the ground to show the cari called Nupurapadika. In Dolapada, the heel is raised and the foot is swung from one side to the other and then firmly placed on the ground hitting it with the heel. In Aksipta, the foot is bent and raised and then the shanks are transposed before hitting the ground with the heel raising the forepart of the foot.

Cari is called Aviddha, in which the feet are transposed at the front foot and is bent and stretched forward and place on the ground touching the place with the heel.

In Udvritta, the foot is raised in a slanting position and held by the hands and then one jumps forward. Turning back repeat the same with the other foot. Bend the foot backwards and extend so as to touch the head and turn round to form the chiri called Udyut Bhranta. The foot is stretched backwards and then brought to touch the ground with the heel. This cari is called Alata. Raise the bent foot so that the thigh which turned becomes triangle. Then turn the hip and the knee. This is called Bhajaya Trasita. In Harina pluta, one leaps up and hits the ground with one foot, raise the other foot backwards bent it and shake it.

22

Abhinaya

Abhinaya means to educate or lead the play towards audience. Abhinaya Darpana says the actors educate the spectator by stimulating in him the latent possibility of aesthetic–experience.

Abhinaya is the synthesis of Aharya consisting of facial make up, costumes, jewellery and settings and vachikabhinaya, which consists of dialogue and also gesticulation.

'Vachikabhinaya' refers to the speeches and songs by the actors.

Angika comprises bodily movements and Satvika, the expression of psychic status, intimately associated with emotional conditions. Satvika manifests itself in terms of joy (Ananda Bashpa), change of voice, trembling, fainting, motionlessness *etc.*

(Natya Sastra, Part I, Chapter VI, Sloka 23, p. 268)

In case of dance dramas, vachika is used by the dancers, for delivering dialogues for singing and for gesticulations also.

Abhinaya is of 4 kinds :

1. Angika
2. Vachika
3. Satvika
4. Mukhajabhinaya

Because the body is the sole medium of expression it is subjected to minute observation. Every movement of the Angas, upangas and pratyangas and their relation to emotion is explored. Thus, a distinct language of hand gestures came into being which was codified in the texts with meticulous care (Sunil Kothari). Satvika deals with the expression of psychic status intimately associated with emotional conditions. A dancer produces 'Rasa' or sentiment in the mind of the audience, by employing all the four types of Abhinaya. Sanskrit scholars call their process as 'Rasabhinaya'. It covers all the nine rasas or aesthetic emotions. They are *Sringara, Vira, Karuna, Adbhuta, Raudra, Hasya, Bhayanaka, Bhibhatsa and Santa.*

For example, Khanditha Nayika is portrayed very aptly by this type of dancing the Nayika expresses her disappointment and anger with sarcasm.

There are Astavidha Nayikas and they express their emotions through different techniques.

Physical movements (Angikabhinaya) are divided into two broad classifications.

One is concerned only with the physical movements which are again divided into Angas, upangas and pratyangas.

The second classification is concerned with physical movements coordinated with the expressions or histrionics, which are again divided into (1) Mukhaja–facial (2) Sarira–Physical (3) Chesta Krita or the movements of the entire body. The second classification of Bharata does not deal with the comprehensive movements of the entire limbs of the body.

The second classification covers the entire gesticulation and any minute movement of the body falls under this division.

Bharata has laid down specifications of each movement, along with the emotional or state evoked by such movement. He has narrated the nature, scope and use of the expression, through physical movements.

Angivabhinaya is derived from Yajurveda or book of sacrifices. It portrays action and reflects emotions through movements of three parts of the body–Anga (hands, legs, head, lips and chest) pratyanga (such as neck, shoulders, back, stomach, thighs, knees and ankles) and upangas (such as lips, mouth, tongue, nose, cheeks and eyes).

In fact abhinaya is gesticulatory expression and is the backbone of Indian classical dance, more so of Kuchipudi style.

Angika Abhinaya

Medieval writers classified Angikabhinaya into 3 more divisions namely :

1. Angas or the major limbs
2. Upangas or the minor limbs and
3. Pratyangas or subsidiary limbs.

They have added some more types of movements to each limb.

According to Sangita Ratnakara and Lasya Ranjana, there are 6 Angas namely the head and hands, chest, side, waist and feet.

Some writers treat the 'shoulder' also as one of the Angas.

The upangas are 15 in number namely, glances, eyelids, eye balls, cheek, nose, breath, lips, teeth, tongue, chin and mouth (these 12 are the gestures of the face). The other three are–the ankle, the sole, and the fingers and toes, the breath, tongue and teeth are not included by Bharata.

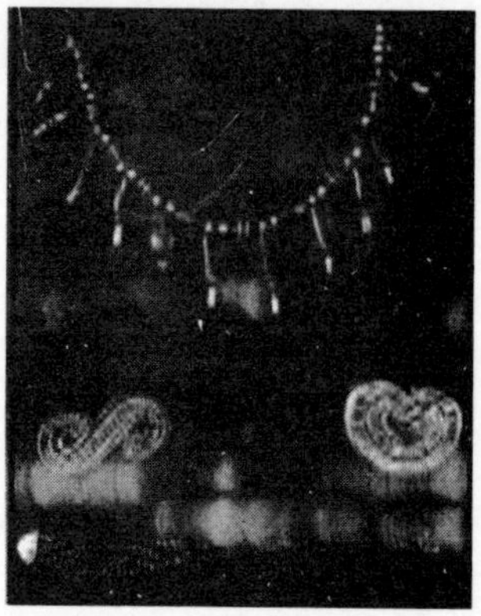

The pratyangas are six namely, neck, arms, cheek, belly, thighs and shanks.

The two main classifications of Angikabhinaya are complimentary to each other.

Vachikabhinaya

It is expression of 'Bhava' by song or speech, *i.e.*, singing or speaking according to the context and mood of the character.

Aharya Abhinaya

It is expression of the mood with the help of appropriate costumes, ornaments, make-up *etc.*, befitting the occasion of the story, song or speech and the status of the character, which the dancer tries to portray. This gives a decorative effect.

Sarirabhinaya : (gestures of the limbs) Uras (chest gestures)

1. Abhugna:-Chest is kept lowered. Back is resided higher, shoulders are slightly bent and left loose at limbs without being stiff. Its application is in embarrassment, despair, fainting, sorrow, cold touch and bashfulness.

2. Nirbhugna:-Chest is stiff, neck depressed shoulders are bent–haughty expression and arrogance is exhibited.

3. Prakampita :-Chest is heave up and down. Its application is in laughter, weeping, terror and misery *etc.*

4. Udhahita:-Its application is in deep breathing, looking at objects placed high above and in yawning.

5. Sama:-All the limbs are in the chaturasana (symmetrical) state and the chest has soustava (excellence).

Another important classification of Angikabhinaya is '*chestakruta*'. Sarirabhinaya deals with the major and minor limbs of the body whereas, Mukhajibhinaya deals with the facial gestures.

These two classifications are of great value in interpretive dance.

The chestakruta deals with the movements of the entire body. It has two aspects. One is the body movement without tempo known as gati prakara, *i.e.*, the different gatis related to different characters, when entering the stage, sitting, standing, reclining and exit from the stage, pertaining to men and women belonging to uttama, madhyama and adhama classes. This discussion will be useful in class drama than in dance. Of course, in dance also, gati prakara is discussed in various circumstances.

The 2nd aspect of cestakruta is Nrittaprakara, *i.e.*, movements or actions of the body followed by a particular tempo. This aspect is purely related to a class of dance.

Thus Nritta prakara is also dealt with in detail, as it is a part of dance technique.

Satwika Abhinaya

Satwikam is 'Sivam' according to our sastras. Nayaka–Nayiki Bhava or sentiment is portrayed in this sort of expression.

It springs from the adharvaveda. Satwikabhinaya consists of two elements complimentary to each other.

(a) Rasa or emotional fervour

(b) Bhava or a mood to suit a particular emotion.

Nandikeswara's Abhinaya Darpana says "where the hands go, the eyes follow. Where the eyes go there the mind goes. Where the mind goes, there is feeling, these is mood of Bhava."

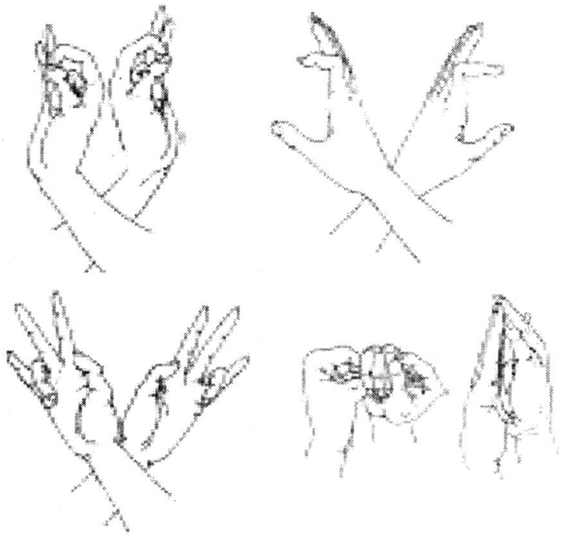

Bhava is complimentary feature to Rasa, which is the primary feature of Nritya. Rasa depends on purely imaginative transfiguration, where as Bhava is more earthly.

Bhava may be of 4 kinds :

1. Vibhava
2. Anubhava
3. Vyabhichhari bhava
4. Satwika bhava–it consists of eight movements to express emotions as joy, fear or disgust.

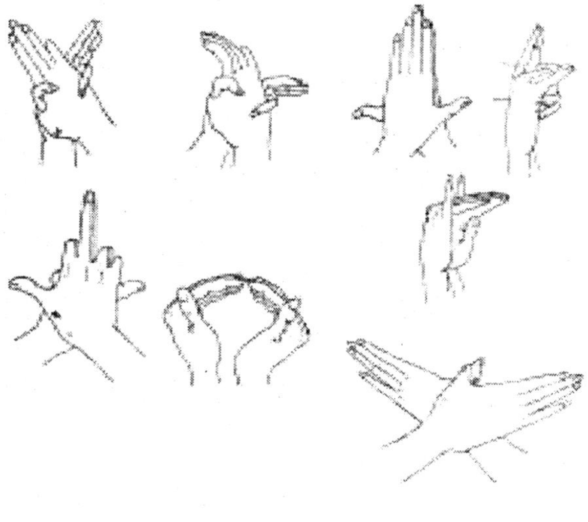

Mukhajabhinaya

Mukhajabhinaya is the first division of the Angikabhinaya. It is the gesticulation related to facial features. Here Bharata coordinates the movements of the gestures with expression. An elaborate discussion of this part reveals how the facial gestures are significant in conveying even minute expressions. The rasa originating in the heart of the performer is expressed viewer through the various gestures of the face or mukha to the viewer, so Mukhajabhinaya is given prime importance because face is the mirror of one's heart and mind. The languages may be different but the meaning and ideas of the lyrics are conveyed through the expression of emotional state combined with the facial gestures. Bharata takes up drsti or glances as the first and foremost attributes of expressive dance. Drstis are divided into 3 parts, they are:

1. Rasa Dristi—The glances with sentiments–8 types.
2. Sthayi Dristi—The glances with permanent states–8 types
3. Sancari Dristi—The glances with temporary states–16 types.

Nandikesvara in his Bharatarnava gives the same classification. But in Sangitaratnakara and Lasya Ranjana 20 types of Sancari Dristis are mentioned.

Darsanas–Eyes

The eyes (balls and lids) eye–brows and lips are the actual life of the face. These are the moving parts of the body and their movements are distinctively visible and can create miraculous change in the expression of the entire face. Bharata speaks about the varieties of glance and names them as additional glances or Darsanas. Apart from the 36 Dristi bhedas or glances, Bharata has given a list of 8 types of Darsanas or looks. Abhinaya Darpana has dealt with only these 8 glances but not 36. As far as 8 types of Darsanas are concerned both the treatises Natyasatra and Abhinaya Darpana discuss similar points. In Lasya Ranjana and Sangitaratnakara there is no reference to the 8 Darsanas.

Eye Balls–Taras

The movements of the pupils put forth by Bharata are of 9 types. Sangitaratnakara and Lasya Ranjana also deal with the same movements. In addition to these nine types Lasya Ranjana mentions 8 more types of the movements of dance.

Eye–lids

The eyelids are the factors which contribute to emphasise the emotions thoroughly. In Natyasastra 9 types of the movements of eyelids are given.

Bhrus–Eye–Brows

There are seven movements of the eyebrows defined in Natyasastra used in various emotional conditions. Sangita Ratnakara and Lasya Ranjana also define similar movements as in Natyasastra.

Nasika–Nose

Bharata has prescribed 6 varieties of expressions with the nose. The same expressions are also described in Sangitaratnakara.

Gandas–Cheeks

Expressions with the cheeks are of six types. Both Natyasastra and Sangitaratnakara deal with similar varieties of cheek movements.

Adhara–Lips

There are 6 types of lip movements defined in Natyasastra Sangitaratnakara and Lasya Ranjana add another 4 types of lip movements. Vivartita, Kampita Visrta, Sandesa, Samudga are common to both the treatises. In addition to these the later works include the following 5 types of lip movements.

1. Nigrhita (drawing the lips inside closing the mouth).
2. Udvrtta (raising the face and lips together).
3. Vikasya (showing the upper teeth and separating the lips).
4. Ayata (opening both the lips while laughing).
5. Recita (expanding the lips upto end).

Cibuka–Chin

The chin does not have independent movement. The chin is dependent upon the movement of the tongue, teeth and lips. That is the reason why Bharata has not dealt with the movements of teeth and tongue separately. According to Natyasastra there are 7 movements of the chin. Sangitaratnakara and Lasya Ranjana give 8 types of chin movements altogether different from those given by Natyasastra. The later works have described the movements of teeth and tongue separately including 8 varieties of tongue movements.

Asya–Mouth

The expression with the mouth is of 6 varieties. Though Sangitaratnakara and Lasya Ranjana mention 6 varieties of mouth movements, there are differences in their description and also names. Bharata says that the movements of the mouth should also use the mouth in conformity with the varieties of glances such as sama and saci and the like mentioned by others.

Mukha Ragas–Colours of the Face

The colours of the face go with the expression of the face. The various sentiments are expressed

through the gesticulation of the face. When the performer on the stage is fully absorbed in emotions, the slightest change in the colour is depicted. Thus the Mukharaga of the face is dependent upon the emotion expressed and the rasa that it has created. According to Bharata the colour is the basis of the state and the sentiments. In Sangitaratnakara and Lasya Ranjana the same varieties of colours of face are explained.

Some of the writers have described the movements of breath in creating various expressions. In Sangitaratnakara 18 types of breathing movements are depicted. In Lasya Ranjana 19 movements are mentioned but only 18 movements are described. There is difference in featuring these movements in these two treatises.

Sirobheda—The Movements of Head

As regards the movements of the head, Natyasastra discusses 13 movements. Abhinaya Darpana discusses 8 movements as in Natyasastra and an extra movement known as 'Sama'. In Bharatarnava 19 movements of head are mentioned. In Sangita Ratnakara and Natyasastra 19 movements are mentioned.

Grivabheda—The Movements of Neck

In Natyasastra 9 movements of neck (the Gruvakarana are explained. With slight differences Sangitaratnakara and Natyasastra Sangraha also follow the Natyasastra tradition. But in Abhinayadarpana only 4 neck movements are described which are different from those mentioned in Natyasastra.

Abhinaya (Gesticulatory expressions)

Abhinaya is the backbone of Indian classical dance. It is divided into four kinds—Angika, Vachika, Aharya and Satwika.

Angika Abhinaya is expression of the Bhava, by using Angas, Pratyangas and Upangas, Karanas and Angaharas (body poses) and Mudras (Gasture of the hand). Facial expressions also come under mudra Abhinaya. Angika Abhinaya is of 3 kinds—(1) Mukhaja—Facial expression, (2) Sarine (poses of the body such as Karanas and Angaharas, (3) Chesta (movements of Angas, Upangas and Pratyangas).

Angas are head, hands, waist, chest, sides and legs. These are main limbs of the body. Upangas are eyes, eye-brows, nose, lower lip, chin and cheeks. The movement of the Angas and upangas are discoverd with details in the Natya Sastra. Hand gestures, otherwise known as Mudras constitute a distinct language by themselves. They are twenty four Asamyutha Hastas (hand gestures or mudras), 13 Samyutha Hastas, 13 poses of the head (sinobhadas), 36 kinds of glances (Dristi Bheda), 7 movement of the eye brows and a movements of Angas, Upangas, and Pratyangas.

Abhinayam

Since the meaning of the songs is communicated through it to the spectators, it is called Abhinaya.

Expression through the body and its limbs is Angika Abhinayam. Expression through voice and speech is Vachika-Abhinayam. Decorating the body with garlands, make-up, costume, jewellery *etc.* is Aharya Abhinayam. Expression through Sathvika Bhavas in Sathvika Abhinayam.

All these four kinds of Abhinayam are essential for both Nritya and Natya. Satvika Bhavas are eight—(1) Stambham, (2) Swedam, (3) Romancam, (4) Swarabhangam, (5) Vepathu, (6) Vaivarnyam, (7) Asru, (8) Pralayam.

Satwika Abhinaya

Four types of this is the most important Abhinayas.

Bharata says that special care should be taken about temperament (Sathva) as it is the basis for a dramatic representation. The Abhinaya with an expression of Sattva is the best one. This Sattwa, though invisible, manifests itself in sentiments like shedding tears *etc.*

Satvika conditions are eight in number.

(1) Stuper, (2) Perspiration, (3) Horripilation, (4) Broken voice, (5) Tremor, (6) Change of colour, (7) Tears, (8) Fairing. In the wider sense all the eight ragas, eight Bhavas and thirty-three Vyabhichary Bhavas consider the category of Sathvika or Sattvi.

Satvika bhinaya deals with the entire situation

Anga-Upanga Pratyangas

Angika Abhinayam is three fold containing :

(1) Angas (2) Pratyangas (3) Upangas.

Angas are 6 : (1) Sinas (2) Hastas (3) Vaksha (4) Parswas (5) Katianal and (6) Padas

Some other consider griva also as ananga. Pratyangas are also six. (1) Shoulders (2) Arms (3) Back (4) Stomach (5) Thighs and (6) Shanks. Some others consider three more *i.e.* wrights, knees and elbows also as pratyangas.

The following twelve are the upangas in the head. (1) Eyes (2) Eyebrows (3) Eye-lids (4) Pupils (5) Checks (6) Nose (7) Jaws (8) Lower lip (9) Lower lip (10) Tongue (11) Chin and (12) Face.

The movement of pratyangas and upangas depend on the movements of angas.

Classification of head movements-Siro-Bhedas

Sirobhedas are nine : (1) Samam (2) Udu (3) Adhomukham (4) Alohitam (5) Dhutam (7) Pari Vritham (8) Utkshiptam and (9) Parivahikam.

Drshti Bhedas

Classification of glances

There are eight Drishti bhedas as explained by our ancient scholars.

(1) Samam (2) Alokitam (3) Saci (4) Pralokitam (5) Nimilitam (6) Ullokitam (7) Amvrittam and (8) Avalokittam.

Bhru and Griva Bhedas

Classification of the movements of eye-brows. The following are the six charming movements of the eye-brows. (1) Sahaja (2) Patita (3) Utkshipta (4) Catura (5) Recita (6) Kuncita.

Griva Bhedas (Classification of movements of neck)

Bharata and others described 9 types of neck movements. They are (1) Sama (2) Nata (3) Unnata (4) Vyasra (5) Recita (6) Kuncita (7) Ancita (8) Valita and (9) Vivrilla.

Now, I shall describe characteristics of hands which are of 2 types (1) Asamyuta and (2) Samyuta hastas.

Bharata described 24 Asamyuta hastas only Nandikuswara added 5 more.

Mandalam Bhedas

Mandalam is a standing posture. They are 10 :

(1) Sthana Mandalam (2) Ayata Mandalam (3) Alidha Mandalam (4) Prenkhana Mandalam (5) Prerita Mandalam (6) Pratyalidha Mandalam (7) Swastika Mandalam (8) Mohita Mandalam (9) Samasuci Mandalam (10) Parswasuchi Mandalam.

Sthanaka Bhedas

Due to variations of the movement of the feet the Sthanakas are of 6 types (1) Samapada Sthanakham (2) Ekapada Stharakham (3) Nagabandha Sthanakam (4) Aindra Sthanakam (5) Garuda Sthanakam (6) Brahma Sthanakam.

Utplavana Bhedas

They are being described as 5 by scholars :

(1) Alaga Utplavam (2) Kartari Utplavam (3) Aswa Utplavam (4) Mohita Utplavanam (5) Kaloga Utplavanam.

Bhramari Bhedas

They are 7 Bhramaris considered by the experts on Natya Sastra :

(1) Utpluta Bhramari (2) Cakra Bhramari (3) Garuda Bhramari (4) Ekapada Bhramari (5) Kuncita Bhramari (6) Akasa Bhramari (7) Anga Bhramari.

Now I shall describe the characteristics of various caris.

(1) Calana cari (2) Camramana cari (3) Sarana cari (4) Vegini cari (5) Kuttana cari (6) Luthita cari (7) Lolita cari (8) Vishama Samchara cari. These 8 are cari Bhedas as described by Nandikeswara. These caris are different from the 16 Bhoumi and 16 Akasiki caris described in Natya Sastra (10th Chapter).

Gati Bhedas

Now the Gati Bhedas are described by Nandikeswara as follows.

(1) Hamsi Gati (2) Mayuri Gati (3) Mrgi Gati (4) Gajalila Gati (5) Turangini Gati (6) Simhi Gati (7) Bhujangi Gati (8) Manduki Gati (9)Vira Gati (10) Manavi Gati.

These are the gatis by experts on Natya Sastra.

In chapter 22, Bharata described the characteristics of 23 types of women. Some of these women are having the characteristics of birds and animals. However, he has not described their gatis.

Bharata says "dance imparts beauty and splendour. People spontaneously love dance and it is said to be auspicious. On occasions like marriage, birth of children, reception of a bridegroom, events of joy and prosperity, dance is employed as an amusement. Lord Maheswara spoke to Tandu thus perform the Tandava dance, before the use of songs. Thus popularise the dance as an ancillary of songs". Mostly performance of dance depends on the ecology of divinities and it is delicately employed in the delineation of the sentiment of love.

The myths or styles of dramatic composition are four-VS2 Bharati, Sattvati, Kausiki and Arabhati which form the foundation of the rules.

There are four pravrithis or regional variations of dramatic performance called Avanti Dahshinatya, Indramagadhi and Panchala madhyama.

Dharmis—the rules of dramatic representation are of two kinds—Lokadharmi (natural) or realistic representation as noticed in the world around, and Natyadharmi (Theatrical performance based on certain conventions).

Abhinaya (representation) is based on real life and hence classification as Lokadharmi is meaningful. Siddhi or Achievement (in performance) is of two kinds as divine and human. The Svaras (musical notes) are seven and are of 2 kinds. Corporeal and those produced by instruments like Vina, Atodya (musical instruments) belong to four kinds with their own characteristics. They are 'Tata' (the stringed instrument), Avanadha (drums), Ghana (used for beating time) and Susira (having holes as in a flute).

There are 4 sentiments which are considered as basic. They are Sringara (the erotic), Raudra (the fusiness), Vira (the heroic) and Bhibhatsa (the destiny).

In the facial mode of representation of the different emotions and sentiments, the action after head is presented. The actions of the head are of 13 kinds. 1. Akampitam 2. Kampitam 3. Dhutaru 4. Kdhatam 5. Parivahitam 6. Adhutam 7. Avadhutam 8. Ancilam 9. Nihancilam 10. Paravritham 11. Utksiptam 12. Adhogatam and 13. Lolitam.

The glanis relating to Rasa or Sentiments are 8 in number as follows. 1. Kanta, 2. Bhayanaka, 3. Hasya, 4. Karuna, 5. Adbhuta, 6. Raudri, 7. Vira, and 8. Bhibhatsa.

The glanis relating to Sthayibhavas or permanent moods are also 8 in number. 9. Shigdha, 10. Hrsta, 11. Dina, 12. Kruddha, 13. Dripta, 14. Bhayancita, 15. Jugupsita, 16. Pulismita the twenty glances relating to Sancharbhavas or transitory feelings are given as 17. Surya, 18. Malina, 19. Sranta, 20. Jajyanvita, 21. Glana, 22. Sankita, 23. Kisanna, 24. Muksula, 25. Kunchita, 26. Abhitapta, 27. Tihma, 28. Lolita, 29. Vitarkita, 30. Ardhamukula, 31. Vibhranta, 32. Vipluta, 33. Akekara, 34. Vikosa, 35. Trasta, 36. and madira are the 36 types of glances on which the dramatic representation is based.

Action of the eyebrows is of 7 kinds as 1. Utiksipa (lifting up) 2. Patana (taking down) 3. Bhrukuti (knilling) 4. Cature (beautiful) 5. Kuchita (contracted) 6. Recita (loosening) and 7. Sahaja (natural).

Actions of the nose are of 6 types as 1. Nata (depressed) 2. Manda (mild), 3. Kikrsta (expanded) 4. Socchvasa (having the respiration) 5. Vikunita (slanted and Svabhavika (normal or natural).

There are six kinds of Ganda (the movement of the cheek), *viz.* 1. Ksama (emacoated) 2. Phulla (Blown up) 3. Purna (full) 4. Kampita (Shaken) 5. Kunchita (contracted) 6. Sama (level or even).

The activities of the lops are classified under six types as 1. Vivartana (rolling) 2. Kampana (tremory) 3. Visarga (spreading out) 4. Viniguhana (concealing) 5. Sandastaka (biting) and 6. Samudga (closed up).

The gestures of the chin are 7 as enumerated. 1. Kullana (clashing) 2. Khandana (cutting) 3. Ecchina (closing) 4. Chakrota (separating) 5. Lehita (licking) 6. Sama (natural) 7. Dasta (biting).

The facial activities are of six kinds as 1. Viniurolla (turned) 2. Vidhuta 3. Nirbhugna (lowering) 4. Blugura (a little about spreading) 5. Vivrta (open) and 6. Udvahi (turned upwards).

The colour of the face is enumerated as 4. 1. Svabhavika (natural) 2. Prasanna (pleased) 3. Rakta (reddish) and 4. Syama (dark or cloudy).

When things are to be represented in a natural way, the colour of the face should be Svabhavika. In the representation of sentiments like Adbhuta, Vira and Sringara, the expression should be prasanna. In the sentiments like vira, raudra and Bhayanaka as also in the emotion of arrogance the Rakta face should be employed. In the sentiments of Bhayanaka and Bhibhatsa, the face should be Syama—dark and moody.

Thus in the representation of the theme delineating emotional moods and sentiments, appropriate facial colour should be employed.

The gesture of the limbs :

The gestures of the chest are enumerated as consisting of 5 types 1. Abhugna (slightly) 2. Nirbhugna (not bent) 3. Prakampita (shaking) 4. Advahita (lifted up) and 5. Sama (level or even).

Abhugna may be understood as the chest, which is kept lowered. The back is raised higher with the shoulders slightly bent and kept at ease. Its application may be used in situations of embrassment, worry, swoon, sorrow, fear, disease, mental agony, cold, rain, and bashfulness. Nirbhugna is that chest with the back bent and shoulders raised and resulting in stiffness. Its application may be understood as in embrassment, arrogance, look of wonder, statement of truth, pride and courage.

In Prakampita, the chest is leaved up and down almost incessantly—a feature to be recognised by the practitioners of drama. They should use this in situations like laughter, weeping, fatigue, fear, cough, sigh, hiccup, sorrow, *etc.*

Advahita is the chest which is kept raised up and its application is in letting a deep breath, looking at an object kept in high place and in agonising.

In Samam, the chest is evenly placed and made attractive due to the symmetrical placement of all limbs. Non-gestures of the sides are of 5 types. 1. Nata (bent) 2. Samurrita 3. Prasarita (extend) 4. Vivartita (turned round) and 5. Apasrta (slightly withdrawn).

In Nata, the waist is slightly bent as also on the sides and a shoulder is drawn away a little.

In minata pose as a result of one side becoming bent the waist side and shoulder of the other side become raised up and result in the variety called unnata. In prasarita, both the sides are stretched out in their respective directions.

In Vivartita, the sacrum is kept turned round. In Apasrta, the side, which had turned fade in the vivartita is brought back to the previous position by a turn.

While approaching some one nata should be employed and unnata, when one goes away. Prasarita is applied when one is delighted and vivartita when one is turning about. Aparita is used in the act of returning.

Gestures of the belly : They are 3 types—1. Ksama (slender or emanciated) 2. Khalla (depressed or hollowed) and 3. Purna (full or inflated).

The Ksama type of belly is employed in the depiction of laughter, cry, sighing, and yawning. The Ksaka type is used in showing disease, revance, fatigue or hunger. The purna variety is resorted to in gasping out stoutness, drapsy and excessive consumption of food.

Gestures of the hip : The gestures of the hip in dramatic performance and dance are of 5 kinds. 1. Cchinna (turned aside) 2. Nivrilla (turned up) 3. Recita (surrounded) 4. Kampita (shaken) and 5. Udvahita (raised).

Turning of the middle of the waist is called Cchinna, and turning to the front from a reverse position is termed Nivrilla. In Recita, one turns about to different directions Prakampita is that in which shivering in the hip occurs (as in the case of a hunch back). In Udvahita the sides of the hip are raised slowly along with the whole waist.

Cchinna is employed when one turns back to look at something in haste or in doing exercises. Vivitha is employed in the act of returning and recita in turning a full circle. In the movements of a hunch back dwarf, or a low type of person, prakampita is made use of. In the gait of a stout person or of women, the hip assumes the pose called Udvahita.

Gestures of the thighs : They are of five types. 1. Kampana (shivering) 2. Valana (turning round) 3. Stambhana (becoming stiff) 4. Udvartana (springing up) and 5. Vivartana (turning away).

Gestures of the feet : Gestures involving the feet are of 5 kinds. 1. Udghattita (with firm heel) 2. Sama (even palms) 3. Agratala Sanchara (on tip toe) 4. Ancita (extended) and 5. Kuncita (bent).

In Udghathita, one stands on the forepart of the feet and then lets the heel touch the ground.

The natural placing of the feet on the ground is called Sama and it is used to represent the natural disposition while representing the natural situation, the feet are held or placed firmly on the ground but they are often moved by the experts to show various Karanas.

Padmasri Vedantam Satyanarayana Sarma

In Agratala Sanchara, the heel is raised, the big toe is stretched out and the other toes are bent. This should be made use of in goading, knocking, standing, thrashing, kicking, turning, removing, as also in various movements including the gait of the person whose heels are wounded.

In Ancita, the heels touch the ground, the forepart remains raised and toes are bent. This is to be employed in movements of persons, whose feet, especially, foreparts are wounded and in turning round, striking of the foot on something and also in various Bhramari movements.

In Kuncita, the heels are raised, the forepart of the heel stressed on the ground with the toes bent. The centre part is also bent in the Kuncita type.

This is to be employed in walking through an edge, in treading one's way on and in the action like jumping over to pass it.

There is a gait called sucipada, in which one stands on the big toe of the right foot keeping the heel raised. The left foot is placed in this in the normal position in dance and in decorating the foot with anklet, this variety of foot is used.

The dancers should employ feet, shanks, thighs *etc.* at the same time for all action of the feet. In all the charis of the foot. They must act together and at the same time.

The simultaneous movements of the limbs like feet, shanks, thighs and lips are technically referred to as cari. This is called vyayama (exercise) when the movements are governed by appropriate ribs and the limbs are in concordance with each other in their activity. The movement involving a single foot is designated as cari and the movement of the two feet is called a karana.

Padma Sri Sobha Naidu

23

Rasa (Sentiments) and Bhava

'Sentiment' or Rasa is the cream or essence of Indian art. It is the underlying force in the expression of painting, sculpture, musical composition, dance and dramatic presentation. The Rasa theory is common to all the Indian fine arts. The Abhinaya is meaningless without the dominant forte of Rasa. In the opinion of many scholars the exact translation or to give the meaning of the word 'Rasa' is very difficult task. In spite of many explanations it has not been possible to express the meaning and contents of Rasa. Rasa can perhaps be experienced and demonstrated with greater ease than explanation.

How is Rasa tasted? It is said that just as, well disposed persons while eating food cooked with many kinds of spices, enjoy its tastes and attain pleasures and satisfaction, so also the cultured people taste durable psychological states while they see them represented by an expression of the various psychological states with words, gestures, and derive pleasure and satisfaction. Brahmananda gave rise to the theory of Rasa. All the human emotions in the poetic form interpreted by inner spiritual sentiments also are Rasa. The emotion that creates a mood and a sense of enjoyment in Bhava which is expressed through the various sentiments known as Rasa. Bhava is compared to an architectural framework which is the body and Rasa is the soul.

There is a controversial opinion among scholars whether Bhava is responsible for creating Rasa or Rasa evokes Bhava. Rasa and Bhava are interdependent. Bhava has no existence unless it promotes Rasa. Rasa cannot be evoked if Bhava is not being expressed. Rasa and Bhava are thus complementary to each other and are represented through the expression of mental status. No poetic meaning is produced without sentiment.

The Rasa or sentiment is produced from a combination of determinants which create emotion called Vibhava, the consequents which types are followed are known as Anubhava and the complementary psychological states which are the transitory states are known as Vyabhicaribhava. Thus the emotion is created and expressed through gesticulation and influenced through the transitory and complementary emotions and create Rasa in the minds of the sympathetic audience into three groups.

(1) The emotions which are static (Sthayibhava) and or 8 types or permanent states.

(2) The emotions which are transitory (Sancaribhava) or 33 types or passing emotions.

(3) The responsive emotions (Satvikabhava) of 8 types.

This brief study of dance techniques forms a base for further discussions. The various Karanas, Caris, Hasta, Sthanus, different rasas are faithfully represented in dance sculptures of Andhra. Even the literature is rich enough in describing the dance techniques of Natyasastra as well as the regional forms of dances. While illustrating every dance sculpture the knowledge of dance techniques enables us to find out the style, form and minute movement adopted by the sculptors. In this regard dance sculptures stand as an important source for tracing the dance traditions through the centuries.

Rasa Theory : Kshetragna's padas on Movva Gopla became very popular on account of "Rasabhinaya' or Satwikabhinaya' and elevated the art to a high degree of excellence. Kuchipudi artists specialized in the Abhinaya of the 'Padas' of Kshetrayya.

A work on Indian aesthetics by name 'Alankara raghava' says "artistic beauty cannot exist unless the heart of the man of good taste is moved to delight by the fascination of its expression". In a dance, the emotion portrayed is impersonal and is shared by all. The dancer's art and skill, makes the audience feel all the emotions, but in each case, the final effect is attainment of ANANDA (the immortal bliss) which breaks down all the fetters of everyday's mundane life and makes the innate nature of man (Atma) to shine.

Rasas are generally accepted as nine :

1. Sringara
2. Hasya (Humour)
3. Krodha (Anger)
4. Karuna
5. Dukha (sorrow)
6. Veera (Heroism)
7. Adbhuta (Astonishment)
8. Bhayanaka (fearful)

Originally there were only eight. Santa is added. Saiva Agamas speak of Navarasas. Only a gifted artist can render padabhinaya in a single rasa generally, vipralambha, sringara and can develop 'Bhavabhinaya' to its highest.

How is Rasa Experienced

The concept of Brahmanada or the inner joy gave rise to the theory of rasa. All the human emotions, in the poetic form interpreted by inner spiritual sentiments are also included in Rasa. The emotion that creates a mood and a sense of enjoyment is Bhava, which is expressed through various sentiments known as Rasa.

A competent writer narrates the pains and pleasures experienced by a human being. The dancer or actor through the four types of Abhinaya brings out the emotion of the poetry and influences the audience with his talent and evokes Rasa Bhava, the attainment of bliss to the individual. Thus the creation of Rasa in a way is a collective effort of the writer, the performer and the spectator.

When we trace the evolution of the traditions of India, we find that art and dance are interwoven and are one with the religious fervour also, to make man enriched with greater ecstasies of joy, which is a very rare combination indeed.

What is rasa and what is rasa swadana ? What is beauty and what is aesthetic emotion ? These matters are discussed in detail by Viswanatha in his Sahitya Darpana. He says that religion and art are thus names for one and the same experience– an institution of reality or identity.

Agni Purana says that Rasa is the life, art and pravrithi are intimately related. As Vishwa Dharmothara Purana says Aharya is dress which is primitive viravinaysa. The three aspects namely Rasa is primitive pranieith (speech, action and senses are all Anubhava are classed as Proudha Charana Bhavas by Bhoja in chapter XIII of his Sringara Pravesa. Singabhupala also followed Bhoja and said in his Rasa I–p. 64 (Dr. Raghavan–some concepts of Alankarasastra) page 175.

A notable feature in the Nritha treated of in Bharatarnava is that Nandikeswara predicts that there is a particular Rasa in each item of pure dance as we have in Abhinaya although the mudras in pure dance are intended only to add grace to the moments of the feet and other parts of the body and do not convey any idea, total effect of the moments of the feature and the expression in the eyes can be ordered as to produce an appeal to a particular Rasa. After postulating this aspect of pure dance, Nandikeswara proceeds to instruct the student of the art of a series of items. First he has given 27 elementary pieces, each consisting of a pose, a step and a look, intended evidently to serve as an alphabet of pure dance with Rasa.

Each Rasa has 2, 3, 4 or 5 forms thus all the nine making up to 27. These 27 simple pieces are called by the name 'Angahara' which is used in a different sense by Bharata, namely, one of 32 finished items in the dance of Lord Shiva, each consisting of 10 Karanas.

Nandikeswara's Angahara is therefore different from the well–known Angahara. After the simple pieces combined pieces are next dealt with in the subsequent chapters in a series.

There are altogether 55 items in the book. All these have gone out of use but with graduated instructions they may be received and taught to students.

After these two standard treatises we do not find in later works of Dattila or Kohala though some extracts of them are to be found in the comments of Sangitaratnakara.

In the eye of Bharata, Rasa is nothing but dance "Natyamcha Rasa evetyutla Prayam"

Bharatha further says :

"Vibhava Anubhava vydhya chari same yogodrasva Nishpathih Bhasa venkata rama/ (bharata 6th chapter says in Andhra Parishat Patrika that Bharata's Natyasastra defines asamarupa and so his text is supposed to be the first treatise of aesthetics of Indian philosophy.

For the traditional Indian artist, artistic creation was the supreme means of realizing the universal being.

The theory of Rasa as conceived by Hindu Aestheticism has two clear aspects.

The first is the eroted state (Rasavastha).

The second is the sentiment—the mood

Bharata says

Dukhartanam sramartanam

Sokartanam Tapaswinam

Visranthi Janane kale

Natyame Tadbhivasthri

Bharata means to say that for a man distressed tired and for a man deeply engrossed, Natya gives solace and pleasure.

"Nane Bhasapa samparria nana vasthantha rathmakam

loka vrithanu Karanam

Natyame Tanmaya Krutham"

Bharata tells natya is replete with display of different kinds of human nature.

It is full of exprcssions.

Narat Jananam Nata lehitpam

Masa vidya Vasa Vala

Nase yogo Natat Varma

Natyasim Yanna Drisyathe "–There is no Knowledge or yoga or karma, which is not found is natya".

Toyam Swabhavo lokasya

Swviha Theyabhi Nayo Peto

Natya Mitrayathi Dhuyate–Bharata tells that this world which is full of happiness and misery is being depicted in the form of dance, with Anga, Pratyanga and Abhinaya.

To evoke Rasa in the spectator is the main object of the Hindu play wright. The term rasa had been translated as 'flavour' (by Coomaraswamy) sentiment, poetic sentiment, aesthetic experience (by Apte and others) and so on, but none of these synonyms bring out the correct idea and meaning of the term. The synonyms, however, are not of much help to anyone unless an explanation is offered, and the nature and characteristic of Rasa will be clear when the relative positions of the spectators and actors are considered. Aesthetic experience (rasaswadana) is the tasting of Rasa, and depends mainly on the innate and acquired sensibility of the spectator. To appreciate the art of India from the standpoint of life it must be studied not only from this point of view, but also as meaning and with reference to use, "We see on the stage, for suitable circumstances of time and place; this affection is intimated by speech and gesture alike, which indicates both dominant emotion of love and its transient shapes in the various stages of love required. The spectacle evokes in the mind of the spectator the impressions of the emotions of love which experience has planted there, and this ideal and generic excitation of the emotion produces in him a sense of joy which is known as Rasa. The fullness of the enjoyment depends essentially on the nature and experience of the spectator to whom it falls to identify himself with the hero of the other character, and thus to experience in ideal form his emotions and feelings. He may even succeed in his effort to the extent that he weeps or laughs, but the sentiment is one of exquisite joy. We may compare the thrill or pleasure which the most terrifying narration excites in us and we are all conscious of the sweetness of sad tales.

Surindra Mohan Tagore defines a Rasa as follows: " when Rati or any other Sthayi–Bhava, being expressed through Vibhava, Anubhava and Sanchari Bhavas, delightfully vibrates over the heartstring of the audience. It is called a Rasa".

Sthayi–Bhava : When a Bhava (mood) is predominant in a man's mind and occupies the mind fully, it is a sthayi-bhava. It is neither influenced nor replaced by any other Bhava.

Sthayi Bhavas are nine as there are nine Rasas, each Sthayi-Bhava having a respective Rasa. They are rati (prem or anurag), has shoka, krodha, utshaha, bhaya, ghrina, ashcharya and shanta.

Sanchari Bhava: Sthayi Bhavas have a few Sanchari Bhavas which have a close relation with Sthayi Bhavas only at times they are at the forefront and show their importance or else they are helping factors. They are always changing and moving about, that is why they are called sanchari. If Sthayi Bhava is an ocean, sanchari Bhavas are its waves or bubbles which take their birth from it and are destroyed in it.

There are thirty three such Bhavas as enumerated in the shastras: Nirveda, (hatred from ones own self), Glani (from tiresomeness), Shanka, Sharma, Dhirty (santosh), Jarata (which arises on hearing any bad message of a beloved), Harsha, Dainya, Ougrya, Chinta, Trasa, Asuya or Irshya (arising from somebody's riches or wealth), Amsrsha, Garva, Smriti, Marana, Mada, Supta, (a particular situation at the time of lying down), Nidra, Vivodha (to awake or to be awakened), Vrira, (Lajja, bashfulness), Apasmara (lunaticism), Moha, Mati (the knowledge of things at their proper places), Alasya, Avega, Trka, Avahitta, Vyadhi, Unmada, Vishada, Autsukya and Chapalya.

Vibhava : The cause of any Sthayi Bhavas which enter into the composition of any poem or drama, are called Vibhava (determinants) Vibhava is of two kinds, viz, Alambana and Uddipana.

Alambana Vibhava : That which is essential to the awakening of Sthayi Bhava is called Alambana Vibhava, such as the hero and the heroine, who are the mutual stay of each other.

Uddipana Vibhava: That which excites a Rasa is called the Uddipana Vibhava. Uddipana Vibhava constitutes the endeavours of the character concerned and his experience of a feeling of similarity as to time and place.

Anubhava: Anubhavas are consequents or deliberate actions. Anubhava is the expression by means of limbs of any sthayi or sanchari bhava.

Anubhava and mudras are the signs of Bhavas in a dance. They are the language by means of which the idea of a dancer is narrated. Every Bhava can be expressed by its particular Anubhava.

The language of a few Bhavas is given below as examples:

Nirveda: Nirveda is insulting one's own self and also thinking to be lowered down in prestige and status by means of Tattawa Gyan, Vipatti, Irsha *etc.* Nirveda can be expressed by the following signs– The Mudra of Chinta, wiping away tears, deep breathing, place–facedness and the Mudras of Uchchas, Dainya and Asahayata.

Shanka: This is a mood of unforeseen frightfulness resulting from one's own ill-doings or by treachery of others. The following outward expressions on a human body detect this Bhava: The shivering of the body, dry lips, the Mudras of Chinta on the eyes, the hand gestures of Vyakulata, colourless body and the change of voice.

Jarata : This Bhava arises on hearing any good or bad news affecting the hearer's beloved. The signs are : sitting quiet, and the Mudras of Nirnimesh Netras.

Many dancers and critics think that it is impossible to depict these Bhavas, but it is not so and it can be well realized from the extract codification of the extant old works how far the dancers in olden times were efficient in this particular branch of knowledge and practice as to exhibit a perfect art.

Sattwika Bhava: The mental condition arising from the Sattwika Guna is called Sattwika Bhava. Still it sometimes assumes different shapes on account of Anubhava. Stambha, Swada, Romancha, Swarabhanga, Vepathu, Vaivarrnya, Asru and Pralaya constitute the Sattwika Bhava. Coomaraswamy speaks of one Sattwabhava as involuntary emotional conditions, but it seems to be meaningless and without any basis. A Sattwika Bhava cannot be itself an involuntary emotional condition unless it is influenced by Anubhava.

The above mentioned Bhavas are expressed by males and also females in both Tandava and lasya, but there are a few Bhavas which seem to be better exhibited by females in Lasya and these Bhavas which seem to be better exhibited by females in lasya and these Bhavas beautify the fair sex. There are twenty such Bhavas and they are divided into three classifications:-(1) Shariraj or which keeps connection with the sharira or body. (2) Ayatnaj or which springs from itself or spontaneous and (3) Swabhavaj or which arises from one's nature.

Shariraj: There are three, Hava, Bhava and Hela.

(1) Hava: When the eyes and eye-brows are changed as a result of Bhava (mentioned below) in a man's mind, it is called Hava.

(2) Bhava: It is the first passionate yearning in a human mind by Rajo and Tamo Gunas. There is no outward expression of this Bhava but it does its work inwardly.

(3) Hela : It exists when there is a linking of shringara with Hava. These three seem to be of vulgar type.

(4) Ayatnaj: There are seven such Bhavas.

Shobha: When the limbs are influenced softly by the desire of genius produced a new art which the word 'Rasa' summarises and symbolises, and which condenses it in one brief formula: the poet does not express but he suggests.

It is evident from his stupendous work Natya Sastra that the sage Bharata had conceived of the imperativeness of the existence of Rasa in a work of art much before dealing with the technicalities of Rasa and Bhava. Rasa is the "niryas" the essence or the extract of any concrete or abstract object. Bharata narrates at the outset the episode of the fight between the gods and the demons over the possession of Amrita or nectar, which in other words is aqua pure water, obtained after churning of the ocean. This battle obviously is over the elixir of life or Rasamrita.

Again Bharata creates the Apsaras or the heavenly nymphs for the womanly or lasya movements. These Apsaras are nothing but containers or receptacles of water, as have been mentioned earlier. Here also Bharata feels the urgent necessity of Rasa and gives shape to it according to his artistic conception.

In other art forms the thinkers and writers could not eliminate the utter necessity of Rasa. Let us take only one example to elucidate our contention.

This example is from "Vishnudharmottara" an ancient compendium on the art and science of Indian sculpture and painting as Bharata's Natya Shastra enfolds Indian drama, dance and music.

At the very beginning of the book which describes the origin of Indian painting to Vajra or Indra. Who approaches him with a request that the former should teach him the principles of the art of sculpture and painting, the commentator narrates a very interesting legend.

He says that once the sage Nara–Narayana was engaged in rigorous peace. Indra apprehended that the sage would obtain power after this hard and rigid penance he sent the Apsaras, who came down to the earth and started dancing in very amorous poses. The sage was standing under a mango tree. When he saw the dancing Apsaras he store away a mango twig and with the juice oozing out from the twig he drew out a picture of woman on his thigh. On seeing the drawing the Apsaras put their hands to cover their faces out of shame and flew away to the heavens. They reported the matter to Indra that the sage had drawn a picture of a woman. Which was so attractive that they had to retire out of shame. They were proud of their own prettiness but when they saw that picture they could realize that it was difficult for them to enamour a man with their physical beauty who had a much better idea of the beautiful features of a woman. Then all the gods and the goddesses peeped at the picture. They came down and slashed away the portion of the picture out of the thigh of Nara–Narayana. They took away that drawing to the heavens, injected life into it, and named it "Urvashi" as it took its birth on the thigh or Uru.

Then there was a conference among the gods and goddesses and it was decided in that conference that they could not keep the created thing with them in the heavens leaving out her creator on the earth below; a creator :

Rasa	*Deity*
Shringara	Vishnu
Vira	Indra
Karuna	Yama
Rudra	Rudra
Hasya	Pramatha
Bhayanaka	Kala
Bibhatsa	Mahakal (a form of Shiva)
Adbhuta	Gandharva
Shanta	Narayana

Colour attributed to Rasa

Rasa	*Colour*
Shringara	Dark brown
Vira	Golden
Karuna	Indian rock dove
Rudra	Red
Hasya	White
Bhayanaka	Black
Bibhatsa	Blue
Adbhuta	Yellow
Shanta	White, like Kunda flower.

The eight Rasas give rise to mental expansion, elation perturbation and withdrawal of mind, *i.e.*, Shringara and Hasya to the first, Vira and Adbhuta to the second, Bibhatsa and Bhayanaka to the third, and lastly Karuna and Raudra to the fourth.

In classic times two commonly girls appeared and removed the two wings of every scene. In the Shringara or Adi Rasa, the white, in the Vira, the yellow, in the karuna the smoke coloured in the

Sringara

Hasya, the partly coloured in Bhayanaka blue in bibhatsa smoke coloured in Adbhuta black. In Raudra the red drop-scene would be used. According to some the red colour is of universal use.

Shringara Adi Rasa or shringara is divided into two parts, Vipralambha and Sambhoga.

Vipralambha: when a lover pines for the sight of his or her beloved it is called Vipralambha. It is divided into four classes: Puvra Raga Mana Pravasa and Karuna.

Purva–Raga : There are three kinds of Purva Raga (i) Nili–Raga, (ii) Kusumbha–Raga and (iii) Manjishtha Raga.

Mana : There are two kinds of Mana, (i) Puranaya Mana and (ii) Irsha Mana. There are six kinds of Irsha Mana: Sham, Bho, Dana, Nati, Upeksha and Rasatmaka.

Vir: There are four classes of Vir Rasa, *viz.*, (1) Dana (2) Dharma, (3) Daya and (4) Yudhdha. The hero of dana is Karna; of Dharma, Judhisthira: of daya, Nimutbahana and of Judhdha, Ramchandra.

Hasya: Hasya Rasa is of 6 kinds, *viz.*, (1) Smita, (2) Hasita, (3) Vihasita, (4) Avahasita, (5) Apahasita and (6) Atihasita.

The good only resort to Smita and Hasita; the indifferent to Vihasita and Avahasita and the vulgar to Apahasita and Atihasita.

Karuna, Vibhatsa, Raudra, Vira and Bhayanaka are hostile to 'Shringara'; Bhayanaka

Hasya

Rauora

and Shanta to 'Vira'; Hasya and Shringara to 'Karuna'; Bhayanaka and Karuna to 'Hasya'; Shringara, Vira, Raudra Hasya and Shanta to 'Bhayanaka'; Shringara to 'Bibhatsa'; Hasya, Shringara and Bhayanaka to 'Raudra'; and lastly Vira, Shringara, Raudra, Hasya and Bhayanaka to 'Shanta'.

Vrittis: In Shringara, Hasya and Karuna, the Kaishiki Vritti; in Vira, Raudra, and Adbhuta, the 'Sattati' and 'Bharati Vritti'; and in Bhayanaka, Bibhatsa and Raudra the 'Arabhati vritti' respectively are employed.

(i) **Kaishiki Vritti:** When the actors and actresses discourse excellent music and perform dancing with amorous accompaniments, it is called Kaishiki Vritti.

(ii) **Sattati Vritti:** The vritti which is replete with Sattwa Guna, heroism, bounty, kindness and simplicity, which has just a sprinkling of Adi Rasa, which is devoid of grief and which excites joy is named Sattati vritti.

(iii) **Bharati Vritti:** That which is full of grave speeches, conducted by great men only and which is mostly carried on in Sanskrit, is called Bharati Vritti.

(iv) **Arabhati Vritti:** Which contains Maya, Jugglery, war, anger, imprisonment, killing *etc.*, goes by the name of Arabhati Vritti.

The look in Shringara Rasa should be cheerful, chaste, graceful and languishing and it should be ardently directed to the beloved object.

Ascharya

Bhaya

In the Vira Rasa the look should be open gave, fixed, dazzling and contracted.

In the Karuna Rasa the eyes should be half shut, the pupils should show grief and the looks should be directed at the tip of the nose.

The raudra rasa requires restless lids and the fixed, red hard, frowning look.

In the Hasya Rasa the pupils should be partly hid and be rolling; at times the lids should be partially closed. The pupils should sometimes be fixed and others active.

The eye lids in the Bhayanaka Rasa should sometimes be started fully and at others closed. The looks should at times be restless and be cast around fearfully, as if searching for the path to fly.

In the Bibhatsa Rasa the eyes should be partially shut and the lids and pupils restless. The side-glance and very contracted look go in as adjuncts.

In the Adbhuta Rasa the look should be cheerful and eyes should be half-shut.

Psychological resources of a mani is the life, the soul, of the entire dramatic representation. Bharata is very much conscious of this fact, which is clear from the importance given by him to 'Rasa' and 'Bhava'.

Under the head satvika Abhinaya Bharata discusses graces or Alamkaras of women. They are of 3 types.

1. Angaja—Physical 2. Sahaja-natural and 3. Ayatmaja (involuntary).

Shanta

Ghrina

'Bhava' the inner idea which causes sentiments arises from Sallwa. 'Hava', the interrupted excitement arising from the mind and manifesting itself in movements of eyes, eye-brows *etc.* and indicative of Sringara-rasa arises from Bhava.

Hela, which depends on Sringara rasa and which expresses itself by Lalitabhinaya by graceful movements arises from Bhava.

Natural graces are ten in number :

1. Lila or sportiveness
2. Vilasa or gracefulness
3. Vicchiti or indifferent attitude
4. Vibhrama or confusion
5. Kilakuncita or mixed feeling
6. Mottayita or manifestation of live
7. Kuttasmita or pretended anger
8. Bibboka or affected indifference
9. Lalita or lolling
10. Vihrita or reservedness

Involuntary graces are seven in number.

1. Sobha or beauty
2. Kanti or charm
3. Dipti or radiance
4. Madhurya or delicacy

Krodha

5. Dhairya or self-control

6. Pragabhya or courage

7. Audarya or dignity

Again various types of Kamopacharas or love—approaches are described by Bharata. This ten are mentioned.

1. Abhilasha (desire) 2. Cinta (worry) 3. Anusmriti (recollection) 4. Gunakivtana (appreciating in qualities) 5. Udvega (excitement) 6. Vilapa (lamentation) 7. Unmada (mental imbalance) 8. Vyadhi (physical discomfort) 9. Jadata (Stupa) 10. Marana (death).

Again eight types of Nayikas are discussed by Bharata and the characteristics of courtesans are also described.

Svakiya or Sviya : She is a woman who is upright and of good character and is of three types—Mugdha, Madhya and Pragalbha.

Mugdha is tender, youthful and young. She is a girl who is unable to give expression to her ideas, shy in love, gentle in anger and silent even though she is offended. Some writers decide Mugdha into two categories 1. Gnata-Yavana and 2. Agnata-Yavana—The young heroine, who is aware and the one who is without knowledge.

Madhya—She is adoloscent and partly experienced. She possesses desire and shyness in equal measure and is intoxicated by her lover.

Pragalbha : She is mature. She is a woman in her full beauty able to express her sentiments.

Apart from Mugdha, the other two types of heroines are again divided into 6 varieties. The 3 kinds of Madhya and Pragalbha belong to Dhira, Dhiradhira and Adhira divisions according to their temperaments. These 3 are again dependent upon their relationship to the hero and divided into Jyeshta, and Kanishta, the older and younger.

Parakiya : The woman who is another's wife is called parakiya. She is of 2 kinds Kakya (Maiden) and Proudha (mature).

An example of the Parakiya in the Javali.

Mogidochi Pilichedu Poyi

Vastura Swami, Maguna Pai Maravakurapriti (My husband calls me. May I go. (Beloved do not forget our love).

Samanya or Sadharana

A woman belonging to anyone, who is a courtesan, well versed in arts, possessed by boldness and seeking to better herself through her lover's attachment.

Vasakasajja : A heroine who is ready to receive the beloved and joyfully decorates herself and the roof or the place where she is to receive her lover.

The heroine is also called Sajjika or Sajjita.

Virohotkantitha

A heroine who suffers by being separated from her lover and is alone. She is disturbed by her lover's absence.

She shows distress, trembles and is exhausted discontented, tearful and expresses her anxiety to her sakhis.

Svadhina Bhartruka : A heroine, whose beloved is captivated and devoted to her. She worships the god of love as her lover is always by her side showing his complete subjection to her will.

Kalahantharita : A heroine who is separated from her beloved by a quarrel and then is filled with remorse. She sighly deeply and is sorrowful and restlessly wonders about, laminating her wilfulness.

This heroine is also called Kupita or abhisaddhita.

Khanditha : A heroine, who engaged and offended jealous of her love, who had been faithless and comes to her with the marks of another woman's caresses upon him.

She breaths deeply, is indifferent playful, sorrowful restless and speaks words of abuse.

Vipralabdha : A heroine who is deceived and disappointed that her lover has not kept his appointment.

She is anxious, sorrowful, depressed, tearful and sighs and faints.

Proshita Bhartruka : A heroine, whose husband has gone abroad. She is sleepless, emanciated neglectful of her appearance, prostrate, inactive and pines for her husband and counts the days of his return.

Abhisarika : A heroine who goes out to meet her beloved. She is anxious and feels harassed. According to the circumstances she goes in the day-time, wears any clothes and pretends to go to draw water or to attend some festival.

Each of these heroines may be again divided into three types : Uttama, Madhyama and Adhama.

The superior, the mediocre and the inferior.

Uttama is balanced and good however her lover behaves. Madhyama retaliates the same way as her lover behaves. Adhama reacts against her lover, in anger, jealousy and indignation.

ASTA VIDHA NAYIKAS

24

Charis or Sthanakas

The whole of chapter X of Bharata's Natyasastra has dealt with charis and sthanaka movements. The harmonised coordination of the foot, calf, thigh and waist is known as charis. All action with one leg are called charis there is no dance without chari action.

According to Natya–Sastra, charis are 32 in number and are divided into two classes (a) Earthly (Bhauma) and (b) Heavenly (akashika). But abhinaya darpana gives only 10 and does not classify them at all. The two works have no names in common in their charis.

Sthanakas begin from sloka 48 but Bharata does not mention in detail the chief characteristics of sthanakas. The body movements are elaborately and exhaustively dealt with in Bharata's Natya Sastra but Abhinaya Darpana fails to narrate them but attaches more importance and attention to hand gestures.

According to Natya Sastra body movements are divided mainly in the following groups—Karanas, Angaharas, Rechakas, and Pindibandhas.

The movements of the limbs such as the waist, the thighs, the shanks and the feet when correlated with a purpose constitute a specific action known as Cari or footwork. Persons practicing the Cari should take up simultaneously the movements of the feet, the shanks and the thighs. The thighs follow the way in which feet are moved, and these two limbs constitute together the Cari of the feet.

The combination of a number of Caris is known as Mandala. The classification of Mandalas go according to that of Caris such as Bhumi Mandalas (earthly) and Akasa Mandalas (Aeriel). The ten Bhumi Mandalas are Bhramara, Aspandita, Avarata, Samotsarita, Elakakridita, Addita, Sakatasya, Adhyardha, Pishtakutta and Casagata.

The ten Akasa mandalas are Atikranta, Vicitra, Lalitasankara, Sucividdha, Dandapada, Vikrta, Alata, Vama Viddha, Lalita and Kranta.

Abhinaya Darpana gives a different list of Mandalabhedas, Sthanaka, Ayata, Aliddha, Pratyalidha, Prikhana, Prerita, Swastika, Motita, Samasuci and Parsvasuci.

Chari is of two kinds:-

(i) Bhoomichari (movement on ground).

(ii) Aakshchary (movement in air above the ground)–Bhoomicharies are of 16 kinds.

1. **Samapada:** Keep both feet in natural pose on the ground which both toes are closer together. Then move the feet in natural way. It is called sampad.

2. **Sthitwarta:**-Keep one foot in same position and the other in Agratala (Toe) position close to it. Then bring the feet in pariyay pose. Repeat the same. It is called Sthitwarta.

3. **Shaktasya:**-Put one Agratal foot in front of other. The whole body and the chest should remain stretched and straight.

4. **Adhiyardika:**-Put the left foot behind the right. Then bring the right foot about one

foot apart and ahead. This is called Adhiyardika.

5. **Chashgati:**-Put right foot ahead and bring it back again. Then spacing the left foot back bring it forward again. This is Chashgati.

6. **Veechya Vacha:**-Take a slight leap from sampad pose and bring both feet facing one another. This is Veechya Vacha.

7. **Adaka Kridita:**-The continuous leaping over the feet is called Baddha.

8. **Baddha:**-To straight the thing sideward in Swastik pose of feet is called Baddha.

9. **Uruddha Vrita:**-Making Agratal pose of one foot, turn it in such a way that the bottom of the foot face outward and bend the second foot. This pose is called the Uruddha Vrita.

10. **Addita** :-One Agratal foot should remain touching the other foot in such a way that the bottom of one foot may touch the heel of other. It is called Addita.

11. **Utsyandita:**-Moving the left foot rightward, bring it back to the same position. Repeat the same with right foot. It is called the Utsyandita.

12. **Janita:**-Keep both feet in Agratal (toe) pose and bring the Musthi of one hand near the chest and stretch the other hand in half moon pose. It is called Janita.

13. **Syandita:**-Dragging one foot away is called Syandita.

14. **Avasyandita** :-The reverse of Syandita is called Avasyandita, *i.e.*, Keeping the other foot away is called Avasyandita.

15. **Mattally:**-Keeping both feet in Agratal (toe) pose and taking about turn. It is called the Mattally.

16. **Warta:**-Moving forward dragging one foot in semi-circular pose is called warta.

The Akash Chari poses are also 16 kinds.

(i) Atikrant:-Raising of foot the height of knee and throwing it on the ground is called the Atikrant.

(ii) Upkrant:-Making Valit of both things and putting one Kunchit foot on the ground with full force is called Upkrant.

(iii) Parshvakrant:-Making one foot in Kunchit pose and raising the other foot sufficiently high and bringing it to its original position is called the parshvakrant.

(iv) Urdhavajanu:-Raising of one foot in Kuchit pose upto the height of chest and bringing it back to ground and further repeating the same with other foot is called the Urdhavajanu.

(v) Soochi:-Bringing one Kunchit foot upto the height of knee and pulling it on the ground by toe is called soochi.

(vi) Noopur Padika:-Raising one Kunchit foot high and striking the other foot on ground is called the Noopur Padika.

(vii) Dolpad:-Raising the Kunchit foot up turn it rightward and then turning it left throw the toe on the ground. The foot in this pose is swang left and right like a pendulum.

(viii) Akshipt:-Raising the right Kunchit foot up, put it right on the other in Anchit pose, it is called the Akshipt.

(ix) Abidha:-Put the left Kunchit foot behind the right and then put this Kunchit foot left in the same position and repeat the same with the right foot called the Abiddha.

(x) Ud Vratta:-Bringing left Kunchit foot forward and raising it to the height of things is called the Ud Vratta.

(xi) Vidyutbhranbt:-Raise one foot back in such a way that the feet may touch the upper part of the back and then spread the foot ahead. The head in this pose is kept moving in circular way.

(xii) Alat:-Raising one foot back touch lower part of the back with feet, then throw it on the ground. It is called the Alat.

(xiii) Bhujanga Trasita:-Raise the left Kunchit foot up and spread the right foot ahead. The left foot in this pose should remain in the level of back.

(xiv) Harinpluta:-Raise the left Kunchit foot up then taking a jump put it on the ground and in the same time bring the right Anchit foot forward. Repeat the same in reverse. It is called the Harinplut.

(xv) Dandpada:-Raising the left Kunchit foot up, put it behind the right at a distance. Then very smartly put it in Anchit pose leftward. It is called the Dandpada.

(xvi) Bhramary:-Raising one foot up and revolving like a top is called Bhramary.

Bhramary is of 4 types:-

(a) Chakra Bhramary–To revolve like a top.

(b) One foot Bhramary–to revolve on one foot.

(c) Kunchit Bhramary–to revolve in bent pose.

(d) Utplant Bhramary–to jump over the revolving pose.

Basic Poses of Feet–There are three basic poses of feet used in modern times.

(b) Poses of full feet

(c) Poses of toe

(d) Poses of heel

The other poses can be formed with the help of the above three poses. The three basic poses are:-

(i) To scale time by throwing the whole foot on ground.

(ii) To scale time by throwing the toe of foot on ground.

(iii) To scale time by throwing the heel on the ground.

(iv) To throw the feet together on the ground.

(v) To throw either foot on the ground.

(vi) Pacing forward or backward to throw the whole foot on ground.

(vii) Bending both feet left and right.

(viii) Keeping both feet apart to throw them left or right.

Poses of Toe

(i) To throw toe on ground taking a pace backward by both feet.

(ii) Taking a pace ahead to throw the toe on ground.

(iii) To throw the toe on ground taking left or right angle.

(iv) Taking left or right turn to throw the toe with other foot.

(v) Taking a leap to throw both toes on ground.

Poses of Heel

(i) To throw the heel on the ground taking or right side.

(ii) To throw heel forward left or right side.

Poses of Feet and Legs

(i) Taking pace forward to get the leg enacted.

(ii) To get the leg stand erect by moulding it back and bending the trunk.

(iii) To make the leg stand in front of the other leg in bent pose.

(iv) To make the leg stand near the opposite thigh.

The Poses of Trunk

The poses of trunk are four, *i.e.*, to bend forward, backward, leftward and rightward.

In Samapada, both the feet are kept close with the nails placed in symmetry. This is used when the actor changes his stance.

In Sthitavarta, the front foot makes a circular movement inwards rubbing the ground before it is set. The same action is repeated by the other foot also.

In Sakatasya, the actor rests on a foot in a sitting position and the other foot is put forward keeping his chest in an erect position. The learned say that in Adhyardhika, the left foot is placed behind the right foot and then it is moved backwards further carigati is described as follows. The right foot is extended forward and placed firmly. The left foot is also similarly set on the ground away from the right foot.

Placing the feet together and assuming the position of Samapada when the right foot is used to pound the ground, it is called vicyava. In Edakakridita, one jumps again keeping the forepart of the feet firmly on the ground. In Badha the shanks are held in a transposed position and turned about with the moving of the thighs. In Uruduritta are stands on Agratala Sancharapada firmly placing forepart of the feet on the ground. One of the shanks is raised with a slant with the turning of the heel outwards. In Addita, the front foot is placed forwards and backwards rubbing against the fore part or back of the other feet. In Utspandita the foot moves gradually in and out and the other hand in the same position is moved about. In this gait called Janita, the feet are kept in Talasanchara position (forepart firmly on the ground. In Syamdota, one foot is put forward five Talas away from the other foot. In Apasyandita, the other foot is also placed similarly (5 talas away). In Samotsarita Mallatti, the front foot is placed with a flourish with a circular movement. This is used in physical exercises. Mallalli is spoken of as that in which a backward step is made with foot with circular movement and the hands respectively assuming the poses of Udvestita and Apaviddha (entwining and separating).

Now I will say something about the aerial varieties of caris. In Atikranta, the foot is raised bent and stretched forward before placing it firmly on the ground with force the foot is bent and raised with the thighs being and turned, the foot is then set down sideways to form this Apakranta cari.

Raise the bent foot high so that the knee is placed in a level with the breast and then place it on the ground hilling the same with the heel to form Parsvakranta.

Raise the bent feet high to place the knee on a level with breast, while keeping it like that emulates the same with the other foot to form Urdhva Janu.

One foot is bent and raised above the knee and stretched toward to place it on the ground with a thud by force to form the cari called suchi.

Fix the heel on the ground and raise the forepart and then hit the ground to show the cari called Nupurapadika. In Dolapada, the heel is raised and the foot is swing from one side to the other and then firmly placed on the ground hitting it with the heel. In Aksipta, the foot is bent and raised and then the shanks are tranposed before holling the ground with the heel raising the forepart of the foot.

Cari is called Aviddha, in which the feet are tranposed at the front foot and is bent and stretched forward and placed on the ground touching the place with the heel.

In Udvirtta, the foot is raised in a slanting position and held by the hands and then one jumps forward. Turning back repeat the same with the other foot.

Bend the foot backward and extend so as to touch the head and turn round to form the chari called Udyut Bhranta. The foot is stretched backwards and then brought to touch the ground with the heel. This cari is called Alata. Raise the bent foot so that the thigh which turned becomes triangle. Then turn the hip and the knee. This is called Bhujanga Trasita. In Harina pluta, one leaps up and hits the ground with one foot. Raise the other foot backwards, bend it and shake it.

Assume the Nupurapada and rule the back foot with the front foot and stretch it forward with a flourish to form Dandapada.

In Bhnamasi jump forward and hit the ground and turn round the sacrum. The other foot may be moved on its sole.

These charis of aerial basis, employing the graceful movements of the limbs may be used in the discharge of bow and arrow thunderbolt sword *etc.* The actors should show poses of hand before or after or even along with the movements of the feet. The hands should move in tune with the feet as the actors deem it to be fit. The hands should move in tune with the feet and the hip should follow the course of the hands. After the setting of the feet, one should appropriately use one's eyes, brows and other limbs. As the feet resume former position in the ground after the dancing steps, the hands should take natural rest on the hips after performing their actions.

Sculpture of Vijayanagara

25

Akasiki Caris

Caris are defined by Bharata as combined movements of the hip, thigh, shank and foot. They are generally movements of a single foot (ekapada pracara). The Caris form one of the important units for Karanas and Angaharas. They are generally used in Nritta, movement (gati pracara), fighting (yuddha) and in the release of weapons. In Natya, only when a situation demands a suggestion of war or has a predominance of rhythm, Cari-s come into play.

The eleventh chapter of Bharata's Natyasastra explains thirty two Cari-s. They are classified into two groups on the basis of the nature of the movement. When the movement of the foot is largely on the ground, they are called Bhaumi (earthly) Cari-s and when above the ground, Akasiki (arial) Cari-s. Each of these groups contains sixteen Cari-s and together they are thirty two in number.

This is the second part of Guru Chinna Satyam's explication of the Cari-s containing the arial movements of the bodily limbs. The first part was published in Nartanam, No. 2 (April-June, 2001).

Atikranta

Kuncitam padamutkshipya puratah samprasarayet
Utkshipya patayeccainam atikranta tu sa smrta

कुञ्चितं पादमुत्क्षिप्य पुरतः सम्प्रसारयेत्।
उत्क्षिप्य पातयेच्चैनमतिक्रान्ता तु सा स्मृता।।

The right foot from Kuncita pada position should be lifted upto the knee and then extended out with toes pointing forwards. This foot is then brought back in the same way to the original position. This movement can be done with the left foot as well.

Apakranta

Urubhyam valanam krtva kuncitam tu samuddharet
Parsve vinikshipeccaivamapakranta tu sa smrta

ऊरुभ्यां वलनं कृत्वा कुञ्चितं तु समुद्धरेत्।
पार्श्वे विनिक्षिपेच्चैचमवक्रान्ता तु सा स्मृता।।

This movement is similar to Atikranta cari, except, after extending the foot forwards, it is moved sideways either in clockwise or anti-clockwise direction, with the body taking a full turn before returning to the kuncita pada position.

Parsvakranta

Kuncitam pada mutkshipya janustanasamam nyaset
Udghatti tena padena parsvakranta vidhiyate

कुञ्चितं पादमुत्क्षिप्य जानु स्तनसमं न्यसेत्।
उद्धट्टितेन पादेन पार्श्वक्रान्ता विधीयते।।

The knee of the right leg whose foot is in Kuncita Pada is held up to the level of the chest. While holding this position, udghattita movement is performed with the left foot.

Urdhvajanu

Kuncitam pada mutkshipya janustanasamam nyaset
Dvitiyam ca kramat stabdhamurdhvqjanuh prakirtita

कुञ्चितं पादमुत्क्षिप्य जानुस्तनसमं न्यसेत्।
द्वितीयं च क्रमात् स्तब्धमूर्ध्वजानुः प्रकीर्तिता।।

This movement is similar to Parsvakranta, except, there is no Udghattita movement with the foot that is on the ground.

Suci

Kuncitam pada mutkshipya janururdhvam samprasarayet
Patayeccagra yogena sa suci parikirtita

कुञ्चितं पादमुत्क्षिप्य जानुरूर्ध्वं संप्रसारयेत्।
पातयेच्चाग्र योगेन सा सूची परिकीर्तिता।।

The right Kuncita foot is raised up and the knee is extended upwards, and then it is dropped down and placed in suci pada position.

Nupurapadika

Prsthato hyanccitam krtva padamagratalena tu
Drutam nipatayed bhumau cari nupura padika

पृष्ठतोह्यञ्चितं कृत्वा पादमग्रतलेन तु।
द्रुतं निपातयेद् भूमौ चारी नूपुरपादिका।।

The right Ancita foot should be lifted and its heel should touch the area behind the left ankle (or the bells when they are worn), and then placed on the ground in suci pada position.

Dolapada

Kuncita pada mutkshipya parsvat parsvamtu dolayet
Patayedancitam caiva dolapada tu sa smrta

कुञ्चितं पादमुत्क्षिप्य पार्श्वात् पार्श्वन्तु दोलयेत्।
पातयेदञ्चितं चैव दोलापादा तु सा स्मृता।।

Lift the Kuncita pada foot upto the knee and then swing it side ways either to the right or to the left. When the foot is brought down it should be placed in ancita pada position.

Akshipta

Kuncitam pada mutkshipya akshipyatvancitam nyaset
Janghasvastika samyukta akshipta nama sa bhavet

कुञ्चितं पादमुत्क्षिप्य आक्षिप्य त्वञ्चितं न्यसेत्।
जङ्घास्वस्तिक संयुक्ता आक्षिप्ता नाम सा भवेत्।।

The right Kuncita pada foot is raised and turned sideways and placed on the ground in the Kuncita pada position behind the left foot. It is then removed and placed next to the left foot in the Ancita pada position.

Aviddha

Svastikasyagratah padah kuncitastu prasaritah
Nipatedancitaviddhamaviddha nama sa smrta

स्वस्तिकस्याग्रत: पाद: कुञ्चितस्तु प्रसारित:।
निपतेदञ्चिताविद्धमाविद्धा नाम सा स्मृता।।

The Agratala feet are first crossed (to form a Svastika) and then uncrossed. The right foot is then raised and extended forwards. This foot is then brought back so that the heel touches the back of the other foot's ankle.

Udvrtta

Padamaviddha maveshtya samutkshipya nipatayet
Parivrtya dvitiyanca sodvrtta caryudahrta

पादमाविद्धमावेष्ट्य समुत्क्षिप्य निपातयेत्।
परिवृत्य द्वितीयं च सोद्वृत्ता चार्युदाहृता।।

This movement is similar to Aviddha cari except, after extending the right leg forwards, it is turned sideways to the right with the body taking a full turn. The body is now back in the original position with the right foot in Ancita pada position.

Vidyudbhranta

Prsthato valitam padam siroghrstam prasarayet
Sarvato mandalaviddham vidhyudbhranta tu sa smrta

पृष्ठतो वलितं पादं शिरोघृष्टं प्रसारयेत्।
सर्वतो मण्डलाविद्धं विद्युद्भ्रान्ता तु सा स्मृता।।

Raise the right foot at the back with the toes pointing toward the head, and then turn a full circle.

Alata

Prsthah prasaritah pado valitabhyantarikrtah Parsni prapatitascaivahyalata sa prakirtita

पृष्ठः प्रसारितः पादो वलिताभ्यान्तरीकृतः।
पार्ष्णिप्रपातितश्चैव ह्यलाता सा प्रकीर्तिता।।

The right foot is placed forward in Samapadam, and the left foot is raised at the back with toes pointing up. In this position the body takes a full turn from the left and ends with the left leg placed in Ancita pada position.

Bhujangatrasita

Kuncitam padamutkshipya trasramuru vivartayet Katijanu vivartacca bhujangatrasita bhavet

कुञ्चितं पादमुत्क्षिप्य त्र्यश्रमरु विवर्तयेत्।
कटीजानु विवार्ताच्च भुजङ्गत्रासिता भवेत्।।

The right Kuncita foot is raised till the knee is in front of the chest, and then the leg is turned sideways to the right with the body taking a full turn while maintaining the raised leg with toes pointing up.

Harinapluta

Atikrantakramam krtva coplutya vinipatayet
Janghanccitoparikshipta sa gneya harinapluta

अतिक्रान्तक्रमं कृत्वा चोत्प्लुत्य विनिपातयेत्।
जङ्घाञ्चितोपरिक्षिप्ता साज्ञेया हरिणप्लुता।।

The right Kuncita pada is raised in front like in Atikranta cari and then quickly alternated with the left foot being extended forwards. The left foot is then brought back with the toes pointing towards the inside of the right knee.

Dandapada

Nupuram caranam krtva puratah samprasarayet
Kshipramaviddha karanam dandapada tu sa smrta

नूपुरं चरणं कृत्वा पुरतः सम्प्रसारयेत्।
क्षिप्रमाविद्ध करणं दण्ड़पादा तु सा स्मृता।।

The right Kuncita pada is raised and used to beat behind the ankle of the left leg.

Bhramari

Atikranta kramam krtva trikam tu parivartayet
Dvitiya pada bhramanattalena bhramari smrta

अतिक्रान्तक्रमं कृत्वा त्रिकं तु परिवर्तयेत्।
द्वितीयपाद भ्रमणात्तलेन भ्रमरी स्मृता।।

The right Kuncita pada is raised up with the knee facing out. It is then brought in with the knee facing the left knee and then turned out again with the foot shaking and in ancita pada position.

(Courtesy—Nartanam)

26

Mudras

"The important role that Mudras play in investing orm with meaning was noticed in describing the igure. The efficiency of gesture to communicate ntensity of feeling and thought in a way that words annot do, has been recognized in India from a emote past. The use of Mudras as definite sign anguage, has come into existence long before the ays of the Buddha (6th century BC)".

It is said that Buddha himself was proficient n this art. The language of Mudras was one mongst the several arts. Mudras have also been nown as Divya–Kriya (divine actions) meaning hereby that they constitute the language of gods. ome of the Mudras are traced to certain significant ctions of gods. Now I would mention about some nportant mudras.

The Rasa or statement is produced from a nfirmation of determinant which creates emotion lled Vibhava (statics) and the consequents which e followed are known as Anubhava. The nfirmatory psychological states, which are the ansitory states are known as Vyabhichari Bhava. Thus the emotion is created and expressed through gesticulation and influenced through in transitory and complimentary emotions and creates Rasa in the minds of the audience.

Bharata has mentioned 49 such emotions in creating Rasa and classified them into 3 groups :

1. Sthayi Bhava—The emotions which are static—they are of 8 types.
2. Sanchari Bhava—emotions which are transitory—they are of 33 types.
3. Satvikabhava—Responsive emotions—they are of 8 types.

Sentiment or "RASA" the essence of art, is the underlying force in the expression of painting, sculpture, musical composition, dance and dramatic representation. (The Rasa theory is common to all the Indian fine arts).

Abhinaya is meaningless without the dominant force of Rasa.

MUDRAS
(Basic Gestures)

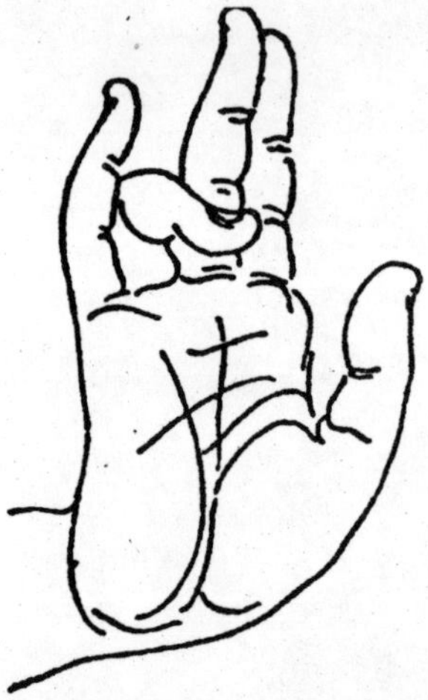

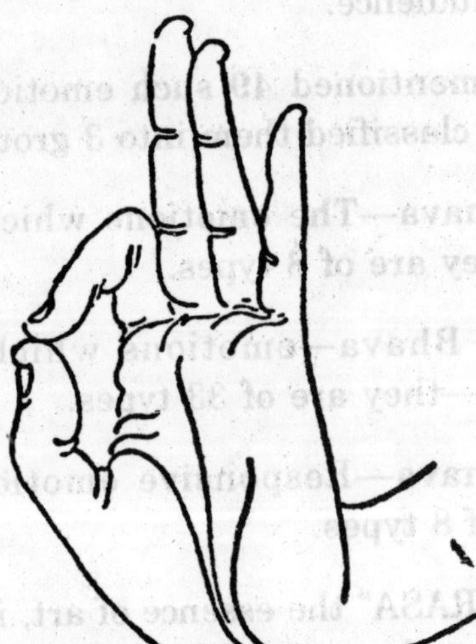
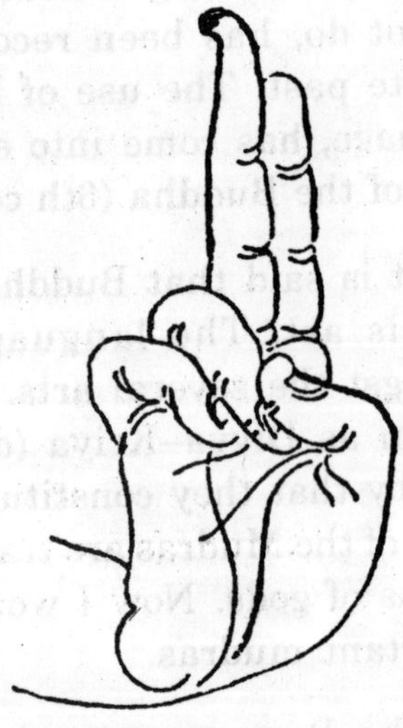
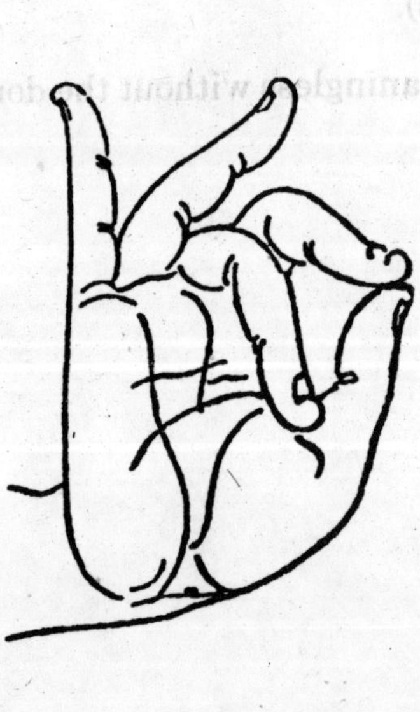
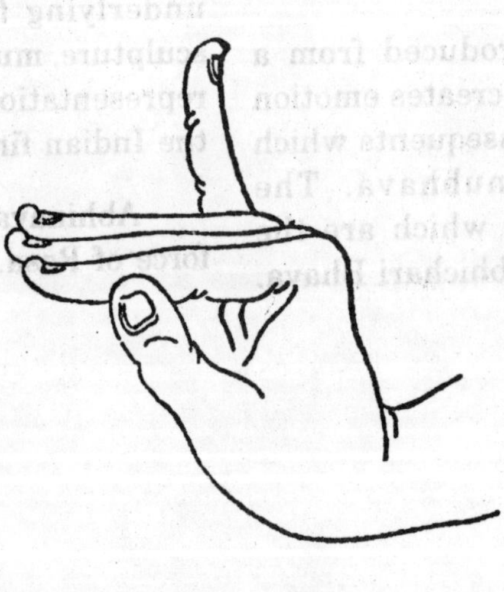
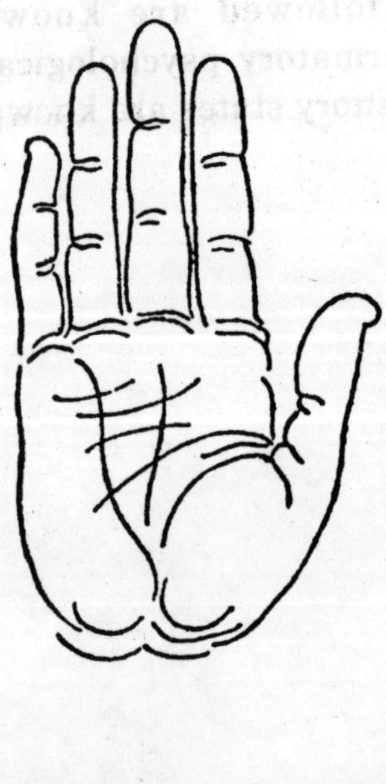

MUDRAS
(Basic Gestures)

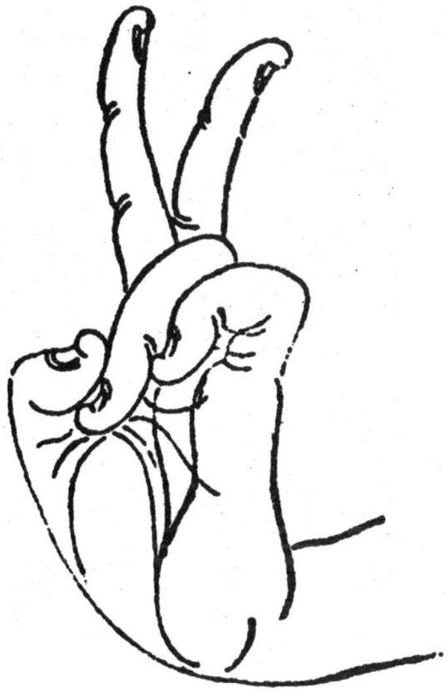

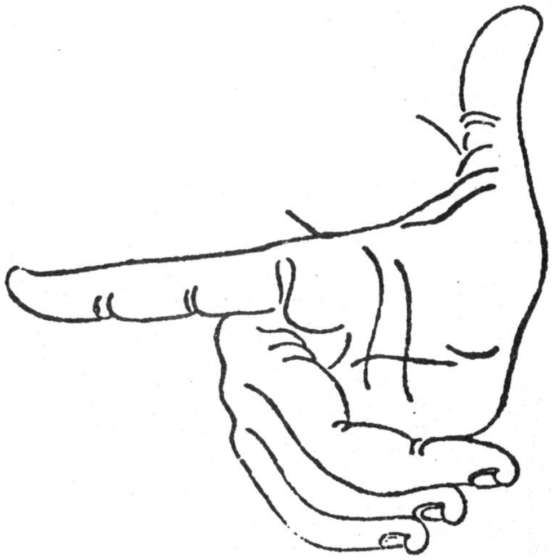

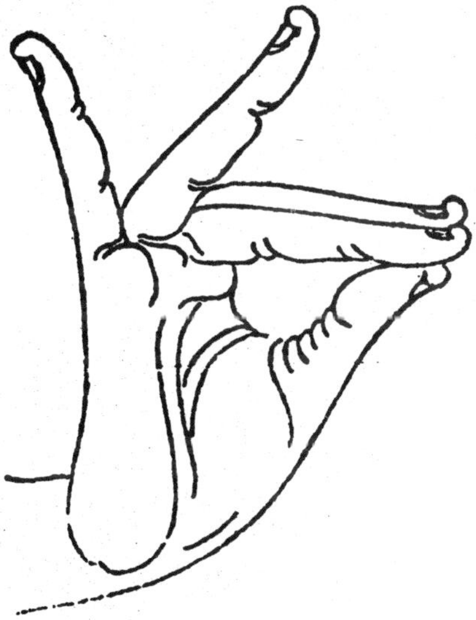

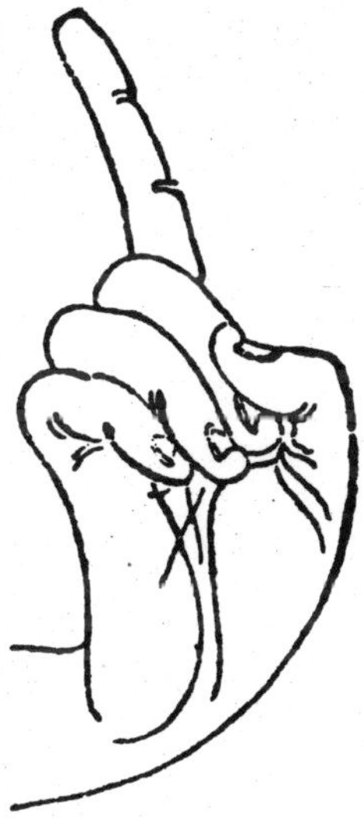

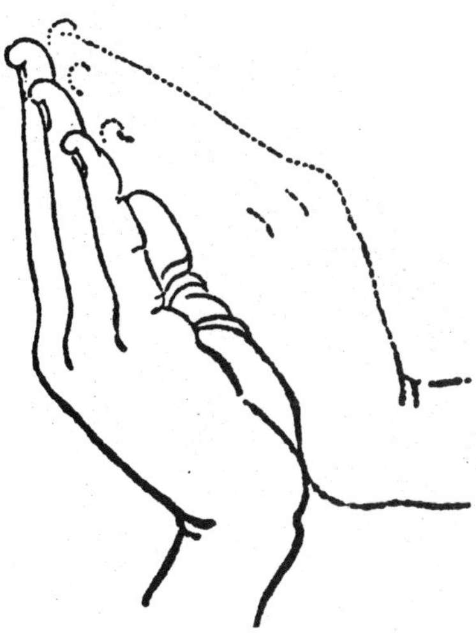

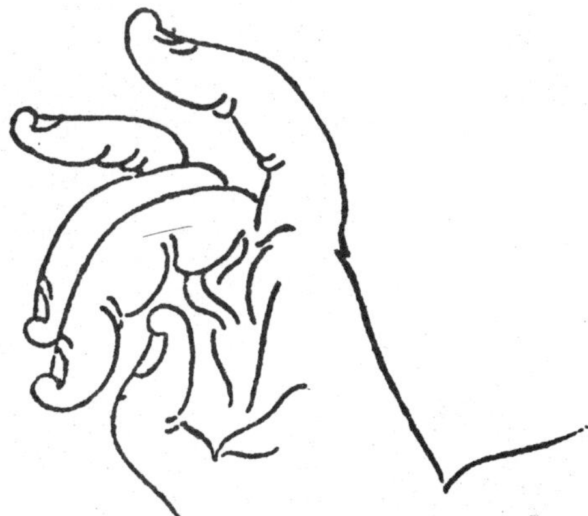

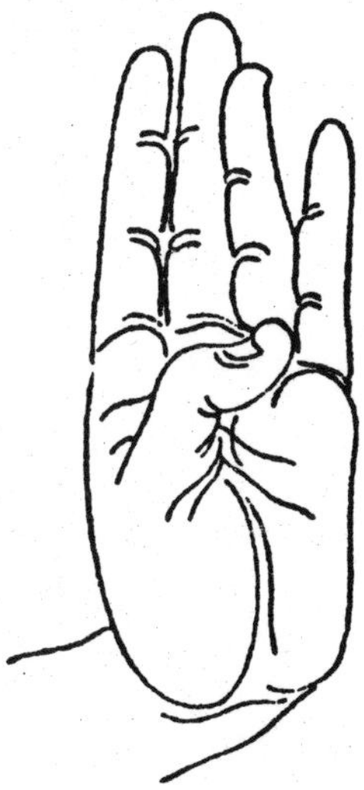

27

Angaharas

One hundred and eight Karanas having been explained, the different Angaharas are being spoken of :

Sthiravasta–Stretch and throw up both the arms–Take up Samapada Sthana, then stretch the left hand upwards from the level of the shoulder. Pratyalidha Sthana is taken up. Then the following Karanas are respectively taken up one after the other–Nikuttita, Urudvitta, Aksipta, Svastika, Nitambha, Karihasta and Katicchanna.

Paryastaka–Employ the Karanas Talapus-paputa, Apaviddha and Vartita. Then take up Pratyalidha Nikuttaka, Urudvrtta, Aksipta, Uromandala, Nitamba, Karihasta and Katicchinna.

Sucividdha–Show Alapalava and Sucimukha gestures employing these Karanas successively–Viksipta, Avartita, Nikuttaka, Urudvrtta, Aksipta, Uromandala, Karihasta and Katicchinna.

Apaviddha–Appaviddha and Sucividdha Karanas are employed and then Udvestita. Turn the Trika and the gesture Uromandala is shown while employing Katic-chinna Karana.

Aksiptaka–Employ the following Karanas, successively *viz.*–Nupura, Viksipta, Alataka, Aksipta, Uromandala, Nitamba, Karihasta and Katicchinna.

Viskambha–Hands to be made Udvestita and one after the other feet successively to Nikuttita and bent and then employ Urudvettakarana–Hands in Caturasra and feet Nikuttita employ Bhujanga Trasita Karana. Then hands in Udevetita employing Chinna and Bhramaraka karanas even as the Sacrum is to be turnd. Employ the Karanas, Karihastra and Katicchinna karanas.

Aparajita–Employ Dandapada Karana hands in Viksipta and Aksipta; then employ the Vyamsita karana the left hand moves along with the left foot hands remaining in Caturasra and feet in the Mikuttaka movement. Employ Bhujanga Trasita karana. Hands in the Udvestita movement. Employ successively the two Nikuttakas, Aksipta, Uromandala, Karihasta and Katicchinna karanas.

Viskambhapasrta–Employ karanas kuttita and Bhujanga Trasita karanas. Recita hand shows Pataka gesture–Employ the karanas Aksiptaka, Uromandala. Lata and Katiccheda successively.

Mattakrida–Turn the sacrum and employ Nupura karana. Then successively Bhujanga Trasita, Recita (right foot) Aksiptaka, China, Bahyabhramaraka, Uromandala, Nitamba, Karihasta and Katiccheda karanas.

Svastikarecita Hands and feet in Recita Employ vrscika karana and repeat this movement of both, then Nikutta karana and Lata gesture alternately with the right and the left hands. Finally Katicchinna karanas.

Parsvastika—Employ Diksvastika from a side. Then Ardhanikuttaka; then repeat all these on the other side. Avrtta hand is placed on the thigh. Employ the following karanas successively Urudvrtta, Aksipta, Nitamba, Karihasta and Katicchinna.

Vrscikapasrta—Employ Vrscika karana holding lata hand, held on the nose. Move the same hand in Udvestita.

Bhramara—The following arenas are employed successively Nupurapada, Aksipta Katicchinna, Sucividdha, Nitamba, Karhasta, Uromandala and Katicchinna.

Mattaskhalitaka—Employ Matalli karanas, move the right hand, bend and place it near the right check. The following karanas in succession–Apavidha, Talasams photita, Karihasta and Katicchinna.

Madavilasita—Moving with dola hands Svastika pasrta feet. Make ancita and valita in the hands. The following karanas in succession. Talasamghattita, Nikuttaka, Urudvrtta, Karhasta and Katicchinna.

Gati mandala—Mandala sthanaka is assumed–hands recita–feet Udghattia. The following successively Matalli, Aksipta, Uromandala and Katiccheda.

Paricchinna—Samapada sthana with Paricchinna karana. Aviddha foot assumes Bahya Bhramaraka–Suci karana in the left foot. The following karanas successively atikranata, Bhujanga Trasita, Katihasta and Katicchinna.

Parivrttaka recita–Hands in losse Svastika held on the head. Bend the body–left hand Recita. Raise the body. Again Recita in the same hands. Hands show Lata gesture. The following karanas–Vrscika, Recita, Karihasta, Bhujanga Trasita and Aksiptaka. Svastika foot–Turn back completely and repeat all. Then Karihasta.

Vaisakharecita–Both the hands made Recita along with the body, repeat this with bent body. Nupura cari Bhujangatrasita, recita, Mandalasvastika—To be employed shoulder is beck then Urudvrtta, Aksipta, Uromandala, Karihasta and Katicchinna karanas.

Paravrtta—Employ janita karana–put forward a foot. Employ alataka karana. Turn the Sacrum afterwards. The bent left hand made nikuttia on the cheek. Employ Katicchinna karana.

Alataka—Employ the following karanas in succession–Svastika, Vyamsita, Alataka Urdhvajanus Nikuncita ardhasuci, Viksipta, Udvrtta, Aksipta, Karihasta and Katicchinna.

Parsvaccheda—Hands in Nikuttia movement placed on the chest employ Urdhvajanu, Aksipta, and Svastika karanas and turn the trika (sacrum). Then employ the karanas Uromandala, Nitamba, Karihasta and Katichinna.

Vidyubhranta—Sucikarana with left foot Vidyubharanta Karana with right foot–Then change the order and karana. Chinna karana then. Turn the trika. Lata and Katicchinna karanas.

Alidha—Employ Vyamsita karana and strike the shoulder with the hands Nupura karana with the left foot. Then Alata and Aksipta karanas with the right foot. Make Uromandala gestures with hands. Employ Karihasta and Katicchinna karanas.

Recita–Showing recita hand bending it on one side and making the same movement–Then repeating this movement after bending the entire body–employ the following karana, successively–Nupurapada. Bhujanga trasita, recita, Uromandala and Katicchinna.

Acchurita–employ Nupura karana turn the trika round–employ Vyamsita karana again turn the trika. Then employ from the left side Ajataka, Suci, Karihasta and Katicchinna karanas.

Aksipta recita–Svastika feet in recita, so too the svastika hands. Then with the same movement they are separated. They are then thrown up. The following karanas are employed successively—Udvrtta, aksipta, Uromandala, Nitamba, Karishata and Katicchinna.

Sambhranta–Employ Viksipta, Karana–throw out the hand with suci gesture. The righthand is placed on the chest–Turn the trika. The following karanas in succession–Nupura, Aksipta, Ardhasvastika, Nitamba, Karihasta, Uromandala and Katicchinna.

Apasarpita–Observe Apakrantacari and employ Vyamsita karana with the hands in Udvesita movement. Then the following karanas are employed successively–Ardhasuci, Viksipta,

Katicchinna, Udvrtta, Aksiptaka, Karihasta and Katicchinna.

Ardhanikuttaka–Observe swiftly Nupurapadika cari. Hands move in harmony with the feet. Trika is turned round. Hands and feet make Nikuttia movement. The following Karanas-Uromandala, Karihasta, Katicchinna and Ardhanikuttaka Karanas.

The Recakas

The thirty-two angaharas have been spoken of the four recakas may kindly be attended to.

Of them the first is the Pada Recaka (of the foot): then Katirecaka (waist) the third Hasta recaka (hand) and the last one Kantha Recaka (Neck).

By Recita is meant moving the limb round separately or its drawing up separately.

Pada recaka–Movement from side to side with the feet wavering or having different movements.

Kati Recaka–Raising up the sacrum and turning the waist or drawing it back.

Hasta recaka–Raising up, throwing out placing forward, turning round and drawing the back to the hand.

Kantha Recaka-Raising up lowering and bending the neck sideways and similar other movements.

On seeing Lord Siva dance with recakas, and Angaharas the daughter of the mountain too danced with delicate features. This dance was followed by the playing of the instruments like, Mrdanga, Bheri, Pataha, Bhambha, Dindima, Gomukha, Panava and Dardura.

After the annihilation of the sacrifice of Daksa, Maheswara performed the dance at the dusk employing Angaharas in conformity with proper beating of the time and the concordance of sounds.

On seeing the Pindibandhas, Mandin Bhadramukha and other Ganas (attendants) gave the names and definitions of Pindibandhas.

Isvara's	Vurspindi
Of Nandin	Pattisi (Padasi)
Of Candika	Simhavahini
Of Vishnu	Tarksya (Garuda)
Of Svayambhu	Padma (Lotus)
Of Sacra	Airavati
Of Manmatha	Jhasa (Fish)
Of Kumara	Sikhi (Peacock)
Of Sri (Lakshmi)	Rupa (Beauty)
Of Jahnavi	Dhara (Current)
Of Yama	Pasa (Noose)
Of Varuna	Nadi (River)
Of Dhanada	Yaksa
Of Bala	Hala (Plough)
Of Bhogins (serpents)	Sarpa (serpents)
Of Ganesvara	Daksayajnavimardini
Of the enemy of	Raudri
Antaka	(In the form of the trident)

The Pind's of the other gods and goddesses shall be indicated through their emblems.

After evolving these Recakas, Angaharas and Pindis Lord Maheswara imparted them to sage Tandu who perfected the art of dance with vocal as well as instrumental music. This art of dance is known as Tandava.

28

Tandava, Lasya, Margi and Desi Types of Dance

Tandava and Lasya

Tandava consists of vigorous movements and is essentially masculine form in character suggesting strength and valour. It characterises intense excitement, heroic mood (Vira Rasa) and also a touch of wrath. Tandava dance also expresses cosmic activity of the divine conquest over evil or the attainment of bliss or *Ananda.*

It is generally performed by males only. The *Prekshani* type of Tandava is described as movement of limbs without any facial expression. *Bahurupa* Tandava includes the exhibition of strong expression.

Seven (7) dance modes of Tandava of Shiva are described in dance treatises.

1. Ananda Tandava or the Joyous dance.
2. Sandhya Tandava is the Evening dance.
3. Uma Tandava–danced by Shiva with his consort Uma.
4. Gouri Tandava–performed along with his consort Gouri.
5. Kalika Tandava–The preventive Kalika form which kills demons of evil and ignorance.
6. Tripura Tandava–which represents the slaying of the demon Tripura.
7. Samhara Tandava–It is dance of death in which Shiva is Lord of the burning ground, meaning that which remains after the annihilation of all forms. His dance symbolizes the release of the sole from the bondage of Maya (illusion).

Tandava is of two kinds–Pebali and *Bahurupa.* Pebali consists of movements of the limbs alone and has no any dramatic element. Bahurupa has dramatic elements such as changing of dress frequently in Bahurupa, the dancer usually sings a song which is composed of certain conventional words such as Ta, Na, Dim *etc.*

Nritta is of three kinds–Vishama, Vikata and Laghu.

"Vishama" consists of many acrobatic feats like that of rope dancing 'vikata' consists of movements of a person in a dress, which strikes awe and terror in the minds of the beholders "Laghu" dance constitutes graceful upward trippings and movements.

The following schools of dancing were prevalent in ancient India.

1. **Karshni :** The dance which was performed by 8 milkmaids, around 8 figures of Krishna with auspicious words.
2. **Jakkani :** The dance which enthused women and men of Turkey bearing bouquets, performed in amorous mood, accompanied with songs.
3. **Saharas :** The dance which the saharas perform with songs.

(Saharas are mountaineers formerly found in the mountains regions of India. This kind of dance still in vogue among the Santals and other people.

4. **Kaurangi :** The dance which men and women in Savari dresses perform with ornaments of Gunja berries, carolling native airs.

5. **Mattavali :** Is the dance performed by the drunken folks of Turkey.

Sri. A.K. Kumaraswamy, the author of "Mirror of Gesture" describes that 'Nicha Nritya' is a dance begun without a prayer *etc.*

Lasya

In Lasya type of dance, the movements are more measured, suggesting grace and beauty and it is considered to be more suitable for female dancers.

Lasya dancing includes amorous expression and graceful movement of the limbs. The Rasa Leela of Krishna with the gopis of Brindavan is of Lasya kind.

Lasya is a graceful feminine dance. In ancient India, this art was learnt in many cultured homes. Princesses living in palaces were good experts in it. Prince Naravahanadatta, the son of Udayana himself played the labor as his consort danced (Katha Sarit Sagara vi. 81.171). Even the dance masters were put to shame as Agnivarma played a flute and watched for a false step of the dancers in his harem (Raghuvamsa xix, 14). Malavika, the young queen of the Sunga Emperor Agnimitra, was an adept in dancing and could bring credit to the high reputation of her master at the art (Malavikagni mitra Act 1, p. 30).

Bharhut sculptures (Cunningham I. Pl. XV. XVI) showing dance scenes, act as commentaries to some of the dance passages of Kalidasa's Malavignimitran. Lasya is divided into two parts–Churita, and Yauvta. It is the dance of the hero and heroin, in a presentation of exciting love. It includes sentiment, passion *etc.* It also bears the appellation of I "Furita or Churita".

Extremely graceful dance of girls accompanied with various movements with a magic to charm and attract the audience–is entitled "Yauvata".

Nandikeswara tells us that Parvathi tought the gentle lasya dance to Usha, the daughter of king Bana. She spread it among the women of Dwaraka. The gopis in turn taught lasya to the women of Sourashtra, who finally spread it to the world.

Marga and Desi

The dance in its original form created by Brahma choosing the good aspects from four Vedas and preserved as a tradition and systematized by Bharata is the type of classical dance called Marga.

In later period, in course of some centuries with the development of regional languages and change of historical and religious facts, some amount of deviation has taken place and the dance which was performed in terms of regional variations is considered as Desi.

References

1. G.K. Bhat (Bhandarkar Oriental Research Institute) (Poona (India) 1983).
2. Indian Sculpture Today, Jahangir Art Gallery Publication.
3. The Hindu Temple I & II–by Stalla Kramrisch.
4. Epic Scenes in Indian Plastic Art by Jayanthika Kala.
5. Classical Indian Dance in Literature of Arts by Kapila Vatsayan.
6. Rhythm in Joy Classical Indian Tradition Text by Leela Samson, Photos by Avinash Pasricha.
7. Dance Dramas of India and the East by Bharata Iyer.
8. Bhavam, Ragam, Talam, Natyam by Ravindranath.
9. Dance as Text–Ideologies of the Baroque body by Marco Franco.
10. Hindu dances (Nrityanjali) by Ragini–Smit Publications (Delhi–110052).
11. Some Dancers of India–by Suseela Misra.
12. Dance Technology–by Judith A Gray.
13. Bharata Natyam–From Temple to Theatre by Anne Marie-Gaston.

14. A hand book of sculptures.
15. His dance–His life–A Portrait of Uday Shanker.
16. Dance in India–by Judy Van Zile.
17. The Natya Sastra–by a board of scholars translated into English.
18. Erotica in Indian Dance by Prajesh Banerjee.
19. Classical Dances and Costumes of India by Kay Ambrose.
20. Ancient India (From the origins to the XIII the century AD).
21. Pre-Harappan Cutters of India–by Sashi Asthana (from the library of central university of Hyderabad).

The Post Gupta Period

29

Sthayi Bhavas

Bharata lists the following eight Sthayibhavas corresponding to eight Rasas.

	Sathayibhava	*Rasa*
1.	Rati (Love)	Sringara (Erotic)
2.	Hasa (Laugher)	Hasya (Comic)
3.	Soka (Sorrow)	Karuna (Pathetic)
4.	Krodha (Anger)	Roudra (Furious)
5.	Itsaha (Heroism)	Vira (Heroic)
6.	Bhaya (Fear)	Bhayanaka (Fearable)
7.	Jugupsa (Disgust)	Bhibhatsa (Odious)
8.	Vismaay (Wonder)	Adbhuta (Marvellous)

The following are the thirty three Vyabhichari Bhavas listed by Bharata :

1. Nirved	Despondency
2. Glani	Weakness
3. Sanka	Apprehension
4. Asuya	Envy
5. Mada	Intoxication
6. Srama	Weariness
7. Alasya	Indolence
8. Dainya	Depression
9. Cinta	Anxiety
10. Moha	Distraction
11. Smriti	Recollection
12. Dhruto	Contactment
13. Vrida	Shame
14. Capalata	Inconstancy
15. Harsa	Joy
16. Avega	Agitation
17. Jadata	Stuper
18. Garva	Arrogance
19. Visada	Despair
20. Autsukya	Impatience
21. Nidra	Sleep
22. Apasmara	Epilepsy
23. Supta	Dreaming
24. Vibodha	Awakening
25. Amarsa	Indignation
26. Avahittha	Dissimilation (concealment)
27. Igrata	Cruelty
28. Mati	Assurance
29. Vyadhi	Disease
30. Unmada	Insanity
31. Trasa	Fright
32. Vitarka	Deliberation
33. Marana	Death

Apart from these types of Bhavas, Bharata lists one more category, which he mentions as sathana Bhavas. They are :

1. Sveda	(Perspiration)
2. Stambha	(Paralysis)
3. Asru	(Tears)
4. Vaivaranya	Change of colour
5. Swara-Sada	Change of voice
6. Pralaya	Familing
7. Romanica	Horripilation
8. Kampana	Trembling

From the above, we may conclude that Bharata did not view the problem of aesthetics as a philosophical exercise. He was not influenced by the concept of Rasa by the philosophy of Upanishads. He was concerned with it as an object, which is responsible for aesthetic experience.

The eight sthayibhavas or permanent moods corresponding to the eight sentiments are as Rati (love), Hasa (Mirth), Soka (Sorrow), Krodha (anger), Utsaha (Courage), Bhaya (Fear), Jugupsa (Aversion), and Vismaya (Wonder). The Vyabhichari Bhawas (transitory moods), are enumerated as thirty-three and they are named as follows. Vivveda (Self-disparagement), Glow (debility), Sanka (apprehension), Asuya (envy), Mada (intoxication), Srama (Weariness), Alasya (Indolence), Dainya (depression), Cinta (reflection), Moha (distracting), Smriti (recollection), Dhruti (equanimity), Vrida (shame), Chapalata (unsteadiness), Harsha (Joy), Avega (flurry), Jadata (Stupe faction), Garva (arrogance), Vishada (despondency), Autsukya (longing), Nidra (drowsiness), Apasmara (dementedness), Supta (dreaming), Vibodha (awakening), Amarsa (Impatience of opposition), Avahitha (dissembling), Ugrata (sternness), Matsya (resolve), Vyadhi (sickness), Unmada (madness), Marana (death), Trasa (alarming), and Ustarka (doubt).

The Sthayibhavas which can be taken generally as involuntary evidences of internal feeling are specified as eight in number. Stamba (Stupor), Sveda (Respiration), Romance (horripilation), Svarabhanga (break of voice), Vipathi (trembling), Vaivarnya (change of colour), Asru (tears) and Pralaya (loss of consciousness).

Dandika Lasyam—Ramappa Temple

30

Aharyabhinaya

Indian dance embodies a harmonious blend of all the arts—acting, dancing, painting, and singing. Of course, Aharyabhinaya plays a secondary role but an important role in the presentation of a performance. Aharyabhinaya makes the performance more impressive.

Aharyabhinaya has mainly three components :

(a) Background or decor

(b) Make–up and

(c) Music

Lighting: Lighting did not play an important part in Indian dancing until recently. In ancient times, the flame from torches sufficed. A *pradipa*, or lamp was used to illuminate an improvised stage. The lamp consisted of cotton threads interwoven and dipped into a vessel filled with mustard oil. The lamp was placed on a high stand.

Modern Stagecraft demands better lighting. Our dancers have learnt to adopt modern stage lighting to suit their art. Floor lights, strip and border lights are used.

Make–up and Ornamentation: Other aids to illusion are make up and ornamentation both of which play an active part in Nritya. It is modern device but a very ancient invention. Of course, it has undergone many changes depending on the mode of dancing.

Music: Since music helps to create the necessary atmosphere for a dance performance, the dancer and the orchestra have to work in union between them, thus creating a mood.

Indian music consists of infinite sound skillfully arranged. Our music based on melody, has innumerable variations, so subtle and with so many twists to each a time measure of 3, 4, 5, 7 and 9. As a result, we have 35 varieties. Each has another time measure of 6, 8, 10, 12 and 16. So, we have another 35 varieties. Altogether there are 70 tales. Each has given again 5 varieties because of the rhythmic divisions; Ragas are nothing but musical patterns.

Bauhinia Adriana lays down the rule that during a dance performance, two cymbal players should sit on the right side of the stage and two

Mridanga players should remain on either side of stage, while the singer must be present with tabmura or drone.

The raga and Tala from the base for music and so the religious quality of Indian music is still preserved.

The Concept of Aharya in Sculpture

The *Aharyabhinaya* is treated par excellence with *Anginka*, *Vacika,* nor *Satvika Abhinayas* or histrionic expressions. *Aharyabhinaya* is the expression through the art of decoration of human figures suitable for the sequence. The major components of *Aharyabhinaya* are the human figure and form. *Natya* is futile even if one of the above components is lacking. When a character or dancer enters the stage or a sculpture or a painting of human form is presented, the costume, head dress, ornamentation, make-up and colour combination appeal to the eyes at the first instance. Then the physical gestures, the speech (in drama) are noticed. Lastly the character's inborn quality is exposed when it evokes 'Rasa' in the heart of the spectators. In the same way a fine piece of sculpture or painting could convey a message to an onlooker through it is dumb and motionless. Thus the concept of *Aharyabhinaya* is always expressed through the jewellery, head dress, costumes and make-up.

Adoring or decorating herself in a pleasing manner and presenting herself in an accomplished way is the natural instinct of a woman. This passion of women has opened a wide gate for the development of the arts such as coiffure, jewellery, cosmetics, textiles, and so on. A dancer and an actor need extraordinary paraphernalia of *Aharya,* as she has to present before public.

Westernization and modernization have least affected the classical dancer and actor on the stage in India. The dress, jewellery, hairstyles and make-up in the presentation on the stage are still based on Hindu ideologies. However, the materials of decoration come through machine and not through handicrafts to the modern artistes.

Every region has its own style in exposing *Aharya.* But it can not be forgotten that from the days of Indus valley civilization to Vedic age and historical times, a considerable degree of uniformity is maintained in presenting accomplished figures which enhanced her to possess deep rooted rich tradition and unique position in the world.

The celestial and human figures in sculptures and paintings throughout India are decorated from top-to-toe in all periods and in all styles. There are many passages in the literary works and hymns dedicated only to the description of the decoration of various parts of the body of men, women and celestials. Even the great sages and saints made use of the Devis *viz.*, Sri (Lakshmi), Saraswati, Sakti, Parvati, Mahishasuramvardhini and others. The Apsaras, celestial dancers and courtesans occupy a major space in decorating temple walls and have a major share in the narration of romantic pieces of literature. They are bedecked with jewels and their headdress adds to the charisma of their figure and form.

The dressing up before a recital or presentation of drama is described by Bharata as *Nepathyavidhi*–the ritual behind the curtain. Bharata has classified the aspects of *Nepathyavidhi* as (1) *Pushta* creation of artificial sets and arrangement of stages; (2) *Angarachana*–decorating face and body by applying paint and grease and formation of various hair styles; (3) *Alankarana*–Decoration of various parts of the body by ornaments and costumes; (4) *Sanjiva*–true to life presentation of animals.

Here the area of speculation in terms of *Aharya* in the sculptors of various periods fall under the aspects of Angarachana and Alankarana which covers head-dress, make-up, jewellery and costume. It would be more appropriate to deal with the decorative aspects one day one in relation to the various dance sculptures belonging to different periods. A thorough examination of minor details would definitely yield valuable and would show a distinctive type of result adoration in every style of sculpture. It appears fashion changed in every century and resulted in depicting different types of decorative items from early Chalukyan to

Vijayanagar times. It is really interesting to note the varieties of decorative patterns exhibited in the sculptures pertaining to dance and music during the span of 1000 years. A close study of the hair styles (coiffure), make-up jewellery and costumes forms a very interesting chapter.

Coiffures

We are amazed at the varieties of hair styles exhibited in the temple premises of early Chalukyan, later Chalukyan, and Vijayanagar periods, it appears that these hair dresses have been adopted since Vedic times. The plaited, bunned, twisted, letting–loose, tufted, knotted hair patterns along with elongated crowns, half crowns, and hair dressed with wreathes of flowers and jewels are found in ample numbers.

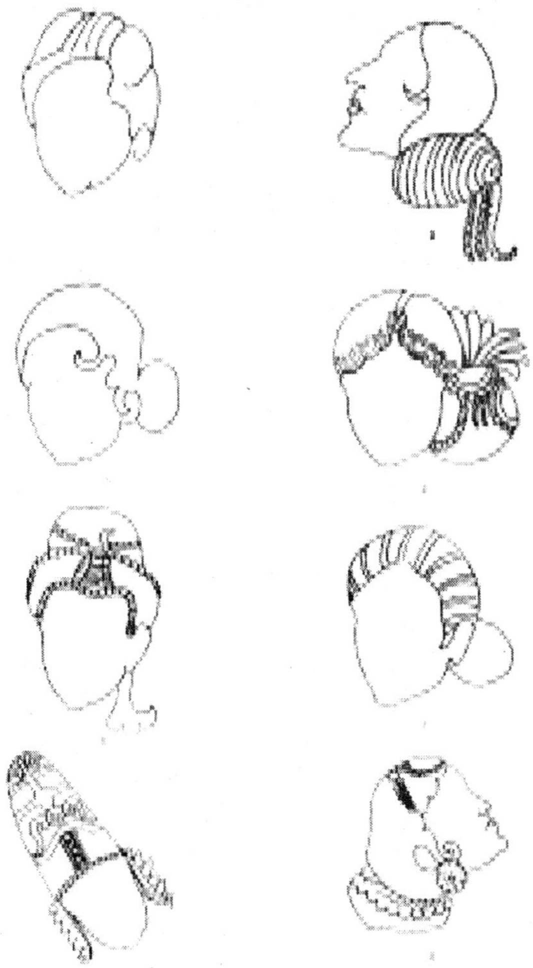

The styles such as Opasa, hair parted into plaits in any number. Kurira–the horn shaped styled for long hairs, kumbha–pots shaped coil set vertically and horizontally, Kopardas–crown shaped coiffure, Siman–parting of the hair on forehead, Sikha–hair set in the manner of tuft or a lock are mentioned in Vedic description of coiffure. Literary references of classical age contain innumerable references to headdresses. In the early centuries of Christian era, the art of hairdressing was cultivated specially by women, and their head dressed according to the occasion and purpose.

There is almost no subject left untouched by Bharata in his Natyasastra. He has mentioned certain hairstyles for certain occasions suitable to the character. It is interesting to know the regional hair dressing in India in times of Bharata. Avantiyuvati, the young woman of Malva dressed her hair with curled locks. The south Indian women arranged their hair in the shape of water vessel (long bunned sikha) help with a beautiful ornament. They also let the locks of hair turned backwards from the forehead. Thus the art of coiffure was an important factor in the presentation of the cultured women of all the regions of India.

The aforesaid references found their expression in the sculptures of Andhra. In early Chalukyan period it appears Kapardas, Kumbha, Sikha and Dhammila were in vogue. The dancers increased their heights by arranging their hair styles by padding with the buns, clips, pins, strings, pendants, broaches, pearls and other jewels were lavishly used in the hairdos.

There are innumerable Jatamukutas in the sculptures and elongated crowns are replaced by the bunned type, tied not over the head but to the ear level. The straight hair in the front is turned to small curled locks. It appears that women in medieval times spent much of their time or there were specialists in setting the woman having small curls.

There is a very charming coiffure available in the dancing sculptures. The hairstyle is set very naturally in all three-bracket figures. The front portion is set with tiny curls with a pendant running over the parting of the hair at the back set to a shape of a big ball by the side of ear. The tuft is decorated with a Jutikabharana and strings of pearls. Flowers are inserted to complete the coiffure (P. No. 78). Fig. 7, a small and simple type of tuft but the front portion is decorated.

There is another elegant coiffure of later Chalukyan times. The sasansundari of jalasanghvi is proudly exhibiting her figure and the coiffure (Pi. No. 138). It appears the cutting of the front hair was a practice among the women of the dancing class. The hair is cut into three parts, two parts set near the ear as curved, side locks and remaining hair over the forehead is cut to a level and trimmed into curls. The forefront is decorated with jewels and at the backside the hair is tied in the shape of an inverted bowl and the lines of twisted golden lace and jewels decorate the coiffure.

Decorated with pearls, studded with precious stones, of jewels and on the top tier a twisted wire like band all in circular form make a disc like head jewel, large in size, set around the bun at the back is commonly found in the bracket figures of Hoysala period. This disc type jewel fixed above the level of

the head on a bun gives the special festive look to these dancers.

Make–up

Women always desired to appear in graceful manner. Beauticians were appointed in the palaces and the houses of harlots to decorate and assist their mistresses to dress up daily and also in a festive manner during occasions. The royal ladies, their attendants, courtesans, ordinary women, all used to decorate their person according to the means at their disposal. This inherent love of personal appearance in the Indian women was made legitimate and compulsory by the Sastraic injunction that a faithfull wife desirous of the longevity of her husband must not forego turmeric, saffron, *kumkum,* red lead, sindura and collyrium.

The colour mark of tilaka on the forehead of a woman indicated *soubhagya.*

Regarding eye make-up, the dancers used collyrium could give an outlook to broader eyes and emphasise the shape of the eyes. Trimming the eyebrow was not new to the dancers Adipurana refers to trimmed eyebrows. The area of the eyes was brightened perhaps by tinting shades. Red Alakataka was used for decorating feet. Even today dancers do not step on the stage without applying Alta to their palms and feet. The literary works describe their love for delicate perfumes, sandal and turmeric pastes, fragrant powers, scented garlands.

The dancers in the medieval times decorated their head and enchantingly to look more attractive. The wavy, loose, glossy and abundant hair with flower strings on it or straight long brain of hair decorated with a string of pearls were considered a part of beauty. Sangita Ratnakara gives an account of good makeup and charming coiffure as 'deep blue profuse flowing hair shall be intertwined with half-bloom flower buds and hand against the back of the body either crooked or straight as occasion may demand. The hair should also be covered by a network of pearls, forehead anointed with Kesar and Sandal. Eyes should be decorated with collyrium and teeth should be

a b c

a b c

enameled white so as to reflect light and face, neck should be powdered with Kasturi leaves.

Jewellery

From times immemorial Indian jewellery has created an aura of charm and grace throughout the world. The Hindu ideals strongly support ornamentation of at least a few minimum items. The elaborately designed jewellery became the aid of beauty and symbol of status. Adornment of makeup with ornaments was considered a necessary adjunct to emphasize the qualities of beauty, courage and wisdom. Most of the sculptures show an almost equal number of jewels on both men and women. Hindu painters and sculptors from earliest times have shown vividly the charm and excellent workmanship of jewels worn through the ages. Our temple sculptures are repositories of variety of jewellery and ornaments.

The history of Indian jewellery has a long tradition. From the time of prehistoric period gold, silver, copper and iron objects that were used as ornaments are known. Neolithic and Chalcolithic sites have yielded a good number of jewellery items.

Sanskrit and Telugu works mention the material of manufacturing ornaments as Swarna, or Kanaka, Rajaka, Vaidurya (dark tinted gems), Vajra (diamond), Pusparaga (Topaz), Pravala or Havala (red coral), Suryakanta and Chandrakanta. Pearls have occupied top position in the ornaments where tassels and danglings are required. The pearl pendants and haras are of innumerable number. The pearl pendants and haras are of innumerable number in sculptures. Someswara confirms that pearls from Simhala and those found in Indian Ocean were of good quality. Yasastilaka an earlier work refers to pearls coming from the Pandya country. It is evident that pearls from Simhala and those found in Indian Ocean were in abundance. The Andhra sculptures and literary works depict a variety of ornaments where pearls were used in ample quantity. Head dress, bangles, lines of pearls decorating neck, ear-rings, dangling of the girdles are the ornaments where pearl is used with gold and other precious stones. Ratnakara's observation is very useful in this connection. He describes a dancer decorated with the ornaments made of pearls such as Tilaka of pearl, pearl pendant and lines, pearl net on the head, pearl stud and nose stud.

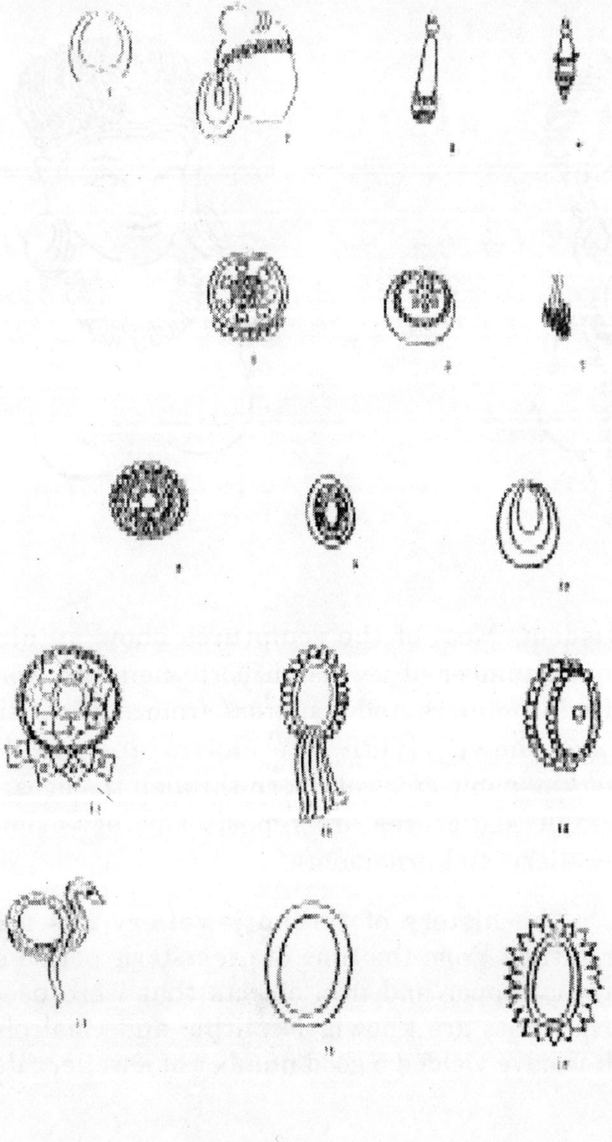

From the Satavahana's to Vijayanagar times Andhra was known for its richness, in the form of gold and precious stones. The sculptures of these periods illustrate innumerable types of ornaments of great variety and novelty. Harsha was fascinated by choice of ornaments, which heightened the shapely figures of ladies. The early Chalukyan jewellery appears to have followed a simple technique in preparing. Pearls and gold were mostly prominent materials that were in vogue. The ornaments of this period appear to be more heavy. Male and female figures are adorned with different types of ornaments. The delicate carving in the gold was the new technique adopted by the Later Chalukyas. The sculptures of this period show very delicate floral designs and beautiful patterns adorning the female figures. The male figures are less ornamented.

The foreign travellers have left behind their description of jewels worn by dancing girls in Vijayanagar period. Abdul Razak opines that these dancing girls were wealthy for each of these women were bedecked with pearls and gems of great value and were dressed in costly ornaments. Domingo Paes also tells us that dancers were wearing ornaments of great value and were dressed in costly dresses. Who can fitly describe to you the great riches these women carry on their person? Calories of gold with many diamonds, rubies, pearls, bracelets, on their arms and upper arms, girdles below and of necessity anklets on the feet. The devotional songs of Devadasis of the period are found with detailed narrations of ornamentation of gods, goddesses, men and women.

Alankarana with Flowers

Bharata in his Natyasastra, calls the adoration of the body as Alankarana by three means–flowers, jewels and clothes. It is evident that flowers were also used for satisfying the love of self-adornment. All ornaments were copied in flower and worn during the rainy season to import a sense of freshness to the wearer. Girls living in the hermitages were not supposed to wear metal ornaments and their ornaments were made exclusively of flowers. Flowers on the head and flower garlands are shown invariably in the sculptures of medieval times. Bharata classified floral decoration into 1. Vistima–Bouquets, 2. Vitatagarlands 3. Sangatya garlands concealing the stalks, 4. Grandhima–making with bouquets and 5. Pralambita or open garland reaching the knees.

The entire jewellery of personal ornamentation is classified into four major heads by Bharata. 1. Avidhya Ear ornaments, 2. Bandhaniya–waist ornaments, girdles, bands *etc.*, 3. Arupya—the ornaments decorating neck and 4. Praksipyaanklets, ornaments on feet *etc.*

Ear Ornaments

Ear ornaments occupy an important place in making the face look more attractive. The shades and the sparkling of the stones illuminate the face. The size and the shape of the ear ornament depends on the shape and complexion of the face. The descriptions in the literary works and the sculptures are the guides in this direction. The ear ornaments selected here from all the four periods range from simple, small ring to delicate and elaborate ear-rings.

There is a simple ear–ring of Early Chalukyan times. It is narrower on top and broader at the bottom. Simple two circular rings of Later Chalukyan times (Fig . 10) large size all very simple circular ear-rings without any special workmanship. The over sized ring is a common northern feature. Figs. 3, 4 and 7 are Kundalas. Nataraja, Devi and dancers of Early Chalukyan period are shown as wearing this type of cylindrical thick ear-ring. A large circular stud with beautiful workmanship is worn as in Mahishasuramardini sculpture. The precious stones are cut into different shapes and set on a circular gold shaped disc. (Pl. No. 54)

Vajragarbha, an ear ornament, worn by royal ladies and dancers had diamonds embedded in the centre. A large bead or pearl set in the centre of a ring is adorned by the male dancers and musicians. The sun-shaped small sized and large sized earrings so well with the male deities, musicians and female dancers of the period.

The Madanikas of the Hoysala period are usually decorated with this type of ear-ring represents an elaborate ear-ring of fine workmanship. Sometimes only disc and the drops are also attached to it. The outer ring of the ornament is stringed with pearls. The beautiful carvings in the central part is studded with precious stones. A large gem is set in the centre. The drops are extra decorative. This ear-ring was best suited for the elongated coiffure of the dancers of the Hoysala times. The Naga Kundalas are the special feature of ornamentation in dancing Siva of Hoysala times.

A peculiar and distinctive type of ear-ring is used by the Nartaki and Darpana Sundari of the National Museum, Delhi of the later Chalukyan period. It appears like Sopanakrama Vinyasta Kundala, *i.e.*, the precious stones are set stepwise and a large ring is attached to it. The step is so big that it has covered the entire ear and appears that the ornament is dangled down from the hair or the edge of the ornament is tucked to the hair. Large pendulous ear-rings of gold, studded with a small bulb sized gem is the middle and double pearl circles as broader as big bangles. This type of ear-rings are used.

By the Madanikas of Belur, Halebid and Kikkeri. A lady setting her large sized ear ornament looking into the mirror is a good example of big circular ear-rings (Pl. No. 99).

Nose Ornament

The female faces in the paintings of Hampi and Lepaksi are decorated with the nose studs. Thus during 15th century itself the nose-ornament was regarded as an essential jewel. The icons of Kanya-kumari, Madurai Minakshi, Kolhapur Lakshmi, Alamelu Mangamma of Alamelumangapura and almost all female deities in temples are decorated with the sparkling gem on the nose.

Bharata who has mentioned a long list of jewels has not mentioned the nose ornament. Even Someswara has not made any reference to an ornament for the nose. From these descriptions we may get an impression that the nose ornament is mentioned only from the fourteenth century. Some historians ascribe foreign origin to this nose jewel as it has been adopted by Malabaris in south from Arabs and that reference to the usage of nose-ring occurs in Sankaracharya's stories like ring in India cannot be later than that of 8th century A.D., the date of Sankaracharya.

Very recently efforts have been made to describe Indian origin to the nose ornament by revising the sculptural, archaeological and literary evidences. K. Krishnamurthy's findings throw light on the existence of nose-rings as early as 2nd century A.D. in India. The evidence of nose stud in some Mithuna figures of Nagarjunakonda and on the nose of a female terracotta figure from Chagtur the nose ornament was known to Indians as early as 2nd century A.D. and the depiction of them in profusion was as late as the 7th century A.D.

Arupya: (The ornaments decorating neck, shoulders, arm and wrist).

The varieties of Kantha (necklace) haras decorating lower neck speak of the grandeur, status and style of the person or image. The intricate workmanship of metal and the assembling of the pearls and beads are note worthy features in making ornaments that adorn neck. The pearl pendants found on the full bosom of the female figures are very expressive and help to emphasize the curves of the bosom and the mid-region. The neck ornaments were used by all the images irrespective of sex.

A plain Kanta abharana was in vogue during early Chalukyan period. It had a line of pearl and stringed pearl patterns. A necklace made of only gold was also used. Necklace lined with or without pendant was favourite ornament in all the periods. Ekavali, Pancavali and Saptavali were the terms used depending on the lines. Beautiful necklaces embedded with the precious stones on gold. The pearls and beads appear in great novelty on the body of female deities and dancers in all times. Depict ornaments which was known as Stanahara and Parvati and other female figures. By the stanahara the form and currings of the figures appear more distinctly. In Later Chalukyan times the pearls are tangled in between the breasts. In Vijayanagara times a large pendant resembling wings of the birds was adorned on accomplished ladies.

The necklaces and neck garlands of Later Chalukyan and Hoysala periods are distinctive when compared to other styles. The heavy bosoms of the bracket figures of these periods are decorated with equally heavy necklaces. The jeweller's art reached high watermark in those days. The gems, beads, pearls and metal were intricately shaped in various patterns. No place in India could give us such rich designs as the Hoysala sculptures. (Later Chalukya) representation a large stone set Kanthahara with five lines of pearls and chains. The long necklaces of Later Chalukyan and Hoysala periods are not found either in Early Chalukyan or Vijayanagar periods.

The Hoysala necklaces are joined with different shapes of padakas at intervals. Three types of necklaces are seen. Firstly, three lines of pearls of medium size; three more lines of small pearls joined with diamond shaped golden pendants, and lastly, large sized pearls, *i.e.*, Muktaphala in the centre are the special features. This is a beautiful representation of Saptavali. The pearls the gems and gold are arranged in a cluster to form the petals of a lotus are the examples of good craftsmanship, which deserve appreciation.

Pearl Yagnopavita is an ornamental piece used to decorate the shoulders and chest of the male figures of the Early Chalukyan style. Brahmansutra is a typical necklace extending up to the navel and is one of the striking features of Hoysala ornamentation.

Ornaments of Shoulder

Keyura and Bhujabhusana are the terms used to designate the ornament that decorates the shoulders. In Early Chalukyan sculptures we hardly come across these ornaments. The shoulders are bare. From Later Chalukyan period onwards the shoulders of male and female figures are decorated with some ornaments. Usually it is the strings of pearls or pendant of pearls and gold beads delicately made to fit the bend of the shoulder. The details of Keyuras from Later Chalukyan period. The Hoysalas added the tassels and cluster of pearls to the simple Keyuras of Later Chalukyan times. Every figure of Hoysala style is adorned with the Keyuras. The details of Keyuras carved on the shoulders of Madanikas. A beautiful tassel with a large pearl is the point of attraction. The central part is filled with a bunch of pearls getting larger at the end. In pendant is the focal point. The pearls are hung around it. The shoulder ornament of Vijayanagar period appears like the one made of metal rather than strings of pearls as it looks more sturdy; A large stone is fixed in the centre. This ornament was also a symbol of status. On occasions it was decorated with peacock feathers and different jewels and pendants. In Hoysala times shoulder ornaments, necklaces, pearl pendants and Brahmasutras covered almost the bare body of the sculptures.

Arm Ornaments

Sculptures exhibit a rich tradition in depicting the armlets or arm ornaments of various patterns from time to time. In all the treatises they are referred to as Angadas. These ornaments were inserted through hands and raised up to arm; in some cases they tied by strings. There were certain arm ornaments, which could be fixed and screwed. We can trace the stage-by-stage development and the new devices in fixing up this ornament. If not tied properly, it becomes a hindrance for the free movements of a dancer.

The early Chalukyan sculptures invariably portray the coiled type of arm ornaments. They appear on the arms of male and female figures. Sometimes the edge is converted into a sheet metal rolled up into several antithetic coils or spirals seemed to have shaped this ornament. These multi-coiled ornaments were possibly flattened to a required breath with a hummer and then coiled round in spirals.

Armlet used by the celestials and Gandharvas of Early Chalukyan times. It is a decorative type using large and small square stones and pearls and a pendant on the top gives a majestic look. The jewellers in medieval times came out with exquisite carvings and settings. The simple coiled were added with lines of pearls, colour stones, delicate cluster of wires, beads of different shapes and colours.

The sculptures of dancers, musicians and celestials on the Hoysala period exhibit elaborate types of armlets. On a sheet metal a colourful, sparkling leaf shaped, oval shaped, round shaped, flower shaped, petal shaped and semicircular pendants were fixed in the centre. Some figures depict various patterns of armlets worn by the bracket figures of Hoysala times. A figure portrays a full-bloomed lotus pattern of armlet. A sculpture from Naggehalli–beauty and the monkey (Pl. No. 142) wears two lined metal ring, as armlet. Decorative tassels flung around are tied to the armlets of this period.

Vijayanagar dancers wore simple types of ornaments (Pl. No. 144). To match with the costume of the frilled lower garment the dancers must have attached the golden colour frills above the elbow.

Bracelets and Bangles

The ornaments that decorated the wrists of the males and females were known as Prakosthavalayas. The thick wristlets were often mentioned as Kadaga and Kankana. Increasing popularity of wrist ornaments can be witnessed in the sculptures of Karnataka. Dancing Siva, Parvati, Vishnu, Copurteans, Madanikas are decorated with single lined bangles to large bands of jewels worn up to elbow. They show high artistic caliber of jeweller's art. In Early Chalukyan period brace to a single piece of metal which appear on the sculptures of female deities and Apsaras.

The bracelets of similar design appear on the sculptures of Later Chalukyan period also. The simple Kadagas have the treatment of superb ornamentation.

Hoysalas have specialized in depicting in Kadagas and Kankanas. Kadagas do not make sound, but kankanas make the tinkling sound of 'kan kan' when the hands are moved. The Hoysala icons both male and female, wear selected varieties of wristlets and bangles. Some are very tight on the wrist; some are embedded with a network of tiny pearls and golden beads. To some the tiny jingles are attached and they are let very loose. Some are just flat and bent. Some are tube like.

The ornamentation of fingers was a necessary aspect of personal decoration of royal persons and dancers. The icons are also decorated with various patterns of finger rings. The rings were usually similar in design to the ear ornaments. Round, diamond shaped rings studded with nine gems; pearls and plain gold rings were in vogue. Multicoiled rings are also seen. Sometimes all fingers are decorated with various types of rings connected by a chain to the wristlet.

Bandhaniya (Waist ornaments, Girdles, Bands *etc.*)

The waist ornaments occupy the central point of the form and gives a balance and elegance to the figure. The dress down the waist is held tight by the waist belts and hands which enable the dancers to have free movements and assure self exhibit their curves and bends. The decorative belts, bands and girdles give a majestic pose to the entire posture. Kalisutra, Kanchidhama and Vodyana are the terms applied while describing these ornaments.

Gold or silver, pearls, gems, wires, pendants, tassels of golden thread, strings, chains, loops of different shapes, bells, jinglings, are the accessories that comprised a waist ornament. The sculptors of all the periods have taken great interest in adorning their sculptures with elaborate waist ornaments. The male dancers and musician's waist ornaments are simple with fewer details than female figures.

The Later Chalukyan foot ornaments are marked with decorative features. This ornament had no singling effect. So the foot is decorated with a chain connected by jingles, which produced sound. Is an anklet, which perhaps had sound effect, as they appear hollow, filled with tiny metal pieces inside? The sound is balanced with foot ornament having a chain with large size jingles. Is a very decorative foot ornament, also having two rows of jingles. Apart from these anklets we find the anduges, the broad and circular ornament for feet in Later Chalukyan sculpture.

The dress and the feet movements of these male dancers appear as the representation of a dance form known as Peranin, described in Sangita Ratnakara. Here the dancer has to tie shining anklet bells upto the shanks and he must be an exponent is the art of timing and tempo (Pl. No. 105, the male figure to left). His dance attracts the audience and he should have been trained exclusively in the art of sound by placing the feet in a particular position in his tempo. The male figures wearing ankle bells upto shanks represent the dance form known as Perani and Ghargare. In contemporary dance forms, Kathak dancer is trained in the technique of sounding the ankle bells. The Kathak dancer covers the shank with brass bells tied with thick thread. In later times South Indian Dance forms must have eliminated the ankle bell technique and it must have remained in north Indian dance forms and absorbed as one of basic factors of Kathak school of dance.

During Vijayanagar times the Addigas were common ornaments that decorated the feet of dancers and royal persons. The toes are also decorated with tiny rings. Mantige and pillie were worn on different toes. The second toe was adorned by a ring called Yamala. The toe rings jingled while dancing and walking. The ornaments that decorated the feet and toes were made of silver.

One figure depicts the ornaments that produced sound when the dancers moved were Kankana (wristlets), Katisutra (girdles), Kinkini (ankle chains) and Anduge (anklets). One example of the bells or kinkini as described in Abhinayadarpana will suffice to point out how much advanced they were in the art of dance and drama. Abhinayadarpana states the qualities of the bells as follows. Tiny bells (kinkini) made of bronze that is kansya should have the stars as their deities and should remain half an inch apart from one another. The dancing girl should bind a hundred of them or two hundred in each of her two feet with blue thread in light knots.

The splendid representation of jewels in the sculptures of Karnataka depicts a glorious tradition in the art of jewellery, which reached a stage of advancement period preferred minimum ornaments. But the later sculptures are profusely decorated with a hoard of jewels on them, which gives an impression that the sculptures or human figures are overburdened with jewels. It looks as though the weight of the jewels has surpassed the weight of the body decorated from top to toe. Bharata warns the dancers to observe propriety in wearing jewellery. Heavy and unrealistic jewellery should not be worn on the stage since it hinders free expressions. So jewels made of light material with shining false gems set in lac (sealing wax) and covered with the gold leaf are advocated. The dance sculptures of medieval times certainly are overburdened with jewellery. But Sangita Ratnakara's description of a dancer's ornamentation prefers minimum jewellery. Chudamani is a jewel worn on the top of the head. Mukuta is to be worn above the forehead. Kundala worn in the lower lobe of the ear, mocka is to be worn in the middle of the ear. Harshaka is a snake shaped ornament, Keyura is worn above the elbow. Anganda is worn above the Keyura. Trisara is a 3–stringed necklace. Tarala is worn below the novel. Sitra worn below tarala. Triveni is ornament worn on the breasts. Govakshi is a head ornament.

Costumes

Another aspect that draws the attention in particular as the chief component of personal decoration is the costumes and clothing. Costume and clothing are not merely the decorative factors but a necessity and one of the three fundamental needs, the other two being food and shelter. As a basic need clothing tops the list of personal decoration. The coiffure, make-up and jewellery are treated as secondary, as far costumes are concerned the sculptures are represented as scantly clothed. From Ajanta to Hoysala period the Gods, Goddesses, celestials, dancers and musicians are illustrated with minimum clothing. But there are examples of fully clothed sculptures in all periods.

The Vedas, mythological works, ancient treatises and literary works speak of various types of dress worn by Indians with beautiful designs and varieties of textiles that existed in India since ages. Textile manufacturing and technique of stitching was known to ancient Indians.

The Concept

According to Bharata the costumes are formed with three types of cloth namely suddha or white, Rakta or coloured and Vicitra or multi-coloured. Thus the Early Chalukyan costumes are formed on the basis of the narration by Bharata. By this time the dancers, actors and royal ladies had picked up different styles in dressing. As witnessed by Yuan Chwang the robes of the women were flowing down to the ground. They completely covered their shoulders. On their heads they wore caps with flower wreathes and jeweled necklets. Dhoti was a common piece of garment worn by the men. The dancers used colourful garments down the waist with decorative pleats, spread between the legs in a more fashionable manner. It appears the females of the western region adopted the use of tailored garments. Thus varieties of sewn dresses are found in the sculptures and painting of this region.

In many sculptures we can notice the edges of duppatta flapping by sides or behind. Early Chalukyan, Later Chalukyan and Hoysala sculptures exhibit different types of lower garments up to knee level with varied designs, and border motifs are woven on them. There are also a few examples of dresses worn below the knee level. For the colours the paintings and literary works provide useful information. The queen Ratnavali used a garment whose ends were dyed orange with saffron for the Madanapuja. By 5th century A.D. we come across with fully developed garments, stitched and modelled into various fashions. Suvasana (splendid garment), Paridhana (dyed garments), Pesa's (embroidered garment of a female dancer), Vadhuya (bridal garment) were the types of ensembles worn for specific purpose and occasions.

The art of weaving, designing and modelling achieved a stage of perfection during Early Chalukyan times. The details of the dress, belt and modes of wearing as represented in the sculptures of Ravalaphadi represent Siva and Saptamatrkas. Dancing Siva is dressed in a variety of lower garment. A well dressed Parvati's lower garments

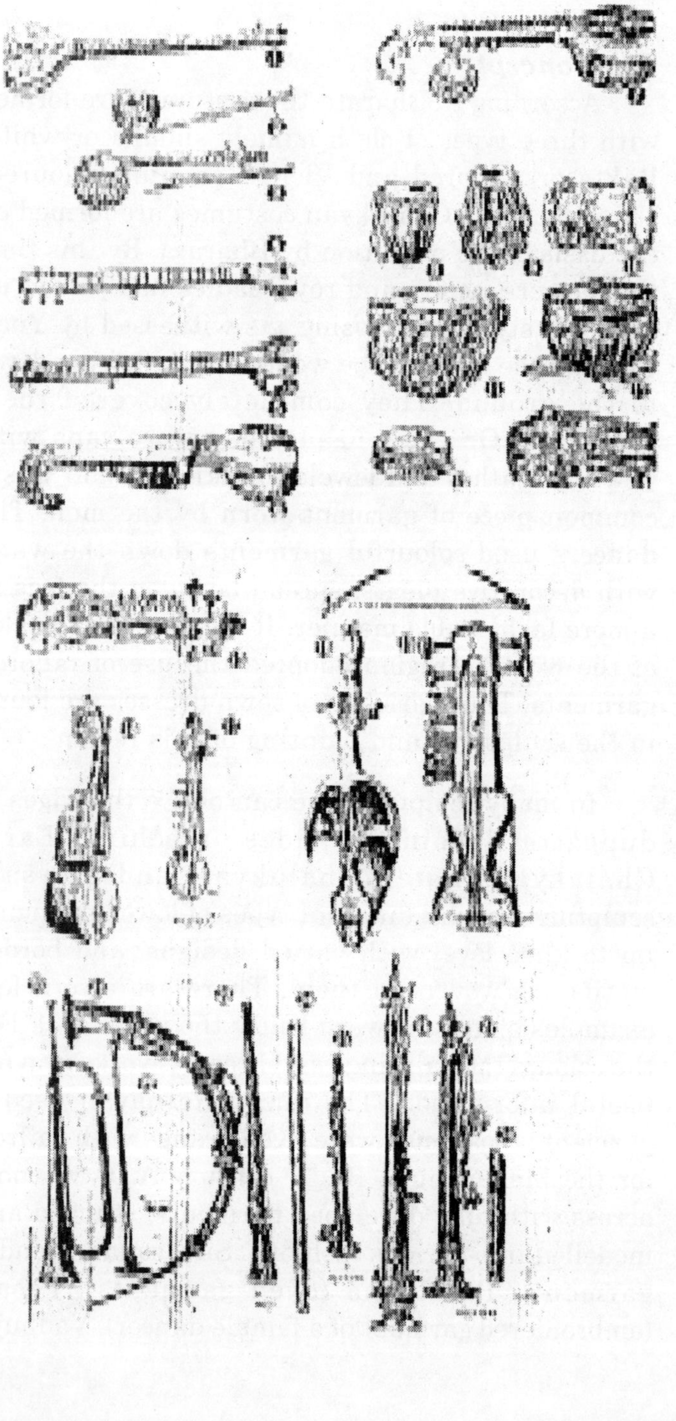

have reached upto the ankle level. It appears like a stitched dress. The frills are neatly arranged between her legs. The plaits of the saree is stitched naturally. The dress of Mahishasuramardini of Aihole is also a stitched one (Pl. No. 54). The dress of a female figure in is a fine example for tight fitting dress and textile design.

In Later Chalukyan period the textile motifs reached good standards. We can see the stitched lower garments like modern tight pant on them. The Darpanasundari of the National Museum, Delhi belonging to Later Chalukyan times has a beautifully designed attire. The entire dress is embroidered with golden flower motifs. The Kuruvatti bracket figures also have similar dresses. The sewn edges near the waist and ankle show the art of dress making.

Hoysala sculptures also demonstrate different types of ensembles. A dress in a figure is a fine depiction of a dress free from girdles and having floral motifs and the dancers and actors developed a technique of wearing the saree like a pair of trousers. The dress was tight fitting and a fan like pendulous pleats helped easy movement of limbs. The shoulders were covered with a dukula, finely woven shawl, especially for dancers.

The literary works have made mention of blouses and brassiers known as Kucavastra. The sculptures do not help us to know the upper garments prevalent in those days. We can see female figure is decorated with a cloth fitting tight covering the upper portion.

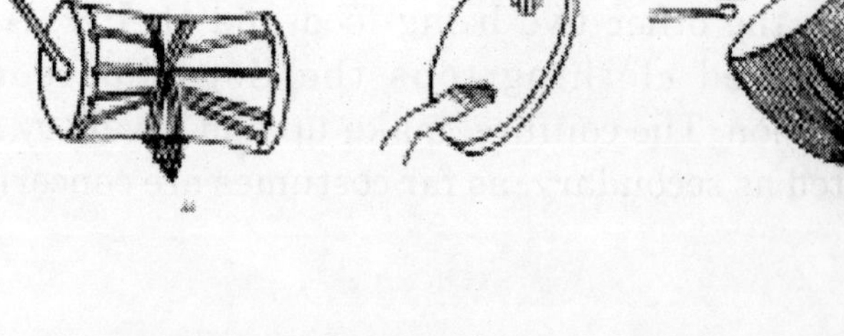

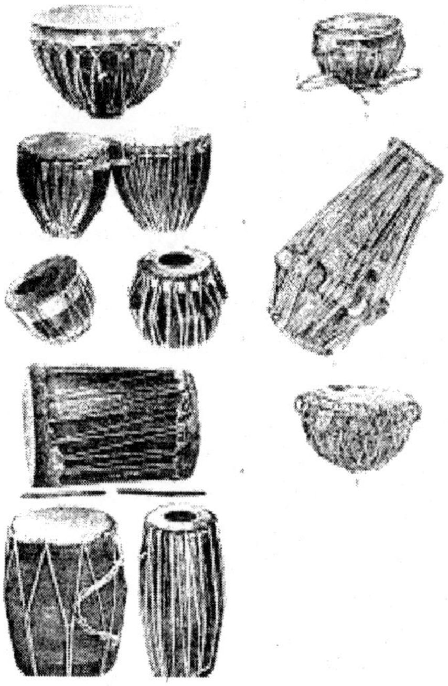

Ratnakara and other contemporary poets of later period have narrated charming dresses of the dancers. It is interesting to note the colour combinations and dress patterns worn during those days. Here a dancer's costume included a green leg sheath, a diamond–studded and gold embroidered yellow shorts known popularly as Kase and Challana, and a brassiere of a network of pearls. Ratnakara describes the shorts and brassiers embedded with precious stones and gems worn by dancers in a number of instances.

Thus Aharya or expression through dress, ornaments and other aids are the essential parts of Abhinaya. Sculptures and paintings exhibit the unparalleled heritage in the jeweller's art. The detailed survey of the coiffure, makeup, jewellery, costumes shows the significant development and aesthetic standards in decoration from time to time. The epigraphical and literary references support frills. A pullow is also shown to the right side.

During Vijayanagar times the dancers used to wear the costume which is still prevailing. The silk material with golden embroidery was stitched and gathered in the centre in the form of frills. The dancing panels of Vijayanagar portray the dresses. Such a dress was worn by the folk dancers of the time. The dancers and actors developed a technique of wearing the saree like a pair of trousers. The dress was tight fitting and a fan like pendulous pleats helped easy movement of limbs. The shoulders were covered with a dukula, finely woven shawl, especially for dancers.

Musical Instruments

Musical instruments accompany the movements of the dancer. Music is of primary importance in virtual (Pure dance). Abhinaya or gesture is in Nritya and music is only secondary (Natyasastra, pp. 188, 288).

Though the subtlety and modulations of the human voice are recognized as being superior to musical instruments, accompaniment to the voice always has been welcomed. The drone of the pipe and the twang of the most primitive of musical instruments with a single of double string form a kind of background even for primitive song. But methods of copying the various modulations of the voice on instruments has from the earliest times engaged the attention of the artistic genius of man and so has brought into being and developed different musical instruments.

The earliest literary works of India as per our most ancient sculptures have preserved descriptions and forms of musical instruments. These have been traditionally classified under four heads, tata which include all stringed instruments, anandha which include all that are struck like drums, sushira which includes all tubular instruments like the flute and the chank, Ghana which includes all cymbal-like resonators. Though the Pali word turiya (Sanskrit turya) which connotes an orchestra. Whether for music alone or as accompaniment to song or dance, should mean only those four, the very name being suggestive of this, atata vitala, atata-vitata, Ghana and sushira are enumerated as making up a turiya pancangika (five limbed orchestra–Vimanavatthu 5, 4). The atatavitata which is a combination of atata (Sanskrit iata) and (Sanskrit Anadhha) must refer to some combination instrument like the tant-ipatahika or stringed drum (Harsha carita, p. 181).

Harp–Type–The first of the talas was the vina, the most famous of Indian musical instruments. The commonest types of vina were bow-shaped and resembled a harp, but there was also another type which was more like a guitar. The former was evolved on the principle of the bow and the resonator, the musical twang of the bowstring being a favourite sound often eulogized by poets as deep and pleasant. The interval between strings tied to the bow-shaped rod immediately above the resonator increased or diminished their length and thus determined the modulation of the note of the note imaging vocal vibrations. (In the story of king Udayana).

Mrudanga

Three kinds of Mrudanga can be distinguished namely Ankya Alingya and Urdhaka. These names denote the positions in which they were held. All these can be seen in Amaravati sculpture, the Ankya is placed on the lap. The Alingya, larger than the Ankya but also placed on the lap. This produces sweet sound (Harsha Charitha p. 131) this and the urdhaka went together. The former, though taller than the modern tabla has to be played in the same fashion.

References

1. The term Aharya can be used as a collective term to denote coiffure, jewellery, costume and make-up.
2. Marg, Vol. XVIII, Homage to Jeweller's Art, p. 2.
3. NS, Ch. XXI.
4. K. Krishna Murthy, Mirrors of Indian Culture, p. 12.
5. NS, Ch. XXI.
6. NS, Ch. XXIII, pp. 64-67.
7. Ratnakaravarni Bharatesa Vaibhava, p. 119, V. 52.
8. JISOA, Vol. III, p. 98.
9. BDCRI, XX, p. 98.
10. Adipurana, Padma, Ch. XI, V. 93.
11. MS, Vol. II, p. 101, Vv. 1175-76.
12. Jyotsna Kamath, Social Life in Medieval Karnataka, p. 27.
13. Prajesh Banerji, Dance of India, p. 169.
14. Enakshi Bhavanani, The Dance in India, p. 169.
15. Jyotsna Kamath, Social Life in Medieval Karnataka, p. 50.
16. Ratnakara, Bharatesa Vaibhava, p. 119, V. 52.
17. *Ibid*, p. 119. V. 54.
18. History and Culture of the Indian People, Vol. III, p. 557.
19. R. Satyanarayana, Studies in Indian Dance, p. 26.
20. R. N. Saletore, VA, 243.
21. *Ibid*, p. 244.
22. Jamila Brij Bhusan, Historical Developments, p. 6 and Marg, Vol. XVIII, No. 4, September 1964.
23. NS, Ch. XXI.
24. *Ibid.*
25. K. Krishna Murthy, Mirrors of Indian Culture, p. 170.
26. Jyotsna Kamath, Social Life in Medieval Karnataka, p. 56.
27. K. Krishna Murthy, Mirrors of Indian Culture, p. 170.
28. Jyotsna Kamath, Social Life in Medieval Karnataka, p. 58.
29. Bharatesa Vaibhava, p. 116, V. 4.
    Kankana dhvani Kanakanane Katisutra
    Kinkini Kinikini enalu //
    Pankajaksiaraidutiddarandugegala
    Jhenkara Jhanarenalu /14/1
30. Prajesh Banerjee, Dance of India, p. 184.
31. P. S. R. Appa Rao, Bharata's Natyasastra, p. 63.
32. NS, V.O.S.
33. Tarlekar, Studies in Natyasastra, p. 63.
34. *Ibid*, p. 319.
35. Jyotsna Kamath, Social Life in Medieval Karnataka, p. 35.
36. Bihubali–Nagakumara Charitam, XXII, pp. 87–89.
37. Bharatesa Vaibhava, p. 119, Vv 42, 49, 53, 54.

Classical Dance—Poses of India
Ravindra Bhavan, New Delhi
Gopinath S. V. Rama Rao
Natana Niketan Publications
Cathedral Road, Madras.
Abhinayadarpanam
Edited by Dr. Manmohan Joshi
6/1A, Bancharam Arkur Lane, Calcutta-12

3. Bharat Natyam
An in-depth study by Natya Kala Bhushani
Siva in dance, myth and iconography
Volume sponsored by Inter-faculty Committee for South Asian Studies
University of Oxford
Saroja Vaidya Nadhan
Bharatavalyam
from temple to theatre
By Anne-Mariee Gaston
Understanding Bharata Natyam
The Maharaja Sayaj Rao
University of Baroda
Baroda (1965).

Yakshagana and its Sanskrit sources
by
Dr. G.S. Hegde

Tibetan Religious Dances
Renedenebesky-Wojkowitz
Pilgrims Book Pvt. Ltd., Delhi-110033
A Study of the technique of Abhinaya
in relation to Sanskrit Drama—Shiveni Pandya

9. The Natyasastra Vol. II
Translated edited by
Dr. Manmohan Ghosh

10. Balasaraswati
by Narayana Menon
(Photographs by Marilyn Silverstone
Published by International Cultural Centre, 16, Hailey Rd., New Delhi-1 (1963).

11. Mohini Attam
The lyrical dance
By Kanak Rele
Nalanda dance research centre
Plot A-7/I, NSRD No. 10, JVPD Scheme
(Vil. Parle W.) Bombay-400049 India

12. The Natya Sastra
of Bharatamuni (Translated into English by a Board of Scholars) Sri Satguru Publications, Delhi.

A Sculpture of Vijayanagara

PART-IV
BHAGWATA MELA AND OTHER TRADITIONS OF ANDHRA PRADESH

31

Birth of Bhamakalapam–A New Technique

"It was in this situation that a group of immigrants from Andhra Pradesh entered Tanjore. In the early part of the 16th century an evolved form called Bhagavatamela or more precisely speaking Yakshagana both as a literary genre and as a theatrical mode took shape. Its development cannot be separated from the growth of Telugu literature. Indeed, the Bhagavatamela of Tamilnadu continues to be a Telugu flowering in Tanjore".[1]

The Telugu's migration cannot be considered to be a simple migration. "What grew up in Tanjore courts under the Naik Kings and the patronage of later Maratha rulers was the result of Telugu migration to Tamilnadu and the subsequent return of the Telugus to Andhra nearly a hundred years later".[2]

"Before narrating this fascinating story of action and interaction, it would be worth while to study Telugu literature of this period, so as to understand how it was natural and logical for literary and theatrical forms in the two regions, to influence each other and evolve a literary genre which moved freely through the "Bhagavathulu", who were the mobile carriers of literary word through visual presentation".[3]

To use the human body as a vehicle of expression and communication was not restricted to what is termed normally as "dance" or movement. It was brought to the aid of "Vak" which primarily was unquestioned art at all levels particularly the village and the urban levels. On the word was superimposed the melodic note. The two together provided the essential prerequisites for interpretation through movement. The colour symbolism of the physical environment, costumes, make-up, head gear, all reinforced the other levels".[4]

We have observed earlier how Palkuriki somanadha in his Pandítharadya charitra described the musical and dance forms which were prevalent in Andhra and how they could attract audience in numbers. Other architectural and inscriptional evidences also tell us about the Andhra Aradhana Nritya in temples.[5]

A rich tradition of literature, music and dance was prevalent in Andhra. Treatises like Abhilashitardha Chintamani of Somasekhara II, Nritta Ratnavali of Jayappa Senani, Vasantha Rejeeyamu of Kumaragiri Reddy and Sangita Chintamani of Pedakomati Vema Reddy bear testimony to the many forms of music and dance which were prevalent in the Telugu land under the distinguished guidance of many Brahmin Natyacharyas.

"What came to be called Kuchipudi was connected both with the literary writings of the medieval period called the 'Desi' forms and the pure dance forms, which were closely associated with temple ritual about which there is ample literary, inscriptional and archaeological evidence".[6] While the devadasis performed Natya in temples, the Kuchipudi Brahmin boys formed itenerant groups in village courtyards.

In the beginning, their stories revolved round Saiva Puranas and after the great wave of Vaishnavism, the popular stories of Bhagavata Purana were given prominence. The performers who were called "Bhagavathulu" migrated to Melattur seeking royal patronage after the decline of the Vijayanagar empire.

Siddhendra Yogi and His Contribution to Dance

For reasons not known, from Melattur, Siddhendra Yogi returned to Andhra. He learnt Kuchipudi style from his guru, Teerdha Narayana Yogi. As the legend goes, Siddhendra yogi composed Parijathapaharanam, out of inspiration of seeing Lord Krishna dancing on the chest of Teerdha Narayana Yogi, when he was singing his 'Tarangas' being a blind man. He followed the literary Yakshagana of the earlier period and his contemporaries like Kshetrayya of movva, Ramadas and Tukaram.

There are several stories about the origin and parentage of Siddhendra Yogi, Elders say that Siddhendra's original name was Siddappa and he was a native of Kuchipudi. Some say he is from 14th century and some others say he belongs to 15th century but it may be apt to say he belongs to the 16th century. Siddayya or Siddapa are the names found in Rayalseema. There is a story which tells that some of the people from Kuchipudi migrated to Kurnool district under the patronage of the Nawab of Banaganpalli. I went to this village personally and enquired about their past history. Siddappa might have been a son of such a Bhagavathar, whose origin was Kuchipudi but migrated to Kurnool Mandalam.

There is also a story that Narayana Teerdha is synonymous with Siddhendra Yogi and both are not different. But, the popular version is that Siddhendra Yogi is a disciple of Nayarana Teerdha and he learnt from his Guru, dance, music and dedication to Lord Krishna.

There are no evidences to show precisely what is what. There is a legend which tells us that Siddappa was an uneducated village boy who was roaming about without aim or purpose in life. But he was associated with the exhibitors of Kuchipudi dance style and he was married also. One day, he realized in his mother-in-law's house that he is uneducated and so humiliated and depressed, he went away to an unknown place. By the grace of God and the patronage of a guru from Udipi he learnt dance and music and returned to Kuchipudi as a scholar. But he could not cross the Krishna river, as it was in floods. So he took to jalasanyasa. Floods stopped and he was thrown to the shores. Thus he came to Kuchipudi and stayed there and taught to Brahmin boys of Kuchipudi after taking an oath from them that every boy born in Kuchipudi should act as Bhama atleast once in his life.

Bhamakalapam is Parijathapa Harana only and the story in short is as follows.

Satyabhama declares herself that she is more beautiful than Krishna. She enters into a pranaya kalaham with Krishna. He leaves her and goes to Rukmini's house. Realising her mistake and out of her love for Krishna, Satyabhama suffers from pangs of love and separation (virahatapa). She also visualizes the incident of Krishna giving parijatha flower to Rukmini. She sends a messenger to Krishna begging him to come back to her. Finally Lord Krishna returns to her.

This is an additional episode of her feelings towards Rukmini in addition to her pride. This results in her realization that she cannot live without the love of the Lord. The linking character in this dance drama is really Vidushaka who plays the dual role of Madhavi (girl messenger) who goes to Krishna and also as Madhava, who gives Rukmini as bride to Krishna.

This dance drama starts with the prologue–a playing of mridanga and maddela accompanied by cymbols. This is followed by a prayer song to Bala Gopala and then comes the flag staff of Indra (Vedic lord of heaven). The sutradhara now sings and announces the theme of play and introduces the characters and invites the audience to enjoy the drama.

Satyabhama now looks over the top of the curtain and performs a beautiful dance full of expression and filled with Rasa. Her movements (Rechakas) foot, waist and neck and hand gestures are eloquent. Towards the end of the song, she takes hold of her magnificent braided plait and throws it over the curtain, as a sort of challenge to anyone to rule out her supremacy in the art. Sutradhara now performs another puja (worship) as the curtain is half-lowered.

Satyabhama sings a song, introducing herself and once again dances pure dance. Sutradhara talks to Narada, the sage, while Madhavi, the girl messenger performs with attractive gait (Charis) and acting the dance movements. Now the curtain is lowered.

Krishna now appears on the stage and receives from Madhavi who is now impersonating Madhava, personifying the wisdom of inner self of Rukmini the real theme now commences.

Satyabhama introduces herself to Madhavi through song and pleads with her to meet Lord Krishna on her behalf, Madhavi asks Satyabhama to describe her lord.

Now the intricate dance of Dasavatarabhinaya commences, in which the ten Avatars of Krishna are depicted–namely, Matsya, Kurma, Varaha, Narasimha, Vamana, Parasurama, Rama, Balarama, Buddha and Kalki.

Madhavi convinces Krishna by her appealing words and succeeds in bringing him back to Satyabhama.

In this context, three kinds of fine dances are performed and followed by full of rasa, between Satyabhama and Madhavi, between Madhavi and Krishna and between Satyabhama and Rukmini. With this there is a happy ending of the story and Krishna gets reconciled with Satyabhama.

There will be wonderful characterization and emotional acting through out the dance drama. It is philosophical and symbolic of the Individual soul yearning for union with god. The story centres round the great love of proud and beautiful Satyabhama for lord Krishna and her suffering in his absence.

This dance drama by Siddhendra yogi, based on Kuchipudi classical dance techniques, won laurels as the best item and it remains as such even today.

This Kuchipudi dance–drama was remodelled in course of time and became "Bhamakalapam", a solo performance. In this new form Satyabhama is highlighted as a character and more emphasis is laid on "abhinaya", her viraha and her sorrow, with new modes of pure dance of classical technique became very popular. Thus Bhamakalapam became the most perfect item in the Kuchipudi repertoire.

In this dance item all the three components of *Bhava, Raga* and *Tala* create a peculiar mood, and melody and create perfect maintenance of a highly technical pure dance with nice interludes. With emphasis on the principles of karanas this style beautifully balances lasya and tandava following the guidelines given in Natya Sastra and Abhinaya Darpana by Nandikeswara, as well as Nritha ratnavali of Jayappa, this dance drama is emotionally fully developed by the usage of hand gestures and language of signs.

In the initial stage only Kuchipudi brahmin boys were enacting all feminine roles, the sutradhara or stage director plays a very important role. He is a Guru, well versed in dance, music and the sastras. He introduces the characters before they enter the stage, provides the necessary humour and sings and enacts Abhinaya.

Bhamakalapam, is a beautiful item, which depicts Vipralambha sringara (pangs of love) of Satyabhama.

There is another popular dance item called Gollakalapam.

2. Gollakalapam

Theme of this kalapam in Kuchipudi style is an ethical, satirical conversation between a Gopi and a Brahmin. This dance drama is a complete form of all that Bharata described for a classical dance. It has added richness of perfect dramatic characterization.

3. Manduka Sabdam

This was a very popular item once. The story was taken from Gajendra Moksham, where the frogs in a pond are described.

Is it Similar to Odyssey

The dance that is in vogue in Orissa is known as Odyssey. Devadasis perform this dance in temples. They also dance before the audiences. The renowned temple of Lord Jagannatha in Puri, is a noted place for music and dance. There were some hundreds of Devadasis serving in this temple and their vocation was to serve the Lord with dance and music at the time of "Kumbha harati".

There is great resemblance between Kuchipudi style and Odyssey. 'Dakkini' was a type of dance that we find in the borders of Andhra State. They also perform 'Bhagavatas', from their dances. They are known as 'Sokkinata', only men take part in this type of dance.

"Dancing was used" says Dharmottara Purana (4th to 7th centuries) "to please the gods in the temples and this art was of greater value than the joy experienced by those who meditated on Brahman, the supreme being". The vedantins compared the experience of contemplation of a work of art, as akin to the highest spiritual attainment. Nowhere in the world has there been such a clear revelation of the inter relationship of philosophic thought and artistic concepts as in India. So also in Odyssey style every image of religious significance is equated with the spiritual duality of god and nature.

In Hindu thought, every ritual was conceived with inspiration, as the quest was for absolute truth. So, it can be well understood how, in a state of exuberant joy in the precincts of temples, amidst devotional fervour of worshippers, and in a pleasant atmosphere of radiance, Indian dance was nurtured.

Tradition, environment and spiritual aspirations gave each style a particular form of its own. The Cholas were a magnificent dynasty, whose contribution to the 4th century BC, was excellent Katyayana, the grammarian mentions about the Cholas. They were prominent till the 13th century. Kautilya, in his *Artha Sastra*, mentions about these Chola kings and we find their names in the inscriptions of the Emperor Ashoka also.

In the 3rd century, the celebrated Sangam Age, they had their centres at Udaipur and Kaveri-pattinam. From AD 846 till 1279, they held sway in Tanjore, their rule ending with the death of Rajendra III. There was a system which continued through the ages judging from the various treatises, that dance was already a systematized and highly technical form, and was called 'Natya' which involved drama, and music. The dancing girls attached to Tanjore temple, were great in number and inscriptions in the temple tell us of their various activities. There were women of culture and proficient in various arts. At this point of time, many of the temples of India, were proud of their Devadasis and their accomplishments. Inscription (1) South Indian Inscriptions, Vol. II part 3, p. 269) shows that in AD 1004, the great temple of Chola King Raja at Tanjore attached to it there were 400 women of the temple, who lived in free quarters in 4 streets round around it and were allowed tax free land out of the endowment.

In the Brahmeswara temple, an inscription of 8th century, tells us of girls, who performed ritual dance and were called 'Maharis'.

The Jagannath temple was the focal point of all such cultural activity and in the 12th century, Chodaganga Deva founded the Ganga dynasty, patronizing the arts, a tradition that continues and which even the later monarchs like the great Kapilendra Deva of the 15th century patronized. His dancers were all from Telangana and Orissa.

There is evidence to show that the Rani herself danced in the 16th century, and she was known as 'Gopisakhi' and later, the King Prataparudra Deva encouraged the dancers to enact the love songs of Krishna, for he was himself a follower of Chaitanya cult. It was he who made the decision that only Gita Govinda of Jayadeva, should be recited in the temple of Jagannath. Chola Kings thus showed great interest in dance and the following paper report about it speaks more vehemently.

Five miles to the south-east of Devanahalli on the Sulebele Road, there is a vacant land, amidst a Tamarind grove, which was a royal city, with palaces, halls mantapas, lofty pinnacles, temple and gilded gates where once the royal horses galloped and damsels danced in the temple courts. According to the legend as sung by the local people in the form of ballad and this Nallur city was destroyed by the treacherous act of a woman. The same is confirmed by Mysore Gazetteer which says "Nallur city was a great extent and was ruled by a lineage of rich and powerful kings". Unfortunately, the Gazetteer throws no light on the period, to which Chodaraya belonged and the dynasty which he represented. The temples that can be seen, resemble in many ways the architectural carvings of the Siva temple of Doddagubbi.

The antiquity of Nallur can be traced to the period of the great Chola kings (12th century).

In the Gazetteer, an inscription (EC-IX dated 1120 AD) gives an interesting account of Nallur and its chief Udaya Marthanda Brahmamarayan. It was he who established dancing schools at Nallur and Sugathur (a place nearby) where dancing classes were held. (S.V. Hillatamani and S. Narayanaswamy in the Hindu dated 31st July 1988- Sunday).

All the evidences though now in ruins, go to show that Nallur was a city of cultural importance, during the period of Cholas and the origin of Nallur may be ascribed to the town established by Rajendra Chola. It was named Veera Rakshasa Nallur, after one of his surnames.

While the 'Maharis' in the temple of Jagannath are dedicated to Krishna, there are Maharis in Bhuvaneswar who worship Siva and Sakti, in the temples of Jhankad and Kakatpur.

The Moghuls came as conquerers and the dancers, who until then danced before the deities in the temple only, took to dance in the courts and Raja durbars. But religious rites in the temple continued as usual and the Maharis, to this day, dance twice in the sacred hall of the temple of Lord Jagannath and also on special festivals. They are called 'Gotipuras'. The superb sculptures on the temple walls, tell us of the quality of this style, which combines both "Tandava" and 'Lasya' and follows closely the rules of Natya Sastra of Bharata. In Bhuvaneswar, in Konark and in other temple dance poses, dance had been immortalized in stone.

The Odyssey dance begins with a song to the earth "Bhumipranam" and then a devotional poem to Ganapati, the remover of all hindrances to all performing arts.

The dance to Siva, the 'Batu Nritya', describes in song the worship to the God, with ritualistic gestures and movements. The 'Ista Deva Bandana' expresses devotion to a particular God and the 'Swara Pallavi Nritya, which follows brings out all rhythmic and musical qualities of this form.

Abhinaya is exquisitely portrayed in the Radha Krishna theme which is well depicted in the lyrics of Jaya Deva.

The similarity of the Odyssey dance with Kuchipudi is striking. Historical evidences and inscriptions in Telugu tell us, that there are fluid movements in Kuchipudi, though stylized. Odyssey is more fluid. Pallavi is there in both. Ragalapana and prevesa Daru is there. Visual representation to a raga, is superb in both the styles, the concept of pallavi is great and it does a fantastic job Krishna cult was mainly instrumental, as observed earlier, for bringing about a major reshuffle of earlier patterns.

'Dasavathara's (Ten incarnations of God) are displayed in both the styles, with dedication and grace.

Kharavela caves have ample evidences of dance poses of Odyssey. The Mardangi pose (Women drummer) is one such, which is very ancient and very exciting.

This sort of fusion of dance with drama is found in both and it can be said, that they conform to traditionalism still. This 'Bhumsuka' tradition (men acting as women) is nowhere found. Kaisiki Vritti or the delicate style in dance is given utmost prominence in the visual representation of a thought, in both Kuchipudi and Odyssey and it is this that keeps them on a separate par with other dance forms of India. The songs of Jayadeva and his love towards Padmavathi, his beloved, became very famous throughout India, on account of this delicate display only.

These dances have their peaks of emotional intensity and movements. They speak to the audience; that is why, Martha Graham, a foreign writer says "every dance is a kind of fever chart, a graph of the heart". A dancer's instrument is his body only, by which, he expresses himself. When we look to the origin of Lasya tradition we find some more interesting details. These two traditions are similar in several respects and when studied in detail, the technique is also identical.

Lasya

Where there is no 'Padatadana' (imprint of foot steps) it is 'Lasya'. Only the 'Hasta Vinyasa' (display of gestures by the hand) is there. The poetic, idea mixed with the Manobhava of the character is well depicted with the help of Angas, Pratyangas and Upangas and their movements. The base of this is 'Sanchareebhava'.

The presiding deity of this 'Lasya' is Sakti, or Parvathi. Tandava is padavinyasa of several types if is performed with Ananda, it is Ananda Tandava and it is performed with Roudra, it is Roudra Tandavam. If it is in the evening, it is Sandhya Tandava; so also Pralaya Tandava. Siva, the layakartha, is the deity for this Tandava. The combination of this Siva and Sakti is Tala.

Abhinaya is of two kinds—sthulabhinaya (the abstract form) and Suksmabhinaya (the delicate form). Sthulabhinaya is displayed with Angika Abhinaya (with costumes, jewellery *etc.*) and Vachikabhinaya (Vacahana, (prose) Padya and Darus). The movements of body with a bhava is Sukshmabhinaya where as the expression of Sukshmabhinaya is nothing but Hastha-Vinyasa or movement of the hands. Unlike in other forms, Odyssey and Kuchipudi give ample scope for display of finer sentiments. Especially, the display of Vipralambha Srinagara is excellent and the Nayika, Satyabhama, pining for love of her Lord.

Vaishnava dances were different from the Saiva, being full of grace and belonging to the Lasya group. While "Ganapathi Koutham", "Siva-Tandava" were prominent in the Saiva dances, the following were the recognized Vaishnava dances. Bhujanga, Bhujanga Trasa, Suddha Kousthubha, Pushpanjali and others. So, the dancers in both the styles begin with 'Pushpanjali' offering of flowers to the Lord. Slokas and Kouthams are explained through "Abhinaya".

"According to a theory, 'Natya' is expressive of 'Rasa', Nritya is expressive of 'Bhava' and Nritta is that which causes beauty perceived by the eye".[2] Natya incorporated all the three features, dance, music and speech-which are so essential for the creation of drama.

Though the art of Natya was created by Bharata for the first time and it is an art, which combines 'Abhinaya' with Nritya, it had no separate, name of its own, nor was it classified as in later years as 'Tandava' and 'Lasya'. It gained the independent name as Natya and was canonized and developed, by 'Kohala'. Some plays were brought into being by Kohala, with his new art or technique.

Kohala's date is supposed to be sometime in between the 3rd century AD and the middle of the 4th century AD. Without deviating from any of the sacred and fondly cherished norms and principles, Abhinaya is being performed even today, by the modern dancers, more especially of Odyssey and Kuchipudi. As per Abhinaya Darpana of Nandikeswara, Abhnaya is the complete term for all techniques of expression of body, face and eyes. It also includes the language of the hands with which the dancer makes poetic comment visible.

When Kakatiya Empire fell, the ruler of Kalinga or Orissa, Bhanu Deva I (AD 1363–1277) ruled Divitaluk in Krishna district and Kuchipudi village was a part of this area and so all other villages like (Movva-Kshetrayya) Avanigadda, which are on the banks of the river Krishna. After the death of Bhanu Deva, Narahari Teera, his minister acted as regent for the young prince. A disciple of Ananda Teera, a great devotee of Krishna, brought the dancers from Orissa to teach the Gita Govinda of Jaya Deva to the Devadasis of Andhra. Gita Govinda, since then has been cherished by the Bhagavatars of Kuchipudi and called it as "Radhakrishna Nrityam". Many songs were composed on this eternal theme of Radha and Krishna and it was in Srikakulam that the celebrated poem Sri Krishna Karnamrutham was written by the poet Leela Suka.

Important items of Kuchipudi are :

(1) Bhama-Kalapam (2) Golla Kalapam (3) Dasavatara Nritya.

Of the techniques that are made use of, the most important are as follows :

(1) Taranga Nritya

(2) Padabhinaya

(3) Sabda

(4) Muktayimpu and Tirmanam

(5) Jakkini Daruvu

(6) Sabda pallavi

(7) Manduka Sabdam

(8) Kandardam *etc.*

Krishna Leela Tarangini was a dance-drama in Sanskrit, written by Tirdha Narayanaswami (14th century). The story opens with Bhudevi (mother earth) praying to Lord Krishna for protection against evil. The story is similar to the theme in Bhagavatham ending with the marriage of Krishna and Rukmini. 7th chapter is especially composed in several 'Talas' for the sake of dancers with musical 'Jathis', a peculiarity of the Kuchipudi technique depicting the Rasa Kreeda.

The name 'Taranga' or wave symbolizes various steps of the dancers. In the 3rd canto of Balagopala, the dancer, execute a typical dance, dancing upon a brass tray, with a pot of water on her head.

There are 12 scenes and each scene is introduced by the Sutradhara and the 'Nati' providing the links in the story. So also in Odyssey.

Bharata Natyam—a Comparison

What is known as Tanjore Bharata Natyam with "Alarippu", "Jatiswaram", "Sabdam" is of recent origin being less than 150 years old. It developed an elegant style and was practiced by Devadasis and courtesans as a solo type of 'Natya' in temples and the durbars of the kings. While Raga-Alapana and singing of the padas in Bharata Natyam were mostly influenced by the Kutchrei music during the last 100 years, the Kuchipudi style resembled the music of pre-Tyagaraja's days, not only in singing but in 'Nritta' and 'Nritya' 'Sabda', 'Muktyayimpu' and 'Tirmanamu'. This Bhagavatha Katha or Bani, I presume, is of great historical importance.

It is claimed by some that the present day Bharata Natyam came to South India from the Andhra Country and it flourished in Tanjore under royal patronage. The claim is made on the ground that much of the literature available on the subject of nattuvars is in Telugu and most of the songs for Varnama, Padams and Sabdams are in Telugu. Some of the famous devadasis in the Tanjore court, were Telugu women. The court language was Telugu and so it is no wonder that writings are in Telugu. "Alarippu" may be a form of the Telugu work "Alarimpu" meaning decorating with flowers.

There is another story that the origin of Bharata Natyam is 'Sadir'. The 'Sadir' was performed by Devadasis, on all auspicious occasions, in temples, palaces and houses of the people also. South India developed this tradition and Devadasis mostly kept up and continued this tradition and technique. Great artists like Chinnaiah, Ponnaiah, Sivanandam and Vadivelu, who were all brothers only, were mainly responsible for spreading it. The Nattuvanars and Devadasis call it 'Kali or Silambu' The old Tamil work is "Koothu" meaning.

Dance-dramas composed by equally great composers developed as a part of Bharata Natyam. These plays were different from Sadir, because there were characters in them. In Sadir, only one individual portrays several characters through Abhinaya. The dance-dramas were performed in temples, almost all by men and as part of the festival and were not performed on private occasions like marriages. These men dancers were called Bhagavatas. Melattur, Soolamanagalam, Oothukadu and other villages near Tanjore were famous for these dance-dramas as we have seen earlier. All the dramas that are now available to us were composed by Sri Melattur Venkata Rama Sastry in early 19th century but they are becoming extinct, owing to lack of proper encouragement and patronage, from any quarter. The stories are all from Ramayana, Mahabharata and Bhagavata. Originally in Sadir Nrityam also, the themes of the songs were religious though 'Nava Stuthi' or praise of the kings and other patrons was common. This led the art, to lower level.

But the dance-dramas of Kuchipudi developed a style of their own.

In Tamilnadu, recitals given by one or two dancers were called 'Sadir' until 50 years ago. This type of Nritya was performed by Devadasis on all auspicious occasions in temples, places and houses of the people. Tamil country specially developed this tradition, which Devadasis kept up.

The word "Natturavanars" (the dance teacher) has been derived from 'Nattuvangam'-Nat-aavi-Angam (dance troupe leader). "There is a theory that Bharata Natyam had originated from Andhra Desa. There is dependable evidence to show that dance was developed at Tanjore under the patronage of Achutappa Nayaka, the 2nd of the Nayak rules (1577-1614) of the place. There is extensive literature on this art in Telugu, dating back to 150 years. The authorship of most of the dance-dramas can be traced to Venkarama Sastry, a Telugu Brahmin".[3]

It is possible that the devadasis of Tanjore Court, who were also Telugu and played a very important part in developing figures on the walls and pillars of old temples of South India were the works of Telugu craftsmen.

The technique of Bharata Natyam, as it stands today was developed by four brothers, as shown above.

The Devadasis were mainly responsible for the preservation of this art. These women were the servants of God who dedicated their lives. In course of time, as the religious sancity of their profession declined, they were treated as merely mistresses of richmen. In consequence, the art also began to decline. But some effort was made by the enlightened classes to lift the art from the stigma attached to it. When girls from respectable families are being trained in this art, in the modern times. One among such luminaries is Dr. Rukmini Arundale, who did yeoman service to this technique of Bharata Natyam. Being born in an upper-strata family, and being a member of the theosophical society, she danced the diving dance and took pains to propagate this art. Her Kalakshetra in Madras, is a living monument to all her efforts, to elevate this art to higher levels. It is attracting the attention of all.

32

Modern Trends, Famous Exponents and Nritya Natikas

Abhinaya Darpanam says "We bow to the supreme divinity who reveals himself through the visible world, the audible music and the ennobled imagination". So, dance is the visible manifestation of inspired soul. The greatness of our ancestors lies in this, they could visualize an Amurtha feeling from a Murtha figure.

Aestheticism, according to Kant, means beauty that in its subjective form pleases the commoner even, without any intellectual, moral or practical advantages or that in its objective form is a thing or an action perceived, without any conception of utility. In 438 B.C. Plato, the Athenian philosopher, propounded a grand theory through his famous dialogues, that beauty in all bodies is one and the same. It is internal and indestructible. Desire for immortality in beauty is love and the human mind is always in love with beauty. That is why our ancestors paid equal attention to both the forms of art-sensuous and aesthetic, emotional and intellectual. Performing arts, thus, give visible satisfaction as they imitate life existing around them and can move the commoner, with the commonality.

Society is changing, Art forms are also changing. Appreciation of various art forms is gaining momentum, as more and more numbers are able to appreciate the stories of the universe. The rhythm and the movement of the spirit can be seen in the rising sun, in the waves of the ocean, in the rotation of the planets and in the lightning thunder. In Kali, Yuga, when people cannot find the time for concentration, easier forms are attracting the attention of people.

Another interesting feature of the modern society is that people are evincing interest in arts; irrespective of their social or economic background. A new culture is being evolved. So, dance especially is not confined to some castes or classes only as before.

The country is progressing in various fields but our arts are still lagging behind, previously the kings and the temple priests could give patronage to the arts. But now, the academies and the government are playing such role. There is imperative need to improve this style keeping in view the tradition and conventions laid down by the authoritative texts.

No doubt parents are taking interest in giving knowledge of fine arts to their children in schools. But, Natya charyas, well trained only should give the necessary training. More and more Kelika Rupas on Bhagavatha paddathi should be evolved. A responsible sound training should be given to youngsters and should take sufficient measures to improve the style of art, according to the needs of society.

Now, I would like to tell about some prominent personalities in the field.

Vedantam Lakshminarayana Sastry, Vempati Peda Satyam, Vedantam Raghavayya, Chinta Krishnamurthy are some of the luminaries in the field.

One must remember the veteran natya charya Vedantam Lakshminarayana Sastri of Kuchipudi. Pendyala, Satyabhama of Pithapuram and Chittajallu Venkataraman of Mareempalli were women dancers of distinction and best exponents of Kuchipudi school of yester years.

Sri Challa Bharatam Lakshmayya of Kota-konda, made his name and fame with his marvellous interpretation of Abhinayam (as Satyabhama other well-known names in the classical dance of Andhra are Vempati Peda Satyam, Vempati China Satyam, Vedantam Raghavayya, Pasumarthi Krishna Murthy, Korada Narasimha Rao, who is a Natyacharya of distinction and danced in the troupe of Indrani in her Kuchipudi centre.

Chinta Krishnamurthy, the greatest authority on Kuchipudi today is the son of the great master Chinta Venkataramaiah. He worked ceaselessly to further the cause of the Kuchipudi and served as the president of the Sangeet Natak Academy of Andhra Pradesh.

Late Banda Kanakalingeswara Rao, who has been responsible for the spread of the Kuchipudi style of dance by introducing to the modern stage is an authority on this subject. He was a writer and an actor of distinction. He was responsible for the establishment of Siddhendra Kalakshetram a dance school at Kuchipudi village which is now teaching to a great number of students in the best traditions. I had an opportunity to see him as producer (drama) in All India Radio, Vijayawada in the early sixties, when I joined service as a Junior Officer in government.

Vedantam Satyanarayana Sarma could win the presidential award for his excellent performance as Satyabhama in 'Bhamakalapam' and as Usha in 'Usha parinayam'. He excels in introducing those characters by his wonderful performance. In fact, his super technique makes him as the best of the exponents of the art.

Sri Vedantam Satyanarayana Sarma, exhibits a female character, very eminently, being a male. His 'Usha' and 'Satyabhama' are living examples. This is something rare and unusual. When I saw him for the first time I was stunned to see a very ordinary simple looking man. But his large eyes and his delicate limbs attract the onlooker's attention. His abhinaya is superb and none can excel him in exhibiting such fine sentiments as he. No woman can exhibit Vipralambha Sringara or pining for love. His performance in the role of 'Satyabhama'. His guru, is his brother whom he showed me in his house at Kuchipudi, a grand old man. Sri Satyanarayana Sarma travelled widely and won laurels for himself and also for the art. He was awarded 'Padmasree' by Government of India in recognition of his talent. Kalidas Academy of Ujjain gave him a sanman of a lakh of rupees and a citation for his exposition of 'Usha'.

Dr. Nataraja Ramakrishna

Dr. Nataraja Ramakrishna is the most respected Natyacharya of Andhra Pradesh. He is the present architect of Andhra Natya, the most ancient classical dance, *i.e.*, natyam performed by the female artistes of Andhra Pradesh. He recreated the Perini Sivatandavam the militant dance tradition of the 10th century A.D. He has revived Navjardanam a great prabandha dance tradition that was being performed in Kunti Madhava. Temple at Pithapuram in East-Godavari District for the last 400 years. Dr. Nataraja Ramakrishna composed and produced Sri Venkateswara Kalyanam (Telugu and Hindi) Kumara Sambhavam, Megha Sandesam and won Swarna. Kalasam at Ujjain for Kumar Sambhavam. He wrote 40 books on dance and six of them got awards from Government of India. His outstanding book is "Andhras and the Art of Dance" covering a period of 2000 years, which will be published very shortly. Dr. Ramakrishna is a dance artiste, guru, scholar, musicologist and he has been propagating classical dance in Andhra Pradesh for the last 35 years.

Dr. Nataraja is an authority on Satwikaabhinaya, the essence of Indian Classical Dance which is a speciality of Andhra Temple

Dance Artistes. Recently he was honoured with Gold Crown, the first of such in the Andhra Cultural History. A.P. Sangita Nataka Akademi conferred on him the title Bharatakalaprapoorna, Andhra University conferred on him the title Kalaprapoorna (Honorary Doctorate). The Andhra Dance Art Lovers conferred on him the title Bharatakala Savyasachi as he is the only performing dance artiste and writer.

He is now establishing a trust to propagate the classical dance of Andhras, to publish books on dance art and to help the dance artistes who are in need.

He was born at Bali Islands fifty years back and now settled at Hyderabad by establishing Nrityaniketan and Perini International.

Vempati China Satyam

Sri Vempati China Satyam, the doyen among the Kuchipudi exponents is the first among the Natyacharayas, who produced very eminent artists. He runs a regular school at Madras by name Kuchipudi Art Academy and gives coaching for hundreds of students. He is also the Secretary of Siddhendra Kalakshetra at Kuchipudi.

His Nritya Natikas like Srinivasa Kalyanam, Chandalika, Parijathapa harnam, Prahlada Vijayam, Gajendra Moksham are very popular. Recently with great skill for organization, he travelled with his troupe to several important towns and cities in Andhra and gave performances. Not only in the country, he has taken the Kuchipudi dance style, to far off lands like United States, South African countries *etc.*

His only aim and purpose in life, seems to be to make the art live with all the honour and dignity that it should have. He feels sorry that it could not get its proper honour or place, along with other styles by the several academies at Delhi level, as there was none to take it to that level and explain in the language that it should be done.

During my discussions with him on several occasions, he told me with anguish and pain and in detail how, this Kuchipudi style was considered by some eminent personalities in the field that it is only of folk type and was thus pushed to the background. This is really unfortunate. There was a time when he was asked to get a certificate from a famous dancer at Madras that his dance also is of the classical type. He felt very sorry to do so but was continuing his efforts to run his dance school, with the hope that a day would come when the world would recognize Kuchipudi style. Though attempts were made by some to draw him to the lucrative cinema field, he was not attracted and was content with running his school, and dedicated his life to dance only. It is now that there is so much of rejuvenation all over, he feels happy and people the world over are recognizing this style, as there are better opportunities. More and more girls from upper strata are coming forward to learn this art and give performances.

Vedantam Lakshminarayana Sastry

I should not forget to mention about late Sri Vedantam Lakshminarayana Sastry, who taught Balasaraswati the subtle grace of 'Abhinaya'. It was he who culled out the 'Solo' from Kuchipudi style. Sri Banda Kanakalingeswara Rao, producer (Drama) in All India Radio, Vijayawada, who was responsible for bringing out this type of dance to limelight by his untiring efforts.

Vedantam Lakshminarayana Sastry who passed away recently was an exponent and also a preceptor of Kuchipudi dance.

Chinta Krishna Murthy

Sri Chinta Krishna Murthy is another fine exponent and the Sangeetha Nataka Academy has honoured him with "Bharata Kala Prapoorna title. Sri Vedantam Raghavayya did tremendous work in the cinema field and was popular as a dance director for many films produced by Vahini Pictures Ltd.

Korada Narasimha Rao

Sri Korada Narasimha Rao, a member of Indrani Rehman's troupe travelled world over and it was he, who danced this style, for the first time on the world stage. He gave excellent performance of Kuchipudi style in the World Dance Festival at Paris and introduced this form of dance to much wider audiences. He exhibited Roudra, Veera, Bhibhatsa, Rasas by himself and none could excel him in this performance and so since then, these rasas took deep root in the style.

Sampatakumar, with his Jalari Nrityam (Fisherman' dance) is another popular exponent.

Ayyanki Tandava Krishna, Swarajyam and Ramana Rao

Mention should be made of Sri Ayyanki Tandava Krishna and dance couple, Srimathi Swarajyam and Ramana Rao who toured widely and gave performances in all the important towns and cities of Andhra Pradesh, in the initial stages so as to give wide publicity to the speciality, and classicism of Kuchipudi style.

Yamini Krishna Murthy

Yamini Krishna Murthy is the first person, who gave performances in the early years of the 19th century, when there were none in the field of Kuchipudi style and gave life to it. Her father, Sri Krishnamurthy, an erudite scholar and researcher and principal of a college gave life to her innate talents by giving her an opportunity to become a dancer. Having drawn from high caste upper strata of society at a time when some traditional values were strictly observed, and women were kept behind the doors; he encouraged her to take to the career of a dancer. When I met her at Delhi and wanted to know about her background, she tells me that her father was instrumental in evolving a dance career for her, and he used to always tell her, to achieve perfection. Now that he is no more, her eyes were wet while telling me about her father and it moved me. She had later been awarded "Padmasree" by Govt. of India. She runs a dance school at Delhi.

Yaminikrishnamurthy is a good artist who has dedicated herself to this ancient art of dance and became an expert in Bharata Natyam, Kuchipudi and Odyssey. Very delicate in her interpretation she portrays the fine and suitable distinction between these three styles of classical dance. While selecting her programme to sallow herself empire scope to show the attainment yamini excels in the interpretation of terms like 'krishna sabdam' showing Nayaka–Nayaki bhava, the "Bhamakalapam" the "Navarasa" and the "Tarangam" from Kuchipudi. Her role as Vishvamohini in Ksheerasagara Madhanam gives her a distinct place in a dance drama, which was once upon a time enacted only by men. She could win a Government scholarship for further studies in dance in the Kalakshetra of Madras run by Rukmini Arundale.

Later exponents were Indrani Rehman, Kumari Swapnasundari, Radha Reddy and Raja Reddy, Sumathi Kaushal, Ratnapapa, who gave performances abroad and won name and fame for the mother land. Unfortunately, I could not get their photos.

Manju Bhargavi

She is of 'Sankarabharanam' fame, a popular Telugu movie, in which she played the major role as a dancer. She is giving performances all over Andhra with a troupe of other eminent colleagues under the able guidance of her guru Sri Vempati China Satyam. She is a good dancer of repute. She is Srinivasa in Srinivasa Kalyanam, by Dr. Satyam with the support of Tirupathi Tirumala

Devasthanam and her performance is superb. The scriptwriter of this highly successful dance drama is Sri Bhujangaraya Sarma, a veteran Telugu scholar, who is no more.

Uma Rama Rao

She worked in the Potti Sriramulu Telugu University at Hyderabad, as head of the Deptt. of Dance. She is the niece of Sri Gora, a famous social reformist of Andhra. I heard she is holding a Senior Fellowship of HRD Ministry, Govt. of India

Sobha Naidu

Sobha Naidu a disciple of Dr. Vempati China Satyam today is one of the most outstanding exponents of Kuchipudi style. Her greatness lies in her total dedication to this exacting genre with classical base. A fiercely uncompromising pursuit, she is highly imaginative with a sense of deep involvement but without losing contact with contemporary taste and sensibility. She is currently working as the Principal of Kuchipudi Art Academy at Hyderabad.

Endowed with a good physique, with all the attractive features—big eyes, slim body, slender waist and delicate hands she gives performances with great competence. She draws innumerable crowds wherever she chooses to give performance. Recently, she had been awarded the title 'Nritya Chudamani' by Krishna Gana Sabha, Madras and the award of Padmasree, from Govt. of India.

Under the auspices of Govt. of India, she led cultural delegations to different far-off countries like Mexico, Trinidad, Venezuela, Cuba, Guyana *etc.* in 1973. She toured Kerala State in 1974 under the sponsorship of Kerala Sangeetha Nataka Academy. In same year, she visited United Kingdom and performed very successfully in London. Again in 1979, she led a cultural delegation to west Asian countries like Iran, Iraq. She gave performance in Mauritius in 1983, with her troupe of 18 members; she gave more than 30 performances in various important cities all over United States from New York to San Francisco. Her recent tour of USSR for one full month was well received and has evoked great interest in the dance lovers of Russia.

She strives for perfection. She is thoroughly convinced that this esoteric facet of India's priceless heritage deserves more support and more and more recognition.

Among the modern and popular dancers mention may be made of Uma Bharati, Uma Rama Rao, Alekya Punjala, Swapna Sundari, Swathi Somanadh, Sumati Kaushal, Vijaya Lakshmi, Jayasri, Ratnapapa, Jonnalagadda Anuradha, Vijayasri Sastry.

Uma Bharati

She is another dynamic rising star of the style of Kuchipudi. She runs a dance school in America and gives performances, in orphanages and several other social organizations. She is able to mix her family life with her dance career, quite successfully. Being a postgraduate, she speaks fine English and introduces her feelings in her performances, by herself.

Usha Gayatri

Gifted with fine attractive physical features, she is able to make a mark in the display of certain subtle feelings and portrays fine sentiments. She may win more laurels in future and bring fame and name to the motherland as well as to her illustrious profession.

Kamala Reddy, Sabita Bala and Others

These are some of the junior, exponents now making a mark on the stage, with their grand performances. Drawn from good academic and social background, Kamala Reddy has established herself as one of the finest exponents of Kuchipudi style and her gestures, and movements have a touch of restraint and refinement, sustained by controlled passion and uncanny precision. Sabita is of Saptapadi fame, a successful movie. Bala's performance as Chandalika is excellent.

Swathy Somanath

Swathy has acquired her Masters Degree in Kuchipudi style from the Central University of Hyderabad. She was the student of her renowned guru Smt. Sumathi Kaushal. She has given several solo performances through out India and abroad. She has the unique honour of being the first dancer from Andhra Pradesh to give performance in United Arab Emirates and won laurels from Cosmopolitan audiences at Dubai, Abudhabi and Sharjah and at Srilankan Embassy. She performed in South and East African countries like Botswana, Shajiland, Tanzania and Mozambique under the auspices of Indian Council for Cultural Relations, Govt. of India in 1998. She also performed during the fourth conference of American Telugu Association at Houston, Texas, USA, Canada in 1996 and at Budapest, Hungary and toured Italy as part of Group study exchange program of Rotary Club of Hyderabad district in 1998. She has choreographed nearly a 100 solo items and 6 Kuchipudi dance dramas.

Pranaya Varudhini is based on Manucharitra, a great poetic work in Telugu literature by Allasani Peddana Matya, a 2 hour dance drama, which highlights the origin of manu and the union of varudhini and pravarakhya.

Rasa Gopalam

This is a one and half hour dance drama based on Gita Govindam by Jayadeva. It depicts the divine concept of Madhurabhakti of Radha towards Krishna through Astapadis.

Sarwagna Sankara

The first dance drama produced from Andhra Pradesh depicting the life of Jagadguru Adishankaracharya. This 2-hour long production

performed with the divine blessings of his holiness Sri Sri Bharati Thirdha Mahaswamiji of Sringeri Sarada Peetham.

Nauka Charitam

It is a one and half hour dance drama based on Tyagarajas Nauka Charitam. It deals with the ultimate union of self with Parabrahma or the Supreme Power through the symbolism of Krishna and gopikas.

Sri Narayana Guru Dharshanam

The first ballet produced in India on the life history of Sri Narayana guru belonging to Varkala in Kerala.

Shakti

This ballet describes the Navarasas with goddess Parvati as the central character and is written by one of the living legends in Karnataka music by name Sri Kollegal Subrahmanyam.

Swati is the head of Nrutya Bharati, an institute dedicated to the ancient forms of classical dance, preserving rich heritage on Gurukul system incorporating Sanskrit literature and vedic knowledge with dance and music.

She has won several awards like Nrutya Choodamani, Natya Rani, Nrutya Mayuri, Natya Parijata, Natya Visharada *etc.* by several noted organisations.

Dr. (Kum) DEMOS GORA M.B.B.S.

Address : Atheist Centre
Benz Circle
Vijayawada 520 010
Andhra Pradesh
Tel: (0866) 2480859,2472330
Cell: 94406 74138
Email: drdemosgora_artistap@rediffmail.com
demosgoraarediffmail.com
"DEMOS" means Democracy in Greek

Family : Grand Parents- Gora and Saraswathi Gora
Parents- Sri G.Niyanta and Smt. Sakala
Aunts– Smt. K. Uma Rama Rao and Smt. Sumathi Koushal
Kuchipudi Artistes

Qualification : M.B.B.S. from Siddhartha Medical College, Vijayawada.
(Campus College of NTR University of Health Sciences)

Studies : Nirmala High School, Maris Stella College and Siddhartha Medical College at Vijayawada

Dance

- Kuchipudi, Bharatanatyam and Folk
- Disciple of Natyacharya Sri Bhagavatula Venkatrama Sarma
- Arangetram-On 23-02-1991 in the presence of Dr.C. Narayana Reddy, the then Vice-Chancellor of Telugu University, Hyderabad.
- Secured First Class in Kuchipudi Certificate Exam. and Bharatanatyam Certificate Exam.
- Grade-A Artiste in Kuchipudi of Deptt. of Cultural Affairs Govt. of A.P.
- Performed more than 500 solo dance recitals and participated in number of Dance Dramas.

Achievements :

— Received a number of 1st and 2nd prizes in Kuchipudi, Bharatanatyam and Folk competitions conducted by Bala Bhavan, Rotary International, Lions *etc.*

Vanaja Uday

Born to Smt. & Sri Hari Vadan Lal, she has distinguished herself in the two classic forms of South India - Bharata Natyam and Kuchipudi. Her committed aim, dedication and endless encouragement from her parents, husband, family and friends, she matured into a well known danseuse in Andhra Pradesh and is being recognized at the National and International levels. She is recognized as 'A Grade National Artiste in 'Doordarshan' an Indian Government Television Channel.

Vanaja is equally strong in the academic field completing her Diploma in Bharata Natyam from Sri Thyagaraja Government College of Music and Dance, Hyderabad, she has been practising dance for more than two decades. After her graduation in Arts, she has done her Masters degree in Arts with subject Sociology and her M.A. in Kuchipudi dance from Telugu University Hyderabad. She has also done her Post Graduate Diploma in Public Relations with a Diploma in Spanish and Tourism.

Performances in India

Vanaja has been actively participating in dance ballets and many cultural events since 1982 in India and abroad. She played in "Thyagaraja Musical Opera" Nauka Charitam, "Annamacharya's Musical

Opera" Alimelu Manga Valasam, Rukmini Hrudayam, Mandakini, Chitra Kuta Mahatyam, Durgasura Samharam, Vigneshwara Kalyanam and Shiva Pallaki Seva Prabhandanam, Girija Kalyanam.

She also participated in the Sur Singar Samsad's Kal-kekalakar Sammelan held at Mumbai, the Pallavothsav Festival held at Mysore, Kalidas Festival held at Ujjain, Central Sangeeth Nataka Academy Festival held at Hyderabad, South Central Zone Cultural Centre Festival held at Nagpur and Gwalior, North Zone Festival held at Kulu, Manali. The Nrityotsav and Natyotsav conducted by the Central Sangeeth Natak Academy held at Hyderabad, The Spirit of Unity Concert for National Integration held at Puttaparthi, The Festival of Hyderabad held at Hyderabad, The Jugal Bandhi Festival conducted by South Central Zone Cultural Centre, Hyderabad, The Indur Festival held at Nizamabad, The Bani Festival held at Hyderabad conducted by P.S. Telugu University.

Performances Abroad

International Youth Dance Festival at Hongkong and Macau, Festival of India held at Srilanka on behalf of ICCR, Performed in ATA (American Telugu Association) at Houston, USA, Performed in TANA (Telugu Association of North America) at New York, USA.

Travelled extensively throughout Mexico on behalf of Rotary International in their GSE (a Group Study Exchange) Program and United States - New York, New Jersey, Connecticut, Philadelphia, Pittsburgh, Detroit, Chicago, Washington, Maryland, Houston, Dallas, Los Angeles, Sanjose, North & South Carolia and Atlanta on behalf of Telugu Association.

In Ugadi Festival held at Mauritius, Indian

Carnival held at Singapore, European—Telegu Association Decennial Celebrations held in London, wherein gave performance of Kuchipudi dance.

Travelled to Canada and performed at-Ottawa, Toronto and Montreal on behalf of South Indian Cultural Association.

Participated in 'Dusshera' Festival held at Sharjah & gave Kuchipudi dance performance.

Family

She is happily married to Sri Uday Kumar a TV. Artiste & Producer who is a source of

Inspiration to her and blessed with a son Mstr. Tanay.

Profession

She is working in Department of Dance of Potti Sreeramulu Telugu University, Hyderabad, INDIA.

Vanaja gave nearly 1800 performances across the Globe under auspicious guidance of her Guru Dr. Uma Rama Rao and Bhagavatila Sethu Ram.

Abhinaya Satyabhama
Dr. G. Padmaja, B.A

Indian mythology, legends and Classical literature provide the themes of the Indian Dance both of the classical and folk variety. The Classical Dance is based on rigid rules and dance discipline. Its forms include BHARATHA NATYAM, KUCHIPUDI, ODDISSI and KATHAK

Andhra Pradesh is well known for the traditional KUCHIPUDI DANCE, which is one of the forms of Classical Dance.

Smt. G. Padmaja is one of the outstanding dancers in Kuchipudi Classical Dance and is in this field for the past 25 years and has to her credit number of awards / titles recognizing her excellent performances not only within India but also abroad by the art lovers, distinguished participants and public wherever the performances are given.

Smt. Padmaja's greatness lies in her total dedication to her exquisite genre, which needs classical base. She is highly imaginative and has a deep sense of involvement. She is successful in achieving a fine balance between the classical and contemporary taste and sensibility, so that the rich Indian Culture is understood and appreciated even by a layman. Her contribution to the art of Kuchipudi Dance conferred on her various titles / awards by various highest dignitaries.

She was participated in the National Level Competition, South Central Zone Nagpur in the year 1980. And also she was qualified the U.G.C. Test for the Lecturership.

Speaking Eyes Mirroring Mirate Shades of emotions with her Forms and Techniques exceeding Incisive sparks of seduction Kuchipudis Oyyari-Padmaja.-Mid Day Daily Newspaper-29-011981.

Padmaja dance with courtesy gifted with a beautiful face dominated by two large and expressive eyes, she gave a memorable interpretation of Othakadu Venakata Subbiers Competition Markatam Mony-Financial Express-Bombay in the year 1982.

Call her a NYMPH a Deer, a Swan or a Peacock she answered an these descriptions-She is Padmaja.-Statesman-New Delhi.

In 1985 she gave a notable and well applauded performances in USA, Canada & Trinidad on the invitation of TANA. She with the name and fame gained also visited Singapore, Thailand, Malaysia in 1988. In 1992 she gave performances in Europe, Australia and Germany and taste of her performance was enjoyed and recognized by the residents there and she is conferred with "NATYA VISHARADHA".

The Indian Council of Cultural Research (ICCR), New Delhi Which is the highest and reputable Institution itself sponsored her to "MAURITIUS" in 1993 and her performance has been well recognized and it has become a significant step for her to go to the heights in this field.

In 1994 itself for her excellent contribution and performance she conferred with the title NATYAVISHARADHA-by His Excellency Shankar Dayal Sarma the then President of India, which is a prestigious title in this field.

Her excellent contribution and performance and her total involvement in Abhinayam gave her title "Natya Visharadha-1994 KALKI KALAKAR 1990, ABHINAYA SATYABHAMA & SAMSKRUTI RATNA in 2001. In one sentence every art lover recognized her an embodiment of Abhinaya.

She was invited for 13th North America Telugu Conference convened from 29th June to 1st July, 2001 at Philadelphia and there her performance enthralled the artistes, dignitaries and other art lovers and it is one of her land marks of her performance of wide, recognition.

She has also given her reputable performance "Road Show" at DUBAI in 2002 organized by respected Mrs. Chandana Khan, Secretary for Tourism Dept., Govt. of A.P.

She did also give her enthralled performance in USA Dallas organized by ATA which gave her further name and fame for her Abhinaya.

In the ETA held at England in November 2002 she got appreciation and her inherent ,talents in her art of Classical Dance were totally recognized by her unbeatable Abhinaya.

The Telugu Association of North America organized a special programme on 21 & 22nd December, 2002 at Ravindra Bharathi, Hyderabad Tana Rajathotsavam and Telugu Janapada Kalasaram which was attended and graced by distinguished dignitaries, Kuchipudi Dance Exponents, Cine producers and actors who got name and fame and who are recognized in the field of traditional arts and who are the outstanding artists and who got highest puraskarams in India and Abroad. Sri N. Chandra Babu Naidu, Hon'ble Chief Minister of Andhra Pradesh, graced this great function. Such a notable programme of the highest degree which needs qualified responsibility with these top dignitaries and distinguished persons was carried out by Smt. G. Padmaja Reddy as a Convener. This is a very big honour and success for her in her career in the field of Promotion of Arts.

She is the first person to touch Kuchipudi Dance on website WWW.teluggone.com

Another added recognition is her participation in Telugu Mahasabhalu convened at Singapore in the Month of November 2002 and where she has an praise and appreciation for her excellent performance.

Now she is the acting Co-ordinator of TANA Programme to be held in June 2003 at Los angles (U.S.A.).

She was represented ETA Celebrations which was held on 25th September 2003 at London, England.

She was invited by the Tourism Department, Govt. of Andhra Pradesh, Hyderabad to performance Kuchipudi Dance and promote Cultural Tourism during World Travel Mart at EXCEL Hall, London from 10th to 13th November 2003.

She for her contribution to promote the art of dance and for the recognition for her outstanding Kuchipudi Dance. She has been honoured by Cinekala Tapaswi Padmabhushan and DADA SAHEB PHALKE Award Graheeta Dr. Akkineni Nageshwar Rao by awarding Gold Medal recently on 19.09.04.

It is also my pleasure to place before you that I have been presented with D. Lit Degree (Hon ru causa) by Sri Krishna Devaraya University on 29th April, 2005.

In another excellent and well said Programme of her in the Brahmostavams of Lord Sri Venkateshwara organized by T.T. Devestanams Tirupathi, on 19.04.04 she gave a memorable performance of Classic Dance "SIVA HELA" which got all appreciations by one and. all This is another milestone which gave her name and fame.

Some of the recent performances by her in this year are "KALYANA SRINIVASA CHARITHAM",-BRUNA HATHYALU",-ANNAMAYA PADA NARTHANA SHOBA".

She is also elected as "OVERSEAS CO-ORDINATOR" for "AMERICAN TELUGU ASSOCIATION" for their programmes for 2005 & 2006.

G. Padmaja Reddy

33

Dance Drama-similarity with Bhajana Sampradaya

China Tirumalayya a follower of Annamacharya wrote about "samkeertana Lakshana Padhati" and the Oriental Manuscripts Library at Tirupathi owns this book. He proves that there is ample similarity between 'Natakam' (play), Samkeertana (chanting) and Harikadha (rendering story of Hari, lord Krishna).

Tiruvothiyur inscription holds good evidence to this argument.

"Prabodha Chandrodayam" a text in 6 parts, written by Krishna Misra also has many references to Bhajana sampradaya and Vema Reddy wrote a commentary on this.

Chaturlakshana Samkeertana Charyulu, was the first man to use the word "Bhagavathulu" speaking about Brahmin boys of Kuchipudi. There were several Bhajan Troupes, even at the time of Muslims. In the temples of Ahobilam (Kurnool District) and Simhachalam (Visakhapatnam District) there was this type of Bhajan singing in praise of the supreme god. They preached the philosophy of "Adwaita" and men only participated (12th century). That was the time when Veerasaivism was in vogue. On account of the influence of Geeta Govinda. Vaishnavism spread throughout India and this line of thought, dominated the Bhajana Sampradaya in the whole of the country. There were several Bhajan troupes, which toured throughout the length and breadth of the country and propagated the Vaishnava culture. Nayaka–Nayaki Bhavana is absent in this and Sringara Rasa has no place.

Varalu was a poet, vocalist and dance master. He did not accept royal patronage and lived in a village called Varahapuri, near Mangalagiri or Kaja in Guntur district before the rule of Krishna Deva Raya, and lands were given to Kuchipudi dancers (1600–1680). He introduced Bhajana Sampradaya. He added : Jathis : to songs. His rendering attracted people and he became the centre of this Bhajan Sampradaya. This tradition was carried on by a long list of people, who were all Telugu Brahmins.

Sada Siva Brahmendra, also a Telugu man Preached Nama Kanvadi or Nama Siddanta as a cult. Siddhendra yogi trained in Udipi, carried on this Bhajan Sampradaya by his writings.

Sreedhara Venkatesa, Bedhendra Sadguru Swamy (one of the pontiffs of Kanchi Kamakoti Peetham) lived in a village called Govindapuram near Kumbhakonam (Mamdalnallur). His original name was Venkataramana.

Then comes Tyagaraja on the scene. Nama Siddhanta is the school of thought which tells by rendering of Nama or the name of the Lord, one can attain bliss. He wrote eight books on Nama Siddanta.

Sahaji Raja Puram was given to 46 families. Sreedhara Venkatesa Aiyar wrote a Kavya called 'Sahendra vilasa'. It is in Praise of Sahaji (1509–1539).

Sanskrit was the base for dance, music, literature, Alankara Sastra in those days.

Yakshagana is a musical play, but need not be a dance–drama necessarily. About 500 years ago, 'Bhagavatha Mela Nataka' flourished and it was popular by that name. Narayana Teerdha and Venkatarama Sastry migrated and took with them to Tamilnadu, this Bhajana Sampradaya.

From this Bhajana Sampradaya, Puja Nrityam Navasandhi Nrityam and Kantuka Nrityam and shodashopachara puja (16th upachara is nrityam) were performed in temples.

Dr. S.S. Janaki of Kuppuswamy Sastry research institute wrote on mudras given in Saiva agamas and I had the proud privilege of discussing with her about these agamas. Rama Bhadramba, Muddupalani (Radhika Santwanam) and some others who lived in Achuthapuram or Unnattapuri (a seat of Venkateswara, a Siva deity) are Telugus.

It was not only entertainment performed in temples. Kuchipudi people came to Tamilnadu during the time of Achuthappa Nayaka, Kshetrayya wrote padams and added a new tradition to Kuchipudi style. "Matsaramuna", "Pralaya Payodhi Jale" and other items of Kuchipudi are from Bhamakalapam and Gollakalapam, which were very popular in those days. So darus in playing Bhamakalapam were prevalent and the rest are from Natya Sastra and mostly from Abhinaya Darpana.

Here, in this context, I would like to mention about the findings of Sri Manepalli Ramakrishna Kavi, a veteran scholar and researcher. He tells us about a type of drama prevalent in Sanskrit literature "Nrittapara". In the prologue to the Bhagavajjuka, a drama of Prahasana kind, ten types of plays are mentioned as modifications of the nataka and prakarana species. The list begins with the name 'NRITTA PARA'.

There are three commentaries to the prakarana and none of the commentators have attempted any enlightening on the word. Certainly, it means one of the rupakas but none of the well-known writers on dramaturgy have used this lord. Then what is this para ? what are its individualising traits"? With this analysis in mind he tried to probe deep into the works on poetics and searched for right interpretation.

Bharata has given us ten types of plays, which all writers on dramaturgy have quietly followed. Dhananjaya even named his word "Dasarupaka" while its commentator called himself as Bahurupa Misra, probably a pseudonym. The ten kinds are 'Nataka', 'Prakarana', 'Dima prahasana', 'samavakara', 'Vyayoga', 'Ihamrija', 'Vidhi', 'Utsrishtikanaka' and 'Bhava'. In the passage refered to all the ten types are armed excluding Nataka and prakarana. But, 'para' and 'Sallapaka' are the two extra words used over the enumeration of Bharata.

"Kohala names twenty while saradatanaya in his 'Bhava Prakasa' gives the usual ten and another twenty of a different species which involve song and dance. Viswanadha gives only twenty eight and vema twenty. In Agnipurana, only twenty seven are named".[1]

These Natikas are corresponding derivatives of Nataka technique but must be of a milder type allowing greater number of feminine, characters. 'Sallapaka' is one among the extra types but is nowhere mentioned.

'Sallapaka' is not one among Bharata's ten plays though it is included in the last given in Bhavadajjuka. It is not in the language of Bharata's admirers a 'Rasaraya' play for the second act of sallapaka must display ascetic feelings in dance, regulated by tala or time. Sallapaka admits a theme found of the puranas or framed by the post or mixed by both. The hero is a calm–minted rich man or a pashanda of passionate and excitable nature. The hero has an unrelenting opponent who invades his peace and dupes him by surprises.

Divine accidents, invasion, fight, capacity, escape and success are the moving incidents of the three parts. In the 1st part, the hero runs away while in the 3rd though surrounded, he exceeds. In the 2nd the dance of Bharata type relieves the excess of craft but recalls the descriptions of the boorish African dance. Thus 'sallapaka' as far as its individual characteristics are known may not deserve a place among the chosen ten.

Bharata assigns to Kaisiki Sringara and 'Haysa' and not ḳaruna. (Kaisiki is the mode of conducting thought and expression in a delicate and graceful form accompanied by natural and delicate and graceful form accompanied by natural and delightful action on the stage. The emotion and sentiment should be exhibited in a mild and elegant form in lovely poses. It is best displayed when female characters exhibit tender emotions. Kohala opines that even emotions of sorrow can be shown by Kaisiki. The authors of standard writers on poetics also supported Bharata.

Sarweswara (1080 AD), a great authority on dramaturgy has assigned 'Bharata' a mode of perfect delivery or pathya as common to all rasas and kaisiki to 'Sringara'. Sattvati to Vira and Arabhati to Raudra and Bibhatsa. The same view is supported by Vishnudharmottara purana, which adds hasya to kaisiki, the rest being the same.

"Abhinav Gupta's reading is based on the psychological analysis or rasa, whereas Bharata's work gives various readings according to different recensions", he further concludes.

Bhagavadjjuka is a drama where Bhagavan and Ajjuka play the role. Bhagavan in this play, is a courtesan. The name may suggest that a questionable union was attempted between a sanyasin and a dancer. But the real story falsifies such import of the name. A pupil to study practical philosophy, sought tuition under a parivrat and the sanysin explains the psychical trans-migrations of soul by entering into the dead body of a courtesan. The authorship of the drama is attributed to Boudhayana by one commentator but to Bharata, by another commentator and the 3rd is silent on the point.

That a poet by name Boudhayana existed is beyond doubt because he is praised by Sukumara in his Raghuvira charita, a play of the 12th century. A fragmentary inscription of Mamandur near Conjeevaram mention about Mathavilasa and Gavadafuka and many more dramas together. In the prologue to Mattavilasa, the authorship is attributed to Mahendra, the ruler of Conjeevaram Manepalli Ramakrishna Kavi says that it may be inferred that in the wornout slab, the letter must have disappeared, before Gavadajjuka and the work may be included among the numerous plays mentioned therein. Another drama mentioned in it that is probably, 'Urvasi madana', along was first published in the Journal of Bihar and Orissa Research Society and then with the commentary of Narayana. The other two commentaries are not now available. Narayana's commentary, which is published, ascribes the drama to Boudhayana.

Nrittapara represents, according to Sri Ramakrishna Kavi, a type of Nataka, in which all types of Nayakas and Nayikas occur in varied situations under a variety of emotions well laid out, presenting all the unities and their angas. Nataka is the best among all classes of plays and para the best of the Nataka types. In the other kinds of Nataka, there is choice in the selection of rasa, nayakas and sandhyangas but in para type, all the 4 varieties and Nayakas and sandhyangas are to be necessarily represented together. That is why it was well known from the time of Subhandha till the days of Mahendra Vikram, and it was considered to be a different type of composition. The type was apparently forgotten and found no place in the later works on dramaturgies. Discovery of a number of lost works on Bharata and Alankara may probably bring to light the full characteristics of the forgotten type of para.

The word Nritta in Nrittapara, is almost a synonym of Natya as used by Abhinava Gupta. The word Natya, according to Bharata means the exhibitor of a play on the stage without song and dance except in the mandir or divine worship. Nritta is natya with song. Nritya is mostly dance with or without song but mostly without delivery of speech which alone, in the opinion of Bharata, creates 'Rasa'.

Is a dance drama similar to yakshagana ?

Sri Korada Ramakrishnayya, who is a researcher of the first generation, on Yakshaganas opines:

"This Veedhinataka in Telugu may be said to be only counterpart of the Malabar Kadhakali, but with this difference that while in Telugu, Veedhinataka the actors speak and take to singing the songs whose meaning they also seek to interpret by means of gestures, *i.e.*, by Abhinaya. The Kadhakali actors enact the whole story by means of mute Abhinaya leaving speeches and songs entirely to the troupe behind them, who supply the musical and other accompaniments necessary for the successful enactment of the drama. The dress, the make-up, the method of performance and all other paraphernalia required for the enactment seems to point towards the identity of their origin, though there may be some minor differences due to later independent developments.[3]

K.R. Pishaorti, on his findings on Kadhakali tells "it shall not be far from the truth if we place this in the latter half of the 17th century. It is quite probable that this new variety must have been devised somewhere in the sixth decade of the 17th century".[4]

"The Raja of Kottarakkara (1578-1650 AD) was the first composer and originator of Kathakali"[5] says Smt. K. Gomathi who did research on the music of the Nrityanatakas of south India.

Sri Korada Ramakrishnaiah, tracing its origin and development says that panditharadhya charitra has ample evidence of song and dance of Yakshagana type and 'Jakkula Kkadha' mentioned in Kreedabhiramam may be translation of the Sastraic word Yakshagana.

It has got some similarities with the 'Desi' type of 'Rupakas'. Sri S. Srinivaschar, further says that "its technique may roughly be compared to the Greek drama in its simplicity of expression and the importance of the element of chorus in it".[6]

"Kama Sutra of Vatsayana (3-4 BC) mentioned about "Yaksha Ratri". Pandits tried to analyse whether it has got any relationship with the present Yakshagana. Yasodhara's Jaya Mangala Vyakhyana tells that it is a Dyutakreeda and so, it may not have anything to do with yakshagana. Hema Chandra (1088-1172) Desinamamala III–430 says that the word "Jakharathee" is the Prakrit rupa and means Deepavali, when the Goddess Lakshmi is worshipped.

But in Kannada Desa, especially in south Canara, every troupe of Yakshagana performers, give their first performance, as a tradition, in the temple of their favourite deity, Mandarthi, Marnakatte, Katil, Dharmasthala, are the temples worth mentioning where the temples had such yakshagana troupes, according to Sri M. Govinda Rao. As a researcher in the type of yakshaganas of Karnataka, he tells "in a study of good number of Yakshagana works, I was not able to come across a work earlier than the end of the 17th century".[7]

But according to Sri Nelaturi Venkataramanayya, "Yakshanagas of Telugu land are the remotest. Yakshaganas of Tamilnadu and Karnataka were written only after the expansion of Telugu. But before 16th century, there is no mention of yakshaganas even in Telugu land. The very word of yakshagans is mentioned in Bheemakhanda and that it is a special type of musical rendering. Prof. Vissa Appa Rao in his article on "The art of dance of Andhras–Kuchipudi Kala Vaibhavam" (1954–Vijayawada Kanaka Durga Kala Samithi 3rd Annual Number) says that 'Kulothunga Chola Deva's inscription speaks of Nattuva Melas giving performance of Yakshaganas.'[8]

Vasantika Parinayam of Kranja Venkatadri and Akkamaha Devi Charitra of Balapapamba are resembling Garudachala Vilasam and Sugreeva Vijayam, which are supposed to be the remotest writings, according to scholars. It is to be noted that the technique of writing yakshagana attracted the attention of some women writers also even in the 16th century and Balapapamba, who is the contemporary of Basaveswara, wrote about Akkamaha devi, who is a great devotee of MahaSiva.

Vishnu Maya Vilasamu of Kakkanti Paparaju, is supposed to be the best among the Yakshaganas that came in the 16th century. He is an employee in Pulicott and is supposed to have lived in 1780 (Viresalingam pantulu).

His writing is suitable for giving performances and includes some padams, a churnika in Sanskrit, two slokas, *etc.* His contemporary by name Tekumalla Ranga Sayi, wrote Janakee Parinayam, in the Yakshagana style. About 1600, one Paramananda teerdha yathi of Dattatreya matt Nellore wrote Muktikanta parinayam and gave it a new name called 'Padachalika' pada chalika or padakelika is, while singing a 'pada', giving Abhinaya to a Bhava. Sabda Ratnakara says 'Pekkana' is a special style of dance. Pekkana is also "Prenkahana", perhaps, it was used for religious propaganda.

"Abhinaya bolu kopu Larudyna teerupul Velayaga Padachaliu vidhimokartu" says Padaraju in his Uttara Charita.

It is evident that by the time of Rudra Kavi, Paparaju, Rangasai, paramanadi yati, several rupakas which won the appreciation of the people, were prevalent in Andhra Desa. As noticed earlier Palkuriki somanadha speaks of several such styles. From the literature available it can be noted that bahurupakas and veedhinatakas were prevalent.

During the times of Reddy kings and Vijayanagara empire there was so much of patronage to dance and music according to Sri Mallampalli soma sekhara sarma.

Those that won the applause of people are some yakshaganas like Siriyala charita, Machala Devi charita; Sammeta Guravaraju charita, and drama of Tajikonda.

The performers of these Natakas are Dora Samudrapu Natulu, Jangamas, and Brahmin Bhagavathuklu of Kuchipudi.

In a Vachana Mallika geetha written by Tallapaka Peda Tirumalacharya who lived in early 16th century, he mentions about the performance of 'Bahurupa'.

"Sanga Bhashnaga Kriyangabhiramya Magu" we find several references to this bahurupa in our literature in the latter part of 16th century. Suranarya, wrote a Margarupaka called Gangavatara. By this, we can conclude that the "Art of dance" in Andhra had Chaturvidhabhinaya and also Geetavadya accompaniments by that time. This was also made use of in Yakshaganas and Veedhinatakas, it may be presumed. The Kelika of Kuchipudi Bhagavathulu before Veera Narasimha Raya in the 16th century is a clear indication, but the pradarsina prakriya of it is not well known.

Vasucharitra of Ramaraja Bhushana (1530-1580) tells about certain stage performances.

"Idi sandhimpaga Velayanchu vasu Rajendrudu Neenandhrinee.

Badavaprati sura Velvadina Tara Bhartha Leetan Lats.

Chada Sanchadika Basi Nilche Nedutan Saranga ragabhinavs.

Nanda Bhrugeeruthi Vandi Magadha Kadha Madhinyaman Dalpagan".[11]

This is similar to the Ranga Pravesa of the Nayaka, in the Yakshagans; It is to be noted that this Pravesha Daru is in Sarangiraga.

"Hari Dambhoruha Lochanal gagana ranga Bhaga

Rangathamo

Bhara Nepadyami Noyya Noyya
Sadalimpan Ratni

Sailushikin

Vasusan Mouktikapattamun Nitatalmu,

Vaktrambu Nudochana

Hrarinanka Kriti Vlche Rekayik,
Sagamelai,

Bimkbamari Toorpunan

(Vasu charitra)[12]

This we know, is a clear tradition of Yakshagana and Kuchipudi Bhagavathulu still present this tradition of removing the curtain.

Kanukuri Appa Rao Kavi of the 17th century, tells about the traits of Yakshagana and it is said that he also wrote a Yakshagana called Ambikavadha but it is not now available. Another two Lakshanamulu by name Ganapa Varapu Vekata Kavi, Pottapi Vekata Ramana Kavi told about the Sangeetha, Tala Lakshana of Yakshaganas. From the above discussion, it may be presumed that by 17th century, Yakshaganas attracted one and all and also the attention of experts in rhetorics and aesthetics. In the latter half of the 17th century came Bhamakalapam written by Siddhendra Yogi.

His mode of performance, rather pradarsina prakriya, is different in style but the mode of writing is in Yakshagana style only. All the characteristics of Yakshagana like Daruvu, Dwipada, Gadya, Vadya are there and there is Natya, in accordance with the guidelines given by the expert in dramaturgy namely Bharata. It is mostly styled by 'Natya' and is Rasika Ramya and Atma Sravya.

When experts of Kuchipudi began to tour the four corners of Andhra Desa, this new technique was propagated and people, till then contented with performances of some Desi cults, began to appreciate and admire the systematic performance of these Kuchipudi Brahmins.

Women were not allowed to participate in these performances.

Towards the end of this century, Parijatha Yakshagana Prabhandha of Purijala Kavi, speaks of men enacting women characters. There is a discussion between Satya and her Sakhi about this proposal whether men can act as women. Why he spoke about this, is not known but it may be presumed that perhaps it was a topic for discussion in those days.

But Cheruvu Belagallu inscription of 1514, tells about, 'Patni' daughter of Tiimayya in Tanjikonda Nataka. Some also draw conclusions from the writings of Sreenadha about 'Bhagothula Buchigadu', 'Pendyala Nagi' and 'Gangi' that there might have been some women participants in the troupe of Bhagothula Buchigadu. But there is controversy about it. The above description is of Rama Kavi of the 18th century but not of Sreenadha (Preface to Kreedabhiramam by Veturi Prabhakara Sastry, pp. 68-69).

Kuchimanchi Jagga Kavi of 18th century, in his Rekhavilasam describes about "Bhagavathulu". From the description Adu Bhagavathuni Jada, Gaddamu, Muthi, Nunnaga Goriginchu Konnanadu". It may be concluded that men were enacting the characters of women.

But there is evidence to show that, in the 19th century, women were participating in Veedhinatakas.

District Gazetters, Visakkhapatnam (Page 130) says 'Janaranjaka Natakamulostreelu Purushulu Veshamulu Vesukuni Vinikidi chesidivaru" (Women and men used to attire and used to give performances to the appreciation of people).

In the first half of the 19th century, a village officer (grama Karnam) of Padakandla village of Atmakur taluq, Nellore district, by name Swamy Raja Kavi used to invite 'Nata Melas' and to provide suitable conditions for their happy living and give dresses and training to give performance of his Yakshaganas, and out of them "Gonudinne Buggasani" used to act as Nayika (Heroine) on his order.

References

1. Works of Manepalli Ramakrishna Kavi–published by Telugu University (p. 184).
2. There are three commentaries to the prahana and none of the commentators have attempted any enlightening on the word. Certainly, it means one of the rupakas (plays).
3. P.19 of Telugu literature outside the Telugu country by K.R.K (Madras University Telugu Series no. 9 (1941) chapter : yakshagana and desi).
4. South Indian Theatre–by K.R.Pisharoti–chapter IX of the "theatre of the Hindus" published by Susil Gupta Ltd., Calcutta–12, 1955.

5. (a) "The music of the Nritya natakas of South India, Thesis by Smt.K.Gomathi for M.Litt. of Madras Univesity.

   (b) 'The language of Kadhakali' by Premakumar Taruma p. 15.

6. "Yakshagana and other plays of "Mysore" an article by Sri S. Srinivasachari, published in the March of India Vol. IV No. 6.

7. S.V. Joga Rao–The story of Yakshagana literature A.O.R.University of Madras Vol. X, Part II, 1952-53. pp. 6-7.

8. Nelaturi Venkataramanayya–History of Andhra literature during the Nayaka kings of Tanjore, p. 88.

9. Madhya Yuga Andhra Desam–Sangeeta Natya Kalabhivridhi Andhra Patrika Chitrabhanu–History of Reddy kingdoms, part–II, chapter VII.

10. T.T.D. Publication, pp. 108-109.

11. Vasucharitra Awani 3, Padya 45.

12. *Ibid*, Aswani 4 padya 17.

Natya Bhangimas—Sculpture of Vijayanagara

34

A Comparative Study of Bhagawata Mela Natakam–Dance Drama of Andhra and Tanjore

Eight miles away from Kuchipudi, lies the village of Srikakulam, on the banks of the river Krishna. It was the seat of Satavahana empire and later a centre of Buddhism. Andhra Vishnu Vardhana (3rd century) was the ruler and built the temple of Vishnu, where Devadasis participated in the religious ceremonies. He gave the Devadasis a village called 'Sanepadu' as gift and so, it was known as the village of the dancing girls.

There is a good Kalyana Mandapa, where Sri Krishna-devaraya wrote Sreekaram to his Amukta Malyada and it was here that he praised the melody of Telugu. (Desa Bhashalandu Telugu Lessa). When I paid a visit to this village, some elders told me that the original temple was washed away in floods of the Krishna River and the present temple was built with the remaining material in the present site. The Gopura also is peculiar unlike other temples.

Vallabhacharya, a famous poet of those times, wrote 108 verses on Sri Maha Vishnu. I wanted to interview some of the dancing girls of the temple. If they were alive, but, I was told that none of them are living in the village now. Most of them are dead and the remaining are living in different places. God here is also known as Ekaratra Mallikarjuna because he gives boons, by a worship of one night.

We have studied earlier that Kakatiya rulers of Warangal patronized the fine Arts and one of the commanding chiefs by name, Jayappa Senani, belonging to the Ganapati Deva, composed Nritta Ratnavali, a treatise on dance. At Warangal, Ramappa temple was constructed under his able guidance, with poses described in his treatise.

Balipeethas, made of black stone slabs, were a feature of the temple, especially constructed for the ritual dance in front of the shrine. Engraved on the sides and on the pillars are the dance poses, as prescribed in detail in Nritta Ratnavali.

When the Kakatiya Empire fell, the ruler of Kalinga, Bhanu Deva I (A.D. 1263–1277) ruled Divi taluk and Kuchipudi village, was part of this area, as were Srikakulam, Ghantasala, Movva, Avanigadda and Challapalli, through which path flowed the Krishna river.

After the death of Bhanu Deva, Narahari Teera, his Minister acted as Regent for the young prince. A disciple of Ananda Teera, the great devotee of Sri Krishna, brought dancers from Orissa, to teach the Geeta Govinda of Jayadeva to the Devadasis of Andhra. The Gita Govinda, since that time has been cherished by the Bhaghavatars of Kuchipudi, called as 'Astapadi Attam' or 'Radhakrishna Nrityam'.

After that, many songs were composed on the eternal theme of Radha and Krishna and it was at Srikakulam, that the celebrated poem 'Sri Krishna Mrutha' was written by the poet Leelasuka.

We have observed earlier that Krishna Leela Tarangini, was a dance-drama in Sanskrit, written by Tirdha Narayana Swami (14th century). The story opens with Bhudevi (Mother Goddess Earth) praying to Lord Krishna for protection against evil. The story is similar to the theme in Bhagavatam, ending with the marriage of Krishna and Rukmini, and the death of the tyrant Kamsa.

The 7th chapter is composed for the sake of the dancers, with musical jatis, a peculiarity of the Kuchipudi technique, depicting the Rasa Kreeda.

The same 'Taranga' or 'Wave' symbolizes the dancers, with various steps (Waves) in the dance art. In the 3rd canto of Balagopala–popularly known as Balagopala Tarangam, the dancer executes a typical dance, dancing upon a brass tray with a pot of water on her head.

There are 12 scenes and each scene is introduced by the sutradhara and 'Nati' provides the mime in the story.

Krishna Deva Raya of Vijayanagar was perhaps one of the most attractive and outstanding personalities of medieval India. He is described as very brave and gallant and "perfect in all things". He was a great patroniser of fine arts. His Bhuvana Vijayam is very famous and the account of the foreign travellor, Paes (about 1537 AD) is worth reading. He describes the Natya mantapa of Raya thus;

"This hall is where the King sends his women to be taught dance. It is a long hall, and not very wide, all of stone, sculpture on pillars, which are at a distance of arms length from the well. In each case, from pillar to pillar, is cross bar, which is like a panel and from pillar to pillar are long panels, at the end of the dance. This is to teach the women, so that, if they forget the position in which they have to remain, they may look at one of the panels to know where the end of that dance is. At the end of the left hand, is a painted recess, where the women cling on with their hands, in order to better stretch and loosen their dancing more graceful. At the other end, on the right, is the place, where the king places himself to watch them dancing".

Solo dancers took items from the Kuchipudi dance-dramas called 'Sabdams' and presented them on the stage as separate items of dance. The most popular were by pandit Kasinadh of Melattur. His 'Manduka Sabdam', 'Prahlada Pattabhishekam' and 'Rama Sabdam', were very popular items. Manduka Sabdam is from the story of Gajendra Moksham, where the frogs in a pond are described. The main 'Rasa' in all Kuchipudi Sabdams is 'Sringara'. This Nayika-Nayaka Bhava is mainly responsible for creating interest in this form of dance in the audience.

When the Empire of Vijayanagara fell, it was the Nayak dynasty of Tanjore that patronized the 'Bhagavatars' of Andhra Pradesh, who migrated to Tanjore in search of patronage and they carried with them the dance traditions of Andhra.

Achutappa Naik (AD 1561-1641) gave land to 500 families at Melattur and Soolamangalam. Raghunadha Nayaka (AD 1614-1633) was a great scholar and patron and poet of Dravidian, as well as Sanskrit literature. He invented a new type of Veena called 'Raghunada Mela', and was the author of 'Parijathapa Haranam'. In his court were great writers, including two women, Ramabhadramba and Madhuravani.

Vijaya Raghava Naik (AD 1633-1673) was the last of the Nayak kings and a devotee of Mannara (Krishna) the deity at the temple of Mannargudi near Tanjore. A patron and composer like his father, Raghunadha Nayak, wrote many Yakshaganas, Natakas and Dwipada Kavyas and 'Mannaru Dasa Vilasamu' is a great composition by a woman by name Rangajamma and Vijaya Raghava arranged Kanakabhishekam in her honour.

Dance dramas were very popular, and following the footsteps of Narayana Teerdha, one of his followers by name Gopala Krishna Sastri composed Dhruvacharitra, Sita Kalyanam and Rukmini Kalyanam. His son, Sri Venkatrama Sastry, who lived at Melattur composed many dance dramas of great brilliance. It is to him that the present form of Bhagavata Mela dance drama is attributed. He was a senior contemporary of the composer/saint Tyagaraja (AD 1759-1847). The dance dramas of Andhra Pradesh, related to the

Bhagavata Mela; though the authors and compositions are different from each other.

The original source of inspiration for the dance and music style of Bhagavata Mela is Kuchipudi, and this seems to have been born from the historical movements of the troops from A.P. to Tanjore. Another evidence is that the lyric is in Telugu and not Tamil. It is certain that Melattur performs close to Kuchipudi and Sulamangalam performs closer to Bharata Natyam.

Melattur's renown is due to the great composer mentioned above. His compositions are remarkable both for their lyric and music. They are fourteen in number :

(1) Prahlada Charitam (2) Markandeya Charitam (3) Harishendra Charitam (4) Usha Parinayam (5) Rukmangada Charitam (6) Golla Bhama (7) Sita Kalyanam (8) Rukmini Kalyanam (9) Dhruva Charitam (10) Bhama Vijayam (11) Kamsa Vadha (12) Vivantha Kalika (13) Bhasmasura Vadha and (14) Vasantha Kelika.

His house, a tiled roof house of the old type can still be seen in East Street, Melattur just in front of the temple.

The Bhagavata Mela took deep root in the village, because of the popularity of Venkatrama Sastry and his compositions are spread to the surrounding villages, but it is only in Melattur that a steadier tradition had been maintained.

Melattur did not survive with a completely unbroken tradition, although it had the stimulus of such great men as Natesa Aiyar and Balu Bhagavatar, to keep up the art. Natesa Aiyar died in Madras in 1931, unable to maintain himself for financial reasons, to continue living in the village. From 1932-1933, Kinjin Kothandarama Iyer tried to keep up the Bhagavata Mela alive, but a few years later, it lapsed completely. In 1936, Balu Bhagavatar formed a troupe with V. Ganesha Iyer's family. This made the village and family proud and faithful to its traditions. Despite the fact that many of the younger members had left the village to earn their livelihood, they feel inspired to return every year and give performances. On the occasion of Nrisimha Jayanthi. Their influence spread to the other villagers, who likewise returned to participate in the Bhagavata Mela performances. But although famous locally, the troupes did not receive much patronage or financial aid from outside. It was in the fifties that Mr. E. Krishna Iyer revived interest in the art. He was Secretary of the Madras Sangita Nataka Sangam, a Govt. cultural organization and raised funds to support the villager's interest in their traditional art. It is well known that V. Ganesh Iyer sold some of his land to place money into the revival movement to set the troupe on its feet again.

I could come across a book edited by the Telugu Pandit of Saraswati Mahal, Tanjore, entitled 'Sabdam alias Tala Solkattu' of Bharatam Kasinadha Kavi, king Sahaji and Narana Kavi.

The poets Bharatam Kasinadha and Bharata Narayanakavi were natives of Melattur. It is known that they belonged to Bhagavata Mela tradition.This publication brings to current knowledge about the traditional Tanjore style. 'Solkkattu' followed in the reign of Maratha kings namely Sahaji, Serfoji, and Prathapa Simha, Tulajaji II, Serfoji II (AD 1984-1832).

These Jathis and Sahityas are mainly in Telugu language. It is quite sure that this 'Solkkattu' will be of great use to the experts in this field. The original manuscript is in Telugu language and script. It might have been possible, in those days, because, the court language was Telugu. Those Sabdas and Sahityas are of 3,000 years old. In order to know the significance of our ancient Natya Sastra, this publication will be of great use to readers and re-searchers.

"Sabda" is a gesture song, a song of praise addressed to a deity or a king. The poetic theme may be devotional, erotic or a narrative episode from the lives of the gods, rendered in expository gestures, facial expression and graceful postures and gaits. The first verse (Pallavi) is sung with rhythm syllabus (Sabdas) and danced in a prelude, refrain and finale".[1]

On a deep study, I could find some more interesting details in the Saraswati Mahal. There is a palm leaf text in the name of one Ramakanta Sastry, who wrote Sita Kalyanam in Prakrit. It was the time of Pratapa Simha. It is not clear whether he was a contemporary to Venkatrama Sastry. The whole script is in Telugu. Some details as regards characters and those who enacted are given as follows:

1. Some Dialects of India – By Ragini Devi

Chikkaji Nayaka	– Ahobilam Sundaram
Dasaradha Maharaj	– Rangayya
Sumanta	– Seshudu
Ramavesham	– Venkatachalam
Lakshmanavesham	– Kannayya
Kausalya	– Subbarayalu
Sakhivesham	– Pedda Vaiddi
Narada	– Seshachalam Subbaiah

From this palm leaf, it is evident that there were some palace dramas.

(dance dramas) even before Venkatrama Sastry.

There is another palm leaf text by name "Garuda-chala Vilasam"–a Yakshagana by Obayya

Natya : Bhagavata Mela Nataka

Manthri. It starts with Sourashtra Ragam, Aditalam:

1. "Patita Jagadadhara–Aganita Bhavadura

   Narahari chatura daitya vihara

   Garudachala Vihara"and

2. "Bhoori Karuna Saramati Visputa Vihara

   Kesava charu satya chara

   Garudachal Vihara" and

3. "Prakata Muni Mandara

   Viswambhara sarira

   Murahari–Sakala Lokadhara

   Garudachala Vihara".

They speak of the style in those days.

There is another text entitled "Daksha Yaga Bharani" of 12th century, belonging to the time of Kulothunga. It is also a dance drama, which starts with Sourashtra Raga. It can be presumed that they followed only one style throughout South India, to bring out integration and cultural synthesis.

To end of the play also, "Mangalam Maha Sri Sri" was added. "Sugreeva Vijayam"–by Guna Rudra Kavi is another drama available with the same ending of "Mangalam Maha Sri Sri" for which Sri Veturi Prabhakara Sastry wrote foreword.

By the above discussion, it can be safely concluded that Telugu dramas flourished in Tanjore.

The original texts like Vasanthika Parinayam, Koravanji Natakam are available. They were written to preach religious sentiments.

It is very interesting to note that "Mannarudasa Vilasam" was enacted only by women. "Narastuti" dramas were by women. But it is not clear whether women could get recognition in Daivastuti or not.

What are the differences between Drama, Yakshagana and a Dance-Drama?

As per Utsava Sampradaya, dance dramas were presented in temples and were more musical. The rest were exhibited in Rajya Sabhas in those days.

There were no women in Bhagavata Mela. There was no place for Srinagara Rasa in the initial stages. Only after Krishna Chaitanya and his Bhakti cult and after Jayadeva, *i.e.*, after 1400 only, Srinagara Rasa could enter. By 14th century, Moghuls became rulers and Ganikas lost their importance.

In Tanjore style, the drama starts with the entry of Ganesha. Kuchipudi people start their prayer with "Amba–Paraku, Devi Praku" (Devi-stuti). But there are some very significant similarities in both the styles.

1. There is music in both dance and drama.
2. There are systematic methods in both the styles.
3. There is nowhere found. Nayika exhibits vipralambha sringara. This, only women can do (Eg., Vasanthi Ka Parinayam).

Differences

But in Bhagavata Mela, there is the hero. The literary values of Mela Sampradaya are in accordance with Bhakti Sampradaya, unlike in a dance drama, where the sringara rasa is given more prominence.

Eminent works like 'Sangita Ratnakara', Nritta Ratnavali', and 'Sangita Parijatham' are brought out in between 12th and 13th centuries. That much of work done by the Reddy Kings and by the Kakatiyas, was not taken up by Vijayanagar Rulers. There are no evidences to show how dance and drama flourished during 14th and 15th Centuries. But from 16th Century onwards, Tanjore Nayak Kings again revived these art forms with much devotion.

'Mannarudasa Vilasa Natakam', a Yakshagana by Rangajamma is one of the plays that was very popular. (It is to be noted here that this Yakshagana starts with the Daruvu in Sourashtra raga and Atatala).

At the time of Raghunadha Nayaka, several Yakshaganas were produced. In the Saraswathi Mahal, Tanjore, as many as 247 texts are mentioned and listed under the head 'Prakrita Telugu Lipi Natakalu'. Many among them are Telugu works. Raghunadhabhyudaya by Vijaya Raghava and Vijaya Raghavakalayanam by Konety Deekshita, are Telugu plays whereas, works by Yagna Narayana Deekshita, Raghunadha Vilasa *etc.* are in Sanskrit.

In those days, it appears, that all Telugu plays are in the form of Yakshaganas, Parijathapaharanam, 'Prahlada Natakam were exhibited as Veedhi Natakas (street plays). Even plays known as Tanjore Natakas are also street plays. In the Raja Durbar, there appears to be a Ranga Mantapa and these plays were exhibited now and then. One such popular play appears to be Raghunadha Abhudaya and it is said that it was exhibited before Raghunadha Nayaka.

The poetry 'Dwipadas', 'Daruvu' and prose narration in these Natakas is three fold and is simpler when compared to the style of Prabandhas. Local costumes, life styles and customs were highlighted in between, wherever necessary according to context. 'Hasya Rasa' also had its place in the narration.

Raghunadha abhyudayam, printed in the British Model Printing Press and published by Andhra Sahitya Parishad and carrying a foreword by the eminent historian Mallampalli Somasekhar Sarma, is in the Saraswathi Mahal and it is dated as "sent on 22nd December 1932".

In the Rajya Sabha of Vijaya Raghava, 'Nattuva roudra'(courtesans) were exhibiting their 'Natya Vidya Vaidushya' and it is evident from Rajagopala Vilasam of Kalakavi. They were all experts in 'Natya' and 'Abhinaya'.

"Chowpada Veliki Roopavati Kanta

Sambi.........Chudamani Chadrakanta

Cheluvagu Jakkini, Jeluva Murthy vadhuti

Korman Gomalavalli Gruru nitamba

Napadamabulu Loka Nayaka Lolakshi

Yala Desi Sasirekha Kabjavadana

Durupadambulu Ratnagiri Nitamba Niyulu

Berinividhamu Bhagiradhiyanu

Madana Bali gootya Navaratna Malikaadi

Bahu vidha Lakshya Natya prapancha mella

Ghanata Vilasilla Dakkina Kanta Lella

Nabhinayinchiri tama nerupu latisayilla"

All the names mentioned in the above stanza seem to be actually working in the Raj Durbar of Vijaya Raghava Nayaka and are not fictitious names.

Now about the different styles they presented :

"Birudu patralu Vijrunbhinehi Yaraja

Varuni Mundara Nila Vaari Lopalanu

Badavali Goriya Rupavathee Vadhuti

Kodaleka perinni gona Chandra Rekha

Mikkili Kopula meravadi Jupi

Jikkini vinipinche Sasirekha yapudu

Nabodiyagu loka Nayika Kanta

Vanaja Lochana Keeravani Lettangi

Dorapadakelika Durusaina Kopu

Varasa Natinchiri vane meeraganu

Koravanji Siva leela Gujarati Desi

Viribondu Kondaru Vinipinchirapudu

(Raghunadhabyudayam)[2]

Chowpadakeli, Jakkini, Koravanji, Navapadas, Desi, Durupadas, Perini, Madanabal Dutyamu are all Natyabandhas.

Vijaya Raghava Maheejani is an expert in the art of dance. He gave place in his Durbar, to Perini, Desi, Jakkini, Danda Lasyamu (Danadalanakamu)

Kanduka-kreeda, chindu *etc.*, and they were all considered to be followed from previous times.

"Valvichi(?) Guhharuvukvedy(?) Dandala

Syamu, Kanduka Kreeda Yallikayunu,

Goravanji Subha leela Gujarati Desi che

Padamu Jikkini Durupadamu Madana

Pada(?Bala) Dantyamunu Jogi (?) go Padachali, Sarada

Samrajyamunu Chindu Savati Macha

Rambulu Natyakambambu Modalaina

Natyamule havaninchina" (Raghunadhabhyudayam)[3]

Further the following narration details about the various styles presented in prose gives somemore

"Mahotsava Mandapamunandu Benolagambundi

Kundali Dandalanaka Prerini Prenkhara Sindhu

Kanduka Dhamali chela mattalle, Halle sakadi

Vrutyampu lavalokinchuchu"

(Bheemakhanadamu)[4]

These Chowpadas, Navapadas, Durupadas mentioned are Nartana Geetas (Charika Karunangahara Rechaka Bhramarikavali). This 'Valvichi', 'Korma' are not clear and we cannot say whether they are correct words or not. We don't know what sort of dance specialties they are and we cannot even fix them up in any category. But, from the descriptions of the Natya-bhedas, we can guess that some of them might be creations of Vijaya-raghava Nayaka, who was an expert.

But 'Padachali', is mentioned in Adibharata. If we look to the Yakshaganas that were prevalent, we find that 'soubhari charitramu' is the first one, according to Sri S.V. Joga Rao, who did research on Yakshaganas. Vipranarayana Charitra—a Jakkulakadha and it happened in Sholingapuram near Tiruttani.

'Banasura Kadha' (Ushaparinayam) 'Samudra Madhanam' (Kheera Sagara Madhanam) were the other popular Yakshaganas, wherein, women's roles were not there. According to 'Saiva Sampradaya', Rama Kadha, Ravan Kadha, Ravanasura Kadha and Tripuranta Kadha were much patronized and titles also indicated male characters and Bhakti culture only. It is only after the introduction of Vaishnava Culture, that female characters got prominence.

When we look to Tamil literature, 'Kalithorai' of the 3rd century seems to be the first available literary piece, in which only male character is mentioned. 'Ahananur', 'Purnananur' are mentioned in Silpadhikaram. 'Paripadal' padas also said to belong to 3rd century, are supposed to be the very ancient available from South India. It is also believed from the words "Tukku" (Telugu) "Pani" (Music dance) that Mahakali, Paravati gave the first performance, as per Sangam literature and studies in the Natya Sastra confirm this idea.

Now let us know more about 'Jakkini',

"Santa Saila Nissantha charana Jcc

Tanta Adi Madhyantha Rahita

Kanta Girija Kanta Kankava

Santa, Sahallarra swantha vasa"

Ellillam, Ellale (Daruvu)

This is Jukkini Daruvu Sahaji was respossible for bringing out Pancharatna Prabandha–He gave 5 Daruvus and Jatis.

For example :

"Kandendu Sekhara, Kundaleela Guna

Madita muruko, Dandahari knoda

Dandita Tripurave, Tanda mukhajanaka

Chandikanadha, Dhanur Gandeevisakha priya"

There are evidences to show that Chikkadeva Rayalu of Sahaji's time wrote this Jakkini. It is Ata Talam (Telugu pandit, Saraswatti Mahal, Tanjore)

Jakkini came on account of the Moghuls.

Navarasa Jakkini Sloka:

"Arya Kooth tulukkachi nga Darwil

Seerya Dahum Dariveni Jakkini

Kerna Nilai peryal

Tanam sadee jagatee

Sindhy Ragam piraka manda

Kurya Ayudham, munnur sul

Nulvanji Kurvanenu".

It is a mixture of Kannada and Prakrita and we cannot say definitely from which part of India, this form of dance came to Tanjore.

"Janakam, prekhya Aprachya Matanga Deepta Tejasam

Kenopayuena Bhagavan Mohitam Sankaram Mama

Adiparva Mahabhaga Rahasyam

Twam Asya Durlabham, Srunuvakhyami Kalyani

Lasyam Bhuvan Mahanam Kundali, Ghoorjari

Chaiva, Jakkina Tridabhavet"

"Kundali Bhagavatayanthuu, Kalpita, Madakarnini

Ayodhya Kritham poorvam, perinir Vayu Sumanea"

(This is supposed to have come from Anjaneya-Swamy)

"Ghoorari Dwaravatyanthu Dideesenaprakalpitham

Kalikayah Kritham poorvam Matangenaiva Jakkini".

It is also believed that Natanga gave this form of dance.

"Bhuja Prakoshtov Jagane

Parswa Jange Drustada

Ketaka Mukha Hasthamcha

Kunchithamcha Yada Kramam".

The dance performed with five types of Instruments namely "Gucheham, Bana (arrow), Soola, knife, Dhakka or Chakravadya (Chakrayudham-Gada)" is known as Jakkini and Devi Kalika, it was believed, gave this form of dance. It is also known as Pancharatra Jakkini Navarasa Jakkini. It runs as follows :

"Kundali Bhagavatyanthu

Matangenaiva Jakkini

Sambhuna Danda Votsave

Apsaeebyam Kritham poorvam

Guruna Syamala Tadha

Premkahneeyuaksha Rajena

Agasthyenathu Jakkini,

Charince Nairutheenam chalva

Bahu cheereeshu Saktinam

Puradevi Mhakalee

Lasithum Sambhu nasah

Janakam prekshya paprachya

Matangam Deepta Tejasam

Kenopayena Bhagavan

Mohitum Sankaram Mama

Adi Seerva Mahabhaga Rahasyam

Tvam Asya Durlabham

Srunuvakshyami Kalyani

Lasyam Bhuvana Mohanam

Kundalee Ghoor jaseechaiva, Jakkini Tridabhavet"

Now a word about Chikkaraya Vilasam. It depicts the Satvika Bhavana of this type of dance.

The dance-drama form gives Navarasas. Because the pada Sahityas are in Kaisiki Vrithi, this soft feeling is created. That is why, people appreciated these themes. People were taken to ecstasy and from the mundane problems and monotony. They were elevated to a state of sublime thought, far away from the routine life. When one saw the dancer performing dance on the stage, he was taken to a dreamy world, where he enjoyed the delicate inner feeling of softness and joy, by which he became a superman, with sense of satisfaction that life is worth living. As the themes also related to subjects which were near and dear to the Indian mind-set from the epics and puranas, they were well appreciated.

That is why dance-dramas written and enacted in simple language, could win the hearts of people and move them. The very cultural life of the nation was moulded by the streams of thought that flowed from these popular themes. In a way fine arts especially dance worked as a linking force and paved the way for the cultural synthesis of various sects of people. Class, creed differences were perhaps forgotten and all sitting in the audience were considered to be a single unit.

Now, I would like to give some of my experiences in Melattur, when I witnessed the performances of Nritya Natikas (14) of Venkatrama Sastry, of all the dance dramas, Prahlada Charita is very popular and the other two are Rukmini Kalyanam and Harischandra.

I came across a radio talk, broadcast in AIR, Madras, written in Tamil, by Dr. Raghavan about Venkatrama Sastry. Sri Ramalingayya, an elderly gentlemen, a landlord of Melattur and the father of the artist of lady characters like Chandramathi, Rukmini *etc.*, read out to me and translated the article into Telugu. Dr. Raghavan describes in one word that Venkatrama Sastry wrote his dance dramas, 'Rasika Jana Ranjakanga' (to the satisfaction of all the elite). He refers to "Sampradaya Priyadarsini" written by one Sahitee Subbaraya Deekshitar, at the time of Pratapasimha Maharaja (1741-1764) and it was traced out in St. George Fort. Therein, he describes for the first time about 'Nayika-Nayaka Bhavana' (the idea of the hero and the heroine). He also mentions about a Devadasi called 'Tiruvarur Kamalam'.

Veerabhadra Iyer wrote 12 'Swarajathis' in the name of Varadaraja Swamy. At the time of Maharashtrian rule Kasi Nathun, wrote in dedication to Siva and with special reference to the temple worship. It was at that time that 'Rudra Kannika' (tradition of dedicating the girl to God) came into existence. In their footsteps, Venkatrama Sastry wrote his dance dramas about Bhagavatha tradition, which were enacted by men only. In fact, he was responsible for writing for enactment of all these Bhagavata Melas. It was at this time that Narayana Teerdha wrote Krishna Leela Tarangini and Saint Tyagaraya wrote several Ragas in praise of Rama. But Bhagavata Mela has Daru, Padyam, Gadyam, which can be played and Abhinaya also can be performed. It is a tradition, which is an admixture of all.

"Vishno rsanancha, Nrityancha, Natanancha Viseshatah

Brahman Brahamana Jateenam Kartavyam Nitya Kasmathi"

-Geeta Govindam[5]

There was Kuchipudi tradition in Andhra Desa, Dr. Raghavan says, and proceeds to add further that there was Bhagavata Mela tradition in Tamilnadu on the lines of Kadhakali. When we critically study some Anandaragas, Raga Lakshanas and some Apurva ragas there are some subtle differences between Geetabhinayam and Yakshagana also. In Tamil and Telugu lands, there was already the tradition of enacting dramas by that time. There was a time when Geeta was sung as Alapana. Harikadha is one of such styles. Telaja Maharaja compared certain Raga lakshanas with the style of Yakshaganas and also the works of Subbaraya Deekshitar.

But Venkatrama Sastry wrote in 'Kaisikivrithi', (*i.e.*, depicting Sringara Rasa). He is Velanati Brahmin, of Srivatsa Gotram and he introduced himself in his writings as the son of Gopalakrishna Arya and a disciple of a Guru called Lakshmana Charya.

In Ushaparinayam, Venkatrama Sastry writes as follows :

"Padika pada Gadya padyadula ma

Natakambugajesi Navarasalokulla

Cheluvamu Ramjilla sreevatsa gotra

Tilakule Lakshmanacharya Krupavalla

Gopala Krishnarya Kumarru dynatti

Prabuche, Kavijana padapadmamula

Ponkamye Madilon Pujinchu

Migula venkatramudu Visadamburanu

Vivarincha Janulella Vinuthis Seyanganu

Dharanilo Achandra Tararkamuganu"

His writings are in the tradition of Subbaraya Dikshitar. Fourteen dramas like Markandeya Charitam, Harischandra, Kamsa Charitam *etc.* are famous but Prahlada Charitam is more popular, Vedanta Sindhu and Anandabhairavi is the 'Raga' practiced as a mother. Previous to Venkatrama Sastry, there was Gollabhama and Radha Charitra in this village of Melattur and Venkanna Kavi has

mentioned about this in his Natakam of Parvati Kalyanam.

"Brindavan, Saranga, Gowri, there is mention, rather description of Mangalagiri, as he was a Telugu man, hailing from Kaza village near Mangalagiri.

There is also a saying that Kaza near Mangalagiri was the birth place of Bhajana Sampradaya. Out of adoration for Sri Panakalaswamy, the deity of Mangalagiri, he must have described his birth place as the origin for this type of sampradaya as Bhajana Sampradaya.

Punnagavarali, Neelambari, Mukhari, Pantuvaralli, Bhairavi, Athana, Kambhoji, Samkarabharanam, Yadukula Kambhoji are the important ragas taken by Sri Venkatrama Sastry. Akhivi in Markandeya Charitra and Anandabhairavi in Rukmangada charitra are prominent.

In Prahlada Charitra nataka Narasimaha Swamy comes only after the midnight. This is a peculiarity. Swarasahityam is Bhairavi, "Mudanuna Janakuni Sarasaksha Harinamama Tarakamani, Madilo Samayam Buchuduraa" preaches the efficacy of Harinama Mantram. Prahlada tells that the 'name of Hari' is 'Brahmananda' in Chapu Tala. Leelavathi's poem 'Inta Kopamela' in Parasurama Raga this is full of Raganubhuthis and these two are specialities of Venkatrama Sastry.

The pious feeling with which the mask of Narasimha is kept in the houses or the temple is to be noted. It is taken out every year only on an auspicious occasion and cleaned. Till such time, no one should touch it. After the performance, Narasimhavatara is taken to the deity and offered 'arati'. Then only, the Roudra Rasa subsides. An ordinary papier mache mask of Narasimha by veneration of people and long years of worship gained particular sanctity.

I was very much distressed to note that such a great soul died an unnatural death in the end, as he fell from the grace of the people. But, there are no specific proofs. In those days, society being highly conservative, that might not have approved of some of his ways of life. He died issueless, it seems. Only his writings are given to the world as his gift. But, he is undoubtedly the creator of the tradition of dance-drama.

Now, I would like to give a detailed description of Bhagavata Mela performance, which I have witnessed during my visit to Melattur in May 1987.

Bhagawatamela–Melattur

When compared to other 5 villages, Melattur has, enjoyed special status. Venkatrama Sastry, the author of the plays was born here and lived and died here. There is the temple of Varadaraja Perumal at Melattur which has importante all 7 its own. This springs from the fact that Venkatrama Sastry composed his most important dance drama "Prahlada Caritam" in honour of the deity of this temple. Venkatrama Sastry wrote 14 plays most popular among them being Harischandra, Markandeya, Usha Parinayam, Rukmini Kalyanam *etc.* The plays are in Telugu and to this day, they are performed in their original language before spectators more than half of the audience who know nothing of Telugu. But this poses no problem, for

hundreds of people come from all around Melattur to witness these plays every year.

The Bhagavata Mela performance at Melattur begins each year with the Narasimha Jayanthi celebrations at the local temple, which takes place in May and lasts for 2 to 10 days. A thatched pandal or covering, about 150 ft long, is constructed in the street facing the temple, the portals of which are open so that the deities within may have a good view of the proceedings and bless the participants as well as those who assemble to witness the plays. The show begins every night at roughly 10 o'clock and ends in the early hours of the mornings. Plays are performed exclusively by local people and none of them is a professional actor or dancer. They come to Melattur at the time of festival. The performers as in Kuchipudi are all men. They are enjoined by convention to observe certain

austerities in their personal and social life. The musicians are also from Melattur and they take part, not for any fees but from a sense of social obligation and dedication to the art.

Performance begins, with the appearance on the stage of Konangi or buffoon. He prances and dances for a while till the attention of the audience is fully arrested. He is followed by the Nattuyanar and other musicians, who recite the Todayamangalam an invocation in the form of interspread with phrases of rhythmic syllables. Then enters a boy disguised as Ganapati and the musicians sing in his honour, while he shuffles his feet, shows a few hastas and makes his exit. Finally appears Kattiyakaran, the herald, who through song and gesture, introduces the play and the characters and exhorts the audience to witness the proceding with patience and understanding. Then begins the play proper which is unfolded strictly as it was written by the author; Venkatrama Sastry. Each principal character enters the stage with a 'daru' which is a song intended to introduce a character. The dance and abhinaya follow the technique of Bhagavata Natyam, mostly with the accompaniment of songs but occasionally, there are prose passages in the form of dialogues or monologues, meant for the main characters and also, Sandhi Vachanas, connecting links and 'Dwipadas', couplets which are Karnatic and the manner in which the author has used various ragas for different situations and

also sometimes, for various parts of the night at which particular sequences of a play are expected to be performed, speaks a lot for this musical genius.

No curtain is used before or during a play. Introduction of the heroine—she executes a dance item, usually Alarippu behind the screen, a cloth held by two volunteers and then it is pulled away, leaving her before the audience—men wear pyjamas kneelong coats or dhotis and some wear turbans *etc.* and moustache masks are used in the representation of Ganapati, Narasimha Brahma and the Rakshasas.

Mask of Narasimha by veneration of people, gained particular sanctity—an ordinary parier mache mask but years of worship for the rest of the time, it remain in a case fixed to the wall above the sacred images. The character finally falls into a trance. He is taken to the temple in a procession with songs all the way. Mask is then removed and ceremoniously replaced in its case, in the temple and only after this, people return to homes.

Venkatrama Sastry a Telugu Brahmin, and a senior contemporary saint-singer to Tyagaraja and who is credited with having created this Bhagavata Mela tradition and art, in the form in which it is recognised today. Kuchipudi has a technique and distinct individuality of its own. It is more accommodative to 'Rasa' like the Sringara, while the Bhagavata Mela is out and out with Bhakti, and Bhakti alone.

In continuation I would like to give a brief description of the performances of the dance dramas, which I have seen actually. On 13th May 1987, 'Harischandra' was enacted on a temporary stage, specially constructed in the fields with hey and fodder at the corner of the village of Melattur.

It started with the traditional 'Tai', 'Dittai'. When the curtain is taken out, Konangi enters, not the Sutradhara. He gives Arati to Vigneswara.

Then the normal invocative prayers "Jayachandra, Jaya Sandra', with all the musical instruments is sung in Sourastra Raga. The man sitting behind the curtain sings and the character on the stage does Abhinaya. For instance, Harischandra, when he entered the stage did a type of dance, when "Rajadhi Raja Martanda Teja etc" was sung in the background. So also the queen Chandramathi dances without any dialogue. Nritya is different from the modern style of solo and Nattuvangam is there. Actually, this drama, I was told, had to be enacted for two days, as per tradition. But, now it is for five hours from 10 P.M. to 3 o'clock.

Even Lohitasya dances in the traditional way, 'Sandhivachana' the linking commentary is not there. It is a Nritya Natika and so its salient features are different from other dramas of the modern stage. The story runs continuously through music in the background.

The story starts with King Harischandra telling about his dream to Chandramathi. There is so much of Nattuvangam in Matanga Kanyas dance also. There is 'Ragada' when Viswamitra sees king Harischandra "Kadupuna Kalagni Kattukunnanu" says Harischandra and Viswamitra delivers his dialogue in pure Telugu. He tactfully takes donation of the kingdom and threatens the Raja, to pay off his debt in one month. Then Nakshatraka his disciple enters.

While singing 'Saketapuramandu', with Saveri Raga, the Abhinaya performed was marvellous. The Soliloquy of Chandramathi, in Todiraga, that she is responsible for all the ills is heart moving.

The 'Dwipada' rendered, while selling the wife by Harischandra is really tremendous–'Ari Neeve-algatti Appu Teerchedanipudu' in beautiful Telugu, is simply moving.

The 'Sandhivachanas' or connecting links, the couplets which are recited by the Prasangi or the prompter are simple prose passages in the form of dialogues or monologues in Telugu.

The music is Karnatic and the manner in which, the author has used various Ragas for different situations and also sometimes for various parts of the night at which particular sequences of a play are expected to be formed, speak a lot of his musical genius.

It is to be noted that all the temples and the themes are Vaishnavite. Varadaraja Swamy is the main deity before whom the performances are given. Unnatapureewsara temple, of course, is a very ancient temple, in the end of the village.

The dance-drama of Andhra Pradesh, Kuchipudi is related to the Bhagawata Mela, although the authors and compositions are distinct from each other. The original source of inspiration for the dance and music style of Bhagawata Mela, is said to be Kuchipudi and this seems to be born out from the historial movement of the troupes from Andhra Pradesh to Tanjore; and another evidence is found in the lyric, which is in pure Telugu, not Tamil. It is certain that Melattur performances are close to Kuchipudi and Sulaimangalam performances are closer to Bharata Natyam, though in course of time a distinct style has emerged purely for Bhagavata Mela inspite of its leanings towards either Kuchipudi or Bharata Natyam.

The youngsters who are keeping up this art need all encouragement and patronage from all corners to make this traditional art live for ever.

Kolata Bhagimas of Vijayanagara Sculpture

35

Development of Dance Tradition of Andhra Pradesh (From Royal Patronage to Classical Excellence)

On a careful study of the epigraphical records of Andhra Pradesh, we can conclude that a place of pride was given to the composite art of 'Dance' in the cultural and aesthetic life of the people of Andhra. A special feature to be noted is the development of this fine art and its close ties with the temple and temple activities. Dance is considered to be one of the "Shoda Sopa" (sixteen) chara pujas offered to God. Badami Chalukyas, Cholas, Hoysalas, Kakatiyas, Pallavas, Vijayanagara monarchs, Kalyana Chalukyas have greatly contributed to the development of dance. The evidence that they have left to future generations as legacy are many in the form of stone inscriptions.

This art form, so to say, is an outcome of man's creative genius.

Some inscriptions record that Rangabhoga was performed as a special item of routine pujas and there are also instances to show that at the time of festivals and utsavas, it was performed as special service.

Archaeological evidences : some excavations conducted by the Archaeological department of Government of India in Andhra Pradesh, reveal rich traditions in the art of dance, since the times of Satavahana emperors of the second century BC.

The findings reveal that there were two schools of dance.

1. Devadasi
2. Kelika

Existing evidences show the patronage of temples and the rulers of the country.

It is said that there were three hundred families of Devadasis at Srikakulam, the original capital of Satavahana Empire in Krishna district.

At Ghanta Sala, before the onset of the influence of Buddhism, an exclusive style consisting of the families of Devadasis and Kelikas existed. Influenced by the above tradition Jayappa Senani, commander of the Kakatiya Elephant Forces, wrote a treatise by name "Nritta Ratnavali" on desi and Margi traditions which is a great contribution of Andhras to this fine art of dance.

There are three lovely dance scenes among the carvings from Amaravathi and another containing single dancers. Two sculptures, one of which is preserved only in a drawing by Col. Mackenzie show "Women dancing to entertain a king in harem."

The third shows the division of the relices at Kusinara where women are also shown as dancing.

In these sculptures, all the dance requirements are satisfactory.

The "Nepathya" or cores of the dancer is as described by Kalidasa. (Malavikagrimitran Act i.p.

23, this can be compared with the danseuse or actress on page 15 of Coomaraswamy and Duggal) just to drape the body without observing its lovely cortons (........... p. 22).

Musical instruments accompany the movements of the dancer.

Music is of primary importance in "Nritya' (pure dance), Abhinaya (gesture) is the soul of Nritya (suggestive dance) and music has only a secondary place says Bharata in his Natya Sastra. (Natya Sastra i.p. 188).

("Yatrabhinayam Gitam Syatlotna Vadyam Na yojryet")

(Abhirama Guptas' Commentary)

There are 3 types of Mridanga–Ankya, Aliyanga and Ordhvaka. Their names denote the positions in which they were respectively held. And these can be seen represented in Amaravati Sculptures.

Amaravati Sculptures in detail—its classical features :

In the Amaravati Sculpture (Pl xiii–Fig. 16), there are four dancers and attitude of the central figure suggests the 'Alarippu' of modern Bharata Natya performance, one movement made by the Nartaki, after she enters the stage (Ranga) Bharata gives an elaborate description of the 'Pravesa' (entry) of the Nartaki. After the Vinyasa of the musical instruments, the Nartaki enters and after different 'Charies' in accordance with the music, she stands in the 'varisakha' basic attitude (sthana) and sways her limbs in all the prescribed movements (Recites or Recakas–loc. Cit i.p. 187 IV 281-282 commentary) she carries a pushpanjali or a handful of flowers. Bharata's great commentator Abhinavagupta describes the 'Karana' for this as 'Talapuspa Puja' and after throwing the flowers all around and bowing to the God, she begins to dance. Abhinavagupta explains the Karana of this as 'Vaisakha Recitava. One of the movements of the hands in 'Pataka' (flag-like) thasta as they are brought in wards, shoulders, elbows and wrists on a level, has been well carved in the sculpture, the movements (Recitas) have to be imagined because a sculpture cannot give a continuous sequence of movements. The 'Sthana' is more like 'Mandala' then 'Vaisakha' (Natya Sastra i.p. 110, y. 65-66, 63-64). The legs are closer and this pose gives the dancer, confidence since Mandala is more appropriate for a graceful feminine dance.

The dancer in front of her is in 'Alidha Sthana' which suggests both a warrior and a wrestler

(Loc. cit ii. P.lll. r, 67-70) The suggestion of 'Malla' means the Malla tribe, as well as 'wrestlers', as the scene is that Kusinara the seat of 'Mallas' by hands are Sikatanda or 'katakamukha hasta' and suggest the drawing of the arrow, the karana appears the 'vyamsita', which is suggestive of a perplexing situation (loc, cit. i. p. 119. IV. 109).

To her left, the dancer is in Sthana known as Ardha Mattalli suggestive of intoxication of youth (Loc. cit, i.p.112. iv sq). The left hand is in 'Recita' and the right is on the hip. The position of the legs here is known as skhalita pasrita. The corresponding figure to the right resembles the precessions one, except in the change of the legs.

In the drawing by Col. Mechanic published by Ferguson (Pt. Ix viii. Fig.1) six dancers are entertaining a king by their art. The central one among the three is more in 'Varisakha' than in the "Mandala Sthana" and her hands are on her waist. To her left the dancer has raised her leg in the 'Bhujanga Trasa' fashion (loc. cit. i.p. 110. iv 101) Her left hand is in the 'Recita' attitude and the right in the "Pataka hasta" near has 8 holder. The dancer to the right of the central figure corresponds to the one on the left.

To the front, there are three dancers, in a row of whom the first stands in the 'Samapada Sthana' (loc. cit. ii. P. 109 & 58) with the hands held in 'Pataka' hasta, while swaying neck, hip and hand the dancer to her right is in the Karana known as 'Lata Vishika' his left hand and leg being in the 'Tala' and vrscika postures respectively.

The pose suggests descent from Heaven. She is balanced on the other side by a corresponding dancer in similar attitude.

The other scene in the harem, where a dancer shows her skill is in a sculpture in the British Museum. (The. iii. Fig.15) She keeps time with her feet and moves in what may be called. 'Atikranta Karana' suggestive of values (loc. cit. i.p. 126., iv 127) she appears to be a perfect dancer, who, while marking the 'tala' (rhythm) with her feet, uses the art of gesture with her eye movements and symbolic postures of the hand, to express the emotions of the song poured out by her sweet voice (Abhinava Darpana, Text 36. p. 5).

One of the sculptures first dug out by Col. Mackenzie, in Amaravati and sent to the Asiatic Society of Bengal (now preserved in the Indian Museum at Calcutta. (Ferguson Pl. 1 xxiv) shows some of the Devas dancing merrily, when some others sound musical in students as the Boddi Sattva descends to the earth from the Tushota heaven for fifth in the royal house of Suddho dana. A Deva towards the extreme right top behind the pavilion is dancing in the famous karana known as 'Mrdhva Jana' (loc. cit. i. P lll. Iv. 86).

Thus, Amaravati sculptures include all the four elements of Abhinaya—Angika, Vacika, Aharyaka and Satwika. Angikabhinaya is seen in various 'Hastas', Karanas and 'Sthanas' that show the attitudes of the dancing figures. Vacika Abhinaya is suggested by the musical instruments, which accompany the vocal music of the dancer. Even 'Aharya Abhinaya' suggestive of the theme can be seen in the cores and ornamentation used for the figures. Satwikabhinaya or suggestion of emotion, the most essential but most difficult element cannot be so easily recognized.

Thus, the movements of the dancer in these sculptures, bring before our eyes the lovely Karanas described by Bharata.

Traditions prevalent in Andhra Desa.

Padabhinaya Tradition

It can be said that this Padabhinaya tradition of south India, had its origin in Khetrayya's Padabhinaya style, perfected by later performers.

Kshetraya is reputed to have written 4,100 padams out of them, 2000 were composed in the court of Tirumalendra of Madura, 1000 in the court of Achuta Vijaya Raghava of Tanjore and 1000 in the court of Golconda Padusha, Abdullah Kutub Shah. Most of them are not known and only those with Achanta Vijaya Raghava are to be found.

Kshetrayya

He seems to have composed some on Tupaki Krishna, commander of Abdullah Kutub Shah. But the Padams which we most favour are those dedicated to Gopala Deva of Movva, a tiny village in Challapalli Samsthanam of Krishna district. They are called Movva Gopala Padas.

200 of these padas were published by Vavilla Ramaswami Sastry and Sons. A printed book published nearly 50 years back contains 20 more Movva Gopala Padas. The Mrs. Sringara Rasa Manjari contains 100 more padas, with Movva Gopala as this makes up a total of 320.

It is very interesting to note that Kshetrayya's Padabhinaya indicates all the lakshanas of the various types of Nayakis *etc.* as detailed by Bhanudatta Misra. This cannot be a pure accident. This must have been properly designed. Kshetrayya must have composed his padas with the specific purpose of imitating Bhanudatta's theory.

The Ms. Sringara Rasa Manjari thus throws flood light on a very important aspect of Kshetrayya's compositions and their eminent place in Telugu Literature on Alankara. His padas contain literary thrust of a very high order.

Perini or Prerana

It is one of the three classical dances prevalent in Andhra Desa—Kuchipudi–a dance done by males in female graph; Perini Shiva Tandavam, a totally warrior dance and a male dance–Lasya Natyam–after mime dance form performed by women. All these forms of dances fall in the parameters of Natya Sastra.

Tandavam is essentially rigorous masculine dance that originated from Lord Nataraja. But perini a dialectical Telugu version of the term of the Sanskrit word 'Prerana' (inspiration).

It appears to be less arithmetic, more elucidated with Hasta Mudras and in tractate foot work, suitable for strong bodied men.

Kakatiya rulers, who ruled our Warangal and some parts of Telengana 600-700 years ago, whose Telugu people and whose men of letters were scholarly.

Ganapathi Deva had only a daughter by name Rudrama and had no male fissions. So, he trained his daughter in martial arts, politics and administration, she ruled the kingdom after her father with great skill and efficiency and shunned all feminine qualities.

Jayappa was the commander-in-chief of the armed forces. ...., he had diverse interests and wrote books on dance, music and literature. His book on dance known as 'Nritta Ratnavali is master piece on dance. His other two works by name 'Gadya Ratnavali', 'Geetha Ratnavali' are not to be traced now.

Kakatiya rulers were followers of Veera Saivism. Jaya Senapathis dance treatise was full of the norms of a baseline type of dance. It is a highly spirited dance, with heroic movements, rigor and masculine footwork.

There is an interesting story about Jayappa's dedication of his wonderful treatise to Ganapathi Deva. He wanted to dedicate his work to the crown princess. She wanted him to give a demonstration of his dance. Accordingly, Jayappa Senani trained some youth who presented this Veera Natya, much to the delight of the princess and her father was pleased with performance, Ganapathi Deva ordered that this type of dance should spread out through the length and breadth of the entire Kakatiya Kingdom. It was also patronized by the successive rulers, with great respect to him. But, with the decline of the Kakatiya dynasty this dance form also went into oblivion.

The famous Natyacharya Nataraja Ramakrishna, could revive their dance form again and bring it to lime light, after 700 years.

Performed in solo and in groups also, this has simple costume–a vesti or dhoti tied above the knees, so as to actuate quick and vigorous movement a few ornaments, and armlets resembling the arman of a warrior of the past years. Its footwork Nattuvangam is also very powerful. Facial expression is long with neck and eye movement and gestures. Mathematical provision and difficult footwork is the high-tech of this ancient art.

The mythological Shiva Tandavam is similar to this form in a way, it immortalise the spirit of combat.

Kala–Krishna, a disciple of Nataraja Ramakrishna is an adept in this art form and has given some thousands of performances both in Indian and abroad and won laurels. He could find a special place for himself and a great name to this form of dance.

This Bhajana sampradaya conforms to the detailed description of Bharata's dance drama. Depending on the political and cultural history of Andhra Pradesh, dance forms envolved in course of time in different modes under the patronage of the rulers.

Kaza near Mangalagiri in Guntur District of Andhra Pradesh is the fifth place of their Bhajana

Samprodaya. Out of his adoration to Sri Panakala Swamy, the presiding deity of Mangalagiri, Venkannakavi, a Telugu man, belonging to Kaza village describes himself as born in this Sampradaya in his Parvati Kalyanam.

'Krishna cult' was mainly responsible for the spread of Nayaka-Nayika Bhava and Sringara became the main story of the dance display. There was progress from Rasabhinaya, from Aradhana (worship to sentimental display).

Kelika Nritya or Andhra Natyam

As in other classical dances of India, Andhra Natyam also consists of Nritta, Nritya and Abhinaya. The Nritha Part, considered as the most important aspect of any classical dance is practiced in the initial training as adverse, 'Aduvas', Jatis and in items like, Vinayaka Kautam, Additachari Vinyasam. Though the three aspects Nritta, Nrutya and Abhinaya are given equal importance in exhibiting padams, Javalis, poems and the Daravus of Navajanardana Parijatam, the Satwi Kashinaya dominates. Nowadays, the dance training stands with advices. Previously the same was a necessity. There are many different patterns of Adavus in Andhra Natyam. The basic position is 'Sama'. From here, the body is made to move. It is also known as 'Saustavam'. Holding two Ardha Chandra Hasthas, on the waist standing in a straight line with feet in 'equal level' is called "Sthanaka of Natya Sastra" says Dr. Nataraja Rama Krishna, the pioneer of Andhra Natyam.

Nritha aspect has to be understood as a technique of body movement. Mrs. Kapila Vatsayan explains thus the Indian dancer is not concerned with musculature of the human form, but rather like the sculptor, takes the joints and fundamental, anatomical bone structure of the human form as its basis. From such a basis, the dancer strives to achieve.

"Dakkini"

Dakkini is a type of dance that we find in the borders of Andhra state. They also perform "Bhagavathas" from their dances. They are known as "Sokkinata", only men take part in this type of dance.

Men acting as women

This tradition of man acting as woman is nowhere found. except in Kuchipudi style. Padmasri Vedantham Satyanarayana Sarma is a famous exponent of Satyabhama and on a fellowship by unesco he had proudly given performance in foreign countries and won applause.

Kaisikivritti

This delicate style in dance is given utmost importance in the visual representation of thought.

Subrahmanya Dikshitar gives an account of himself. He was a Telugu Brahmin, who lived during the reign of Sarabhaji and Sivaji of Tanjore. He wrote several padams in Kaisiki style and he has defined and adorned the plays of Venkatarama Sastry, as well as Telugu language, which was official language of Nayak Kings.

Dance–Drama

There is dependable evidence to show that dance was developed at Tanjore under the patronage of Achutappa Nayaka, the 2nd of the Nayak rulers (1577-1614) of the palaces, there is extensive literature on this art in Telugu. The authorship of most of these dance–dramas can be traced to Venkatarama Sastry, a Telugu Brahmin, working as Telugu pandit in Pudukkottai Samsthanam.

He wrote 14 dance dramas—Rukmini Kalyanam, Harischandra, Prahlada Charitham, Seeta Kalyanam, Usha–Parinayam, *etc.*

Those who take part in these dance–dramas are still called Bhagavatars.

These dramas are being presented in Melattur in May, at the time of Nrisimha Jayanthi. They are all men working in different high professions and they perform as a religious duty to keep up their family tradition.

Venkatarama Sastry introduces himself, in his plays as the son of Gopalaraya Sastry and 'Srivatsa' is his Gotram. He was a contemporary of saint Tyagaraya, who lived in Tiruvathiyur, 16 kms. away from Melattur. I was simply thrilled to see his house in Melattur, which is just opposite to the temple dedicated to 'Siva' by name Varadaraja Swamy.

Devadasi Nrityam

It is not beyond truth to say that it is these devadasis, who are responsible for the presentation of the art of dance. These women, who are supposed to be servants of God, dedicated their lives to the fine art. In course of time, when the religious sanctity of this profession declined, they were treated as concubiness of rich men. As a consequence, this art also began to decline.

But a sincere effort was made by some interested Natyacharyas to lift this art from the image attached to it. When girls from respectable families also began to learn this art and began to give stage performances in public, it retained its importance as a divine art. Dance schools have been started in every city and many performing artists have come up into lime light.

Kuravanji

Dance of Kuravanji is for the lower castes. Even today, a piece in Raga 'Nada Nama Kriya' opening with the words "Taluku–Beluku" is available the melody type is known as chindu–a variety of folk songs are two varieties. 1) Vandana Chindu–represented by one or two .... as in 'Nandana Charitam' composed Chindu, that forms the sine–qua–non of the modern music halls and is the most important and necessary asset of the modern professional writing about Music and Dance Vaggeyakaras.

Sabdam : Solo Dance : solo form of dance is culled out from Kuchipudi dance dramas called 'sabdams' in (Bharata Natyam) and they are being presented on stage as separate items of dance, the most popular are by Pandit Kasinadha Sastry of Melattur, this "Mandukasabdam," "Prahlada Pattabhishekam" and "Rama Sabdam" are famous, Manduka Sabdam is from the story of Gajendra Moksham where the frogs playing in a pond are described. Words are spoken like the sound of jumping frogs, the main Rasa in all these sabdams is 'Sringara'.

Bhagawata Mela

The traditional dance drama Bhagawata Mela is performed annually at Nara Simha Jayanthi festival in Melattur village in Tamilnadu. It uses the classical gesture language with Karnatic musical fabric the tradition that was earlier practiced in six villages around Tanjore, Melattur, Salimangalam, Ethukadu, Nallur, Saliya-mangalam, and Theperamanallur–have shrunken and taken the form of a ritual at Melattur in the service of God Narasimha.

The tradition which was richly followed during the Nayak and Maratha Kings of Tanjore, has declined. Today, the form is abbreviated and has been reclaimed as a traditional dance–drama style. Bhagavatha mela has been given a new life by the composer Venkatrama Sastri (1759-1847) a contemporary of Tyagaraja, the great saint singer of south India. Sastri composed marvellous dance dramas in the Telugu language and enriched reporting the most famous of his immortal work in Prahlada Charitham.

At the annual festival, held in May–June, the deity is taken out in an evening procession and ceremoniously installed in the Gopuram Passage, the actors perform through the night on a platform before the presiding deity.

The opening benediction (Todaya Mangalam) is followed by Konangi (the clown) who capes and tumbles. Then the courier of the Royal Place appears on the stage and announces the hero. The Phaganatha leads the chorus and reads out a description of each character and the singer offers the introduction song called "Daru" (Bharata Muni called this introduction Daru as Pravesika Daru, these Darus are excellent raga compositions in slow rhythm ideally suited for interpretative acting.

The Daru gives the idea of the character, the mood, the background. Singers sing according to the rhythm of the character.

The Bhagavatha reads connecting links by chanting prose pieces. The character do's a brief

dance as the Bhagavatha sings the introduction. The play goes on all night, using a language accompanied by a strong dance and music.

The names of several Vaggeyakaras of those times are also to be found. They are not very popular. They never spoke about themselves and remained unseen and unsung but their efficiency can be observed with due respect. Tallapaka Chintayya, Jatapalli Varu, Sobhanagiri Varu, Veerabhadrayya, Mathra bhutha kais, Inukonda Varu, Sivarayapuram Varu, Ghanam Seenayya are some of them. But unfortunately, their works are not available.

Thus various traditions of dance forms developed in Andhra Desa and took deep roots in other traditions also.

Artists of Telugu land carried their rich traditions to their land of migration. It is unfortunate that such fine traditions have not found due place of publicity in the history and nowadays, an attempt is being made to bring them to light.

It appears to be proper to say that rich traditions mentioned above were patronised by the rulers as well as the people and they developed into more sophisticated stage, with some innovative ideas of different Natya Charyas. The point to be noted is also fine—that the traditions are all on the lines suggested by authoritative texts or treatises and people honoured those rich traditions and that is why, they are living today even after lapse of centuries.

Maids attending on Parvati—A Sculpture from Lepakshi Veerabhadra ceiling

36

Summing Up
How People Patronised Arts in Different Times

Andhra Pradesh has a rich tradition and a hoary past in the world of fine arts, especially dance. From 1000 BC to 4th Century, there flourished a great stone culture similar to that of Sindhu Valley culture. Recent excavations in Phani Giri in Nalgonda district have proved beyond doubt that the Toranas and sculptures dug out by the dept of archaeology are just similar to those taken out at Amaravati and Nagarjuna Konda. Several sculptures depict stories of lives of Buddha and Jataka Kathas have been taken out from them after several centuries. They are all in Brahmi Script. Santamoola, the first emperor of Ikshvaku dynasty had got them prepared. It was he who developed Nagarjuna Konda also.

Out of the eight acres of land available in Phanigiri only one acre had been recently excavated. When once the other seven acres are also covered, many more such wonders may be found.

Now a beautiful sculpture depicting Siddhartha going on the chariot and studying the life of people before his becoming Buddha is found. In addition several sculptural constructions are taken out from Phanigiri, which speaks of the then culture. Historians speak of this as a rare phenomenon.

The Cult of Worship

The cult of worship of objects or phenomena has been one of the traits of mankind from very ancient times. The early form of such practice has come down to us in the course of some centuries, in the form of traditions and material relics.

We have glimpses of Gods and spirits worshipped by the common man as religious practice even before the advent of religions like, Buddhism, Hinduism and Jainism.

Worship of local gods and spirits inhabiting trees, rivers and hills, lakes and tanks were similar in principle. The worship of the trees was once very popular. These spirits were associated with trees like Banyan, Arasu (Pipal), Neem *etc.* From archaeological evidence, the concept of tree worship appears to be very ancient, dating back to Harappan times.

Man in ancient times appears to have danced in ecstasy, when he saw rain falling and seeds germinating. He also began to ask for boons like fertility from the invisible god and worshipped him, in the name of supernatural force. Offering of flowers, garlands, bathing for the sake of purification with sacred water became common.

Construction around 'sacred tree' was also taken up to meet the needs of worship like performing some rituals. It also took some definite architectural shapes in course of time. (Buddhist sites, dating back to 2nd century are clear evidences of this method of worship. This deep-rooted and very ancient cult of worship appears to have been continued even after the organized temple worship.

Even before the Buddhist times, the abode of 'Devata' or 'Divine Being' was prayed for giving boons to man.

Bodhi–Ghara is represented as a high gallery and the area surrounding the 'Bodhi tree' and Vajrasana at its foot with definitely made entrances, into the sacred area, the Buddha–mantapa.

Asoka, the great emperor, so as to fulfill his vow, is stated to have poured scented water from a thousand vessels by mounting on an enclosure, which he had constructed on all the four sides of Bodhi Ghara at Buddha–Gaya. By the two Amaravathi versions of the Bodhi-ghara in south India, one is in fact (partly preserved) and the other is fragmentary.

The large Maha Chaitya of Nagarjuna Konda, which was built in early Ikshaku times belongs to the class of uncased stupas.

Temples were built in course of time, with platforms, cult objects, or ionic representation.

Recent excavations in Gudimallam temple in Chittoor district (on Tamilnadu–Andhra border) have revealed that the "LINGA" with its pitha (bottom) both of sand stone were originally hypaethral in the 2nd century BC. A brick shrine enclosing it came up in the 1st-2nd century AD and it was replaced by a stone apsidal, one much later. (Dr. J.K. Sarma).

—DG Archaeology

The excavations in Nagarjuna Konda have revealed large non-Buddhist—Temple complexes of the Ikskhaku Kings (3rd and 4th Century) dedicated to Siva, Vishnu, Kartikeya and Devasena. They are mostly four sided.

Garbha grihas were built over an elevated plinth area with a large pillared mantapa in front of them a raised platform at the forefront of the mantapa, indicating a ranga–mantapa. The pillars of the Mandapa were made from Palnad limestone.

Similar brick–temples of the post-Ikshvaku and pre-Chalukyan period have been excavated in the submersible Sri Sailam Project area. Fortunately there are apsidal shrines of this period of original Buddhist dedication and subsequent conversion to Hindu creed. They are still existing in their entirety.

They are the Trivikrama Temple at TER in western Deccan and the Kapoteswara Temple at Chejerla in Guntur District. Both are dated earlier than AD 600.

There arose a movement at the time of Ashoka, which resulted in series of temples, being made of more permanent material. They have survived to the present day.

Cave temples of Andhra Pradesh and dance poses of painting—Eastern Chalukyas of Vengi have constructed over a dozen cave–temples on the banks of river Krishna. They are to be found in Vijayawada and Moghalrajapuram on the north bank of Krishna river and in the hills of Undavalli, Penamaka, and Sitarampuram on the South Bank in Guntur district Akkanna–Madanna cave at Vijayawada is ascribable to the middle of this century. Cave I to IV of Mogalrajapuram, the Undavalli and other caves in a series ending with Bhairavani Konda are datable to the middle of the 8th century. These cave temples consist of a rock-cut hall or "Mandapa" with one or more, often three shrine–cells behind. The Mandapa is sometimes multi-pillared. While most of the cave temples are dedicated to Siva, two are dedicated to Durga and a few to Vishnu. Here, in this context, mention may be made of Tandava-Siva. The Ananta–sayanagudi cave temple at Undavalli, is the largest of the group and is a 3–storied structure similar to the Ellora Buddhist caves 11-12.

Bhairavanikonda temples are excavated in the hills at Kottapalli in Nellore district. There are two rock-sculptures of dancing Siva and Harihara.

Image worship in some form or other existed among the non-Aryans, in all our ancient literature the epics, the Sutras, Arthasastra, temples are referred to as "Devalaya" or "Devayatana". Temples might have originated as soon as image worship came into vogue in India.

Andhra Pradesh was stronghold of Buddhism for about six hundred years (300 BC to 300 AD).

Mode of worship in Andhra–Till the introduction of the image of Buddha, around AD 150 in the Krishna valley, symbols that represented the Buddha, such as the Bodhi tree, Throne, Dharma Chakra, Triratraswastika, Buddha Padas and Chaitya or stupa were worshipped. The emergence of Mahayana during the 2nd century AD and the introduction of Buddha image, brought about a revolution in the aims of the Buddhists and the methods of achieving them.

Worship of Dhatus

Andhra started with worship of the relics of Buddha. The major Stupas of Andhra Desa such as those of Dhanyakataka and Bhattiprolu were built on the genuine coppered relics of the great teacher. Manjusri Multanantra says that the 'Caitya' at Dhanyakataka at Bhattiprolu State the Dhatu of Jina, another name of Buddha. According to Lalita Vistara, Buddha was in the crystal in the womb of Mayadevi to avoid defilements.

Chaitya Worship

As a result, chaityas became all the more sacred and there developed the Chaityaka sect among the Andhra with Chaitya as the cult object. The Chaityakas believed that offering of flowers, garlands, lamps and incense to Chaityas were considered to be meritorious acts. Many sculptures from Buddhist sites show man, Yakshas and Gandharvas adoring and worshipping stupas.

A sculpture from Amaravathi, which has been assigned by Ananda Kumara Swamy to about 200 BC reveals that temples were built with stupa as the artic of worship. In the excavations at Nelakonda Palli was discovered a marble stupa, which was probably intended for installation in a shrine.

The rock–cut Chaitya gruha of Guntupally is in fact the earliest chaitya griha in Andhra Pradesh and it dated back to Mouryan period. There are more than 35 brick built stupas at Guntupalli. Several motive stupas are found on the hills of Ramatirtam and Salihundam (Srikakulam).

The Hindus appear to have adopted this practice and especially at Saivaite Kshetras we find monolithic votive temples.

A posture of kneeling before the object of worship was the most popular way expressing one's devotion, which suggests self-surrender, which became an important concept of Vaishnavism.

Image Worship

From about the middle of the 2nd century AD the image of Buddha became popular.

The image thus consecrated was decorated with jewels. Amaravati inscriptions of the Pallava King Simhavarma, who visited the Buddha Kshetra about AD 550 speaks of jewels wonderfully, worked in gems, gold and silver.

During 5-6th centuries AD, devotionalism became the more predominant feature of Indian religious life, both Buddhist and Brahmanical. After the 6th century, Buddism declined and Buddha became an integral part of pantheon of Vishnu as 9th incarnation.

A highly interesting Dasavatara sculpture of about 10th–11th century is in the ceiling of the sun temple at Alampur in Mahaboobnagar District. In this the central position is occupied by Buddha in Yogamudra and the other Avataras are shown around him.

Almost a replica of the sculpture is in the Sangameshwara temple outside the town of Alampur on the bank of Tungabhadra. With this the Vishnu Buddha identification is complete.

Gangadhara was a Brahmin minister of Kakatiya Rudra. Bekkalu inscription belongs to AD 1171. Mallareddy built 4 shrines in which he installed the image of Siva, Vishnu, Jina and Buddha. Such was the catholicity of common people.

According to Amaravati pillar inscription dated AD 1182, Kota Kataraja II gifted three villages, Kanteru, Medikonduru and Dokiparru to Buddha Deva. His queen Prolama and concubine Surama Devi gifted 55 sheep each to the same God for perpetual lamps. A Natavadi princess Buyya Mahadevi also gifted 55 sheep to Buddha Deva and in Telangana also, temples were built as is known from Karimnagar inscription of Gangadhara and Bekkallu inscription of Mallareddy.

What was creative in man, he offered in worship to the creator of all.

Art Tradition brought down to the level of common man :

To keep the premature society intact some unifying force was invented. Vedic sayings like "Satya Meva Jayathe", "Dharmam Chera" are considered to be the ideals of human life. They are said in a preaching style and they are taken as sanctions by the humanity.

But the intellectuals of the growing society, preached them in a pleasant manner, in the shape of Puranas, interesting stories and attractive themes in the form of art forms like visual performance to the common man. In the initial stages, it appears that there was no common platform. But after the invention of image worship and temple culture, there was a place, a place of congregation for all the people of the village to sit and enjoy the performance, irrespective of their caste or creed, in the temple corridors or Rangamatapas.

The Upakhyanas, the Samvadas (discussions) and music *etc.*, found in the Vedas might have paved the way, for the invention of "Natakeeyata", or the visual performances in the form of Veedhi Natakas, Kolatas, Bhajana Kirtanas, giving entertainment to the onlooker, and also preaching him the ideals of life. It is of course very difficult to trace the origin of the dance of how and when it was invented and by whom.

In Andhra, during Mouryan's time, there appears to be a male dance, the earliest form of dance. Females are prohibited to participate. Even while narrating the Jataka Kathas, our sculptures reveal, that 'Midhunas' are included not only to popularize the themes but to make the stories more interesting. But, when we trace the evolution of society, we can find the art forms emerging from social life. Narration and dance forms are not to be found in Hinayana cult.

Mouryans were succeeded by Satavahanas in the South. Texts from the Jatakas and Buddhas life as legends indicate the themes of the panels of those times. For example there is mention of the names of the famous celestial dancers like Oorvasi,

Padmavathi, and others and of the Yakshas, Yakshis and Nagas like Supavasa Yakshi Chakravaka Naga, Siranna Devata and the Kuherayarisha. The beliefs and the rituals of the day worship of the tree spirit, Nagas, river–Gods and goddesses and the celestials like Indra all expressed.

At a later stage, when Ramayana and Mahabharata came to be honoured as standard people learnt to think in terms of the ideals of those Heros as they come nearer to their heart. Words like "Nata", "Nartaka", "Rangasthala" in Ramayana, words like "Rangasala", "Nata", in Mahabharata indicate the above fact.

Writers like Bhasa, Kalidasa, have added glory to the art of dance by their writings. There is another word for Natya–Sastra, as a synonym of Natya veda, which is considered to be the Panchama Veda' Yama–Yami Sukta, Urvasi–Pururava Sukta, Sarama–Pani Sukta are very interesting.

Panini in his grammar says "Parasarya silali Bhyam".

Bhikshu Nata sutra Yoh".

This sutra in which the word "Nata sutra" is found for the first time indicating "Natya".

"Ye Ye Swabhavole Kasya Sukha Dukha Samanvitah.

No Gadya Bhi Nayo Petah Natya Mityabhi Dhuyate"—which means "that which speaks of loka swabhava, which consists of joy and misery and which is expressed through the limbs of human body, may be called Natya, confirming this idea Dhanika the communicator of "Dasa rupaka", says that word "Natya" originated from Nata-Avaskanda. In other words that which is moving is 'Natya'.

"Dharmo Dharma Pravittanam"

Kamah Kmopa–Sevinam

Easwaranam Vilasascha

Sthairyam Dukharjtha Swacha

Ardhopa Jeefina mordhah Dhruti

Rudusigne Cheta sam

Nana bhava Sampannah, Nanavasthamtha ratnakam

Loka Vrithan Karanam Natyame Tanmaya Krithrur"

Dhanika said,-Natya Sastra.

In Dasarupaka

"Avasthanu Kruthirnatyam"

Vidyadhara Said

"Dheero Datta Dyavasthanu Kruthir natyam Rasasrayah".

Art is a wonderful window, through which one can see a new world.

In the place of vedic ritualism, more ways of Bhakthi were invented in the changed environment of society, by the influence of Puranas.

"The institution of temple played a major role in the evolution of Purana culture. The Puranas are very liberal in the aspect of dedicating temples to any god of one's liking, unlike Buddha, Chaityas, which were built to commutate only the Buddha. It stands as a symbol of religion of the society. The Vishnu Dharmottara Purana gives some principles regarding construction of temples, which are elaborated in the Agama works (V. V. Parabrahma Sastry–page 95).

So, it can be safely concluded that the simple language of the Puranas was easily understood for worship in temples, which was within reach of the common man. There was thus a marked change in the religious, as well as cultural life of the society. I think, it was during this period that dance–dramas and other art forms were invented to bring puranic themes nearer to common man. Perhaps worship in the temples was made more accessible and easier to common man, when it was mixed with art. Dance was one of the forms of attraction.

"The Puranas constantly advocated the cult of Bhakti and for that purpose provided worship of images of innumerable gods like Siva, Vishnu, Kartikeya, Durga, Ganesha and so on, according to the liking of the devotee. This kind of worship became very close to the simple ways of propitiating the primitive gods of the indigenous people in fact, a large number of indigenous deities which were being worshipped by the common folk have been taken into the puranas under different sanskritised names.

"Continuously the vedic Brahmanas did not try to propagate their religion among the common folk. In fact, these little in the Vedic scriptures which can be conveniently adopted in the daily life of the common people. It was all confined to the cult of Sacrifices and Upanishadic philosophical discourses useful for the intellectuals alone. Not even temples were constructed for the worship of deities of the common people. So Buddhism naturally gained the upper hand in attracting the masses"

(V. V. Parabrahma Sastry)

Cultural Integration in India through Puranas

When such was the situation in which society was placed Buddhism, endeavoured to maintain social contacts irrespective of caste or creed, with a missionary spirit and a majority of common families traditionally in the coastal Andhra and Telangana districts followed Buddhism. So, according to the latest count, there are more than seventy Buddhist centres discovered in Andhra so far and many of them yielded structural as well as epigraphical evidences datable to a period as late as 12th Century AD. (The Bekkallu inscription dated 1195 AD) inscription of Andhra Pradesh, Warangal District. No 20 refers to Buddhism as a living faith in Andhra. In fact Buddhism had enormous influence over society, for more than a millennium, beginning from the time of Ashoka and declining in the 7th Century as noticed by Huian Tsang.

The dates given to puranas vary and historians differ on this A.L. Basham in his book "The Wonder that is India" has stated that the puranas are compendia of legends and religious instructions.

"Indian art is the expression of a world of thought and feeling very different from European. Nowhere has European art attempted to portray the same kind of relationship between God and man as there is in Indian sculpture".

India's conception of life, has subtle systems of metaphysics, and philosophy had been evolved through more than 5 thousands from the rest of the world...Her influence had been profoundly felt by the world outside. The Buddhist art in ceylone, Burma, Siam, Indo-China, China and Japan. The south Indian colonizers of Java took with them Hindu mythology, sculpture and the dance.

Indian influence has been traced in Rome and Alexandra and we know that traffic between the west coast ports of Malabar and in Roman Empire were very considerable.

The earliest culture we know of in the sub-continent is megalithic. There are curious survivals of it among some of the aboriginal tribes even today–the Gonds, Todas and Nagas, says Winifred Holmes.

Thus there is a cultural development between the megalithic period. With its tentative expressions of a developing peoples mind and the next phase was development of the highly civilized cities of Harappa and Mohenjadaro in the Indus Valley. From among the ruins, the mother Goddess, the torso of a male dancer, the figurines of the dancing girl were found as evidences.

How People's Patronage Triumphed

Buddhism, with the encouragement by the Mouryan Emperor Ashoka, could flourish in Andhra, and Monasteries and stupas were built.

Emperor Ashoka's edicts were meant for the local governors and teachers to read and interpret to the uneducated common man. There was story telling in stone. Thus holy places were developed as places of pilgrimage.

Peak Stupa sculpture was developed in Amaravathi in the Second Century A.D. under the powerful dynasty of the Andhra ruler of Deccan and it is considered to be the "Most voluptuous and delicate flower of Indian sculpture". It was also produced in the cave temples built in the southern area of Vindhya hills. The people who appear on the cave walls are more elegant, they were more clothes, their surroundings are more luxurious. The earliest cave temples and monasteries were Buddhistic but later cave temples were excavated or adopted to Hinduism, as Buddhism lost its hold on people and disappeared from the land in course of time.

During Gupta or early medieval period Jainism, Buddhism and Brahminism existed side by side. This is known as the classical period or the Golden age.

From cave to temple change over, from cave to structural temple building took place during their period.

Between 400 AD and 750, Pallava dynasty became followers of Siva and built structural temples in his honour. Pallava King by name Mahendra Varma, was responsible for construction of a remarkable group of temples; Radhas were carved from granite at Mamallapuram during his time.

The medieval period (8th to 12th) centuries saw Hindu culture at its heights, with the Chalukyan, Chola and Rajaput dynasties, patronizing and developing the fine arts. They maintained peace and civilization on orthodox Hindu lines, till they were swept away by the Mohammedans.

Fabulously rich Hindu Court of Vijayanagar patronized fine arts and literature. A foreign traveller described Vijayanagar court as being "Full of courtesans, dancers, jugglers and performing elephants. People were attracted towards the various forms of art but after the fall of this empire, Hindu arts flickered and died down in A.P.

Several writers, pandits and musicians for instance Tyagaraja, Narayana Teerdha, Kshetrayya migrated to Tamilnadu, seeking royal patronage after the fall of the empire. They carried with them the traditions of Andhra Pradesh.

On careful study of the situation, some new ideas totally related to the life of the people and based on their involvement and patronage took shape. Fine arts, Natya took deep roots.

These Natyas continued for hundreds of years because of their unquestioned and unparalleled popularity. Even today they attract thousands of people, who watch them with total involvement.

For a meaningful assessment of those traditions. It is necessary to understand their roots in the life of the people. They have been the vehicles of basic values and beliefs of Indian life. In fact they played a leading role in keeping different classes of people united and related in maintaining a constant dialogue among them. They imbibe the brilliance acquired through the practice of some centuries and on the other hand, display immense vitality on account of their being closely related to life at many levels. The stories are drawn from Indian historical episodes, folk tales and events, women came to stage by the middle of 20th century.

The spirit of these forms provides fundamental unity and continuity.

The dances of the tribal groups can be classified on the basis of anthropological ethical and racial factors. Nearly thirty-eight million people of India, belong to this category. Their dance and music are examples of vigorous folk and classical style. Like their society their artistic forms are also highly structural.

Kapila Vatsayan says "there is the original village society whose origin can be killed with the vedic concept of 'Grama' 75 per cent of the population of this country. Have lived and continue to live in this social structure. These villages have been analysed from many points of views–both historical and sociological. Here, music, dance and drama have been woven into agricultural functions and are integral to the daily and annual routine of the peasant. Many survivals and continuities of tribal society can be discerned in the agricultural rites connected with sowing, reaping, and harvesting. The origin of these along with many dances of propitiation of magic and sorcery, goes back to an unknown antiquity. Thus, after a contemporary community dance contains in it elements of the original tribal life..... co-existent with the manifestations which are integral to the agri. cycle of the life of the peasant are artistic manifestations based on the two epics and the many Jatakas and Puranas of Buddhist, Jaina and Hindu origin. The many pageants and tableaux and local forms of dances and dance dramas developed from both the pure recitative word and its consequential interpretation through gestures, mime and song. Local variations of them have been considered as the permeation of the regional forms in turn shaped many literary versions of the epics. A history of the development of the Rama theme will make this amply clear.

Close to the village community, but a class apart is a group of professional singers, dancers, musicians and actors, who are differently classified. This is a group for whom the performance is a vocation not a social, tribal or agricultural function. They are in and out of society, a community or group recognized since the days of Panini. They move from place to place. It is this group of people which have been responsible for the mobility of ideas, forms and styles between the villages and the urban centres. They have also been carriers of reform movements and articulators of satire and social comment and thus the instruments of social–cultural change.

This is finally the urban city-based culture, which has grown up from the tribal/village culture, and in turn has affected it. Forms which developed within the framework of agricultural and other life functions and particularly social organizations, are carried forward and taken over in an urban milieu, though only after they have been disassociated from their original agricultural functions. Into the old form is now introduced a new literary content and a musical score. Class city is the result. A mannerism and stylization are achieved through chiselling of the earlier forms and structuring them in relation to the word and sound. This then has been the secret of the highly esoteric arts, which have not lost their links with the earth and have in them the potential of continued rejuvenation through successive ages.

At this level, the same epics, the Puranas and the themes received a different treatment. The performers are professional or non-professional in terms of economic vocation but they are all dedicated academicians, committed to the arts as discipline of life and as means of release.

This multi-layered pattern can be observed practically in every region of India. It can be also discerned in many parts of Asia, particularly Java, Bali, some parts of Thailand, and Burma.

The distinctive style and technique of each form gives each a personality unique and autonomous with an inner life and external methodology of communication. Thus, Smt. Kapila Vatsayan established the fact that people were responsible to transform society and fine arts out of their patronage. But who are the audiences and how do they differ. Hardly there is any distinction between the participator, the actor–dancer, musicians, and the audience all join in, she says.

Thus, the performing arts worked as a unifying force and were appreciated by the people in the earliest times. Arts developed as people developed.

Kings and rulers patronized these art forms in course of time and they developed into a classical level par excellence, as per the sastraic traditions.

Indian art and its forms have seen several ups and downs. After her gaining independence, she is undergoing biggest changes of her history. Whatever maybe the effect of the change, Indian Art, especially its dance, is not simply an art of the drawing room. It is a part of the man's constant attempt to reach the unknown or unattainable.

Through Dance–dramas written in Kaisiki Vritti, soft feeling was erected. People appreciated these themes. People were taken to ecstasy from the mundane problems and monotony. They were elevated to a sublime thought far away from routine life. They were taken to a dreamy world, when they saw the dancer, dancing on the stage. In fact, the audience enjoyed the delicate inner feeling of gentleness, softness and joy. Perhaps man became a superman, with a sense of satisfaction that life is worth living. All the themes were also related to subjects, which were near and dear to the Indian mind–mostly from epics and Puranas. People very well appreciated these stories.

Thus dance–dramas written in simple language and enacted by actors on the stage, could win the hearts of people and move them. The very cultural life of people and in a larger sense, the nation, was moulded by some currents and cross–currents of thoughts created by the popular themes. Arts especially dance worked as a linking force and paved the way for the cultural synthesis of various sections of people. Class, creed differences were forgotten and all sitting in the audience were considered as a single unit with simple legends called Sthala Puranas being incorporated in them. The origins of the great pilgrim centres like Sri Sailam, Tirumala and Ahobhilam in Andhra, according to the respective Sthala-Puranas are connected with the tribal people. Goddess Brahmaramba, the consort of Mallikarjuna at Srisailam till recent times was worshipped on certain occasions by the local tribals called Chenchus in their way of offering animals before the deity.

(V.V. Parabrahma Sastry, p. 92)

This clearly indicates the deities of pre-historic, say the neolithic period have been conveniently transformed into puranic Gods like Siva, Narasimha, Durga and so on.

Dance thus is a composite art. It is the art of the stage, drama, music, poetry, colour and rhythm. Its key note is the dance, which includes all the arts and its message is not only to the senses and through them to a purely eternal enjoyment.

It is also a divine art. In this universalistic and comprehensive approach to life, Hindu faith is included among the manifold expressions of the divine dance which includes music, drama, and all the other creative arts. Abhinaya is one of the most important aspects of this histrionic art, conjuring up a fascinating world of imagination Abhinaya Darpana mentioned "it is a synthesis of Aharya, Vachika referring to the speech and songs by the actors and Angika, comprising of bodily movements and Satvika, the expression of psychic styles intimately associated with emotional conditions". All the above characteristics are found in Kuchipudi style.

(a) Music in Various dance Styles

'Bhagavathulu' who experimented this style followed the classical Karnatik traditions. The musical instruments used are, Mridangam, flute, violin, and cymbals. The Nattuvanar recites jathis and the vocalists render the darus. The various talas are used in solo performances also.

Brisk passages of jathis adorn certain compositions in Sanskrit operas like Krishna Leela Tarangini by Sri. Tirdha Narayana Yathi.

Bhagavatamela came into existence as a result of Bhakti movement. The dance drama forms, which developed in Andhra and Tamilnadu are thus a continuation of the traditions of Gita Govinda. Inscriptions of the 8th, 9th and 10th centuries support the existence of this dance–drama tradition in south India. Two devotee poets, Tirdha Narayana Yathi and Siddhendra Yogi skilfully employed the art of dance, music, song and drama, using themes from Srimadbhagavatha and other puranas, to extol the principle of Bhakti. The artists who practiced this art, used this mighty weapon, to propagate religious sentiments as well as eternal enjoyment and encouraging thus the spirit of Bhakti.

"Of the two traditions of Brahman Melas, the Kuchipudi dance drama tradition appears to be an earlier one".

(b) Rasa in different Style

The theory of Rasa as conceived by Hindu aesthestics has two aspects—the first is the evoked state. Rasavastha and the second is the sentiments the moods, the permanent and the transitory states, which were the object of presentation.

Saiva Agamas speak of Navarasas. The function of all arts, more especially dance, is to evoke 'Rasa' (Rasavastha). The aesthetic value is to be achieved through the human body, gestures, movements, rhythms and sentimental expressions. In Indian ancient treatises like 'Saranga Ratnakara' not a single part of the human anatomy is denied expressions".[2] We learn from this classic example the great immortal essence of all important earlier treatises on the subject. So minute and accurate is the analysis of the expressive powers of the human body made by our theorists 13 varieties of pratyanga, 36 rasa dristi Bhrdas, 7 varieties of eye-brow movements, 6 of the eye-lids, 9 of the eye-balls, 6 of the cheek, 19 varieties of breathing, are mentioned.

Desire of sambhoga is created by Ritu 'Malya', 'Anulepana', 'Alankara', 'Istajana', 'Vishaya', 'Varabhanana', 'Upabhoga', Vanagamana, Anubhavana, Sravana, Dasana, Kreeda, Leela etc, as per the texts. The dancer creates the above conditions through his skill of Abhinaya.

Bharata mentions that this Abhinaya should be exhibited through 'Nayanachatura', 'Bhukshepa', Katahsha, samachara lalitha Madhyrangahara 'Vakyadi', experiences. Vipralamba sringara is to be shown through 'Giant', 'Nirveda', 'Sanka', 'Asvya', 'Srama', 'Chinta', 'Outsukya', 'Nidra', 'Supta', 'Swapna', 'Vibodha', 'Vyadhi', 'Unmada', Apasmara', 'Jadya', 'Marana' *etc.* It creates sorrow.

The ancient Rishis asked Brahma, how the Rasas are to be enacted and shown in Natya.

"ye Rasa iti Pathyanthe Natya Natya Vichkshanaihi, Rasatvam Kenavya Tesha Metha Dakhyatu Marhasi".[4] from the four Vedas, four constituents of Natya have been evolved and "Pathya and Geetha" are the famous parts of it. "Abhinayam" is taken for representing the meaning of words.

Some feel that 'Rasa', 'Bhava', 'Abhinaya', 'Geeta' and 'Adhyatma', is Natya. The above sloka speaks of eleven Angas whereas, some feel that 'Upachana' and 'Mandapa' are combined with the above Upangas (altogether 13) (Natya Sangraha.) 10 lip movements, 8 of the teeth, 6 of the tongue, 8 of the chin, 5 of the ankle, 8 heel movements, 7 finger movements, 5 toe movements etc are described in detail not to speak of several other poses, postures, gaits mobile patterns, revolutions and spinnings *etc.*[3]

The sages asked Bharata "What is Rasa", "How can Rasathwa Siddhi be achieved".

Bharata replied

"Nahi Rasa Drute Kaschidardhan Pravarthathe"

Without rasa, there is no meaning, without rasa there is no use.

"Vibhavanubhava vyabhichari samyoga drasa Nishpathin"

Several commentators like Bhatta, Lollata have defined rasa in several ways.

Lollata says on account of the sayoga of sthayeebhava with vibhava, rasa is created.

"Rasa poorna Katwam Bhavanam"

Bhava Poornakatwam rasasya" says Natyaveda.

"Rasah" "Rasysta is Rasah" Because it is being swallowed, it is Rasa.

Nine rasas are mentioned. Out of them sringara is the most prominent, which elevates the human mind to ecstasy. That is why sringara is called Rasaraja.

"Sukha prayestha sampanna Ritu malyadi sevakah purusha pramada yuktah sringara iti sampathi".

"Rutu malayalankaraihi priyojana Gandharva kavya sevabih.

Upavanagamana viharaihi sringararasa samudbhavabi".

"Nayana vadana smita madhura Vacho Dhruti Promodaischa this sringara is of two kinds (1) sambhoga and (2) Vipralambha (Pining for love).

Many talented artistes have developed this Rasabhinaya tradition very interestingly and they also perform Abhinaya for a Padam, Slokam, Poem and Javali *etc.*, and exhibit histrionic expressions, according to the guidelines given by ancient texts. Main purpose is to educate the masses about mythological themes epics, and culture. Scope of dance is considered immense.

Dance being a supreme art, is a form of worship, its scope is explained by Bharata as embracing all the terms in life. Dance has a message for the audience that man should live an ideal life in the path of righteousness prosperity and fame. Natya is ageless and originates with the desire of man to express himself.

Depending on the social, political and cultural transformation of society in Andhra Pradesh, dance forms evolved in course of time in different ages of the rulers. People also appreciated the various forms. Several themes were switched from mere prayer to Rasabhinaya, from Aradhana (Worship) to sentimental display through Nayaka Nayakiabhinaya.

Kuchipudi style is now a popular dance form in Telugu land, evolved on the basis of vachikabhinaya with special emphasis on presentation of samcharibhavas along with sprightly foot work as V. Patanjali says. It can be also said that Kshetrayyas padabhinaya tradition has been perfected by the Kuchipudi performers. They deserve all praise for their role of Satyabhama".

I feel proud to present these great forms of dance, evolved as classical forms. These delicate styles in dance given utmost importance in the visual representation of thought. This tradition of men acting as women is nowhere found as in Andhra Pradesh.

It is not beyond truth to say that it is the Brahmin families of Kuchipudi that are responsible for the presentation of the Kuchipudi dance. Sincere effort was made by some Natyacharyas to lift this fine art to a greater level to win name and fame at the international level. In spite of their ups and downs, they could preserve the rich tradition with their dedication.

Dance schools have been started in towns and cities and many performing artists have come to lime light. Girls from respectable families also began to learn this fine art and to give stage performances. This trend is really to be appreciated by one and all.

Solo forms of dances are culled out from Kuchipudi dance dramas and they are being presented as separate items of dance.

Vedokta dharmas like "satyamevajate" "satyam vada", "Dharmam chara" are being shown through nritya" which is a drisya Kavya and filled with it will have its due place among the other classical forms.

Conclusion

I made a systematic study of the development of dance traditions in Andhra Pradesh in the light of literary, archaeological and sculptural evidences available. I visited important places like Tanjore, Warangal, Kuchipudi, Amaravathi, Movva Melattur (Tamilnadu) and several established libraries including Bhandarker Oriental Library, Poona and Sangit Natak Academy, New Delhi, Saraswati Mahal in Tanjore *etc.*

I attempted to make a critical analysis of the process of development and laid stress on the artistic talent and aesthetic sense of Andhras during the several phases. The literature produced in the past gave me enormous information on the contribution of Andhras to the divine art of dance.

Mainbody of my work was divided into four different parts and 32 chapters.

Many Gurus and Natyacharyas and friends in the field gave me several ideas and gave valuable suggestions during my study, which spread over five years. I attempted to write on dance out of divine inspiration and out of my interest in fine arts, though I am not a dancer. I hope this work of mine, written in simple English, would be readable and useful to the student, and to the general reader as well and would provide some base material for a researcher on the subject in future. I included mythological stories wherever possible and depending on the political and cultural history of Andhra Pradesh. I traced the reminiscenes of the past glory.

References

1. Ananda K. Swamy—The Origin of the Buddha Image, pp. 112-13.
2. B.S.L. Hemantha Rao—Religion in Andhra, pp. 28-37.
3. C. Siva Rama Murthy—Amaravati Sculpture.
4. Guru Raja Rao—Megalithic culture in South India.
5. Art in worship—Dance traditions and their development in Andhra Pradesh.

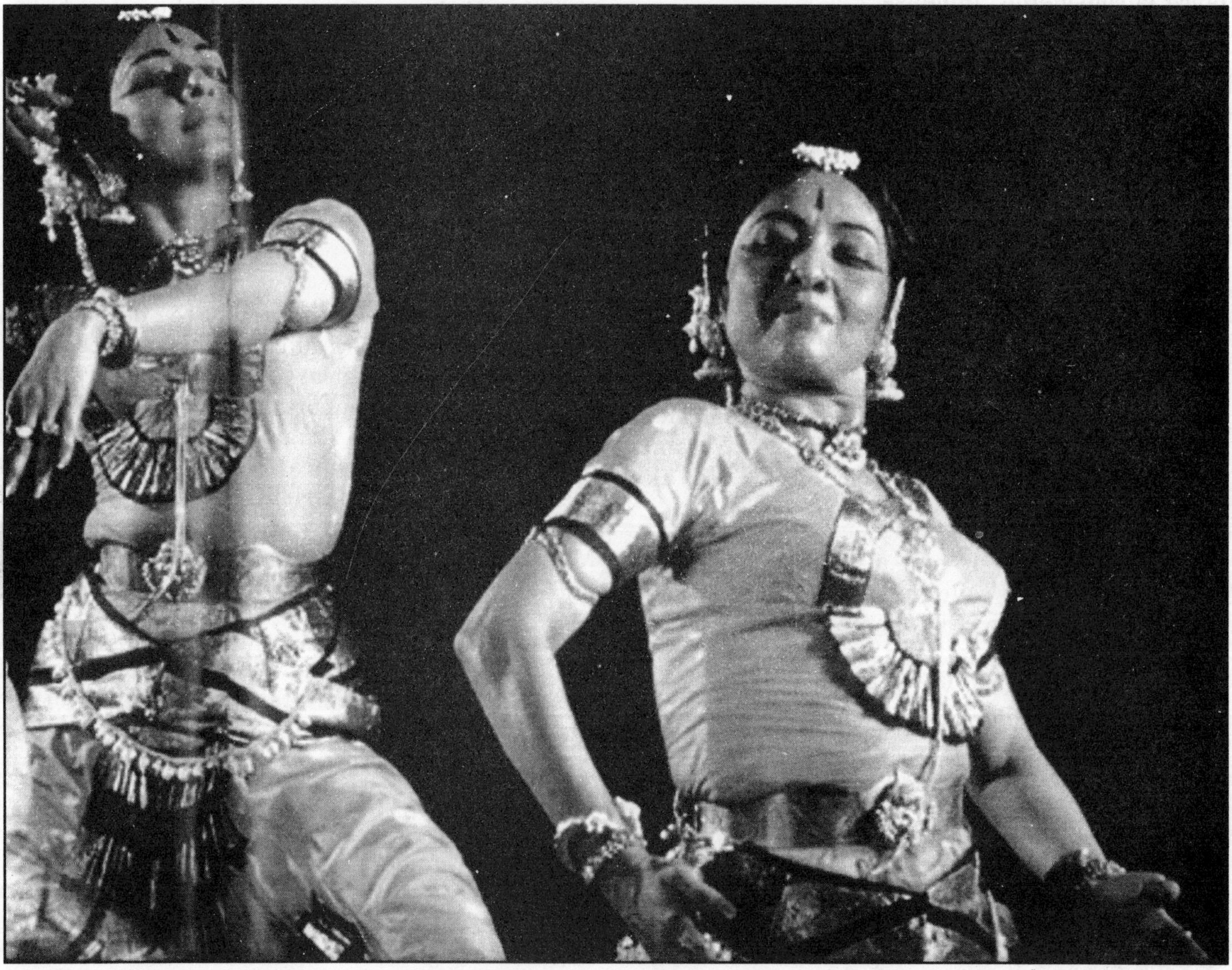

Yamini Krishna Murthy

Annexures

THE AUGMENTATION OF INDIAN DANCE ART

I. NATURE

↓

Arts

↓

Fine Arts

- Mārga (Nāṭyadharmi)
- Dèsi (Lŏkadharmi)

II. FINE ARTS

- Music
- Painting
- Sculpture

III. MUSIC

- Vocal Music (Gītham)
- Instrumental Music (Vādyaḿ)
- Drama & Dance (Nāṭyakaḷa)

IV. NĀṬYAKALA

- Nāṭyam
- Nrityam
- Nrittam

NĀṬYAM

- Yakshagānam Nrityanāṭakam
- Gēya, Vachana nāṭakam

NRITTAM

- Vishama
- Vikaṭa
- Laghu

NRITYAM

- Lāsyam
- Tāṇḍavam

LAASYAM

- Churita
- Yavvarita

TAANḌAVAM

- Pebāli
- Bahurūpa

NRITTAM

- Rasa Prādhānya
- Gatīprādhanya
- Jati prādhānya
- Śabda prādhānya

NRITYAM

- Kathāprādhānya
- Gīthaprādhānya

NATYAM

- Nāṭakamulu (Dramas)
- Tólu Bommalāṭa
  Bommalāṭa
  VeedhiBhaagavatamu

VEEDHIBHĀGAVATHAMU

- Nattuvamèla (female oriented)
- Bhaagavatamèla (male oriented)

ĀLAYA KAḶALU (Temple Arts)

TEMPLE

- Archakulu
- Pauraṇikulu
- Haridāsulu
- Bhajanakūtamulu
- Vichitravèshamulu
  - Pagaṭi Bhāgavatulu
    Pagaṭi Veshamulu
- Yakshagānamulu
  - Bahupaatra (Nāṭyam) Characterisation
  - Èkapatra
    - Kalāpam

TEMPLE (DANCERS) DANCE

↓

- **Mārga** (to dance for Gods following the Āgama Śāstra According to Tradition) Ritual Dance
- **Dèśi** (Dance compositions with regional effect) Kelika Dance

TEMPLE DANCERS

↓

- **Vaishṇava temple dancer**
- **Śaiva temple dancer**

COURT DANCE

↓

- **Kèḷika**
- **Mèjuvāni**
- **Mèlam**

NATTUVA MELAM

↓

Yakshagānapaddhati (Dance drama)

↓

1. Jakkula purandhri (Andhra)
2. Kuravanji (Tamil)
3. Lāvaṇi, Lalit, Tamāsha (Maharashtra)
4. Keertana (Bengal)
5. Sokkhināta (Orissa)

Kacchèri style (solodance)

↓

1. Dāsi Āttam(Tamil)
2. Bhōgamāta (Andhra)
3. Mōhiniāttam (Kerala)
4. Kalāvanthanritya (Mahārāshtra)
5. Kathak (Uttar Pradesh)
6. Khènta (Bengal)
7. Odissi (Orissa)

BHAGAVATAMELAS

Nāṭyamèla

↓

Veedhi Bhāgavathamu ↓ | Kalāpamulu ↓ (Which are developed only in Andhra)

I. Veedhi Bhāgavatamu

1. Kūchipūdi Brāhmana Bhāgavatulu
2. Kōta Konda Kapatrāla Bhāgavatulu
3. Yanādi Bhāgavatulu
4. Chenchu Bhāgavatulu
5. Golla Bhāgavatulu
6. Nakkala Bhāgavatulu
7. Dāsari Pāṭakulu
8. Bahu Rūpulu

II. Brāhmana Bhāgavatulu (Tamil Nadu)

Mèlattur, Oottukādu, Shūlamaṅgaḷam

III. Yaksha Gāna Nartakulu(Karṇātaka)

IV. 1. Kathākaḷi
2. Chakkiyār Kūttu
3. Kutiyāttam (Malabar)

— Kèrala

V. 1. Rāmaleela
2. Nautanki
3. Bharatulu

— Uttar Pradesh

VI. 1. Gajan(Shiva Leela) — Bengal

VII. 1. Dandōra — Maharastra

Kalāpamulu

↓

Bhāmā Kalāpam
Golla Kalāpam
Radhā Mādhavam

↓

Kūchipūdi | Dèva gaṇika

Troup of Nattuva Mela

1. Naṭṭuvāngam - Āchārya - Guru
2. Pātra or Nartaki
3. Naṭudu (helper vayasyudu or a comedian)
4. Vantapāṭakulu (play back singers)
5. Vādyakulu (players of musical instruments)

Musical Instruments used for Indian Dances

1. Mrudangam, Tabala, Śuddha Maddela etc. are called as Charma Vādyamulu
2. Vènuvu(flute) Mukhavīna etc. are Galivādyamulu
3. Vīna, tambura, Violin etc., are called tantri(stringed) Vadyamulu
4. Jalatarangini, Jalavādyam.

Recognised Classical dance traditions of India

1.	Āndhra Pradesh	Āndhra Nātyam & Kūchipūdi
2.	Tamil Nādu	Bharatanāṭyam & Bhāgavatamèla
3.	Kèrala	Móhiniāttam & Kathākaḷi
4.	Orissa	Odissi & chchau
5.	Uttar Pradesh	Kathak
6.	Maṇipur	Maṇipuri

Source - Dakshinatyula Natyakala Charitra - Dr. Nataraja Ramakrishna

Vijayanagar Penukonda Ramachandra—Outer wall- Dancing Vishnu

Goddess flanked by dwarf attendants. Bracket projection of a pillar in Cave 21 (Ramesvara) at Ellora (Deccan). Vakataka, fifth-sixth century A.D.

Side View of Padmini Jati Stree—Lepakshi

A Pillar figure—Ellora

Mahishasuramardini—Ellora

Buddhist Relic-casket. Gold Repousse, set with Rubies. Bimaran, Afghanistan. c. 2nd century A.D.

Indian Ivory Statuette, found at Herculaneum. 1st century A.D.

Ivory Plaque. Begram, Afghanistan. 2nd century A.D.

Tondo from a cross-bar from the railing of the stupa at Amaravati. Second century A.D. London, British Museum.

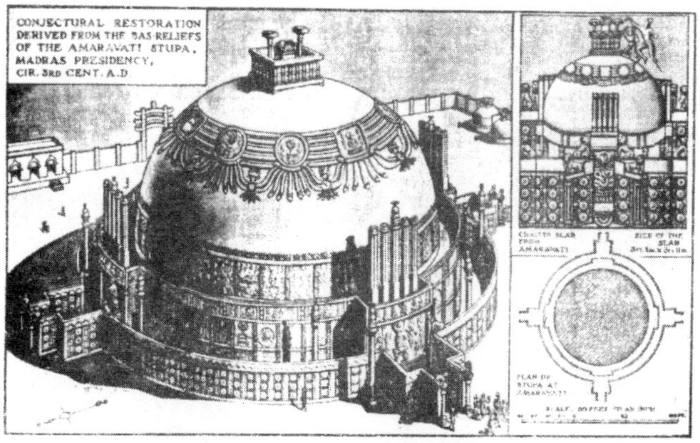

Amaravati, stupa, conjectural reconstruction

Inner and outer faces of a railing pillar from the stupa at Amaravati. Second century A.D. London, British Museum.

Index

E

L

M

N

U

V

W

Y

Z